DICTIONARY
OF MARY

MARY — QUEEN OF HEAVEN AND EARTH

As the daughter of the Father, Mother of the Son, and Bride of the Holy Spirit, Mary was crowned Queen of Heaven and Earth by the Triune God.

DICTIONARY OF MARY

"Behold Your Mother"

REVISED AND EXPANDED EDITION

With Complete References to
The Catechism of the Catholic Church

Catholic Book Publishing Co.
New Jersey

NIHIL OBSTAT: Francis J. McAree, S.T.D.
Censor Librorum

IMPRIMATUR: ✠ Patrick J. Sheridan, D.D.
Vicar General, Archdiocese of New York

This book is a *greatly expanded* version of a work originally written by Members of the Editorial Committee of the French magazine *Cahiers Marials* (Marian Notes) under the general direction of Father Alphonse Bossard, S.M.M. It was originally published by Desclée de Brouwer. The English translation was made by the Rev. John Otto. (Material included from the Italian edition was translated by Anthony Buono, general editor of the English edition.)

(T-367)

THE first Edition of this *Dictionary of Mary* appeared in 1985 and has been warmly received. It has aided many with its presentation of a doctrine on Mary that is genuine in a language that is understandable by and accessible to all.

However, the veritable explosion of Marian material in the last decade and the continued interest in all things relative to Mary pointed to the need for a revised and expanded Edition. The present volume is the result.

Some forty new entries have been included as well as a Table of the Collection of Masses of the Blessed Virgin Mary (Appendix 8) and a series of Classic Prayers of the Saints to Mary (Appendix 9). In addition, the Select Chronology of Major Marian Events (Appendix 10) has been updated through 1995. Also, handy references to *the Catechism of the Catholic Church* appear in brackets next to each entry.

Among the more important new entries are the following:

Angels and Mary outlines Our Lady's view of Angels, in keeping with the great current interest in these heavenly beings. The *Catechism of the Catholic Church and Mary* gives a summary of the Marian teachings in the first official Universal Catechism that has appeared in 400 years.

The *Collection of Masses of the Blessed Virgin Mary* provides a brief description of an unparalleled liturgical book containing 46 new Masses in honor of Our Lady that can be celebrated on open liturgical days. The *Crowning of an Image of the Blessed Virgin Mary* summarizes the teaching put forth in the revised liturgical rite in honor of Mary's Queenship.

The *Cult of Mary* reviews briefly the Church's Marian Liturgy, showing Our Lady's place in each of the rites. The *Feasts of Mary* comments on each Feast of Mary in the present Universal Calendar and indicates some of the past feasts that have been deleted.

The *Infancy Narratives* casts a brief look at the role Mary is given by Saints Matthew and Luke in the Infancy Gospels, which have retained enduring interest both for scholars and for the average person. *Judaism and Mary* attempts to sketch the prevailing Jewish attitude toward Mary in this day of greater interfaith contact and understanding.

The *Life of Mary* outlines the important stages of Mary's life as found in the Gospels. *Prayer(s) to Mary* gives a brief history of the most well-known and quasi-official Marian prayers.

Among the other new entries are the significant Magisterial Documents on Our Lady: *Ad Caeli Reginam; Ad Diem Illum Laetissimum; Adiutricem Populi; Fulgens Corona; Homily of Paul VI at the Closing of the 3rd Session of Vatican II; Ineffabilis Deus; Inter Sodalicia; Laetitiae Sanctae; Lux Veritatis; Marialis Cultus; Munificentissimus Deus; Octobri Mense; Redemptoris Mater; Signum Magnum.*

Also added are entries on incidents in the life of Mary not fully covered in the previous edition: *Coronation of Mary; Death of Mary; Ephesus; Mark, Gospel of Saint; Resurrection and Mary; Words of Mary.* Still others focus on Mary's relationship with Jesus and her parents: *Immanuel; Parents of Mary.*

The Church's teaching about Mary also gives rise to other entries: *Dogmas, Marian; Full of Grace; Knowledge, Our Lady's; Lectionary, Marian; Presence of Mary in the Eucharist.*

The last division concerns specific Marian themes for Catholics today; it includes *Apparitions after Vatican II; Marian Classics; Medjugorje; Novenas and Mary.*

May this new Edition contribute in some way to increased knowledge of Mary and her mission as well as to the joyful veneration of her about which Pope Paul VI spoke:

"The Church's reflection on the Mystery of Christ and on her own nature has led her to find at the root of the latter the same figure of a Woman: the Virgin Mary, the Mother of Christ and the Mother of the Church. . . .

"Thus our own time, faithfully attentive to tradition and to the progress of theology and the sciences, will make its contribution of praise to her whom, according to her own prophetic words, all generations will call blessed" (MC, Intr.)

In that way, this *Dictionary of Mary* will continue to help all Catholics go *through Mary to Jesus,* the Way, the Truth, and the Life.

The Publishers

INTRODUCTION TO THE FIRST EDITION

A Cross and a Mother

ALL Catholics are surely aware that we are in the midst of a new Marian springtime which is filling hearts with genuine hope. A rediscovery of Mary is taking place among church groups, popular devotion is blossoming under the impetus of pilgrimages to Marian Shrines, and both personal and collective consecrations to Mary are being renewed after the example of Pope John Paul II, whose motto is *"Totus tuus—All yours, [O Mary]."*

The Pope's coat of arms is also becoming the emblem of contemporary Catholics: a luminous cross flanked by a smaller "M" growing out of it—A Cross and a Mother, Christ and Mary. It illustrates the riches of mercy and salvation that are ours through Christ who comes to us in Mary.

Authentic Doctrine and True Devotion

However, there is a pressing need for materials that will provide authentic devotion to Mary without hint of sentimentalism or affectation. Priests, religious, catechists, and parents are seeking to present Mary to their listeners in her true light—in a way that combines the traditional with the contemporary so that Marian theology will be understood and appreciated by people today. They seek to portray Mary within the framework laid out by the Second Vatican Council in its *Constitution on the Church (Lumen Gentium)* and by Pope Paul VI in his *Apostolic Constitution on Devotion to the Blessed Virgin Mary (Marialis Cultus).*

This is the precise reason for this book—to present a doctrine on Mary that is genuine in a language that is understandable by and accessible to all. Created by a Committee of some of the best Marian scholars who are themselves devoted clients of Our Lady, it is made up of a listing of words in alphabetical order that speak of Mary or have some reference to her.

But it is a *Marian Dictionary* that does not intend to say everything on the subject of Mary. It deals with the most important Marian themes and those most relevant to our day.

The subtitle "Behold Your Mother" reveals the ultimate purpose of the Dictionary: to serve as an echo of the solemn and moving words that Christ hanging on the Cross addressed to His beloved disciple. They are words of revelation that define the mission of Mary in the Church: to collaborate maternally in the birth of the children of God and to accompany them on their journey from earthly Baptism to heavenly glory.

This Dictionary wishes to advance the progress of authentic Marian spirituality, that is, to help Catholics accept Mary as our Mother with an attitude of filial love and openness so that they may attain a closer union with the Blessed Trinity.

Use of the Dictionary

This *Marian Dictionary* is ideal for meditation, study, and evangelization. To facilitate its use, we have provided a "Guide for a Systematic Reading" which puts Marian entries in their logical order. We have also included the helpful section "Marian Celebrations of the Liturgical Year" in the spirit of Pope Paul VI's *Apostolic Exhortation "Marialis Cultus"* as well as a list of themes for a "Month of Mary." Other appendices include three listings of Marian liturgical readings, ideas for celebrating Advent and Christmas with Mary, a table of the development of the cult of Mary in the Roman Liturgy, and a "Select Chronology of Major Marian Events in the Church."

We trust that this new and unique book will enable all who use it to walk with Mary in an authentic fashion, for as John Paul II has said, "she must be found in all the Church's daily ways of life." Only if we get in tune with the Mother of Jesus—indeed, only if we become one with her—will we live the new Advent of this last part of the second millennium. For where Mary is, Christ will also be born anew!

The Publishers

ABBREVIATIONS

AA	*Apostolicam Actuositatem*
AAS	*Acta Apostolicae Sedis* (The official organ of publication for the Holy See)
Acts	Acts of the Apostles
A.D.	*Anno Domini* (In the year of Our Lord)
Am	Amos, The Book of
Bar	Baruch, The Book of
B.C.	Before Christ
c.	*circa:* about; or: century
CCC	*Catechism of the Catholic Church*
cf.	*confer:* compare
1 Chr	Chronicles, The First Book of
2 Chr	Chronicles, The Second Book of
Col	Colossians, The Epistle to the
1 Cor	Corinthians, The First Epistle to the
2 Cor	Corinthians, Second Epistle to the
Dn	Daniel, the Book of
DS	New edition of Denziger-Schoenmetzer, *Enchiridion Symbolorum,* 1965
Dt	Deuteronomy, The Book of
Eccl	Ecclesiastes, The Book of
e.g.	*exempla gratia:* for example
EN	*Evangelii Nuntiandi*
Eph	Ephesians, The Epistle to the
Est	Esther, The Book of
Ex	Exodus, The Book of
Ez	Ezekiel, The Book of
Ezr	Ezra, The Book of
f/ff	following
G	Gospel
Gal	Galatians, The Epistle to the
Gn	Genesis, The Book of
Hb	Habakkuk, The Book of
Heb	Hebrews, The Epistle to the
Hg	Haggai, The Book of
Hos	Hosea, The Book of
ibid.	*ibidem:* in the same place
i.e.	*id est:* that is
Is	Isaiah, The Book of
Jas	James, The Epistle of
Jb	Job, The Book of
Jdt	Judith, The Book of
Jer	Jeremiah, The Book of
Jgs	Judges, The Book of
Jl	Joel, The Book of
Jn	John, The Gospel According to
1 Jn	John, The First Epistle of
2 Jn	John, The Second Epistle of
3 Jn	John, The Third Epistle of
Jon	Jonah, The Book of
Jos	Joshua, The Book of
Jude	Jude, The Epistle of
1 Kgs	Kings, The First Book of
2 Kgs	Kings, The Second Book of
Lam	Lamentations, The Book of
LG	*Lumen Gentium*
Lk	Luke, The Gospel According to
Lv	Leviticus, The Book of
Mal	Malachi, The Book of
1 Mc	Maccabees, The First Book of
2 Mc	Maccabees, The Second Book of
MC	*Marialis Cultus*
Mi	Micah, The Book of
Mk	Mark, The Gospel According to
Mt	Matthew, The Gospel According to
Na	Nahum, The Book of
NCE	*New Catholic Encyclopedia*
NEH	Nehemiah, The Book of
Nm	Numbers, The Book of
no(s).	number(s)
Not	*Notitiae,* periodical of the Sacred Congregation on Divine Worship
Ob	Obadiah, The Book of
OT	*Optatam Totius*
PC	*Perfectae Caritatis*
Phil	Philippians, The Epistle to the
Phlm	Philemon, The Epistle to
PO	*Presbyterorum Ordinis*
Prv	Proverbs, The Book of
Ps(s)	Psalms, The Book of
1 Pt	Peter, The First Epistle of
2 Pt	Peter, The Second Epistle of
q.v.	*quod vide:* which see
RI	Reading I
Rom	Romans, The Epistle to the
Ru	Ruth, The Book of
Rv	Revelation, The Book of
SC	*Sacrosanctum Concilium*
Sir	Sirach, The Book of
1 Sm	Samuel, The First Book of
2 Sm	Samuel, The Second book of
Song	Song of Songs
Tb	Tobit, The Book of
1 Thes	Thessalonians, First Epistle to the
2 Thes	Thessalonians, Second Epistle to the
Ti	Titus, The Epistle to
1 Tm	Timothy, The First Epistle to
2 Tm	Timothy, The Second Epistle to
Wis	Wisdom, The Book of
Zec	Zechariah, The Book of
Zep	Zephaniah, The Book of

AUTHORS OF THE ARTICLES

BILLET, BERNARD: Benedictine, Director of a French magazine about Lourdes.

BOSSARD, ALPHONSE: Montfort Missionary, Editor of "Marian Notes" ("Cahiers Marials"). He is also the Editorial Director of this Dictionary.

BOULET, ANDRE: Marianist, Theologian.

BUONO, ANTHONY: Layman, Doctor of Theology, Editor of both English Editions.

CAROL, JUNIPERO: Franciscan, founder and past president of the Mariological Society of America and Editor of *"Marian Studies."*

CASTEL, R.: La Salette Missionary, Member of the Pastoral Committee of La Salette.

CAZELLES, HENRI: Sulpician, Professor of Exegesis at the Catholic Institute.

CHENOT, A.: Rector of Beauraing.

DE FIORES, STEFANO: Montfort Missionary, Professor of Marian Spirituality and Contemporary Mariology at the Gregorian University and the "Marianum."

DELESALLE, AGNES: Daughter of Wisdom, Member of the Editorial Committee of "Marian Notes."

DU BUIT, M.: Dominican, Scripture Scholar.

DUMONT, A.: Priest of the Order of Mary Immaculate.

GIENS, JEANINE: Laywoman, Member of the Editorial Committee of "Marian Notes."

GONTHIER, J.: Vincentian, Expert in Pastoral.

HOLSTEIN, HENRI: Jesuit, Theologian.

LAURENCEAU, JEAN: Dominican, Secretary of the French Society for Marian Studies.

LE BORGNE, OLIVIER: Montfort Missionary, Expert on Spirituality.

MANTEAU-BONAMY, HENRI-MARIE: Dominican, Theologian.

MEXICAN PRIEST: Member of the Pastoral Committee of the Shrine of Guadalupe.

PINTARD, JACQUES: Priest, Patrologist.

POINT, R.: Priest, Member of the Pastoral Committee of Lourdes.

POULAIN, P.: Rector of Pontmain.

PREVOST, JEAN-PIERRE: Montfort Missionary, Doctor of Biblical Theology.

RUM, ALBERTO: Montfort Missionary, Director of the Italian "Mother and Queen" ("Madre e Regina").

TOSTAIN, ANDRE: Missionary of the Sacred Heart, Director of the French "Annals of Our Lady of the Sacred Heart."

VALENTINI, ALBERTO: Montfort Missionary, Expert in Biblical Studies.

VAN LOON, M.: Rector of Banneux.

ZBUDNIEWEK, J.: Priest of the Order of St. Paul the Hermit, Member of the Pastoral Committee of the Shrine of Jasna Gora.

ZOBEL, PHILIBERT: Benedictine, Theologian.

GUIDE FOR A SYSTEMATIC READING

- A -

AD CAELI REGINAM [971]

SEE   *Church and Mary*
       Crowning of an Image
         of the Blessed Virgin
         Mary
       Cult of Mary

Feasts of Mary
Litany of the Blessed Virgin
Magisterium (Documents of)
Queen
Vatican II and Mary

O N October 11, 1954, at the conclusion of the Marian Year and as a crowning achievement of his devotion to Mary, Pius XII published an Encyclical entitled *Ad Caeli Reginam* ("To the Queen of Heaven") to announce the liturgical feast of Mary's Queenship. The Pope indicates his belief that this teaching—although not knew—should be presented to the Christian people together with a summary of texts from Tradition for the praise of our Heavenly Mother and the spiritual benefit of the faithful.

The Encyclical sets forth texts from the Fathers of the Church connected with Sacred Scripture, taken up by theologians, and confirmed by the Supreme Pontiffs—from St. Martin I to Benedict XIV—as well as references to the Liturgy and popular prayers plus the contributions of Christian art and the custom of crowning images of Mary. Then it proceeds to illustrate the reasons for Mary's Queenship that flow from these documents: (1) Mary's Divine Motherhood; (2) her collaboration with Christ in our salvation; and (3) her fullness of grace.

The Pope goes on to say that Mary enjoys a Queenship of Excellence: "Mary is raised by her dignity above all creation and comes first after her Son." She also enjoys a Queenship of Efficiency: "Not only has she been given the highest degree of excellence and perfection after Christ, but she also shares in the power that her Son and our Redeemer exercises over the minds and wills of human beings."

In the light of all these reasons, the Pope then makes known his decision to institute a new feast of Mary. Although such an act is not equivalent to a dogmatic definition as in the case of the Assumption, it unquestionably forms part of the Ordinary Magisterium of the Church. It is set forth with a certain solemnity and with the declared intention of proposing to clergy and faithful a truth belonging to the doctrinal patrimony of the Church.

The Encyclical establishes the feast on May 31 together with the consecration of the human race to the Immaculate Heart of the Blessed Virgin. In the renewed Liturgy of Vatican II, the feast of the Immaculate Heart of Mary is assigned to the Saturday following the 2nd Sunday after Pentecost, and the feast of the Queenship of Mary is established on August 22, one week after the Assumption.   *A. Buono*

AD DIEM ILLUM LAETISSIMUM   [491-493]

SEE   *Church and Mary*   *Immaculate Conception*
      Cult of Mary   *Magisterium (Documents of)*
      Feasts of Mary   *Vatican II and Mary*

O N February 2, 1904, the fiftieth anniversary of the proclamation of the Dogma of the Immaculate Conception, St. Pius X issued an Encyclical entitled *Ad Diem Illum Laetissimum* ("On That Happiest of Days"). The Pope hastens to indicate that many blessings have flowed from that definition: the convoking of Vatican Council I, the promulgation of the dogma of papal infallibility, the fervor of the faithful toward the Vicars of Christ, and the Blessed Mother's appearances to Bernadette at Lourdes together with its numerous graces and miracles.

The Pope then goes on to indicate the chief reason why the fiftieth anniversary of the Proclamation of the Dogma should excite a singular fervor in the souls of Christians: the restoration of all things in Christ. "There is no surer and more direct road than by Mary for uniting all humankind in Christ and obtaining through Him the perfect adoption of children, that we may be holy and immaculate in the sight of God. . . .

If, as Christ said, *'Now this is eternal life: That they may know You, the only true God, and Jesus Christ, Whom You have sent'* (Jn 17:3), and if through Mary we attain to the knowledge of Christ, through Mary also we most easily obtain that life of which Christ is the source and origin."

Indeed, Mary is regarded as the one who, after Christ, is the most powerful safeguard of the Catholic Faith. The Pope gives the reasons for this function as well as the privileges of the Virgin. Only through Mary can we come to know many Mysteries of the life of Christ that were known solely to her. Since Christ is the Head of the Mystical Body, which is the Church, Mary is also the Mother of believers, and all Christians have been given spiritual birth by her.

Mary offered Jesus the matter of her flesh, participated in His Passion, and presented Him as a Victim to the Father. Hence, she became the Mediatrix, between God and human beings, of the graces of the Redemption. "It cannot be denied that the dispensing of these treasures is the particular and supreme right of Jesus Christ . . . Who is the Mediator between God and human beings. Nevertheless, by this union in sorrow and suffering that existed between the Mother and the Son, it has been allowed to the august Virgin to be the most powerful Mediatrix and Advocate of the whole world, with her Divine Son."

As consequences of such truths, the Pope stresses that the fiftieth anniversary of the Dogma must signify a more perfect knowledge of Jesus in a renewed spiritual life. The Dogma of the Immaculate Conception will then teach us to flee from sin and strengthen our faith in the truth of original sin and the Redemption, which are basic truths of our Faith.   *A. Buono*

ADIUTRICEM POPULI   [971, 2678, 2708]

SEE   *Church and Mary*   *Magisterium (Documents of)*
     Cult of Mary   *Rosary*
     Ecumenism (Mary and)   *Vatican II and Mary*

ON September 5, 1895, Pope Leo XIII issued one of his many Encyclicals on the Rosary entitled *Adiutricem Populi* ("Helper of the People"). In it he urges the faithful to pray to the Lady of the Rosary, who is the Mother of the Church, for a favor that was especially close to his heart: the reunion with the Catholic Church of the Separated Brethren and in particular the separated Eastern Churches. He sets forth the precise reasons why the patronage of the Blessed Virgin is so opportune in this matter.

Mary was entrusted with the special mission of maintaining the Church in the unity and integrity of the faith. When Jesus returned to heaven she remained on earth to guide the first steps of the Church and to animate the Apostles in the spread of the Gospel. Upon her entrance into heaven, she continued this function, as she has demonstrated many times in the history of the Church by intervening to revive the faith of believers and to overcome dangerous heresies.

The Pope stresses that the faithful should pray to her because today special reasons move her to supplicate God for the return of the Eastern Churches. At the Council of Ephesus, the Christians of the East and the West gathered around Mary in perfect unity of faith and zealous participation in identical worship. Moreover, the nations cut off from unity with the Church have done prodigious things for her honor in the past, especially in the East. To them is due much of the credit for propagating and increasing devotion to Mary, and from them have come some of her greatest champions and followers.

He concludes with a warm exhortation to all Christians to pray to the Blessed Virgin to bring together all her children into the one Church.

A. Buono

AIN KARIM

Sᴇᴇ   *Holy Land and Mary*, 2a

AKATHIST HYMN

[2678]

SEE   *Prayer(s) to Mary*

1. Origin and Author

THE Akathist Hymn is the most widespread expression of the Marian devotion found in churches of the Byzantine Rite. Historically, it is connected with the defense and liberation of Constantinople. During the siege of 626, in fact, the Patriarch Serge consecrated his city to Mary, making the Akathist Hymn a chant of victory and thanksgiving.

The popularity of this form of prayer was immense both in the East and in the West, where it inspired Marian piety and the Litany of Our Lady. It is called "Akathist" (=to be recited "without sitting down") out of reverence for the Incarnation of the Son of God, announced by an Angel, in the same way that we stand when listening to the Holy Gospel.

Originally composed for the Annunciation, the hymn is chanted in the Byzantine Office for the Fifth Saturday of Lent and it habitually serves as the Little Office of the Blessed Virgin in a spirit that is much akin to our Rosary or the Litany of Our Lady.

"The origin of the Akathist Hymn remains a mystery" (D. Guillaume). Many attribute it to Saint Romanos the Melodist who died about 556 at Constantinople. B. Emmi has stated: "The Akathist Hymn was composed as a hymn of thanksgiving after the rebellious factions of Circo were put down (532); it became popular after the liberation of the Avars (626) and was completed at the time of Photius IX (9th century) and enriched with various additions in succeeding times."

2. Structure and Content

The Akathist Hymn is an alphabetic acrostic of 24 strophes, each of which is a letter of the Greek alphabet, in which it was written. The first 12 strophes sing of the Gospel of the Infancy (Annunciation, Incarnation, Visitation, Disturbance of Joseph, Visit of the Shepherds and the Magi, Flight into Egypt, Presentation). The other 12 strophes contemplate the Mystery of the Incarnation and Mary's virginal Motherhood.

"The stanzas alternate the Marian framework with Christianized themes, fusing both Son and Mother together: some breaking out in praise of the Virgin and others giving acclaim to the Lord. All begin with the presentation of a fact or a theme, which fixes the mind on the Mystery. The Marian strophes—the odd numbered ones—then prolong the contemplation, which has become verbal, in a succession of alternating choirs, and binary forms of concise thoughts and lapidary assertions. These are couched in graphic images taken from the Scriptures and from all creation as a commentary on the proposed themes, and they conclude with a spontaneous solemn ovation: Rejoice (or Hail), Virgin and Bride!" (E. M. Toniolo).

3. Contemplative Prayer

The Akathist Hymn possesses "a lyrical richness completely unknown to the liturgical seasons of the West as well as a theological profundity that is rarely found in texts consecrated to the praise of the Mother of God. As such it can elicit in readers the impression of satiety and it can appear to be nothing more than a repetition of the same praise because of its ever new images and ever differing expressions. However, the defect lies not in the hymn but in those who read it. The hymn is the expression of a love that neither can nor knows how to impose limits on itself. Above all, it is the testimony of a prayer that is contemplative and magnificently preserves that aspect.

"The vision that the soul contemplates is ever new and ever the same. The logical narrative procedure in the even strophes seems to be continually annulled by the flood of lyrical sentiment that pours forth in the uneven strophes. The reprise of the former in their sobriety continually renews the prodigy of an explosion of love in the latter that, in their litany-like form, seem to demand active participation on the part of an acclaiming multitude" (D. Barsotti).

As an invitation to read and make use of this "contemplative prayer," we give below the first strophe of the Akathist Hymn.

Rejoice (or: Hail), through you joy rings out again.
Rejoice, through you sorrow is put to flight.
Rejoice, O resurrection of fallen Adam.
Rejoice, O redemption of the tears of Eve.
Rejoice, O sublime peak of human intellect.
Rejoice, O profound abyss even for Angel eyes.
Rejoice, for in you the King's throne was elevated.
Rejoice, for you bear the One Who sustains everything.
Rejoice, O star that go before the Sun.
Rejoice, O womb of the Incarnate God.
Rejoice, for through you all creation is renewed.
Rejoice, for through you the Creator became a baby.
Rejoice, O Virgin and Bride!

J. Laurenceau—A. Rum.

ALPHONSUS LIGUORI (Saint)

SEE   *Servants of Mary, 4*

ANGELS AND MARY

SEE   *Assumption*   *Matthew (Gospel of)*
       Litany of the Blessed   *Queen*
       Virgin Mary

1. Familiarity with the Notion of Angels

Mary grew up in a world in which Angels were commonplace. She learned that they had intervened in the history of the Jewish people from time to time.

They had helped promulgate the Law (see Acts 7:38; Gal 3:19) and protected God's faithful as avengers (Ex 23:20; 2 Kgs 19:35; Ps 78:49; Dn 10:13). They also watched over human beings (Tb 3:17; Ps 91:11; Dn 3:49f), presented their prayers to God (Tb 12:12), and presided over the destinies of nations (Dn 10:13-21).

Mary also no doubt learned that since the time of Ezekiel Angels explained to the Prophets the meaning of their visions (Ez 40:3f; Dn 1:5-19; 9:21ff; Zec 1:8f). They received names corresponding to their functions: Raphael, "God heals" (Tb 3:17; 12:15); Gabriel, "Hero of God" (Dn 8:16; 9:21); and Michael, "Who is like God?" (Dn 10:13, 21; 12:1).

Hence, Mary was well aware of the existence of the Angelic world and its presence in the world of human beings. She was also familiar with the idea of the Angel of the Lord, present in the ancient Biblical narratives (Gn 16:7; 22:11; Ex 3:2; Jgs 2:1), Who is no different from Yahweh Himself and manifested Himself on earth in visible form (Gn 16:13; Ex 3:2). For God could not allow creatures to see His face (Ex 33:20) since He lives in light inaccessible.

At the same time, Mary was also familiar with two Old Testament Messianic texts that had to do with a Woman who was to help overthrow God's ancient enemy (a fallen Angel) by giving birth to the Messiah King while remaining a virgin (Gn 3:15; Is 7:14).

2. Mary's Experience with Angels

In her own life Mary experienced the coming of Angels as messengers from God and helpers on earth. She did so first during the Conception and Infancy of her Son Jesus. At the Annunciation, the Angel Gabriel announces to her that she will be the Mother of the Messiah Who will be the Son of God. In the light of her knowledge that Angels were from God, she believes the Angel's message and consents to become the Mother of God's Son.

She then hears from Joseph of the messages he receives via the Angel of the Lord concerning her mode of conception and, later, the way to outwit the wicked Herod. At the Visitation, Mary meets her cousin Elizabeth who also benefited from an Angelic mission. After the birth of Jesus, shepherds alerted by an Angelic choir come to meet the Child and to tell Mary and Joseph what had been told to them about Him. *"Mary treasured all these things and reflected on them in her heart"* (Lk 2:19f)—including the appearance of the Angels!

Mary was also familiar with Angels by the fact that Jesus alluded to them at various times in His preaching. In addition to having intimate dealings with Angels (Mt 4:11; Lk 22:43), Mary's Son mentioned them as real and active beings.

He showed that they watch over human beings and always view the face of His Father (Mt 18:10), which no human can do. Moreover, their life escapes subjection to the flesh (Mt 22:30).

They are at Christ's service, and He can demand their intervention at the time of His Passion (Mt 26:53). They will also be the executors of the Last Judgment (Mt 13:39, 49; 24:31), and they always share in the Divine Joy when sinners repent (Lk 15:10). Hence, Mary was well versed on the subject of Angels.

3. Borne Up by Angels

Perhaps Mary's fullest encounter with Angels took place at the Assumption. The Apocryphal Books about the Assumption assign an important place in the event to Angels, especially Michael. The Ethiopic *Book of Rest* states that many Angels accompanied Jesus and Michael to the scene of Mary's death. Her soul was entrusted to Michael, and her body was buried. After three days, Our Lord and Michael returned, accompanied by countless Angels. Then Christ gave a sign and Michael spoke with the voice of the faithful Angels.

"The Angels came down in three clouds, and their number above the cloud appeared to be ten thousand before the Savior. And Our Lord told them to bear Mary's body in the clouds. . . . And when they had reached paradise, they placed Mary's body by the tree of life. And they brought her soul and placed it on her body. And the Lord sent the Angels back to their own place."

Other versions of this Book have Mary in conversation with Michael, who links to Mary's person the paramount event in Jewish salvation history—the Exodus. The preservation of the bones of the Patriarch Joseph are seen as a type of her bodily glorification.

4. Testimony of Tradition, the Magisterium, and the Liturgy

From the 8th century onward, we have further evidence of Mary's relationship to Angels.

An 8th-century liturgical antiphon for the feast of the Assumption reads: "The holy Virgin Mary is exalted above the choirs of Angels to the heavenly kingdom." The same subject appears in such hymns of the 11th century as *Regina Caeli* ("Queen of Heaven"), *Ave Regina Caelorum* ("Hail, Queen of the Heavens"), and *Ave Domina Angelorum* ("Hail, Mistress of Angels") as well as in the title "Queen of Angels," pioneered by Saint Fulbert of Chartres and Saint Anselm.

By the 14th century, Nicholas Cabasilas calls Mary the Mediatrix between God and Angels, and Theophanes of Nicaea adds that Mary surpasses all the orders of Angels. And in the 17th century, Saint Lawrence of Brindisi describes Mary as exalted above all the Angels by Christ.

The Church in official documents from the modern Popes has characterized Mary as "exalted above all the choirs of heaven" and as "Queen of Angels." In the *Constitution on the Church* of Vatican II, Mary is described as "surpassing all other creatures, both in heaven and on earth" (LG 53), "exalted by the Lord as Queen of the universe" (LG 59), and "exalted by God above all Angels and human beings" (LG 66).

Finally, in the revised Liturgy of Vatican II, Mary's Queenship of the Angels is clearly affirmed.

In the Liturgy of the Hours, she is termed the "Queen of heaven and earth" (Invitatory for the Queenship of Mary, August 22) as well as hailed as "Queen of heaven" and "by Angels Mistress owned" (Marian Antiphons *Regina Caeli* and *Ave Regina Caelorum* at the conclusion of Night Prayer). In the Order of Crowning an Image of Mary, the bishop prays: "[Mary] is exalted above the choirs of Angels."

She is called "Queen of Angels" in the Litany of Loreto and the Litany of the BVM in the Order of Crowning an Image, and in the latter she is also called "Queen of the universe." Lastly, in the Collection of Masses of the BVM, one of the Prefaces states: "You exalted [Mary] above all the choirs of Angels to reign with Him in glory and to intercede for all Your children, our advocate of grace and the Queen of all Creation" (Preface P 29 for the Mass of Mary, Queen of All Creation).

5. Biblical Basis of Mary's Queenship of the Angels

Sometimes we are tempted to believe that Jesus became incarnate only to save human beings who had fallen into sin. Angels and demons would seem to be outside the Mystery of Christ. Their creation, their trial, and their consequent state would all have been antecedent to and independent of the Incarnation.

However, the Bible indicates otherwise. The prologue to John's Gospel and the Christological hymns that begin the Epistles to the Ephesians and the Colossians clearly state God's plan: *"[Christ] is the firstborn over all creatures. In Him everything in heaven [Angels] and on earth [human beings], things visible and invisible . . .; all were created by Him and for Him"* (Col 1:15-19). Therefore, even the creation of pure spirits came about in Christ and for Christ, and in Him all these were reconciled in God, those in heaven (Angels) and those on earth (human beings), through the blood of His Cross (cf. Col 1:19f).

Some theologians believe that only by the merits of Christ have the Angels been admitted into communion with the Mystery of the Trinity. Many of the Fathers made interesting statements in this regard, as for example Saint Athanasius who does not hesitate to say that even the Angels owe their salvation to the Blood of Christ.

In the light of the above, even the role of Mary with respect to Angels and demons becomes real and direct as a result of her participation in the Incarnation of the Word. Mary's title as Queen of heaven has more than merely an honorific ring. It expresses a real relationship that the Bible brings to light even though theology has yet to plumb its depths.

A. Buono

ANGELUS

Sᴇᴇ   *Liturgy*   *Prayer(s) to Mary*
      Marialis Cultus

IN the Apostolic Constitution on Devotion to the Blessed Virgin Mary (*Marialis Cultus,* no. 41), Pope Paul VI strongly recommended preserving the custom of reciting the Angelus three times daily (morning, noon, and evening). This devotion consists of three Hail Marys with versicles and a concluding prayer. Its name comes from the first word of the opening versicle in Latin. The text is as follows:

℣. The Angel of the Lord declared unto Mary,
℟. And she conceived of the Holy Spirit.
   Hail Mary ...
℣. Behold the handmaid of the Lord.
℟. Be it done unto me according to your word.
   Hail Mary ...
℣. And the Word was made flesh,
℟. And dwelt among us.
   Hail Mary ...
℣. Pray for us, O holy Mother of God,
℟. That we may be made worthy of the promises of Christ.

Let us pray. Pour forth, we beg You, O Lord,
Your grace into our hearts:
that we, to whom the Incarnation of Christ Your Son
was made known by the message of an Angel,
may by His Passion and Cross
be brought to the glory of His Resurrection.
Through the same Christ our Lord. Amen.

1. The Thousand-Year History of the Angelus

"The Angelus, in reality, began in that transcendent moment of the world's history when the Angel Gabriel appeared in the light of a celestial vision to a young girl of Nazareth and greeted her with the words 'Hail Mary' " (R. Panetta). Thus, we can say that the Angelus is in a way the story of the Hail Mary.

The Angelus attained its present form only gradually. At first it was recited solely in the morning. The Franciscan Chapter of Assisi (1269) prescribed that the Brothers exhort the faithful to greet Our Lady after Compline with a Hail Mary or so and recall the Mystery of the Incarnation at the ringing of the bells. At the same time, Brother Bonvesin of Riva (c. 1260-1315) introduced the evening ringing of the "Hail Mary bell" at Milan and in its environs.

Little by little, this practice became widespread in Christianity. On October 13, 1318, Pope John XXII approved the custom of reciting the Hail Mary at the curfew hour and on May 7, 1327, he wrote his Vicar General at Rome to have the evening bell of the three Hail Marys rung even in the Eternal City. It is surely to this evening Angelus that Dante Alighieri alludes in canto VIII of his *Purgatorio.*

The 15th century witnessed the establishment of the custom of ringing the bell and reciting the Hail Marys also in the evening, with special remembrance of Mary's sorrows.

Last to become solidified was the practice of the Angelus at midday. In 1456, Callistus III prescribed the daily ringing of the bells at midday with the recitation of three Hail Marys for the success of the Crusade. King Louis XI of France had the "Angelus of Peace" rung at midday. Upon hearing the bell, the saintly King dismounted from his horse and knelt to pray.

Finally, in the 16th century, the various devotions of the Angelus acquired the unitary form that in 1724 Pope Benedict XIV definitively approved, while prescribing that during Easter Time the Angelus be replaced by the *Regina Caeli.*

2. Value and Freshness of the Angelus

In the Apostolic Exhortation on Marian Devotion (*Marialis Cultus*), Pope Paul VI stated that "despite the passing of centuries [the Angelus] retains an unaltered value and an intact freshness." Hence, it "does not need to be revised," because its essential elements are always valid:

● *Simple structure:* announcement of the Angel; response of Mary; Incarnation of the Word;

- *Biblical character:* composed of verses taken from the Gospel;
- *Historical origin:* linked with the prayer for peace and safety;
- *Quasi-liturgical rhythm:* sanctification of different moments during the day;
- *Remembrance of Paschal Mystery:* recalling the Incarnation of the Son of God, we pray that we may be led "through His Passion and Cross to the glory of His Resurrection."

3. A Pause for Prayer

Even though "a few practices traditionally linked with the recitation of the Angelus have disappeared or can only with difficulty be continued in our day," nothing prevents us from finding a little time for this Marian prayer. It is true that we no longer have the ringing of bells, which have been muted by the routine of modern life. But we can hear the voice of our hearts inviting us to the silent recitation of the Angelus—habitually possible even in the full rhythm of work—with a brief *contemplative glance* at the Mystery of the Incarnation, a faithful invocation to Mary, and an offering of our day to God.

All understand that "it is useful to recall the importance of these times of contemplative reflection, not to decrease our work but to make it more conscious and attentive. . . . We will work more speedily and happily" (Archbishop Carlo Martini of Milan, "Pastoral Letter on the Contemplative Dimension of Life," 1980/1981).

Most of us are familiar with The Angelus by J. F. Millet (1814-1875), which artfully portrays the religious poem of that daily greeting to Mary. "The farmer and his wife interrupt their work at the first sounding of a distant bell. The triple tolling at twilight spans the infinite from earth to heaven, like a blessing on the hard labor already finished and like a reminder of the one thing necessary" (M. Vloberg).

Most of us also know that every Sunday, from the window of the Apostolic Palace, Pope John Paul II follows the heritage of his "venerable predecessors" and continues "with great joy" to recite the Angelus, to which he loves to add the doxology "Glory be to the Father" and a prayer for the faithful departed. The Pope's Sunday Angelus is preceded—as the same Pontiff himself stated at the shrine of Jasna Gora on June 5, 1979—"by a brief meditation and also a remembrance of the events that should be especially recommended to God in prayer, and is concluded with a blessing."

4. Alternative Concluding Prayer

Pope Paul VI in a note to number 41 of the Apostolic Exhortation allows an alternative concluding prayer to be used in the Angelus. The usual prayer is taken from the Opening Prayer for the Fourth Sunday of Advent. The alternative prayer is the Opening Prayer for the Feast of the Annunciation of the Lord (March 25). The latter prayer expressly names the one who one day was taken up into dialogue with God and gave her active and responsible consent to the work of the ages, that is, the Incarnation of the Word:

O God,
You willed that Your Son should truly become Man
in the womb of the Virgin Mary.
We confess that our Redeemer
is both God and Man.
Grant that we may deserve to be made like Him
in His Divine Nature. Amen.   *A. Rum*

ANNUNCIATION (Luke 1:26-38)

SEE   *Feasts of Mary   Rosary*
       Fiat   Servant of the Lord
       Mother of God

THE announcement to Mary (Lk 1:26-38) has ever been a preferential source of Christian thought about Mary. The Liturgy, even as theology and exegesis, points to its primordial and normative importance for understanding the mystery of Mary, and draws from it *both the new and the old* to celebrate her exceptional role in the History of Salvation. By the use of literary forms familiar to readers of the Old Testament and a constant play of Biblical allusions, Luke manages to convey, within the limits of his account, the first Christian communities' reflections regarding Mary.

The very construction of the account already indicates Luke's fundamental theological purpose. For one thing, he draws upon other "announcements of miraculous birth" to show the transcendence of the Mystery of Jesus, manifested by the exceptional character of the Divine intervention at the time of His conception. In addition, by fashioning the account in the pattern of the announcement to Zechariah, Luke wants to bring out the continuity from John to Jesus but also the superiority of Jesus in comparison with John, as well as the contrast between the vocation of Mary and that of Zechariah. And by its broad footing in Biblical tradition, the account asks us to construe the Mystery of Jesus, and therefore the vocation of Mary—all-dependent on this Mystery—as fulfilling the promises made to Israel.

1. A revelation about the Mystery of Jesus

The account of the announcement to Mary depends for its Biblical understanding on a more extensive literary form much in evidence in the Old Testament: that of *announcements of miraculous birth* (Isaac: Gn 17:15-22 and 21:1-7; Samson: Jgs 13:2-24; Samuel: 1 Sm 1:9-20; Immanuel: Is 7:14ff).

Hence it is not unexpected to find here several elements characteristic of this literary form: (a) situation of Mary (young woman, virgin, and betrothed: v. 27); (b) appearance of an angel sent by God (v. 26); (c) revelation of an approaching birth (fruit of the benevolent and free intervention of God), of the name of the child and his destiny (vv. 31-33); (d) expression of astonishment and question about the "how" of the birth (v. 34); (e) gift of a sign (vv. 35-37).

As in all accounts of this kind, the *central message bears on the person who will be born and on his mission*. This indicates that the announcement to Mary is first of all an announcement of Jesus: *"You shall conceive in your womb and bear a Son and call His Name Jesus"* (v. 31). It is in fact the first *glad tidings* concerning Jesus, Son of God and Messiah.

Certainly the messenger, the form of the message, and its recipient are also important but always in proportion as they concern the person and the mission of the one whose birth is being announced. Their purpose and their greatness are to be of service to the mystery that is revealed.

To present this Mystery of Jesus, Luke projects on his account the light of Messianic faith through an accumulation of titles taken from the Old Testament. But, at the time when Luke wrote, these Christological titles could assume new depth, owing to the maturation of the first Christian communities' reflection in light of the Resurrection.

The mere mention of Gabriel to open the account is enough to place us in a *Messianic* and eschatological context (cf. Dt 9: the seventy weeks): the revelation that will follow has something to do with the *"end of the ages."* The name itself of the child, revealed by Gabriel, contains a whole program and leaves no doubt as to His mission: JESUS, i.e., *"the Lord saves"* (cf. Mt 1:21). It is in Him that the salvation promised by God to His people will be fulfilled in definitive manner.

Luke then places in the mouth of Gabriel a series of titles that are so many professions of the Messiahship of Jesus and the unique and transcendent character of His relation to God:

He will be *"great"* (after the manner of God Himself, in an absolute way: Ps 48:2; 76:2; 86:10; 96:4; etc.).

"He will be called Son of the Most High" (an expression that, at the very least, puts Jesus in the line of Davidic heir: 2 Sm 7:14; Ps 2:7).

"The Lord God will give Him the throne of David His father; He will rule over the house of Jacob forever, and His reign will have no end" (formulation absolutely classic of Davidic Messiahship, drawn from the prophecy of Nathan: cf. 2 Sm 7). The perspective does not yet transcend the national horizon; it will be left to Simeon at the Presentation to reveal the universalist aspect of Jesus' mission.

He will be *"holy"* (again after the manner of God and in an absolute way: Lv 19:2; Ps 71:22; 89:19; 99:5).

He *"will be called the Son of God"* (this, according to Luke, is the pinnacle of the revelation brought by Gabriel and the strongest affirmation of the transcendence of Jesus, as evidenced by three other uses of the same title in the Gospel of Luke: 3:22; 9:35; 22:69-70).

It is within and in function of this Christological revelation that Luke and the first Christian communities understood the vocation of Mary. To be sure, they had not attained the level of the theological explication that was to mark the Council of Ephesus. But it is interesting—and important—to note how this perception of Mary's role originated and was expressed in strict correlation with faith in the Divine Sonship of Christ.

2. A Revelation about the Vocation of Mary

The great originality of Luke, no doubt, is to have integrated with his basic literary genre the characteristic themes of another important genre: that of *accounts of vocation* or calling. The way in which Mary is called, her dialogue with the Angel, and her response place her, by exceptional title, in the line of those whom God summons to a specific mission within the History of Salvation.

Mary learns from the Angel Gabriel that she has *"God's favor,"* favor that is a sign of both a personal quality and a Divine choice in view of a mission (Noah—Gn 6:8; Abraham—Gn 18:3; Moses—Ex 33:13, 16, 17). The term used here assumes a connotation of permanence and excellence. It is the new name given to Mary: *you who have God's favor.*

The second part of the salutation also has a properly vocational tenor: *"The Lord is with you"* (this is how God assures His presence with those whom He chooses in view of a particular mission, promising to act with them in behalf of His people: Gn 28:15; 31:3; Ex 3:12; Dt 31:23; Jos 1:9; 3:7; Jgs 6:12; 6:16; Is 41:10; Jer 1:8, 19; 15:20).

Mary's reaction to the situation is that of the Patriarchs and Prophets before God Who calls: she is *"troubled"* and asks the messenger to explain the *"how"* of her mission (as Abraham and Gideon had done: Gn 15:8 and Jgs 6:15). The Angel's reply, *"Do not fear, Mary,"* is the immediate preparation for the announcement of a mission (Gn 15:1; 21:17; 26:24; Jgs 6:23; Is 10:24; Dn 10:12, 19): Mary will bear a Son and it is she who will give Him His name.

Mary thus receives a vocation or calling to motherhood, but motherhood that will be entirely under the sign of the "Holy Spirit," and will be the manifestation of God's active presence with His people (*"the power of the Most High will overshadow you"*: cf. Ex 40:35; Nm 9:18, 22, 10:34). The sign that Gabriel then gives appears as confirmation of Mary's vocation.

Lastly, Mary's response indicates free and complete acceptance of the vocation just revealed to her: *"I am the handmaid (servant) of the Lord"* in fact marks acceptance of a change of destiny (Ru 3:9; 1 Sm 25:41) and total dedication to God's plan of salvation for His people (it makes use of the name the Bible gives to Abraham, Moses, David, and the Servant of Yahweh).

3. Fulfillment of the Promises Made to Israel

Luke, as we have seen, finds to his purpose accounts of miraculous birth in the Old Testament and accounts of vocation. These serve him to present the mission of Jesus and the vocation of Mary as the culmination and full realization of the promises made to Israel. What Luke means to say is that the God Who intervened at the conception and birth of Jesus is the same God Who intervened at the time of the Patriarchs, the Judges, the Monarchy, and the Prophets. It is in Jesus that the initial promise made to Abraham finds its fulfillment, *"for nothing is impossible with God"* (v. 37; cf. Gn 18:14). The Son of the promise is Jesus.

Likewise, Mary's vocation has to be understood in reference to the collective history of Israel: she herself will say it in her *Magnificat,* but it is already discernible in the words employed by Gabriel to greet her: *"Rejoice, O highly favored daughter"* (v. 28). Mary personifies the Daughter of Zion (cf. Zep 3:14-17). Symbol of the "Remnant" that has remained faithful to Yahweh, she is invited to rejoice in the coming of the Messianic age and the presence in her of the Messiah.

The Annunciation is the First Joyful Mystery of the Rosary.

J. P. Prevost

APOCALYPSE 12

SEE   *Revelation 12*

APOCRYPHA AND MARY

SEE   *Holy Land and Mary, 2 b*

1. Importance and Types of Apocrypha

THE word "apocrypha" comes from the Greek for "hidden" or "secret." It is a name given to a wide body of works written on the margin of the Sacred Scriptures and often manifesting some connection with those Scriptures. The basic meaning is that books so called were noncanonical—that is, not accepted as Sacred Scripture by the Church or allowed to be read during the Liturgy (although some of them are cited in the New Testament and in the Liturgy).

A secondary meaning is that such works are of spurious origin or are unorthodox and esoteric in content, although originally the term was one of dignity and respect. The apocryphal book was "too sacred and secret to be in everybody's hands and thus must be *reserved for the initiate*, the inner circle of believers" (M. Rhodes Montague).

This accounts for the fact that among the Apocrypha we have three different types of writings comprising: (1) *ecclesiastical literature*, such as the *Epistle to Barnabas, Pope Saint Clement's First Epistle to the Corinthians,* and the *Shepherd of Hermas*—works that are part of a group called the Apostolic Fathers; (2) *personal doctrinal teaching and authoritative data,* such as the *Gospel According to the Hebrews,* once used by the Church Fathers and later set aside; and (3) a *blend of popular piety, folklore, and authentic traditions,* such as the *Protevan-gelium of James, Gospel of Pseudo-Matthew,* the *Gospels of the Infancy,* the *Gospel of Nicodemus,* the works on the *Passing of Mary,* and the *History of Joseph the Carpenter.*

2. The "Gospel of Mary"

It is this last type of writing that contains information about Mary. The works herein attempted to fill the gaps in the story of Mary told by the Gospels. The most important of the Apocrypha for Marian details is unquestionably the *Protevan-gelium of James* (also known as the *Book of James*). Indeed, we could call it the "Gospel of Mary," for it has rightly been termed "the first Christian writing to exhibit an independent interest in the person of Mary."

Dated about the middle of the 2nd century and of un-known authorship, this Gospel acted as the main source for similar infancy Gospels, such as the *Gospel of Pseudo-Matthew* and the much later *Gospel of Mary's Nativity.* "Because of its literary form, marked by some degree of beauty, the direct and serious manner in which the tale is set forth and the deeply de-votional spirit it expresses, this work seems certainly outstand-ing among all the apocryphal texts. If we overlooked a detail here and there, this work may be described as being of all the Apocrypha closest to the high level of the canonical writings" (H. Daniel-Rops).

The *Protevangelium* gives (1) the miraculous birth of Mary after its announcement by an Angel to her aged parents Joachim and Ann; (2) the presentation of Mary in the Temple at three years of age; (3) Mary's betrothal to Joseph, an old man lined up with a group of youths all vying for Mary's hand, who is pointed out as the husband favored by God through a sign (a dove flies out of his rod and alights on his head); (4) the Annunciation with added details (see below); (5) Joseph's doubt; (6) the birth of Jesus in a cave outside Bethlehem; (7) the midwife's testimony to Mary's virginity and Mary's vindi-cation before the High Priest; (8) the slaughter of the innocents and John the Baptist's escape from Herod's fury; and (9) the murder of Zechariah by Herod's soldiers.

The book is filled with little details that throughout the centuries turned up in Marian art and literature, such as: (1) Mary is a descendant of David; (2) her birth is miraculous; (3) the "brothers of the Lord" are sons of Joseph by a former marriage; and (4) the Annunciation takes place in Jerusalem.

3. Other Marian Details

1. *Mary's virginity.* Many apocryphal works mention or allude to this point. In addition to the already noted *Protevangelium*, other works that are important in this regard are the *Odes of Solomon*, a Jewish-Christian psalmbook of the 1st or 2nd century; the *Acts of Peter*, written about 180/190 in Asia Minor or Rome; the *Sibylline Oracles*, a Jewish-Hellenist work from the 2nd century; the *Ascension of Isaiah*, a 2nd-century Christian revision of a Jewish writing; and the *History of Joseph the Carpenter*, a narrative dating from the 4th or 5th century and extant in Arabic.

2. *Mary's intercession.* Some of the works hint at Mary's power of mediation and intercession with Christ. The *Sibylline Oracles* state that God allotted seven periods for penance to straying humans "thanks to the Holy Virgin." A late compilation, the *Arabic Gospel of the Infancy*, recounts two miracles of the Infant Jesus worked for women who appealed to Mary. The 3rd or 4th century work, *Book of the Resurrection of Christ*, has the Apostles asking Mary to pray to the Lord to reveal to them the things that are in heaven.

The *Assumption of the Virgin*, a group of works from the 3rd or 4th century, has many texts concerning Mary's intercession. Finally, the *Apocalypse of Paul*, dated in the 3rd or 4th century, describes the coming of Mary in glory before her Son's coming in glory.

3. *Mary's feasts.* The most important work in this regard is the already mentioned *Protevangelium*, which gave rise to three feasts: the Conception of Mary, the Nativity of Mary, and the Presentation of Mary in the Temple. One could also say that the Assumption apocrypha had a hand in propagating the teaching of Mary's Assumption that ultimately culminated in the feast.

4. *Mary's titles.* Some of the Apocrypha have what amount to titles of Mary. The *Book of the Resurrection of Christ* calls Mary the "Highly Favored One," "Tabernacle of the Most High," "Salvation of the World," "Mother, Queen, and Servant," and "Mother of the Heavenly King."

5. *Mary and the Passion.* The 4th-century *Gospel of Nicodemus* or *Acts of Pilate* gives details about Mary during the Passion of Jesus. It mentions Mary's meeting with Jesus on the way to Calvary (4th Station of the Cross) as well as Veronica wiping the face of Jesus (6th Station). At the Cross, Mary is portrayed as overwhelmed with grief, weeping, and crying aloud—all aspects that were depicted by the artists of the Middle Ages. The *Gospel of Gamaliel,* which forms part of this Apocryphal book, describes an appearance of the risen Jesus to His Mother.

6. *Other Details.* In the *Protevangelium,* Mary at the Annunciation sees the Angel Gabriel twice—first when she is drawing water at the well and second when she is busy spinning at home. The *Sibylline Oracles* add nice touches to the Annunciation scene: Mary laughs, and her cheeks become flushed; she rejoices and is touched in her heart with shame—but she takes courage. Finally, the *History of Joseph the Carpenter* (4th to 7th century) portrays Mary as comforting Joseph in his old age and dying agony and urges that Joseph be invoked by the poor.

A. Buono

APPARITIONS   [67]

SEE *Apparitions*	*Guadalupe*	*Mount Carmel*
after Vatican II	*La Salette*	*Notre Dame du Cap*
Banneux	*Loreto*	*Pontmain*
Beauraing	*Lourdes*	*Rue du Bac*
Czestochowa	*Medjugorje*	*Syracuse*
Fatima	*Miraculous Medal*	

THE place that certain shrines of Marian apparitions have in the life of the Church is well known. Lourdes and Fatima, to mention two of the most prominent, are centers of pilgrimage renowned the world over.

An apparition may be termed "a manifestation of God, Angels or the dead (Saints or not) appearing under a form that surprises the senses" (L. Bouyer). What this definition says, among other things, is that the mode of perception in an apparition is of the sensory order, whereas the reality that makes an appearance either is not sensible in itself (God, Angels, nonresurrected dead) or is not sensible under the ordinary conditions of our present mode of knowledge (the case of the glorified bodies of Christ and Mary).

An authentic apparition, therefore, is not a purely subjective experience. It results from a real, "objective," intervention of a higher power that enables the beneficiary to make true contact with the being that appears and makes itself known. But the important thing here is not how to define the modalities of such a "perception" (modalities that, at least in some of their aspects, are necessarily beyond the scope of our usual experience). The important thing is rather to be able, on the basis of a number of criteria, to establish the authenticity of the supernatural intervention.

The apparitions of Mary testify to her active presence in the life of the Church. They are a special manifestation of the "maternal love" by which "she cares for the brothers and sisters of her Son who still journey on earth" (LG 62). Their purpose is not to bring a new revelation but to recall and focus attention on this or that aspect of the Gospel teaching. Mary can only repeat, in all her messages, what she said to the waiters at Cana when directing them (and us) to Jesus: *"Do whatever He tells you"* (Jn 2:5), sometimes with reference to this or that aspect especially needed in a given time or place.

If the message or messages of an "apparition" are at variance with a revealed doctrine or the teaching of the Church, that is a clear sign of nonauthenticity, or conscious or unconscious falsification. It is for ecclesiastical authority (and first of all for bishops in their respective dioceses) to determine if an apparition attributed to Mary meets the guarantees of authenticity. Only then may public veneration in the place of apparition and promulgation of the message be authorized.

The decisions of ecclesial authority in this matter are not infallible and do not command the inner assent of faith. Nevertheless, when the authority "interdicts"—says no—the external compliance demanded of the faithful binds the conscience to obedience. In no way could Mary work against the Church of her Son.

The extraordinary or "miraculous" aspect of an apparition has its importance, but it ought not to become the principal object of attention. Instead, we should be intent on the aspects of the Gospel message pointed out by Mary (conversion, prayer, penance, etc.) for our life as children of God or the needs of the Church and the world. This is the response desired by her whose mission is to lead us, maternally, to her Son so that we might live by Him.

J. Giens

APPARITIONS AFTER VATICAN II   [67]

SEE			
	Apparitions	*La Salette*	*Mount Carmel*
	Banneux	*Loreto*	*Notre Dame du Cap*
	Beauraing	*Lourdes*	*Pontmain*
	Czestochowa	*Medjugorje*	*Rue du Bac*
	Fatima	*Miraculous Medal*	*Syracuse*
	Guadalupe		

THE Church always has the same attitude toward apparitions: prudence in every case, frequently strong reservations, and at times even hostility accompanied by prohibitions. Such an attitude is also the primary reflex of priests: from Father Peyramale of Lourdes in the 1800's to Bishop Zanic Mostar, who has manifested in an energetic manner his opposition to Medjugorje.

This severity is in line with the word of Christ: *"Blessed are they who have not seen and have believed"* (Jn 20:29), since faith is precisely to believe God *at His word.* In addition, the recipients of the apparitions, those seers who seem to have a direct line to heaven, overshadow somewhat the official authority, which can lead to conflicts. Finally, within the last few decades other causes have slowly led to reservations and apprehensions: critical currents in theology, the vogue in psychoanalysis all too ready to explain mystical phenomena by neurosis, and the rationalist or idealist philosophies that relativize and subjectivize faith.

At the conclusion of the Second Vatican Council, someone wrote: "Good-bye apparitions. Lourdes will have to shut down. And religion, finally accommodated to modernity, will dispel the last vestiges of the mythological era."

However, nothing of the sort has taken place. Instead, after the Council, the number of pilgrims to Lourdes has regularly continued to increase until it has become twice that before the Council, even though new apparitions have taken place elsewhere.

The Church had combated many of these new apparitions and seemed to have renounced forever the recognition of others. Indeed, the last recognitions were of the apparitions in 1932-1933 for the events at Beauraing and Banneux in Belgium.

1. Change of Attitude toward Apparitions

However, in 1987 everything changed. On November 21, feast of the Presentation of Mary, Pio Bello Ricardo, Bishop of Los Tequel in Venezuela, recognized as authentic the ongoing apparitions of the Blessed Virgin at Finca Betania, within the territory of his diocese. What makes the recognition even more noteworthy is that the Bishop was a theologian who had pursued higher studies as well as a psychologist who had taught at the University of Caracas and specialized in religious and mystical phenomena.

Other new events also took place. Numerous bishops, in various forms, granted recognition not to *apparitions in themselves* that took place in their dioceses but to the *cult* that resulted from the apparitions.

At Cuapa (Nicaragua), the bishop wrote a preface to a book that recounted the apparitions of the Blessed Virgin to a fifty-year-old layman, Bernardo, from May 8 to October 13, 1981. And he invited the faithful to participate in the discernment in prayer.

At Kibeho (Rwanda), on August 15, 1988, Bishop Gahamanyi authorized the cult connected with the apparitions that had not yet been terminated.

In Akita (Japan), in the diocese of Niigate, a statue of the Blessed Virgin had emitted tears and blood. A national commission believed that the phenomenon could be attributed to ectoplasmic influence of the seer on the statue. Bishop Ito was not satisfied with such bizarre explanations that were deprived of all scientific value. He had rigorous medical and physiochemical tests performed on the blood, the tears, and the sweat. Then he approved the cult with expressions that were favorable to the apparitions in themselves. (In 1984 he set down in a pastoral letter the reasons for his acceptance of events at Akita as supernatural.)

At San Nicolas (Argentina), apparitions of the Blessed Mother were witnessed by Gladys, the mother of a family. And an official act equal to a recognition of the cult has been posited: the bishop has laid the first stone of a Marian shrine to receive pilgrims, among whom there abound graces and conversions (which for that matter also occur in the places cited above).

In the case of Medjugorje, the bishop of Mostar had more than once announced his negative judgment concerning the apparitions. But when he went to propose it at Rome (at the end of April 1986), Cardinal Ratzinger did not accept it. Instead, in the first case of its kind, the Cardinal transferred the responsibility for deciding about the apparitions to the Yugoslavian Episcopal Conference.

2. Status of Apparitions in the Church

Why is there such a sharp difference of opinion about apparitions? The answer is that it stems from the ambiguous position of these events in history and law.

Apparitions have a status in the Church that is very modest and precarious. The Magisterium (or Teaching Office) of the Church maintains a reserve because in this matter it possesses a competence that is rather limited. When it teaches Revelation and the Creed, things are completely different, because in that case the Magisterium speaks in the name of God and can anathematize whoever refuses to believe. But when apparitions are at issue, the Teaching Office never becomes formally involved.

It is true that Church authority has recognized the apparitions at Guadalupe, Lourdes, Knock, and Fatima: and John Paul II has visited these four shrines. However, the Church does not oblige her members to believe in such apparitions. In these cases, in fact, the Church says only that there are good reasons to believe, that such places have borne fruits; but she never demands belief. Everyone remains free to believe or not.

What is the reason for this largesse? The Church has received authority and infallibility to transmit the Revelation given once and for all by Christ. But particular revelations or apparitions are something else. They are "news items" in the life of the Church, and they bring into play hypothesis and conjecture. In this case or that, is it true that Jesus appeared? Did Mary really appear? On this point, no one can pronounce infallibly, not even the highest authority. The Pope has always avoided proffering judgments in such cases.

Hence, in these cases, we can arrive at merely conjectural discernment, which is customarily the task of the bishop of the place (or the episcopal conference in our time) and proceed necessarily by gropings in accord with criteria that are not always easy to apply. In substance, one asks: "Is this event in harmony with or contrary to Revelation, or to faith and morals? Are the seers sincere persons or hypocrites, healthy or sick, saints or sinners?"

Furthermore, "Are there signs, such as healings, that are scientifically recognized?" Finally, there is the fundamental criterion: "Are there spiritual fruits or not?" This is the measuring stick that Jesus recommends: *"You can tell a tree by its fruits. . . . A sound tree cannot bear bad fruit any more than a decayed tree can bear good fruit"* (Mt 7:16-20). These are the criteria of discernment established in 1977 by Cardinal Seper, prefect of the Congregation for the Doctrine of the Faith.

3. Message of the Apparitions

Already at the Council, the Church had distanced herself from a certain ecclesiastical juridicism that looked with severity upon apparitions from the outside, without interest for their fruits. After the Council, in 1970, Paul VI abolished Canon 1385 of the old Code of Canon Law, which prohibited "books and pamphlets that speak of new apparitions, revelations, visions, prophecies, and miracles." And John Paul II, man of openness and discernment, has inaugurated in the Church a more open attentiveness to the inspirations of the Spirit.

If we turn to the apparitions that seem in conformity with the fundamental criteria of the Church, we can establish that their total message presents notable agreements that can be summarized as follows. Our world has tranquilly abandoned itself to sin and is self-destructing; indeed, it is digging its own grave. (When the apparitions at Medjugorje and Kibeho began, the two Great World Powers were continuing to seek peace through the armaments race and the balance of terror.)

But above all, these messages insist on the scourge of moral degradation. We are witnessing the worldwide erosion of the family, with a spectacular diminution of marriages and the increase of divorces and free unions. The consequences are grave above all for children, who represent the future of humankind.

And the remedies that the apparitions suggest are precisely evangelical invitations: return to God through faith, conversion, and fasting. In a world in which satanism is raging, even though in disguise, the apparitions echo the words of Christ in the Gospel: *"This kind of demon does not leave but by prayer and fasting"* (Mt 17:21).

Thus, the convergent message of recent apparitions is the sin of the world, the evangelical remedy, and Mary's maternal exhortation for peace and reconciliation of human beings through the only way possible, which is the loving acceptance of God in the prayer of the heart.

[The above is a digest of a lengthy article by René Laurentin, the noted international authority on apparitions of Mary, which appeared in the February 1990 issue of the Italian magazine "Jesus."]

A. Buono

ARCHEOLOGY (AND MARY)

SEE   *Holy Land and Mary, 2*

THE science of archeology in its many forms can be of great help to Mariology. Any facts it throws on the life and work of Jesus necessarily influence Marian studies. In addition, archeology sometimes unearths sites directly related to Mary as described in the article on the *Holy Land and Mary.* At other times, digs that are unconnected with either Christ or Mary have yielded significant contributions to our knowledge of Our Lady and devotion to her. The following are only some examples.

Excavations at Nazareth at the site of the Basilica of the Annunciation have brought to the surface some *thirty inscriptions and graffiti* in Greek, Hebrew, Aramaic, Syriac, and Armenian. These inscriptions offer sure proof that the Judeo-Christians of Palestine believed in the Divinity of Christ before the Council of Nicaea and practiced devotion to the Martyrs and to Mary as early as the 3rd century.

A Jewish-Christian cemetery in Jerusalem has yielded numerous evangelical names in Hebrew (among them, *Mary* and Simon Bar Jonah) and in Greek (Jairus and Zaccariah) as well as Christian symbols. This fact has a bearing on the historicity of the Gospel that mentions a certain "Mary" as well as the events in which she took part.

The *Roman Catacombs* also provide important information on the Blessed Virgin. Inscriptions and graffiti under

Saint Peter's Basilica stemming back to the 2nd or 3rd century portray Mary as a Protectrix for the Christian departed and their Mediatrix with Christ. In the *Catacombs of Saint Priscilla,* there are frescoes with the same theme.

The *Inscription of Abercius,* discovered by W. M. Ramsay in 1883, is the epitaph of Abercius Marcellus, Bishop of Hieropolis in Phrygia Salutaris (d. 200). It records his travels to Rome and Nisibis and with the use of early Christian symbolism renders testimony to the Eucharist. At the same time, it also states: "I followed Paul and was led everywhere by faith who gave me the nourishment of fish from a powerful and pure spring. A *spotless Virgin* took it up into her hands and gave it to her friends to eat forever, having sweet wine and extending the mixed cup with bread." Mariologists see this as a very early reference to Our Lady, indicating her virginity and holiness as well as her relationship with the Eucharist.

A *Jewish burial inscription* found in Egypt and stemming from the first century serves to reinforce the Tradition of Mary's perpetual virginity. It uses the word "firstborn" in the very same way Luke applied it to Mary and her child without prejudice to her perpetual virginity. It describes a woman as having given birth to a firstborn child although that woman died in childbirth and *would have no others.* This fact helps answer objections to Mary's virginity based on Luke 2:7.

A. Buono

ASSUMPTION   [966f]

SEE *Cult of Mary*   *Intercession*
     Dormition, Holy Land   *Motherhood, Spiritual*
       and Mary, 3h   *Munificentissimus Deus*
     Feasts of Mary   *Rosary*

"**B**Y the authority of Our Lord Jesus Christ, of the Blessed Apostles Peter and Paul, and by our own proper authority we pronounce, declare, and define as Divinely revealed dogma that Mary, Immaculate Mother of God ever Virgin, after finishing the course of her life on earth, was taken up in body and soul to heavenly glory." By these words Pope Pius XII, exercising Pontifical Infallibility, "declared" on November 1, 1950, that the Assumption was a dogma of faith and was henceforth to be believed as such by the faithful (*Bull Munificentissimus*).

1. Content of the Dogma

(a) The language of the Definition is very precise as to its object: "having finished the course of her life on earth," Mary was "glorified in body and soul." That is to say, Mary is *already* in the state that will be true of the elect *after* the "resurrection of the dead." This implies a *transition* from the bodily state proper to life on earth to the state, mysterious but real, proper to eternal life.

In the case of Mary, how was the transition realized? Was it by an immediate transformation without going through death, i.e., without prior separation of the soul from the body? Or was it by an anticipated resurrection, which presupposes that Mary was dead?

The Definition purposely does not take a position on this point. It remains a question that theologians may freely debate. Discussion aside, let it simply be said that the opinion that Mary, like her Son, passed through death in order to be raised up, immediately or after a short interval, has by far the stronger support in tradition.

Also noteworthy is the expression, Mary "was taken up to heavenly glory" (whereas the Ascension means that Jesus "went up to heaven"). Mary received what God alone can give.

(b) Pius XII defined the Assumption as a dogma of faith after assuring himself of the "universal, certain and firm consent of the Church's Ordinary Magisterium," together with its corollary: the concordant belief of the faithful. Such belief flows from the people's adherence to the Magisterium's teaching, but in the course of history the people also have influenced the Magisterium. The "sense of the faithful" (*sensus fidelium*) is a "theological source" (*locus theologicus*).

(c) In no way was there question of a new revelation. Hence, if the Assumption was to be declared a "Divinely revealed dogma," it had somehow to be contained in the established sources of Revelation. The Bull *Munificentissimus* takes note of this, saying that the "ultimate basis" of the defined truth was found in Sacred Scripture. However, in referring it to the Bible the papal document does not mean to suggest that the Assumption can be "read" there in an immediate and explicit manner. In the present state of Biblical scholarship, it seems difficult to go beyond this statement: that the dogma of the Assumption, "Divinely revealed," is really contained in Revelation in an implicit manner.

2. The Meaning of the Assumption for Mary

(a) *A culmination. "Blessed is she who has believed . . ."* (Lk 1:45). The promises of the Lord were fulfilled for Mary, and as always, beyond all expectation.

Her glorification in body and soul results from the Divine munificence. But it also came, so to speak, as the logical conclusion of her vocation on earth and the way she lived it. Her Divine Motherhood is in utter harmony with her Assumption, as are her Immaculate Conception and Perpetual Virginity, both called for by the supernatural motherhood. How could the body of her in whom *"the Word was made flesh"* to save the flesh have known the corruption of the grave? Or the body of her who totally escaped the power of sin? And the body of her who, by her virginal consecration, belonged to her Son and His mission in a perfect and exclusive way?

The association of Mary with her Divine Son is one of the leitmotifs of the Second Vatican Council's *Constitution on the Church*, chapter 8. Mary was "predestined from eternity, by the decree of Divine providence that determined the incarnation of the Word, to be the Mother of God. . . . Above all others and in a singular way, she was on earth the generous associate and humble handmaid of the Lord" (LG 61). We can say, therefore, that in the Divine mind—so far as revealed to us—Mary is indissolubly linked with the Word Who became flesh in her. She has no purpose except in Him and for Him.

This union, founded on the Divine Motherhood, extends to constant and "unique" association in the work of salvation. From the "Yes" of the Annunciation to the sorrowful assent of Calvary, Mary, "embracing God's salvific will with a full heart . . . devoted herself totally to the person and the work of her Son" (LG 56). If anyone has "followed Christ" to the utmost, without the least failing, it is Mary. How, then, could He not but gather her with Him, body and soul, to the glory to which the Cross is the way and the portal? What other "recompense" could be imagined for Mary than this immediate and total participation in the life of the Risen Lord?

(b) *A beginning.* Mary is now *in* eternal life. For her, on the personal level, this means the joy and blessedness that comes from loving and beholding the God Who is Light, Life, Love. It also means fullness of communion with all who love God, with all whom God loves—and God loves everything He has made, creation being the effect of His love. But though the blessedness of eternal life is true of all elect in heaven, it is true of Mary in a very special way, not only because she is in perfect "glory" but also because her Assumption enables her even now to live her blessedness in the fullness of her glorified humanity.

And it does not mark the end of her "service." On the contrary, her service could now assume its universal dimensions: "Taken up to heaven, she did not lay aside her salvific duty. . . . By her maternal love she cares for the brothers and sisters of her Son who still journey on earth" (LG 62).

Yes, Mary is now in a position to exercise fully her "Motherhood in the order of grace," without interruption "until the eternal fulfillment of all the elect" (LG 62). And it is not immaterial, here as always, that Mary's "maternal love" for us engages not only her soul but all the powers of her human nature lifted up to glory.

3. The Assumption and Us

(a) Anything that "happens" to Mary concerns the Church, of which she is a member, a type and Mother. What the Lord did for Mary in her Assumption is for the Church a sign and promise of the total glory.

(b) By His Incarnation in the womb of Mary, Christ wanted to take upon Himself everything human so as to restore it to the Father through the Spirit. Consequently, nothing "human" should escape His influence. The road He asked His Mother to travel to arrive at the glory of the Assumption, pursuant to her exceptional vocation, is the road for us to travel according to our vocation. Far from inviting withdrawal from the needs of the world, the Assumption of Mary calls us to positive service in daily life, for the Lord and fellow humans.

(c) For Mary the Assumption is truly a "privilege"—not a privilege that separates her from us but one that brings her nearer and makes her more present. The kinship of faith that unites us with our Mother "in the order of grace" takes its quality and strength in part from the fact that her glorified Heart is immersed in it.

The Assumption is the Fourth Glorious Mystery of the Rosary.

A. Bossard

AVE MARIA

SEE   *Hail Mary*

- B -

BANNEUX (Belgium) [67]

SEE *Apparitions*   *Apparitions after Vatican II*

THE apparitions of the Virgin of the Poor took place in 1933 at Banneux, a small town about 15 miles from Liège in Belgium.

Mariette Beco, to whom the Virgin appeared, was 11 years old. She was the eldest of seven children. The family was poor and lived along the edge of a pine forest.

There were eight apparitions in all, from January 15 to March 2, 1933. And all occurred about seven o'clock in the evening.

The particular veneration of Mary at Banneux, the coming of pilgrims and contingent of afflicted, and the spread of the Virgin's message all had their origin in the visits of the Virgin to little Mariette and the words she spoke to the child.

It is for us to seek the graces of the Virgin's visiting and to heed the message that comes like an echo from the Gospel.

The Church took note in the person of Bishop Kerkhofs of Liège, who, in 1949, officially recognized the reality of the apparitions at Banneux. Hence, an account of the apparitions is of more than passing interest:

Sunday, January 15, 1933
The Holy Virgin, in resplendent light, prays, smiles on Mariette and motions her to come closer.

Wednesday, January 18, 1933
This time the Holy Virgin, after praying at some length, leads the child to the Spring and says: *"Dip your hands in the water. This Spring is set apart for me. Good evening. Good-bye for now."*

Thursday, January 19, 1933
Mariette asks: *"Who are you, my Beautiful Lady?"* The Virgin replies: *"I am the VIRGIN OF THE POOR,"* and then,

46

for the second time, leads the child to the Spring and says: *"This Spring is set apart for all countries, to help the sick. I will pray for you. Good-bye for now."*

Friday, January 20, 1933
Mariette asks: *"What is your wish, my Beautiful Lady?"* The Virgin replies: *"I would like a small chapel."* Then she blesses the child with an imposition of the hands and the Sign of the Cross.

Saturday, February 11, 1933
A third time the Holy Virgin leads the child to the Spring and says: *"I come to relieve suffering. Good-bye for now."*

Wednesday, February 15, 1933
Mariette says: *"Holy Virgin, Father told me to ask a sign from you."* The Virgin replies: *"Trust me. I will trust you."* Then she confides a secret to her and adds: *"Pray much. Good-bye for now."*

Monday, February 20, 1933
A fourth time the Holy Virgin leads Mariette to the Spring, and says: *"My dear child, pray much. Good-bye for now."*

Tuesday, March 2, 1933
"I am the MOTHER OF THE SAVIOR, MOTHER OF GOD. Pray much. Farewell!" But before disappearing for good the Holy Virgin blesses the child as on January 20, with an imposition of hands and the Sign of the Cross.

M. Van Loon

BEAURAING (Belgium)   [67]

SEE *Apparitions*   *Apparitions after Vatican II*

"HERE, under the hawthorn, in the course of her latest apparitions, the Virgin manifested her Immaculate Heart."
After Fatima, another "sign for this generation" is provided at Beauraing in the year 1932. The 33 apparitions of the Blessed Virgin covered the period from November 29, 1932, to January 3, 1933.

Five children were beckoned by the smile of Our Lady. They belonged to two families, weak in the practice of their faith: two sisters and a brother from one family and two sisters from another, whose third daughter never saw the apparitions.

Four of the children are still living, as is the mother of one of them. The fifth died in June 1978. One of the four survivors is a widow. All five married and raised a family, while exhibiting prudence, courage, and complete selflessness. They have remained completely loyal to Our Lady and the place of the apparitions, called "the Garden."

The Garden was the recreational ground of a school the children attended. Beginning with the third evening of the apparitions, the Holy Virgin was seen along the road, by the hawthorn of the Garden. The children were skeptical and could not imagine themselves to be other "Bernadettes."

In 1942 Bishop Charve (d. 1977) gave provisional approval to special veneration of Mary at Beauraing, and in 1949 acknowledged the facts as authentic.

The Immaculate Heart of Mary, the most prominent feature of the last six evenings that she appeared, is a sign and messenger of the values of the heart, for a life of faith and family life today.

The Virgin identified herself to the children:

"I AM THE IMMACULATE VIRGIN" (12/21/32).

"THE MOTHER OF GOD, QUEEN OF HEAVEN" (1/3/33).

On three occasions there was this distinct request: "PRAY MUCH. PRAY ALWAYS."

Mary was calling to the Church when she asked for "A CHAPEL" (12/17/32) and "FOR PEOPLE TO COME HERE IN PILGRIMAGE" (12/23/32).

She refers us to the Gospel: "I WILL CONVERT SINNERS."—"DO YOU LOVE MY SON? DO YOU LOVE ME? THEN SACRIFICE FOR ME. FAREWELL" (1/31/33).

The annual pilgrimage day is August 22. The number of pilgrims and visitors from year to year is about 200,000. At least two cures have been recognized as miraculous.

A. Chenot

BERNARD (SAINT)

SEE   *Servants of Mary*

BETHLEHEM

SEE   *Holy Land and Mary, 2b*

BIRTH OF CHRIST

SEE   *Infancy Narratives*   *Rosary*
       Life of Mary

BIRTH OF MARY

SEE   *Feasts of Mary*   *Holy Land and Mary 2*

"THE present Feast forms a link between the New and the Old Testament. It shows that Truth succeeds symbols and figures and that the New Covenant replaces the Old. Hence, all creation sings with joy, exults, and participates in the joy of this day.... This is, in fact, the day on which the Creator of the world constructed His temple; today is the day on which by a stupendous project a creature becomes the preferred dwelling of the Creator" (Saint Andrew of Crete).

"Let us celebrate with joyful hearts the birth of the Virgin Mary, of whom was born the Sun of Justice.... [Her birth constitutes] the dawn of hope and salvation to the world" (Mass of the Feast).

As these texts so clearly indicate, an atmosphere of *joy and light* pervades the Birth of the Virgin Mary.

1. Historical Details about the Feast

The origin of this Feast is sought in Palestine. It goes back to the consecration of a church in Jerusalem, which tradition identifies as that of the present basilica of St. Ann.

At Rome the Feast began to be kept toward the end of the 7th century, brought there by Eastern monks. Gradually and in varied ways it spread to the other parts of the West in the centuries that followed. From the 13th century on, the celebration assumed notable importance, becoming a Solemnity with a major Octave and preceded by a Vigil calling for a fast. The Octave was reduced to a simple one during the reform of Saint Pius X and was abolished altogether under the reform of Pius XII in 1955. The present Calendar characterizes the Birth of Mary as a "Feast," placing it on the same plane as the Visitation.

For some centuries now, the Birth has been assigned to September 8 both in the East and in the West, but in ancient times it was celebrated on different dates from place to place. However, when the Feast of the Immaculate Conception (which has a later origin than that of the Birth) was extended to the whole Church, the Birth little by little became assigned everywhere to September 8: nine months after the Solemnity of the Immaculate Conception.

2. At the Heart of Salvation

As we know, the Gospels have not transmitted to us anything about the birth of the Virgin Mary. Their attention is completely centered on the mystery of Christ and His salvific mission.

The birth of Mary is recounted by the *Protevangelium of James* (5:2), an apocryphal writing from the end of the 2nd century. Subsequent tradition is based on this account.

The description—although in the manner of an apocryphal document—obviously presents an important historical event: the birth of the Mother of the Lord.

But the problem that concerns us here is the significance of this event. In the case of all the Saints, the Church commemorates their birthday on the day of their return to the Lord. However, in the cases of Saint John the Baptist and the Blessed Virgin, it also celebrates the day of their earthly birth. This is a singular fact already emphasized in ancient times, for example, by Paschasius Radbertus (d. about 859).

The reason for this fact is not found primarily in the greatness or the privileges of the persons involved but in the singular mission that was theirs in the History of Salvation. In this light, the birth of the Blessed Virgin is considered to be—like that of John the Baptizer—in direct relationship with the coming of the Savior of the world. Thus, the birth and existence of Mary—similar to and even more than those of the Baptist—take on a significance that transcends her own person. It is explained solely in the context of the History of Salvation, connected with the People of God of the Old Covenant and the New. Mary's birth lies at the confluence of the two Testaments—bringing to an end the stage of expectation and the promises and inaugurating the new times of grace and salvation in Jesus Christ.

Mary, the Daughter of Zion and ideal personification of Israel, is the last and most worthy representative of the People of the Old Covenant but at the same time she is "the hope and the dawn of the whole world." With her, the elevated Daughter of Zion, after a long expectation of the promises, the times are fulfilled and a new economy is established (LG, 55).

The birth of Mary is ordained in particular toward her mission as Mother of the Savior. Her existence is indissolubly connected with that of Christ: it partakes of a unique plan of predestination and grace. God's mysterious plan regarding the incarnation of the Word embraces also the Virgin who is His Mother. In this way, the Birth of Mary is inserted at the very heart of the History of Salvation.

3. Christological Orientations

The Biblical readings of the Feast have a clear Christological-salvific orientation that forms the backdrop for contemplating the figure of Mary.

Micah 5:1-4a. The Prophet announces the coming of the Lord of Israel Who will come forth from Bethlehem of Judah. The Mother of the Messiah, presented as one about to give birth, will give life to the prince and pastor of the house of David Who will bring justice and peace. She will work with the Messiah to bring forth a new people.

Romans 8:28-30. This passage does not speak directly about Mary but about the believer justified by the grace of

Christ and gifted with the indwelling of the Spirit. He or she has been chosen and called from all eternity to share Christ's life and glory. This is true in a privileged manner for Mary, Spouse and Temple of the Holy Spirit, Mother of God's Son, and intimately united with Him in a Divine plan of predestination and grace.

Matthew 1:1-16, 18-23. The meaning of this seemingly arid genealogy is theologically profound: to place Jesus, the Messiah-Lord, within the dynastic tree of His people. He is a descendant, and in fact "the descendant," of Abraham (cf. Gal 3: 16) and the Patriarchs in accord with the promises, and He is the semi-heir of the Prophets. The ring that united Christ with His people is Mary, Daughter of Zion and Mother of the Lord.

The virginity stressed by the Gospel text is the sign of the Divine origin of the Son and of the absolute newness that now breaks forth in the history of human beings.

The Christological-salvific purpose and tone dominate not only the Bible readings but also the Eucharistic Celebration and the Liturgy of the Hours.

It has been observed that, although the texts of this Feast's celebration are less rich than those of other Marian feasts, they do have one outstanding characteristic: "The number of themes is rather restricted, [but] there are extremely numerous invitations to joy" (J. Pascher).

Indeed, joy pervades the whole of this Feast's liturgy. If many "will rejoice" at the birth of the precursor (cf. Lk 1:14), a much greater joy is stirred up by the birth of the Mother of the Savior. Hence, this is a Feast that serves as a prelude to the "joy to all people" brought about by the Birth of the Son of God at Christmas and expressed by the singing of hymns and carols.

Added to this theme of joy on this Marian Feast is that of light because with Mary's birth the darkness is dispersed and there rises in the world the dawn that announces the Sun of Justice, Christ the Lord.

A. Valentini

- C -

CALVARY

SEE *Cross (Mary at the)*

CANA (John 2:1-12)   [2618]

SEE *Calvary*   *Holy Land and Mary, 2f*
      Faith   *Motherhood, Spiritual*

THE *beginning of the signs of Jesus* has always fascinated commentators. The reason is not only the enigmatic character of the dialogue between Jesus and His Mother, but also the fund of Johannine themes that punctuate the account. Everyone agrees that this first sign is eminently theological and symbolic: the changing of water into wine marks the transition from the old economy to the new economy. There remains, however, great diversity in the interpretation of the central dialogue between Jesus and Mary, as well as in regard to Old Testament influences on the account.

In recent years, moreover, exegetical thought regarding Cana has taken a practically new direction and has benefited from new insights owing, in large part, to the study of traditions found in early extra-Biblical Judaism. This newer interpretation is followed here because of its current attraction and the extremely interesting perspective it opens up for understanding the sign of Cana.

1. A New Reading: Cana and the Experience of Sinai and the Covenant

Given the importance in the Old Testament of Israel's experience at Sinai, it is not surprising that early Jewish traditions devote extensive commentaries to accounts of it (particularly those in Exodus). It appears that John—who read and interpreted the Bible according to the tradition and formation he received from Judaism—not only was familiar with these traditions concerning Sinai and the Covenant but drew upon them for his account of the first sign of Jesus and the first manifestation of His glory.

In the main, the proposed analogy between Sinai and Cana rests on the following considerations:

(a) The immediate context already offers a parallel between Jesus and Moses: *"For while the law was given through Moses, grace and truth came through Jesus Christ"* (1:17).

According to John, then, the work of Jesus is to be understood as the introduction of a new economy. Jesus is the new Moses, bearer of a new Covenant and source of a new order of grace and truth.

(b) The Evangelist presents the sign of Cana explicitly as a *manifestation of Jesus' glory*. Jesus manifests His glory and His disciples believe in Him, just as Yahweh had manifested His glory (Ex 24:16-17) and accredited Moses as His Prophet (Ex 19:9) at the theophany on Sinai.

(c) In rabbinic tradition, wine is a common symbol for the Mosaic Law and the teaching of the Messiah.

(d) Mention of the *"six stone water jars"* prescribed for Jewish ceremonial washings (v. 6) could well be an echo of the purification ordered by Yahweh prior to manifesting Himself to the people: *"Have them wash their garments and be ready for the third day. . . ."* (Ex 19:10-11; cf. also 19: 14-15 and 24:5-8).

(e) Similarly, the opening reference in the Johannine account to the "third day" could be understood in allusion to the Biblical chronology of Sinai and its developments in extra-Biblical Jewish traditions. It was on the third day that Yahweh manifested Himself to Israel: *"Go to the people and consecrate them today and tomorrow. Have them wash their garments and be ready for the third day; for on the third day the Lord will come down on Mount Sinai in the sight of all the people"* (Ex 19: 10-11; cf. 19:6).

(f) The words of Mary to the waiters *"Do whatever He tells you"* (v. 5), correspond perfectly to the words of the people promising to adhere to the Covenant: *"We will do everything the Lord has said"* (Ex 19:8; 24:3, 7; Dt 5:27).

By integrating with his account so many motifs characteristic of the Sinaitic Covenant, John makes evident the recapitulative import of the sign performed by Jesus. The most original and most profound experience of ancient Israel finds here
its peak and completion. Jesus appears as *the Prophet preeminent,* the bearer of a definitive revelation, symbolized by the
new wine, of better quality than the old. Jesus is the new
Moses, promised and awaited: *"I will raise up for them a
prophet like you from among their kinsmen; will put My words
in His mouth, and He will tell them all that I command Him"*
(Dt 18:8; cf. Acts 3:22).

It is clear, however, that John is not slave to a literary
model. At every level of the account one finds a properly Johannine note: the *hour* of Jesus, the *signs,* manifestation of the
glory, the *faith* of the disciples. The presence of these themes
reveals another aspect of the sign of Cana: its prospective significance. The manifestation of the glory of Jesus, at Cana, is
not only the crown and recapitulation of Israel's experience.
According to John, it also has the force of a beginning; it inaugurates the properly Messianic Age and effects the transition
to an absolutely new economy, at the same time that it points
to the coming of the supreme Hour of glorification through the
Cross.

2. The Mother of Jesus and the
Beginning of the Signs

John quite plainly attaches special importance to Mary's
presence and intervention at Cana. But his interest in her is
not simply as an individual person (he does not call her by her
given name, only by her title of *"Mother of Jesus"* or
"Woman"). He presents her more for purposes of the twofold
aspect—recapitulative and prospective—of the first sign performed by Jesus.

By making use of the words of the people declaring their
adherence to the Covenant, Mary becomes the representative
and personification of the Messianic people. By her total recep-
tiveness to the word of her Son, Mary expresses the faith of the
whole Messianic people disposed to receive the revelation

brought by Jesus. It is perhaps in this sense that Jesus addresses Himself to her as to the *Woman* (symbolic name often applied to the people of Israel: Ez 23:2; Is 54:6; Hos 2:4; Jer 3:1, 20).

But Mary does more than represent the people. Her intervention, in fact, is directed to acceptance of the sign that will be performed by her Son. Mary's faith precedes the sign and prepares for it: *"Blessed are they who have not seen and have believed"* (Jn 20:29). Because of her faith Mary is destined to play a role in the creation of the new people, the Messianic community that will form around Jesus, beginning with Cana. Her role is to point the way to Jesus by preparing the acceptance of signs.

The *beginning of the signs* of Jesus also marks an important development in the relationship between Jesus and Mary. The reply of Jesus to Mary's intervention calls into question the relationship that had bound them to each other (v. 4). Jesus asks Mary not to cling to her role of mother but to redirect her life to the service of His mission, to the service of the *signs* and the *Hour.* Mary does not hesitate in the least to make the change her Son wants of her:

"Mary, entirely receptive to the orientation indicated by Jesus, makes a sort of conversion. She relinquishes the former level of her relationship with her Son and adopts a different and extremely positive level. Her influence is no longer exercised on Jesus but is directed to the service of Jesus" (A. Vanhoye).

Mary, in short, accepts the vocation of the *Woman,* which will know its utter fulfillment when the Hour of the supreme Sign arrives, at the Cross (Jn 19:25-27). (SEE *Woman* and *Cross.*)

J. P. Prevost

CARMEL, MOUNT

SEE *Apparitions*   *Feasts of Mary*
   Apparitions after Vatican II

THE liturgical celebration of "Our Lady of Mount Carmel" was extended to the Latin Church in 1726 and is in the new calendar as an Optional Memorial (July 16). It commemorates the cult of Mary on Mount Carmel, the Marian spirituality of the Carmelite Order, and the gift of the scapular.

1. Mount Carmel

Twenty miles from Nazareth, on the border between Samaria and Galilee, Carmel (from the Hebrew *Karem el* = garden and vine of God) is the symbol of grace, blessing, and beauty because of its luxurious vegetation (Is 35:2; Jer 50:19). For the Bible, it is above all the mount of the renewal of the Covenant and of God's interventions through Elijah the Prophet (9th century B.C.). After the challenge by fire, the Israelites return to the one God and renew the Covenant with Him (1 Kgs 18:20-40). Similarly, at Mount Carmel Elijah prays seven times for the life-giving rain eagerly awaited after a long drought and announced by a little cloud rising from the sea (1 Kgs 18:41-46).

In this little cloud carrying the rain of benediction we see a symbol of Mary, Mother of Christ the Savior. Already in the 5th century, Chrysippus of Jerusalem greets the Blessed Virgin as "Hail, Cloud of Rain that offers drink to the souls of the Saints." With the eremeticism of the 12th century, Carmel becomes a place of veneration toward Mary. A book for pilgrims, written about 1220, states: "On Mount Carmel there is a delightful spot, the residence of the Latin hermits called Brothers of Carmel. There is a small church dedicated to the Blessed Virgin."

In the feudal mentality, dedication of a church to Mary signified not only to place oneself at the service of a temple but also to give oneself completely to Mary's disposal with a personal consecration ratified by an oath. Therefore, the Brother Hermits of Carmel chose our Lady as Patroness and their official name became "Brothers of the Blessed Virgin Mary of Mount Carmel."

This title is not limited to indicating Mary's protection over the Carmelites or even their dedication to the Virgin; it also expresses the Gospel similarity existing between Mary and the Carmelites based on their choice of virginity.

Carmel thus becomes Mary's mount where the brother hermits follow the spiritual footsteps of the Blessed Virgin and profess devotion to her. In the 17th century the Sanctuary of Our Lady of Mount Carmel arose with the large monastery of the Carmelites.

2. Marian Spirituality of the Carmelite Order

The commemoration of Our Lady of Mount Carmel calls for a rediscovery of the contemplative dimension of life. Nothing indeed is more foreign to Carmel and to Mary than an exteriority bereft of any intimate union of love with God.

Mount Carmel recalls the Prophet Elijah the man of insistent prayer and the programmatic motto *"The Lord of Hosts lives, and I serve Him . . . today"* (1 Kgs 18:15), and it summons us to encounter God and renew the Covenant with Him. There is no more profound and urgent need for people today—who are in danger of losing themselves in a frenetic chaos without a definitive meaning—than the need to experience God in their own lives.

The great mystical Carmelite authors have had an acute sense of the spiritual life as a "way of perfection" (Saint Teresa of Avila) or "ascent of Mount Carmel" (Saint John of the Cross) or "little way" (Saint Theresa of Lisieux). On this journey Mary is present as Mother and Model of contemplatives, that is, of Christians attuned to the filial listening to the Father through Christ in the Spirit.

A devout Carmelite writer, Arnold Bostio (d. 1499), recommends: "No day, no night, no journey, no study, no conversation, no joy, no labor, and no rest must take place without the resemblance of Mary. In the very vestibule of memory, let her be the first. . . . Every day you will become greater, more interior, stronger, more enlightened, and purer—you will become better because she teaches the ways of God" *(Patronage of the Blessed Virgin Mary)*.

Among the other Carmelite Marian authors a singular place is held by Michael of Saint Augustine (d. 1684) with his celebrated treatise on *"The Marian and Marian-Formed Life,"* which proposes a life of intense communion with Mary as a "new way" of living for God. He bases this constant attitude not on particular visions but on the teaching of the Church concerning Mary's Mediation and Spiritual Motherhood.

The reference to Mary as Mother, Sister, and Patroness pertains to the charism of the Carmelite Order, which can affirm: "The Order of Carmel is totally Marian."

3. The Scapular

The main reason behind the "Solemn Commemoration of Our Lady of Mount Carmel" was gratitude for the benefits granted to the Carmelite Order. Among these were the apostolic approval of the victory gained at Cambridge in 1374 regarding the legitimacy of the Marian title to be attributed to the Order itself.

A special grace of the Virgin toward the Carmelites that was to shine in the Christian people is thus reported by the *Viridarium* of John Grossi (written about 1400): "Simon Stock begged the glorious Virgin, Mother of God, Patroness of the Order, to grant some privilege to the Brothers who bear her name. And one day, while he was devoutly reciting a prayer, the glorious Virgin Mary, Mother of God, appeared accompanied by a multitude of Angels, and holding in her hand the scapular of the Order she said: 'Here is the privilege that I grant to you and to all the children of Carmel. Whoever dies clothed in this habit shall be saved.' "

Under the form of a historical account we have the transmission of a conviction of the Carmelite Order: Whoever perseveres in belonging to the Order, symbolized by the habit, will gain eternal salvation. Obviously, it is not a question of a grace deriving from the simple investing of the scapular. Eternal life depends on living the Carmelite ideal of contemplation or hearing of God's Word and zealous service of one's brothers and sisters, an ideal rendered more easily realizable by the protective presence of the Blessed Virgin.

The Christian people are right in preserving the values inherent in the devotion to the scapular as well as trust in the intercession of the Mother of God in the important problem of salvation. However, we must avoid all temptations for magical results and combine such trust with the imitation of Mary's actions in the Gospel.

S. de Fiores

CATECHESIS (CATECHETICAL ACTIVITY) AND MARY [6-10, 426-429, 906, 1074-1075, 1698, 2226]

SEE *Catechism of the Catholic Church and Mary*

THE *General Catechetical Directory* issued by the Sacred Congregation of the Clergy in 1971 describes catechesis or catechetical activity as one of four forms of the ministry of the word that devolves on the Church and every Christian. (1) The *evangelization* form has as its purpose the rousing of the beginnings of faith so that human beings will adhere to the word of God. (2) The *catechetical* form is intended to make people's faith become living, conscious, and active through the light of instruction. (3) The *liturgical* form takes place within the setting of a liturgical celebration, especially that of the Eucharist (e.g., the Homily). (4) The *theological* form is the systematic treatment and the scientific investigation of the truths of faith.

Thus, catechesis is "an education of children, young people, and adults in the faith, which includes especially the teaching of Christian doctrine imparted, generally speaking, in an organic and systematic way, with a view to initiating hearers into the fullness of Christian life" (John Paul II, *Catechesi Tradendae*, 18).

1. A Living Catechism and Model of Catechists

In the 1977 Synod on Catechetics, Mary was called "a living catechism" and "the Mother and Model of catechists" (which category includes directors of religious education, catechists, and parents). These two phrases nicely summarize Our Lady's relationship to catechetical activity.

A Living Catechism. Mary manifests Christ's Spirit in an altogether singular manner because she is *"full of grace"* (Lk

1:28) and a "Model of the Church" (LG 63). The Holy Spirit has fully manifested His gifts in her, for she was preserved from all stain of original sin, remained freely and fully faithful to the Lord, and was assumed body and soul into heavenly glory and completely conformed to "her Son, the Lord of lords, and the Conqueror of sin and death" (LG 59).

Mary is the Mother of God and "Mother to us in the order of grace" (LG 61), the type of the whole Church's virginity and motherhood (LG 63-65), and the sign of a sure hope and solace for the pilgrim people of God (LG 65). Hence, Mary "in a certain way unites and mirrors within herself the central truths of the faith" and she summons believers to her Son and to His sacrifice as well as to love for the Father (LG 62).

Mother and Model of Catechists. By a unique vocation Mary formed her Son—Who was *"the only Son from the Father"* (Heb 10:5) and *"full of grace and truth"* (Jn 1:14)—in human knowledge of the Scriptures and of the history of God's plan for His people, and in adoration of the Father. It was by Mary's side that Jesus progressed steadily in *"wisdom and age and grace"* (Lk 2:52).

Mary was also His *first disciple in time.* When she found her adolescent Son in the Temple, she received from Him lessons that she kept forever in her heart. She was also His *first disciple in devotion.* No one else has been *"taught by God"* (Jn 6:45) to the same extent that she has been. Indeed, Mary was "both Mother and Disciple" in the words of Saint Augustine, who added that her discipleship was even more important for her than her motherhood (Sermon 25).

2. Place in Salvation History

Hence, religious instruction should lead students to see Mary as singularly blessed and relevant to their own lives and needs. Following the Christian Tradition as continued in the Second Vatican Council, catechists should explain the special place of the Virgin Mary in the History of Salvation and in the Church.

Mary should be shown to be in the Church in a place highest after Christ and proper to our spiritual Mother. There should be explanations of her special gifts from God (e.g., being the Mother of God, being preserved from all stain of original sin, being assumed body and soul into heaven). Finally, the special veneration that is owed Mary—Mother of Christ, Mother of the Church, and our spiritual Mother—should be taught not only by word but also by example.

A. Buono

CATECHISM OF THE CATHOLIC CHURCH AND MARY

See   *Catechesis (Catechetical Activity) and Mary*

The new *Catechism of the Catholic Church* issued by Pope John Paul II on October 11, 1992 (and in an English translation in 1994), has much to say about the Blessed Virgin Mary. Some of the important Marian themes are the following.

(1) *Mary has an important role in God's plan of salvation.* She was chosen by God from all eternity to be the Mother of His Son (no. 488), and the mission of many women of the Old Testament, among them, Eve, Sarah, Hannah, Deborah, Ruth, Judith, and Esther, *prepared* for her. After a long period of waiting, the times were fulfilled in her, the exalted Daughter of Zion, and the new plan of salvation was established (no. 489).

In addition, Mary was enriched by God with gifts appropriate to her role: she was full of grace, so that she could give the free assent of her faith to the announcement of her vocation (no. 490). From the first moment of her conception, by a singular grace and privilege of Almighty God and by virtue of the merits of Jesus Christ, Savior of the human race, she was preserved immune from all stain of *original sin;* thus, she was redeemed in a more exalted fashion by reason of the merits of Christ (nos. 491-492). And by the grace of God Mary remained free from every *personal sin* her whole life long (nos. 411, 493).

(2) *Mary was the first among all believers with an obedience of faith.* She is the perfect embodiment of someone submitting freely to the Word of God, Who is Truth itself (no. 144). It is for this faith that all generations have called her blessed (no. 148). Throughout her life and until her last ordeal

when Jesus died on the Cross, Mary's faith never wavered. She never ceased to believe in the fulfillment of God's word (no. 149). Mary believed that *"nothing is impossible with God"* (Lk 1:37) and was able to magnify the Lord (no. 273).

(3) *Mary's life was intertwined with that of her Son, Whom she conceived in love*, especially during His hidden years and His Death on the Cross (nos. 485, 525ff, 721ff), and it culminated in her presence at the birth of the Church at Pentecost in the Upper Room (no. 965) and her Assumption (no. 966).

(4) *Mary is an example and model of holiness for Christians* (nos. 273, 2030) *as well as a model of prayer.* She teaches us what Christian prayer is: to be wholly God's because He is wholly ours (no. 2617).

(5) *Mary is both the Model of the Church* (nos. 507, 829) *and the Mother of the Church.* She is clearly the Mother of the members of Christ since she has by her charity joined in bringing about the birth of believers in the Church, who are members of its Head (no. 963). She aided the beginnings of the Church by her prayers (no. 965).

(6) *Mary's virginity is attested to by the Church from the first formulations of her faith*—confessing that Jesus was conceived solely by the power of the Holy Spirit in the womb of the Virgin Mary, while affirming also the corporeal aspect of this event: Jesus was conceived by the Holy Spirit without human seed (no. 496ff).

The reasons why God in His saving plan wanted His Son to be born of a Virgin are as follows. (a) Mary's virginity manifests God's absolute initiative in the Incarnation. (b) Jesus is conceived by the Holy Spirit in the Virgin Mary's womb because He is the New Adam, Who inaugurates the New Creation. From His fullness as the Head we have all received grace upon grace. (c) By His virginal conception Jesus ushers in the *new birth* of children adopted in the Holy Spirit through faith. (d) Mary is a Virgin because her virginity is the sign of her faith unadulterated by any doubt and of her undivided gift of self to God's will (nos. 502-506).

(7) *Mary is the masterwork of the union of the Son and the Spirit in the fullness of time.* In her began to be fulfilled the

wonders of God that the Spirit was to announce in Christ and the Church (no. 721). (a) The Holy Spirit prepared her by His grace, so that she was full of grace (no. 722). (b) In her the Holy Spirit *fulfilled* the plan of the Father's loving goodness, and by the power of the Spirit and her faith her virginity became uniquely fruitful (no. 723).

(c) In Mary, the Holy Spirit *manifested* the Son of the Father now become the Son of the Virgin; she made the Word visible in the humility of His flesh (no. 724). (d) Through Mary, the Holy Spirit began to bring human beings, the objects of God's merciful love, *into communion with Christ* (no. 725).

(8) *Devotion to Mary is intrinsic to Christian worship* (no. 971). The Church rightly honors her "with special devotion. From the most ancient times the Blessed Virgin has been honored with the title 'Mother of God,' to whose protection the faithful fly in all their dangers and needs. . . . This very special devotion . . . differs essentially from the adoration that is given to the Incarnate Word and equally to the Father and the Holy Spirit, and greatly fosters this adoration" (LG, 66).

The liturgical feasts dedicated to the Mother of God and Marian prayer, such as the Rosary, an epitome of the whole Gospel, express this devotion to the Virgin Mary (MC, 42).

(9) *Mary is the Mother of Grace* (nos. 968-970), as a mediator not a source of God's grace. "In a wholly singular way she cooperated by her obedience, faith, hope, and burning charity in the Savior's work of restoring supernatural life to souls. For this reason she is a Mother to us in the order of grace" (LG, 61). However, she is an intercessor before God only through the mediation of Christ (no. 970).

(10) *Mary is the perfect prayer, a figure of the Church.* When we pray to her, we are adhering with her to the plan of the Father, Who sends His Son to save all human beings. Like the beloved disciple, we welcome Jesus' Mother into our homes, for she has become the Mother of all the Living. We can pray with and to her. The prayer of the Church is sustained by the prayer of Mary and united with it in hope (no. 2679).

A. Buono

CENACLE

SEE *Holy Land and Mary, 2g*

CHAPTER 8 OF LUMEN GENTIUM

SEE *Vatican II and Mary*

CHILDREN OF MARY

THIS name was attached to a number of pious unions of the laity (confraternities and sodalities) devoted to Mary. Their purpose was to enable their members to attain a virtuous Christian life by fostering devotion to the Blessed Virgin. The oldest stemmed back to the Middle Ages and many were associated with the archsodality (called *prima primaria*) established in Rome in 1584.

In the 12th century the fraternity of Sons and Daughters of Mary was established at Ravenna by Blessed Peter de Honestis. In the 16th century a similar society originated among the students of the Roman College and became open to all in 1751. In the early 17th century, a Marian sodality was founded in France by Saint Peter Fourier. In the 19th century, the Society of the Children of Mary was canonically established at Rome and the Society of Mary Immaculate began among girl students of the Sisters of Charity and was opened to all in 1876.

After the Second Vatican Council, these sodalities adopted a rule of life and spirituality in accord with the Council and became part of the new designation "Christian Life Communities." The new group and program were approved by Paul VI in 1971, and the American headquarters are in St. Louis, Missouri.

A. Buono

CHRIST (MARY AND)

SEE *Life of Mary*   *New Testament*
     Mother of God   *Trinity*

CHURCH AND MARY [963-972]

TO understand the relationship between Mary and the Church three things affirmed by Vatican Council II must all be considered: (1) Mary is prototype of the Church; (2) Mary is part of the Church as "preeminent member" of the Mystical Body; (3) Mary is Mother of the Church.

1. Mary—Prototype of the Church

This aspect was much favored in the first centuries of the Church and also attracted considerable attention in the Middle Ages. Mary represents and signifies the Church. In Mary, personally, we discover what constitutes the greatness of the Church that Christ desired and established.

For the source of this delineation, we must look in chapter 12 of the Book of Revelation. Presented there in one and the same scene are both Mary, "*mother of the male child*" pursued in vain by the devil's hatred, and the Church, mother of the "*reborn*" in Christ and mother who must flee into the desert so long as there exists the persecution from which God ultimately delivers the faithful.

We can assimilate to this parallelism of Mary and the Church another theme, dear to Saint Irenaeus: Mary is the New Eve untying by her obedience the knot of Eve's disobedience.

Alongside Christ, Head of the New People that is His Body, Irenaeus places Mary in counterpoint to the original sinful pair. Mary, the New Eve, personally assumes care of the new race of the saved. Her obedience and faith are those of the Church. Mary, who is, properly speaking, more model of the Church than its mother, expresses in herself the holiness of the Church, which Christ loved and by giving His life sanctified.

Everything the Church is, Mary is first, personally and perfectly. In the 13th century a disciple of Saint Bernard,

Abbot Isaac of "Stella," a monastery in Poitou (France), could say to his monks:

"Everything said in the Scriptures universally of the Church, Virgin and Mother, is singularly true of Mary. . . . The same expressions apply to both. Both are mothers, both are virgins. Both give to God the Father a posterity. Mary furnishes the Body its Head; the Church gives this Head a Body. Both are mothers of Christ, but neither gives birth to Him completely without the other."

The Second Vatican Council speaks in comparable terms: "By contemplating Mary's hidden sanctity and imitating her charity, the Church becomes herself a mother. . . . She brings forth to a new and immortal life the sons and daughters born to her in Baptism, conceived of the Holy Spirit and born of God. She herself is a virgin, who keeps the faith given to her by her Spouse whole and entire" (LG 64).

2. Mary—Member of the Church

Model of the Church, Mary nevertheless remains a member of the Church, albeit, in the words of the Council, "a preeminent and singular member" (LG 53). She is a redeemed creature, beneficiary of the Redemption, which came to her through a remarkable anticipation: the Immaculate Conception. The effect of this application to Mary of the redemptive act was to immunize her against the sin of her race. Yet descendant of Adam like us, she belongs to the people of the redeemed whom Jesus reconciled with His Father.

Mary in fact, while with us, wanted no privilege. From the day of the Ascension she is found "in the company of the Church" together with some saintly women. And on Pentecost she receives the Holy Spirit in the Church, in which until her glorious Assumption she lived a life of humble prayer.

The point should be stressed: Mary is a member of the Church because she receives all that she gives. If every grace passes through her hands, the grace is implored and obtained from the liberality of her Son. That is why we always ask her to pray for us. As the cooperatrix and Mother of her Lord, Mary rejoices in her dependence on the Divine Source. In the glory of heaven she is "suppliant omnipotence" (in the classic words of Saint Bernard), and "by her constant intercession she continues to bring us the gifts of eternal salvation" (LG 62).

Nevertheless, it is in Mary that the Church finds its fulfillment and its fullness, since it was in Mary that God, in the Person of the Word, entered into union with humankind. And this is why she announces and represents the Church, i.e., a permanent union and communication between God and human beings. The words of Isaac of Stella bear repetition: what the Church, the people of the redeemed, is collectively, Mary is personally because she, creature most favored, is the one who gave to the Son of God the human nature that made Him like unto us. Masterwork of God, Mary was very much part of the community of God's children, and by her loving and filial perfection helped to realize the wondrous, unforeseeable destiny that it pleased God to ordain for her Son.

3. Mary—Mother of the Church

An anonymous monk of the 8th century, in a commentary on the Book of Revelation, concluded that Mary was both "daughter and mother of the Church." Mother of the Head, would she not also be mother of the entire Body? And Jesus, from the height of the Cross, did entrust to her, in the person of Saint John, the whole people for which He gave His life.

During the Middle Ages, from the moment that the interpretation of *"Behold your son"* became evident and indisputable, Mary was recognized as loving mother of all human beings. But not so with the title "Mother of the Church." Only later, and after a great deal of hesitation, was it found fitting to call the Mother of Jesus "mother" of a Church to which she was daughter. The Second Vatican Council left to Pope Paul VI the joy of proclaiming the title, November 21, 1964, at the close of the Council's third session:

"We proclaim the Most Blessed Virgin Mary *Mother of the Church*, i.e., of the whole people of God, faithful and pastors, and we call her most loving Mother."

In the view of the Council, the Church is not strictly confined to baptismal membership. All who believe in Christ, or who are still groping for God sincerely, are not totally alien to the Church. Declaring Mary Mother of the Church is not restricting her protection but bringing it in line with the eternal plan of the God Who "calls all human beings to be part of the people of God."

In this plan of universal salvation Mary holds a privileged place, that of mother. Having given us the incarnate Son of God, she extends her maternal mission to the entire Mystical Body. It is not a hierarchical mission, as Paul VI pointed out, three times noting that Mary is the mother of pastors and faithful. It is a mission of goodness, solicitude, and attentive and affectionate love. For centuries Mary has inspired trust and confidence, and attracted the prayers of the faithful ("God wants to give us nothing that does not pass through the hands of Mary," says Saint Bernard). The title "Mother of the Church" expands the horizon of her patronage and goes to the heart of it. The whole people of God, in its universality, and not only an undefined fraction of suppliants, has the Blessed Virgin for mother and is the object of her care.

In the Church of which she is part (since "the Mother of the Word Incarnate," said Paul VI, "is our sister by the bond of human nature"), Mary occupies the place of mother. And the whole Church invokes the Mother of its Lord as its own mother.

Paul VI expressed the hope that this title would lead "Christians to honor Mary even more and to call upon her with still greater confidence." To her the people of God turn spontaneously, in moments of joy as well as in time of need. It is fitting that the Pope's proclamation should have been the crown to the magnificent theology of the Church produced by Vatican II.

H. Holstein

COLLECTION OF MASSES OF THE BLESSED VIRGIN MARY

SEE   *Crowning of an Image of*   *Liturgy*
          the Blessed Virgin Mary   *Month of Mary*
       Cult of Mary   *Presence of Mary in the*
       Feasts of Mary   *Eucharist*
       Lectionary, Marian   *Saturday of Our Lady*

ON the Assumption in 1986 the Congregation for Divine Worship issued a decree promulgating the *Collection of Masses of the Blessed Virgin Mary.* The Latin text appeared the following year, and the English text of some of the Masses was available in America in early 1988. The total collection in English was published in 1992.

1. Mary's Place within the Mystery of Christ and His Church

Following the Church's teaching on the place of Mary within the Mystery of Christ and His Church by the Second Vatican Council, churches and Religious Institutes composed new Mass Propers from ancient liturgical sources and the writings of the Fathers of the Church. These Propers are outstanding because of their piety, teaching, and the significance of their texts. To promote properly the devotion to the Mother of God, the Roman Liturgy integrates commemorations of her into the Liturgical Year, to indicate her connection in the annual cycle of Christ's Mysteries.

In celebrating the Sacred Mysteries, the Church is aware of the entire work of salvation. Since Mary was intimately involved in the History of Salvation, actively present during the Mysteries of Christ's life, the *Collection of Masses* has special meaning and purpose, commemorating her role as the Mother of the Lord in the work of redemption, as it celebrates the events of salvation in which the Blessed Virgin was involved in view of the Mystery of Christ. By honoring the Mother of God in this way, the Masses actually celebrate the action of God in our salvation, indicating Mary's intimate connection with her Son.

As Christ is present in our celebrations of the Liturgy, so also is Mary, now exalted in heaven at the side of her Son, where her intercession continues to obtain gifts for our salvation. She is ever present as the Mother of the Church and her advocate. Mary is considered the exemplar of the Christian life. She is considered a *figure,* because she exemplified how one should live as a virgin, spouse, and mother. She is referred to as an *image,* since she was perfectly fashioned after her Son, and thus as a flawless image, she is one to be emulated.

2. Nature of the Collection

Most of these texts are from local churches and Religious Institutes or are already in the *Sacramentary.* They would be intended primarily for the Marian shrines where Masses in her honor are celebrated frequently, but also for all Church communities, especially on Saturdays in Ordinary Time. In other words there are no changes in the rubrics governing such Masses as stated in the *General Instruction of the Roman Missal.*

3. Structure of the Collection

Forty-six of the Marian formularies are distributed over the seasons of the Liturgical Year: three in Advent, six in Christmas, five in Lent, four in Easter, and twenty-eight in Ordinary Time. The last mentioned are subdivided into three sections, the first (11 formularies) celebrates her under titles derived from Sacred Scripture, or shows especially her bond with the Church; the second (9 formularies) honors her under titles that indicate her cooperation in fostering the spiritual life of the faithful; the third (8 formularies) celebrates her under titles that indicate her compassionate interceding on behalf of the faithful.

Published in two volumes, the first comparable to our *Sacramentary,* the second to our *Lectionary,* the collection, in

volume 1, contains a liturgical, historical, and pastoral introduction to each formulary, so that one may prepare properly
for the Eucharistic celebration.

4. Use of the Collection

The seasons of the Liturgical Year are to be respected,
though there may be occasions to use certain Masses during
another season for a just reason. Thus, Mary, Mother of Reconciliation, assigned to Lent, might be used during Ordinary
Time to arouse a spirit of reconciliation. However, others, such
as Mary and the Lord's Resurrection, would not ordinarily be
allowed outside of the Easter Season.

The Marian shrines will benefit the most from this collection because of their privilege to have more frequent celebrations of Masses in her honor. Even though a shrine might be
dedicated to a specific title of Mary, the liturgical season ought
to be respected and the Biblical readings from those specific
seasons should be proclaimed during such times. Even when
there is a proper Mass of a shrine, during specific liturgical
seasons, that same Mass should not be said every day and
more than once the same day, in order to allow the faithful an
overview of the entire History of Salvation. Even a pilgrimage,
especially one that would spend several days at the shrine,
should celebrate a variety of such Marian Masses.

Dedicating Saturday to the Blessed Mother is an ancient
custom recognized by the recent liturgical reform, which bestowed new vigor on this type of celebration. These Masses
allow a wide variety of ways for the ecclesial communities to
honor Mary as a kind of introduction to the Lord's day. Genuine Marian devotion is not merely a multiplication of such
Masses but a celebration of a vital liturgical spirit accomplished with care and propriety.

5. Biblical Readings

In the *Lectionary* there are many readings relating to the
life or mission of the Blessed Mother, or concerning prophecies
about her. Some events, figures, or symbols foretell or suggest

her life and mission; some readings may not refer specifically to Mary but extol virtues that flourished in Mary, who was the most perfect disciple of Christ. Although only two readings are provided, on some occasions three readings may be used, taken from the Common of the Blessed Virgin Mary or the appendix to the *Lectionary.* There may be occasions when the celebrants will want to replace certain readings with more appropriate ones from these listings. (*See also Appendix* 8.)

A. Buono

COMMUNION OF SAINTS   [946-948, 953]

SEE   *Church and Mary*   *Queen*
       Intercession

IN patristic times this expression generally referred to common participation of the faithful in "sacred things" (*sancta,* in the neuter), meaning the sacraments. Among these "sacred things" the Eucharist occupies a central place, uniting participants who receive Christ in truth: "*Because the bread is one, we, many though we are, are one body, for we all partake of the one bread*" (1 Cor 10:17).

This importance of the Eucharist no doubt explains the more personal sense of the expression that arose in the Middle Ages and has prevailed for centuries since, namely, community of life in Christ by all baptized (*sancti,* in the masculine): "In various ways and degrees all who are in Christ are in communion in the same charity of God and neighbor. . . . All who are in Christ, having His Spirit, form one Church and cleave together in Him" (LG 49).

What is the place of Mary in the "Communion of Saints"? The answer cannot be simple. A number of things enter into consideration and contribute to the total picture.

(a) *Mary forms part of the Communion of Saints.* Redeemed daughter of Adam, self-effacing and full of love, Mary is pleased to belong forever to the immense multitude of elect described in Revelation (ch. 7), to be with them in their blessedness as she had been in their tribulation. Mary is the first of believers and, as Paul VI said, "the perfect disciple of Christ." Her presence on Pentecost, with the infant Church, is significant.

(b) *Mary, in heaven, receives a glory that exalts her above all Saints:* all of them do homage to the Mother of their Lord. But, as has been said, "Mary is crowned for her humility." Her greatness is the greatness foretold in the *Magnificat: "He has ... raised the lowly to high places"* (Lk 1:52). Mary alone, among those who have come through *"the great period of trial"* (Rv 7:14), is glorified in her body, and that places her above all others, still waiting for the Resurrection. Prototype of the Church, she anticipates in her person the total eschatological victory of the Body of Christ.

(c) *The full powers of Mary are expressed in her intercession and mediation.* The vitality of the Body of Christ, to which she gave the Head, is in some way the fruit of Mary's motherhood. Nevertheless, Mary is not the Source. She beseeches and intercedes, and receives from the Divine Source whatever she shares with her children. One can, in fact, speak of a continual dispossession or celestial "poverty" of Mary, who, holding nothing back, passes on the spiritual treasures that the Father in His love showers upon her.

H. Holstein

COMPASSION

SEE   *Cross*   *Sorrows of Mary*
      Motherhood, Spiritual

CONCEPTION, VIRGINAL

SEE   *Virginal Conception*

CONSECRATION   [438, 901, 916, 931ff,]

SEE   *Devotion(s)*   *Louis-Marie de Montfort (Saint)*
      Kolbe (Saint Maximilian)

1. To Consecrate, to Consecrate "Oneself"

IN the strict sense, and especially as concerns persons (the only case in point here), "consecration" is determined by God. Only God can appropriate a being so as to make it sacred by communicating to it a participation in His holiness. And if human beings can "consecrate themselves" so that they really belong to the Lord in a new way, it must be understood that this is in fact a response, and acquiescence, by which they bind themselves personally to a consecration that comes from God. Here applies literally the expression: "Become what you are."

The example of Christ in this regard is particularly enlightening. At the solemn moment when He enters upon the Passion to live His "Hour" to the full and complete His mission of salvation, He says: *"I consecrate Myself for their sakes now, that they may be consecrated in truth"* (Jn 17:19). The immediate reference was to the Apostles, His privileged hearers, but according to the context the words extend to *"those who will believe in Me through their word"* (Jn 17:30). To consecrate "oneself" for Jesus is to do what He was sent to do by the Father, the work to which His Sacred Humanity was "ordered" by the very fact of the Incarnation, from the first moment of His existence in the womb of Mary.

By the Incarnation, in and of itself, the Humanity of Jesus is consecrated, so that in becoming Man Jesus is *ipso facto* constituted Savior, Prophet, King, Priest and Victim of the one sacrifice that was to save the world. He is the "Anointed" par excellence, the "Christ" totally belonging to God, His Humanity being that of the Word and indwelled by the Holy Spirit. When, by a free act of His human will, He accepts what He is, doing what He was sent to do, He can say that He consecrates "Himself." In Christ, therefore, what might be called His "subjective" consecration is a perfect response to the "objective" consecration produced in His Humanity through the Incarnation.

And what Christ does brings with it a "consecration" for His disciples, a very special belonging to God, since He imparts to them His own life precisely by making them participants in His own consecration.

Through Baptism Christians also are consecrated and *"anointed"* by the power of the Spirit. They share, in their measure, in the essential consecration of Christ, in His character of King, Priest, and Prophet (cf. 1 Pt 2:9; 2 Pt 1:3-4; Rv 5:9; etc.). With Christ and through Christ they are "ordered" to the glory of God and the salvation of the world. They do not belong to themselves. They belong to Christ the Lord, Who imparts His own life to them. (Among the effects of this consecration we must distinguish between those that sanctify personally the subjects through the communication of grace, and those that "order" or prepare them for a mission by enabling them to be instruments of Christ.)

The vocation of those who have been baptized is to "live" this consecration by a voluntary adherence—and one that is as perfect as possible—to what it has made of them. Living as "children of God," they fulfill subjectively their objective consecration; like Jesus, they consecrate themselves. This is the deeper meaning of vows and baptismal promises, together with the actual way of life corresponding to them. The baptismal consecration is the fundamental one, constitutive of the Christian. All consecrations that come after it presuppose and are rooted in it, be they the consecration of religious, or those that order and prepare the subject for a special, sacramental ministry (like the ministerial priesthood).

2. Consecration to Mary

If, in the strict sense in question here, consecration makes one belong to God—and Christ is God—how is it possible to speak of consecrating oneself to Mary? It is possible because by God's will Mary has something to do with our Christian life, with our sanctification. She is certainly not, like Christ, the source of salvation but she is maternally ordered to our life as children of God—always, however, in perfect union with her Son and subordinate to Him: "our Mother in the order of grace" (LG 61). Hence, in the full sense of the word a consecration to Mary includes at least implicitly a real and essential reference to Christ and to the Baptism that binds us to Him. In the words of Saint Louis-Marie de Montfort: "Jesus Christ our

Savior, true God and true Man, must be the ultimate end of all our other devotions; otherwise they are false and deceiving."

But Saint Louis is not satisfied with an implicit reference when he proposes his perfect practice of devotion to Mary. For him it is then explicitly a question of consecration that has Jesus Christ for ultimate terminus: "We consecrate ourselves at one and the same time to the Most Blessed Virgin and to Jesus Christ: to the Most Blessed Virgin *as to the perfect means* by which Jesus chose to unite Himself with us and to unite us with Himself; and to Our Lord as to *our ultimate end,* to whom we owe all that we are as to our Redeemer and our God." Obviously, for him this consecration must be more than words, becoming in reality "a perfect renewal of vows and the baptismal promises."

The consecration is perfect because it is made through Mary, "perfect means," *and* because of its "totalism," in the sense that everything, absolutely everything that we are and that belongs to us, must be surrendered. Since, moreover, this act of consecration requires an attitude that corresponds to it in deeds, it pledges those who so consecrate themselves to strive to "perform all actions through Mary, in Mary, and for Mary in order to perform them more perfectly through Jesus Christ, with Jesus Christ, in Jesus and for Jesus." In the view of Father de Finance, the idea of consecration attains here its perfect expression (*Dict. de Spiritualité,* art. *Consécration,* fasc. XIII, col. 1583).

3. Consecrating Others to Mary

Pope Pius XII consecrated the whole world to the Immaculate Heart of Mary on October 31, 1942. In some places parents have their children consecrated to Mary when they are baptized. What is the justification for such acts, in which the "subject" does not necessarily have a say? Mostly, it is that the persons who make the consecration have a "power," a responsibility toward those whom they consecrate.

This power, which ultimately comes from God, must be exercised in the service of those who have been entrusted to them. Basically, the act of such persons is a recognition of the intrinsic finality of their service, namely, to bring to the Lord, "to make belong" to Him, those in their care. To the extent of their power they can give; and the Lord receives: this means that their action is not without effect on those who are so consecrated. Consecrating others to Mary is possible for the same reasons and in the same sense as consecrating oneself to her. And here also Mary "receives." Hence, the consecration is not without importance.

Primarily responsible, however, for putting the consecration into practice are the parents (or sponsors). This should be brought out in any pastoral ministry of consecrating little children to Mary. Parents (or sponsors) acknowledge and assume the place and role of Mary in the life of the newly baptized so as to bind the child more closely to Christ. Normally this means that they will inculcate devotion to Mary as part of their task as Christian educators of the child.

A. Bossard

CO-REDEMPTRIX [968-970]

SEE *Mediatrix*   *Motherhood, Spiritual*

THE title "Co-Redemptrix," which originated in the 14th century, has been widely used by Catholic Bishops, theologians, and popular writers ever since. In more recent times it has been employed even in documents of the Holy See. Hence, no one should question its legitimacy.

But more important than the title itself is its doctrinal content. What does the word "Co-redemptrix" mean? For some theologians, it refers to Mary's cooperation in the Redemption in the sense that she knowingly and willingly gave birth to the Redeemer (indirect, remote cooperation), and that she dispenses to us the fruits (graces) of the Redemption already accomplished by Christ alone (technically: cooperation in the *subjective* Redemption). The majority, however, believes that, besides the two types of cooperation just mentioned, Mary also contributed to the Redemption itself, i.e., to the redemptive action of Christ that was consummated on Calvary (called *objective* Redemption). Specifically: Together with Christ (though in total subordination to Him and in virtue of His power), Mary atoned or satisfied for our sins, merited every grace necessary for salvation, and joined the Savior's sacrifice on Calvary to appease the wrath of God. It was in view of this joint operation of Son and Mother that God was pleased to cancel our debt and take us back into His friendship broken by sin.

The aforementioned opinion of the majority is based on various pronouncements of the Magisterium. Thus, e.g., Benedict XV stated that on Calvary, Our Lady "to such extent . . . immolated Him [Christ], in so far as she could, in order to appease the justice of God, that *we may rightly say that she redeemed the human race together with Christ*" (*Inter Sodalicia:* AAS 10 [1918] 182). And according to Pius XII, Mary cooperated in our Redemption "in such a way that our salvation flowed from the love of Jesus Christ and His sufferings *intimately joined with the love and sorrows of His Mother . . .*" (AAS 48 [1956] 352). Substantially the same thing is taught by John Paul II in his 1980 encyclical *On the Mercy of God (Dives in misericordia)*. The Second Vatican Council made repeated references to Mary's cooperation in the Redemption, but they are not as explicit as those already mentioned (LG 56, 58, 61, 68).

But are not all the members of the Church supposed to contribute to the work of Redemption by *"filling up what is wanting in the sufferings of Christ"* (Col 1:24)? Yes, but the Church contributes nothing to the *objective* Redemption (as Mary did); only to its *subjective* phase (cf. Pius XII's encyclical *On the Mystical Body, Mystici Corporis*, in AAS 35 [1943] 213).

When we, therefore, say that Christ *alone* redeemed us, we are referring to His primary, universal, infinite, and self-sufficient causality in the redemptive process. We do not mean it in a sense that would exclude Mary's secondary, finite, and totally subordinated share, which drew all its efficacy from the merits of her Son. While Mary did not (could not) enhance the value of Christ's redemptive merits and satisfactions, God was pleased to accept her share therein together with (but subordinated to) Christ's sacrificial action and for the same purpose, namely, the redemption of the human race. Only in this restricted sense can we say that Mary "redeemed the human race together with Christ," as Pope Benedict XV boldly stated.

Bibliography. Every aspect of this question is treated extensively and with abundant bibliography in the essay *Our Lady's Coredemption,* published in J. B. Carol, O.F.M. (ed.), *Mariology,* vol. 2 (Milwaukee, Wis., Bruce, 1957), pp. 377-425. See also the entry *Mediatrix of All Graces* in NCE 9 (1967).

J. B. Carol

CORONATION OF MARY   [966-970]

SEE   *Assumption*   *Mother of God*
       Crowning of an Image   *Queen*
          of the Blessed Virgin *Rosary*

THE Coronation of Mary is the Fifth Glorious Mystery of the Rosary. It is intended to highlight the bodily aspect of the Assumption and to record the final moment of Our Lady's Assumption into heaven, most likely resulting from the allegorical interpretation of a few Scripture texts.

In the *Liturgy of the Hours,* the Church has included the magnificent words of Saint Amadeus of Lausanne (c. 1110-1159): "When the Virgin of virgins was led forth by God and her Son, the King of kings, amid the company of exulting Angels and rejoicing Archangels, with the heavens ringing with praise, the prophecy of the Psalmist was fulfilled in which he said to the Lord: '*At Your right hand stands the Queen, clothed in gold of Ophir*' (Ps 45:10).

The text of the Song of Songs 4:8 in the Vulgate reads: "*Come from Lebanon, My bride, . . . and you shall be crowned. . . .*" The text of the Book of Revelation 12:1 reads: "*A great sign appeared in the sky, a woman clothed with the sun, with the moon under her feet, and on her head a crown of twelve stars.*"

Pope Pius XII stated in the Encyclical *Ad Caeli Reginam* ("To the Queen of Heaven"): "Sacred art, founded on Christian principles, faithfully expresses the simple and spontaneous piety of the faithful. Ever since the Council of Ephesus [431 A.D.] it has pictured Mary as Queen and Empress, seated on a royal throne, adorned with royal emblems, crowned with a diadem, surrounded by Angels and Saints, and dominating not only the forces of nature but also the evil influence of Satan."

The coronation of Mary was discussed by Bishop Melitus of Sardis (d. 381) and by Saint Gregory of Tours (c. 540-594), but it became a frequent theme only in the Middle Ages when the cult of Mary was at its zenith.

In the 12th century Christian art portrayed Mary as seated at her Son's right hand with a crown on her head. And by the next century the more common picture developed: Mary being crowned Queen by Christ the King. At times Mary is shown kneeling before God the Father to receive the crown or being crowned by all three Persons of the Trinity.

A. Buono

CROSS (MARY AT THE)

SEE   *Cana*   *Motherhood, Spiritual*
      Church and Mary   *Rosary*
      Co-Redemptrix   *Sorrows of Mary*

"**N**EAR *the cross of Jesus there stood His mother*" (Jn 19:25; verses 25 to 37 of John 19 should be considered as a whole).

1. The Hour of Jesus and the Hour of the Woman

We know how much John (and Jesus Himself) dwells on the "Hour" of Jesus. From Cana (2:4) to the great "preface" that precedes the sacrifice (13:1ff), mention of the Hour that only the Father knows (cf. Mt 24:36) directs attention to the mystery of Christ's glorification on the Cross (cf. Jn 12:27, etc.). *"The Hour has come"* when the glorification of the Son will bring glory to the Father by the saving of humankind (17:1ff).

This Hour, in which the new Humankind is born, is also the Hour of the Woman whose offspring crushes the devil (cf. Gn 3:15), who rejoices *"that a Man has been born into the world,"* according to Jesus' own words (Jn 16:21), and who becomes the mother of all the living (cf. Gn 3:20).

At Cana the "Woman" is mentioned in connection with the Hour of the Savior. On Calvary Mary is present "in keeping with the Divine plan" (LG 58) and by personal will (since her sister also is there, and other relatives of Jesus).

Under the Cross Mary assures in a very special way the presence of the Church (and humanity), receiving salvation and entering into it with all her being (cf. LG 58, 61, 65).

2. The "Accomplishment" of All Things and Mary's Oblation

Two times (Jn 19:28 and 30), once by Jesus Himself, it is noted that "the work" assigned by the Father is finished, *"accomplished"*(cf. Jn 4:34; 6:38; 13:1; 17:4). Human disobedience (cf. Gn 3) is redeemed by the Son of Man's obedience (Jn 14:30). And the sign of salvation is the gift of the Spirit, Whom Jesus *"hands over"* or *"passes on"* (19:30; a word proper to John). We receive *"the new heart and the new spirit"* that had been promised (Ez 36:26-38).

Renewed in this Spirit, Mary reaffirms the Yes of the Incarnation (Lk 1:38) and, by a consent of love, "unites herself with the sacrifice of her Son" (LG 58). Her obedience is joined with that of the Son. She is the *New Eve* at the side of the New Adam (cp. patristic exegesis from Saint Irenaeus on).

3. The Gathering into One of God's Dispersed Children and the Motherhood of Mary

It is in Jerusalem (and particularly in the Temple) that the Lord, like a shepherd leading His People in a new Exodus, was to gather the "dispersed" recalled to life (cf. Is 35:10;

51:18-20; 52:11; 54:11-12; 60:17; 60:20-21; Jer 3:17-18; 31:9; 50:5; Ez 22:17-22; 37:25ff; Zec 2:14-15; etc.).

The tremendous motherhood of Zion-Jerusalem is one of God's "marvels." The barrenness of sin is made fertile (cf. Is 49:21 and 66:7-8) by Him to Whom *"nothing is impossible"* (Lk 1:37; cf. Gn 18:14), and a New Covenant (Jer 31:31-34; Ez 34:25; 37:26) is inaugurated by the Servant (Is 42:6-7; 49:5-7; 50:5-9; 52:13—53:12), in Zion-Jerusalem, future mother of all nations (Ps 87).

In the Hour of Jesus when all, dispersing, have left him *"quite alone"* (Jn 16:32), and even the few *"disciples"* are not at hand except imperfectly, the Good Shepherd will give His life for His sheep (10:15). Christ *"will draw all people"* to Himself (12:32) and make them one with Him in His own unity with the Father (10:30; 17:22-23), Who is, as it were, the "place" of gathering for the dispersed of the New Covenant (cf. 11:52). No more on the mountain is God to be found and worshiped but in the Spirit and truth of Jesus, new Temple *"not made by human hands"* (Mk 14:58) but clad in flesh by Mary.

The Woman who is "flesh of the flesh" of the new Adam (cf. Gn 2:23), the Wife-Virgin of whom God is the *"architect"* and Husband (Is 62:4-5; cf. Hos 1 and 2), the beloved City to which gather the redeemed and all nations (Is 62:11-12 and 61:9), the barren woman who gives birth to a people in one day (Is 54:1 and 66:7-8)—this is now Mary; this is now the Church.

In the Hour of Jesus "His" Mother Mary (Jn 19:25), renewing her consent and again overshadowed by the Spirit (19:30; cf. Lk 1:35-38), sees fulfillment of the mysterious announcement at Cana and hears solemn declaration of the motherhood she had already felt in her heart: motherhood both as regards the type-disciple ("your" mother from now on, 19:27) and motherhood toward all who are one with Jesus.

The mention of the Hour, the solemnity of the moment, the designation of John as the "typical" disciple "whom God loves," the designation of *"water"* (19:34) and the *"Spirit"* (19:30; cf. 3:5) do not permit us to regard the words of Jesus only as a simple domestic gesture to ensure the future of His

Mother. They are a "declaration" of the motherhood of Mary toward all "whom God loves" (cf. Lk 2:14). It is by the express will of Jesus, in virtue of the Spirit given by Jesus as fruit of His salvific Death (Jn 7:39), that the Mother "of Jesus" becomes the Mother "of disciples."

"In a singular way Mary cooperated by her obedience, faith, hope, and burning charity in the work of the Savior in giving back supernatural life to souls. Therefore she is our Mother in the order of grace" (LG 61).

The principal "exercise" of Mary's Motherhood will be, as at Cana (Jn 2:5, "*Do whatever He tells you*"), to lead all "disciples" to the same obedience as the Son's.

On Calvary, then, Mary is a "type" of the Church as beloved Spouse, and Mother both of Christ the Lamb whose contemplation saves us (Jn 19:36-37) and of the disciples "gathered" by the obedience of the Son and vivified by His Spirit in order to be brought to the Father (Jn 17:9-10).

4. Reception by the Disciple and Reception by the Church

"*From that hour onward, the disciple took her into his care,*" or "*received her into his own*" (Jn 19:27b).

"The" disciple is a type of those whom Jesus loves because they participate, in faith, in His obedience to the Father and keep the Commandments, that of love first of all (Jn 14:21).

Among the good things that Jesus and His Father bestow on us to make our joy complete (Jn 15:11), there is thus also Mary. As "disciples" it behooves us to receive her Motherhood as the dying gift of Christ. Receiving Mary "into our own" will be to extol her with all generations (cf. Lk 1:48). But it is also to join her in exalting the God Who does great things (cf. Lk 1:46-49), and to enter with her into the obedience of faith (cf. Lk 1:38) and into the love that begets for God children-disciples "*acknowledging His glory*" (cf. 2:11).

5. Fountain of Life and Community of the Redeemed

Mary sees the fountain springing up from the right side of the New Temple (Jn 19:34; cf. Ez 47:1-12), the river of grace that purifies (even the Dead Sea, symbol of sin!) and fecundates the new Jerusalem (Rv 22:1-12). To it come the redeemed of all nations, washed by a pure and loving flowing water from the Heart of Christ (cf. Ez 36:25-26).

"Looking on Him Who was pierced" (Jn 19:37; cf. Zec 12:10—13:1 and Rv 5:6b), Mary could give testimony, along with the beloved disciple, *"so that we might believe, we also"* (Jn 19:35) and have life. Christ is the Lamb of the true Passover (Jn 19:36; cf. Ex 12:46). *"With Your blood You purchased for God holy ones of every race and tongue, of every people and nation. You made of them a kingdom"* (Rv 5:9-10), an anointed, filial people.

The Woman-Church who gives birth to this filial people (cf. Rv 12:5ff) is still in the desert. But (like Mary) the Church is at work, through the word of God, through the Spirit *"handed on,"* through the water of Baptism *"and the blood"* (Jn 19:34) of the Eucharist, looking on Him Who was pierced and uniting human beings in His obedience. She thus prepares the Day when *"the power and kingship of our God and the power of His Christ"* will be manifested, the Day when the "dispersed" will form *"the immense people that no one can number"* and that sings *"the song of the Lamb"* in the *"midst"* of the New Jerusalem (cf. Rv 14—15; 19—22).

The Carrying of the Cross and the Crucifixion are, respectively, the Fourth and Fifth Mysteries of the Rosary.

A. Tostain

CROWNING OF AN IMAGE OF THE BLESSED VIRGIN [966-970]

SEE   *Collection of Masses of the*   *Litany of the Blessed*
       Blessed Virgin Mary   *Virgin Mary*
       Cult of Mary   *Queen*

The crowning of an image (picture or statue) of the Blessed Virgin is an honorific rite that may be carried out only with authoritative permission. Both in the East and in the West the practice of depicting the Blessed Virgin wearing a regal crown came into use in the era of the Council of Ephesus (431 A.D.). Since then Christian artists have often portrayed the glorified Mother of the Lord seated on a throne, dressed in royal robes, and surrounded by a court of Angels and Saints. In many such images Christ is shown placing a crown on His Mother's head.

It is especially from the end of the 16th century that in the West the practice became widespread for the faithful, both religious and laity, to crown images of the Blessed Virgin. The Popes not only endorsed this devout custom but on many occasions, either personally or through bishop-delegates, carried out such a coronation.

The growth of the custom led to the composition of a special rite for crowning images of Mary, and in the 19th century it was incorporated into the Roman Liturgy. In 1981, the Sacred Congregation for Divine Worship issued an updated version of this rite under the title *Order for Crowning an Image of the Blessed Virgin* (English edition, 1987).

By means of this new rite the Church proclaims that Mary is rightly regarded and invoked as Queen for the following reasons. (1) She is the Mother of the Son of God, Who is the Messianic King. (2) She is the chosen companion of the Redeemer, Who made us a kingdom to our God (cf. Rv 5:10). (3) She is the perfect follower of Christ, who was taken up into heavenly glory and exalted by the Lord as Queen of all (cf. LG, 59). (4) She is the foremost member of the Church, who is rightly invoked as Queen of Angels and of Saints, as our Lady and our Queen.

The rite of crowning is fittingly held on Solemnities and Feasts of Mary or on other festive days. But it is not to be held on the principal Solemnities of the Lord or on days having a penitential character. It may take place within Mass, within the Liturgy of the Word at Evening Prayer, or within a celebration of the Word of God suited to the occasion.

The whole sense of the rite rests on the idea of the exaltation of the lowly chanted by Mary in the *Magnificat*, and it contains great theological and spiritual riches. Foremost among these is a new Litany of the Blessed Virgin, which combines faithfulness to Biblical tradition and conformity with the spiritual sensibility of our times.

A. Buono

CULT OF MARY [971,1172]

SEE   *Collection of Masses of the*
          Blessed Virgin Mary
       Crowning of an Image
          of the Blessed Virgin
       Feasts of Mary
       Lectionary, Marian
       Litany of the Blessed
          Virgin Mary

Liturgy
Marialis Cultus
Presence of Mary in the
   Eucharist
Redemptoris Mater
Signum Magnum

MARY was involved in the Mysteries of Christ. As the most holy Mother of God she was, after her Son exalted by Divine grace above all Angels and human beings. Hence, the Church appropriately honors her with a special cult or devotion.

1. Cult from Most Ancient Times

Indeed, from most ancient times the Blessed Virgin has been venerated under the title of "God-bearer." In all perils and needs, the faithful have fled prayerfully to her protection. Especially after the Council of Ephesus (431) the cult of the People of God toward Mary wonderfully increased in veneration and love, invocation and imitation.

This cult differs essentially from the cult of adoration that is offered to the Incarnate Word as well as to the Father and to the Holy Spirit. Yet devotion to Mary is most favorable to this supreme cult. While honoring Christ's Mother, her cult causes her Son to be rightfully known, loved, and glorified and all His commands to be observed.

Without a doubt the Mysteries of Redemption and the Eucharistic celebration must be at the center of worship; but according to the *Constitution on the Sacred Liturgy* (LG 103, 104, 108, 111) there is a consonant and perfectly subordinate place for the veneration of the Virgin Mary. The Church's devotion to the Blessed Virgin is an intrinsic element of Christian worship. It is firmly rooted in the revealed Word and has solid dogmatic foundations.

This devotion is based on (1) the singular dignity of Mary, Mother of the Son of God, and therefore beloved Daughter of the Father and Temple of the Holy Spirit; (2) the part she played at decisive moments in the History of Salvation that her Son accomplished; (3) her holiness, already full at her Immaculate Conception yet increasing all the time as she obeyed the Father's will and accepted the path of suffering; (4) her mission and the special position she holds within the People of God as preeminent member, shining exemplar, and loving Mother; (5) her necessary and efficacious intervention for those who call upon her; and (6) her glory that ennobles the whole of humankind.

Saint Louis Grignion de Montfort notes that this devotion to Mary is the ardor to serve her, the better to serve God. True Marian devotion must be (a) *interior,* more in the heart than in practices; (b) *steadfast,* based on faith and not fluctuating with moods and feelings; (c) *disinterested,* more intent on God than the graces to be obtained (though the prayers of petition and thanksgivings are important elements in the general devotion that moves us to serve God); (d) *oriented toward Christ,* in Whom we are brought to the Father; and (e) *confident and heartfelt,* since in us the spiritual itself is fleshly, i.e., communicates through the flesh.

2. Liturgical Cult

The Blessed Virgin Mary occupies a prominent place in the Liturgy of the Church. The liturgies of both East and West bear witness to this fact by the ample space allotted to her memory in the Eucharistic Prayers, in the Sacramental euchology, and in the diverse expressions of prayer. Her presence is especially evident in the Marian feasts that have grown over the years.

The Roman Rite, with its traditional sobriety, has reserved to Mary a specific remembrance in the very heart of the Eucharistic Prayer—in the "Communicantes" of the Roman Canon. It has also gradually come to include a whole series of feasts that run throughout the Liturgical Year.

As Pope John Paul II has put it, "Mary is present in the *memorial* because she was present in the *event!* . . . She is continuously united both with Christ the High Priest and with the Church, the worshiping community, in the saving event and in its liturgical memorial" (Not. 20 [1984], pp. 173f).

Consequently, she does not have a different cult but occupies a special place in the unique "Christian" cult, capable of making the Church community relive mysteriously in the present the historical past of the saving actions of Christ and (because of this) not dissociate the united action of Christ and His Mother even in its cultural-ritual-liturgical re-evocation. This enables the Church to celebrate the memorial of the Blessed Virgin not in her own special liturgical cycle but within the unique liturgical cycle of the Mysteries of Christ.

3. Model in the Celebration of the Mysteries

In addition to this aspect of the indissoluble union between Christ and Mary in the economy of salvation and in its Sacramental realization, there is another aspect. Mary is united to the Mystery of the Church as her model in the celebration of the Mysteries. First of all, Mary is the *attentive Virgin* with respect to the Word of God; she thus appears as the model of the Church who meditates, is attentive to, accepts, lives, and proclaims the Word that became incarnate in Mary.

Secondly, Mary is the *Virgin in prayer,* because of her prayerful attitude as well as the sentiments that the Holy Spirit infused in her heart and that coincided with the grand divisions of ecclesial prayer, which has its roots in the Eucharistic Prayer: the *praise* and *thanksgiving* found in the *Magnificat,* the *intercession* at Cana, and the *petition* for the coming of the Spirit in the Upper Room.

Thirdly, Mary is the *Virgin presenting gifts* in the Temple of Jerusalem and on Calvary. This experience both in its active aspect (*Mary offers*) and in its passive aspect (*Mary is offered*) becomes the exemplar for the Church in her sacrificial offering of the Eucharist and prayer.

Fourthly, Mary is the *Virgin-Mother.* As such she is the model of that active collaboration with which the Church also labors, through preaching and the Sacraments (especially Baptism, Confirmation, and the Eucharist) to transmit the new life of the Spirit to human beings.

In this sense, every liturgical celebration must be *implicitly Marian,* insofar as it must be celebrated by the Church with the sentiments that were in Mary. The Marian note characterizes every celebration of the sacred Mysteries and makes liturgical spirituality an authentically Marian spirituality in the best sense of the word.

Finally, Mary is not only an example for the whole Church on the exercise of Divine worship but also a teacher of the spiritual life for individual Christians. She is an example of the worship that consists in making one's life an offering to God. Her Yes is for all Christians a lesson and an example of obedience to the will of the Father, which is the way and means of one's sanctification.

Thus, at every liturgical celebration, Mary the Mother of God is with us—as our Model, our Intercessor, and our Mother. And she is even more each of these things in the Marian celebrations.

Each Marian celebration is also intended to give us a better understanding of Mary's part in our salvation, a true catechesis of Mary. As the Liturgy honors Mary over the course of a year, the Mysteries of Christ become present to us in their relationship with her.

4. Mary in the Eucharist

Mary is prominently mentioned every day in the Ordinary of the Mass in the Introductory Rites at the Confiteor, in the Liturgy of the Word at the Nicene Creed, and in the Eucharistic Prayer. Admittedly, the Roman Rite does not possess the admirable euchology of the Ethiopian Rite, which enjoys two Marian anaphoras, and the Byzantine Rite, which reserves a special memorial for the Mother of God immediately after the epiclesis. However, it does offer a valid synthesis of all the possible links between the celebration of the Eucharistic Mystery and the Blessed Virgin.

The Preface of Eucharistic Prayer II recalls the Incarnation of the Word through the power of the Holy Spirit in the Virgin Mary: it is an ancient, universal, and essential mention because it unites the Eucharistic Mystery with the moment of the Incarnation, of which the Eucharist is also the recapitulation. The same remembrance is found in Eucharistic Prayer IV after the *Sanctus*. Eucharistic Prayer I solemnly expresses the union with Mary in the *Communicantes* in which her title of perpetual Virgin and her essential role as Mother of God are also recalled.

In a similar way, Eucharistic Prayer III expresses with intense supplication the desire of those praying to share with the Mother the inheritance of the children: "May He make us an everlasting gift to You [the Father] and enable us to share in the inheritance of the Saints with Mary, the Virgin Mother of God." Mary is also mentioned in each of the other seven approved Eucharistic Prayers.

5. Mary in the Sacramental Rites

References to Mary in the Sacramental rites are restrained but important. In the *Rite of Ordination* there are prayers of supplication to Mary on behalf of the bishops, priests, and deacons over whom the Litany of the Saints is invoked. In the *Rite of Penance* Mary's help and intercession are invoked for sinners in the Confiteor and at the absolution, and the *Magnificat* is suggested as a prayer of thanksgiving.

In the *Rite of the Pastoral Care of the Sick* the sick person, before receiving Communion, makes a profession of faith in Jesus the Son of God, born of Mary; in the recommendation of the dying, Mary the Mother of God is invoked and a prayer asks God to grant the dying person an eternal dwelling with her in the new Jerusalem. In the *Rite of Marriage* one of the Gospel readings is the passage from John 2:1-11 wherein Mary's intercession for the bridal couple comes to the fore. In the *Rite of Baptism* the Church invokes the Mother of grace before immersing candidates in the saving waters of Baptism. In the *Rite of Confirmation* the confirmands make a profession of faith in the Son of God, born of Mary, just before they are confirmed.

In the *Order of Christian Funerals* the Church asks that the grief of parents over a dead child may be assuaged by the maternal presence of Mary who stood by her dying Son on Calvary, and the Opening Prayer for the Mass of [Deceased] Parents, Relatives, and Benefactors asks that those who have passed from this world may through Mary's intercession enjoy perfect happiness in heaven.

In the *Rite for the Dedication of a Church and an Altar* Mary's intercession is invoked in the Litany of the Saints and in the prayer that follows; the Preface speaks of the true temple in which there dwells the fullness of the Divinity, that is, the humanity of the Son born of the Virgin Mary. Finally, in the *Rite of Religious Profession* Mary's intercession is invoked in the Litany of the Saints and her example for those who consecrate themselves to God by a life of perfect chastity, obedience, and poverty, which was chosen by Christ the Lord and His Virgin Mother.

The *Order of Crowning an Image of the Blessed Virgin Mary* is completely Marian throughout. It provides a short summa on the theology of Mary after the Second Vatican Council and is filled with riches of Marian spirituality, including a new Litany.

6. Mary in the Liturgy of the Hours

The *Liturgy of the Hours* also contains outstanding examples of the liturgical cult of Mary. These are found in the Latin hymns—which include several masterpieces of universal literature, such as Dante's sublime prayer to the Blessed Virgin— and in the antiphons that complete the daily Office.

To these lyrical invocations there has been added the well-known prayer *Sub Tuum*, venerable for its antiquity and admirable for its content. Other examples occur at Morning Prayer and Evening Prayer, prayers that frequently express trusting recourse to the Mother of mercy. There are selections from the vast treasury of writings on Our Lady composed by authors of the first Christian centuries, of the Middle Ages, and of Modern Times. Finally, the Church makes use of the *Magnificat* every day at Evening Prayer, using our Lady's words to give thanks for the wondrous gift of salvation.

7. Mary in the Liturgical Seasons

The *Season of Advent* has a typically Marian character, underlined especially in the *Liturgy of the Hours* where the hymns and antiphons frequently contain the name of Mary. There are many liturgical references to Mary besides the Solemnity of December 8, which is a joint celebration of the Immaculate Conception of Mary, of the basic preparation (see Is 11:1, 10) for the coming of the Savior, and of the happy beginning of the Church without spot or wrinkle. In the Proper for the United States, there is also the Feast of Our Lady of Guadalupe showing Mary's love for her children.

Such liturgical references are found especially on the days from December 17 to 24, and more particularly on the Sunday before Christmas, which recalls the ancient prophecies concerning the Virgin Mother and the Messiah and includes readings from the Gospel concerning the imminent birth of Christ and His Precursor.

The *Christmas Season* is a prolonged commemoration of the Divine, virginal, and salvific Motherhood of her whose inviolate virginity brought the Savior into the world. On the Solemnity of the Birth of Christ the Church both adores the Savior and venerates His glorious Mother. On the Solemnity of the Mother of God (January 1), the Church commemorates the part Mary played in the Mystery of Christ's Birth.

On the Feast of the Holy Family, the Church meditates upon the holy life led in the house at Nazareth by Jesus, the Son of God and Son of Man, Mary His Mother, and Joseph the just man.

On the Epiphany when she celebrates the universal call to salvation, the Church contemplates the Blessed Virgin, the true Seat of Wisdom and true Mother of the Redeemer, who presents to the Wise Men for their adoration the Redeemer of all peoples.

On the Feast of the Presentation (February 2), the Church highlights Mary's part in the suffering on Calvary, bringing the season to a close.

The *Season of Lent,* because of its preparatory character, has few references to Mary. It thus presents Mary as a model for us in living the preparation for Easter as disciples of Christ in such a way as to arrive with her at the Cross and the Resurrection. It does contain the Feast of St. Joseph, Spouse of Mary (March 19), in which Mary has a great part, and the Feast of the Annunciation of the Lord (March 25), in which Mary is also highly involved.

During the *Easter Triduum,* Mary is also seen in various texts that serve to keep her before us. In the Office of Readings for Holy Thursday, the Easter homily of Melito of Sardis is read, which refers to Mary and calls her "the fair ewe." She is also mentioned in the hymn sung at the reposition of the Blessed Sacrament, *Pange Lingua:* "From a noble womb to spring. / Of a pure and spotless Virgin / Born for us on earth below."

In the Veneration of the Cross on Good Friday, the other hymn *Pange Lingua* recalls the Incarnation and the role of Mary in the History of Salvation: "From a virgin's womb appearing, / clothed in our mortality. / All within a lowly manger, / lo, a tender Babe He lies! / See His gentle Virgin Mother / lull to sleep His infant cries! / while the limbs of God incarnate / round with swathing bands she ties." The Passion according to John also contains the passage on Mary at the Cross.

On Holy Saturday, Mary is invoked in the Litany of the Saints and mentioned in the profession of baptismal faith as well as the *Communicantes* of the Canon. At Morning Prayer there is a reference to the sorrowing Mother standing by Jesus at His Death and burial.

During the *Easter Season,* beginning with Holy Saturday the *Liturgy of the Hours* is concluded at Night Prayer with the joyous *Regina Caeli,* the hymn that exults with Mary at the Resurrection of her Son. The Common of the Blessed Virgin

(Mass no. 6) points to the Apostles who "were continually at prayer together with Mary" (Entrance Antiphon) and thus reminds us that we should be too, for her Son "has arisen from His grave" (Communion Antiphon).

During this season there is also the great joy of the Month of Mary (May) and (when Easter comes late) the Feast of the Visitation (May 31) with its joy that anticipates the joy of the Resurrection. All this is topped off by the vigil of prayer in union with Mary that ends with the coming of the Holy Spirit at Pentecost.

In *Ordinary Time*, Mary is always before us—in the Ordinary but also in the Proper feasts that occur throughout this time as well as the celebrations of Mary on Saturday. She is there as the Mother showing continual interest in her children (Our Lady of Lourdes, February 11), as the praying Virgin teaching us to ponder God's Word in our hearts (Immaculate Heart of Mary, 3rd Saturday after Pentecost), as the "garden-paradise" leading us to Christ (Memorial of Our Lady of Mount Carmel, July 16), and as the temple of God and the new Jerusalem calling us home (Dedication of St. Mary Major, August 5).

Mary is with us as the image and the commanding proof of the fulfillment of our final hope (Assumption, August 15) and as the Queen and Intercessor sitting beside the King of Ages (Queenship of Mary, August 22). She is with us as the hope of the world and the dawn of salvation (Birth of Mary, September 8) and as the suffering Mother (Our Lady of Sorrows, September 15).

Mary is with us in the victories of the History of Salvation (Our Lady of the Rosary, October 7) and as the exemplar of dedication to God (Presentation of Mary, November 21).

The *Collection of Masses of the Blessed Virgin Mary* adds 46 new Masses and Mass texts that can serve to aid Mary's clients carry out their devotion to Mary through the Liturgy. (See Appendix 8 for more specific information.)

A. Buono

CZESTOCHOWA (Poland) [67]

SEE   *Apparitions*   *Apparitions after Vatican II*

THE history of Our Lady of Czestochowa is inseparable from a venerable icon honored at the monastery of monks of Saint Paul the Hermit on Jasna Gora (Hill of Light). A whole legendary halo surrounds its origin. In the people's mind the icon was none other than the Madonna of Saint Luke, carved into the top of a table built by Saint Joseph for the Holy Family. Historical studies, on the other hand, place its origin between the 5th and the 8th century. But the popular belief followed the wondrous travels of this sacred Image, from Palestine to Byzantium, then in Hungary, and in Ruthenia, to the castle of Betz. Here begins the history of this icon that is verifiable.

1. Historical Notes and Their Importance

The icon was brought to Czestochowa by Prince Ladislaus Opolczyk, as booty of war, and offered to the monks of Saint Paul in 1384. It suffered severe damage, in 1430, at the hands of brigands. King Ladislas Jagiello had it restored by artists of the court of Augsburg, who imposed a mélange of Byzantine and Western style. The Madonna of Czestochowa belongs to representations of the Virgin known as "Hodigitria," i.e., Mary pointing with her right hand to the Holy Infant held in her left.

The mysterious and dramatic history of this Image only served to increase the popular veneration and the flow of pilgrims. First reports of miracles, in 1402, marked the beginning of grateful testimonies to her who was called "Healer of the sick, Mother of mercy and Queen of Poland." By 1957, some 1,500 testimonies had been counted, in registers of intentions and in ex-votos, all extolling the miraculous beneficence of the sacred Image. (Ex-voto refers to pictures, figures, or other objects hung in chapels and churches in token of a vow or a favor received.)

From the very beginning, this icon of Mary attracted monarchs and knights in time of political misfortune, as well as the sick in quest of healing and separated Christians who came to pray for the unity of the Church. Rulers of Poland laid their crowns and scepters at its feet, made vows to the Virgin, commended to her their burdens, and acknowledged her as queen and mistress of the realm.

In the 15th century golden tablets began to appear among the ex-votos, and in the 16th the Virgin and Infant were capped with royal crowns, a donation of Ladislaus IV. The first coronation in the name of the Pope took place in 1717, and a second in 1910.

Pilgrimages experienced a revival in 1655, when the monks of Jasna Gora repulsed the attack of the Swedes, thanks to an apparition of Our Lady. The statutes of the Diet proclaimed the people's gratitude to the monks for this feat, and in 1764 the Diet decreed Poland's perpetual indebtedness to the Virgin.

In the 18th century, when Poland lost her independence, the Virgin became the patroness of every resistance and the protectress of liberty and the national sovereignty; hence the aversion of the Russian and Prussian occupiers, who tried to prevent pilgrimages and to do away with the sacred Image. At this time writings in its honor, as well as pictorial reproductions, began to appear in increasing numbers. At this time also, the first churches to bear its title were built. Today there are about 270 worldwide, 27 of them in the United States, which has the largest Polish population outside of Poland. And it is estimated that some 10,000 altars the world over show a reproduction of this famous icon of the Virgin.

Group pilgrimages began as early as the 14th century. By the 17th, pilgrims numbered from 40,000 to 60,000 annually. About 200,000 people gathered for the coronation in 1717. The numbers grew in the 19th century when Poland again lost her independence and the monastery became the rallying center of patriotism. Between the two World Wars people came in organized groups as the hostility of the Nazis inflamed the attachment to the national Shrine. The Virgin and the Church were the principal strength of the Polish people. For the Consecration of the nation to the Mother of God a million and a half pilgrims flocked to Czestochowa. During the nine years prior to 1966 a tour of images of Our Lady served as preparation for the special rite of Servitude of Love for the service of Mary.

The number of pilgrims on foot, which had fallen off, rose when political chicanery hampered the usual means of travel. In 1979 more than 40,000 people made their way to Warsaw by foot. In spite of everything, the total number of pilgrims that year came to two million and a half. Increasingly, foreign dignitaries have been among them, like the Kennedy brothers, La Pira, Aldo Moro, and special groups such as one from Italy representing the movement "Communion and Liberation."

For centuries the monastery has been considered the spiritual capital of the Polish nation. Held there are ecclesial Synods, meetings of the Episcopal Conference, various Congresses and most national symposiums. Of particular interest to visitors are the old chapel of the miraculous Image, the basilica of the 15th and 17th century, the monastery of the 17th and 18th century, and the towering campanile built in the 20th century.

J. Zbudniewek

2. American Celebration

On August 22, 1982, Americans joined in celebrating the 600th anniversary of the arrival of the Icon at Jasna Gora. In ceremonies in honor of Our Lady of Czestochowa at the National Shrine of the Immaculate Conception in Washington, more than 2,000 Polish-Americans and friends of Poland marched in procession.

On the same day 5,000 people flocked to the tiny Texas hamlet of Cestohowa, settled by Polish immigrants 109 years ago and named after Czestochowa in Poland.

At an evening Mass in Panna Maria, Texas, known as the oldest Polish settlement in the United States, John Cardinal Krol delivered the homily and recalled that even the Nazi governor of Poland during World War II wrote in his diary that "the greatest strength of Poland resides in the Church and the Saint of Czestochowa."

3. The Words of John Paul II

With the election of Karol Cardinal Wojtyla, Metropolitan Archbishop of Krakow, as Supreme Pontiff on October 16 1978, the Shrine of Our Lady of Czestochowa suddenly vaulted to the attention of the whole world, especially after the Pilgrimage that John Paul II made there in June 1979. At that time, the Pope declared how close the celebrated shrine was to his heart and to the heart of his country Poland as well as how it was a sign of inspiration and faith for the whole Church.

(a) *The Pope's devotion to the "Black Madonna" of Jasna Gora.* "The call of a son of Poland to the Cathedral of Peter contains an evident and strong link with this holy place, with this Shrine of great hope: *Totus tuus* (I am all yours), I had whispered in prayer so many times before this Image" (June 4, 1979).

(b) *Poland's devotion to the "Shrine of the Nation."* "Jasna Gora is not only a goal of pilgrimage for the Polish people of the motherland and of the whole world but it is also the *Shrine of the Nation.* We must lend an ear to this holy place to hear *how the heart of the nation beats in the heart of the Mother.* This heart indeed pulses, as we know, with all the appointments of history, with all the events of the life of the Nation. . . . The history of Poland can be written in various ways; especially the history of the last few centuries can be interpreted in divers keys.

"Yet if we want to know how the Polish heart interprets this history, we must come here, we must lend an ear to this Shrine, we must perceive the echo of the life of the entire Nation in the heart of its Mother and Queen! And if this heart beats with disquieting tones, if there resound in it the solicitude for and the call to conversion and restrengthening of consciences, we must accept this invitation. It is born of a motherly love that in its way forms the historical processes of the Polish land" (June 4, 1979).

"The person who had once spoken in the *canticle* (of the Bogurodzica: 'Mother of God') also spoke with this *Image* (of Czestochowa), manifesting with it her maternal *presence* in the life of the Church and the Motherland. The Virgin of Jasna Gora has revealed her maternal *solicitude* for every soul; for every family; for *every person*" (June 4, 1979).

"The most recent decades have confirmed and made more intense a close union between the Polish Nation and its Queen. Before the Virgin of Czestochowa there was pronounced the consecration of Poland to the Immaculate Heart of Mary on September 8, 1946. Ten years later, there were renewed at Jasna Gora the vows of King Jan Kazimierz on the 300th anniversary of his proclamation of the Mother of God as the Queen of the Polish Kingdom after a kind of 'deluge' (invasion by the Swedes in the 16th century). . . . And finally in the year of the millennium (of the Baptism of Poland) on May 3, 1966, here in this place there was proclaimed by the Primate of Poland the act of total servitude to the Mother of God for the freedom of the Church in Poland and in the whole world" (June 4, 1979, Homily at Jasna Gora).

(c) *Czestochowa, sign of Mary's presence in the Church.* "The heavenly Mother is particularly present here. She is present in the Mystery of Christ and the Church. . . . She is present for all and for each of those who make a pilgrimage to her. . . . Always more and more people from all of Europe and beyond come here" (June 4, 1979).

"White-clothed Mother of the Church! Once again *I consecrate myself to you* 'in your maternal servitude of love': *Totus tuus!* I am totally yours! I consecrate to you the whole Church—even to the ends of the earth! I consecrate to you all humankind; I consecrate to you all my brother and sister human beings. All Peoples and all Nations. I consecrate to you Europe and all the continents. . . . Mother, accept us. Mother, do not abandon us. Mother, guide us!" (June 4, 1979, in the Assembly at Jasna Gora).

A. Rum

- D -

DAUGHTER OF ZION [722, 2676]

SEE *Marian Titles*

THROUGH the words of the Angel to Mary, the Evangelist Saint Luke (1:28-30) seems to suggest the words God used in Zephaniah (3:14-17) to speak to a new people, *"humble and lowly"* (v. 12), *"the remnant"* (v. 13), named *"daughter of Zion"*: *"Shout for joy, O daughter of Zion. . . . Be glad and exult. . . . The Lord has removed the judgment against you [i.e., forgiven you]. . . . The King of Israel, the Lord, is with you; you have no further misfortune to fear. . . . Fear not. . . . The Lord, your God, is with you, a mighty savior."*

Originally, the "daughter of Zion" appears to have been a dependency of Jerusalem, established and fortified, near the Temple, for refugees from Samaria (Mi 4:8-10). But from the beginning of the 7th century B.C. (Is 1:8), it was a section of Jerusalem that symbolized the most religious aspects of the city.

Jeremiah frequently uses the expression in reference to the people of Jerusalem, doomed to the calamity of invasions and ruin because of the infidelity of its kings. After the Exile, disciples of Isaiah set forth the characteristic of the new Israel: it comes into being with a new name (65:15), a new longevity (65:20), a new priesthood (66:21), in a new earth and under new heavens (66:22). These disciples repeat the *"Shout for joy. . . ."* of Zephaniah, addressed this time to Jerusalem/Zion. She brings forth a new people, a new nation, in one day (66:8): *"Before she comes to labor, she gives birth; before the pains come upon her, she safely delivers a male child"* (66:7).

On the basis of these texts the New Testament, and in particular Revelation 12, depicts Mary both as the one through whom Zion gave birth to a new people whose victorious Head is the "male child" (12:5) and as the one who among this new

101

people exercises the maternal function toward the "rest of the offspring" (12:17).

H. Cazelles

DEATH OF MARY

[966]

SEE   *Assumption*
      Dormition, Holy Land
      and Mary, 2h

Munificentissimus Deus
Tomb of Mary, Holy Land
and Mary, 2m

1. Question of Mary's Death

TECHNICALLY speaking, the question of whether Mary died before her Assumption into heaven is still open. Some theologians have held that she did not die, while many more hold the opposite. In defining the doctrine of the Assumption, Pius XII did not settle the question but deliberately left it open: "When the course of her earthly life was finished, [Mary] was taken up body and soul into heavenly glory and exalted by the Lord as Queen over all things, so that she might be the more fully conformed to her Son, the Lord of lords and conqueror of sin and death" (*Munificentissimus Deus*).

However, few if any still hold the notion that Mary did not die. Death is the door through which all of us must pass in accord with our human condition. Jesus, like us in all things except sin, as stated in the Epistle to the Hebrews (4:15), subjected Himself to death. It is hard to understand why Mary would want to do otherwise.

Furthermore, Catholic traditions, cult, and archeology concur on this point. From the most ancient times, the Orthodox celebrated the "Dormition" of Mary, that is, her death and her Assumption. The death of Our Lady is described in an apocryphal work of the 4th century, *The Dormition of the Holy Mother of God*, which is authoritative by its antiquity: it contains information and Jewish-Christian literary forms that reveal an original source dating to the 2nd century.

Two sites are preserved in which the Marian cult precedes the Byzantine epoch. On Mount Zion, near the Upper Room, in the crypt of the Basilica of Saint Ann, a tradition indicates the house in which Mary spent her last years and in which she died. (In 1898 this house was purchased by Kaiser Wilhelm II of Germany and donated to German Catholics for the erection of the Church of the Dormition.)

Most of all, on the slopes of the Mount of Olives, next to the Basilica of Gethsemani, there is preserved the tomb in which the body of Mary is said to have been buried. Archeologists verify that it is a tomb from the 1st century, that it was for a single person, and that it was preserved in a simple grotto. The fact that it was the object of a cult confirms the other data of the tradition.

2. Account of the Dormition

The account of the Dormition says that when Mary was about sixty years old, she was visited by an Angel (who is thought by some to be Gabriel since the event was parallel to the Annunciation and by others to be Michael since it is he who guides souls to heaven). He presented her with a palm from heaven to be carried before her bier and told her that she would die within three days.

The Apostles were miraculously transported to her deathbed, where she lay with a candle in her hand. After taking leave from them Mary had a vision of her Son, Who came accompanied by Angels, Patriarchs, and Prophets to carry her soul to heaven. The Apostles escorted her body on a bier to Gethsemani (other versions say the Valley of Jehoshaphat) and Saint John carried the palm.

When Mary's body was laid in the tomb, her soul was reunited with her body and she was carried up (assumed) into heaven for her Coronation. Roses fluttered down to the empty sepulcher, while her girdle went into the hands of St. Thomas the Apostle, who in keeping with his skeptical nature had questioned the fact of her Assumption.

A. Buono

DEVOTION(S) [971, 1172]

1. Devotion

IN the first sense (and always in the singular) devotion means ardor to serve God. It is the interior act of the will giving itself to God with generosity and fervor; the interior dispositions correspond to this will and maintain the soul in it. Devotion leads to exterior acts, but essentially it is interior. Although based on faith, it has its principal source in theological love and sometimes can be identified with it.

Saint Thomas Aquinas deals with "devotion" in the *Summa Theologica* (II-II, q. 82) where he writes that "devotion is an act of the virtue of religion." It is readiness of the will to serve God, readiness that comes from the will (hence the whole person) offering itself for the service and worship of God. Saint Thomas points out that devotion is a gift of God but also a work of human beings, particularly as exhorted to pray, to meditate, to contemplate, all of which inspires love and engenders devotion. Devotion should mark our whole life, and constantly. And where it does, it radiates interior joy.

In sum, devotion is the joyous *dedication* of the whole self to God (and to others for the sake of God), in living response to the gift He makes of Himself.

2. Devotions

Devotions are the exterior acts of devotion (in the first or generic sense, spoken of above). Customarily, however, "a devotion" or a "special" devotion means a body of religious acts proposed or at least authorized by the Church, acts inspired by a special object (that to which the devotion is directed). Likewise the attachment to these acts is part of the devotion.

A devotion consists of acts. In their beginning at least, devotions serve as means of giving oneself totally to God (which is devotion in the generic sense).

A devotion requires a special "object." This may be a Mystery of God, a definite person (the Saints), sometimes things (images, places, etc.). Centering around this object are both the spiritual activity of the devotion—whose origin must be attributed to the Spirit—and the spiritual attraction that accompanies it.

A devotion also signifies a spiritual attraction, an attachment of love both to its object and to the acts or "practices" by which it is expressed. Hence a devotion (whether created for oneself, or adopted from some existing one) includes a "personal" element, a choice and decision by the self—but the Holy Spirit must not be absent.

Devotions are legitimate. Indeed, devotion (in the generic sense) affects the whole person, and "the spiritual itself is fleshly," as Péguy said. The multiplicity of devotions is explained by the "unfathomable richness" of the one God, Whom we discover through successive and ever partial approaches. But the diversity also comes from the differences among people and even from differences in individuals according to the times of their human and spiritual development.

Devotions are judged by their fruit. A devotion without devotion (in the generic sense) invites adverse judgment on the "devotee." A devotion implies devotion. Its purpose must be to serve God and grow to *"the full maturity of Christ"* (Eph 4:15-16).

A devotion, or devotions, spring up and grow, and can deviate and die. A devotion deviates when it tends to superstitions the quest of magical efficacy rather than conversion of the heart. It also deviates when it focuses on gratification of the self (the old authors spoke of "spiritual epicurism") and ignores the essential, the desire to serve God and fellow humans.

Nevertheless, and because devotion without devotions languishes, we must not prejudge any devotions, however ingenuous or "popular." A simple gesture like wearing a medal or reciting a favorite prayer-formula can be an act of true devotion. It is the pastoral function of the Church to watch over and, if need be, to reform and redirect the fundamental tendency of devotions of the faithful.

Judgment concerning devotions lies within the authority of the Church. It approves, corrects, and sometimes must condemn them. Saint Louis-Marie de Montfort notes that a "true" Marian devotion must be: (a) *interior,* more in the heart than in practices; (b) *steadfast,* based on faith and not fluctuating with moods and feelings; (c) *disinterested,* more intent on God than the graces to be obtained (though the prayers of petition and thanksgiving are important elements in the general devotion that moves us to serve God); (d) *oriented toward Christ,* in Whom we are "brought to the Father"; and (e) *confident and heartfelt,* since in us the spiritual itself is fleshly, i.e., communicates through the flesh.

These earmarks represent the ground rules of "good usage" on which the Church relies for helping the faithful to recognize the working of the Spirit in a given age or need.

3. Devotion and Devotions to Mary

Devotion to Mary is the ardor to serve her, the better to serve God, whereas "devotions" are the acts by which this devotion is expressed.

Mary, the Woman, the Virgin, and the Mother most blessed of God, associated by Him in the work of the Son to an extraordinary degree, and even now sharing in His risen glory—Mary is for us a "sign," because our relationship to Mary says something about God, and something about ourselves. Our contemporaries have come to recognize this.

The Church very early kept the "memory" of Mary, and was led to say something about Mary (e.g., at Ephesus) in the intent to say something about Christ. Moreover, the Church very soon placed itself under the protection of Mary, calling upon her in its needs (by the prayer *Sub tuum,* in the early part of the 3rd century).

Throughout the history of the Church, it is Mary who has summoned all to give praise (Lk 1:46-55) and to practice devotion (Jn 2:5). She is also the one who at the foot of the Cross shows the heights that fidelity must reach. Finally, she is the one who in the Upper Room indicates how prayer tends above all to ask for the Spirit and to gather the community of believers.

Wearing a medal of Mary, praying to her, making pilgrimages to her or, more generally, "consecrating" oneself to her *in order to* consecrate oneself to Christ and to God—fundamentally what all this means is that we "devote" ourselves with joy to the service of God and the Church.

"After the Synod of Ephesus the cult of the people of God toward Mary wonderfully increased in veneration and love, in invocation and imitation" (LG 66).

Veneration and love for Mary lead to God and redound to His glory: "Blessed are You, O Lord, in the honor that we render to the Blessed Virgin Mary" (Cl. Rozier).

The invocation of Mary acknowledges that within the Communion of Saints she "occupies, after Christ, the highest place and the one that is closest to us" (LG 54) and also unites herself to Christ Who is *"forever living to make intercession for us"* (Heb 7:25).

The imitation of Mary leads not to abject servitude but to the praise and joyous service of God (and others for love of God).

"True devotion consists neither in sterile or transitory affection nor in a certain vain credulity. It proceeds from true faith, by which we are led to know the excellence of the Mother of God, and we are moved to a filial love toward our Mother and to the imitation of her virtues" (LG 67).

Misguided feelings and "vain credulity" are the pitfalls of devotion, manifested in bizarre practices or attachment to unfounded traditions (unrecognized apparitions, for example). Excesses have led some people to frown on devotion and devotions alike. But a devotion to Mary drawn from the Bible and the Liturgy could, as Paul VI observed, find ready acceptance among all (even among "separated brethren") and lift the faithful to total "practice" of the Christian life.

To sum up, there are these hortatory words of the Council: "The Virgin in her own life lived an example of that maternal love by which all should be animated who cooperate in the apostolic mission of the Church for the regeneration of human beings" (LG 65).

A. Tostain

DOGMAS, MARIAN

[88ff, 471-492, 495, 496-507, 966]

SEE *Assumption*   *Magisterium (Documents of)*
Icons and Images of Mary *Mother of God*
Immaculate Conception *Munificentissimus Deus*
Ineffabilis Deus   *Virginity, Perpetual*

The *Catechism of the Catholic Church* states: "The Church's Magisterium exercises the authority it holds from Christ to the fullest extent when it defines dogmas, that is, when it proposes truths contained in Divine Revelation or having a necessary connection with them, in a form obliging the Christian people to an irrevocable act of adherence.

"There is an organic connection between our spiritual life and the dogmas. Dogmas are lights along the path of faith; they illuminate it and make it secure. Conversely, if our life is upright, our intellect and heart will open to welcome the light shed by the dogmas of faith" (nos. 88-89).

The following truths about Mary have been formally defined or declared by the Church.

1. The Two Early Dogmas

(1) *Divine Motherhood.* The Council of Ephesus (431) declared that in Christ there were two natures (one Divine and one human) but only one person. It also approved the second letter of Saint Cyril to Nestorius and through this approval officially confirmed the attribution to Mary of the title Mother of God: "Thus, [the holy Fathers] have unhesitatingly called the holy Virgin 'Mother of God.' "

The Council went on to condemn anyone who "does not confess that the Emmanuel is truly God and, therefore, that the holy Virgin is the Mother of God [since she begot according to the flesh the Word of God made flesh.]"

The normative decision taken at Ephesus was then explicitly promulgated as a dogma in 451 by the Council of Chalcedon: "Following the holy Fathers, we unanimously teach to confess one and the same Son, Our Lord Jesus Christ, the same perfect in Divinity and perfect in Humanity, the same truly God and truly Man composed of rational soul and body, the same one in being with the Father as to the Divinity and one in being with us as to the Humanity, like unto us in all things but sin (cf. Heb 4:15). The same was begotten from the Father before the ages as to the Divinity and in the latter days for us and our salvation was born as to His Humanity from Mary the Virgin Mother of God."

(2) *Perpetual Virginity.* From the first formulations of her faith, the Church has confessed that Jesus was conceived solely by the power of the Holy Spirit in the womb of the Virgin Mary, affirming also the corporeal aspect of this event: Jesus was conceived "by the Holy Spirit without human seed ... and without any detriment to her virginity, which remained inviolable even after His birth" (Council of the Lateran, in 649).

Although this Council of the Lateran was not a General one, the deepening of faith in the virginal Motherhood led the Church to confess Mary's real and perpetual virginity even in the act of giving birth to the Son of God made man. In 681, the Third General Council of Constantinople stated: "By the power of the Holy Spirit [Jesus Christ] was born of the Virgin Mary."

Here the term "Virgin" is connected with the person of Mary appositionally and not adjectivally or attributively. The syntax of the Greek text is: "Mary the Virgin," and doctrinally it indicates the essential characteristics, the significative elements, of the human contribution to the Annunciation. Mary is the Virgin by antonomasia (the giving of a proper name that is made up of a leading quality): the determining qualification of her contribution to the Annunciation in itself and to the salvation that follows.

Through the ages there has been such unanimity about Mary's perpetual virginity that there was no need for direct action on the part of the Magisterium. The Second Vatican Council, for example, had over 30 references to Mary as Virgin, Virgin Mother, or ever-Virgin. It stated that Christ's birth did not diminish His Mother's virginal integrity but sanctified it (cf. LG 57). And so the Liturgy of the Church celebrates Mary as the "Ever-Virgin" (Ibid.) (See CCC 496-511.)

2. The Two Modern Dogmas

(3) *Immaculate Conception.* In 1854, Pope Pius IX defined the dogma that Mary was conceived free from original sin—a belief totally in accord with the belief of the Church from time immemorial.

(4) *Assumption into Heaven.* In 1950, in accord with the belief of the Church throughout the ages, Pius XII defined the dogma of the Assumption, that Mary was taken up body and soul into heaven at the end of her earthly life.

Two main corollaries flow from these four dogmas concerning Mary—her sinlessness and her veneration.

Mary's Sinlessness. The Council of Trent (1547) stated that the Church holds that through a special privilege Mary once justified was able to avoid all sins, even venial ones, throughout her entire life (Canon 23 on Justification).

Veneration of Mary. The Council of Trent also declared that "it is a good and useful thing to invoke the Saints [including the Queen of all Saints] humbly and to have recourse to their prayers and to their efficacious help to obtain favors from God through His Son Jesus Christ Our Lord Who alone is our Redeemer and Savior" (DS 984). At the same time, honor and veneration are to be paid to images of the Virgin Mother of God (DS 986).

3. Deepened Understanding after Vatican II

After the Second Vatican Council, the attention of theologians was turned toward the central truths of the Faith (Christological, ecclesiological, and anthropological) to seek to apply the eternal truths to changing conditions of this world and to express them in a way that people of the modern world will understand (OT 16).

Reflection in this vein on Marian themes soon followed, leading to a large literary production of the finest quality. The result was significant for the whole of Mariology, but the Marian dogmas reaped particular benefit from it.

The Divine Motherhood of Mary received a fuller understanding. It is no longer presented solely in the genetic moment of conception and birth. Rather, consideration is taken of its historical and human character, and it is presented with a greater focus on the continuous and progressive relationship of Mary with her Son, from His conception to His Resurrection and Ascension into heaven.

The rediscovered soteriological vision also had a positive influence in the manner of presenting Mary's virginity. This dogma is approached from three aspects. In its Christological aspect, it indicates that Jesus is the truly new Being, the uncollectible gift of God. In its salvific aspect, it reveals the plan of God Who selects lowly means to accomplish salvation. In its existential aspect, it expresses the total option for God on Mary's part.

The dogmas of the Immaculate Conception and the Assumption used to be considered as particular privileges that reveal the greatness and glory of Mary considered as an isolated person. Today, they are presented within the context of far vaster contexts such as Christological, anthropological, and eschatological ones.

Thus, the Immaculate Conception calls attention to the need of every human for redemption but also to the image of the one who remained totally free—by reason of her fullness of grace—from all stain of sin. Hence, it calls attention to the full and definitive victory of Christ over evil.

The Assumption is closely linked with the anthropological truths of the dignity and the vocation of the human body. As such, it is a sign that confirms the fulfillment of the promises of Christ and of the faith in the resurrection of the body.

Seen in this context, the Marian dogmas acquire a profoundly ecclesiastical meaning. The figure of Mary reveals itself at the same time as a typical member and Mother with respect to the Church. Before the Church appears, Mary is already holy and immaculate; before the Church appears, Mary is united with Christ and forms with Him one sole body, one sole life, and one sole love; before the Church appears, after Mary has been in communion with her sufferings, she participates body and soul in the glory of the Risen Christ. Yet, these anticipations are not foreign to the Church, because in all this Mary is already Church.   *A. Buono*

- E -

EASTERN CHURCH AND MARY [818, 838]

SEE *Ecumenism (Mary and)*   *Icons and Images of Mary*

1. Historical Contributions to Marian Teaching and Devotion

THE Eastern Church may rightly be regarded as having originated the teaching about Mary and devotion to her. It was the Eastern Church that gave rise to the Apocrypha (specifically the *Protevangelium of James* and its adaptation, the *Pseudo-Matthew* and the *Transitus (Passing) of Mary)*. The traditions concerning Our Lady were contained in these books and prompted devotion to her.

At the same time, we also have evidence that devotion to Mary was practiced in the East as early as the beginning of the 3rd century. A Greek papyrus found in Egypt and dating from the early 3rd century has the Marian prayer *Sub Tuum Praesidium (Under Your Patronage)*. It thus provides proof that the "Theotokos," Mother of God, was venerated even before the Council of Ephesus in the 4th century.

We can also show that the words "Hail Mary" in Greek are inscribed on a column of the Byzantine Church of the Annunciation at Nazareth. This comprises a prayer to Our Lady that goes back to the 4th century.

The efforts of Saint Athanasius and Saint Cyril of Alexandria in behalf of the Blessed Virgin culminated in the official bestowal of the title *Theotokos* (Mother of God) upon Mary by the Council of Ephesus. From this key title there flowed all the other titles heaped on her by East and West in subsequent centuries.

The Eastern Liturgy played a major role in this Marian tradition. At an early stage, Feasts were celebrated in honor of the Marian events—and these passed on to the Western Church through their celebration at Rome in the 7th century.

These were the Feasts of the Hypapante or Presentation of Our Lord (4th century); the Dormition or Assumption (5th century); the Annunciation (date not established); and the Nativity of Mary (7th century). Later, other Feasts arose, such as the Conception of Mary and the Presentation of Mary.

The hymns and prayers found in the Liturgy also had an effect on Marian devotion in the West. Two of the most celebrated prayers in the Liturgy of the Hours were the *Sub Tuum Praesidium* and the *Akathist Hymn,* which placed much spiritual power in Mary's hands and rendered true praise to her as the Mother of God.

Moreover, Mary holds a privileged place in the Eastern Liturgies. There are a wide-ranging series of Marian insertions in them, such as the so-called Ethiopian Anaphora of Mary.

The Byzantine Liturgy of the Eucharist makes reference to Mary's prayers on several occasions and voices four "remembrances" of Mary after the conclusion of litanies and invocations: "Remembering our all-holy, spotless, most blessed and glorious Lady, Mother of God and ever-Virgin Mary," and *refers to her prayers.*

The principal mention of Our Lady occurs after the invocation of the Holy Spirit at the Consecration: "We offer You this worship in spirit on behalf of our forebears . . . and especially our all-holy, spotless, most blessed and glorious Lady, Mother of God and ever-Virgin Mary." Then a hymn is sung to Mary. Mary is called "sinless" and "Mother of God," exalted above cherubim and seraphim, and described as having "brought forth the Word of God." It concludes with the words: "We magnify you, Mother of God in truth."

2. Present Attitude toward Mary

Present-day Eastern Orthodox Christians have continued this tradition of love and honor toward the Mother of God. In this they are united with the teachings of the Catholic Church except for the doctrine of the Immaculate Conception. Orthodox theologians hold that the Immaculate Conception would have set Mary too far apart from the other members of the human race. They therefore regard Mary as being sanctified at the Incarnation.

Some also reject the doctrine of the Assumption, although it is a teaching that originated in the East.

There is little doubt that the rejection of these two doctrines was influenced by the acrimony that was sometimes present in the past relations of the two Churches. The ecumenism engendered by Vatican II has paved the way for a balanced discussion about differences, including differences about Marian teaching. Unquestionably, devotion to the Mother of God never waned in the Orthodox Church.

Paul VI paid tribute to this love for Mary on the part of Orthodox Christians when he declared: "In venerating with particular love the glorious Theotokos and in acclaiming her as the 'Hope of Christians,' Catholics unite themselves with their brothers and sisters of the Orthodox Churches, *in which devotion to the Blessed Virgin finds its expression in a beautiful lyricism and in solid doctrine*" (MC 32).

And it is no doubt this devotion to Mary that is both a harbinger of and a spur to Christian unity. The cause of Christian unity "properly pertains to the role of Mary's Spiritual Motherhood. For Mary did not and cannot engender those who belong to Christ, except in one faith and one love" (MC 33).

A. Buono

ECUMENISM (MARY AND) [820-822]

SEE   *Eastern Church and Mary*   *Judaism and Mary*

NEAR to the center of the Mystery of Salvation by her maternal relation to the Word incarnate, Mary is in close relation with the Mystery of the Church and its unity. In the conflicts that have divided and continue to divide Christians, cultic and doctrinal expressions of this relation between the Church and Mary play an important role. If at times this role appears to be negative, a factor of oppositions, fundamentally it cannot but serve a positive end, lighting the way that is leading Christians unceasingly to unity in Jesus Christ.

1. "Mary, Mother of God" at the Council of Ephesus

One of the first great disputes that have divided Christians since the 5th century had to do with Christological doctrine, the nature and person of Christ. Antiocheans emphasized the distinction between the Humanity and the Divinity in Jesus Christ. Nestorius went so far as to assert an absolute separation between the two "natures" of Christ, denying in effect the real union between them. In contrast, Alexandrians stressed the fact that there was no common measure between the Humanity and the Divinity and tended toward absorption of Christ's Humanity by His Divinity ("One only nature of the incarnate Son of God"—Cyril of Alexandria), a tendency which led logically to the heresy of Monophysitism.

In proclaiming Mary "Theotokos," Mother of God, the Council of Ephesus restored and expressed the unity of the Church regarding its belief in the Word incarnate. This Marian teaching—that Mary is the Mother of God—became a touchstone of orthodoxy and unity.

2. Mary in the Western Controversy between Catholics and Protestants

To the extent that Western Christianity was organized around the Church of Rome, not only art but spiritual doctrine and in time theology itself sought to express the privileges of Mary and her role in the economy of salvation. In addition, her place in the Church's worship and belief was extolled and made secure.

Yet it was not this place of Mary in worship and belief that played a determining role in the first disputes of the 16th-century Reformation. We can cite passages and prayers of Luther, of Zwingli, and of Anglican theologians that show a high regard for and a fervent attitude toward Mary as the woman whom *all ages to come shall call blessed.* But in spite of this, and rather soon, there arose points of controversy between the Reformers and Catholics on the subject of Mary. Among these points were: the veneration of Mary, the prayers addressed to her, the prominence given to her active participation in the Redemption, and beliefs relating to Mary's conception and bodily assumption, which were challenged as nonscriptural. It can be said that today still the basic contentions of the Reformation find application in Mary:

- *"Soli Deo gloria"* ("to God alone the glory")—hence the veneration accorded to Mary runs the risk of becoming idolatry.
- *"Jesus Christ as only Mediator between God and human beings"*—hence what place is there for a Marian mediation, for the intercession sought in prayer addressed to her. . . .
- *"Sola fide, sola gratia"* (by faith alone, by grace alone)—the fundamental principle of justification by faith alone, to the exclusion of works, calls into question Mary's active participation in the work of our salvation.
- *"Scriptura sola"* (Scripture only)—which is to say, only what is found in Scripture can be made a belief for Christians. The appeal to Tradition as in some way additional to Scripture is declared unacceptable. But the Church believes a number of things about Mary that are not explicitly taught in the New Testament.

The impassioned character of the controversies in regard to Mary made dialogue rather difficult. This was especially true with Protestant fundamentalists and Evangelical conservatives. On the other hand, where currents of High Church and Low Church coexisted within the same communion, it was possible to see fruitful dialogue taking place.

Such was (and is) the case with the Anglican Church, in which since the Reformation "Catholics" and "Evangelicals" have been in constant interrelation and have maintained unity as to Sacraments and Liturgy.

Not only are there in the Anglican Liturgy Marian expressions, Marian feasts, and Marian names of churches (Church of St. Mary the Virgin, Feast of the Purification of Mary the Blessed Virgin, etc.). There have been as well in every period of the Anglican Church theological currents in favor of Marian devotion and traditional Marian belief (Carolinian Fathers of the 17th century; Oxford Movement of the 19th; contemporary Anglo-Catholics). And as for theologians of Evangelical bent, today we see many of them in renewed study of Mary's place in the New Testament and substantiating the inseparable link between Mariology and Christology (cf. John de Satgé, *Mary and the Christian Gospel,* London, 1976).

Dialogue along this line between Roman Catholics and representative non-Catholic groups has now been created. In the more friendly and trustful contemporary climate there is reason to hope for positive results in regard to Marian doctrine and prayer. On the Catholic side, it can be said that there has been a return to the Scriptural supports, owing to a greater interest in Biblical theology. This in turn has led to a recentering of Marian doctrine on Christ. Chapter 8 of the *Constitution on the Church (Lumen Gentium)* is typical of this orientation. In a related development, a growing number of Protestants have begun to take a closer look at the Scriptural evidence concerning Mary and are finding in Jesus Christ the key to a truly spiritual understanding of the Mystery of Mary.

3. Mary in Eastern Christianity

If it was possible for such a dialogue to be created in the West, the reason in large part was that Orthodox (Eastern) Christians had entered into ecumenical dialogue as early as 1920. In the view of the Orthodox, the Marian teaching transmitted by the Tradition of the Church belongs to the very essence of the faith. A Christianity deprived of the Blessed Virgin would be a mutilated Christianity with a nature different from that of established teaching.

This insistence of the Eastern Church is maintained in dialogue, and its Liturgy leaves a marked place for the Mother of God in the celebration of every mystery of Christ. Hence, contact with the liturgical prayer of Eastern Christians offers the possibility of seeing more clearly what is the place of Mary in relation to her Son and the Holy Spirit, as well as her place in the domain of faith, prayer, and the communal life of the Church.

Dialogue with the Eastern Church on the subject of Mary may also show Catholics the way to a better balance, through Christ and the Holy Spirit, between various levels of life in the Church—personal, local, and universal.

4. Toward a Conciliar Community

The way to Christian unity seems today to lie in the pursuit of a "conciliar" community embracing various Christian Churches. We have seen that while Mary may have been a sign of discord, dialogue concerning her has now made possible a growth of this conciliar community. Mary is at the heart of the living memory of the Church, which receives the present gift of the Holy Spirit. By this gift the Church continuously imparts renewed being to the Body of Christ in the present world and directs the hope of all believers toward the Lord Who is coming: *"Do whatever He tells you"* (Jn 2:5).   P. Zobel

EMMANUEL

SEE *Immanuel*

EPHESUS   [466, 495]

SEE *Assumption*   *Mother of God*
     Dogmas, Marian   *Motherhood, Spiritual*
     Lux Veritatis

EPHESUS was a Greek city located on the western shore of Asia Minor. Strategically situated between the eastern and the western world, it was a city of world importance in New Testament times, both politically and economically with a population of some 250,000. Paul preached at Ephesus during his 2nd and 3rd missionary journeys (until he was forced to leave following a riot instigated by the silversmith Demetrius).

Nonetheless, a large Christian community quickly developed in Ephesus.

There is a tradition (mentioned by Saints Justin and Irenaeus) that John the Apostle lived in Ephesus for a long time. Since Mary had been entrusted to John by the dying Christ, it was natural for the idea to spread that she too had lived in Ephesus. In fact, there exist the remains of a house in which she is supposed to have lived. Unfortunately, corroboration for such a tradition is lacking.

However, Ephesus has another connection with Our Lady. It was the Council of Ephesus (431) that first approved the expression "Mother of God" with reference to Mary after it had decreed that in Christ there was one person but two natures (human and Divine). This title of Mary paved the way for her singular place in the Redemption and in Christianity.

In 1931, Pope Pius XI issued the Encyclical *Lux Veritatis* ("The Light of Truth") to commemorate the 15th centenary of the Council of Ephesus and instituted the new feast of the Motherhood of Our Lady for the whole Western Church.

A. Buono

EPHREM (Saint)

SEE   *Servants of Mary, 1*

EVANGELIZATION AND MARIAN PIETY   [849ff, 927, 2472]

SEE   *Popular Religion and Marian Piety*

MARIAN piety is a stimulus and support to evangelization. Saint Louis-Marie Grignion de Montfort was both an untiring popular preacher of the Gospel and an ardent promoter of true devotion to Mary. Closer to our time, Abbé Godin, one of the pioneers of modern evangelization, was a man of deep and tender Marian piety.

Among the movements stirring in the Church today, in the spirit of the Second Vatican Council, are the effort to preach the Gospel to people of our time and a renewal of

Marian piety. But it seems that the two movements have little in common, to judge from pastoral activity and even from the theology of the day. Often, "those dedicated to the apostolate" and "those devoted to Mary" are at odds with one another.

"Could it be that the Holy Spirit would inspire at the same time this rediscovery of Mary and this apostolic renewal unless there were a basic rapport between the two movements?" (Cardinal Suenens).

The purpose here is to point out some aspects of this relationship and some inferences to be drawn from it. Our sources are two Apostolic Exhortations of Paul VI: *Devotion to the Blessed Virgin Mary (Marialis Cultus,* 1974) and *Evangelization in the Modern World (Evangelii Nuntiandi,* 1975).

1. Union with Jesus-Savior

To evangelize is *"to announce the Good News of the Kingdom of God"* (Lk 4:43), the salvation manifested by the miracles and Resurrection of Jesus and offered in His Name to all people. To evangelize is, more pointedly, to make known the personal Mystery of Jesus, Son of God become man to make us adopted children of God (cf. Gal 4:4-5).

We can therefore say that to evangelize is to continue the work of salvation for which Jesus was sent by the Father.

Mary, from the moment of the Annunciation, is the perfect model of faith in the Good News of salvation through the Incarnation of the Son of God. And, "as 'handmaid of the Lord,' she devoted herself totally to the person and work of her Son" (LG 56).

Mary brought Jesus to Elizabeth and to John the Baptist. She "evangelized" the shepherds and the Magi. At Cana, by her faith in Jesus, she obtained the sign that confirmed the faith of the disciples. By confiding—no doubt to the beloved disciple—the memories long kept and reflected on in her heart, she enlightened the faith of the Church in Jesus, Son of God *"born of a woman"* (Gal 4:4).

The Church (and every Christian), contemplating Mary, enters more deeply into the Mystery of the Incarnation and feels impelled to give testimony of it.

From Mary, it is clear that evangelization springs from personal faith in Jesus and union with Him; that its object is the Mystery of Christ; and that it is cooperation with the very mission of Jesus.

2. Power of the Holy Spirit

"Evangelization will never be possible without the action of the Holy Spirit. The Spirit descends on Jesus of Nazareth at the moment of His baptism (Mt 3:17). . . . Jesus is 'led by the Spirit' to experience in the desert the decisive combat and the supreme test before beginning His mission (Mt 4:1). It is 'in the power of the Spirit' (Lk 4:14) that He returns to Galilee and begins His preaching at Nazareth, applying to Himself the passage of Isaiah: 'The Spirit of the Lord is upon Me' (Lk 4:18; Is 61:1). . . . To the disciples whom He is about to send forth He says: 'Receive the Holy Spirit' (Jn 20:22)" (EN 75).

All through the Acts of the Apostles it is the Holy Spirit Who inspires and guides evangelization, through extraordinary "charisms" (gift of tongues, "prophesyings," healings, etc.) but also through a constant, less palpable presence that inspires filial prayer, preaching, fraternal communion. It is with the assistance of the Holy Spirit that the Church is born and spreads (Acts 9:31). In the Cenacle, Mary is present with the Apostles: "By her prayers she implored the gift of the Spirit, Who had already overshadowed her in the Annunciation" (LG 59).

The similarity between Pentecost and the Annunciation is suggested in the texts of Luke. To the Apostles Jesus says: "*You will receive power when the Holy Spirit comes down on you; then you are to be My witnesses . . .*" (Acts 1:8). To Mary, the Angel had announced: "*The Holy Spirit will come upon you and the power of the Most High will overshadow you*" (Lk 1:35). The Incarnation of Christ in the heart and flesh of Mary and the birth of the Church through the witnessing of the disciples are both the work of the Holy Spirit. They escape all human might and constitute "*wonders*" of the Power of God to Whom "*nothing is impossible.*"

With Mary, "temple of the Holy Spirit" (MC 26), the Church understands that evangelization is not a human work but a bringing to birth of the Body of Christ through the power of the Spirit of God.

For our work of evangelization to bear fruit we must, as in the Cenacle, "pray faithfully with Mary, Mother of Jesus," and implore the Holy Spirit. We must enter ever more deeply into "the mystery-laden bond between the Spirit of God and the Virgin of Nazareth, and their action in the Church" (MC 27).

True Marian piety is infused with the Holy Spirit, the Spirit of Pentecost Who impels us to evangelize.

3. Motherhood of the Church

"It is the whole Church that receives the mission to evangelize. . . . Evangelization is for no one an individual and isolated act; it is one that is deeply ecclesial . . . in communion with the Church and her pastors" (EN 15 and 60).

Evangelization is a projection of the motherhood of the Church, of the fecundity inherent in the Communion of Saints. That is why union with the Church and obedience to the hierarchy in evangelization are critical.

Jerusalem, sign of the unity of God's people, and spouse of God called to become mother of a multitude of children (cf. Is 54 and 66; Ps 87, etc.), has its fulfillment in the Church our Mother (Gal 4:26-27; cf. Rv 12:17). It is in the Church and through the Church that we are born of God and grow to the image of Christ. Evangelization is an active participation in the motherhood of the Church to bring to birth the Body of Christ. It does not bear fruit except in communion with the Church visible and its pastors, and more mysteriously with the whole Church of heaven and earth. It is an essential aspect of the *Communion of Saints*.

On Calvary, Mary was proclaimed by our Savior Mother of the beloved disciple and—according to the deep conviction of the Church—Mother of all disciples whom Jesus loves, Mother of the whole human race for which Jesus gave His life.

Mary never ceases to exercise this Motherhood of grace: "Taken up to heaven, . . . she continues by her constant intercession to bring us the gifts of eternal salvation. By her maternal charity she cares for the brothers and sisters of her Son who still journey on earth" (LG 62).

Mary is the personal image, the perfect realization, of the motherhood of the Church/Communion of Saints. She is "our Mother in the Communion of Saints" (MC 29).

"The action of the Church in the world can be likened to an extension of Mary's concern. The active love she showed at Nazareth, in the house of Elizabeth, at Cana and on Golgotha . . . finds its extension in the Church's maternal concern that all people should come to knowledge of the truth" (MC 28). This cooperation, this deep conjunction between Mary and the Church to produce the Mystical Body of Christ, prompted the Second Vatican Council to say: "The Virgin in her own life lived an example of that maternal love by which all should be animated who cooperate in the apostolic mission of the Church for the regeneration of human beings" (LG 65).

4. A Few Corollaries

Marian piety (understood as meditation on the role of Mary in the Gospel and the life of the Church, prayer with Mary and through her intercession, imitation of Mary, etc.) is a stimulus to and an incomparable support for evangelization. It also helps us understand and live more fully the profound reality: union with Christ, docility to the Holy Spirit, communion with the whole Church, demonstration in our lives of God's motherly love (cf. EN 29).

True Marian piety makes the apostle of the Gospel more receptive to the *"fruit of the Spirit, which is love, joy, peace, patient endurance, kindness, generosity, humility"* (Gal 5:22). It presses him or her to go to the most abandoned, the most helpless, and to those who seem most impervious to the Good News of Jesus the Savior.

"The Spirit-inspired encounter of the Marian movement and the apostolic movement is not a chance happening. It is a prodigious grace both for Marian piety, which thus reaches its full potential, and for apostolic action, which becomes rooted in the Spiritual Motherhood of Mary" (Cardinal Suenens).

J. Laurenceau

- F -

FAITH OF MARY [144, 273, 494]

SEE   *Annunciation*   *Presentation of Mary*
        Cana   *Servant of the Lord*
        Cross (Mary at the)   *Visitation*
        Fidelity

IN Hebrew, "to believe" is expressed by two words: *"Aman"* which connotes firmness (from which derives our "Amen") and *"batah,"* which puts greater emphasis on trust and enlightenment. These two words represent the two poles of the act of believing: *faith-illumination* (which is the light received) and *faith-adherence* (which is the personal response).

Faith, therefore, is not an ossified state, or an act elicited once for all. Faith is total trust in someone, and this means readiness to accept all the surprises that can come from God, Who never ceases to arouse and enlighten faith for the sake of continual movement forward. The believer is "built" gradually and advances by the responses given to God, Who calls.

With regard to Mary's faith, we should note the comparative reticence of the Gospels. When Luke or John writes, it is to inform Christians of the important points that concern them, and not to produce a biography. This is why in regard to Mary they do no more than underline key points, to show us more clearly the depth and progression of her faith and to contribute to our understanding of the Mystery of Salvation.

These key points are so many insights into the revelation of God's plan and Mary's growth. At the Annunciation, the light received by Mary from the Most High shattered all her plans for herself and put her on a course in which the gift of herself attained, and would attain, a fullness unequaled. Her adherence of faith brought her the praise of Elizabeth, speaking by the Holy Spirit: *"Blessed is she who believed . . ."* (Lk 1:45).

The first "beatitude" of the Gospel serves to underline Mary's faith, a faith that made her direct her whole being to the Lord to sing His praise and tell Him her gratitude in the *Magnificat*.

Faith is progression in the knowledge we have of someone. Even Mary knew the uncertainties and gropings inherent in the life of every believer. After the *"how"* of the mysterious and sorrowful prophecy of Simeon, came the *"why"* of the Finding in the Temple (Lk 2:28).

Cana marks an important transition and John makes note of it. The quasi-refusal of Jesus enlightens her heart; hence she makes a decision: *"Do whatever He tells you."* Cana underlines the transition to another kind of relationship with her Son, to Whom pertains the initiative whenever there is question of accomplishing the work for which He has been sent. Whenever necessary, Jesus undertakes to dispel the excessively terrestrial conceptions entertained by *"His own,"* who, because of this, do *"not accept Him"* (Jn 1:11). But Mary, in the fullness of her faith and trust, knows how to be completely at His service, even when intervening to secure His response as at Cana.

And when, at the beginning of His ministry, the relatives of Jesus want to halt His mission (Mk 3:21), Mary is even more made to realize that the bond with the Creator, formed by adhering to His word, prevails over bonds of the flesh with the creature: indeed, none is absolute save God (cf. Mk 3:31-35; LG 58).

The Cross strikes a final blow to terrestrial triumphs. It is then that Mary makes her most total dispossession of the gift of her Son. It is the acme of her act of faith, which prepares her for the fact of the Resurrection and for participation in the painful birth of the Church.

The growth of Mary's faith, in the wake of the events in her life, is the very type of the growth for which every faithful believer must strive. That is why Mary merits the name of first believer, "first and most perfect disciple of Christ" (MC 35). This she is not only because she was the first to have complete faith in Jesus Christ but also because she yielded herself constantly to be formed by God. Her conduct is exemplary and typical for everyone and for the Church:

"The Blessed Virgin advanced in her pilgrimage of faith, and faithfully persevered in her union with her Son unto the Cross, where she stood in keeping with the Divine plan . . ." (L G 58). "As Saint Ambrose taught, the Mother of God is a type of the Church in the order of faith, charity, and perfect union with Christ" (LG 63).   *A. Delesalle*

FAMILY LIFE AND MARY   [2201-2231]

SEE *Devotion(s)*   *Woman*
    Single People and Mary   *Youth and Mary*
    States of Life and Marian Devotion

IN their excellent 1973 Pastoral Letter entitled, *Behold Your Mother* (129-142), the Bishops of the United States offered a good summary of this topic. The following is taken from their text.

The Mother of Jesus is the Exemplar for the whole Church and she is also the Model for all Christians regardless of life situation or vocation. Thus, Mary has much significance for family life and all families. As the Mother of the Holy Family, she is *the Mother and Queen of every Christian family.*

"The perfect example of the spiritual and apostolic life [in the world] is the most Blessed Virgin, Queen of Apostles. While leading the life common to all here on earth, one filled with family concerns and labors, she was always intimately united with her Son and in an entirely unique way cooperated in the work of the Savior" (AA 4).

1. Mother of Every Christian Family

Human motherhood reached its greatest achievement when Mary conceived and gave birth to Jesus. From the moment of the Annunciation, Mary was the living chalice of the Son of God made Man. In the tradition of her people she recognized that it is God Who gives life and watches over its growth. *"Just as you do not know the way of the wind or the mysteries of a woman with child, no more do you know the work of God Who is behind it all"* (Eccl 11:5; cf. Ps 139:13; 2 Mc 7:22).

This reverence for human life from its beginnings is bound up with the correct understanding and use of sexual love. Christians following in Mary's footsteps will look upon abortion with the same horror as the slaughter of the Innocents in Matthew's Gospel. They will regard Elizabeth's words to Mary, "Blessed is the fruit of your womb," as true in a real sense of every unborn child.

God called Mary and Joseph to sublimate the consummation of their married love in exclusive dedication to the holy Child, conceived not by a human father but by the Holy Spirit. When Mary said to Gabriel, *"How can this be since I do not know man?"* (Lk 1:34), the Angel told her of the virginal conception. Joseph received the same message in a dream. Christian tradition from early times has seen Saint Joseph as protector of the Christ Child and of his wife's consecrated virginity throughout their married life.

Christian marriage is a sign of the union between Christ and His Church. Man and wife in mutual love, and in the children they welcome from God and care for, are a witness to the world of love of God and of their fellow humans. The offering of the bride's bouquet at Our Lady's statue is an American Catholic custom that invites the Blessed Virgin into the life of the newlyweds. The conjugal chastity of a holy marriage is an answer to the neo-pagan degradation of human sexuality by pornography and by the glorification of promiscuity, divorce, and perversions.

Parents and children will find renewed strength in the grace of Christ and in the example and assistance of the Blessed Virgin, model of perfect purity and of self-surrender to God and neighbor. Christ was "Man of Sorrows," tortured and executed for the sins of men. Mary was "Mother of Sorrows," sharing her Son's sufferings even to Calvary. But there were also the joyous years at Nazareth, as her Son grew to adulthood, and something of the happiness of the Holy Family comes through in the Gospel preaching of Jesus with His tender examples from home life.

2. Queen of the Home

Mary is Queen of the home. As a woman of faith, she inspires all mothers to transmit the Christian Faith to their children. In the setting of family love, children should learn free and loving obedience, inspired by Mary's obedience to God. Her example of concern for others, as shown at the wedding feast of Cana, will exercise its gentle influence. *"He went down with them ... and was obedient to them. ... [Jesus] progressed steadily in wisdom and age and grace before God and humans"* (Lk 2:51-52).

This obedience of Jesus is emphasized throughout the New Testament: at Nazareth, throughout His ministry in which He sought only to do His Father's will, even unto death. The Gospel makes clear also Mary's obedience to the Law and to the traditional prayer life of her people. This is evident, for example, in her annual trip to Jerusalem for the Passover. Faithful to the Law of Moses, the holy couple brought Jesus to the Temple, His Father's house, for the presentation. Such obedience was the flower of Mary's faith. Because of it, God found her worthy to be the Mother of His Son.

In her appearances during the public life, Mary showed the same generous response to the will of the Father made manifest in her Son. At the marriage feast of Cana, after her Son's mysterious reference to the "hour not yet come," Mary's reaction was to advise the waiters, *"Do whatever He tells you"* (Jn 2:5). Family love builds on the Fourth Commandment, and in Jesus, Mary, and Joseph, parents and children have a powerful example of obedience to the will of God.

3. Mother of the "Domestic Church"

Family prayer, in whatever form it takes—meal prayers, night prayers, the family Rosary, attending Mass together—provides opportunities for prayer to the Blessed Virgin. Children forget many things when they grow up. They do not forget the manly piety of the father, the gentle devotion of the mother, and the love of Jesus and Mary as the support of the home, in sorrow and in joy.

Because of the primacy of the spiritual in all that makes for renewal, top priority should be given to whatever may produce a sound "family spirituality": family prayer, above all that which derives its content and spirit from the Liturgy and other devotions, particularly the Rosary.

In this way, the Virgin Mary, who is the mother of the Church, also becomes the mother of the "Domestic Church" (the "church of the home"). Thanks to her motherly aid, each Christian family can really become a "little church" in which the Mystery of the Church of Christ is mirrored and given new life. The family members will take the Handmaid of the Lord as an example of humble and generous acceptance of the will of God. And the Sorrowful Mother at the foot of the Cross will comfort the sufferings and dry the tears of those in distress because of the difficulties of their families.

A. Buono

FATHER (MARY AND THE)

SEE   *Trinity (Mary and)*

FATHERS AND MARY   [8, 11, 78, 688]

SEE   *New Eve*

1. Role of the Fathers

THE *Fathers of the Church* is a title conferred on ecclesiastical writers of the East and West who (1) lived in the early centuries of the Church, (2) led a holy life, (3) taught with wisdom and truth, and (4) have received the approval of the Church. They can be divided in many ways, among which is the following. The *Apostolic Fathers* are those who wrote in the first and second centuries and had some connection with the Apostles whose teaching they reflect. The *Early Fathers* (including the Apostolic Fathers) wrote in the first centuries. The *Later Fathers* are those who wrote in the 4th through the 8th centuries. Saint Gregory the Great (d. 604) is the last Father in the West and Saint John Damascene (d. 749) is the last Father in the East. The acceptance by the Fathers of a teaching indicates that it belongs to the "deposit of the faith" that Christ left to the Apostles.

In the case of Mary, the Fathers provide a fruitful source of doctrine as well as a barometer of the Church's attitude toward her. Their works are still being mined for Marian teaching, an early Patristic researcher into Marian teaching offers a nice summary: "Saving a very few differences on points of lesser moment, the Fathers of the first six centuries unanimously held Our Blessed Lady in the same high appreciation as she has been held by Catholics of all subsequent ages. . . . Everything that the Church has at any time defined or sanctioned with regard to her privileges and the honor that is due her—together with all that Saints and theologians of medieval and modern days have uttered in her praise—*is to be found substantially, and at least in principle or germ,* in the writings of the great Fathers" (T. Livius).

It is little wonder then that both Popes and Councils have consistently appealed to the Fathers as corroborative elements in their teaching on Mary. In his solemn definition of the Immaculate Conception as a doctrine of the faith, Pius IX frequently refers to the "Fathers" (although he does not name anyone). In defining the Assumption, Pius XII quotes from three Fathers: John Damascene, Germanus of Constantinople, and Modestus of Jerusalem. And in his encyclical that established the Feast of Mary's Queenship for the whole Church, Pius XII referred to ten Fathers.

The Second Vatican Council in its Marian chapter in the *Constitution on the Church* cites fourteen Fathers. Paul VI in *The Great Sign (Signum Magnum)* has six references to the Fathers while in *Devotion to the Blessed Virgin Mary (Marialis Cultus)* he has twenty.

2. Major Emphases of the Early Fathers

Mary's position in the theology of the Fathers of the first three centuries is quite small—and this is altogether natural. It flows from the picture of Mary that comes down to us from the Sacred Scriptures. There are no formal treatises on Mary in Patristic writings. The Fathers had other matters of a more pressing nature to engage their attention. They had to establish and set forth in detail the primary truths of Christian revelation: on the nature of God, His unity of being and trinity of Persons; the Incarnation and Divinity of the Word; the personality of the Holy Spirit; the unity and catholicity of the Church; the Communion of Saints; the doctrines of original sin and grace. They were also occupied with commentaries on Scripture and with all sorts of occasional writings such as sermons and homilies, exhortations, epistles, poems, historical, moral, and philosophical works.

Thus the Fathers speak of Mary only when, in Cardinal Newman's words, "[Mary's] own story is necessary for [Christ's]." This happens especially in their struggles against heresies. When Christ's humanity is attacked by the Docetists, it is emphasis on Mary's Divine Motherhood that repulses such a teaching, and her virginal conception of Christ that vindicates His Divinity in the face of the Adoptionists (who claim God merely adopts Him as His Son).

Accordingly, some of the Apostolic Fathers are silent about Mary—for example, the *First Epistle of Clement to the Corinthians*, the *Didache*, the *Epistle of Barnabas*, the *Shepherd of Hermas*, the *Epistle of Polycarp*, and the *Epistle to Diognetus*. However, Saint Ignatius of Antioch is quite explicit in his letters (110-115). He cries out: "Do not listen to those who refuse to confess that Jesus Christ, the son of David, was born of the Virgin Mary." The Saint has four other references to Our Lady as a Virgin and Mother in accord with God's plan.

The Apologist Aristides of Athens (c. 145) also cites the Virgin Mary in a text akin to a creedal formula: "He is confessed as the Son of the High God, coming down from heaven for the salvation of human beings through the power of the

Holy Spirit; and born of a holy Virgin without seed and in purity, He took flesh."

Saint Justin Martyr (d. 165) may be regarded as the first to write fully about Mary. He cited the Eve-Mary typology. This was picked up by Saint Irenaeus (d. 202): "Eve's disobedience was untied by Mary's obedience; what the virgin Eve bound through her unbelief, the Virgin Mary loosened by her faith." Irenaeus identified Mary as the person at the threshold of the new humanity—the Mother of the new humanity in whom God made a new beginning.

The Fathers of the 3rd century (Clement of Alexandria, Saint Hippolytus, and Saint Cyprian) as well as the ecclesiastical writers (Origen and Tertullian) go further and deal with the Divine Motherhood. They assert that Mary cannot be fully understood except in the light of her perpetual virginity—a virginity existing before, during, and after the birth of Jesus. By the end of the 4th century the two Marian characteristics of *motherhood* and *virginity* had become part of the authorized teaching.

Saint Cyprian (d. 258) stressed the confidence we should have in Mary and extolled her virginity. He calls her: "the tree that produced the marvelous fruit, the house possessed by the Holy Spirit, the door of the Savior, the guarded sanctuary of the Holy Spirit, the abode of Christ's humanity, the house of sanctity that the Third Person of the Most Blessed Trinity willed to adorn, and the vessel of election in which the Divinity poured the fullness of grace."

Clement of Alexandria provides a fine explanation of the spiritual implications of Our Lady's virginity: "Mary's fruitful virginity is comparable to that of the written Word of the Lord. The Scriptures are fruitful because of the light that shines from them and the truth that they bring to the world; but they still remain virginal as they enclose the Mystery of the Truth in a pure and holy vessel."

3. Major Emphases of the Later Fathers

From the 4th century on, the Fathers focus on Mary's holiness and her role of exemplar for Christians. In the West,

Saint Ambrose (d. 379) holds her up as a model for girls and women to follow as well as a type of the Church in the order of faith, charity, and perfect union with Christ. Saint Augustine proclaims Mary's freedom from original sin as well as her status as Virgin and Mother. Not only is Mary Mother of our Head but she is also the "Mother of all the members of the Divine Head," that is, Mother of the Mystical Body.

In the East, Saint Gregory of Nyssa (d. 394) chronicles the first apparitions of Mary recorded—to Saint Gregory the Wonderworker—thus demonstrating the beginnings of devotion to Mary reigning in power and glory. Saint Ephrem (d. 397) in his many prayers and hymns devoted to Mary calls upon Our Lady's powers of mediation with her Son and the Father and foreshadows the *Memorare,* as the following indicates: "O immaculate Virgin, protect us and guard us beneath the wings of your tender pity."

These notions culminate in the definition of Mary as the Mother of God (*Theotokos*) by the Fathers of the Council of Ephesus (431) under the leadership of Saint Cyril of Alexandria, (d. 444). After this there is no longer any question of Mary's personal purity: "After the Council of Ephesus the cult of the people of God toward Mary wonderfully increased in veneration and love, in invocation and imitation, according to her own prophetic words: 'All generations shall call me blessed, because He Who is mighty has done great things for me' " (LG 66).

By the 6th century, Mary's Assumption is being affirmed by the Fathers. Saint Germanus of Constantinople (7th-8th century) considered the fact that the body of Mary the Virgin Mother of God was incorrupt and had been taken up into heaven to be in keeping not only with her Divine Motherhood but also with the special holiness of her virginal body.

The arguments in favor of the Assumption are nicely summed up by Saint John Damascene, the last Father in the East: "It was fitting that she, who had kept her virginity intact in childbirth, should keep her own body free from all corruption even after death. It was fitting that the spouse, whom the Father had taken to Himself, should live in the Divine mansions.

"It was fitting that she, who had seen her Son upon the Cross and who had thereby received into her heart the sword of sorrow that she had escaped in the act of giving birth to Him, should look upon Him as He sits with the Father. It was fitting that God's Mother should possess what belongs to her Son, and that she should be honored by every creature as the Mother and as the handmaid of God."

Hand in hand with this view of Mary comes the belief in her heavenly intercession—which had already been circulating and was exemplified by the prayer *Sub Tuum* ("Under Your Protection"). Mary thus receives the title of Mediatrix from the pen of Saint Andrew of Crete (d. 740).

Hence, with the end of the Patristic Age, so to speak, we find that the place of Mary in the theological, liturgical, and devotional life of the Church has become solidly established both in the East and in the West. The seeds have also been planted for a Mariology that will sprout and one day flourish into the theological science that it is today.

A. Buono

FATIMA (Portugal)   [67]

SEE   *Apparitions*   *Apparitions after Vatican II*

THE famous apparitions of the Virgin Mary to the children of Fatima took place during the First World War, in the summer of 1917. The inhabitants of this tiny village in the diocese of Leiria (Portugal) were mostly poor people, many of them small farmers who went out by day to tend their fields and animals. Children traditionally were assigned the task of herding the sheep.

The three children who received the apparitions had been brought up in an atmosphere of genuine piety: Lucia dos Santos (ten years old) and her two younger cousins, Francisco and Jacinta. Together they tended the sheep and, with Lucy in charge, would often pray the Rosary kneeling in the open. In the summer of 1916 an Angel appeared to them several times and taught them a prayer to the Blessed Trinity.

On Sunday, May 13, 1917, toward noon, a flash of lightning drew the attention of the children, and they saw a brilliant figure appearing over the trees of the Cova da Iria. The "Lady" asked them to pray for the conversion of sinners and an end to the war, and to come back every month, on the 13th.

Further apparitions took place June 13 and July 13. On August 13 the children were prevented by local authorities from going to the Cova da Iria, but they saw the apparition on the l9th. On September 13 the Lady requested recitation of the Rosary for an end to the war. Finally, on October 13, the "Lady" identified herself as *"Our Lady of the Rosary"* and again called for prayer and penitence.

On that day a celestial phenomenon also took place: the sun seemed to tumble from the sky and crash toward earth. The children had been forewarned of it as early as May 13, the first apparition. The large crowd (estimated at 30,000 by reporters) that had gathered around the children saw the phenomenon and came away astounded.

Official recognition of the "visions" that the children had at the Cova da Iria came on October 13, 1930, when the Bishop of Leiria—after long inquiry—authorized the cult of Our Lady of the Rosary at the site. The two younger children had died: Francisco (who saw the apparition but did not hear the words) on April 4, 1919, and his sister Jacinta on February 20, 1920. Lucy, the sole survivor, is a professed nun.

1. The Message of Fatima

The public message of Fatima recalls that of Lourdes. Through the children Mary urges prayer for sinners, recitation of the Rosary, and works of penance. On October 13 she said: *"I have come to exhort the faithful to change their life, to avoid grieving Our Lord by sin, to pray the Rosary. I desire in this place a chapel in my honor. If people mend their ways, the war will soon be over."*

But Mary also confided several "secrets" to the children, some of which Lucy subsequently transmitted. Presumably there was prediction of another war in the near future and a request for special veneration of the Immaculate Heart of

Mary. The final secret Lucy is thought to have entrusted to Pope John XXIII.

As at Lourdes, the "apparitions" of Fatima have brought crowds of visitors. Pilgrimages, which began in the summer of 1917, have experienced growing success, not only among the Portuguese themselves but also among people from other countries, including the United States. The national pilgrimage following ecclesiastical recognition of the apparitions (May 13, 1931) is said to have drawn more than a million participants.

Popes have shown exceptional favor toward Fatima, Pius XII, Paul VI, and John Paul II in particular making a visit to the shrine. The papal interest has helped to swell the summer pilgrimages to Fatima and the basilica built at the site of the apparitions. Crowds comparable to and sometimes larger than those at Lourdes are not uncommon. In a rustic setting, pilgrims hear the message repeated that Mary spoke to the children: prayer, works of penance, recourse to her Immaculate Heart.

H. Holstein

Fatima and the Popes

As a proof of the "exceptional favor" with which Pius XII, Paul VI, and John Paul II have looked on the Shrine of Our Lady of Fatima, we can cite the following among many testimonies.

1. Pius XII

Consecration of the World to Mary's Heart. On October 31, 1942, Pius XII sent a radio-message to pilgrims who had journeyed to "the holy mount of Fatima" for the 25th anniversary of the apparitions (and the 25th anniversary of his episcopal ordination). After exhorting them to thanksgiving, fidelity, and prayer, the Pope consecrated the world to the Immaculate Heart of Mary.

Importance of Fatima Event Underlined. On May 13, 1946, the same Pope sent a radio-message for the crowning of the Image of Our Lady of Fatima. In it he recalls how "the prodigy of Fatima" is the work of the "maternal and compassionate Heart of the Blessed Virgin Mary, the Immaculate Queen," and also makes note of Mary's continued protection over Portugal. The Pope exalts Mary's heavenly and universal Queenship, "a Queenship that is essentially maternal and exclusively beneficial," and he underlines the importance and significance of the Fatima event:

"Is it not this Queenship that you are experiencing? Is it not the infinite benefits, the graces with which the maternal Heart of this august Queen has favored you, that you are here proclaiming today with a lively sense of gratitude? The most tragic war that has ever laid waste to this world has touched your borders but has never come over them because of the protection of Our Lady above all."

2. Paul VI

Human Family Entrusted to Our Lady. In the closing discourse to the third session of Vatican Council II (November 21, 1964), Paul VI addressed an ardent prayer to the Blessed Virgin that she might bless the Ecumenical Council and the Church and cast her glance "on the endless horizons of the whole world, the object of the most lively care of the Ecumenical Council, and which Pius XII of venerated memory, not without inspiration from on high, solemnly consecrated to the Immaculate Heart of Mary."

The Pope goes on to say: "Today we consider it particularly opportune to recall this act of consecration. Bearing this in mind, we have decided to send a special mission to Fatima in the near future in order to carry the Golden Rose to the sanctuary of Fatima, more dear than ever not only to the people of the noble Portuguese nation—always, but particularly today, dear to us—but also known and venerated by the faithful throughout the entire Catholic world. In this manner we intend to entrust to the care of this heavenly Mother the entire human family, with its problems and anxieties, with its legitimate aspirations and ardent hopes."

Call for Renewal of Personal Consecration. On May 13, 1967, on the occasion of the 50th anniversary of the Apparitions of Our Lady at the Cova da Iria, Paul VI went to Fatima on a pilgrimage of prayer and peace. For that occasion he published an Exhortation directed to the whole Church on the veneration and imitation of the Blessed Virgin entitled *Mary, Mother of the Church (Signum Magnum)*. In it Paul VI invites all Catholics to renew personal consecration to the Immaculate Heart of the Mother of the Church:

"It was 25 years ago that our predecessor Pius XII addressed the people of Portugal (October 31, 1942) by radio and solemnly consecrated the Church and the whole human race to the Immaculate Heart of the Virgin Mary. We repeated this consecration on November 21, 1964. So now we urge all members of the Church to consecrate themselves once again to the Immaculate Heart of Mary, to translate this pious act into concrete action in their daily lives. In this way they will comply ever more closely with God's will and, as imitators of their heavenly Queen, they will truly be recognized as her offspring."

3. John Paul II

Message of Fatima and Teaching of Christ. On May 12, 1982, John Paul II made a pilgrimage to Fatima to celebrate the 65th anniversary of Mary's appearance, to give thanks for the Virgin's intercession in saving his life a year earlier, and to consecrate anew the people of the world to Our Lady's Immaculate Heart. Then on May 13, 1982, on the anniversary of Our Lady's first appearance, the Pope celebrated Mass at the Shrine and gave Communion to the 75-year-old Carmelite Sister Lucia dos Santos, the only living member of the three children who witnessed the apparitions. He then placed the message of Fatima within the framework of the teaching of Christ:

"The Church has always taught and continues to proclaim that God's revelation was brought to completion in Jesus Christ, Who is the fullness of that revelation, and that no new public revelation is to be expected before the glorious manifestation of Our Lord. The Church evaluates and judges private revelation by the criterion of conformity with that single public revelation.

Summons to Conversion. "The Church has accepted the message of Fatima . . . because that message contains a truth and a call whose content is the truth and the call of the Gospel."

" '*Reform your lives and believe in the Gospel*' (Mk 1:15). These are the first words that the Messiah addressed to humanity. The message of Fatima is in its basic nucleus a call to conversion and repentance, as in the Gospel. This call was . . . addressed particularly to this present century. . . . The message of Our Lady of Fatima is a motherly one [yet] it is also strong and decisive. It sounds severe. It sounds like John the Baptist speaking on the banks of the Jordan. It invites to repentance. It gives a warning. It calls to prayer. It recommends the Rosary."

At the end of the Mass, John Paul II reconsecrated the world to Our Lady. He asked that she intercede for its deliverance from hunger, sins against life, injustice in social, national, and international life, and from nuclear war, incalculable destruction, and every kind of war.

A. Rum

FEASTS OF MARY

[971]

SEE *Annunciation*
  Assumption
  Birth of Mary
  Carmel, Mount
  Collection of Masses of
   the Blessed Virgin Mary
  Crowning of an Image
   of the Blessed Virgin
  Cult of Mary
  Guadalupe
  Immaculate Conception
  Immaculate Heart of Mary

Lectionary, Marian
Litany
Lourdes
Month of Mary
Mother of God
Presence of Mary in the
 Eucharist
Presentation of Jesus
Queen
Saint Mary Major
Saturday of Our Lady
Visitation

WITH the reduction of the Sanctoral Cycle in the revision of the Roman Calendar various feasts in honor of the

Blessed Virgin were eliminated. Thus, the Church endeavored to strengthen the concept of Mary's Christocentric role as the Mother of our Redeemer, stressing her vocational role with Mother-Son feasts, such as the Annunciation (March 25) and the Presentation of the Lord (February 2), which now is not really considered the feast of her purification.

1. Solemnities

On the other hand, other feasts may be considered personal, such as Mary's Immaculate Conception, Divine Motherhood, and Assumption. These are the highest ranking Marian celebrations and also Holy Days of Obligation in the United States.

Immaculate Conception. By the 8th century, there was a feast in honor of this title in the Eastern Church. In the 11th century, it appeared in the Western Church and was celebrated in England. Two centuries later in Scotland, Blessed John Duns Scotus clarified the distinction whereby, though Mary deserved original sin like all other human beings, she was preserved from it at the moment of conception by a pre-redemption.

This feast was included in the calendar of the Universal Church in the 14th century and made a feast of obligation in 1708, with an Opening Prayer that declared: "God prepared a worthy dwelling place for [His] Son through the Immaculate Conception of the Virgin, preserving her from all sin in view of the foreseen Death of [His] Son." Finally, in 1854, Pius IX defined this prerogative as a Dogma of Faith and used practically the very words of the Liturgy.

The Immaculate Conception is more than just Mary's preservation from evil. It is her fullness of grace. Like her privilege of the Assumption, it is based on Mary's Divine Motherhood. Under this title, Our Lady is the Patroness of the United States. *Liturgical celebration:* December 8 (Solemnity); *theme:* purity of life before God.

Mary, Mother of God. This feast recognizes Mary as the physical parent of Christ, the God-Man, defined at the Council of Ephesus in the 5th century. The third Mass of Christmas reflects the role of Mary in the Redemption; so her role has always been connected with the Christmas Mystery. Later, from the 5th to the 7th century, the feast was transferred to the Octave Day of Christmas, January 1.

Prior to the time that this feast occurred on January 1, New Year's Day was observed as a day of prayer to offset pagan practices, since there were many riotous pagan celebrations. From the 5th century until the Middle Ages, it honored Mary and her Divine Maternity. Then it was observed as the Octave of Christmas, which developed into the feast of the Circumcision. From 1961 to 1969 the title changed back to the Octave of the Nativity. Finally, in 1969 the ancient Marian character was restored, so that we have its present title.

Liturgical celebration: January 1 (Solemnity); *theme*: veneration of Mary, Mother of God, and adoration of her newborn Son.

Assumption. This feast probably originated from the feast of the dedication of a church of Mary in Jerusalem before the middle of the 4th century; it was also celebrated at Antioch in the 4th century and at Palestine in the 5th century. It was then adopted in the 7th century at Rome through the influence of the Eastern Church in the nature of an anniversary of death similar to that of other Saints. The date of August 15 seems to have originated in Asia Minor. In Egypt and countries with a Gallican liturgical tradition, it was assigned to mid-January. Over the centuries, the Assumption has remained one of the greatest feasts of Our Lady in the Church.

Liturgical celebration: August 15 (Solemnity); *theme*: Mary's assumption into glory foreshadows our own entry, body and soul, into heaven for all eternity.

2. Feasts

Two events in the life of Mary are celebrated by the Church with the rank of Feast: the Birth and the Visitation.

Visitation. This feast commemorates Mary's visit—under the Holy Spirit—to her cousin Elizabeth before the birth of

Saint John the Baptist (Lk 1:39-56). It was instituted by Urban VI in 1389 after the Franciscans had celebrated it on July 2 from 1263 on. Sixtus IV (1471-1484) had a new Mass composed for it. The present calendar celebrates it on May 31, the last day of the month traditionally assigned to Mary and three weeks before the Solemnity of the Birth of John the Baptist (June 24). *Liturgical celebration*: May 31 (Feast); *theme*: sharing feelings of joy by praising God.

Birth of Mary. This feast derives from the dedication of the Church of Mary's Nativity (said to have been built on the house of St. Ann) at the end of the 5th century. In the 7th century it spread to Constantinople and Rome. From the 15th century on, the celebration assumed notable importance, becoming a Solemnity with a major Octave and preceded by a Vigil with fast. The Octave was reduced to a simple one during the reform of Pius XII in 1955. The date of celebration differed from place to place, but after the feast of the Immaculate Conception (which has a later origin than that of the Birth) was extended to the Universal Church, the Birth came to be assigned to September 8, nine months after the conception. *Liturgical celebration*: September 8 (Feast); *theme*: joy at the birth of her who is the dawn of our salvation.

Our Lady of Guadalupe. In the Proper of the United States, there is also another Marian Feast, that of Our Lady of Guadalupe, which commemorates the apparition of the Blessed Virgin on December 9, 1531, to an Indian convert named Juan Diego on a hillside at Tepeyac outside Mexico City. She left with him a picture of herself impressed on his cloak and asked that a church be built in her honor. The Shrine of Our Lady of Guadalupe is one of the most celebrated places of pilgrimage in North America.

Guadalupe is to Mexico and Americans what Lourdes and Fatima are to France and Portugal. She becomes the sign of God's presence and grace in the Americas and represents for all Americans the inculturation of the Gospel in the New World. It was from Mexico that the missions of Texas, Arizona, New Mexico, and California developed. These Christian landmarks are honored as a rich legacy from Mexico, and consequently the Feast of Our Lady of Guadalupe was chosen to be part of the Proper Calendar for the United States in 1971 and raised from a Memorial to the status of Feast in 1988. *Liturgical celebration*: December 12 (Feast); *theme*: the Mother of God is the Mother of the Americas and symbolizes the solidarity of the United States' Catholics with their compatriots of Mexico as well as Central and South America.

3. Memorials

There are also eight Memorials of Mary in the calendar, some Obligatory and others Optional. They are inspired by episodes in the life of Mary or by theological ideas or by places venerated by the faithful. In the order of their appearance in the Liturgical Year they are as follows.

Our Lady of Lourdes. Instituted by St. Pius X in 1907, this feast celebrates the appearance of Mary to St. Bernadette in 1858. The history of devotion and consolation that Lourdes conjures up can lead to the contemplation of Mary as the Health of the Sick and the Comforter of the Afflicted. *Liturgical celebration*: February 11 (Opt. Mem.); *theme*: overcoming human weakness through the intercession of the Mother of God.

Immaculate Heart of Mary. This feast stems from the efforts of Saint John Eudes to inspire devotion to the Heart of Mary. In 1646 he won approval for a Mass of the Immaculate Heart of Mary to be celebrated locally. In 1855 the Congregation of Rites approved a Mass for the feast, and in 1880 Leo XIII extended it to the whole diocese of Rome. After the appearances of Mary to three children at Fatima in 1917, Pius XII consecrated the world to the Immaculate Heart of Mary in 1942 and in 1944 established the feast for the Universal Church on the octave day of the Assumption (August 22). *Liturgical celebration*: Saturday following the 2nd Sunday after Pentecost (Mem.); *theme*: becoming worthy temples of God's glory through devotion to the Immaculate Heart.

Our Lady of Mount Carmel. This feast was instituted about 1380 by the Carmelites in thanksgiving for the Order's successful establishment in the West after having been forced to leave their place of origin (Mount Carmel in the Holy Land). Benedict XIII extended it to the Universal Church in 1726. It is also connected with the scapular and consecration to Mary. *Liturgical celebration*: July 16 (Opt. Mem.); *theme*: reaching Christ through the prayers of His Mother.

Dedication of Saint Mary Major. This feast recalls the 4th-century dedication in Rome of a replica of the basilica of Mary's Nativity in Bethlehem. In the 5th century Sixtus III offered the Church to the People of God, and it became a monument to the dogmatic definition of Mary as the Mother of God handed down by the Council of Ephesus (431). Saint Pius V placed it in the Universal Calendar in 1568. *Liturgical celebration*: August 5 (Opt. Mem.); *theme*: Mary is the temple of God and the new Jerusalem who will obtain our salvation through her prayers.

Queenship of Mary. This feast was inserted in the calendar for the Universal Church by Pius XII in 1954, the centenary of the proclamation of the Immaculate Conception as a dogma, and assigned to May 31. It is now more felicitously assigned to August 22: "The Solemnity of the Assumption is prolonged in the celebration of the Queenship of. . . Mary, which occurs seven days later. On this occasion we contemplate her who, seated beside the King of Ages, shines forth as Queen and intercedes as Mother" (MC 6). *Liturgical celebration*: August 22 (Memorial); *theme*: by honoring Mary our Queen, we honor Christ the King and obtain eternal life in the heavenly kingdom.

Our Lady of Sorrows. This feast recalls the sorrows of Mary at the foot of the Cross. Originally granted to the Order of Servants of Mary in 1667, it was introduced into the Roman Calendar in 1814 and assigned to the third Sunday of September. In 1913 the date was changed to September 15. Until the recent reform, it was also anticipated on the Friday before Palm Sunday. Occurring on the day after the Triumph of the Cross, it is "a fitting occasion for reliving a decisive moment in the History of Salvation and for venerating, together with her Son lifted up on the Cross, His suffering Mother" (MC 7).

Liturgical celebration: September 15 (Memorial); *theme*: union with Christ in His sufferings.

Our Lady of the Rosary. This feast was instituted in 1573 as a special commemoration of the victory gained at Lepanto on Sunday, October 7, 1571, over the forces of Islam threatening to invade Europe. Prescribed by Gregory XIII for certain churches, it was inserted into the Roman Calendar by Clement XI in 1716 and assigned to the first Sunday of October. In 1913, it was assigned to October 7. *Liturgical celebration*: October 7 (Memorial); *theme*: following Christ by living His Joyful, Sorrowful, and Glorious Mysteries in union with Mary.

Presentation of Mary. This ancient feast was based on a pious tradition, recounted by the apocryphal Gospel known as the *Protevangelium of James,* that Mary was presented in the Temple of Jerusalem at the age of three where she lived with other girls in the charge of holy women. This event was already commemorated in the 6th century in the East. Gregory XI in 1372 heard of the feast, kept in Greece on November 21, and instituted it at Avignon. In 1585, Sixtus V extended it to the Universal Church. *Liturgical celebration*: November 21 (Memorial); *theme*: total consecration to the Lord through Mary.

4. Other Feasts

In keeping with the principle to leave to particular calendars Marian feasts that do not possess universal interest, the new Liturgy suppressed the universal celebration of certain feasts. The *Seven Sorrows of Mary* on Friday before Passion Sunday had been part of the Universal Calendar since 1727. However, since it duplicated the Memorial of Our Lady of Sorrows on September 15, it was dropped from the Calendar.

The *Holy Name of Mary* had been inserted on September 12 as a counterpart to the Feast of the Holy Name of Jesus (January 2). However, once the latter was eliminated and made a Votive Mass because it was part of the Solemnity of Mary, Mother of God on January 1, the *Holy Name of Mary* was also deleted and made a Votive Mass.

The feast of *Our Lady of Ransom* was celebrated on September 24 and was linked to a devotion spread by the Order of Mercedarians, which worked for the liberation of slaves. It was deemed to be of lesser interest for the Universal Church today and so returned to particular calendars.

5. Local Feasts

Many other feasts of Mary were celebrated in some dioceses and Religious Congregations from the 17th century to the reform of Vatican II. Some of these were: Translation of the Holy House of Loreto (December 10); Our Lady of Guadalupe (December 12); Expectation of the Childbirth of Mary (December 18); Marriage of Mary and Joseph (January 25); Our Lady of Good Counsel (April 26); Mary, Help of Christians (May 24); Most Pure Heart of Mary (3rd Sunday after Pentecost); Our Lady of Perpetual Help (Sunday before June 24); Motherhood of Mary (2nd Sunday of October); Purity of Mary (3rd Sunday of October); Patronage of Mary (2nd Sunday of November); and Manifestation of the Miraculous Medal (November 27).

6. Common

The Common of the Blessed Virgin Mary in the *Roman Missal* comprises six Mass formularies and one Prayer formulary. These are used in the feasts mentioned above that do not have a complete formulary of their own. They are also utilized for the Mass of the Blessed Virgin on Saturday when there is no feast with a higher rank than Optional Memorial. They can also be used as Votive Masses. (See also entry on the *Collection of Masses of the Blessed Virgin Mary* and Appendix 8.)

The Common of the Blessed Virgin Mary in the *Liturgy of the Hours* contains complete formularies for all the Hours. These are used in the feasts mentioned above that lack a complete formulary. They can also be used as Votive Offices.

A. Buono

"FIAT" IN THE NAME OF HUMANITY   [488-494]

SEE *Annunciation*   *Church and Mary*
       Cana   *Cross (Mary at the)*

IN three entries of this Dictionary we find the following statements:

"In lending Mary the words of the people declaring their adherence to the Covenant, John makes her the *representative and personification of the Messianic people.* . . . She expresses the faith of the whole Messianic people disposed to receive the revelation brought by Jesus" (J. P. Prevost; SEE *Cana*).

"Under the Cross Mary *assures in a very special way the presence of the Church* (and humanity), receiving salvation and entering into it with all her being" (A. Tostain; SEE *Cross*).

"Mary *represents and signifies the Church*. In Mary, personally, we discover what constitutes the greatness of the Church, that Christ desired and established" (H. Holstein; SEE *Church and Mary*).

In what does this role of representation consist, a role attributed to Mary in regard to the Messianic people, the Church, and humanity? There can be no thought of putting it on the same level as that which is proper and exclusive to Christ the Head, preeminent "representative" of the human race, which He recapitulates in Himself, which He redeems, gathers into one, and restores to the Father. Mary is entirely among the redeemed, receiving the Savior, absolutely free Gift of the Father's Love (cf. Jn 3:16). She receives her all from Him. But she is "the Virgin Mother of the Redeemer, His generous associate . . . who cooperated in a singular way in His work" of Redemption (LG 61). On this twofold count of Mother of the Redeemer and exceptional Associate in His mission, Mary, through the perfection of her response, attains a universal dimension that embraces the whole Church and each one of us.

The same is true of her "Fiat" ("Let it be done") at the Annunciation. It committed her, personally, to active acceptance of service. But, as Saint Thomas notes, it went beyond the personal engagement: "The Annunciation asked the consent of the Virgin *in the name of all human nature" (Summa Theologica,* III, q. 30, art. 1). Mary is the one in whom and through whom human nature as such, in virtue of her consent, acceded to the realization of God's gift in the Incarnation, "event of the ages." Seen in this light, the "Yes" of the Daughter of Zion recapitulated and brought to their maximum all the "yeses" to the Lord that preceded it and made possible, for its part, all those that would follow it.

The "Fiat" of the Virgin Mary is not for a day. It expresses a fundamental and permanent attitude of Mary, who defines herself as *the servant of the Lord.* On Calvary especially, she lives it with all the intensity demanded by her participation in the *Hour of Jesus.* The texts of the *Constitution on the Church* point out the exceptional merit and significance of her actively consenting presence at the foot of the Cross and the quality of her unfailing faith, which enables her to bring to the work of the Redeemer a cooperation absolutely without compare (cf. LG 61). In the "Virgin presenting offerings" (MC 20) is condensed in some way the faith of the whole Church receiving salvation and, like Mary, cooperating with it.

In this role committed to Mary by the Lord we can see and admire the consideration that it shows, or what might be called God's respect for His creature. He did not simply want mankind to be general beneficiary of the Redemption that would follow upon the Incarnation of the Word. He also willed that—through Mary and in Mary, redeemed creature entirely docile to the Holy Spirit—each of us should receive the Savior more perfectly and give Him the full "consent of love" (LG 58). The New Adam, transcendent Head of the new humankind, associated His whole Body with His sacrifice in the person of Mary, New Eve, who is member, Mother, and type of the Church.

The permanent "Fiat" of Mary, faithful Virgin of the Annunciation as she stood on Calvary, is truly given "in the name of all humanity." But this does not dispense us from entering personally into receiving the Savior and cooperating with salvation. On the contrary, in a total dependence on Christ from

Whom she receives all, Mary by her "yes" contributes to making it possible for us to cooperate and she invites us to commit ourselves ever more effectively by the fact that she has already given consent for us.   *A. Bossard*

FIDELITY   [144, 494]

SEE   *Faith of Mary*

F IDELITY, both the word and the reality, derives from faith. It presupposes trust and, like faith, denotes life and growth. Far from being pure receptivity and passivity, it participates actively in the will of the One on Whom it relies.

"Mary kept all these things in her heart" (or "memory," Lk 2:51), not to bring about a withdrawal into self but to discover the hidden demands of words and events whose full meaning would become clear only gradually.

Fidelity is an important element in the constitution of the subject, who is not shackled or immobilized by it but projected toward the future. Although it maintains its bond with the past on which it is founded, this is a dynamic maintenance that makes possible new tomorrows.

Mary's fidelity involved more than one act of acceptance. It was a source of progression in faith that brought her to understanding the "refusals" of her Son, the surprises He reserved to Himself. Faithful to the end, she found them springboards to advance in the comprehension and fulfillment of her vocation.

A splendid pastoral illustration of Mary's fidelity is offered by John Paul II in the Homily he gave in the Cathedral of Mexico City on January 26, 1979:

"Among all the titles given to the Virgin through the centuries for her motherly love of Christians, there is one that stands out: *Virgo Fidelis* (Faithful Virgin). What does this fidelity of Mary mean? What are the dimensions of this fidelity?

"(1) The first dimension is *searching*. Mary was faithful when she searched for the profound meaning of the will of

God in her life. '*Quomodo fiet?*' ('How can this be?') she asked the Angel of the Annunciation. In the Old Testament this searching is already translated into an expression of rare beauty, of profound spiritual meaning: 'To seek the face of the Lord.' There can be no fidelity if there is not this deep-seated searching, if we cannot find in the human heart the question to which only God is the answer.

"(2) The second dimension of this fidelity is called *acceptance*, to accept. The '*quomodo fiet*' is transformed on the lips of Mary as a '*fiat*' ('let it be'). Let it be, I am willing, I accept. This is the moment of truth for fidelity, the moment in which human beings come to realize that they can never fully understand the why, that there are in God's design more areas of mystery than explanations, that no matter how hard they try, they will never be able to accept everything.

"At this point, human beings are ready to accept this mystery and give it a place in their heart, as Mary kept all these things in her heart (Lk 2:19; cf. Lk 3:15). It is the moment in which humans open themselves to this mystery, not in the way some give up facing an enigma or the absurd, but rather with the openness of people letting themselves be possessed by something—someone—bigger than their heart. This acceptance is fulfilled through faith that is the union of our being with the mystery that is revealed.

"(3) *Coherence* is the third dimension of fidelity. To live in accordance with what one believes. To adjust one's life to what one adheres to. To accept misunderstanding, persecutions, before we break with what we believe in, before there is a break between life and convictions: that is coherence. Here we find perhaps the most intimate nucleus of fidelity.

"(4) But fidelity must stand the most difficult test: *perseverance*. That is the fourth dimension of fidelity, perseverance. It is easy to be coherent for a day or even a few days. It is difficult, however important, to be coherent through an entire life of faith. It is easy to be coherent at the hour of elation, but difficult in the hour of tribulation. And we can call it fidelity when it lasts a lifetime.

"The 'fiat' of Mary at the Annunciation finds its fulfillment in the 'fiat' at the foot of the Cross. To be faithful is to remain faithful in private to what we proclaimed in public. . . .

"In this solemn hour I invite you to grow in that fidelity. I invite you to translate it into a strong and intelligent fidelity to the Church of today. Are not those the same as the characteristics of Mary's fidelity?"

A. Delessale

FINDING IN THE TEMPLE (Lk 2:41-52)   [531-534]

SEE   *Infancy Narratives*   *Rosary*

AS a sign of respect for tradition and submission of Jesus to His parents, the account of the Finding of Jesus in the Temple seems at first sight to report nothing more than a miscellaneous fact pertaining to the family history rather than the unfolding of the revelation concerning Jesus. It is true that for one of the few times in the Gospel of the Infancy the narrative part is developed much more than the dialogue or the commentary. But it is not less evident that Luke wanted to make this scene the crown of the Gospel of the Infancy and the anticipation of the public ministry of Jesus.

The principal themes are: importance of Jerusalem and the Temple, allusions to the Paschal Mystery, religious faithfulness of the parents of Jesus, and the anticipation of Our Lord's public ministry. In fact, everything in this account is ordered to the first words of Jesus and points us to the heart of the Mystery: Jesus, obedient to His parents and experiencing normal growth, makes known the unique and absolute character of His relation to the Father (2:49).

1. Anticipation of the Paschal Mystery

Luke's temporal and spatial notations in the account combine in a remarkable convergence. In the foreground we find mention of Jerusalem (2:41, 43, 45) associated with celebration of the Passover feast (2:41). In Luke's Gospel mention of Jeru-salem is either a prefiguration or an evocation of the Passion-Resurrection of Christ (9:31, 51; 13:33 . . .), whereas the feast of the Passover is the immediate setting (Lk 22:1, 7, 8, 11 . . .). The very words of Jesus (*"I HAD to be in My Father's house:"* 2:49; cf. 9:22; 13:33; 17:25 . . .) imply a reference both to the liturgical presence of God giving Himself to His people and to God's plan of salvation that was to be realized by the one sacri-fice of Christ.

In addition, it is quite possible that the mention of *"three days"* (2:46; cf. 13:33) also has the function of pointing the reader toward the Paschal Mystery. Whatever the detail of the interpretation, there is no doubt that this Mystery was already looming up over the horizon. Jesus placed Himself squarely in this perspective, and all His ministry sought to bring about an understanding and full acceptance of this "necessity" of God's plan.

2. Jesus Reveals and Declares Himself

Up to this point in the Gospel of the Infancy, revelation of the Mystery of Jesus has come through intermediaries: Gabriel, Elizabeth, Mary, an Angel of the Lord, Simeon, and Anna. But now Jesus takes the initiative in revealing Himself. His first public words assert the transcendent character—pri-mordial and absolutely unique—of His filial relation to the Father. He is the only One in the whole New Testament Who could literally say *"My Father"* (2:49) when speaking about God or addressing Him (cf. Lk 23:46; 24:49; Jn 20:17). By this fact He is also the only One Who can make known the Father: *"No one knows the Father but the Son—and anyone to whom the Son wishes to reveal Him"* (Mt 11:27; cf. Jn 1:18).

What is striking in the initial and normative utterance of Jesus is the exertive aspect: *"I HAD to be in My Father's house."* Jesus did not speak of His relation to the Father in ab-stract or essentialist terms but in words of a task to accom-plish, a mission to assume. The whole thrust of the Incarnation is here in play, and Jesus from the moment of His human consciousness accepted all of its demands: *"I have come to do Your will"* (Heb 10:9).

3. Mary's Faith

Preceding scenes in the Gospel of the Infancy have served to extol—rightly so—the faith of Mary. In the scene of the Finding, Luke does not retreat from anything he has said, but he makes clearer another aspect of her faith: its insertion in the flow of time and its progressive nature. For Luke there is no contradiction in his praise of Mary's faith, despite her astonishment here, her search for Jesus *"in sorrow,"* and her failure to grasp immediately what Jesus says. This view of the account has been captured by René Laurentin:

"The notation of Luke 2:50 shows more pointedly what is already apparent from the rest of the Gospel of the Infancy: Mary has lived under conditions that are the common lot of people, conditions of lowliness, poverty.... She has experienced the obscurity of faith, seeing 'indistinctly, as in a [clouded] mirror' and not face to face, as Saint Paul says (1 Cor 13:12). Her life has not been without anguish (2:48), or trials, or the inner labor of pondering (1:29), of deliberating and meditating (Lk 2:59, and especially 2:19). Her faith has thus obeyed the law of progress" (*Jesus in the Temple*, Paris: 1966, p. 176).

The Finding in the Temple is the Fifth Joyful Mystery of the Rosary.

J. P. Prevost

FULGENS CORONA   [491-492]

SEE   *Church and Mary*   *Immaculate Conception*
      Cult of Mary   *Magisterium (Documents of)*
      Feasts of Mary   *Vatican II and Mary*

ON September 8, 1953, Pope Pius XII issued an Encyclical entitled *Fulgens Corona* ("The Radiant Crown") in commemoration of the one hundredth anniversary of the Dogma of the Immaculate Conception. In this Encyclical the Pope invited the Catholic world to celebrate in a worthy fashion the Marian Year proclaimed for the centenary.

He adverted to the exultation of the faithful when Pius IX solemnly defined the new dogma, which received incontrovertible confirmation by the wondrous apparitions of the Blessed Virgin at Lourdes. And he indicates that the authentic reasons for the dogma are found in Sacred Scripture and Tradition. He then set forth the texts that prove the validity of the arguments adduced in favor of the Immaculate Conception.

The Pope took pains to stress that to affirm that the Blessed Virgin is Immaculate does not lessen the Redemption in any way, regardless of what some may aver. To the contrary, the infinite dignity of Jesus Christ and His office of universal redemption is not diminished or lowered by this tenet of doctrine; rather it is greatly increased.

For it demonstrates how Christ, precisely through this work of salvation, wills to have a Mother exempt from original sin. Indeed the doctrine is confirmed by the Eastern Christians who each year celebrate the feast of the Immaculate Conception.

The Pope then alluded to the joy that reverberated in himself and in all Catholics when on November 1, 1950, he defined the Dogma of the Assumption, which he viewed as a worthy crowning of that definition of Pius IX and a reason for serene hope in Our Lady's protection. But the commemoration of these centenary feasts would be all for nought unless they led to an increase in spiritual and moral life. Therefore, the Pope expressed the firm desire that the Marian Year should find an adequate celebration in every diocese and in every parish.

In closing, the Pope asked Our Lady for the gift of peace for all peoples. For it is only in the Divine Redeemer that Christians can find a hope for a serene life and promote a real progress in civil society.

A. Buono

"FULL OF GRACE"

[490-493]

SEE *Annunciation*　　　　*Immaculate Conception*
　　Hail Mary　　　　　　*Trinity (and Mary)*
　　Holy Spirit (and Mary)

1. God's Eternal Blessing

AT the Annunciation, the Angel Gabriel addressed Mary as "Full of grace" (Lk 1:28). In fact, as Pope John Paul II stated in his Encyclical *Redemptoris Mater* ("The Mother of the Redeemer"), "he calls her thus as if it were her real name. He does not call her by her proper earthly name: *Miryam* (=Mary), but by *this new name: 'full of grace'* " (no. 8).

This manner of address is unique in the Bible and is reserved exclusively for the Blessed Virgin. Its importance with regard to Mary led Pope John Paul II in the above-mentioned Encyclical to give a detailed analysis of it. The following points are made by the Pope.

God the Father of Our Lord Jesus Christ has blessed us in Christ with every spiritual blessing (cf. Eph 1:3). His Divine Plan, which was fully revealed to us with the coming of Christ, is eternal and eternally linked to Christ. It includes everyone, but it reserves a special place for the "Woman" who is the Mother of Him to Whom the Father has entrusted the work of salvation.

As the Second Vatican Council says, "she is already prophetically foreshadowed in that promise made to our first parents after their fall into sin (cf. Gn 3:15). Likewise she is the Virgin who is to conceive and bear a Son, Whose name will be called Emmanuel (cf. Is 7:14)" (LG 55).

Mary is "full of grace" because of that blessing with which God the Father has filled us "in the heavenly places with Christ." It is a *spiritual blessing* that is meant for all people and that bears in itself fullness and universality. It flows from the love that, in the Holy Spirit, unites the consubstantial Son to the Father. At the same time, it is a blessing poured out through Jesus Christ upon human history until the end: upon all people.

This blessing, however, refers *to Mary in a special and exceptional degree*: for she was greeted by Elizabeth as "blessed among women" (Lk 1:42). In the soul of this Daughter of Zion, there is manifested, in a sense, all the glory of grace, the grace that the Father has given us in His beloved Son.

In the language of the Bible, grace means a special gift, which according to the New Testament has its source precisely in the Trinitarian life of God Himself, God Who is love (cf. 1 Jn 4:8). The fruit of this love is the "election" spoken of in Ephesians 1:4-6. On the part of God, this election is the eternal desire to save humankind through a sharing in His own life (cf. 2 Pt 1:4): it is a salvation through a sharing in supernatural life.

2. God's Special Blessing of Mary

When we read that the messenger addresses Mary as "Full of grace," the Gospel context, which mingles revelations and ancient promises, enables us to understand that among all the "spiritual blessings in Christ" this is a special blessing. In the Mystery of Christ, she is *present* even before the creation of the world, as the one whom the Father has chosen to be the Mother of His Son in the Incarnation. And, what is more, the Son has chosen her, entrusting her eternally to the Spirit of holiness.

In an entirely special and exceptional way, Mary is united with Christ, and similarly she is eternally loved in this beloved Son, this Son Who is of one being with the Father and in Whom is concentrated all the glory of grace. At the same time, she is and remains perfectly open to this gift from above (cf. Jas 1:17). As Vatican II teaches, Mary "stands out among the poor and humble of the Lord, who confidently await and receive salvation from Him" (LG 55).

In the context of the Angel's announcement, the greeting and the name "Full of grace" refer first of all *to the election of Mary as Mother of the Son of God*. But at the same time, the "Fullness of grace" indicates all the supernatural munificence from which Mary benefits by being chosen and destined to be the Mother of Christ. If this election is fundamental for the accomplishment of God's salvific designs for humanity, and if the eternal choice of Christ and the vocation to the dignity of adopted children is the destiny of everyone, then the election of Mary is wholly exceptional and unique. So also is the singularity and uniqueness of her place in the Mystery of Christ.

Mary is "Full of grace" because it is precisely in her that the Incarnation of the Word, the hypostatic union of the Son of God with human nature, is accomplished and fulfilled. As the Council says, Mary is "the Mother of the Son of God. As a result she is also the favorite Daughter of the Father and the Temple of the Holy Spirit. Because of this gift of sublime grace, she far surpasses all other creatures, both in heaven and on earth" (LG 55).

The Epistle to the Ephesians speaks of the *"glory of grace"* that *"God the Father . . . has bestowed upon us in His beloved Son"* and adds: *"In Him we have redemption through His blood"* (1:7). This *"glory of grace"* is manifested in the Mother of God through the fact that she has been "redeemed in a more sublime manner" (LG 53). By virtue of the richness of the grace of the beloved Son, by reason of the redemptive merits of Him Who willed to become her Son, Mary was *preserved from the inheritance of original sin.*

In this way, from the first moment of her conception— that is, of her existence—Mary belonged to Christ, sharing in salvific and sanctifying grace and in that love that has its beginning in the "Beloved," the Son of the Eternal Father, Who through the Incarnation became her own Son. Consequently, through the power of the Holy Spirit, in the order of grace, which is a participation in the Divine Nature, Mary *receives life from Him to Whom* she herself *gave life* as a Mother.

3. Mary's Holiness

Theologians mention that this fullness of grace exists in three different degrees. There is first of all the absolute fullness of grace that exists in Christ, the Savior of the world. Taking into consideration only God's ordinary power, there can be no greater grace than this. It is the inexhaustible source of all the grace that human beings receive from the Fall till the end of time. It is also the source of the beatitude of the just, for Jesus has merited all the effects of our predestination.

Secondly, there is the fullness of superabundance that is Mary's special privilege. It is named thusly because it is like a spiritual river that has poured out its abundance upon the souls of human beings throughout the ages.

Thirdly, there is the fullness of sufficiency common to all the just and which makes them capable of performing those meritorius acts that lead them to eternal life.

Our Lady's fullness of grace did not cease to increase up to the time of her death. Hence, theologians speak of (1) her initial fullness or plenitude; (2) her second sanctification at the moment of the Savior's conception; and (3) her final fullness at the instant of her entry into glory.

A. Buono

- G -

GENEALOGY [488]

IN keeping with the paucity of the information that has come down to us about Mary, there is no extant genealogy of the Mother of Jesus. However, the Church has always taught that Mary was of the line of David, based on the words of the Angel to her at the Annunciation: *"The Lord God will give Him the reign of David* His father" (Lk 1:32). This Davidic descent of Jesus is also alluded to by Paul in Romans (1:3) and Second Timothy (2:8). Since Jesus was born of Mary alone (by the power of the Holy Spirit, Lk 1:34-35), Mary had to be of the Family of David.

Thus, in the *Liturgy of the Hours* (Morning Prayer for the Birth of Mary), we find the antiphon: "We commemorate the birth of the blessed Virgin Mary, a descendant of Adam, born of the tribe of Judah and of David's seed."

For a time, Scripture scholars thought that the genealogy given for Christ by Matthew (1:1-16) was really the genealogy of Mary, for it differed from the genealogy presented by Luke (3:23-38), which they regarded as that of Joseph. Matthew would then enable us to draw up a list of Mary's ancestors culminating with Abraham. However, this theory seems to have gone into decline; most scholars now regard the two genealogies as referring to Joseph but based on different schemes, while others consider the genealogies to be artificial, in keeping with the custom of the time.

In sacred art, Mary is also depicted as part of Christ's family tree—the Jesse tree, named after Jesse, the father of David and founder of the Davidic line. *A. Buono*

GUADALUPE (Mexico) [67]

SEE *Apparitions*   *Apparitions after Vatican II*

1. The Apparitions and Their Historical Context

IN discussing the apparitions of the Virgin of Guadalupe one must bear in mind the conquest of Mexico by the Spaniards in 1521. It was only ten years later that the miracle of Tepeyac took place: the Blessed Virgin appeared to an Indian native, a recent convert to Christianity who was on his way to catechetical instructions given by the missionaries from Europe.

Juan Diego—the name of the seer—went to tell the bishop, Juan de Zumarraga, who lent him no credence at all. So, in a subsequent apparition Juan asked the Blessed Virgin for a sign that he might convey to the bishop. The Blessed Virgin asked him to pick some roses at the place of the apparition. This seemed impossible, given the season—the month of December—and the place, a rocky mass. But Juan Diego found roses and filled his cloak. When he unrolled it to show them to the bishop, the image of Mary was seen imprinted on the cloak. Ever since, this image has been venerated at Guadalupe. In 1754, Benedict XIV authorized a Mass and Office in honor of Our Lady of Guadalupe on December 12. These were added to the Proper of the United States as a Memorial in 1971 and as a Feast in 1988.

It is important to understand that the apparition of the Blessed Virgin took place at the beginning of a new people's formation and their adherence to Christianity. The apparition was accompanied by a message: Juan Diego was to proclaim who she was, "the Mother of the true God Who gives life," and to ask for "the construction of a shrine where she could show her motherly love."

2. Importance of the Apparition of the Blessed Virgin at Guadalupe

The fact that the apparition occurred at the beginning of a new people's history is a clue to what it was to mean for the Mexican nation. It has left its mark on the consciousness of the Mexican. The Virgin of Guadalupe has figured in all the stages of the national history as well as in the simple, unhurried life of the Mexican people. Guadalupe, apparition and all, has become one of the established values of Mexico, jealously guarded by everyone as a national treasure.

The reason for this can be found in a number of significant details:

"In the image, miraculously imprinted on the *tilma* of Juan Diego, Our Lady wore a cincture marking her pregnancy. The Aztecs took this as a sign that Mary came to them with her Son not yet born. They interpreted the whole image in a symbolic manner. It was like a book that showed them the way to the true God. The missionaries could point out and explain, with the help of the image, many truths of the faith and use it as a guide to introduce the Indians to religious ideas that were new to them yet in some respects similar to their own.

"At Guadalupe, Mary took pains for detail. The place she chose, the hillside of Tepeyac, had a special meaning for the Indians. Tepeyac was the site of a temple built to honor the mother of a pagan god. Our Lady's desire was for construction of a temple to the Mother of the true God.

"The place she chose, her cincture, the name she gave herself; her love and attention expressed in the gift of her image on the garb of one of their own; the revelation of her motherly care: all this let the Indians know that she truly was their Mother. They called her 'Tonantzin,' i.e., 'Our Mother,' and sometimes 'Teotenantzin,' i.e., 'Mother of God' " (Christopher Rengers, O.F.M. Cap.).

3. Present Situation

The shrine of Guadalupe is home to all Mexicans. There they can find the most loving Mother who intercedes for all her children. Every Mexican visits it as often as possible.

Today at Guadalupe there is a modern basilica in accord with the liturgical guidelines of Vatican II. It permits better handling of visitors and pilgrims, as well as allows more adequate pastoral care.   *Mexican Priest*

4. The Pilgrimage of John Paul II

It is worth recalling the "pilgrimage of faith" that John Paul II made to Mexico in January 1979—it was his first apostolic journey—"to invoke on [his] pontificate the motherly protection and assistance of Our Lady of Guadalupe; to repeat to her with greater vigor prompted by new and immense obligations: '*Totus tuus sum ego*! [I am all yours!],' and to place in her hands the future of the evangelization of Latin America" (January 25, 1979, at Fiumicino Airport).

In the homily pronounced at the Cathedral in Mexico City (January 26), the Pope asked the Virgin of Guadalupe to bestow on the Mexican people who "love her with deep devotion" the gift of fidelity in the dimensions of searching, acceptance, coherence, and perseverance that once animated her own fidelity.

In the homily during the Mass at the Basilica of Our Lady of Guadalupe (January 27), John Paul II gave this historical summary: "Ever since the time that the Indian Juan Diego spoke of the sweet Lady of Tepeyac, you, Mother of Guadalupe, have entered decisively into the Christian life of the people of Mexico."

At the conclusion of the address given at Puebla on January 28, 1979, for the Opening of the Third General Assembly of Latin American Bishops, the Holy Father said: "The fact that this meeting of ours is taking place in the spiritual presence of Our Lady of Guadalupe, who is venerated in Mexico and in all the other countries as the Mother of the Church in Latin America, is for me a cause for joy and a source of hope. May she, the 'star of evangelization,' be your guide in your future reflections and decisions. May she obtain for you from her Divine Son: the boldness of prophets and the evangelical prudence of pastors; the clearsightedness of teachers and the reliability of guides and directors; the courage of witnesses, and the calmness, patience, and gentleness of fathers."

Finally to the workers of Guadalajara (January 30), the Pope addressed these words: "I come to you bearing in my eyes and in my soul the Image of Our Lady of Guadalupe, your Protectrix. You bear a filial love toward her which I have been able to spot not only in her shrine but also while passing through the streets and cities of Mexico. Wherever there is a Mexican, there is the Mother of Guadalupe. Someone recently told me that 96 out of 100 Mexicans are Catholic but 100 out of 100 are Guadalupeans!"

A. Rum

- H -

HAIL HOLY QUEEN (Salve Regina) [971]

SEE *Prayer(s) to Mary*

THIS choral anthem is a beautiful testimony to the flowering of Marian devotion in the 11th century, first under the form: *Hail, Holy Queen of Mercy*, which at Cluny became: *Hail, Holy Queen, Mother of Mercy*. Since the 13th century, it has been the last evening chant in many communities.

After greeting our Queen and our Mother, full of mercy and tender love, we cry out our misery. For she is our Advocate. We ask that when our time comes, she show us Jesus born of her womb. This prayer of praise and supplication is a jewel that scarcely needs comment. The text is as follows:

> Hail, holy Queen, Mother of mercy;
> hail, our life, our sweetness and our hope.
> To you do we cry,
> poor banished children of Eve.
> To you do we send up our sighs,
> mourning and weeping in this valley of tears.
> Turn then, most gracious Advocate,
> your eyes of mercy toward us.
> And after this our exile
> show unto us the blessed fruit of your womb, Jesus.
> O clement, O loving, O sweet Virgin Mary. *J. Laurenceau*

HAIL MARY [435, 2676-2678]

SEE *Annunciation*   *Rosary*
    Prayer(s) to Mary

THE Hail Mary is the Marian salutation without compare. The part from the Gospel was used very early in the Liturgy and apart from it. By the beginning of the 12th century it had become a common prayer in the West. Added in time (mostly in the 15th century), was the second part, a prayer of supplication: "Holy Mary . . . pray for us," etc.

163

Hail, Mary,
full of grace,
the Lord is with you.
Blessed are you among women
and blessed is the fruit of your womb, Jesus.

(Lk 1:28, 42)

Holy Mary,
Mother of God,
pray for us sinners,
now and at the hour of our death.

1. The Evangelical Salutation (Lk 1:28 and 42)

The Angel, messenger of God, says to Mary: *"Rejoice!"*
We may see in this the equivalent of the common greeting in
Greek, and translate by *"Hail, Mary."* But, viewed in the Biblical context, it is normal to take it as an indication of the
Messianic joy announced by the Prophets to the *Daughter
of Zion*, personification of the Remnant of Israel: *"Shout for
joy, O daughter of Zion! sing joyfully, O Israel. . . . The Lord,
your God, is within you, a mighty savior"* (Zep 3:14-17; cf. Zec.
9:9).

The name of *Mary*—Myriam—recalls the sister of Moses
and Aaron, who led the singing and thanksgiving at the crossing of the Red Sea (Ex 15).

"Full of grace." This new name expresses God's permanent favor toward Mary. She is greeted as the Beloved of God,
personification of the People chosen and loved by God.

"The Lord is with you." To Moses fearful of the task en-
trusted to him, God says: *"I will be with you"* (Ex 3:12). To
Gideon about to receive the mission of saving the Israelites, the
Angel begins by saying: *"The Lord is with you, O champion!"*
(Jgs 6:12). The task entrusted to Mary for the salvation of the
world is beyond all human power, but God is with her.

*"Blessed are you among women and blessed is the fruit of
your womb."* This benediction spoken by Elizabeth, *filled with
the Spirit*, appears to be modeled on the benediction addressed
to Judith by the people whom she had just saved in decapitat-

ing Holofernes: *"Blessed are you, daughter, by the Most High God, above all women on earth; and blessed be the Lord God"* (Jdt 13:18). Mary is the woman chosen by God to give birth to the One Who was to bring salvation. On Mary and the Child rest the Divine blessing and the praise of human beings. In Jesus the Church recognizes, with Mary, the Blessed One in person.

2. Supplication of the Church

First in the list of Saints in the litanies of the Church is *"Holy Mary, Holy Mother of God."*

Mary, *All Holy,* as Eastern Christians say; Mary, *full of grace* and preserved from all stain of sin; Mary, "temple of the Holy Spirit."

Mother of God. This is a title that expresses the Church's belief in the reality of the Incarnation, the Son of God born of Mary for our salvation. The Council of Ephesus (431) solemnly approved it. She is *"Mother of God"* not only by the virginal conception of God the Son but by her generous participation in the work of the Savior.

"Pray for us." Mary, in union with Christ, intercedes for us. The Communion of Saints finds its supreme fulfillment in the maternal love of Mary, who prays and cares unceasingly for the brothers and sisters of her Son (cf. LG 62).

"[Pray for us] sinners." This brings to mind the prayer of the tax collector: *"Be merciful to me, a sinner"* (Lk 18:13).

"Now and at the hour of our death." These concluding words, added in the 19th century, lend point to our petition. Amid daily preoccupations, we keep an eye of faith on our eventual passing through death, in the strength of Christ, to the Father's house. Mary was at the foot of the Cross, refuge of hope.

3. Repetition of the Hail Mary

From the 11th century on, we find ascetics and other devout persons repeating the Hail Mary in sets of 50 (50, 100, 150 . . .), often accompanied by genuflections or prostrations.

These devotions were a forerunner of the Rosary as we know it.

"The litany-like succession of Hail Marys becomes in it-self an unceasing praise of Christ, Who is the ultimate object both of the Angel's announcement and of the greeting of the mother of John the Baptist" (MC 46).

J. Laurenceau

HOLINESS

S<small>EE</small>   *"Full of Grace"*

HOLY LAND AND MARY   [80ff]

S<small>EE</small>   *Archeology (and Mary)*

1. The "Holy Land"

THE Holy Land does not reveal itself easily. Often visitors find therein only an echo of their own thoughts and what they bring to it. Hence, one must know how to query this Land.

(a) *What is no longer seen in the Holy Land.* Only a gener-ation ago the traveler would still find in Palestine an oriental Middle Ages bordering on Antiquity. A *fellah* (farmer) working the land with his wooden plow and yoke of cows brought to mind the Patriarchs and the Parables. So did the Bedouin in *keffieh* and *abaye* (cloak and hood) leading his flock. And a veiled woman with a little child represented the Virgin Mary. All had a quiet dignity in their bearing and activity that gave them each the role which the pilgrim had expected.

But today visitors spend most time in the city, among peo-ple clothed and working in the modern style, whom they never have time to get to know well and who make little impression at first sight.

(b) *What one must make an effort to see.* Age-old scenes are still to be met, but one must keep an eye out to catch them. Chances are best on the interior roads along the mountains of

Judea, Samaria, and Galilee. The time spent traveling these roads is essential on a pilgrimage. The opportunity should not be missed despite the necessary effort.

Pilgrims need not betray themselves along the way, if they guard their tongue. Nor is it the time to sing canticles or recite the Rosary. Given a chance to visit the Land of Mary, we do not speak to her to tell her our troubles. That can be done just as well without setting foot from home. But we watch for the scene that might call to mind Mary and her way of life, and provide food for future prayers.

Keeping interior silence, like the hunters on the alert for prey, is itself a discipline and in its own way a kind of prayer.

(c) *What should be borne in mind.* Many things have changed, but not the people of the countryside. The larger views command more interest than the details. Events of Sacred History can be tied to them with certainty.

With regard to Mary, we will be reminded that the *Daughter of Zion* embodied the highest spiritual values of God's people: such as the Consecration that the Bible calls holiness, Fidelity, Faith, humble Obedience of the Handmaid, and the Charity of the Visitation. That was not all. Mary bore the entire history of her people and recounted it to her Son, sometimes in sight of the very place where an event took place.

Traveling through the Holy Land is in many ways a journey through the Old Testament. The whole experience can find place in one's devotion to Mary.

2. "Biblical Places" and Mary

(a) AIN-KARIM, or EN-KEREM

"Fountain of the Vines" is one of the places where the ancient Near East still comes to life, with its simple and uncomplaining poverty. One has only to look down from the ridge and its large modern buildings that dominate the town.

It matters little that the pilgrimage in honor of Saint John the Baptist dates only from the 6th century and is historically questionable: For those at leisure to draw up their own schedule, Ain-Karim would be a place to spend a little more time, preferably in reading and meditating on the Gospels of the Infancy and the Beatitudes of the poor.

The two churches, of the Visitation and the Birth of Saint John the Baptist, are large enough to accommodate groups and are quite attractive yet not pretentious. The church of the Visitation—of more immediate interest to a Marian pilgrimage—is even surrounded by a terrain where it is possible to read Luke 1:39-56 undisturbed.

The town with its old Levantine homes is inhabited by an unassuming Jewish population that tends its gardens and small plots and goes to work in Jerusalem. Toward the lower edge of the town stands the convent of the Sisters of Zion. It is an old stone building whose interior offers a cool contrast to the outdoor climate. The view from the convent is beautiful, and an air of peace and kindliness prevails.

(b) APOCRYPHA AND SHRINES OF THE HOLY LAND

The location of several churches follows indications of apocryphal Gospels or other similar works. The two principal ones are:

- *Protevangelium of James*, for the church of the Birth of Mary in Jerusalem and the church of the Annunciation at Nazareth;
- Cycle of the *Transitus Mariae* (passing of Mary), for the church of the Dormition of the Blessed Virgin and her Tomb in Jerusalem.

These writings are of Palestinian origin and date probably from the 2nd century, or in any case from the time of persecution. Intruding upon profoundly contemplative scenes are childish adjuncts of no value. But this need not come as a shock. Works of this kind represent a semiclandestine people's Christianity in which the ebullient heart escapes cultural restraint. They are legendary accounts varying in quality from one line to the next.

Protestants and Catholics attached to the letter of the New Testament disdain them; yet it is well to remember with Saint Paul that *"the letter kills, but the Spirit gives life."* The content of a book need not be rejected en masse simply because it has not been found canonical and inspired throughout.

These works offer scenes of contemplation on the spiritual privileges of Mary and their manifestations. Churches of East and West with direct roots in Antiquity ratify these scenes. To this extent, at least, the works can be safely recommended to Christ's faithful. But no historical value should be attributed to those details—some topographical, others picturesque or anecdotal—that are the weak points of the Apocrypha.

(c) BETHLEHEM AND ITS ENVIRONS

Today Bethlehem is a suburb of Greater Jerusalem with some 15,000 inhabitants, most of whom work in the capital. It is a rundown locality and has nothing expressive to show.

The Basilica. This is the only church in Palestine that has preserved its original architecture: the columns of Constantine (325) and the trilobate apse of Justinian (540). The raised choir is over the Grotto that Origen already knew in the 3rd century. Several decorative elements of the Crusaders are easily recognized.

The Grotto is not well suited for more than private prayer. To celebrate Holy Mass arrangements have to be made well in advance, and the hour is not open to choosing. It may be questioned whether pilgrims have all that much to gain in the bargain.

For quiet reading and meditation (on Luke 2:1-7 and 15-20, for example), the Franciscan monastery adjoining the Basilica is an excellent retreat. Its crypts, where Saint Jerome lived while translating the Bible into Latin, offer good opportunities for celebrating Mass with a group.

The *Herodion* (Mt 2:1-18). A visit to the Herodion, 14 miles from Bethlehem, is first of all an occasion to get a taste of real wilderness. It was the palace-fortress of Herod the Great, intended to be his tomb as well. Excavations at the site reveal a good deal of this energetic king, talented but cruel and unscrupulous.

Rachel's Tomb (Mt 2:17-18). Coming from Jerusalem, one necessarily passes by this ancient Biblical site, which today is in the hands of the Israelis (Gn 35:19). It is at the fork of the Hebron and Bethlehem roads. Saint Matthew no doubt had it in mind when citing Jeremiah 31:15, in connection with the slaughter of the Innocents.

There is not much to see inside, but the site ought to have its place among memories of a Holy Land visit.

Shepherds' Field. In the Christian period processions formed here before going up to the Basilica. No doubt the spot was chosen as a common ground between the cultivated areas to which Bethlehem owes its name (House of Bread) and the Wilderness, hence a place for ethnic groups of the region to come together. This consideration for natural differences should not be lost on us.

Besides the Gospel of Saint Luke, one might read here the accounts of the young David (1 Sm 16; 17), the prophecy of Micah foretelling the restoration of Israel through a return to the God of its origins (Mt 5:1-14), and the delightful Psalm 23.

Shepherds' Field would be a good place to meditate on the person of David in a Marian spirit (cf. 1. The "Holy Land"). For this purpose it is well to have a scientific Bible and look for Psalms marked "of David." These in fact are adapted to the great episodes of his adventurous yet always loyal and fundamentally faithful life.

(d) BIRTH AND PRESENTATION OF MARY

According to the apocryphal *Protevangelium of James,* the Virgin Mary was born to Ann and Joachim in Jerusalem, in the neighborhood of the Sheep Pool close by the Temple (cf. Jn 2:2). These particulars, which are probably legendary, convey something deeper: the Daughter of Zion's close association with the Temple.

On a similar note, the *Protevangelium* says that Mary was presented in the Temple at the age of 12, to live there in seclusion while learning the Law and beginning to serve God with her weaving and embroidery.

It was these considerations that determined the site of the St. Ann church, not far from the ruins of the Sheep Pool. The visit to the church and vicinity is best combined with the visit to the Temple.

Built on Byzantine foundations of the 6th century, the present church was vaulted in Roman style perhaps at the time of the Crusaders or even before, since pilgrimages had begun earlier. Some ornamental features, like the beautiful window of the main facade, were the work of Kings of Jerusalem, who established there a community of nuns. The church is one of the most captivating sights in Palestine, by the purity and simplicity of its architecture. If at all possible, a visiting group should experience the celebration of Mass there.

(e) CALVARY

The visit to the Basilica of the Holy Sepulcher, or of the Resurrection, as the Greeks say, should be made most of all for its own sake. A good guide can expound its history, which is a résumé of the Church's history.

The Virgin Mary has only a guarded place in the mysteries commemorated by the Basilica. For Saint John's testimony, see what is said under the entry "Cana."

(f) CANA

In all probability the true site of the Cana of the Gospels was at Khirbet Qana in Upper Galilee, now in ruins and hard to get to. As for the wedding of Cana, it has become customary to mark it with a festival in the town of Kafr Kenna. This is the road from Nazareth to Tiberias, over which most pilgrims travel. Not too much importance should then be given to what guardians of the Latin and Greek churches here point out.

But time would be well spent meditating on the text of Saint John, as dense as it is difficult.

Jesus takes His distance from His Mother. The words *"Woman, how does this concern of yours involve Me?"* should not be softened. They can even be reinforced by another scene of distance-taking (Lk 8:19-21) and other words of breaking away (Lk 14:25-27).

But there is also a promise: the ruptures will end in rediscoveries (Lk 18:28-30).

In Saint John the words *"Woman,"* *"My Hour,"* and *"His glory"* foreshadow the cycle of the Passion (Jn 13:1ff; 17:1ff; 19:25-27). At the last moment Jesus reunites those whom He had never ceased to love: His Mother and His disciple.

It may be better to meditate on this cluster of texts in a longer halt at Cana rather than while staying in Jerusalem, where there are too many things to see and occupy the mind.

(g) CENACLE (UPPER ROOM)

The Chapel of the Cenacle was part of a very large basilica of the 4th century, the Mount Zion, whose remains unfortunately are impossible to trace. It was located in an upper story, in conformity with indications of the New Testament (Mk 14:15, etc.).

Its present state goes back to the 14th century. At that time it was rebuilt and decorated in the style of a monastic refectory or chapter hall that incorporated a somewhat florid Gothic. Commemorated there, in addition to the Last Supper of Holy Thursday, were the gatherings of the primitive Church in Jerusalem and the miracle of Pentecost (Acts 1:13; 2:1).

In this latter cycle, which derived from the earliest Judeo-Christian community, the Virgin Mary played a modest but essential role. Around her gathered two groups that were divided while Jesus was on earth. One was the disciples and the women (Lk 6:14-16; 8:1-3; 23:49). The other was the "brethren," i.e., the extended family of Jesus (Lk 8:19-21; Jn 7:1-5). The separation begun at Cana came to an end. The reunion begun on Calvary had its every effect.

The Church exists when those who had been separated are reunited, and the Spirit will soon inspire them to bear witness before all sorts of people. This, in my opinion, is the thought conveyed by contemplatives who assert that the Spirit of Pentecost rested first on the Virgin Mary. He had come once for all at the Annunciation, and now His secret presence in Mary prepared for His fulgurant coming at Pentecost.

The Descent of the Holy Spirit is the Third Glorious Mystery of the Rosary.

(h) CHURCHES OF THE HOLY LAND

Prayer and meditation. "One can pray to God anywhere, even in churches of the Holy Land," it has been said. Indeed, travelers welcome these havens where they can rest themselves and gather their thoughts.

To those who can follow their own itinerary, my advice would be to keep the visit of churches for the end of the journey. After you have traveled over and viewed the Land, you might do well to pause and do some reading on what has been seen, write down impressions gained, engage in meditation, and tell God about new ideas or new desires that may be coming to mind.

Visit and culture. Churches of the Holy Land generally are of little artistic interest but often of great historical interest. Many retain, quite visibly, foundations that stem from the first century of Christian freedom, the century following the Edict of Constantine (312), which saw the beginning of the tradition of pilgrimages. Frequently there appear upon these original foundations the traces of reconstructions and later embellishments. The churches rising from them not only have the nobility of a monument but they figure as condensations of Christian history, with its centuries of good fortune and bad. They are witnesses to the persevering devotion of Christians coming back time and again to pray at the very places where Salvation came about.

This is true more especially for the church of the Annunciation at Nazareth, and the churches of Bethlehem, of Calvary, of the Birth of Mary, and of her Tomb.

Guidebooks to these churches are indispensable. They provide noteworthy historical and archeological information, and Christians in particular are helped to make their visit in the spirit of devotion to Mary.

(i) DORMITION OF THE VIRGIN MARY

Jesus more than once referred to death as a kind of sleep and indicated that those in this sleep are actually alive in God (Mk 5:29; Jn 11:11-14; Mk 12:24-27). Saint Paul speaks similarly (1 Thes 4:13, for example).

Accordingly, Christians gave the name *Dormition* (Latin *dormire*, to sleep) to the passing of the Virgin Mary from this world to God. Byzantine tradition places the occurrence not far from the Cenacle, in another chapel of the Basilica of Holy Zion.

This whole quarter has been ravaged by time. The present Basilica was rebuilt in 1898 by German Benedictines, who also are its guardians.

It is not difficult to meet there and celebrate Mass (cf. Tomb of Mary).

(j) JERUSALEM

It is not at all easy to mark off the Jerusalem of the New Testament from the modern city, which extends beyond it on all sides.

Pilgrims tend to confuse it with the old city surrounded by walls. This, unfortunately, is completely inaccurate. The Old City looked more like a medieval shantytown, built on the remnant of the Romano-Byzantine Jerusalem.

The city over which Jesus wept and whose destruction He foretold was beautiful, new, and built in the grand style (Lk 19:41-44; 21:20-23).

To see for oneself, a close visit should be made to the esplanade of the Wailing Wall and the excavations that stretch between it and the medieval wall.

For a large number of pilgrims nothing compares with an interpreted examination of the model of Jerusalem on display in the gardens of the Hotel Holyland. The model is drawn on the plans of an eminent Israeli archeologist, and while not every detail is necessarily guaranteed, one gets an adequate view of the terrain and the ancient City. But perhaps most interesting of all is its probable reconstruction of the Temple.

(k) NAZARETH

Nazareth, unknown to the Old Testament and from which nothing good, it seemed, could come (Jn 1:45-46), was the place of the Lord's Annunciation, of His Infancy, and lastly of His Rejection.

Today it is a bedroom community of 20,000 to 30,000 inhabitants, many of whom work in Haifa. Its poverty is obvious and contributes to its lack of distinction. A visit, to be fruitful, requires a good deal of effort.

Church of the Annunciation (Lk 1:26-38). This large basilica is built on a site certainly visited by pilgrims as early as the 4th century, the beginning of juridical freedom for Christians. In the crypts can be seen vestiges of the first Byzantine church, which was superseded by the large church of the Crusaders. An added attraction is the little Grotto of the Annunciation, still venerated today. An interesting detail of the grotto is a Greek graffito: Khaire Maria (= Hail Mary), traced in an awkward hand by a very early visitor.

Connecting with the underground church are grottos and caves that, according to archeological findings, date to the 1st century. Many of the old homes stood over shelters of this kind, desirable for their even temperature.

Not to be neglected as well is the Greek Orthodox church of Saint Gabriel, located near the public Fountain to accord with the apocryphal *Protevangelium of James*. The church has neither date nor style. But it does have charm, and its decor of icons is a delight, especially if a good guide is at hand to explain the symbols. Visitors might also use the occasion to acquaint themselves with the local Christian population, which more than any other has retained its character.

Infancy of Jesus (Lk 2:39-52). The crypt called Workshop of St. Joseph (at the Sisters of Nazareth) stands little chance of being historical. It features a tomb sealed with a rolling stone, suggesting the Resurrection of Jesus (Mk 16:3).

To meditate on the Infancy of Jesus, it is best to find a spot above town, such as the school of the Salesians. Or one might opt for a point about half a mile below town, far enough to take one into the country, where the view is ample and pleasant and a perfect setting to read the Biblical account of creation or the Psalms (e.g., 8; 19; 33; 65; 104).

It is historically and spiritually allowable to think that Mary, tending her sheep with her little Boy, recited to Him and made Him learn by heart these sacred Texts.

Rejection of Jesus (Lk 4:16-30; Mk 6:1-6). The synagogue where Jesus spoke to His townspeople has not been found. What is today pointed out as the synagogue is no more than a vault without age or style, having nothing historical or of real interest. But the weary traveler can rest there, and it is a place for celebrating Mass. It is maintained by Greek Catholics as an annex to their church.

Mary had no active role in this scene. We are not even told if she was present, though it may be presumed.

But, Daughter' of Zion, she was the obstacle at which stumbled the faith of her neighbors and relatives, who said of Jesus: *"Is this not the carpenter, the Son of Mary?"* (Mk 6:3).

The meditation of Christians devoted to the Virgin Mary almost inevitably turns in the direction of this scandal: *"His own did not accept Him"* (Jn 1:11), and their prayer will ask for understanding, and ultimate reconciliation.

(l) TEMPLE

The promenades of the ancient Temple of Jerusalem, today Haram esh-Sherif, the Noble Shrine, are not an appropriate place for public acts of prayer. Travelers from the West must remind themselves that they are not at home.

The Temple is the only monument of Palestine that achieved great art.

After the ruins caused by the Romans in the year 70 after Jesus Christ, and the Moslem reconstructions beginning in 690, the appearance of the Temple in Jewish times is hard to visualize. A visit to the Model of Jerusalem is strongly recommended. But in any case. the visitor should want a spiritual understanding of what is seen today.

For example, the sacred Rock venerated under the great cupola, or Dome of the Rock, was the basement of the Holy of Holies, or perhaps of the Altar of Holocausts. Archeologists are divided on the matter. At the time of the Gospels, tradition identified it with Mount Moriah, where Abraham offered Isaac in sacrifice (hence Jn 8:56).

Isaac was the firstborn son of Sarah (i.e., she had no child before him). The ritual consecration of a firstborn son truly was an offering, a kind of sacrifice. As the Jews were to say, they themselves would be "bound" by the commandments as Isaac had been bound on the altar (cf. Ex 13:2).

This and more could be reflected on in reading the Presentation of Jesus in the Temple and seeing why Simeon's prophecy ends in prediction of the Passion (Lk 2:22-38; Ex 13:2; Lv 13:1-8).

(m) TOMB OF MARY

The Apocryphal *Transitus Mariae* (Passing of Mary) conveys the early Palestinian tradition that the Virgin Mary, after her Dormition in the Lord, was buried in a tomb found empty three days later.

The tradition names the areas of Gethsemani, at the bottom of the Valley of Jehoshaphat, i.e., Valley of God-Who-judges (Jl 4:2; Zec 14:4). Implied is that the Assumption of Mary, like the Resurrection of Christ, of which it is an echo, addresses all people, past, present, and future. This may explain why early churches of East and West approved of and made their own the tradition in question.

A first church was built in 455. Construction came in the wake of the Council of Chalcedon and the devotion to Mary that developed with the Council's definition of the title Mary Mother of God (*Theotokos*).

This church can still be visited. But the rise in the ground level at the bottom of the valley led to building a superstructural Byzantine church, then a large Gothic church that survives only in the ornamentation of the entrance steps. When the original church was built, it barely penetrated the rock-ribbed ground. Today it has all the appearance of a subterranean crypt.

(n) WAY OF THE CROSS

The Way of the Cross in Jerusalem (*Via Dolorosa*) grew out of the processions made by pilgrims at the time of the Crusades. Over the centuries both the route and the number of stations have varied. Fourteen stations gradually became the accepted number. European pilgrims were largely responsible for this, since that was what they were accustomed to in their own churches and wanted to find on their pilgrimages.

As concerns historical fact, most authorities by far dispute the claim that Pontius Pilate resided at the Antonia fortress, the starting point of the procession. They contend, with good reason, that Pilate's residence was in the palace-fortress of Herod. Its remains are seen in the medieval Citadel of Jerusalem.

Making the Way of the Cross, on the spot or in the devotion by that name, should be understood most of all as an act of the Church. Either way, it testifies to the desire of Christians of all countries to honor their God in the City where He willed to give His life for the world.

In the arrangement of a Marian pilgrimage the Fourth Station, where Jesus meets His Mother, is often the best place for meditating on John 19:25-27.

M. du Buit

HOLY SPIRIT (AND MARY)   [721-726]

SEE   *Trinity (Mary and)*   *Rosary*

ON two occasions the New Testament brings Mary into relationship with the Holy Spirit. At Pentecost, there is scarcely more than the suggestion: Mary is present in the Upper Room (Cenacle) praying with the community prior to the election of Matthias and the outpouring of the Spirit (Acts 1:14). But when speaking of the Messiah's conception in the womb of Mary, both Matthew and Luke stress the point.

In Matthew, Mary is found with child *"through the power of the Holy Spirit"* (1:18); hence the notification to Joseph: *"It is by the Holy Spirit that she has conceived this Child"* (1:20). In Luke, the Angel announces to Mary that her Son will be called *"Son of the Most High"* and that *"the Lord God will give Him the throne of David His father"* (1:32). Then, after Mary's query, the Angel adds: *"The Holy Spirit will come upon you and the power of the Most High will overshadow you; hence, the holy Offspring to be born will be called the Son of God"* (1:35).

It is therefore in consequence of the Holy Spirit's action upon Mary that the Heir to the throne of David, with a reign declared eternal (Lk 1:33), will bear the title of Son of God. Son of the Most High, He inherits the throne of David (1:31-32), and is Son of God because the power of the Most High *"will overshadow"* Mary at the same time that *"the Holy Spirit will come upon"* her.

From the beginning of the Israelite monarchy the title *"Anointed of the Lord,"* i.e., Messiah (which is Hebrew, as "Christ" is Greek, for "anointed"), was associated with the coming upon the elect of the Spirit of the Lord (1 Sm 10:6; 11:6; 16:13) or Spirit of God (1 Sm 10:10). In neighboring monarchies kings were "anointed" in the name of a superhuman power. For example, the great emperors of Mesopotamia, Sargon and Naram-Sin, were said to be the "anointed of Anu," supreme god. The so-called kings of Canaan, like Taku, were "anointed" in the name of their suzerain, the Pharaoh, himself considered a god.

If Saul could save Israel from the Ammonite peril, and David could do the same as regards the Philistines, it was because they had received from God a superior power that the Bible calls the *ruah* and we translate by *Spirit*.

For contemporaries of Saul and David the *ruah* was the atmospheric space between heaven and earth, and was both invisible and impalpable yet necessary for life. With the pagans this element became Divinized.

In the Bible the *ruah* is entirely subject to the Lord. The Lord can withdraw *"His"* spirit from human beings (Gn 6:3) at the end of a certain period of time, and their life is then limited. According to Psalm 104 (29-30), when God withdraws it, people expire; when He imparts it *"they are created and the face of the earth is renewed."*

It was this Spirit of life that the Lord gave to Saul and then took back, leaving him at the power of an evil spirit (1 Sm

16:14). David on the other hand kept it to his very last words (2 Sm 23:2). On certain Judges it acted only passingly, but more durably in Joseph (Gn 41:38).

After the fall of the monarchy this Spirit was imparted to Prophets like Ezekiel. By command of God the Prophet ordered the Spirit to revivify Israel (Ez 37). He will be poured out upon the whole house of Israel (Ez 39:29) and, in the latter days, upon all flesh.

But, according to Isaiah and his school, this happens because the Spirit will rest upon the shoot of Jesse, with the gifts of wisdom, understanding, counsel, strength, knowledge, piety, and fear of the Lord, gifts that enable Him to make human beings rest in the fear of the Lord (Is 11:1-3), *"the earth being filled with knowledge of the Lord as water covers the sea"* (Is 11:9).

According to Isaiah 42:1, the Spirit is upon the *"Servant of the Lord,"* Who will make known the revealed law to the nations and bring them its hope (Is 42:4). Finally, in Isaiah 63:11, this Spirit is called Holy Spirit (as God is Holy). Grieved by the people when He was in Moses, He it is Who will lead this people to rest (Is 63:14), since God wants His people to be holy as He is holy (Lv 19:2), by loving their neighbors as themselves (Lv 19:18 and 34).

In the Old Testament, therefore, the Messiah and His mission of sanctifying the people are closely linked with the action of the vivifying Spirit of God. As for the Mother of the Messiah, whatever her role would be, there is no mention of the Spirit of God in that regard. Furthermore, in the Old Testament the Messiah is Son and heir of God through enthronement (2 Sm 7:14; Ps 2:6-7; 89:21, 27), and in Psalm 110:3-4 this sonship is joined with a priesthood according to Melchizedek, whose God is precisely the Most High (*upsistos*, Gn 14:18). In the Gospel, on the other hand, this sonship is referred to the motherhood of Mary.

In describing the action of the Spirit of God upon the Messiah the Hebrew Bible often changes the verb. For Judges like Samson (Jgs 14:6), and for kings like Saul and David, the Bible speaks of *"penetrating"* (*"rushing upon"* in many translations). For the Judge Gideon it speaks of *"enveloping"* (Jgs 6:34).

The Spirit can also *"seize"* the Prophet or *"fall"* upon him, or *"carry him away"* (like Elijah, 2 Kgs 2: 16). For Elisha (2 Kgs 2: 15) and for the shoot of David (Is 11:2) the Bible indicates the permanence of the Spirit by saying *"rest on."* More simply, the Spirit is *"in"* Joseph (Gn 41:38) and *"in"* Moses (Is 63:11). But in Numbers 11:25 He is *"on"* the Judge Othniel (Jgs 3:10) and *"on"* the Servant of the Lord (Is 42:1). Lastly, in Ezekiel 37:10 the Spirit *"comes"* into the dead bones of Israel, which He restores to life.

It is this verb that Luke chooses to describe the coming of the Spirit upon Mary, perhaps by way of suggesting the vivifying and redemptive role of this consecration of the Messianic birth.

The *"power of the Most High"* could be an intended allusion to the priesthood of Melchizedek, *"priest of the Most High,"* which is one of the themes in the Epistle to the Hebrews. Luke makes allusion to the *"Divine protective shade."* This beautiful and ancient image (cf. Nm 14:14) had been revived in the Psalms (121:5) to portray the gentleness of the Divine protection and to avoid seeing in the "power" of the Most High a violent action. The coming of the Spirit was sometimes conceived as a violent and fearsome wind. The *"holy Offspring"* born of Mary sanctifies His people in peace.

In particular, Luke may have had in mind Psalm 17:8: *"Hide me in the shadow of your wings,"* the more so in view of the new symbolism of the Holy Spirit descending upon Jesus in the form of a dove when the Father proclaimed His Divine sonship. The woman in the Book of Revelation would also be surrounded by enemies. The Evangelist might also have been thinking of Psalm 91:1-4, where God protects His faithful one with His *"shadow"* and *"covers him with his wings."*

H. Cazelles

HOMILY OF PAUL VI AT THE CLOSING OF THE 3RD SESSION OF VATICAN II

[963]

SEE   *Church and Mary*   *Mother of the Church*
      Cult of Mary   *Vatican II and Mary*
      Magisterium (Documents of)

ON November 21, 1964, Pope Paul VI gave a closing homily for the 3rd session of the Second Vatican Ecumenical Council in which he proclaimed Mary "Mother of the Church." Like all the homilies opening and closing conciliar sessions, this too is closely connected with the acts of the Council. Indeed, it has even more importance inasmuch as it expresses the intention of Paul VI to clarify and combine the Papal Magisterium and the Conciliar Magisterium, the latter of which had on that very day approved *Lumen Gentium*, the *Dogmatic Constitution on the Church.*

In that Constitution, chapter 8, dedicated to Mary Most Holy in the ministry of Christ and the Church, was the fruit of a lengthy and laborious elaboration during which Paul VI had on various occasions pointed to the opportunity to speak of Mary as the Mother of the Church. The Council Fathers had accepted the papal invitation and made an equivalent affirmation in this regard. The primary reason for their hesitancy to use the papal phrase was their ecumenical proccupation, the wish not to disturb the Separated Brethren.

However, the Pope, because of personal conviction and devotion as well as the requests of theologians and pastors, believed it opportune to solemnly attribute to the Blessed Virgin the title Mother of the Church and to ask that she be venerated by the Christian people hereinafter under this title.

Obviously, this was not an ex cathedra definition but an act of great prominence of the Papal Magisterium, analogous to that of Pius XII with the proclamation of the Queenship of Mary. In fact, it was even more binding than the latter because it took place in an ecumenical council with the obvious intention to complete the declarations of the Council Fathers and with the explicit assertion that the new title "expresses in an admirable synthesis this Council's recognition of the privileged place of the Blessed Virgin in the Church," and that the Conciliar Constitution on the Church is, as it were, "sealed" by the proclamation of Mary as Mother of the Church.

The Pope's justification for the title is based on the Divine Motherhood of Mary, through whom the Word became flesh and united to Himself as Head His Mystical Body, which is the Church.

A. Buono

HYPERDULIA

SEE   *Devotion(s)*

ADORATION is an act of religion in which the human mind and will acknowledge God's infinite sovereignty and supreme dominion over His creatures. It is expressed externally by an attitude of reverence and by words of praise.

The highest type of worship is reserved for God alone and is called *latria* by theologians.

The honor paid to Mary and the Saints is on an infinitely lower plane. When it refers to the Saints, it is called *dulia,* and when it refers to Mary it is called *hyperdulia.* This latter is indeed less than that given to God but it surpasses the honor accorded to the Saints and Angels combined. Mary deserves this veneration because of her unique position as Mother of God.

"Among the Saints in heaven the Virgin Mary, Mother of God, is venerated in a special way. Because of the mission she received from God, her life is most closely linked with the Mysteries of Jesus Christ, and there is no one who has followed in the footsteps of the Incarnate Word more closely and with more merit than she. Neither is there anyone who has more grace and power over the Most Sacred Heart of the Son of God and through Him with the Father.

"Holier than the cherubim and seraphim, she enjoys unquestionably greater glory [and deserves greater veneration] than all the other Saints, for she is full of grace (Lk 1:28), she is the Mother of God, who happily gave birth to the Redeemer for us. . . . She teaches us all the virtues; she gives us her Son and with Him all the help we need—for God 'wanted us to have everything through Mary' (Saint Bernard)" (Pius XII: *Mediator Dei, Encyclical on the Sacred Liturgy,* no. 169).

This veneration given to Mary—as varied and intense as it is—remains far removed from idolatry because of two reasons: (1) It is an honor rendered to a creature who has carried out a unique role in the History of Salvation and has through grace attained the heights of sanctity and glory, but remains a creature nonetheless; she remains, for Christian tradition, the "servant of the Lord." (2) The veneration of Mary is neither a substitutive for, nor something independent from, nor an alternative to the worship owed to the Trinity. It is willed by God and has God as its end.

The Second Vatican Council summed this point up very nicely: "This cult, which always existed in the Church, although it is altogether singular, differs essentially from the cult of adoration that is offered to the Incarnate Word, as well as to the Father and the Holy Spirit, and it is most favorable to it. . . . As she is proclaimed and venerated, Mary calls the faithful to her Son and His sacrifice and to the love of the Father" (LG 66, 65).

A. Buono

ICONS AND IMAGES OF MARY [1159-1162]

IMAGES of Mary are countless: frescoes, icons, mosaics, bas-reliefs, statues, paintings, medals, and more. What is their connection with the faith of the Church? How do they help us to pray?

1. "Born of a Woman" (Gal 4:4)

For fear of idolatry (= worship of images), the Old Testament prohibited in principle every human or animal representation (Ex 20:4; 32). The true God is invisible. Humans cannot see the face of God (Ex 33:18-23).

But in Christ *"the fullness of the Godhead resides in bodily form"* (Col 2:9). *"He is the image of the invisible God"* (Col 1:15). The glory of God shines on the face of Christ (2 Cor 4:6).

This became fact through the Son of God's being born of a woman, Mary. Because His Mother was truly human, we are assured of the reality of the Incarnation and the nearness to us of the Son of God. It is normal, therefore, that in addition to images of the Face of Christ or His Transfiguration, images of the Mother of God should be the most ancient and the most venerated.

2. In the West

On the walls of the catacombs a young mother is shown holding up her son to the star prophesied by Balaam (Nm 24:15-19) or to the adoration of the Magi representing pagan nations. It is Mary.

When the Roman Empire adopts Christianity, emphasis shifts to the Divinity of Christ in opposition to the dying idols, and the Mother of God is clothed in the mantle of empresses.

At the time of Saint Bernard, Christians again look to Mary as evidence that the Lord of glory also is a man like them, and like them has known suffering—the suffering that brought the blessedness of salvation. Gothic Virgins appear: Virgin with an apple, Virgin with grapes or birds.

The Renaissance also leaves its mark, in representations of Mary that are more and more "human," and minus her Son. This gives impetus to the Protestant opposition against images.

Modern Catholic piety leans to the privileges of Mary (Immaculate Conception, Assumption), reflected in images like the Miraculous Medal of Bac or the medal of Our Lady of Lourdes.

3. In the East

Veneration of images has a large place in the piety of Eastern Christians, especially since the Iconoclastic Controversy of the 8th century. The Second Council of Nicaea (787) resolved the controversy on the basis of Saint Basil's principle that "honor paid to an image redounds to the original model."

The icon as expression and support of prayer is the result of long contemplation, in an atmosphere of obedience, fasting, silence, and chastity. Images reflect definite traditions. The Mother of God is often represented. Among the most common types are:

Hodigitria, "she who shows the way," i.e., Christ.

Elêousa, Mother of God of tenderness, head inclined toward her Son.

The *Déésis,* she who intercedes, standing with hands lifted heavenward.

The *Veil:* Mother of God, figure of the Church, covering with her protection her multitudinous children.

The *Sign:* Mary represented with the Child-God in her arms surrounded by a circle or oval signifying the Divine glory.

4. Today

In this audiovisual age Christians need images that by their beauty can lead them to the Son of God born of Mary.

We ought to take the time to study and admire images of Mary from the past. But we ought also to create new ones that speak of salvation to the heart of our contemporaries.

J. Laurenceau

IMITATION OF MARY

[2030]

SEE *Consecration*   *Value of Marian*
     States of Life and   *Devotion*
     Marian Devotion

IT would be hard to find a spiritual writer on the Christian life who does not recommend imitation of Mary. Eminent passages in point could be cited from Saint Ambrose, Saint Bernard, Saint Louis-Marie de Montfort, Saint Pius X, and many others.

The Second Vatican Council continues this long tradition, saying: "True devotion to Mary proceeds from true faith, by which we are led to know the excellence of the Mother of God and are moved to a filial love toward our Mother and the *imitation of her virtues*" (LG 67).

In the same chapter 8 of the *Constitution on the Church* the Fathers of the Council show Mary as "*the* model" and the "type" of the Church "in the order of faith, charity, and perfect union with Christ . . . the exemplar both of virgin and of mother" (LG 63, 65).

Paul VI devotes the entire second half of his important Apostolic Exhortation *Signum Magnum* (May 13, 1967) to "imitation of the virtues of the Most Blessed Virgin."

What, precisely, is being proposed?

1. Take Mary as a Model

To imitate someone is to take that person as a model, to follow his or her example. This can range from copying externals (physical posture, speech, gestures), as an actor might do, to adopting the thoughts, opinions, likes, and dislikes of another.

In the case of Mary, what is proposed for imitation are her virtues, especially her faith, her charity, her humility, her docility to the Holy Spirit, her love of Jesus, her union with Him, etc. For each virtue the Evangelists provide help for meditation: for example, the Annunciation, Cana, Mary at the foot of the Cross, and Mary in the Cenacle.

Admittedly, this seems simple enough. Nevertheless, it can stand a word of explanation to prevent Marian devotion from going in the wrong direction and ending in frustration.

First, even while imitating the "virtues" of Mary, we do not try to reproduce, literally, the life she led. This would be an illusory archeologism and a fruitless pursuit because, among other things, the sociocultural context today is far different from the one known to Mary and in addition her personal vocation is unique (cf. MC 35ff).

What we try to do is center on her fundamental attitude of self-giving to the Lord and commitment to His service as well as the service of our fellow humans. It is this attitude that we must cultivate so that it will become part of us.

Thus, we should learn from Mary, the first and perfect Christian, how to live as children of the Father, as disciples of Christ, in docility to the Holy Spirit, each according to our personal vocation, even as she lived according to hers, every moment of her life. Far from being a literal "copying," our imitation of Mary should lead us to "discover" and "apprehend" what constitutes our own fidelity day by day—just as she did in her time.

2. Be Formed by Mary and by the Holy Spirit

Moreover, the exemplarity of Mary must not be conceived as something static, with Mary having a purely passive role, like the "model" that a painter interprets and reproduces as closely as possible. If Mary were a model in this sense, and if Christians had to find within themselves the means of imitating her, let us say at once that this itself would require a very advanced state of virtue.

What really happens when we strive to imitate Mary is that we yield our lives, consciously or not, to her action as Mother and teacher; we place ourselves under her direction. Desiring to imitate her faith, her charity, etc., we are saying to her: "Teach me to believe, to love, and to be united with Jesus as you did. Form me to resemble your Son." In short, we call upon her Spiritual Motherhood.

That is not all. Every time we turn to Mary in contemplation and take her as model, or simply have recourse to her protection (*"Sub tuum praesidium*—We fly to your patronage"), we yield ourselves to the Holy Spirit as well. Mary is entirely "fashioned and formed by the Holy Spirit" (LG 56), Who does nothing in a soul without Mary cooperating in His action.

Only the Holy Spirit can sanctify us, but He does so through the maternal influence of Mary and her pedagogic action. It is a perpetual rule that the Christian is born and grows in the Divine Life "by the power of the Holy Spirit . . . [through] the Virgin Mary."

Hence, the more we are united with Mary, particularly in our efforts to imitate her, the more also are we given to the action of the Holy Spirit. And by Him we are made to grow in faith and Divine charity and are filled with the mind of Jesus Christ Himself, our first and primary model.

Only the conjoint action of the Holy Spirit and Mary can reach us in the mysterious sanctum of our heart and liberty. But this action is generally accomplished through multiple intermediaries such as the pedagogic action of the Church and cells within the Church: family, spiritual groups, parish, religious communities, etc., as well as the *example of saintly persons* whom we cultivate and their concern for us. Accordingly, the exemplarity of Mary frequently operates through the exemplarity and devotedness of members of the Church already deeply imbued with grace.

Mary, it should be noted, is the archetype of the Church. This means that something of Mary's holiness is spread abroad in the Church by the Holy Spirit and is diffused, through the medium of the Church and Church members, into our heart so that we might live according to the Gospel and build up the Body of Christ.

This is to say that Mary's exemplarity for the Church is not static. It is comparable to that of God, exemplary cause of all things in the sense that all things receive from Him whatever resemblance they bear to Him.

A. Boulet

IMMACULATE CONCEPTION [491-492]

SEE   *Feasts of Mary*   *"Full of Grace"*

1. Mary, All Holy

THE Mystery of the Incarnation gave rise, from earliest times, to the Church's conviction of Mary's holiness. Chosen by the Father to be the Mother of His Son, and accepting this mission by characterizing herself as the *"servant of the Lord,"* Mary could never have consented to an offense against God. According to an expression favored by Eastern Christians, she is the "all-holy," *panagia*. The proclamation in the 5th century (Council of Ephesus, 431) of her title "Mother of God" reinforced this persuasion of her exceptional holiness.

The Church, as a consequence, sees in Mary one who never denied God the least sign of love.

Mary was the object of special attention on the part of God, Who prepared her to become the Mother of His Son. From birth she was filled with the Holy Spirit, which accounts for the wonderful display in her life of the theological virtues.

Her faith enabled her to consent without hesitation to the "word of God" sent through the Angel of the Annunciation; her faith was the source of the obedience by which throughout her life she kept in such accord with her Son's mission as to be, by singular and unique title, His associate in the work of the Redemption. Her hope nothing could undermine, not even the death on Calvary. And her Divine charity, which is universal, embraced and still embraces us in the boundless love she has for her Son Who is her God. Mary was indeed *"full of grace,"* as Gabriel said in greeting her.

"From the first instant of her conception she was adorned with the radiance of an entirely unique holiness" (LG 56).

All holy, Mary obviously was exempt from sin, because sin always means denial that leads away from God, as in the case of the prodigal who strayed from the father's house. Mary was never away from God. Like the servant of Psalm 123, she kept her eyes on her Lord to do His will at the least sign of it.

2. Immaculate from Conception

In the East the Feast of the Immaculate Conception was celebrated as early as the 7th century. In the West it was adopted several centuries later (Saint Thomas Aquinas attests to its existence in churches of his day: *Summa theologica*, III, q. 27, art. 2, ad 3). The Feast proclaims the total immunization from sin in the soul of the Virgin Mary and, consequently, the exceptional grace bestowed on her. To say that this grace goes back to the moment when Mary began to exist is to prove, as it were, her perfect impeccability, demanded by the holiness that the Church acclaims in the Mother of God.

Indeed, if at sixteen or eighteen this humble maid of Nazareth could declare herself "servant of the Lord" with such apparent confidence, it was because no sin ever touched her from the beginning of her life. In other words, God had filled her with grace in view of what He would one day ask of her.

When theologians of the Middle Ages were prompted by Saint Augustine's theology to delve into the question of original sin—an hereditary trait transmitted at conception to descendants of Adam—they also pondered over the exact nature of the privilege accorded to Mary. For the Greeks, initiators of the Feast, the expression "Immaculate Conception" meant that Mary, from the first moment of her life, was preserved from sin. Did it also mean that she was spared even original sin?

Latin theology was firm on two things: (a) every human being is infected with original sin and bears its consequences; (b) this hereditary sin is remitted through the merits of Christ, Redeemer of the entire human race.

That Mary was preserved from personal sin, Latin theologians admitted without question, faithful in this to the thought of Saint Augustine: "The honor of Christ forbids the least hesitation on the subject of possible sin by His Mother" (*De natura et gratia*, cited by Saint Thomas, *Summa theologica*, III, q. 27, art. 4). But that Mary should have been the beneficiary of a preventive immunization posed a problem as to the universality of the grace of the Redeemer. Saint Thomas hesitated and, in the end, felt constrained to deny Mary a privilege that would, as he thought, be a "derogation of the dignity of Christ as Savior of all" (III, q. 27, art. 2, ad 2). For him, as for his contemporary Saint Bonaventure, Mary inherited the legacy of Adam and contracted original sin. But she was sanctified in her mother's womb.

The question, however, continued to be asked as late as the 18th century: Was Mary absolutely preserved from original sin? Or was she touched by this contagion and then cured by the grace of her Son, even before birth?

The Franciscan theologian Duns Scotus (last quarter of the 13th century) had struck an original position, defending Mary's privilege in its fullness from the beginning of her life. He pointed out that rather than detracting from the Redemption, the privilege of a total immunization, preserving Mary from all sin, even original, would represent the most glorious result of Christ's work. A modern theologian summarizes the argument of Scotus as follows:

"There are two kinds of ransom: one is ransom paid for an individual already prisoner, redemption by *liberation*; the other is ransom paid even before the acquired right of servitude is exercised, redemption by *preservation*. In making to His Mother an anticipated application of His merits to preserve her from the taint of original sin, which as a daughter of Adam she had naturally to incur, Jesus Christ became more fully her Redeemer. Far from being diminished, the excellence of Redemption is enhanced by Mary's privilege" (X. Le Bachelet).

3. The Definition of 1854

The position of Duns Scotus—prevenient Redemption by immunization from original sin—gradually prevailed, overcoming the doubts and hesitations of the great Scholastic masters. The Immaculate Conception of Mary, it was seen, does not escape the universality of the Redemption and does not constitute an "exception" that would diminish the value of the salvific act of Calvary. On the contrary, it manifests the very fullness of that salvific act.

Already at the Council of Trent (session V), no theological objection was found to undermine the Scotist thesis. But the Fathers of the Council felt that the question was not ripe for them to take a decisive stand. With the centuries, the theological debate subsided, and when Pius IX queried the Bishops of the world, it was apparent that a "definition" of Mary's privilege would express the common sentiment of the Catholic Church—on condition that the connection of this privilege with the Redemption be affirmed. As a daughter of Adam, Mary was included in the Redemption, and if she had the wonderful gift of total immunity, of complete holiness from the first moment, it was only because she received it from her Son.

Adopting the theological position of Duns Scotus, Pius IX, on December 8, 1854, proclaimed Mary preserved from original sin, beginning with the moment of her conception. The privilege is the source and basis of the Mother of God's essential impeccability, acknowledged since the first centuries of Christianity.

Said the Pope: "We declare, proclaim, and define that this dogma is revealed by God and therefore to be firmly and unremittingly believed by all the faithful: namely, the dogma that holds that the most Blessed Virgin Mary, from the first moment of her conception, by a singular grace and privilege from Almighty God and in view of the merits of Jesus Christ, was kept free of every stain of original sin."

Three things may be noted in this definition:

(1) *The nature of Mary's privilege.* It is, properly speaking, an immunization. Original sin is depicted as a sort of contagion that affects all human beings (except the God-Man, Jesus) and "soils" them. From this comes the attraction to evil that resides in each of us. Nothing of the sort was found in Mary, who did not experience the disorder introduced by the first parent into his descendants.

(2) *The ground of the privilege.* The definition takes account only of the singular grace accorded to Mary "in view of the merits of Christ." But Tradition, much cited in considerations of the privilege, finds reason for this singular grace in the Divine plan that destined Mary to become the Mother of God

and therefore could not tolerate her being, even for an instant, in the power of the devil.

(3) *The mode of preservation.* It was by a "preventive" (one is tempted to say "retroactive") effect of the Redemption gained on Calvary that Mary was preserved from original sin. Jesus is Redeemer of all human beings, and there is no sanctifying grace imaginable apart from His one, universal act of Redemption. This law applies *also* to Mary, even though she was accorded the grace "in view of the merits of her Son," i.e., before the fact, and not subsequent to it as with the rest of us.

4. Conclusion

Despite the wording of the definition, the Dogma of the Immaculate Conception does not have a negative content. It does not define an absence, nor a mere "immunization," health being something more and better than the absence of sickness. The dogma of 1854 declares positively, and from her beginning, the exceptional holiness of Mary and thereby her constant union with the sanctifying Spirit.

Mary's holiness should encourage us to seek her help and protection in our continual effort to overcome sin and sanctify our lives. Like her, we ought to respond generously to the suggestions of the Spirit so as to live as our Baptism requires. Mary is indeed an incomparable model but also a Mother attentive to the needs of her sinful children. The devotion of the Saints to the Immaculate Conception teaches us to entrust our own striving for holiness to the all-holy Virgin.

H. Holstein

IMMACULATE HEART OF MARY   [478, 487, 2669]

SEE   *Feasts of Mary*   *Sorrows of Mary*
      Joys of Mary

1. From the Gospel of Luke to Our Day

THE devotion to the Heart of Mary is founded on the Gospel. On two occasions Saint Luke the Evangelist observes: *"Mary treasured all these things and reflected on them in her heart"* (2:19) and *"His mother [Mary] meanwhile kept all these things in memory [heart]"* (2:51). But *"the mouth speaks what ever fills the mind [heart]"* (Mt 12:34). Hence, the *Magnificat* reveals to us the wondrous riches of Mary's humble and regal heart.

Mary's heart is one "that sings the praises of God, and its song is not the solitary song of the history of a soul, but the song of the History of Salvation for all God's People. . . . It is a heart that sings of the liberation of the Poor of Yahweh, because in her all the mendicants of God acclaim the Lord of glory and mercy. . . . In virtue of this ecclesial dimension, the *Magnificat* will be the autonomous song of thanksgiving in the liturgy of the New Testament and in Christian piety" (L. Deiss).

With Saint Anselm (d. 1109), Eadmer (d. 1141), Saint Bernard (d. 1153), and Hugh of Saint Victor (d. 1140) the devotion to the Heart of Mary flourishes in a true and proper private cult. This cult is advocated above all in the works of Saint Mathilda of Hackeborn (1241-1298), Saint Gertrude the Great (1252-1302), and Saint Brigid of Sweden (1303-1373). But it is Saint Bernardine of Siena (1380-1444) who can be called the "Doctor of the Heart of Mary." In that Heart he sees, as it were, seven burning furnaces that give rise to seven flames, which are the seven acts of love expressed in the seven "words" of Our Lady found in Gospel.

After a brief decline in the 15th century, the cult of the Heart of Mary attains renewed vigor in the 16th century to such a point that it becomes in the 17th century well known to contemplative souls and those devoted to the Mother of Jesus. Saint John Eudes (d. 1680) is, in the words of Saint Pius X, "the Father, Doctor, and Apostle of the *liturgical cult* of the Sacred Hearts of Jesus and Mary." After him, the devotion to the Heart of Mary enjoys a continuing crescendo, with particularly favorable periods owing to the Miraculous Medal (1830) and the Appearances at Fatima (1917). On October 31, 1942, the 25th anniversary of Fatima, Pius XII consecrates the worldwide Christian Family and the whole human race to the Im-

maculate Heart Mary, and on May 4, 1944, he extends the
Feast of the Immaculate Heart of Mary to the Universal
Church.

2. Theological Reflections

Liturgically, the cult of the Immaculate Heart has an opti-
mum reason for existing. It recognizes and honors the Heart of
Mary as the symbol of the reality of her love: her act of putting
her entire conscious, intelligent, and free personality completely at the disposal of the salvific love of God and the Redemption of the world. For this reason, the devotion to the
Heart of Mary has great spiritual value to draw and direct our
wills and our lives toward Christ and toward others: as an efficacious sign of grace. Therefore, such a devotion deserves to be
cultivated by our age that requires full "Christian maturity"
and responsibility toward our brothers and sisters and toward
history.

The pages of Sacred Scripture, the texts of the Fathers,
and the teaching of the Church's Magisterium provide valid
theological foundations for the devotion to the Immaculate
Heart of Mary. The Second Vatican Council states that "at the
message of the Angel, Mary received the Word of God in her
heart and her body and gave Life to the world" (LG 53). In the
Encyclical on the Redeemer of the Human Race (*Redemptor
Hominis,* no. 22), John Paul II notes that "the Mystery of the
Redemption was formed, we might say, under the Heart of the
Virgin of Nazareth, when she pronounced her 'fiat.' From that
moment this *virginal and at the same time maternal Heart*,
under the special action of the Holy Spirit, always follows the
work of the Son and goes out toward all those whom Christ
has embraced and continues to embrace in His inexhaustible
love."

To be devoted to the Immaculate Heart of Mary means to
contemplate this maternal love that the Mother of God injects
into the Mystery of the Redemption and into the life of the
Church. It means to acknowledge therein a more comprehensi-
ble and accessible sign of the Father's love. It means to cast

ourselves on the Heart of Mary, Mother of Christ and Mother of the Church, to live the Mystery of the Redemption in all its vivifying depth and fullness, and to place ourselves at the service of our brothers and sisters on earth.

3. Consecration to the Immaculate Heart of Mary

We might fittingly conclude this brief note by indicating some of the special fruits that devotion to the Heart of Mary cannot fail to produce in the souls of those who practice it. They are (in the words of F. Arragain): "(1) a unified and profound understanding of the mystery of Mary; (2) a serious spiritual commitment, sustained by consecration to her Immaculate Heart; and (3) a greater facility for and assurance of reaching union with Christ Who lives in the Immaculate Heart of His Mother."

A. Rum

IMMANUEL   [712]

SEE   *New Testament*   *Old Testament (Mary in the)*

1. The Great Messianic Sign

IMMANUEL (or Emmanuel, as in the Vulgate), the personal name of the future Messiah given in Isaiah 7:14 (and repeated in 8:8), is part of what has been termed the great Messianic sign: *"Therefore the Lord Himself will give you this sign: the Virgin shall be with child, and bear a Son, and shall name Him Immanuel."*

This sign was given by the Prophet Isaiah to the incredulous Ahaz, King of Judah (736-728 B.C.). When the king refused a sign offered by the Prophet, he was told that Immanuel (that is, "With us [*humanity*] is God [*deity*]") would be born of a virgin. Because of the future appearance of this Immanuel, the kingdom of Judah would not be totally destroyed by the Assyrians (Is 8:8-10).

In reality, this sign was given to the house of David ("you" is plural) and concerned the perpetuation of that house

till the preeminent sign of the ages should be realized. This had
been promised by God to David (2 Sm 7:12-16) and would be
fulfilled by the coming of Immanuel as the ideal king (cf. Is
9:5-6; 11:1-5). The Hebrew for "virgin" here is *almah,* which
means "young woman" and not necessarily a virgin, but the
Septuagint translated it as "virgin" in Greek (*parthenos*).

2. Applied to Christ and Mary

Writing for Jewish-Christians, Matthew quoted this text
from the Septuagint and declared that it was fulfilled in Christ
(1:23), because God is with us through His assistance and
through His Incarnation.

The Church has always followed Matthew in seeing the
transcendent fulfillment of this verse in Christ and His Virgin
Mother. The Prophet need not have known the full force latent
in his own words; and some Catholic writers have sought a
preliminary and partial fulfillment in the conception and birth
of the future King Hezekiah, whose mother, at the time Isaiah
spoke, would have been a young, unmarried woman.

The Holy Spirit was preparing, however, for another Nativity, which alone could fulfill the Divinely given term of Immanuel's mission, and in which the perpetual virginity of the
Mother of God was to fulfill also the words of this prophecy in
the integral sense intended by Divine Wisdom.

3. Meaning

The Gospel passage concerning this verse reveals two
things to us. Jesus is God-with-us prophesied by the Prophet.
All of Christian Tradition is unanimous on this point. Jesus is
God-with-us not only because of His Divine mission but also
because of His Incarnation. At the Annunciation, the
Archangel Gabriel indicated that the Child to be born of Mary
was to be called Jesus, which means Savior. And this was carried out by Joseph.

The second point is that the Virgin Mary in whom the
prophecy was fulfilled remained a virgin before giving birth

and even in giving birth. The miraculous character of the sign lies precisely in the fact that a woman who is a virgin is likewise a mother.

4. Casts Light on the Role of Mary

The figure of Immanuel contributes to showing the role of Mary in the economy of salvation. In this connection, the words of Vatican II are completely appropriate:

"The Sacred Scriptures of both the Old and the New Testament, as well as ancient tradition, show the role of the Mother of the Savior in the economy of salvation in an ever clearer light and propose it as something to be probed into.

"The Books of the Old Testament recount the period of the History of Salvation during which the coming of Christ into the world was slowly prepared for. These earliest documents, as they are read in the Church and are understood in the light of further and full revelation, bring the figure of the Woman, Mother of the Redeemer, into a gradually sharper focus.

"When looked upon in this way, she is already prophetically foreshadowed in that victory over the serpent promised to our first parents after their fall into sin (cf. Gn 3:15). Likewise she is the Virgin who is to conceive and bear a Son, Whose name will be called Immanuel (cf. Is 7:14; Mic 5:2-3; Mt 1:22f). She stands out among the poor and humble of the Lord, who confidently await and receive salvation from Him.

"With her, the exalted Daughter of Zion, and after a long expectation of the promise, the times were at length fulfilled and the New Dispensation established. All this occurred when the Son of God took a human nature from her, that He might in the Mysteries of His flesh free human beings from sin" (LG 55).

A. Buono

INCARNATION

SEE   *Annunciation*   *Mother of God*

INEFFABILIS DEUS

SEE   *Church and Mary*   *Immaculate Conception*
      Feasts of Mary   *Magisterium (Documents of)*
      Fulgens Corona

ON December 8, 1854, Pope Pius IX issued an Encyclical entitled *Ineffabilis Deus* ("Ineffable God") that has become celebrated with good reason. It contains the dogmatic definition of Mary's Immaculate Conception. The text of the definition is accordingly a document of the Supreme Magisterium of the Church exercised by the Pope "ex cathedra" with the assistance of the Holy Spirit Who renders it infallible.

The Encyclical sets forth the reasons for the definition, starting with the argument that it is repugnant to the holiness of God and the dignity of Mary that she should ever have been subject—even for an instant—to the power of Satan because of original sin. However, this reason alone would not suffice.

Hence, the Encyclical deals with the teachings of Scripture and Tradition. It shows that the truth of the Immaculate Conception was known and believed by the faithful from the earliest days of the Church. The strongest manifestations of this important tradition are found in the liturgical cult of the Immaculata, in the teachings of the Fathers of the Church, and in the acts of the Popes. The latter favored the cult of the Immaculata, explained its meaning and doctrinal content, and prohibited any public teaching against it.

The thought of the Fathers is given at length by a kind of florilegium of their praises in honor of the Immaculate Virgin. The citations are particularly important because they interpret Scripture in those passages that refer to Mary with at least an implicit allusion to the Immaculate Conception.

The Pope stresses that the Fathers, to vindicate the original innocence of the Mother of God, not only compare her with Eve while the latter was still a virgin, innocent, and undefiled, not yet deceived by the death-dealing snares of the treacherous Serpent. They also give her precedence over Eve, using a wonderful variety of expressions of praise. For it was Eve's sad lot to obey the Serpent, to fall from her state of original innocence and become his slave. The Blessed Virgin, on the other hand, constantly added to the gift that was originally given her. Not only did she never give ear to the Serpent but by a power from above she completely destroyed his strength and might.

The Encyclical also goes out of its way to point out that the Council of Trent, when it promulgated the dogmatic decree concerning original sin, decreed and defined that all human beings are born infected with original sin. Nonetheless, it solemnly declared that it had no intention of including the Blessed Virgin Mary in this decree. Thus, by this declaration the Fathers of Trent sufficiently intimated that the Blessed Virgin was free from the original stain.

After citing the enthusiastic adherence of the whole Catholic world to the doctrine of the Immaculate Conception and to the numerous requests for its definition, the Encyclical concludes with the view that the moment for its pronouncement has arrived and gives the solemn definition of the dogma.

It concludes with an ardent exhortation to all the faithful to place all their trust in the Immaculate Virgin.

A. Buono

INFANCY NARRATIVES [522-534]

SEE *Luke (Gospel of Saint)* *New Testament*
   Matthew (Gospel of Saint)

1. A Well-Known Literary Form

THE term "Infancy Narratives" designates the Gospel accounts of the Birth and Childhood of Jesus found in Matthew and Luke. They represent a literary form that was known from the Old Testament as attested by the stories of Isaac (Gn 18:1-15; 21:1-7), Samson (Jgs 13), and Samuel (1 Sm 1—3). Judaism also knew of an allegorical type of reflection called the Midrash, which often took as its object the birth and childhood of the great personages of Israel in order to show how their life and mission were already found in germ in their origins, such as the Midrash of the little Moses that inspired Matthew.

The two narratives do not depend on one another nor do they depend on a common source. Each of the accounts is complete in itself, and one should not try to combine them in order to present a history of the infancy of Jesus. Each author arranges his material according to a fixed pattern. Matthew uses a series of incidents each of which ends in an Old Testament quotation. Luke utilizes a double diptych composed of annunciation and birth stories of John the Baptist and Jesus. Joseph is dominant in Matthew's account, and Mary in Luke's account.

2. Matthew's Infancy Narrative (1:1—2:23)

Matthew begins by establishing the genealogy of Jesus to show that he is from the lineage of David by Joseph, his adoptive father (1:1-17). He then produces five accounts centered upon a Prophetic word of the Old Testament (1:8—2:23). One of these delineates the role of Joseph; three concern the visit of the Magi and Herod's opposition to the Child fashioned after Pharaoh's opposition to Moses (Ex 1—2); and the last one sets forth Jesus returning to Nazareth.

Matthew emphasizes five titles of Jesus: Immanuel (1:23), Chief Shepherd (2:6), Son of God (2:15), Israel fulfilled (2:18), and Nazorean (2:23). At the same time, he also uses the genealogy to shed light on God's plan and Mary's role in it.

While the genealogy shows the continuity of God's providential plan from Abraham on, discontinuity is also present. The women Tamar (1:3), Rahab and Ruth (1:5), and the wife of Uriah, Bathsheba (1:6), bore their sons through unions that were in varying degrees strange and unexpected. These "irregularities" culminate in the supreme "irregularity" of the Messiah's birth from a Virgin Mother; the age of fulfillment is inaugurated by a creative act of God.

3. Luke's Infancy Narrative (1:5—2:52)

Luke presents a parallel between John the Baptist, resuming prophecy in Israel, and Jesus, the Son of the Father, basing itself on the infancy accounts of Samuel. After the two annun-

ciations and the meeting of the two mothers (1:5-56), he recounts the two births with the visit of those close by and the circumcision (1:57—2:21). These are followed by the presentation of Jesus in the Temple (2:22-38), the return to Nazareth (2:39-40), and the finding amidst the doctors (2:41-50).

In this section, Luke announces many of the themes that will become prominent in the rest of the Gospel: (1) the centrality of Jerusalem and the Temple; (2) the journey motif, (3) the universality of salvation, (4) joy and peace, (5) concern for the lowly (6) the importance of women, (7) the presentation of Jesus as Savior, (8) Spirit-guided revelation and prophecy, (9) the fulfillment of Old Testament promises, and (10) emphasis on Jesus as the Son of God and on the role of Mary His Mother.

In the parallelism between Jesus and John, Luke stresses the ascendency of Jesus over John. (a) John is the Prophet of the Most High (1:76); Jesus is the Son of the Most High (1:32). (b) John is great in the sight of the Lord (1:15); Jesus will be Great (an attribute used absolutely of God by the Septuagint) (1:32). (c) John will go before the Lord (1:16f); Jesus will be Lord (1:43; 2:11).

4. Themes Common to Both Narratives

The two narratives have the following points in common. (1) When Mary, the Mother of Jesus conceives Him, she is betrothed to Joseph (Mt 1:18; Lk 1:27). (2) The birth of Mary's Son is foretold by an Angel (Mt 1:20-23; Lk 1:30-35). (3) Joseph is a descendant of David (Mt 1:20; Lk 1:27). (4) Joseph has no say in the conception of Mary's Child (Mt 1:18; Lk 1:38). (5) The Child's conception is brought about by the Holy Spirit (Mt 1:18, 20; Lk 1:35).

(6) The Child's name, Jesus, is given to the parents by an Angel (Mt 1:21; Lk 1:31). (7) An Angel states that Jesus is to be a Savior (Mt 1:21; Lk 1:31). (8) Mary and Joseph are united in marriage at the time of Jesus' birth (Mt 1:24—2:1; Lk 2:5). (9) Jesus' birth occurrs in Bethlehem (Mt 2:1; Lk 2:6f). (10) After the early events of the infancy, Jesus' family settles in

Nazareth (Mt 2:23; Lk 2:39). (11) Jesus' infancy is located in general history by the explicit reference to Herod (Mt 2:1; Lk 1:5).

(12) Constant appeal is made to the Old Testament: by direct quotations in Matthew and by verbal similarities in Luke (e.g., Mt 2:6; Lk 1:46-55). (13) Isaiah 7:14 is cited: directly in Matthew and indirectly in Luke (Mt 1:23; Lk 1:31). (14) Abraham is named: in the genealogy in Matthew and in the canticles by Luke (Mt 1:1; Lk 1:55, 73). (15) The Godhead is evoked: by the title Emmanuel ("God-with-us") in Matthew and by the title Son of God in Luke (Mt 1:23; Lk 1:31). (16) A heavenly sign is recorded at the birth of Jesus: a star in Matthew and an angelic choir in Luke (Mt 2:2; Lk 2:8-14).

(17) The universalism of Jesus' mission is indicated: in Matthew by the coming of the Magi (2:1-12) and then the establishment of Jesus in Galilee (2:22f; see 4:15: *heathen Galilee*); in Luke by the prayer of Simeon (2:32: "*a revealing light to the Gentiles*"). (18) The Passion is prefigured: in Matthew by the flight to Egypt and massacre of the infants (2:13-18); in Luke by the prophecy of the "sword" and Jesus' going up to Jerusalem at Passover time (2:35, 41).

5. Mary in the Matthean Account

Compared with Luke, Matthew says relatively little about Mary. Although he mentions her presence at events in the infancy of Jesus, he is quite reticent about her inward experience.

There is no account of her calling, or of her reaction or prayer following the announcement of the Incarnation. He presents the infancy of Jesus primarily from the standpoint of Joseph.

It is Joseph who is summoned and guided by heavenly visions; it is he who gives Jesus His name and who takes and leads *the Child and His Mother* where he is told to take them. However, Matthew makes it equally clear that Joseph is a just man who acts in the service of the Child and His Mother, under the promptings of the revelation received.

Nonetheless, we can draw several aspects of Mary's role from the Matthean Infancy narrative, which is clearly preoccupied with demonstrating the juridic origin of the Messiah from the family of David and to defend His virginal conception in Mary's womb.

(1) Mary is in continuity with the chosen people: (a) with the long line of intermediaries (1:1-17) that prepared the coming of Jesus; (b) with the women who stand out in Israel's history because of God's free and unmerited intervention in their favor, beyond every anticipation and every frontier (Tamar, Rahab, Ruth, and the wife of Uriah); (c) by reason of the fact that in her was fulfilled historically the prophecy of Immanuel (Mt 1:23), which conveyed the whole Messianic hope of Israel; and (d) through the experience, which she relived in a close association with the destiny of her Son (sojourn in Egypt and "exodus").

(2) At the same time, Mary represents a break with the experience of Israel: by the fact that her participation in the Mystery of Christ is linked with a gift of God and the Spirit; just as Jesus is the fruit of God's gift and of the Spirit (1:18, 20), so Mary's association with Christ in making the Incarnation a reality is a mystery of grace.

(3) Although Matthew stresses the role of Joseph, it is clear from his account that Joseph himself is in the service of the Child and His Mother: "*Have no fear about taking Mary as your wife*" (1:20). Possibly, this fact is even clearer in the words of the Magi episode: "*They found the Child with Mary His Mother*" (2:11).

6. Mary in the Lucan Account

The Lucan account has its bases in circles of the Poor of Yahweh, among Mary's relatives, probably at Nazareth. It wishes to show that Mary, as the Daughter of Zion (Zep 3:14ff; Jl 2:21ff; Zec 9:9f) and the Ark of the Lord (Ex 40:35), is full of grace and overshadowed by the "power of the Most High," because of which the One born of her will be called the holy One and the Son of God in accord with Nathan's prophecy (2 Sm 7:12).

Recognized as the Mother of the Lord by Elizabeth and John the Baptist, Mary bursts out with the *Magnificat* through which she gives thanks to the God Who exalts the Poor of the Lord and brings down kings (Lk 1:39-45). Returning to Nazareth, she marries Joseph with the intention of remaining a virgin (Lk 1:34, 56; 2:5). She goes to Bethlehem because of the decree of Quirinius and brings forth her firstborn Child, Who belongs to God (Ex 13:12; 34:19), in a manger (Is 1:3) because room in the inn is lacking.

Rejected by His own people, the Child is accepted by pious shepherds and Simeon and Anna, who discover in Him the salvation for all peoples and the redemption of the Poor of the Lord but also the scandal and the ruin of many Israelites. As a result a sword will pierce the heart of Mary. To accomplish His mission the twelve-year-old Jesus consecrates Himself totally to the work entrusted Him by His heavenly Father, breaking the human link with His earthly family. This causes Mary some concern and leads her to unceasing reflection on her Son's mission.

René Laurentin has stated that the approximation of Jesus to Yahweh is the final word in Luke's Christology. All this redounds implicitly to Mary. At the same time, she is highly praised in her own right. She is God's *"highly favored daughter" [that is, "full of grace"]*, is told *"the Lord is with you,"* and is called *"blessed among women"* (1:28, 42).

Mary *"has found favor with God"* (1:30), is *"the servant of the Lord"* (1:38), and is *"blessed"* for having *"believed"* (1:45). *"All ages to come"* will call her blessed, for He Who is mighty has done great things for her (1:48f); she *"shall be pierced with a sword—so that the thoughts of many hearts will be revealed"* (2:35). Mary responds fully to God's call in the Annunciation and takes the initiative in the dialogue (2:48). She is also the recipient of the Spirit of God (1:35).

A. Buono

INTER SODALICIA

[968-970]

SEE *Church and Mary*   *Mary at the Cross*
      Co-Redemptrix   *Mediatrix*
      Documents of Vatican II   *Sorrows of Mary*
      Feasts of Mary   *Stabat Mater*
      Magisterium (Documents of)

ON March 22, 1918, Pope Benedict XV wrote a brief Apostolic Letter to the Association of Our Lady of a Happy Death, which became a foundation piece in the Church's teaching on Mary as Co-Redemptrix. Pope Leo XIII had already written about "Mysteries of our Redemption in which [Mary] not only shared but also took part" (Apostolic Letter *Parta Humano Generi* of September 8, 1901), and Saint Pius X had stated: "Since [Mary] surpassed all in holiness and union with Christ in the work of Redemption, she, as the expression is, merits *de congruo* ["congruently"] what Christ merits de condigno ["condignly"], and is the principal minister in the distribution of graces" (Encyclical *Ad Diem Illum Laetissimum* of February 2, 1904). (Condign merit is based on God's justice and fidelity to His promises; congruous merit depends on God's goodness.)

Echoing his predecessors, Benedict XV pronounced himself for the first time in the history of the Papal Magisterium in a clear and formal manner in favor of the teaching that upholds Mary's cooperation in the Redemption of Christ accomplished on the Cross by means of her mystical participation in her Son's immolation on the Cross to appease the Divine Justice.

"It was God's design that the Blessed Virgin Mary, apparently absent from the Public Life of Jesus, should assist Him when He was dying nailed to the Cross. Mary suffered and, as it were, nearly died with her suffering Son. For the salvation of humankind, she renounced her Mother's rights and, as far as it depended on her, offered her Son to appease the Divine Justice. *Hence, we may rightly say that she with Christ redeemed humankind."*   A. Buono

INTERCESSION OF MARY   [969, 975, 2617-2619]

SEE   *Mediatrix*   *Spiritual Motherhood*
        Queen

A S understood in much devotional literature, Mary's intercession reduces to a "transmission" of our prayers and petitions. "Mary's intercession," writes one theologian, "is realized through an act of supplication addressed to Christ, to obtain various graces for us."

But this is an impoverishment of Mary's prayer and our
association with it, which she desires. Mary's prayer is first and
foremost one of praise and thanksgiving: the *Magnificat*. By
inviting us to join her in her *Magnificat*—a hymn of thanksgiving of the Church, declares Saint Irenaeus—she places on our
lips a praise that ought never to cease in the heart of a child of
God. In the Gospel Mary is the perfect example of grateful joy,
full admiration for the great work of God. What is more fitting, then, than to learn from her the secret of her *Magnificat*,
an authentic "eucharistic" prayer, to make it our own?

At the same time, it is true that most often our recourse to
Mary takes the form of petition. Knowing the suppliant power
of the Mother of God to whom her Son wants to refuse nothing, we as Christians readily if not habitually come to her as
mendicants. In this, moreover, we are encouraged by the Tradition of the Church and the confidence of the Saints: "Never
was it known . . ." (part of the *Memorare* prayer).

1. Confidence in Mary's Prayer

This confidence rests on the efficacy of Mary's intercession. "Mary intercedes with her Son, in all the power of her
maternal prayer," declares Pius IX in the Bull defining the Immaculate Conception. And Paul VI (in *Marialis Cultus*, no. 18)
recalls "the *prayerful presence* of Mary in the early Church
and in the Church throughout all ages, for, having been assumed into heaven, she has not abandoned her mission of intercession and salvation."

An ancient testimony of confidence in Mary is the prayer *Sub tuum,* which historians place in the 3rd century. Its mention of the title "Mother of God" (*Theotokos*) makes it contemporary with the great Trinitarian and Christological Councils:

> We fly to your patronage,
> O holy Mother of God;
> despise not our petitions in our necessities,
> but deliver us always from all dangers,
> O glorious and blessed Virgin.

The prayer achieves its effect by its childlike simplicity. It is a plea for Mary's help "in danger." The "Mother of God" is besought for her maternal care and invoked as Mother of Jesus, Who can refuse her nothing. With this Mother close by, the anxious child always has safe and loving refuge.

2. Ground for This Confidence

If Christians have confidence in Mary, it is because she was and remains totally united with Christ. Devotion to her is a tribute to the power of a mother over the heart of her Son, but even more it is a recognition of the Virgin's union with Jesus for the salvation of the world.

Through Mary, the Christian implores Christ. Recourse to the all-powerful prayer of Mary lends weight to our own prayer. But it is not a question, as is sometimes supposed, of having the Mother appease the anger of her Son, Who is imagined to be irritated with us. Rather, we are confident in Mary because of her close union with Jesus.

The "subordination" of Mary to Jesus, of which the Second Vatican Council speaks (LG 62), is a loving subordination, without prejudice to the depth and perfection of their union. Because of her consent to the work of mercy of Jesus, *"come for sinners,"* Mary's prayer has unique access to the Heart of Jesus. Knowing her Son and the mission of mercy given Him by the Father, she asks our obedience, with confidence in the result: *"Do whatever He tells you"* (Jn 2:5).

There is, then, this twofold basis for the power of Mary's intercession, namely, her union with the work of the Redemption and the maternal task entrusted to her, without limits or restriction. Hence, every sincere prayer qualifies for presentation by Mary to Jesus. And through Mary, uniting it with her maternal worship, every sincere prayer can be offered in the expectation of its being heard.

No more, however, than at the Annunciation does Mary take the initiative. *"Servant of the Lord,"* she received and accepted the mission for which she was singled out. At the foot of the Cross she received the maternal trust. When we come to her in prayer, she responds to it in fulfillment of her mission. At the side of Jesus, in the glory of heaven, she bears in her heart the suffering and sinfulness of her children.

Most assuredly, Mary in heaven is not insensitive to our afflictions. "The state of glory enables her in fact to sympathize with them more completely, since this state opens wide her Heart to the dimensions of God's love. Ever since her passage to the beyond, our sufferings and our needs reverberate all the more in Mary. Her intercession proceeds from genuine compassion toward us, and the feelings of pity and mercy that we attribute to her are not pure metaphor" (J. Galot).

3. Does Mary's Prayer Influence God?

This is a troublesome point with some people. Their difficulty takes the form of a dilemma: Either Mary changes God's mind, or her intercession is without substance, a formality.

The difficulty implies in Mary and Jesus the competitive spirit that characterizes the business world. Even more than to Mary, this is an injury to God because He is imagined as an intractable despot but one whose decisions can be modified through maneuvers of one kind or another.

Mary is completely obedient to the will of God, but this will is all love and mercy. To appreciate her intercession in heaven, we should carefully consider her obedience while on earth, such as is shown in the Gospel.

"In her own particular life Mary fully and responsibly accepted the will of God because she heard the Word of God and acted on it and because charity and a spirit of service were the driving force of her actions. . . . She was the first and most perfect disciple of Christ" (MC 35).

This attitude of obedience, which Mary in glory retains in her heart, comes from a joyous consent to God and not from servile fear or self-interest. To us who are sinners, God's will sometimes seems hard and painful in its demands. Sin clouds the understanding and hardens the heart, and in some situations it is only with great difficulty that we bring ourselves to say: *Yes, Father, Your will be done.*

But not Mary. In fact, it can be said that in her case there was a "spontaneous coincidence" with whatever God wanted—because He wanted it. One finds this in human love, which may lead to spontaneous acquiescence in the preferences of those we love, for no other reason than that such are their preferences. And the Gospel itself shows instances of disciples declaring themselves unconditionally, as in Luke 9:57: "*I will be Your follower wherever You go*" (cp. Mt 8:19). All the more was this true of Mary, the most perfect disciple who loved God perfectly with the purity of a virginal heart completely in the possession of the Holy Spirit.

Mary can only want what her Son wants because it is the same love of us—love that moved the Father to "*give His only Son*" (Jn 3:16)—that united them in a Redemption consented to as one. Her intercession does not derive its efficacy from positional power, like the power of "mother over the king," but from the union of the Mother with the salvation work of the Son. If Mary is glorified, it is because she is "co-redemptrix": "Lovingly consenting to the immolation of the Victim she herself had brought forth, . . . she was given as Mother to His disciple" (LG 58).

The omnipotent property of Mary's intercession flows from her association, freely accepted, with the redeeming Passion. For this reason Mary, eternally glorified as Mother and Associate of the Savior, has the authority and credibility of preeminent witness of God's love, Who "*loved [us] and gave Himself for us*" (cf. Eph 5:2; Ti 2:14).

H. Holstein

ISLAM AND MARY   [841]

MARY is given place in the Koran as virginal mother of
Isa, Jesus, the "Messiah" in the sense that Moslems give
to this term, i.e., a "prophet" among the greatest—but still inferior to the one recognized as "the" prophet, Mohammed.
This indicates the depth of the chasm that divides Moslem
thought about Jesus from Christian thought. To the faithful of
the Koran the Divinity of Christ is literally unthinkable.

But the Koran does keep and integrate some elements of
the Christian tradition concerning Jesus, and first of all His
virginal conception through the intervention of almighty God.
And it uses the name of Maryam as title for its chapter 19.
What is found there is closer to the Apocrypha than to the
Gospels recognized as canonical by Christians. The same
is true of chapters 3, 4, 33, 43, 57, 66, which also speak of
Mary.

In chapter 4 we see how the Koran presents the Annunciation of Jesus:

(42) "Behold, the Angels said: 'O Maryam, God has truly
chosen you; He has purified you; and He has chosen you over
all women in the world.'

(43) " 'O Maryam, be devoted to your Lord; kneel and
bow with those who bow. . . .' "

(45) "And behold, the Angels said: 'O Maryam, God announced to you the Good News of a word about Him having
the name of Messiah, Isa, Son of Maryam, illustrious in this
life and in the next, numbered among those closest to God.

(46) " 'He will speak to human beings from His cradle
and as a perfect adult; He is one of the holy ones.' "

(47) "She said: 'My Lord, how can I have a child without
any man having touched me?' It was said to her: 'It is possible
because God creates what He wants. When He has decreed a
thing, He says: Be, and it is.' "

Elsewhere in the Koran:

"And she who had remained a virgin. . . . We have
breathed our Spirit upon her. We have made of her and her
Son a Sign to the world" (Sura 31, v. 91).

"And Maryam, daughter of Imran, who kept her virginity, We have breathed our Spirit upon her; she declared veracious the Word of her Lord and His Books. She was numbered among those fearing God" (Sura 66, v. 12).

In principle, Koranic orthodoxy rules out all cult properly speaking toward any creature—Mohammed himself included. Nevertheless, the Koran acknowledges a certain intercessory role of prophets in behalf of their various communities on the Day of the Last Judgment. And, in practice, the person and role of Mohammed have known a certain glorification. Also, the attraction of the figure of Mary for Moslems—and not only for their women—is an observable reality in many places. At Ephesus, for example, pilgrimages to the "House of the Virgin" number almost as many Moslems as Christians. The virginal Mother of Jesus, "chosen over all women in the world," is an important reality for Islam.

A. Bossard

- J -

JERUSALEM

SEE   *Holy Land and Mary, 2 j*

JOHN AND MARY

SEE   *Cana*   *Motherhood, Spiritual*
      Church and Mary   *New Testament*
      Cross (Mary at the)   *Revelation*
      Intercession of Mary   *Sorrows of Mary*
      Knowledge of Mary   *Stabat Mater*
      Mother of the Church

JOSEPH AND MARY   [437, 488, 497, 530, 534, 583]

SEE   *Infancy Narratives*

JOSEPH, name of the noted son of Jacob, was a common patronymic at the time of Our Lord. It occurs even in the genealogy of Christ's ancestors. And Christ Himself was known in His public life as *"son of Joseph"* (Lk 4:22 and Jn 1:45—but not in Mark). The two genealogies of Luke 3 and Matthew 1 do in fact make Jesus the son of Joseph. Matthew's genealogy shows it was through Joseph that Jesus of Nazareth was heir to the royal rights of David, founder of the chosen dynasty. Luke shows it was through Joseph that Jesus of Nazareth was son of Adam and therefore stood for all humanity.

Matthew's Gospel tells us most about Joseph. The community or communities for whom he wrote it were wondering how Jesus could be the expected Messiah of the Scriptures, given current traditions that told of his virginal birth by Mary. The answer was that Joseph, knowing the facts and supernaturally enlightened, took Mary as wife and accepted Jesus as son for purposes of the Law—"*born of a woman, born under the Law*," Paul will say (Gal 4:4).

Thus, in the eyes of the people and the Law Joseph was responsible for the birth and education of Mary's Son, until He came of age and was a full member of the people of God whom He was to save and over whom He was to rule. Not only did Joseph assume paternity of the Child but he decided to take Him away to Egypt, to bring Him back after Herod's death and, instead of remaining in Judea where the rule of Archelaus posed a threat, to settle in Nazareth. Hence, Jesus became known as the "Nazarene" or "*Nazorean*," a term that for a time, it seems, described all Christians in the eyes of the Jews.

Luke expressly mentions the presence of Joseph ("*parents*") not only at the Presentation in the Temple but also in Christ's first pilgrimage to the Temple at the age of twelve, as required by the rites of adolescence. In addition, and despite the possible meanings of "*son of the carpenter*," it seems clear that Jesus was not only a carpenter but the son of a carpenter, i.e., was taught the trade by His father, which identified Him at Nazareth. A metaphorical sense (= "educated") seems very unlikely, since this rabbi was thought not to have made His studies.

Wherever Joseph appears it is as the close partner of Mary. He is truly the "*man*" (Greek: *aner*), i.e., husband of Mary. After the contract of betrothal had run its course (in Galilee usually one year), he took her as wife. It was "*the Child and His Mother*" that he led away to Egypt. And it was with Mary that he presented the Child in the Temple and brought Him at the age of twelve to Jerusalem. Because of his toil, his presence and protection, Mary could live her private life with the Son of God Who grew in her, then with her, in stature, grace, and wisdom. Thanks to Joseph, Mary could bring up the Child and meditate in her heart on all that was said of Him.

But if Joseph had this role with the Mother and Child, it was, Saint Matthew tells us, because he was a "just" man. The vernacular renders but imperfectly the sense of the Hebrew, which in the books of the Bible written after the Exile designates individuals who were completely faithful to the moral teaching and religious practices of the Old Testament. It was a justice that went beyond mere equity in that it retained an aspect of generosity and royal munificence.

Joseph may well have been *"just"* in the sense that at first he did not think he could take for his own a woman who had conceived her Child without him. He was *"just"* in the sense that he did not want to transgress any of the laws pertaining to a situation of this kind. He was also *"just"* in not wanting disgraced the woman whom he nevertheless felt compelled to repudiate secretly. It is here that we see a *justice* adorned with respect and love toward the woman whose husband he agreed to become, for the protection and upbringing of the Child to Whom he transmitted his rights. Everything suggests that he died, his work finished, before the Public Ministry of Mary's Son began.

H. Cazelles

JOYS OF MARY

SEE   *Rosary*   *Sorrows of Mary*

DEVOTION to the *Joys* or *Delights* of Mary comes from the Gospel through the medium of the Liturgy.

1. Gospel

Even if some hesitate to translate the message of the Annunciation by *"Rejoice,"* the joy brought by Jesus the Savior is mentioned several times in Luke 1—2. *"The baby [John the Baptist] leapt in my womb for joy"* (Lk 1:44). *"My spirit rejoices in God my savior"* (Lk 1:47). *"I bring you Good News of great joy that will be for all the people. This day in David's city a Savior has been born to you"* (Lk 2:10-11).

In Mary God produces the joy promised by the Prophets to the *Daughter of Zion* (Zep 3:14; Zec 9:9; Is 54:1, etc.). Mary treasures and ponders over her memories: joy of the Annunciation, joy of the Visitation, joy of the Nativity. And with the disciples she experiences the intense joy of the Resurrection and glorious Ascension of her Son (cf. Lk 24:41, 52).

2. The Liturgy and Piety

In the West, beginning with the 11th century, the joy of Mary is celebrated in private devotion by saying two anthems of Byzantine inspiration, *Gaude, Dei Genitrix* (Rejoice, Mother of God) and *Ave Maria* (Hail Mary), both taken from the votive Office of the Virgin and both very popular at the time.

Rejoice, Mother of God, Virgin Immaculate.
Rejoice, you who received joy from the Angel.
Rejoice, you who conceived the brightness of eternal
    Light.
Rejoice, Mother.
Rejoice, Holy Mother of God and Virgin.
All creation extols you.
Mother of Light, pray for us.

In recitation of the *Ave Maria* (Hail Mary) it was the words *"The Lord is with you"* that were thought to express the essence of Mary's joy.

By recalling to Mary the Mystery of the Annunciation, the source of her joy on earth, people felt they were preparing themselves for sharing her eternal joy of being with the Lord.

3. Devotions

Toward the end of the 11th century arose the idea of pairing each *gaude* (rejoice) with a joyful event in the life of Mary. The great liturgical feasts provided the events, and the list of the five joys soon became fixed: *Annunciation, Nativity, Passion-Resurrection, Ascension and Assumption*. The Ascension was deemed a joy of Mary because on that day the Flesh born of Mary and our human nature were glorified. The forms of this devotion to the five joys were numerous and could vary greatly. Often they were accompanied by a set number of Hail Marys.

In the 12th century many of the faithful added the *Adoration of the Magi and the Sending of the Holy Spirit*. This made *seven joys,* as many as there were Hours of the daily Office and days of the week. Later, some preferred the *Purification* or the *Visitation,* thought no doubt more "Marian" than the Ascension and Pentecost.

In the 13th century Franciscan spirituality, from its beginning, encouraged devotion to the *Seven Delights* of Mary. Saint Bernardine of Siena (1444) and his disciples preached this devotion in its definitive form: *the garland of delights,* or *Chaplet of 72 Hail Marys.* The purpose was to honor both the seven joys of Mary (Annunciation, Visitation, Birth of Jesus, Adoration of the Magi, Finding in the Temple, Resurrection, and Assumption) and the years of Mary's life on earth.

The meditations on the *fifteen joys* of Mary by Stephen of Sallai (diocese of York, between 1225 and 1250) are a good example of Cistercian devotion to Mary, nourished on Scripture, the Liturgy, and the works of Saint Bernard, and entirely centered on living with Christ.

Each of the joys comprises a meditation, then a "joy" addressed to Mary (*Gaude, quae*—Rejoice, you who . . .), and lastly a petition followed by a somewhat amplified Hail Mary. The fifteen joys are divided into three groups of five:

1. Misery of the sinful world and birth of Mary.
2. Most holy life of Mary, who "drew" to us the Son of God.
3. The Archangel Gabriel comes to greet the Virgin.
4. The work of the Trinity: God the Father sends His Son in the flesh.
5. Mary goes to greet Elizabeth and ministers to her.

Pause: Excellence of the Virgin, in whom Jesus dwelled for nine months.

6. The virginal birth and Mary's joy at home with Jesus.
7. The Magi come from the East.
8. Mary brings Jesus to the Temple to offer Him to the Father.
9. The admirable life of the Child Jesus and "Mary keeps all these things in her heart."

10. The miracles of Jesus, the changing of water into wine.

Pause: The joys of Mary in seeing all that Jesus did, from His Baptism to His Passion.

11. The Son of God offers Himself to His Father on the altar of the Cross.
12. Mary learns of the Resurrection of Jesus and sees her risen Son.
13. The glory of the Ascension of the Lord.
14. The company of disciples wait in prayer and receive the gift of the Spirit.
15. The completion of the Virgin's joys in this life and her elevation to heaven by her Son.

Going through these valuable texts, which have been edited by Dom Willmart, one cannot but be impressed by their spiritual depth and fullness. The joys of Mary are celebrated, but it is the *Mysteries* of the Word Incarnate that lie at the heart of the devotion.

The *fifteen joys* of Mary were also popularized in simplified form through the Book of the Hours (in France since the end of the 14th century). We cite the eleventh joy according to the Hours of René of Anjou:

"Gentle Virgin, for the great joy in your life and the bitter compassion you had when your dear Son Jesus Christ suffered death and agony on the Cross for our sake, Gentle Virgin, pray Him that the death He suffered may deliver me from the death of hell. Hail Mary. . . ."

As for the celestial glory of Mary, it had been more or less implied in various Salutations of Mary: *Hail, Queen of Angels—Hail, Queen of Heaven—Hail, praise of all Saints,* etc. But in the 13th century, in reaction to a too historical tendency, appeared a special devotion to the *seven celestial joys* of Mary, which may be summarized as follows:

1. The glory of Mary surpasses that of all the Saints.
2. The great brightness of Mary illumines heaven.
3. Mary is Queen of heaven.

4. Her prayer is always heard.
5. God rewards those who honor her.
6. Mary is the one closest to the Trinity.
7. The celestial joys of Mary are eternal.

We still find an echo of this devotion in the *Regina caeli, laetare, Alleluia,* and in the Mystery of Mary's coronation in heaven.

Sometimes *five terrestrial joys* and *seven celestial joys* of Mary were combined in one devotion, named *Crown of Twelve Stars* (cf. Rv 12:1).

Beginning with the 13th century, these various devotions to the *joys of Mary* were complemented by meditations on the *sorrows of Mary.* This abundant tradition of Marian piety was recapitulated by the Dominican Alain of Roche (1435) in the 15 Mysteries of his *"New Psalter of the Virgin"* (the Rosary), a number that then began to prevail largely through the efforts of Confraternities of the Rosary.

4. Spirituality

As we have seen, devotion to the *joys of Mary seems to have originated with the five gaude's* of the anthem *Gaude, Dei Genitrix.* This is an important finding, since the whole meaning of the hymn, a poetic echo of the *Hail Mary,* derives from the central fact of the Incarnation. It was in her dependence on the Mystery of Christ that Mary was hailed and implored.

Through Mary's joys of motherhood the Middle Ages praised the Mysteries of the Word Incarnate. Behind it all lay a desire to enter more deeply into our union with Christ the Savior. Mary was the first to enjoy this union, with a joy she would share with all who came to her to find it.

As a consequence of the tendency to make Marian joys coincide with the great events in the life of Christ and Mary, devotion became less directly centered on the Motherhood of Mary, source of a joy in which the physical presence of Christ was the determining factor. Even the idea of joy tended to give way to that of *"Mystery."* But all in all the desire to encounter the Son of God in His Incarnation remained at the heart of Gospel-based devotion to Mary.

"Near to Christ, Mary recapitulates all joys. Mother filled with holy joy (*Mater plena sanctae laetitiae*), she experienced the perfect joy promised to the Church. With good reason do her children on earth turn to her, *Mother of hope* and *Mother of grace*, invoking her as *cause of their joy*" (Paul VI).

J. Laurenceau

JUDAISM AND MARY [839-840]

SEE *New Testament*   *Old Testament (Mary in the)*

1. New Era in Catholic-Jewish Affairs

THE Second Vatican Council inaugurated a new era in Catholic-Jewish affairs. Calling for "fraternal dialogue and Biblical studies" with Jews, it ended a centuries-long silence between Church and Synagogue. An age of dialogue was begun. Conversations between Catholics and Jews proliferated rapidly in many forms. Productive meetings took place on every level, from the highest intellectual exchanges to the most popular types of social gatherings.

John Paul II has said: "Our common spiritual heritage [with Judaism] is considerable. To assess it carefully in itself and with due awareness of the faith and religious life of the Jewish people as they are professed and practiced still today, can greatly help us to understand better certain aspects of the life of the Church" (March 6, 1982).

Indeed, it is a sad fact, as the Bishops of the United States stated, that Christians have not fully appreciated their Jewish roots. Early in Christian history, a de-Judaizing process dulled our awareness of our Jewish beginnings. The Jewishness of Jesus, *of His Mother,* of His disciples, of the primitive Church, was lost from view. That Jesus was called Rabbi; that He was born, lived, and died under the Law; that He and Peter and Paul worshiped in the Temple—these facts were blurred by the controversy that alienated Christians from the Synagogue. (Cf. Statement on Catholic-Jewish Relations, November 20, 1975).

The Bishops go on to say that most essential concepts in the Christian creed grew at first in Judaic soil. Uprooted from that soil, these basic concepts cannot be perfectly understood. It is for reasons such as these that Vatican II recommends joint "theological and Biblical studies" with Jews. The Vatican Guidelines of 1975 encourage Catholic specialists to engage in new research into the relations of Judaism and Christianity and to seek out "collaboration with Jewish scholars."

This, of course, is especially true of Mary, the Mother of Jesus. Unfortunately, research in this area is just beginning. In time, much more will be done and lead to a better understanding of Mary from both a Catholic and a Jewish point of view.

2. A True Daughter of Israel

The *Constitution on the Church* speaks of Mary as the "exalted Daughter of Zion" (LG 55), a new title in the documents of the Magisterium and one that is almost lacking in the theological manuals. This fact is regarded as indicating a greater contemporary awareness of our Hebrew roots, an awareness that leads us to rediscover in the Mother of the Lord an authentic daughter of the people of Israel.

It remains true, however, that the Church from the earliest of times was called the Israel of God (Gal 6:6), and Christians had always revered Abraham as their spiritual father in the Faith. And Mary had from the earliest times been regarded as foreshadowed by the women of the Old Testament and called *"the glory of Jerusalem, the surpassing joy of Israel, . . . the splendid boast of [her] people"* (Jdt 15:9).

Mary is not only the Daughter of Zion but also the remnant of Israel, the servant of the Lord (Yahweh) as were the Patriarchs (Dt 9:27), Moses (Nm 12:7f), the Prophets (Am 3:2), and Israel itself (Is 41:8; 44:21). In Mary it is all of Israel that responds to the call of the Lord. Mary is also the voice of the Poor of Yahweh as well as the holy Ark as indicated by Luke's usage of the word *overshadow* with respect to her (1:35). It is the same word used in the Old Testament to indicate God's dwelling with human beings (Ex 40:35).

Yet despite this de facto relationship between Mary and Judaism, she hardly figures in the Jewish consciousness. There is no official Jewish position about her for there is none about her Son. The early Fathers spoke of Jewish texts that fashioned tales about Jesus and His Mother because they could not accept the Virgin Birth. During the Middle Ages, there was the *Toledoth Jeshu* ("Stories of Jesus"), which in a crass manner tried to present Mary as the innocent victim of a ruse resulting in her pregnancy, although she was a scrupulous observer of the Torah.

3. Common Marian and Jewish Themes

A few basic themes of the Marian tradition are found in the Jewish sources attributed to individual women of the Old Testament and even to Israel itself, regarded as the spouse of the Lord. Their sources run from the Talmudic period (3rd-6th centuries A.D.) to the Middle Ages.

The vicissitudes of Yokebed, cast away from her husband Amram when she was already pregnant and then taken back, present some affinity with the Gospel accounts. When she is taken back by her husband she regains the youthful look. Her giving birth is without pain, a sign of the Messianic age; she gives birth to all Israel.

Miriam, Moses' sister, occupies a position with him that is not dissimilar to Mary's position with Jesus. The difference between Moses and Jesus is reflected also in the two women. Nonetheless, even Miriam is a virgin, also of her it is said that the Spirit comes upon her, and she prophesies the birth of and mission of her brother.

Miriam is also connected with the theme of water in the desert: the wells vanish when she dies. John's Gospel is framed around two "water-events": Cana, where the turning of water into wine takes place (Jn 2:1-11), and Calvary, where blood and water flow from the pierced side of Jesus (Jn 19:25ff). In both of these Mary has a special part.

The "mothers of Israel" also have a large role in the story of their people. The purity of Sarah and the women of the generation in the desert obtains Israel's redemption; the miracles worked in Egypt are due to the fact that they abstained from incontinency. Indeed, because of the holiness of the mothers 190 years are taken away from the time of oppression.

Similarly, Mary is connected with the whole community of Israel. When that community is before Sinai, it presents itself as a spouse without stain, and she emerges from the desert shining brightly.

In recent times, there has been a notable change in attitude toward Jesus among such Jewish writers as Joseph Klausner, Germain Levy, C.G. Montefiore, Stephen Wise, H.G. Enelow, and Martin Buber. Similarly, there is beginning to be a change toward Mary. Sholem Asch's 1957 book about Mary has been described as a kind of ample midrash on her life, framing her in the context of Jewish life and piety, beginning in her adolescence and reaching to the Resurrection of Jesus. Ben Chorin, a disciple of Martin Buber, has authored a trilogy whose first volume is dedicated to the "brother of Jesus," the second to Paul, and the third to "Mother Mary." He describes Mary as a Jewish mother at the time of Herod, constantly referring to Jewish practices, to tradition, and even folklore, which we are familiar with through the Jewish literature that is closest to the New Testament.

A. Buono

- K -

KNOCK (Ireland)

SEE *Apparitions*   *Apparitions after Vatican II*

1. The Apparition

AMONG the many appearances of Our Lady, the one at Knock in Ireland is unique—for no words were spoken. It was just fifty years after the passing of the Catholic Emancipation Act (1829) by which the Catholic Church ceased to be legally proscribed when this manifestation of the Divine goodness occurred. It thus strengthened the faith of the people of that obscure and remote village in County Mayo (now called Cnoc Mhuire) and provided consolation in especially hard times.

On August 21, 1879, which was the eve of the Octave of the Assumption at that time, at about seven-thirty in the evening, Mary appeared at the south gable of the wall of the village chapel. The vision lasted for a full two hours and was seen by fifteen persons. Although it was raining quite heavily, the figures in the vision and the spot where they appeared were perfectly dry. This is what the witnesses saw:

The Blessed Virgin was clothed in white garments and wore a large brilliant crown on her head. Her hands were raised as if in prayer and her eyes were turned heavenward.

On her right was Saint Joseph with his head inclined toward her. On her left stood Saint John the Evangelist, vested as a bishop with his left hand holding a book and his right raised as if in preaching. To the left of Saint John was an altar on which stood a cross and a lamb about eight weeks old. The gable wall that formed the background for the tableau was bathed in a cloud of light.

2. The Message

Although Our Lady spoke not a word, the most common interpretation of this vision has been that it wanted to confirm

225

the Irish people in their "way." Mary personified personal holiness; Saint John, the defense and spread of the Church; Saint Joseph, charity; the Cross, sacrifice; and the altar (on which the Lamb of God is sacrificed), the source of the strength necessary for a Catholic life.

"The first lesson of the apparition is the Mass. Everything seems to point to that—the altar with the sacrificial Lamb, the gesture of Our Lady, the presence of Saint John in vestments, and the respectful attitude of Saint Joseph.

"But we may also see in the vision a reminder of another great truth *connected with the Mass—the necessity of Mary's mediation and intercession and the unique character that the latter acquires because of Mary's glorious Assumption and Coronation.* We use bodily relics of the Saints when we wish to obtain our requests, but we have no bodily relics of our heavenly Mother. We have, however, something infinitely more powerful—we have the continuation on our altars of the Sacrifice in which her Son was immolated.

"We have His very Body and Blood on the altar and, at the same moment, in heaven at the right hand of the Father, and with it is the human source from which it was taken—the assumed body of Mary. If the dead bodies of the Saints move the Heart of God on our behalf, how much more the living body of the Immaculate One who crushed forever the enemy of mankind!

"Let us see, then, in the manifestation of Knock, an invitation to have recourse ever more to the Blessed Virgin, *Mediatrix of All Graces and Queen of Heaven and Earth,* to pray to her and to take into our lives the consciousness of her full gentle presence in heaven" (Michael O'Carroll).

3. The Shrine

Knock soon became a place of pilgrimage and eventually a large church was built for the crowds in addition to the Old Church with the Apparition Gable. Thousands of cures were recorded, although there was no Medical Bureau before 1936 to evaluate them. Even more wondrous, however, are the countless spiritual cures to which John Paul II alluded when he visited the Shrine on September 30, 1979, to join in celebrating the centenary of Mary's appearance:

"From that day of grace, 21 August 1879, until this very day, the sick and suffering, people handicapped in body or mind, troubled in their faith or their conscience, all have been healed, comforted, and confirmed in their faith because they trusted that the Mother of God would lead them to her Son Jesus. Every time a pilgrim comes up to what was once an obscure bogside village in County Mayo, every time a man, woman, or child comes up to the Old Church with the Apparition Gable or to the new shrine of Mary Queen of Ireland, it is to renew his or her faith in the salvation that comes through Jesus, Who made us all children of God and heirs of the Kingdom of heaven."

The Pope conferred the status of a Basilica on the New Church and offered a Rose of Gold to the Shrine.

A. Buono

KNOWLEDGE, OUR LADY'S   [144, 148, 149, 492, 494]

SEE   *Annunciation*   *New Testament*
      Faith of Mary   *Poor of Yahweh and Mary*
      Finding in the Temple

1. Traditional Catholic Teaching

TRADITIONAL Catholic teaching concerning the knowledge had by Mary distinguished three types: acquired, infused, and beatific. (1) Acquired knowledge referred to the whole series of ideas and facts that she derived from her cultural environment through education and personal experience. (2) Infused knowledge referred to the truths she received directly from God and that concerned her vocation, which gave her a unique relationship with the Trinity. (3) Beatific knowledge referred to a vision that some believe was hers at least in certain moments of her life on earth.

The question that keeps popping up about Mary's knowledge is whether she knew at the Annunciation that her Son would be Divine. The best modern answer is that this cannot be known from the Bible alone. Some exegetes like Stanislaus Lyonnet are convinced that Mary knew her Son was Divine; others like René Laurentin believe this may be the case.

2. First Modern View

The first point of view believes that Mary, as a child of her people, inherited a unique way of looking at history. Israel was a people of "listening," or "memory." Her whole life consisted in retaining in its heart the events of the salvific history, to listen to and accept the commands, laws, and norms that the Lord had given revealing Himself in them.

With her *Fiat* ("yes") of the Annunciation, Mary accepts to "serve" the plan of God the Savior. From that day onward, the story of Jesus becomes also her story. Jesus' words and deeds become the material for her contemplation. The events that concern Him, the words that He utters, and the deeds that He accomplishes are the fulfillment of the Scriptures.

She shows that she has questioned the Scriptures that speak of Israel's past as the People of God and of the future toward which its Lord was leading her in the penumbra of faith. Mary too has a twofold attitude toward the events and words of Jesus. On the one hand, she *conserves* their remembrance (Lk 2:19, 51); on the other hand she shows that this remembrance is not a static one, for she seeks to *deepen her understanding of them, "reflecting on them in her heart"* (Lk 2:19).

In this way, the Virgin matured in her faith by means of the Word of God. She did this not by proceeding from an affirmation to a negation but by going from a lesser to a greater, from a minor light to a greater light. John says that the relatives of Jesus did not believe in Him (7:5). Never is this said of the Virgin. Concerning her, the Gospel says (at least once: Lk 2:50) that she did not understand but that she surpassed this obscurity of faith by her remembrance and assiduous penetration into what Jesus said and did.

In this tradition Mary is first and foremost the Mother of the Messiah, and she and the other Poor of Yahweh who await the consolation of Israel recognize this as the significance of her own virginal Motherhood. This holds true for the visit to Elizabeth (Lk 1:39-45) and Mary's own *Magnificat,* to the accounts of the Birth of Jesus at Bethlehem (cf. Mt 1:18-25; Lk 2:1-20), the visit of the Magi (Mt 2:1-12), the purification and canticle of Simeon (Lk 2:22-35), the flight into Egypt (Mt 2:13-15), and the return to Nazareth (Mt 2:19-23).

3. Second Modern View

The second view is that Mary was incompletely aware of the significance of the events in question. It says that this incomplete knowledge of Mary can be seen in three Gospel episodes.

(1) The *Finding in the Temple* (Lk 2:41-52). In this episode Mary is shown to be confused by Jesus' word to her about having to be in His Father's house: " *'Son, why have You done this to us. Behold, Your father and I have been searching for You in sorrow.' He said to them, 'Why did you search for Me. Did you not know that I had to be in My Father's house?' But they did not grasp what He said to them."*

(2) *The Marriage at Cana* (Jn 2:1-11). In this episode Mary does not know that Jesus has a Divine timetable from which to accomplish His life work of redemption.

(3) *Mary's Seeking of Jesus* (Mk 3:31; Lk 8:19-21). In this episode Mary seeks Jesus during His Public Ministry (possibly to divert Him from His mission) and fails.

4. Teaching of the Magisterium

Throughout the ages the great Doctors of the Church have all taken for granted that Mary had knowledge of her Son's Divinity. Saint Bernard, for example, always returns to the idea that Mary was asked to become the Mother of God's Son.

The response of the Popes on this theme can be arrived at by citing the words of Saint Pius X in the Encyclical *Ad Diem*

Illum Laetissmum: "Who more than His Mother could have a far-reaching knowledge of the admirable Mysteries of the Birth and Childhood of Christ, and above all of the Mystery of the Incarnation, which is the beginning and the foundation of faith? She not only *'kept in her heart'* (Lk 2:19-51) the events of Bethlehem and what took place in Jerusalem in the Temple of the Lord, but sharing as she did the thoughts and the secret wishes of Christ, she may be said to have lived the very life of her Son."

The Second Vatican Council made statements about Mary that take for granted her knowledge that her Son was Divine. "The Father of mercies willed that the consent of the predestined Mother should precede the Incarnation, so that as a woman contributed to death, so also a woman should contribute to life" (LG 56). "At the message of the Angel, the Virgin Mary received the Word of God in her heart and in her body, and gave Life to the world" (LG 53). "For believing and obeying, Mary brought forth on earth the Father's Son" (LG 63). "This union of the Mother with the Son in the [Divine] work of salvation was manifested from the time of Christ's virginal conception up to His Death" (LG 57).

It is clear from these brief statements that the Church regards Mary as having a knowledge of faith. She was blessed because she believed that what the Lord had promised her would be accomplished (Lk 1:45). This faith combined with her familiarity with the promises about the coming Messiah in Scripture and Jewish tradition and the vision of Divine things promised to the pure of heart (Mt 5:8) as well as conversations with Her Son. The result was that Mary had a supernatural knowledge of Christ and His mission, which increased from the Annunciation to Pentecost.

A. Buono

KOLBE (SAINT MAXIMILIAN)

SEE *Servants of Mary, 5*

- L -

LAETITIAE SANCTAE

[971, 2678, 2708]

SEE   *Church and Mary*   *Rosary*
Magisterium (Documents of)

ON September 8, 1893, Pope Leo XIII issued an Encyclical entitled *Laetitiae Sanctae* ("Holy Joy") concerning the value of the Rosary as a remedy for the three principal evils present in modern society.

The first such evil is *the distaste for a simple life of labor.* It generates envy for those who have more goods, abandonment of rural areas and flights to the pleasures of the large cities, and rash hopes of an equal distribution of wealth. The quest for these dreams brings with it both individual and social delusions, disturbances, and uneasiness. Contemplation of the *Joyful Mysteries* of the Rosary teaches us instead to seek joy in leading honest and work-filled lives in accord with our state.

The second evil is *the repugnance toward suffering of any kind*: "the determined will to avoid suffering, to use every means to avoid suffering and to reject adversity." Without the light of faith suffering is viewed as an injustice or a disorder that can be eliminated and give way to chimerical earthly paradises. The *Sorrowful Mysteries* show us the sufferings of the Innocent One and aid us to understand the reason for suffering and to accept it from the hands of God, thus giving it a redemptive power for us and for others.

The third evil is *the forgetfulness of future goods, the object of our hope.* People pursue the perishable goods of this world so avidly that they lose sight of the memory of a better homeland in eternal beatitude. The *Glorious Mysteries* unveil these heavenly treasures and beauties to us; they keep before our minds the true happiness that awaits us in the next life.

The Pope concludes that if the Rosary of Mary is recited assiduously and understood by the faithful, it will bear consoling fruits of even social renewal.

A. Buono

231

LAITY AND MARY

SEE   *States of Life and Marian Devotion, 2*

LA SALETTE (France)

SEE   *Apparitions*   *Apparitions after Vatican II*

ON September 19, 1846, a "Beautiful Lady" appeared to two children who were grazing sheep near La Salette in the French Alps, at an altitude of almost 6,000 feet. The children, Maximin Giraud, 11 years old, and Melanie Calvat, 14 years old, were from the region of Corps (Isère). Seated at first and all in tears, the "Lady" stood up and spoke to them in French and in the local dialect, weeping still. Then she walked up a steep path and disappeared in a bright light. The brightness in which she was enveloped seemed to come from the Crucifix on her chest, which was surrounded by a hammer and nails, by chains and roses.

On September 19, 1851, after a thorough inquiry covering the event, the witnesses and the content of the message, Bishop Bruillard of Grenoble, in a memorable letter of instruction, determined that the apparition "bore in itself all the marks of truth and that the faithful are justified in believing it to be certain and indubitable."

From the beginning, pilgrims crowded the rough paths leading up toward her whom they spontaneously named "Reconcilatrix of sinners." Amid these solitary heights there soon rose the basilica, then the first units for lodging.

It is hard to imagine, today, the impact of the apparition on public opinion and the press of the time. A Christian renewal transformed first the region. From France, and from beyond, organized pilgrimages came in ever increasing numbers. It was at La Salette, in 1872, that nationwide pilgrimages began to be formed.

Born of La Salette was a great movement of prayer, of conversion, and of commitment. The movement gained convents, monasteries, congregations, and archconfraternities.

Christians everywhere saw or felt its influence. Chaplains of the Shrine became a religious and missionary Congregation that has spread throughout the world: the Missionaries of Our Lady of La Salette. The Sisters of La Salette had a similar evolution.

Saints, pastors, writers, and others have been marked by La Salette: people like Don Bosco, the saintly Curé of Ars, Peter Eymard, Madeleine Sophie Barat, Father Prévost, and Bishop Dupanloup as well as Bloy, Huysmans, Maritain, Psichari, Claudel, and Mauriac. Today, more than ever, at La Salette itself and in all the "little La Salettes" around the world, the Mother of Jesus Christ attentive "to all His people," whose pilgrimage is not yet finished, draws to "her Son" all who find in her tears the expression of God's love.

Her message speaks to us from the perspective of the Cross. At first it seems a frustrating message because it is deeply "imbedded" in a bygone environment, rural France of the 19th century. But it is a challenging message nonetheless, because it recalls to us the realities and demands of faith, the Good News we had forgotten as well as the fact that the Son Who offers His salvation cannot save us without ourselves. It tells of the futility of Mary's mediation, "*if you do not value it.*"

Our Lady's message appeals to our liberty, safeguarded by the seventh-day rest. It asks us to place our trust "*in the Name of the Son,*" "*in His outstretched arms,*" Who saves us but Who also "*deposes the proud.*" It exhorts us to read the signs of the time and see in them the urgent call to conversion of life (Luke 12 and 13). It inculcates the necessity of daily prayer, of the Sunday Eucharist, of the yearly Lent. And it sends us on mission "*to all my people.*"

The message traces the "*narrow road that leads to life*" (Mt 7:14), like the steep and narrow path the Beautiful Lady climbed before melting away in the light. The Biblical resonances and the Evangelical quality of the message bespeak the usual manner of the Beautiful Lady. She always comes to implore us: "*We implore you, in Christ's name: be reconciled to God*" (2 Cor 5:20). The Virgin in tears is the ambassadress of a vulnerable God, made known in Jesus Christ but Who respects our free will. Her message goes to the core of the insistent spiritual needs of our time. These needs are spoken in the pastoral ministry to pilgrims and in the French periodical devoted to the Lady, *Annals of Our Lady of La Salette.*

R. Castel

LECTIONARY, MARIAN   [1154]

SEE   *Collection of Masses of the*   *New Testament*
         Blessed Virgin Mary   *Old Testament*

ONE of the major pluses of the new Liturgy is the "Marian Lectionary," comprising the readings that are used in Marian celebrations. The previous *Lectionary* made only partial and disordered use of the Biblical material that has to do with Mary. A few readings (like Lk 1:26-38 and 11:27-28) were repeated too much while others (like Jn 2:1-11 and Acts 1:12-14) were never used in a Marian context. The non-Gospel readings made almost exclusive use of pericopes from the Wisdom Books of the Old Testament (Sir 24 and Prv 8) or the Book of Revelation of the New Testament (chs. 11 and 21).

Following the lead of Vatican II (LG 11), the new *Lectionary* includes texts that describe the preparation for salvation, which, read in the Church and interpreted in the light of complete revelation, aid our understanding of the Mystery of the Mother of the Savior. New Testament texts then evoke the ecclesial traits of Mary. Thus, the *Lectionary* contains a larger number of Old and New Testament readings concerning the Blessed Virgin (around 55).

This numerical increase has not been based on random choice. Only those readings have been accepted which in different ways and degrees can be considered Marian, either from the evidence of their content or from the results of careful exegesis, supported by the teachings of the Magisterium or by solid tradition (MC 12).

Thus, the new *Lectionary* utilizes from the Old Testament the Protoevangelium (Gn 3:15), a few historical texts (Gn 12: the promises to Abraham, and 2 Sm 7: the prophecy of

Nathan—both of which are alluded to in the Annunciation): 1 Chr 15 and 16 (the transferral of the Ark), and a certain number of prophetic oracles (Is 7: the virgin mother, and Is 9: Emmanuel—both of which are also alluded to by the Angel to Mary; Is 61: the spouse, as well as Mic 5: Immanuel: God-with-us; Zep 3 and Zec 2: on the Daughter of Zion).

The Gospel texts are also better used. The accounts of the Infancy show Mary's person and function in relation to the events of the Savior's life. Luke also brings out Mary's personality and her spiritual journey. He shows her faith, obedience, complete openness, acceptance and interiorization of the Word of God, Who becomes flesh in her. She is the point of arrival for the faith and expectation of the just of the Old Testament, the place where God becomes man amid the poor.

Then John completes the portrait by the account of Mary standing by the Cross, showing how she becomes the Model and Mother of the Messianic People of the New Covenant.

Among the other New Testament pericopes the most important ones are those from the Book of Revelation (chs. 11 and 12: the Woman, and 21: Jerusalem); Acts 1 (Mary with the disciples) and four Pauline texts (Rom 5 and 8; Gal 4; Eph 1). These consistently bring out Mary's role in Salvation History, that is, her relation to Christ and to the Church.

A. Buono

LEGION OF MARY
[971]

THE Legion of Mary was begun in 1921 by a Dublin layman, Frank Duff, together with a small group of lay people. Its purpose is the sanctification of its members by prayer and active cooperation in the work of Mary and the Church to advance the reign of Christ. Its principles come from those of the Mystical Body and the book by Saint Louis Grignion de Montfort on *True Devotion to the Blessed Virgin Mary*.

The Legion spread quickly all over the world and has grown into one of the largest lay organizations in the Church.

It can be used by the bishop or clergy of a diocese for any form of Catholic Action except the collection of money. It requires its members to lead a devout Christian life, attend a weekly meeting of prayer, spiritual reading, and instruction by a priest director, and allot at least two hours a week to apostolic work.

The Legion has a highly organized structure and is patterned on divisions used in ancient Rome. The smallest unit is termed a praesidium; two or more praesidiums are called a curia; a regional governing body is a senatus; and the supreme governing body is the concilium.

One of the Legion's most effective practices for individual growth in holiness is the annual consecration of the legionaries to Mary, called the *Acies*. In its own words, "the essential idea of the Legion . . . is that of *working in union with and in dependence on Mary, its Queen*. The 'Acies' is the solemn declaration of that union and dependence, the renewal—individual and collective—of the legionary promise of fealty."

Perhaps the most effective practice used by the Legion in its apostolate is the practice of visiting the homes of people and encouraging Bible Study, which is called the *Pilgrimatio pro Christo* ("Pilgrimage for Christ").

A. Buono

LIFE OF MARY   [525ff, 721ff, 2097]

SEE *Annunciation*   *New Testament*
     Infancy Narratives   *Visitation*
     Marian Chronology

1. A Woman of Her Time

IT is the teaching of the Church that Mary of Nazareth was an obscure Jewish maiden chosen from all eternity and formed to the Divine Plan from the first moment of her existence. She was kept free of the stain of original sin and throughout her lifetime was without stain of any fault or transgression. She cooperated perfectly and in all respects with the will of God for her own unique destiny—to be the Mother of God's Son become Man to achieve the salvation of the human race.

According to the New Testament, Mary belonged to the tribe of Judah and the house of David (Lk 1:32, 69; 2:4; cf. Rom 1:3). According to an early tradition accepted by most of the Fathers of the Church and based on the *Protevangelium of James,* her parents were named Ann and Joachim. This apocryphal work has led to the growth of legends about her early years. One such is that Mary was presented in the Temple by her parents when she was very young. However, the legal prescription bound only firstborn males, inasmuch as they belonged to the Lord by law (Ex 13:2-12).

Apart from the announcement of the Angel (Lk 1:26-38), there is nothing of the miraculous about Mary. She is described as a woman of people with lowly origins, a sharer in the joyous or sad events of the daily life of her time. She becomes engaged, conceives a child, visits an aging relative, bears a son in Bethlehem, makes the customary pilgrimages to Jerusalem, is present at a wedding feast and at the cruel death of her Son, and is part of the apostolic community.

All of this shows that Mary is not an invention. Rather, she is a real woman who knows how to reflect and speak, listen or take the initiative, weep or rejoice.

2. The Childhood of Jesus

There is very little said about Mary in the New Testament—statistically she appears in only approximately 200 verses out of those found in the 27 Books. Everything said of her is in relation to her Child, Who is the Son of God. And she appears mostly in connection with His Childhood. (1) In the account of the Conception of Jesus (Mt 1:18-25), she is clearly shown to be the only human parent of Jesus, Who is declared to be conceived by the Holy Spirit and the Savior of God's people. (2) In the account of the Annunciation (Lk 1:26-38), this same idea is affirmed together with the fact that the Messianic Child of Mary will be the Son of God.

(3) In the account of the Visitation (Lk 1:39-56), the Child's Messianic character appears again as well as Mary's commitment to the Poor of Yahweh. (4) In the account of the Birth of Jesus (Lk 2:1-20), Mary travels to Bethlehem with Joseph her husband and brings forth her firstborn Son, laying Him in a manger because of lack of space at the inn; after hearing the shepherds' report of Angels singing about the birth of a Redeemer, she keeps all these things in her heart.

(5) In the account of the Circumcision (Lk 2:21), the Child is circumcised and given the Name Jesus in accord with what had been told to His father and His Mother (Mt 1:21, 25, 31; Lk 1:31). Through this rite, a Jew became the son of Abraham (cf. Rom 4:11) and subject to the Law (Gal 5:3). According to the Divine Plan, Christ was born under the Law that He might redeem those who were under the Law (Gal 4:4).

(6) In the account of the Presentation (Lk 2:22-39), on the 40th day after childbirth Mary goes to the Temple to fulfill the requirements of the Law: the purification of the Mother (Lv 12) and the presentation of the firstborn Son (Ex 13:2, 12, 15). Mary hears from the lips of the aged Simeon about her Son's universal salvation and about her singular association with it: "*And your own soul a sword shall pierce*" (Lk 2:35).

(7) In the account of the Adoration of the Magi (Mt 2:1-12), Mary is the parent mentioned when the Magi find the Child and adore Him: "*On entering the house, they found the Child with Mary His Mother*" (Mt 2:10). (8) In the account of the Flight into Egypt (Mt 2:13-15), Mary flees with the Child and Joseph because of an Angel's warning of Herod's evil designs against the Child Whom he regards as a rival for the throne.

(9) In the account of the Return from Egypt and Settling at Nazareth (Mt 2:19-23), Mary returns to Israel with her Son and Joseph and settles in Nazareth of Galilee. There in combination with Joseph she rears her Son in the ways of God, the customs of her people, and the practices of her town. (10) In the account of the Finding of Jesus in the Temple (Lk 2:41-52), Mary learns that her Son is growing up and beginning to think of His ultimate mission given Him by His heavenly Father. Al-

though she does not understand completely what is happening, she keeps His words in her heart and constantly seeks to learn from them.

(11) In the account of the Hidden Life of Jesus (Lk 2:51-52), Mary returns home with Jesus and notes His obedience to her and Joseph. She also sees Him advance in wisdom and age and grace before God and humans. In time, Joseph teaches Jesus the trade of carpenter and dies, leaving Mary alone with Jesus until the time for His Public Ministry has come.

3. Mary during the Public Ministry

Mary was the wife of an artisan in a provincial town. Her life was naturally associated with caring for the home and looking after her husband and her Son. Accordingly, the Gospels focus upon Jesus and place Mary in the picture only when her exalted mission requires her presence. During the Public Ministry it seems that she may have accompanied Him at times when He was preaching in Galilee, which suggests that by then Joseph was dead. This definitely seems to be the case in the incident found in Mark 6:3 and possibly in that of Matthew 13:55, where Joseph's name is not mentioned, although one would expect it to be if he were living.

Mary appears on the occasion of Christ's first miracle when at her suggestion He changes water into wine at the Marriage Feast of Cana (Jn 2:1-5). She then goes to Capernaum with Her Son, a possible indication that she no longer resided at Nazareth (Jn 2:12).

She also appears in the account of the Coming of Jesus' Relatives (Mk 3:20-21) inserted within the account of the Unbelieving Scribes from Jerusalem who attribute Jesus' power over demons to Beelzebul (Mk 3:22-30). Some of His relatives are shown to not yet believe in Jesus and to actually regard Him as "out of His mind." This is in keeping with Mark's emphasis on the Messianic Secret (on the incomprehension of Jesus' greatness). Thus Mary participates in a family without glory and unable to explain the wisdom of the Rabbi from Nazareth (Mk 6:3).

Jesus is then alerted that His Mother and His relatives are looking for Him, which is the occasion for Him to show that one who does the will of His Father is as close to Him as to His nearest relatives (Mk 3:31-35 and parallels Mt 12:46-50; Lk 8:19-21). By these words, He shows that His Mother (who has been shown to do always the will of God: Lk 1:38) is the closest to Him both naturally and supernaturally.

Mary also appears in Matthew 13:55 (and parallels Mk 6:3; Jn 6:42) where she is mentioned as His Mother and as one well known to the people of Nazareth. And she is alluded to in the account of the Woman in the Crowd Who Praises Jesus' Mother. Jesus stresses that faith and obedience to God come before all else, showing again that Mary is to be praised even more for her spiritual greatness than for her physical Motherhood (Lk 11:27f).

4. Mary during the Passion / Resurrection

The Gospels say nothing about Mary meeting Jesus as He was led to Calvary for execution. They say nothing about the pain and sorrow that she shared with Him at this point, although they hint at it by the words *"Near the Cross of Jesus there stood His Mother"* (Jn 19:25). Then Jesus entrusts her care to John the Apostle (Jn 19:27). This clearly shows that there were no relations with whom she could live.

The final mention of Mary in the New Testament is in the Cenacle awaiting the Coming of the Holy Spirit, together in constant prayer with the disciples and the brethren (Acts 1:14), where *"all were filled with the Holy Spirit"* (Acts 2:4).

From that time on, when Mary was still less than sixty years old, we have no more information in Scripture about her life. The reticence about Mary as well as about the entire life of Jesus and His family and village connections before the Baptism seems to suggest a deliberate attempt to avoid making kinship the basis of special claims. A by-product of this reticence is our almost total lack of genuine information concerning the life of Mary.

Tradition, of course, has given us some information about Mary's death and Assumption, much of it based on the apocryphal books, which have to be gauged carefully. (SEE Assumption; Death of Mary.)   *A. Buono*

LITANY OF THE BLESSED VIRGIN   [971]

SEE   *Litany of Mary, Biblical   Prayer(s) to Mary*

1. History and Content

THE Litany of the Blessed Virgin was originally approved in 1587 by Pope Sixtus V. It is also known as the Litany of Loreto from the famous Italian Shrine where its use is attested for the year 1558 (but its existence far antedates this year). The last five invocations (Immaculate Conception, Assumption, Rosary, Peace, and Mother of the Church) are later additions made by the Holy See itself, as occasion warranted. There seems little doubt that the Litany dates from between 1150 and 1200, and was probably of Parisian origin, or its environs.

The list of praises to Mary (51 titles) owes much to prayers of the Greek Church, in particular to the *Akathist Hymn* (translated into Latin and first circulated at Venice, about the year 800). Originally, the Litany counted some 15 more invocations, among which were: Our Lady of Humility, Mother of Mercy, Temple of the Spirit, Gate of Redemption, and Queen of Disciples.

The form of supplication comes from the Litany of Saints, in wide use in Europe as early as the 7th /8th century, no doubt through the efforts of Irish missionary monks. In it Mary heads the list of Saints and is invoked three times: *Holy Mary, pray for us; Holy Mother of God, pray for us; Holy Virgin of virgins, pray for us.* These invocations are retained in her own Litany.

The alternation of admiring contemplation and confident supplication makes the Litany a prayer at once simple and complete.

2. Text of the Litany

Lord, have mercy.
Christ, have mercy.
Lord, have mercy.
Christ, hear us.
Christ, graciously hear us.
God, the Father of heaven,
have mercy on us.
God the Son, Redeemer of the world,
have mercy on us.
God the Holy Spirit, *have mercy on us.*
Holy Trinity, one God,
have mercy on us.
Holy Mary, *pray for us.**
Holy Mother of God,
Holy Virgin of virgins,
Mother of Christ,
Mother of the Church,
Mother of divine grace,
Mother most pure,
Mother most chaste,
Mother inviolate,
Mother undefiled,
Mother most amiable,
Mother most admirable,
Mother of good counsel,
Mother of our Creator,
Mother of our Savior,
Virgin most prudent,
Virgin most venerable,
Virgin most renowned,
Virgin most powerful,
Virgin most merciful,
Virgin most faithful,

Mirror of justice,
Seat of wisdom,
Cause of our joy,
Spiritual vessel,
Vessel of honor,
Singular vessel of devotion,
Mystical rose,
Tower of David,
Tower of ivory,
House of gold,
Ark of the covenant,
Gate of heaven,
Morning star,
Health of the sick,
Refuge of sinners,
Comforter of the afflicted,
Help of Christians,
Queen of angels,
Queen of patriarchs,
Queen of prophets,
Queen of apostles,
Queen of martyrs,
Queen of confessors,
Queen of virgins,
Queen of all saints,
Queen conceived without original sin,
Queen assumed into heaven,
Queen of the most holy Rosary,
Queen of families,
Queen of peace,
Lamb of God, You take away the sins of the world; *spare us, O Lord.*

* *Pray for us* is repeated after each invocation.

Lamb of God, You take away the sins of the world; *graciously hear us, O Lord.*
Lamb of God, You take away the sins of the world; *have mercy on us.*
℣. Pray for us, O Holy Mother of God.
℟. *That we may be made worthy of the promises of Christ.*

Let us pray.

Grant, we beg You, O Lord God,
that we Your servants
may enjoy lasting health of mind and body,
and by the glorious intercession
of the Blessed Mary, ever Virgin,
be delivered from present sorrow
and enter into the joy of eternal happiness.
Through Christ our Lord.
℟. Amen.

During Advent

Let us pray.

O God,
You willed that, at the message of an Angel,
Your Word should take flesh in the womb of the Blessed Virgin Mary;

grant to Your suppliant people,
that we, who believe her to be truly the Mother of God,
may be helped by her intercession with You.
Through the same Christ Our Lord.
℟. Amen.

From Christmas to the Purification

Let us pray.

O God,
by the fruitful virginity of Blessed Mary,
You bestowed upon the human race
the rewards of eternal salvation;
grant, we beg You,
that we may feel the power of her intercession,
through whom we have been made worthy
to receive the Author of life,
Our Lord Jesus Christ Your Son,
Who lives and reigns with You forever and ever.
℟. Amen.

During Paschaltime

Let us pray.

O God, Who by the Resurrection of Your Son,

Our Lord Jesus Christ, granted joy to the whole world, grant, we beg You, that through the intercession of the Virgin Mary, His Mother, we may attain the joys of eternal life.

Through the same Christ Our Lord.

℟. Amen.

J. Laurenceau

3. Two New Invocations: "Mother of the Church" and "Queen of Families"

On March 13, 1980, the Prefect of the Congregation for the Sacraments and Divine Worship (Cardinal Knox) declared that the invocation "Mother of the Church" was to be inserted in the Litany of the Blessed Virgin after the invocation "Mother of Christ" and before "Mother of Divine Grace." This insertion was to take place in each country as soon as the National Bishops' Commissions rendered approval.

Well known are the circumstances in which Paul VI on November 11, 1964 at the close of the Third Session of Vatican II made the official declaration of this new Marian title: "For the glory of the Blessed Virgin and our consolation, we proclaim Mary most holy as 'Mother of the Church,' that is, of the whole People of God, both of the faithful and of the pastors who all call her their most loving Mother."

John Paul II, in response to urgent requests from all over the world, gave permission for the insertion of this title in the Litany. He determined that not only does it express the will of the hierarchy but it also responds to a felt need of the Christian people: "The insertion of this new invocation in the Litany after 'Mother of Christ' reflects the Marian schema in the Constitution on the Church [*Lumen Gentium*] and stresses the complete motherhood of Mary toward Christ and toward the Church, as Mother of the Head and Mother of the members of the Mystical Body."

On December 31, 1995, the Congregation for Divine Worship and the Discipline of the Sacraments sent a Letter to the Episcopal Conferences indicating that the Supreme Pontiff empowered them to insert the invocation "Queen of families" in the Litany of Loreto after "Queen of the most holy Rosary" and before "Queen of peace." This invocation flows naturally from the fact that Mary is "Mother of the Church." She is also Mother of the Domestic Church—the family.

John Paul II concluded his 1981 Apostolic Exhortation *The Christian Family in the Modern World (Familiaris Consortio)* with the words: "May Christ the Lord, the Universal King, the King of Families, be present in every Christian home as He was at Cana, bestowing light, joy, serenity, and strength."

By the side of the *King of Families* shines forth the *Queen of Families.* And it is once again John Paul II who gives us the meaning of this new invocation: "Mary called herself the *'Handmaid of the Lord'* (Lk 1:38). Through obedience to the Word of God she accepted her lofty, yet not easy vocation as wife and mother in the family of Nazareth. Putting herself at God's service, she also put herself at the service of others: a service of love. Precisely through this service Mary was able to experience in her life a mysterious but authentic 'reign.' It is not by chance that she is invoked as 'Queen of heaven and earth.' The entire community of believers thus invokes her; many nations and peoples call upon her as their 'Queen.' For her 'to reign' is to serve! Her service is 'to reign.'

"This is the way in which authority needs to be understood both in the family and in society and the Church. . . . The maternal 'reign' of Mary consists in this. She who was, in all her being, a gift for her Son has also become a gift for the sons and daughters of the whole human race, awakening profound trust in those who seek her guidance along the difficult paths of life on the way to their definitive and transcendental destiny" (*Letter to Women*, June 29, 1995).

A. Rum — A. Buono

4. A New Litany in Honor of Mary's Queenship

On March 25, 1981, the Church promulgated the *Order of Crowning an Image of the Blessed Virgin Mary,* replacing the rite that had been inserted in the *Roman Pontifical* in the 19th century in response to the Church's devotion to Mary from the earliest ages.

The new Rite indicates that Mary's Queenship is an outgrowth of her Motherhood of the Word Incarnate, her role as the new Eve associated with the new Adam (Christ) in the work of the Redemption, as the perfect follower of her Son and preeminent member of the Church. The prayers highlight the relationship between Mary's Queenship and her participation in the Paschal Mystery. They indicate that Queenship is to be understood in the Gospel sense of discipleship, service, and love. They thus summon all the faithful to a more fervent commitment to the Christian life.

One of the most innovative features of the rite is a new "Litany of the Blessed Virgin" that is especially suitable to be prayed privately and meditated upon. It has been drawn up especially with the people in mind, and includes well-known *traditional elements* that appeal to us at once: the opening sevenfold invocation, *Lord, have mercy . . . Holy Trinity, one God;* the beloved response, *pray for us;* the first three invocations to Mary, *Holy Mary, Holy Mother of God, Holy Virgin of virgins;* and the triple imploration of the *Lamb of God* at the end.

The heart of the Litany lies in its emphasis on Mary's Queenship. It defines the *specific area* of her Queenship: she is Queen of *charity,* because she excels in *charity* (and charity is essential for the follower of Christ). And she influences the souls of the faithful so that they may attain *charity.* Finally, as Queen of charity, Mary is also *Queen of mercy* and *Queen of peace,* for mercy and peace flow from charity.

The Litany also sets down the *groups* (angelical, Old Testament, and New Testament) over whom Mary is Queen because of the depth of her service and the purity of her love. These are: *Angels, Patriarchs, Prophets, Apostles, Martyrs, Confessors, Virgins, and All Saints.*

Lastly, the *boundaries* of Mary's Kingdom are delineated and they are the same as those of her Son's Kingdom: she is *Queen of the world, of heaven, and of the universe.*

This modern and inspiring Litany is based on the *finest sources* and they are clearly evident as we voice the invocations: (a) Sacred Scripture: *Virgin Daughter of Zion; Handmaid of the Lord; Woman crowned with the stars*. (b) Formulas of Previous Litanies: the first three invocations are from the Litany of the Saints; the group of invocations from *Queen of Angels* to *Queen conceived without original sin* are from the Litany of Loreto. (c) Documents of Vatican II: *Most excellent fruit of the Redemption* (SC 103); *Queen of the universe* and *Associate of the Redeemer* (LG 59, 61). (d) Liturgical Texts: *Advocate of grace* (Preface for Dec. 8), *Queen of heaven, Queen of the world,* and *Queen of mercy*.

Lord, have mercy.
Christ, have mercy.
Lord, have mercy.
God, the Father of heaven,*
God the Son, Redeemer of the world,
God the Holy Spirit,
Holy Trinity, one God,
Holy Mary,**
Holy Mother of God,
Holy Virgin of virgins,
Chosen Daughter of the Father,
Mother of Christ the King,
Glory of the Holy Spirit,
Virgin Daughter of Zion,
Virgin most pure and lowly,
Virgin most meek and obedient,
Handmaid of the Lord,
Mother of the Lord,
Associate of the Redeemer,
Full of grace,
Fount of beauty,
Summit of virtue,
Most excellent fruit of the Redemption,
Perfect follower of Christ,
Most pure image of the Church,
The new Woman,
Woman clothed with the sun,
Woman crowned with the stars,
Lady most benign,
Lady most clement,
Our Lady,
Joy of Israel,
Splendor of the Church,
Glory of the human race,
Advocate of grace,
Minister of devotion,
Helper of the People of God,
Queen of charity,
Queen of mercy,
Queen of peace,
Queen of Angels,
Queen of Patriarchs,
Queen of Prophets,
Queen of Apostles,
Queen of Martyrs,
Queen of Confessors,

* *Have mercy on us* is repeated after each invocation.
** *Pray for us* is repeated after each invocation.

Queen of Virgins,**
Queen of All Saints,
Queen conceived without original sin,
Queen assumed into heaven,
Queen of the world,
Queen of heaven,
Queen of the universe,
Lamb of God, You take away the sins of the world; *hear us, O Lord.*
Lamb of God, You take away the sins of the world; *graciously hear us, O Lord.*
Lamb of God, You take away the sins of the world; *have mercy on us.*

℣. Pray for us, O Holy Mother of God,
℟. *That we may be made worthy of the promises of Christ.*
O God of mercy,
hear the prayers of Your servants.
We acknowledge Your holy handmaid Mary
as our Mother and Queen.
Help us to serve You and one another on earth
and obtain a place in Your eternal Kingdom.
We ask this through Christ Our Lord.
℟. Amen.

** *Pray for us* is repeated after each invocation   *A. Buono*

LITANY OF MARY, BIBLICAL   [971]

SEE   *Litany of the Blessed Virgin   Prayer(s) to Mary*

IN addition to the Litanies in honor of Mary approved for liturgical or public use (Litany of Loreto and Litany for the Crowning of an Image of Mary), other litanies have been drawn up from time to time for private use. One of the most relevant private litanies today is a litany consisting of Bible phrases—a Biblical Litany.

It is possible to compose a long list of praises of the Virgin Mary by using God's own Word. They are concrete titles, attributed to her and emphasizing the Most Blessed Virgin's "function" in the mystery of the Word made flesh and the Mystical Body. When we call upon Mary by these titles we are praying with the Word of God, which has been from time to time interpreted by the Church's tradition in a clearly Marian sense. The litany that follows was composed by A. M. Roguet, O.P., and was published by *La Vie Spirituelle*, no. 553, pp. 213-217.

GREETED by the Angel Gabriel: Lk 1:28.
Full of grace: *ibid.*

Mother of Jesus: Lk 1:31.

Mother of the Son of the Most High: Lk 1:32.

Mother of the Son of David: *ibid.*

Mother of the King of Israel: Lk 1:33.

Mother by act of the Holy Spirit: Lk 1:35; Mt 1:20.

Handmaid of the Lord: Lk 1:38.

Virgin, Mother of Emmanuel: Mt 1:23, citing Is 7:14; cf Mt 5:2.

You in whom the Word became flesh: Jn 1:14.

You in whom the Word dwelt amongst us: *ibid.*

Blessed amongst all women: Lk 1:41; cf Jdt 13:18.

Mother of the Lord: Lk 1:43.

Happy are you who have believed in the words uttered by the Lord: Lk 1:43.

Lowly handmaid of the Lord: Lk 1:48.

Called blessed by all generations: *ibid.*

You in whom the Almighty worked wonders: *ibid.*

Heiress of the promises made to Abraham: Lk 1:55.

Mother of the new Isaac: Lk 1:37 (Gn 18:14).

You who gave birth to your firstborn at Bethlehem: Lk 2:7.

You who wrapped your Child in swaddling clothes and laid Him in a manger: *ibid.*

Woman from whom Jesus was born: Gal 4:4; Mt 1:16, 21.

Mother of the Savior: Lk 2:11; Mt 1:21.

Mother of the Messiah: Lk 2:11; Mt 1:16.

You who were found by the shepherds with Joseph and the newborn Child: Lk 2:16.

You who kept and meditated all things in your heart: Lk 2:19.

You who offered Jesus in the Temple: Lk 2:22.

You who put Jesus into the arms of Simeon: Lk 2:28.

You who marvelled at what was said of Jesus: Lk 2:33.

You whose soul a sword should pierce: Lk 2:35.

Mother who were found together with the Child by the Wise Men: Mt 2:11.

Mother whom Joseph took into refuge in Egypt: Mt 2:14.

You who took the Child Jesus to Jerusalem for the Passover: Lk 2:42.

You who searched for Jesus for three days: Lk 2:46.

You who found Jesus again in His Father's house: Lk 2:46-49.

Mother whom Jesus obeyed at Nazareth: Lk 2:51.

Model of widows: cf Mk 6:3.

Jesus' companion at the marriage feast at Cana: Jn 2:1-2.

You who told the servants, "Do whatever He tells you": Jn 2:5.

You who gave rise to Jesus' first miracle: Jn 2:11.

Mother of Jesus for having done the will of the Father in heaven: Mt 12:50.

Mary who chose the better part: Lk 10:42.

Blessed for having heard the Word of God and kept it: Lk 11:28.

Mother standing at the foot of the Cross: Jn 19:25.

Mother of the disciple whom Jesus loved: Jn 19:26-27.

Queen of the Apostles, persevering in prayer with them: Acts 1:14.

Woman clothed with the sun: Rv 12:1.

Woman crowned with twelve stars: *ibid.*

Sorrowful Mother of the Church: Rv 12:2.

Glorious Mother of the Messiah: Rv 12:5.

Image of the new Jerusalem: Rv 21:2.

River of living water, flowing from the throne of God and the Lamb: Rv 22:1; cf. Ps 45:5.   *A. Buono*

LITTLE OFFICE OF THE BLESSED VIRGIN MARY

[1176-1178]

SEE   *Cult of Mary*   *Liturgy*

THE *Little Office of the Blessed Virgin Mary* is an orderly arrangement of daily prayer in honor of Mary that arose in the 9th or 10th century. It was patterned after the *Divine Office* (now more usually called the *Liturgy of the Hours*) consisting of seven hours. The Little Office was an abridgment of the "Common of the Blessed Virgin Mary" found in the Office and was possibly meant to coincide with the "Votive Masses of Our Lady on Saturday" that had just been composed by Alcuin. Revised and recommended by Saint Peter Damian (d. 1072), this Little Office was adopted by the Cistercians and Camaldulensians and later utilized by the secular clergy. The form varied from place to place, but the standard form was determined in 1585 after Saint Pius V in 1568 removed the obligation of saying it under pain of sin.

The Little Office became part of the *Books of Hours* in honor of Mary and was used by many lay people. Many congregations of women made its use mandatory for their members, and it also became the prayerbook of Third Orders. In 1952, this Office—which had very little variety according to the liturgical seasons and the days of the week—was revised and given psalms, canticles, hymns, responsories, short readings, antiphons, and prayers for each of the six periods of the liturgical year. It totalled 28 feasts of Our Lady with proper antiphons for the *Benedictus* (Canticle of Zechariah) and the *Magnificat* (Canticle of Mary). The Second Vatican Council made this Office a part of the public prayer of the Church (LG 98).

With the publication in 1971 of the newly revised four-volume *Liturgy of the Hours* the Church urged that those not obliged to the recitation of the full Office should say at least one or two hours of the new Office, for example, Morning Prayer or Evening Prayer. Accordingly, short one-volume Offices appeared in various languages and they were immediately adopted by congregations not bound to the whole office. As a result, the *Little Office of the Blessed Virgin Mary* initially lost some of its popularity. However, recent attempts to revise it have somewhat restored its fortunes.

The major revisions concern a notable variety of psalms, hymns, and Biblical and patristic readings with the addition of texts for intercessions that are in harmony with the official prayer of the Church and with the needs of today's faithful who are immersed in many daily activities.

Like the *Liturgy of the Hours*, the *Little Office* has the *purpose of sanctifying the principal moments of the day*. Thus it has Morning Prayer and Evening Prayer as well as a Midday Prayer (composed of Midmorning, Midday, and Midafternoon parts suitable for 9:00 A.M., 12:00 P.M., and 3:00 P.M.) and Night Prayer before retiring. Each hour comprises a hymn, some psalms, one or two readings, intercessions, and a concluding prayer. A moment apart is constituted by the ancient Matins now called Office of Readings, the nocturnal prayer transformed into a brief time for meditative prayer.

The *elements* of the *Little Office* are also the same as those of the *Liturgy of the Hours:* Biblical texts with more or less direct reference to the Mystery of Mary, with psalms with proper antiphons, responsories, intercessions, and prayers—all Marian in character. The originality lies precisely in this emphasis given to the person of Mary, who nonetheless never appears in isolated fashion. She is always portrayed as part of the History of Salvation, as the admirable fruit of the Divine Power, as the Mother of the Lord, or as the Image of the Church.

Hence, the *Little Office* is a way of living—in praise and reflection—the principal moments of each day with Mary, who spent her life alongside her Son in ardent love, in joyous praise, and in deep faith.

A new edition of the *Little Office* based on the *Liturgy of the Hours* was published in 1988 by the Catholic Book Publishing Co. and has proven to be very popular.

A. Buono

LITURGY   [971]

THE Catholic Church gives a distinctive place to the Virgin Mary in her Liturgy. She honors her with a special cult.

Historically, it was most natural for Christians to re-sound the greetings of the Angel and Elizabeth or the praises addressed to Mary, such as preserved in the Gospels. Already in the first centuries she is venerated under titles like *the Holy One; the Holy Virgin; the All-Holy*.

At the beginning of the 4th century we find two principal expressions of the Church's cult toward Mary. One was the *"Memory of the Blessed Virgin Mary, Mother of God"* in the Roman Canon of the Mass; the other, a direct recourse to her intercession in the very ancient prayer *Sub Tuum* ("We fly to your patronage . . .").

Very early, too, the Church adopted the Canticle of the *Magnificat* to sound her own worship of praise to the Father through the Son in the Holy Spirit.

In the Office of the Blessed Virgin especially, but also in the spiritual interpretation of various Psalms and the Book of Revelation, the Church identified herself in some way with Mary by seeing her as the Daughter of Zion, the Mother of peoples, the Wife, the Woman, Jerusalem, the Temple—all fig-ures that designate the Church herself.

Accordingly, the cult of the Virgin Mary began with a *recognition* of her role in the work of salvation and in the life of the Church herself. And it was furthered by *an experience* of communion in the Mystery of Christ, a communion in which Mary holds the first place through the special bond that joins her to her Son as Mother of God and also to the Church as her most eminent member, her Mother in the Spirit.

In addition, the Church finds in Mary the most perfect ex-pression and the exemplary referent of the worship in spirit and in truth that the Church is to render to God when she cel-ebrates the Divine Mysteries. In this sense already, one could say that the whole Liturgy is Marian, even if this character is not always explicit.

In the Church's Marian cult properly speaking, the refer-ence to Mary is spelled out. To see it we have only to examine the prayer of the Church in this regard, which can be classified under three principal heads.

1. Prayer to God with Mary

Here the Church makes place for Mary in her own prayer to God. The Church may take cognizance of Mary hearing and receiving the Word of God, or cognizance of what the Scriptures tell us on this point. Or she may repeat Mary's canticle of thanksgiving, or identify herself with her in the offering of Christ's sacrifice on the Cross, or have recourse (at least indirectly) to her intercession in heaven.

The Preface of the Blessed Virgin II is the perfect example of this first type of prayer. In the Ordinary of the *Roman Missal* we find moreover the "Memory" of the Virgin already spoken of as well as the mention of the Virgin in the Creed, in some other Prefaces, and with variants in the new Eucharistic Prayers.

The liturgical Seasons of Advent (especially from December 17 onward) and Christmas give a place of choice to the Virgin Mary, both in the Readings and in the texts of the Mass and Office.

Furthermore, some feasts of the liturgical Calendar, like the Presentation and the Annunciation, are as much "Feast of the Lord" as of the Virgin Mary. The same is true of the Feast of Mary, Mother of God (January 1), since it also commemorates the naming of Jesus. Mary has her place in the formulary of a number of other feasts besides Christmas and Epiphany and the Feast of the Holy Family: for example, Saint Joseph (March 19 and May 1), Saints Ann and Joachim (July 26). She is mentioned as well in some Masses for special occasions, like the Mass for the Consecration of Virgins, for Religious Profession, for Christian Initiation, for the Funeral of Children, and for Migrants. And there is mention of her in a number of Sunday and weekday readings (15 new readings in the Common or the Feasts of the Blessed Virgin).

2. Prayer to God in Honor of Mary

The Church "celebrates" the Virgin Mary by praising the Lord for the participation of the Mother of Jesus in the major events of her Son's life, such as we know them from the Gospel and Tradition. The Church also gives praise to God for the special graces that prepared the Virgin Mary for her mission, and praise to God for the rewards heaped upon her in body and soul, as well as for a number of events in the life of God's people where Mary's action was particularly evident. Each time, also, provides the Church with an occasion for recourse to Mary's intercession so that we might follow her example or enjoy her protection.

Here belong the Marian Feasts properly speaking, together with their Prefaces: *Solemnities* of the Immaculate Conception (December 8), of Mary, Mother of God (January 1), and of the Assumption (August 15); *Feasts* of the Birth of Mary (September 8) and of the Visitation (May 31) as well as Our Lady of Guadalupe (December 12); *Memorials* of the Immaculate Heart of Mary (Saturday after the Feast of the Sacred Heart), of the Queenship of Mary (August 22), of Our Lady of Sorrows (September 15), of Our Lady of the Rosary (October 7), and of the Presentation of Mary (November 21); *Optional Memorials* of Our Lady of Lourdes (February 11), of Our Lady of Mount Carmel (July 16), and of the Dedication of Saint Mary Major (August 5).

To be added are the seven formularies of the Common of the Blessed Virgin Mary, with their corresponding lectionary (11 readings from the Old Testament, 7 second readings from the New Testament, 5 Psalms or Canticles, 12 proper Gospels). These 35 passages, for the most part, are also used in other Masses with a Marian character, but the lectionary for Marian Feasts offers yet another 15 texts.

Lastly, special mention should be made of the Solemn Blessing recommended by the Missal for Solemnities of the Virgin. The three invocations that precede the formula of blessing relate in some way to the two types of prayer to Mary described above: invocation of God with mention of Mary by way of praise to the Lord, plus Mary's canticle of thanksgiving, but also a special call to love Mary and honor her in celebration for the sake of communion with her Son.

3. Prayer to Mary

In this third case the Church speaks directly not to God but to Mary herself, to praise her, to congratulate her in words of the Gospel referred to above, but also in direct recourse to her intercession.

This third form of liturgical prayer is more closely connected with private devotion. It is already in evidence at the beginning of the 11th century in Hymns (*Ave Maris Stella*—Hail, Star of the Sea) and Anthems (*Salve Regina*—Hail, Holy Queen, etc.) dedicated to Mary and in the somewhat later *Stabat Mater* (At the Cross Her Station Keeping) not to mention its expression toward the 12th century in the *Confiteor* (I Confess) of the Mass. Not until then can one speak in all propriety of a "special cult toward the Virgin Mary" rather than simply a "special place of Mary in the liturgical worship of the Church." Frequently also the formularies of Marian Feasts included Acclamations at the Gospel or Canticles addressed directly to the Virgin Mary.

From the ecumenical standpoint, it is especially this third form of Marian prayer (liturgical or not) that must be clearly differentiated from the worship paid to the three Divine Persons and to which it must remain subordinate. In none of its forms can the cult given to the Virgin be considered as an end in itself. Yet it remains eminently suitable to serve the worship owed to the true God alone. The Father receives honor and praise for the wisdom of His purposes revealed in Mary. Through the honor paid to His Mother, the Son is better known and loved. And the action of the Spirit in Mary and the Church also is extolled and proclaimed. Marian cult is "at the center of the worship rendered to God."

Even prayer addressed directly to Mary, invoked as Advocate, Auxiliatrix, Help of Christians, or Mediatrix, finds in God its ultimate terminus. Mary's mediation is not additional to that of Christ, since Mary and Christ are but one in the Mystery of His Mystical Body. But to those who pray to her, she brings the motherly help of her own prayer, which merges with the supreme prayer of Christ the Mediator.

Without lapsing into sentimentalism or maudlin piety, authentic cult toward Mary brings a very human complementary note to the worship we render to the Father through Christ in the Holy Spirit, a note of loving contemplation, interior silence, joyous giving, and spiritual promptitude. Although subordinate to Divine worship, the cult of Mary is not therefore optional. "It is right and just" to praise and venerate Mary, the true Mother of God and of our Redeemer Jesus Christ; "right and just" to give thanks for the exceptional grace that places her above all creatures in heaven; "right and just" to thank the Lord for giving her as Mother to us as well as to the whole Church, and for letting us have the benefit of her intercession with her Son in heaven.

It is a duty for us to pay honor to the eminent dignity of Mary and the unique character of her maternal mission in God's plan; a duty also to have recourse to her intercession and invoke her as the "Woman who in a hidden manner and in a spirit of service watches over the Church and carefully looks after it until the glorious day of the Lord" (MC, Introd.). We ought, then, to seek her help in our apostolate as priests, religious, or laity.

The cult of the Virgin Mary is by no means unproductive, since it leads to imitation of the example of Mary, "the perfect model of the disciple of the Lord: the disciple who builds up the earthly and temporal city while being a diligent pilgrim toward the heavenly and eternal city, the disciple who works for that justice which sets free the oppressed and for that charity which assists the needy; but above all, the disciple who is that active witness of that love which builds up Christ in people's hearts" (MC 37).

Add to this that the liturgical cult given to the Virgin Mary serves a regulatory function in regard to private devotion and the "pious exercises" by which the faithful express their piety toward the Blessed Virgin. This private devotion should have the same Trinitarian, Christological, and Ecclesial imprint that is essential to the liturgical cult of Mary.

B. Billet

LORETO (Italy)   [67]

SEE *Apparitions*   *Apparitions after Vatican II*

1. Origin

L ORETO is one of the most famous and venerated Marian Shrines in Italy and in the world. "For centuries, Christian piety has intimately linked it with the ineffable mystery of the Incarnation of the Word" (John Paul II). Indeed, according to an ancient tradition, the Holy House—where the Word became flesh—arrived on the hill of Loreto (via sky or sea?) seven centuries ago, after a stay at Tersato in Dalmatia in 1291 (in remembrance of this stay there still exists at Tersato a minor basilica dedicated to Mary, Mother of Grace, the goal of pilgrimages since the 13th century) and in 1294 at Recanati, in a woods belonging to a nobleman named Loreta. The existing iconography in the Shrine—two 400-year-old bas-reliefs—would seem to confirm the tradition of transport by sea.

Investigations conducted soon after the appearance of the Holy House of Loreto showed that its dimensions were identical to those of the House of the Holy Family that was missing from its place of enshrinement in a basilica at Nazareth. Markings found in the stones of this House are similar to those found at Nazareth. Also, the Holy House has no foundations and stands on a public way (as was ascertained by the latest excavations in 1962-1965).

In the opinion of experts, these and other elements weigh in favor of a translation of the Shrine. It was in referral to this translation of the Holy House "by the hands of Angels" that on March 24, 1920, Our Lady was declared by Benedict XV to be the "principal Patroness of all aviators."

This is apparent from the special blessing approved by the same Pontiff for the "machines destined for aerial flights," which is as follows: "O merciful God, You have consecrated the house of the Blessed Virgin Mary with the Mystery of the Word Incarnate and placed it in the midst of Your children. Pour forth Your blessing on this vehicle so that those who take an aerial trip in it may happily reach their destination and return safely home under Mary's protection."

2. A Brief History

The historical archives of the Holy House yield these details. On October 23, 1315, the Church of St. Mary of Loreto was mentioned for the first time in the acts of a penal process held at Macerata. On November 2, 1375, Pope Gregory XI (1371-1378) by his Brief *Dum Praecelsa* granted the first indulgences to the Loretan Church. In 1468 construction was cited as being under way for the church desired by the Bishop of Recanati (Nicola delle Aste) and on May 8, 1728, it was raised to the rank of basilica by Benedict XIII.

On March 7, 1586, by the Bull *Pro Excellenti Praeeminenter* Pope Sixtus V raised the town of Loreto to a city and granted cathedral status to the church. He noted that the City of Loreto was "the most famous in the world" because it guarded the Holy House that was consecrated by the Divine Mysteries of salvation. In it the Lord daily multiplied His prodigies and to it pilgrims flocked "from every corner of the world."

Subsequent to the Concordat between the Holy See and Italy (1929), the Basilica of the Holy House, with its attached edifices and works, was ceded to the Holy See. On June 24, 1965, by the Constitution *Lauretanae Almae Domus* (Holy House of Loreto) Paul VI suppressed the Pontifical Administration of the Holy House and substituted the Pontifical Delegation of the Shrine and the prelature of the Holy House, erecting the episcopal cathedral in the basilica.

3. Effect on All Christians

From its very origins, Loreto had the character of a worldwide center of prayer. In the 16th century devotion to the Holy House flourished in all of Christendom. Pilgrims flocked to the Shrine and on their knees dug for furrows of faith and filial love toward the Virgin of Loreto. Some litany-like prayers gained a distinctive place at the Shrine and around 1400 took the name of "Litany of Loreto."

It would be difficult to estimate the countless number of Saints and pilgrims who prayed at the Holy House throughout the centuries as well as the innumerable artists who lent their profuse talents (even gratuitously) to it. Religious congregations also were drawn to the House of Loreto and contributed various works of charity. Among these were the Carmelites, Capuchins, and Friars Minor.

On October 4, 1962, Pope John XXIII visited the Shrine of the Holy House on the vigil of the Second Vatican Council. On the Feast of the Birth of Mary, September 8, 1979, John Paul II went to Loreto as a pilgrim "to ask light and assistance" from Our Lady for his imminent trip to New York to speak at the United Nations (on October 2, 1979).

The *Universal Congregation of the Holy House* was founded on May 27, 1883. It summons all Christian families to take as their model the Holy Family of Nazareth and publishes a monthly magazine in Italian entitled *The Message of the Holy House.*   *A. Rum*

LOUIS-MARIE GRIGNION DE MONTFORT (SAINT)

SEE   *Servants of Mary, 3*

LOURDES (France)   [67]

SEE   *Apparitions*   *Apparitions after Vatican II*

1. Place and Date of the Apparitions

L OURDES in 1858: a city of about 5,000 inhabitants, located along the river Pau, at the entrance to the high valleys of the Pyrenees.

—Grotto of Massabielle (from the French *"vieille masse,"* ancient mass): to the west of the city, some yards from the river, at the foot of the rocky mass of Espelugues (from *spelunca*: cave).

—February 11, 1858, about three years after the dogmatic definition of the Immaculate Conception, a 14-year-old girl of

Lourdes, Bernadette Soubirous, and two companions go looking for dead wood along the left bank of the river. The two
companions cross over, leaving Bernadette temporarily
stranded on the other side. She tarries there before the Grotto
of Massabielle, when suddenly she is in the presence of a
"Lady in white." The Lady is praying the Rosary and smiles
on Bernadette.

—February 14, second apparition, in the presence of some
smaller companions of Bernadette. The Lady smiles again but
says nothing.

—From February 18 to March 4: the Lady appears 13
times and gives her "message."

—March 25, Feast of the Annunciation, the Lady reveals
her name. She appears two more times: April 7 and July 16.

—In all, 18 apparitions.

2. The Seer

—Bernadette Soubirous is born January 7, 1844, at
Lourdes, of a very Christian family. Her parents are millers.
The family has fallen on hard times but maintains its dignity
and an atmosphere of love and understanding. In 1858 they
move into the "Jail," an abandoned municipal prison put at
their disposal by a kindly cousin.

—Sickly: Bernadette has had cholera and is asthmatic.

—As the eldest child, she helps her mother and often
misses school. She can neither read nor write and speaks only
the Burgundian dialect. It is in this dialect of Lourdes that the
Virgin delivers her message. Because of lack of preparation,
Bernadette has not yet made her First Communion. To help
this preparation along, she returns from Bartrès, where she has
been put out to nurse and where she has lived from September
1857 to January 1858. All in all, she belongs to the poorest of
the poor: penniless, powerless, and unlettered.

—But she possesses the primordial quality for a witness.
She is transparent. Moreover, she has much good sense and a
remarkable tenacity coupled with unselfishness beyond her
years. Hence she is a capable instrument for transmitting the

"message" entrusted to her, without adding or suppressing anything.

—These messages of prayer and penitence Bernadette lives out, particularly during her religious life at Nevers, a life of suffering but also of generosity and happiness. She died at Nevers, in the convent, April 16, 1879. Her body is preserved intact. She was canonized December 8, 1933.

3. The Message

—Personal message: *"Do me the favor of coming here for 15 days"*; *"I do not promise to make you happy in this life but in the next."* Bernadette, in effect, is told that the apparitions will gain her no advantage or special treatment. The message is rounded off with a prayer and three secrets that Bernadette never revealed. There is no reason to think that they contained anything extraordinary, probably some information reserved for Bernadette but in line with the message we do know.

—Penitential message:

"Pray to God for sinners."
"Penitence! Penitence! Penitence!"
"Kiss the ground for the conversion of sinners."
"Drink from the spring and wash in it."
"Eat of the grass which is there."

Prayers, penitential exercises, and especially conversion of life, with a sign of this conversion: the spring discovered at the foot of the grotto, February 25. It is a reminder of the necessity of purification and also of the fountain *"leaping up to provide eternal life"* (Jn 4:14). But the Lady also wanted to bring help for bodies. Several sick people were cured at the very beginning by washing or being immersed in this water.

—Ecclesial message:

"Tell the priests that people should come here in procession and that a chapel should be built on the site."

This is a summoning of the People of God for building up the Church, the material edifice being sign of the building up of "God's Temple," the spiritual edifice made of "living stones."

—Signature of the message: On March 25, at the insistence of Bernadette, the Lady of Massabielle reveals her name: *"I am the Immaculate Conception."*

To those whom she calls to conversion the Virgin presents herself as the "highly favored of God." She is the figure of the Church. She is also Mother of the Church, who continues her motherhood in the Mystical Body of her Son.

—Her message echoes the Gospel:

"Be on guard and pray" (Mt 26:41; cf. Lk 18:1).

"Reform your lives! The kingdom of heaven is at hand" (Mt 4: 17).

"Whoever drinks the water I give him will never be thirsty" (Jn 4:14).

"You are 'Rock,' and on this rock I will build My Church" (Mt 16:18).

"I am with you always, until the end of the world" (Mt 28:20).

4. Repercussions

—Commission of inquiry formed by Bishop Laurence. Bernadette is questioned and the cures are investigated. The conclusion is announced on January 18, 1862, that the Mother of God has indeed appeared 18 times to Bernadette Soubirous, at the Grotto of Massabielle.

—May 1866: blessing of the Crypt and first Mass celebrated at the Grotto.

—August 15, 1871: blessing of the Church of the Immaculate Conception (upper basilica).

—1872: first national expression, a pilgrimage with "flags and banners." First torchlight procession.

—1873: first nationwide pilgrimage, organized by the Assumptionist Fathers.

—1874: first pilgrimages from outside of France, originating in the United States and Belgium.

—1876: coronation of Our Lady of Lourdes.

—1889: opening of the Church of the Rosary.

—March 25, 1958: centenary of the apparitions; consecration of the Basilica of Saint Pius X.

—Several international Eucharistic and Marian Congresses (the most recent being the International Eucharistic Congress of 1981, held at Lourdes).

—Several throngs of more than 100,000 people, in particular the pilgrimages of ex-Servicemen and ex-Convicts.

5. Today

—Each year: about 4 million visitors pass through Lourdes, among which are over a million pilgrims in planned contingents.

—All French and Belgian dioceses, with very few exceptions, sponsor annual pilgrimages. The great national pilgrimages are: the Montfortian, the "National," and the Rosary. The military pilgrimage is international.

—Each year: 650,000 sick received in three reception Centers and ministered to by a complete service of "Hospitality."

—Each day: from Easter to mid-October, several "festive" Masses with Eucharistic and torchlight processions.

—Twice a week: international Mass in honor of Saint Pius X, concelebrated by bishops and several hundred priests (800 for the Mass of Requiem for Paul VI).

—Importance of individual confessions (Chapel of Reconciliation), but also communal penitential celebrations with general absolution in strict conformity with the norms of the Ritual.

—Frequent, and at least twice a week: communal anointing of the sick.

—Importance unfailingly given to prayer and conversion of life: places of prayer like the Grotto and Crypt, where the Blessed Sacrament is exposed every day. Way of the Cross always a prominent feature. Strategic locations for viewing events and comparing them with the Gospel, and to produce

"a collective effort of renewal" (Encyclical of Pius XII for the Centenary of the Apparitions, 1958).

—Reception of tourists, of individual pilgrims and groups (this last service was begun in 1979, with the possibility of "One-day Pilgrimages").

—Reception of unbelievers and those who are searching: "Open Door."

—Service for young people: reception, lodging, orientation: Camp for the Young.

—Reception for the elderly.

—Vision of the universal Church, with the "Missionary Pavilion."

—A witness to the charity of the Church, with the St. Peter City of Catholic Relief and the Service for mutual aid of Shrines.

—Places for dialogue on the cures and miracles (medical bureau), on vocations ("Vocation" Pavilion), on problems of couples (family pastoral service), on problems of peace (Pax Christi), etc.

Thus, Lourdes has joined hands with the Second Vatican Council and aims to bring to the world the Good News of Jesus Christ. This it does, today as from the beginning, by living the Message of Our Lady transmitted through Bernadette.

R. Point

LUKE (GOSPEL OF SAINT)

SEE *Annunciation*   *Jerusalem*
     Cenacle   *Knowledge, Our Lady's*
     Daughter of Zion   *Nazareth*
     Faith of Mary   *New Testament*
     "Fiat" in the Name of Humanity *Presentation of Jesus*
     Finding in the Temple   *Servant of the Lord*
     Hail Mary   *Virginal Conception*
     Infancy Narratives   *Visitation*

LUMEN GENTIUM, Chapter 8

SEE   *Vatican II and Mary*

LUX VERITATIS   [466, 495]

SEE   *Church and Mary*   *Magisterium (Documents of)*
      Cult of Mary   *Mother of God*
      Feasts of Mary

ON December 25, 1931, Pope Pius XI issued the Encyclical
Lux Veritatis ("The Light of Truth") to commemorate the
15th centenary of the Council of Ephesus, which perfected
Christological teaching and proclaimed the Divine Motherhood of Mary. The Pope outlines the history of this third Ecumenical Council: the essence of the Nestorian heresy; the work
of the papal legates; the acknowledgment of the primacy of
Peter; and the condemnation of the heretic.

He then reaffirms the central doctrine of the Council:
Jesus Christ is at the same time true God and true Man by
means of the hypostatic union; in the name of the family of believers he renews Peter's profession of faith: "*You are the Messiah, the Son of the living God*"; and he states that this faith is
preserved pure and whole in the one true Church of Christ,
which is the Roman Catholic Church.

In the third part of the Encyclical, the Pope deals with the
Dogma of the Divine Motherhood of Mary as a corollary of the
teaching about her Son: "From this Dogma as from a hidden
spring of gushing water flows the singular grace of Mary and,
after God, her great dignity." He goes on to justify devotion to
Mary, who is the Mother of Christ's brothers and sisters and
hence their refuge as well as the pledge of Christian unity and
a model of family life.

The Pope concludes the Encyclical by indicating that he
has directed the Congregation of Rites to issue a Mass and
Office of the Divine Motherhood to be celebrated by the
Universal Church. Originally celebrated on October 11, in
the renewed Liturgy of Vatican II this feast is assigned to
January 1.   *A. Buono*

- M -

MAGISTERIUM (DOCUMENTS OF)

SEE *Dogmas, Marian* *Redemptoris Mater*
Ineffabilis Deus *Signum Magnum*
Marialis Cultus *Vatican II and Mary*
Munificentissimus Deus

DOCTRINAL declarations concerning Mary (e.g., "Mother of God," Immaculate Conception, Assumption) are the result of long development in the life and faith of the Church, guided by the Holy Spirit *"to all truth"* (Jn 16:13) and faithfully adherent to the teaching of the Apostles (Acts 2:42).

This progressive explicitation of the Mystery of Mary, as it relates to the life of the Church through the centuries, is a very significant aspect of the living Tradition in its continuity with the Apostolic deposit of faith. The mission and charism to verify and attest to the continuity with Tradition belong to the Apostolic Magisterium (Popes, Councils, etc.).

Marian piety, even in its most fervent expressions, must always be ready to let itself be validated and guided by the pronouncements of the Magisterium.

1. Indispensable Basic Documents

(a) The "Apostles' Creed," a baptismal profession of faith going back to the 2nd-3rd century (". . . and in Jesus, His only Son Our Lord, Who was conceived by the Holy Spirit, born of the Virgin Mary . . .").

(b) Vatican Council II, Dogmatic Constitution on the Church (*Lumen Gentium*), promulgated November 21, 1964, Chapter 8: *"The Blessed Virgin Mary, Mother of God, in the Mystery of Christ and the Church."* Condensed in this chapter, beginning with the Biblical data, is the entire teaching of Tradition on Mary, Mother and Model of the Church. Mary's mediation is formulated along the lines of maternal love and intercession. The deep analogy between Mary and the Church is underscored.

(c) *Marialis Cultus,* an Apostolic Exhortation of Paul VI on Devotion to Mary, signed February 2 and published March 22, 1974. In the context of the liturgical renewal inspired by the Second Vatican Council, the Pope shows the place of Mary in the prayer life of the Church and recalls the principles and norms of devotion to Mary, which must be centered in Christ, in the Holy Spirit, and in the Church. He gives some guidelines for renewal of Marian devotion, with reference to the Bible, the Liturgy, Ecumenism, and human Sciences (particularly as regards women of today).

By way of illustration Paul VI speaks of the Angelus and, at greater length, of the Rosary, both Gospel-based and both the object of the Church's continuing regard. He concludes by pointing out the theological value of devotion to Mary and its pastoral effectiveness for renewing the Christian way of life.

(d) *Redemptoris Mater,* an Encyclical of John Paul II on *The Mother of the Redeemer* issued March 25, 1987. It gives a comprehensive treatment of Mary's part in the Mystery of Salvation and in the life of the Church on her pilgrimage of faith.

Mary is the Mother of the Church, which is the Body of Christ prolonged throughout the ages. Hence the Church "looks to" Mary through Jesus, just as she "looks to" Jesus through Mary. As the Servant, Mother, and Disciple of the Lord, Mary is the model, guide, and strength of the pilgrim people of God, especially through the most important stages of their journey through life.

2. For Additional Study

Among the major texts:

—*Council of Ephesus* (431): Letter of Saint Cyril to Nestorius, officially approved by the Council, with the name *Theotokos* (Mother of God) recognized for Mary because of the union of the Divine and human nature in the one Person of Christ.

—*Council of Chalcedon* (451): "begotten of the Father before all ages according to His Divinity but born in these latter days for us and for our salvation, of the Virgin Mary, Mother of God, according to His human nature . . . one and the same Christ the Lord."

—*Letter of Pope Siricius* (392) and *Council of the Lateran* (649) on the perpetual virginity of Mary.

—Bull *Ineffabilis Deus* of Pius IX for the definition of the Immaculate Conception (1854).

—Apostolic Constitution *Munificentissimus Deus* of Pius XII, defining the Assumption of Mary (1950).

—For the period 1743-1957, from Benedict XIV to Pius XII, there is a collection of numerous pontifical texts on *Mary,* by the monks of Solesmes. Also by the same monks is a collection of similar texts on the *Rosary,* and another on *consecration to Mary.*

—*Homily of Paul VI* at the closing of the 3rd session of the Second Vatican Council (November 21, 1964). On this occasion the Pope proclaimed *Mary Mother of the Church* and at the same time offered some observations on Ecumenism: "Mary, perfect figure of the disciple of Christ . . . humble servant of the Lord, completely ordered to God and to Christ . . . ," etc.

—Apostolic Exhortation *Signum Magnum* of Paul VI (May 13, 1967) on the meaning and purpose of devotion to Mary. Her Spiritual Motherhood is exercised through her intercession with her Son by the Evangelical example of her holiness.

It is clear that the Magisterium of the Church will continue to speak to us of Mary, exhorting us to a devotion ever more inspired by the Word of God and Tradition, in worship rendered with Mary to the Father, through Christ, in the Holy Spirit (MC 25).

J. Laurenceau

MAGNIFICAT (Lk 1:46-55)   [2097, 2619]

SEE   *Annunciation*   *Prayer(s) to Mary*
       Poor of Yahweh and Mary *Visitation*

1. Text and Sources of the Magnificat

*M*Y *soul proclaims the greatness of the Lord,* [1 Sm 2:1]
my spirit rejoices in God my savior, [Is 61:10]
for He has looked with favor on His lowly servant.
                          [1 Sm 1:11; Ps 113:7; Zep 3:12]

From this day all generations will call me blessed: [Jdt 15:10]
the Almighty has done great things for me, [Ps 71:19; 126:2f]
and holy is His name; [Ps 111:9]

He has mercy on those who fear Him
in every generation. [Ex 20:6; Ps 85:9; 103:17]

He has shown the strength of His arm, [Ps 98:1; Is 40:10]
He has scattered the proud in their conceit.
                          [Jb 5:12; Ps 33:10; 138:6]

He has cast down the mighty from their thrones
and has lifted up the lowly. [Jb 5:11; Ps 75:8]

He has filled the hungry with good things; [Ez 34:29]
and the rich He has sent away empty. [1 Sm 2:5; Ps 34:10f; 107:9]

He has come to the help of His servant Israel [Is 41:9]
for He has remembered His promise of
    mercy, [Ps 98:3; Jer 31:3, 20]
the promise He made to our fathers,
to Abraham and His children forever.
                          [Gn 13:15; 22:18; Ps 132:11]

Spontaneous songs of praise like the *Magnificat* (which
gets its name from the first word of its Latin translation meaning "magnifies") were part of the Old Testament tradition.
Mary's song brings together the major themes of Old Testament piety as shown by the references given in the text printed

above: (1) Salvation is accorded to the Poor of Yahweh (the lowly). (2) The salvation to be accomplished by Mary's Son will be another (and greater) Exodus and Return from the Exile. (3) The Suffering Servant of Isaiah (the Poor of Yahweh par excellence) will be upheld in remembrance of the promises made to Abraham, the father of the nation and especially of the Poor of Yahweh.

Thus, the *Magnificat,* totally imbued with the faith and hope of Israel, has become the Church's song of predilection for praising the ineffable gratuitousness of the Lord's salvific intervention toward the poor and lowly.

2. Movement of the Magnificat

For us, the importance of the *Magnificat* is found most of all in the event that, according to Luke, Mary celebrated: the conception of Jesus. This is by far the most striking and most decisive of the *"great things"* that God has done for the salvation of His people. It is also the reason why Christian generations have made the *Magnificat* the favored expression of their own experience of salvation in Jesus Christ. The movement of soul that called forth Mary's song of thanksgiving is in fact the same sort of inward movement that issues in the faith of the Christian. In Mary's case, the actual experience of God's beneficent presence served to illuminate her future as well as her past.

(a) *The present of the personal experience.* In the Bible, expressions of thanksgiving always flow from an actual, personal experience of salvation. Heads of people, war heroes, prophets, and psalmists recount, each in a personal way, their wonder over God's active presence at the center of history and the center of human life. See, for example, the canticle of Moses and the children of Israel celebrating their deliverance from the hand of the Egyptians (Ex 15), or the canticle of Anna (1 Sm 2:1-10) singing her joy and gratitude to the Lord Who heard her prayer (cf. also Jgs 5; Jdt 16).

The entire first half of the *Magnificat* (1:46-50) tends to express the unique experience of Mary from the moment that the conception of Jesus was announced. Mary *"proclaims the greatness of the Lord*" because she realizes it is He Who is active *here and now* at the core of her life. She gives thanks for being *favored* by the God Who "*has looked with favor on His lowly servant*" and Who, for her, "*has done great things.*" The God Whom she extols is the same One Who has intervened so many times in behalf of His people.

But Mary can call Him her *Savior* in a sense that surpasses everything it was possible to discern or hope for from the prefigurative and preparatory manifestations under the Old Covenant. In her *Magnificat* Mary celebrates the salvation revealed in fullness and brought to completion in the very Person of Jesus.

(b) *An experience open to the future.* Turning her attention to the future ("*all generations will call me blessed*"), Mary focuses on the absolute newness and the normative character of the Incarnation. What is in prospect is the birth of a new people, a delivered people, no more centered on the Law but on the Spirit. *Henceforth,* it is the Incarnation that will reveal, more than any other sign or marvel of God, the *holiness* of His *Name* and His mercy . . . *in every generation.*

This also tells the realism and profundity of the Incarnation. The salvation given by God in Jesus Christ is not automatically inscribed in the unwinding course of history or human development. It has to be received anew "*in every generation,*" in the period of history that is ours, between the Resurrection of Christ and His Parousia, period of the Church's apostolate.

(c) *From yesterday to today.* The second part of the *Magnificat* (1:51-55) shows the equilibrium and the depth of *Mary's faith.* Far from thinking only of herself, she expands the horizon of her thanksgiving to include the whole people of God and its history. Consciousness of God's gift made her particularly sensible of the mystery conveyed in the history of Israel: mystery of the extraordinarily faithful love of the God of the Covenant.

Likewise, as *humble servant,* she can more easily reflect on the habitual ways of God and discover His preference for the poor and lowly in the Psalmic sense. Rich with God's gift, rich also with the experience of her people, Mary does not merely add one more testimony in praise of the God of the Covenant. Her song is a thoroughly new and original meditation on the history of Israel—and of all humankind called to salvation—history illuminated in a *definitive* manner by the prodigious event that is taking place: God Who-is-love coming to save His people by making Himself one of us, Jesus.

J. P. Prévost

MARIALIS CULTUS

[971]

SEE   *Church and Mary*   *Magisterium (Documents of)*
     Cult of Mary   *Redemptoris Mater*
     Feasts of Mary   *Signum Magnum*
     Lectionary, Marian   *Value of Marian Devotion*
     Liturgy   *Vatican II and Mary*

ON February 2, 1974, Pope Paul VI published an Apostolic Exhortation on *Devotion to the Blessed Virgin Mary* entitled *Marialis Cultus* ("Marian Devotion"). It is one of the most important documents of his pontificate and of the whole Marian Magisterium of the Roman Pontiffs. The document sets forth the reasons and the means for devotion to Mary in a manner attuned to the needs of the mentality and custom of our age. To do so, it draws upon the liturgical reforms of Vatican II and the great psychological and sociocultural changes that have overtaken the world.

Part One deals with devotion to Mary in the revised Liturgy in the unfolding of the various seasons of the Liturgical Year and in the special celebrations in honor of Mary (Feasts and Memorials), both universal and particular. It treats references to Mary in the Eucharistic Prayer, the theological and spiritual richness of the prayers, readings, hymns, and the like in the *Sacramentary, Lectionary, Liturgy of the Hours,* and *Ritual.*

It speaks of the spiritual attitude with which the Church celebrates and lives the Divine Mysteries, taking as her Model Mary, who is the *attentive Virgin,* the *Virgin in prayer,* the *Vir-*

gin-Mother, and the *Virgin presenting offerings* in perfect union with Christ. And with the Church as a whole, individual Christians are also called to imitate Mary in piety, spiritual life, and worship.

Part Two sets forth the reasons, norms, and means for the renewal of Marian devotion. It grounds them all on the Biblical, patristic, conciliar, and theological Magisterium of Christian Tradition.

First it illustrates the Trinitarian, Christological, and ecclesial basis of Marian devotion and gives a valuable passage on Mary and the Holy Spirit. It then adds four orientations for the devotion itself: it should be Biblical, liturgical, ecumenical and anthropological in harmony with the best Tradition of the Church and with the most genuine needs of today's spirituality.

A. Buono

MARIAN CHRONOLOGY   [525ff, 721ff]

See   *Life of Mary*   *New Testament*

THE chronology of Mary's life depends completely on the chronology of her Son Jesus' life, which is in itself sparse in the New Testament. Therefore, at best a chronology of Mary can be only indicative rather than conclusive.

Nonetheless a chronology—even a tentative one—is a potent aid in our visual age in bringing a person to life for us. Hence, the following chronology has been drawn up to provide a more graphic idea of the life of Our Lady.

B.C.

23/20	Birth of Mary to Ann and Joachim
20/17	Presentation of Mary in the Temple
11/8	Betrothal to Joseph (Mt 1:16; Lk 1:27)
7	Annunciation of Christ's Birth to Mary (Lk 1:26-38)
	Mary's Visitation of Elizabeth (Lk 1:39-56)
	Mary found with Child (Mt 1:18-25)

7/6   Birth of Jesus in Bethlehem (Lk 2:1-19)
        Circumcision of Jesus at 8 days of age (Lk 2:21)
        Purification of Mary after 40 days (Lk 2:22-24)
        Prophecy of Simeon concerning Jesus and Mary (Lk 2:25-35)
        Prophetess Anna speaks of Jesus (Lk 2:36-38)
        Return to Nazareth (Lk 2:39)

6/4   Adoration of the Magi (Mt 2:1-11)
        Flight into Egypt to save Jesus from Herod (Mt 2:13-14)

4-?   Return to Nazareth after Herod's death (Mt 2: 19-23)

A.D.

6   Finding of Jesus in the Temple at Jerusalem (Lk 2:41-50)

6-?   Life of Mary and Joseph with Jesus at Nazareth (Lk 2:51)

27/28-
30   Mary at the Marriage Feast of Cana (Jn 2:1-11)
        Mary with Jesus during His Public Life (Mt 12:46-50; Mk 3:31-35; Lk 8:19-21; Jn 2:12-13)
        Jesus' indirect praise of Mary for her faith (Lk 11:27-28)

30   Mary at the Cross (Jn 19:25-27)
        Mary with the Apostles in the Cenacle after Jesus' Ascension (Acts 1:14)
        Mary is assumed to heaven to rejoin her Son.

A. Buono

MARIAN CLASSICS [971]

SEE *Devotions(s)*   *Servants of Mary*

IN modern times, a huge amount of Marian material has been printed. This is especially true of the Marian apparitions and messages with their promises and warnings in their confrontations with society, which captured the attention of many of the faithful. All of this material is spread in books, magazines, and pamphlets that run into huge numbers worldwide. The figures experienced a decrease after the Second Vatican Council, but they have now rebounded with far greater numbers than before the Council. Much of this increase is due in no small part to the Marian devotion and preaching of Popes Paul VI and John Paul II.

However, this article is concerned only with delineating what might be termed classics among the best-known Marian spiritual works, prayers, and periodicals.

1. Spiritual Works

(1) *The Protevangelium of James* or *The Gospel of Mary.* This noncanonical work, written in Greek about 150 A.D. can rightly be termed the first Marian classic. It had a very wide circulation in the early Church and was translated into many languages. In twenty-four chapters it treats the period from the birth of Mary to the massacre of the Innocents by Herod. The birth story comprises at most one-third of the narrative. The real narrative interest is in Mary. Central to the narrative as a whole are the circumstances of her birth, the years of her infancy and childhood, and the announcement of her conception as well as her relationship to Joseph and Jesus. (SEE *Apocrypha and Mary,* 2.)

(2) *The Glories of Mary.* Written by Saint Alphonsus Liguori over the course of sixteen years in a life crowded with other activities, this book is the best-seller par excellence, having gone through some 800 printings in various languages since its publication in 1750. Divided into two parts (Volume I: Explanation of the *Hail Holy Queen,* and Volume II: Exhortations on the Feasts of Mary), it follows a tripartite pattern.

Saint Alphonsus gives: (a) a doctrinal part that highlights a privilege or title of Mary and supports it with references from the Fathers and theologians; (b) an illustration or edifying story, such as to attract the popular imagination; and (c) a prayer that translates Marian doctrine into Marian devotion. Thus, the work shows Mary as a living person and loving Mother who intervenes in the lives of sinful men and women and helps us overcome discouragement while leading us to the Sacraments and to the performance of works of charity. (SEE *Servants of Mary,* 4.)

(3) *The Imitation of Mary.* Written by the French Jesuit Alexandre Joseph de Rouville and published anonymously in 1768 (since the Jesuit Order had been suppressed at that time), the book quickly won wide readership in France and Belgium and was translated into many languages. In this book, patterned after the *Imitation of Christ*, the author follows the Blessed Virgin through the Mysteries and circumstances of her life, from her Immaculate Conception to her Assumption into heaven. At each point he reflects on her conduct and her sentiments, thus providing instructive insights that will help every Christian in the varying situations of his or her own life.

If we judge by the devotion and solid piety toward God and His Blessed Mother that fill these pages, we must say that the author has not been unworthy of his more famous forerunner, Thomas a Kempis.

(4) *A Treatise on True Devotion to the Blessed Virgin.* Written by Saint Louis-Marie Grignion de Montfort in the 18th century, this magnificent work was published posthumously only in 1843. Set forth in it is a spiritual way for living in full the life of Christ with and through Mary. It is a work intended for all states of life with the overriding theme of the apostolic aspect of the Christian life.

From the day of its publication to the present, this work has become a best-seller of the first rank, translated into fifty languages. Indeed, one can say that the principal Marian movements of the last century arose through meditation on this impassioned work. Father G. Roschini has said: "If an international referendum were taken concerning the question: What is the most beautiful writing about Our Lady, I am sure that the greater part of the responses would give the preference to this little book. It is a truly classic work, a small summa of Marian theology."

A second Marian classic by the same author is associated with the Treatise. It is the little booklet entitled *The Secret of Mary.* Written in the form of a letter of spiritual direction, it deals with a method of personal union with Jesus through Mary.

2. Prayers

The principal Marian prayers are for the most part by unknown authors and all are given separate entries in this Dictionary. They bear witness to the devotion of all the subsequent
Christian centuries. They appeared spontaneously like the
various flowers in each season.

In the 3rd century, there appeared the Greek text of the
prayer *Sub Tuum Praesidium* ("We Fly to Your Patronage"—
p. 457). This is a popular prayer to ask for the intercession of
the Mother of God in our needs and dangers.

In the 10th century, the hymn *Ave Maris Stella* ("Hail,
Thou Star of Ocean"—p. 285) implores her who as our Mother
hears our prayers and will in turn be heard by her Son. The
antiphon *Regina Caeli* ("Queen of Heaven"—p. 398) sings of
the joy of the Blessed Virgin on the day of Easter.

In the 11th century, the antiphon *Alma Redemptoris
Mater* ("Mother Benign of Our Redeeming Lord"—p. 284) is
an address on the part of the sinful people striving to rise to
the Virgin who is accessible despite being so elevated because
she brought the light of day to her Creator. The antiphon *Salve
Regina* ("Hail Holy Queen"—p. 163) petitions her who is our
sweetness and our life to show us her Son Jesus after our exile
in this valley of tears.

In the 12th century, the antiphon *Ave Regina Caelorum*
("Hail, O Queen of Heaven"—p. 284) celebrates the glory of
the Queen of heaven, who gave birth to Christ, the Light of the
world.

In the 14th century, the *Stabat Mater* ("At the Cross Her
Station Keeping"—p. 447) is the great heart-shattering hymn
of the sufferings of Compassion endured by the Blessed Virgin
at the foot of the Cross. The *Angelus* ("The Angel of the Lord
Declared unto Mary"—p. 22) commemorates the great moment of the Incarnation when, through Mary's "Yes," the Son
of God became Man in her womb.

In the 15th century, there comes into being our version of
the *Litany of Loreto* (p. 241), the litany of the Mother of Christ
and Virgin for the world, a Helper for us and a Queen for the
Angels. At the same time, the *Rosary* receives its actual form,

in which we ask the Blessed Virgin to unite with her own and immerse in the joys, sorrows, and victories of her Son: our poor sorrows, so that they will not be bitter; our poor victories, so that they may always be magnanimous. (See p. 405.) At the same epoch, there appeared the touching popular prayer of the *Memorare* ("Remember . . ."—p. 324).

In the 16th century, the *Hail Mary* (p. 163) was finalized. The first part, which is in the Gospel, was most likely used as a prayer from the very 1st century and eventually appeared in an Entrance Antiphon of the Mass around the 6th century. It began to spread among the faithful beginning with the 12th century.

The second part ("Holy Mary . . ."), whose elements pre-existed in a separated state, was put together beginning with the 15th century and became current among the faithful a little after 1500.

3. Journals

There are many Marian periodicals and journals. The following are only a few of the more authoritative ones.

(1) *Marianum.* A Mariological review published since 1939 by the Servants of Mary at Rome. It contains articles, reviews, news, and documents of the Magisterium concerning Mariology.

(2) *Ephemerides Mariologicae.* A review analogous to Marianum, begun in 1951 by the Claretians in Madrid to develop and diffuse Mariological studies.

(3) *Marian Studies.* The journal of the Mariological Society of America begun in 1950.

(4) *Etudes Mariales.* The Bulletin of the French Society for Marian Studies, published annually since 1935.

(5) *Estudios Marianos.* The organ of the Spanish Mariological Society published since 1941.

(6) *Cahiers Marials.* A more popular type of publication with the purpose of offering aids and studies to promote Marian catechesis and pastoral. It was a group of workers from the staff of this publication that produced the French book that forms the basis for this English *Dictionary of Mary.*

In addition to the above the following list of books are well-known aids to Marian study and instruction.

Enchiridion Marianum Biblicum Patristicum, ed. D. Casagrande, Rome, 1974.

H. Graef, *Mary, A History of Doctrine and Devotion,* London, Vol. I, 1963, II, 1965.

R. Laurentin, *Court Traité de Théologie Mariale,* Paris, 1953.

—— *Court Traité sur la Vierge Marie,* Paris, 1968.

Mariology, ed. J Carol, O.F.M., Milwaukee, 1956-1961.

Mary in the New Testament, ed. R. E. Brown, K. P. Donfried, J. A. Fitzmyer, S.J., J. Reumann. New York, 1978.

McHugh, J., *The Mother of Jesus in the New Testament,* London, 1975.

Papal Teachings: Our Lady, ed. at Solesmes. English translation, St. Paul Editions, 1961.

Roschini, G. M., O.S.M., *Maria Santissima nella Storia della Salvezza* (4 vols.), Rome, 1969.

Second Vatican Council, *Lumen Gentium,* Chapter 8, December 4, 1963.   *A. Buono*

MARIAN CONFRATERNITIES   [971]

SEE   *Children of Mary*

CONFRATERNITIES are religious associations of lay people whose members practice a special form of public devotion or worship and may also perform some apostolic work. They possess a corporate structure and the officers guide the common activities. When confraternities reach the stage where they give rise to similar affiliates that embrace their rules, they become archconfraternities. Usually, a religious order or congregation is connected with each confraternity.

Over the years many Marian confraternities have existed in the Church. One of the first on record goes back to 11th-century Greece and some contemporary confraternities can trace their roots to the Middle Ages. However, most confraternities stem from the Counter-Reformation, and a good number of them are patterned after the sodalities started by the Society of Jesus.

Among some of the more well known confraternities are those of Our Lady of the Miraculous Medal; Our Lady of Mount Carmel; Our Lady of Perpetual Help; Our Lady of Prompt Succor; Confraternity of the Immaculate Conception of Our Lady of Lourdes; Confraternity of the Most Holy Rosary; Association of Marian Helpers; and the Blue Army of Our Lady of Fatima.   *A. Buono*

MARIAN CONGRESSES   [971]

MARIAN Congresses are assemblies of clergy and laity for the study of topics relating to Mary. During their sessions, papers are read and discussed and religious services are held in honor of Our Lady. The Congress may be international, national, or regional. The Congress at Livorno, Italy, in 1895 is regarded as the first national one, while the Congress at Lyons in 1900 is regarded as the first International one.

The second took place at Fribourg in 1902, the third at Rome in 1904, the fourth at Einsiedeln in 1906, the fifth at Saragossa in 1908, the sixth at Salzburg in 1910, the seventh at Trier in 1912, and the eighth at Rome in 1950 (this also became the first Mariological Congress). It was followed by the ninth Congress at Rome in 1954, the tenth at Lourdes in 1958, the eleventh at Santo Domingo in 1963, the twelfth at Lisbon in 1967, the thirteenth at Zagreb in 1971, the fourteenth at Rome in 1975, the fifteenth at Saragossa in 1979, and the sixteenth at Anchipel, Malta, in 1983.   *A. Buono*

MARIAN CROWNING

SEE   *Litany of the Blessed Virgin Mary, 4*

MARIAN DOCTORS

SEE   *Servants of Mary*

THE name "Marian Doctor" can be given to any one of a few great Saints and Doctors who have borne that label over the years: Alphonsus, Anselm, Bernard, and Blessed John Duns Scotus.

Saint Alphonsus, as can be seen under *Servants of Mary,* more than earned this title by his loving and learned writings about the Mother of God, especially his masterpiece *The Glories of Mary.*

The same can be said about Saint Bernard, another *"Servant of Mary,"* because of his beautiful Marian prayers and writings, especially *The Song of Songs.*

Another candidate for the title is Saint Anselm (1033-1099) Archbishop of Canterbury, Doctor of the Church and Father of Scholasticism. His literary works abound with Marian references and allusions as well as beautiful and devout prayers in honor of Our Lady. These prayers spread far and wide and made Catholics aware of Mary's intercessory power.

Although Anselm lived long before the formal definition of the Immaculate Conception and did not arrive at the point to embrace its teaching, he did pave the way for its acceptance in the Church by setting forth the principle on which the teaching came to be based (as quoted by Pope Pius IX in his Encyclical *Ineffabilis Deus*: "On the Immaculate Conception"): It was fitting that Mary should possess more purity than anyone imaginable below God for she was to be the Mother of His Son Who was equal to the Father—thus He was to be Son both of the Father and of the Blessed Virgin. This was Anselm's greatest contribution to Mariology.

However, the candidate most usually called the Marian Doctor is Blessed John Duns Scotus (1265-1308). First of all, he is one of the greatest Scholastics and Doctors of the Church. His theological system is pervaded by subtle yet first-rate metaphysical analysis and makes the Incarnation its major theme. For him, the Incarnation is decreed from all eternity even apart from the Redemption. It is the supreme created manifestation of God's love. Thus, Mary is linked to her Son in the eternal decrees. This idea served to revolutionize the theological thinking about Mary.

Second, Scotus accepted the Immaculate Conception long before its definition by the Church and he set forth the theological arguments in favor of this privilege for Mary. Against the prevailing theological opinions of his day, the Franciscan theologian demonstrates that the preservation of the Mother of God from original sin not only is not opposed to Christ's dignity and excellence but also exalts that dignity and excellence to the utmost. The Mother of God was redeemed in the most sublime way, through the infusion of grace in the first instant of her conception.

"The most perfect mediator can make use of a most perfect act of mediation with regard to the person for whom he mediates. Therefore, Christ had the most perfect degree of mediation for the person for whom He was Mediator. But He had no greater degree of perfection with regard to anyone other than Mary. . . . This would not have been the case unless He had merited to preserve her from original sin. I show this in three ways: first, by comparison with God, with Whom Christ reconciles; second, by comparison with the evil from which He reconciles; and third, by comparison with the obligation of the person whom He has reconciled."

Scotus's theological teaching did not take hold immediately. It was accepted and defended by the Franciscans, however, and in the 15th century it became the prevailing opinion after the Council of Basle. He can thus be called the Doctor of one of Mary's most exalted privileges—the Marian Doctor par excellence.

A. Buono

MARIAN HYMNS   [971]

SEE   *Angelus*   *Salva Regina*
      Prayer(s) to Mary   *Stabat Mater*
      Regina Caeli   *Sub Tuum Praesidium*

HYMNS may be termed sacred poetry set to music and usually sung in public worship. This broad definition encompasses Biblical hymns based on the Psalms as well as antiphons (or anthems) for the Divine Office. There are of course a vast number of hymns in honor of Mary that have been sung in the Church for centuries. Here we can point out only the most celebrated ones.

1. Antiphons or Anthems

The designation "Marian antiphons" is usually reserved for four rhymed prayers that have habitually been sung at the end of Night Prayer in the Divine Office or Liturgy of the Hours.

Alma Redemptoris Mater (Mother Benign of Our Redeeming Lord). The title comes from the first three Latin words of the antiphon assigned to be read from Advent to February 2. The Latin text is attributed to Herman the Cripple (1013-1054) and there are many fine English translations like the following.

Mother benign of our redeeming Lord,
Star of the sea and portal of the skies,
Unto your fallen people help afford—
Fallen, but striving still anew to rise.
You who did once, while wondering worlds adored,
Bear your Creator, Virgin then as now,
O by your holy joy at Gabriel's word,
Pity the sinners who before you bow.

Ave Regina Caelorum (Hail, O Queen of Heaven, Enthroned). This antiphon is made up of a series of acclamations honoring the Blessed Virgin assigned to be recited from February 2 to Holy Thursday exclusive. Its author is unknown and it dates from the 12th century. The following is only one of the translations that are used.

Hail, O Queen of heaven enthroned!
Hail, by Angels Mistress owned!
Root of Jesse, Gate of morn,
Whence the world's true Light was born:
Glorious Virgin, joy to you,
Loveliest whom in heaven they view:
Fairest where all are fair,
Plead with Christ our sins to spare.

Regina Caeli (Queen of Heaven). See p. 398.
Salve Regina (Hail Holy Queen). See p. 163.

2. Hymns

The list of hymns in honor of Mary is, of course, quite lengthy. For example, J. Vincent Higginson in his *Handbook for American Catholic Hymnals* (The Hymn Society of America, 1976) lists more than 180 Marian hymns found in American hymnals. The following are a few of the more popular ones.

Ave Maris Stella (Hail, O Star of Ocean). This liturgical hymn is used for Evening Prayer on Feasts of Mary. Its author is unknown and it dates to the 9th century.

Hail, thou star of ocean,
God's own mother blest,
Ever sinless Virgin,
Gate of heavenly rest.

Oh! by Gabriel's Ave,
Uttered long ago.
Eva's name reversing,
'Stablish peace below.

Break the captive's fetters,
Light on blindness pour;
All our ills expelling,
Every bliss implore.

Show thyself a Mother;
May the Word Divine,
Born for us your Infant,
Hear our prayers through thine.

Virgin all excelling,
Mildest of the mild;
Freed from guilt preserve us
Meek and undefiled.

Keep our lives all spotless,
Make our way secure,
Till we find in Jesus,
Joy for evermore.

Through the highest heaven
To the Almighty Three,
Father, Son, and Spirit,
One same glory be.

Corcordi laetitia (United in Joy). This Paschaltime hymn of unknown origin formed the basis for the hymn *Maiden-Mother, Meek and Mild* of Cecilia Caddell.

Maiden-Mother, meek and mild,
Take, oh take me for thy child;
Ever Virgin Mary!

Throughout life, oh let it be
My sole joy to think of thee;
Ever Virgin Mary!

(There are four other verses.)

Lourdes Hymn. The original hymn of Abbé Gaignet had eight stanzas, but it was later extended to sixty stanzas to accommodate the large processions while recounting the Lourdes story.

Immaculate Mary, thy praises we sing,
Who reignest in splendor with Jesus, our King.
Ave, ave, ave, Maria! Ave, ave, Maria!

In heaven, the blessed thy glory proclaim,
On earth, we thy children invoke thy fair name.
Ave, ave, ave, Maria! Ave, ave, Maria!

Thy name is our power, thy virtues our light,
Thy love is our comfort, thy pleading our might.
Ave, ave, ave, Maria! Ave, ave, Maria!

We pray for our mother, the Church upon earth;
And bless, dearest Lady, the land of our birth.
Ave, ave, ave, Maria! Ave, ave, Maria!

Mother Dear, Oh Pray for Me. A ballad and later hymn written in 1850 by Isaac B. Woodbury and revised by an unknown editor. Although this hymn has been criticized as being too sentimental and has fallen into disuse after Vatican II, it previously enjoyed enormous popularity. Higginson states: "This hymn and *Holy God, We Praise Thy Name* were likely two of the best-known hymns of the late 20th century."

Mother dear, oh pray for me
Whilst far from heaven and thee
I wander in a fragile bark
O'er life's tempestuous sea.

O Virgin Mother, from thy throne
So bright in bliss above,
Protect thy child and cheer my path
With thy sweet smile of love.

Mother dear, remember me
And never cease thy care
Till in heaven eternally
Thy love and bliss I share.

O Sanctissima (O Most Holy One). This Hymn is regarded
as a cento, a literary work made up of parts of other works. It
is also known as the "Sicilian Hymn" because it was a favorite
of Sicilian sailors—doubtless on account of its catchy tune.
The following is one English translation.

O most holy one,
O most lowly one,
Dearest Virgin, Maria!
Mother of fair Love,
Home of the Spirit Dove,
Ora, ora pro nobis.

Help in sadness drear,
Port of gladness near,
Virgin Mother, Maria!

In pity heeding
Hear thou our pleading,
Ora, ora pro nobis.

Mother, Maiden fair,
Look with loving care,
Hear our prayer, O Maria!
Our sorrow feeling,
Send us thy healing,
Ora, ora pro nobis!

Quem Terra, Pontus, Aethera (The God Whom Earth and
Sea and Sky). An 11th-century hymn attributed to Saint For-
tunatus erroneously, it formed part of the Breviary of 1632.
The following is a popular translation.

The God Whom earth and sea and sky
Adore and laud and magnify,
Whose might they own, whose praise they tell,
In Mary's body deigned to dwell.

O Mother blest! the chosen shrine,
Wherein the Architect Divine,
Whose hand contains the earth and sky,
Vouchsafed in hidden guise to lie.

Blest in the message Gabriel brought;
Blest by the work the Spirit wrought;
Most blest, to bring to human birth
The long-desired of all the earth.

O Lord, the Virgin-born, to Thee
Eternal praise and glory be,
Whom with the Father we adore
And Holy Ghost for evermore.

Salve Regina (Hail Holy Queen Enthroned Above). See Hail Holy Queen. This translation is of unknown authorship and appeared in 1884.

Hail, holy Queen enthroned above, O Maria!
Hail, Mother of mercy and of love, O Maria!
    Refrain: Triumph all ye Cherubim,
    Sing with us, ye Seraphim,
    Heaven and earth resound the hymn,
    Salve, salve, salve Regina.

Our life, our sweetness here below, O Maria!
Our hope in sorrow and in woe, O Maria! (*Refrain*)

To thee, we cry, poor sons of Eve, O Maria!
To thee we sigh, we mourn, we grieve, O Maria! (*Refrain*)

Turn, then, most gracious advocate, O Maria!
Toward us thine eyes compassionate, O Maria! (*Refrain*)

When this our exile's time is o'er, O Maria!
Show us thy Son for evermore, O Maria! (*Refrain*)

Virgin Wholly Marvelous. English translation and adaptation of a hymn by Saint Ephrem the Syrian (307-373) that is a good indicator of what can be done with ancient hymns in modern dress.

Virgin wholly marvelous,
Who didst bear God's Son for us,
Worthless is my tongue and weak
Of thy holiness to speak.

Heaven and earth, and all that is,
Thrilled today with ecstasies,
Chanting glory unto thee,
Sing thy praise with festal glee.

Cherubim with fourfold face
Are no peers of thine in grace,
And the six winged Seraphim,
'Mid thy splendor shine but dim.

Purer art thou than are all
Heavenly hosts angelical,
Who delight with pomp and state
On thy beauteous Child to wait.   *A. Buono*

MARIAN SYMBOLS   [375, 694ff, 753ff, 1101, 1145]

1. Christian Symbolism

SYMBOLS may be defined as visible objects that represent abstract ideas. Hence, symbolism is a system of actions whose reality is accompanied by a *hidden* meaning. It is found especially in religion and is transmitted primarily in cultic memorials, in paintings, and in sculptures, and is termed the symbolism of religious art.

Christian symbolism derives from the Bible and Tradition. The Old Testament makes use of *symbolic language*—in narratives, anthropomorphisms, expressions about the Covenant, rites of Hebrew religion (Passover, feasts, sacrifices, etc.), places and signs of God's presence in the world (the Ark of the Covenant, the Tent, the Temple), and objects of worship, among others.

The New Testament continues the Old Testament attitude of seeing all reality and all history in strict relationship with God. It shows Christ fulfilling the types and promises of the Old Testament. Thus, supper, baptism, and imposition of hands take on added meaning in reference to Christ.

Christian symbolism was also enhanced by its intrinsic relationship to the community of the faithful, the perdurance of the Biblical traditions and mentality, and the influences of the various cultures in which Christians lived. For the most part, Christian symbols were Biblical in inspiration: images, graphic signs, representations, actions, attitudes, objects, and liturgical signs.

Gradually, Christian symbols became fuller and more prevalent. They transmitted details of the truths of the Faith, of our Savior, of His Blessed Mother, and of the Saints, as well as other aspects of the Faith. They became indispensable aids to imparting religious truths and—in the words of Saint Augustine— "books for the unlettered."

2. Marian Symbolism

Particularly in the Middle Ages, a wealth of Marian symbolism arose that was part of many paintings of Our Lady. Thus, the symbol of *Mary with extended arms* represents her as the glorious Virgin, symbol of the new Eve and Mother of all humanity; the symbol of *Mary kneeling before the Child Jesus* highlights the adoring Mother of God. The symbol of a *lily* in Mary's pictures denotes her purity, and a star on her cloak recalls two of her exalted titles: Star of the Sea and Morning Star.

The following are only a few of the more popular symbols used by the Church in reference to Mary.

- The wine; the oil poured out; the odor of ointments (Song 1:1-3)
- The tents of Kedar; the curtains of Salma (Song 1:5)
- The sun; the vineyard (Song 1:6)
- The sachet (bundle) of myrrh (Song 1:12)
- The flower of Sharon; the lily of the valley (Song 2:1)
- The dove in the clefts of the rock (Song 2:14)
- The column of smoke of aromatical spices (Song 3:6)
- The doves' eyes (Song 4:4)
- The tower of David (Song 4:4)
- The dripping honeycomb (Song 4:11)
- The pillar of marble (Song 5:15)
- The army set in array (Song 6:3)
- The dawn; the moon; the sun (Song 6:10)
- The mouth of the Most High (Sir 24:3)
- The pillar of a cloud (Sir 24:4)
- The light that never fails (Sir 24:6, Vulg.)
- The vault of heaven; the bottom of the deep (Sir 24:8)
- The cypress tree on Mount Hermon (Sir 24:13)

- The fair olive tree in the fields; the plane tree by the water (Sir 24:14)
- The cinnamon and fragrant balm (Sir 24:15)
- The best myrrh (Sir 24:15)

A. Buono

MARIAN TITLES   [963-971]

SEE *Daughter of Zion   Mother of God*
     Immaculate Conception   Motherhood, Spiritual
     Intercession   Queen
     Mother of the Church   Servant of the Lord

THE word "title" has many definitions and uses in English. As used here, it means an appellation of dignity, honor, distinction, or preeminence attached to a person by virtue of rank, office, precedent, privilege, or attainment. In this sense, the titles of Mary are almost endless. The most used title in the Church is "Blessed Virgin Mary." This is how she is named by the Church in official documents of any kind—doctrinal, liturgical, legalistic, and the like.

Offshoots of this Marian title are found in many languages. In English, we speak of "Our Blessed Lady," "Our Blessed Mother," "the Virgin Mary." Other languages speak of the "Holy Virgin," "Most Holy Virgin," and "Mother of God." Finally, there are the Italian "Madonna" ("My Lady") and the French "Notre Dame" ("Our Lady").

These might be termed her "name" titles. There are also others connected with her "function" (associate of Christ in His Redemption). Some of the more important ones are: Advocate, Associate, Blessed Mother, Daughter of Zion, Exemplar, Handmaid (Servant) of the Lord, Help of Christians, Immaculate Conception, Mediatrix, Mother of the Church, Mother of God, Mother of Mercy, Queen of Peace, and Seat of Wisdom.

1. Advocate

The term "advocate" stresses Mary's intercession with her Son or with the Father. It goes back to the early Church, Saint

Irenaeus portraying Mary as advocate of Eve and Augustine calling the Saints our "advocates" because they share Christ's *advocacy.* It is found especially in the Middle Ages in the prayer "Hail Holy Queen" (q.v.) and in Saint Bernard's writings.

In modern times, it was used by Popes Pius VII, Pius X, Pius XI, and Pius XII. The Second Vatican Council made use of it together with "Mediatrix" in its Marian Chapter: "By her maternal charity, Mary cares for the brothers and sisters of her Son, who still journey on earth surrounded by dangers and difficulties, until they are led into the happiness of their true home. Therefore, the Blessed Virgin is invoked by the Church under the titles of Advocate, Auxiliatrix, Adjutrix, and Mediatrix. This, however, is to be understood in such a way that it neither takes away from nor adds anything to the dignity and efficaciousness of Christ the one Mediator."

The Council also gives an official explanation of how this title is to be understood: "No creature could ever be counted as equal with the Incarnate Word and Redeemer. Just as the priesthood of Christ is shared in various ways both by the ministers and by the faithful and as the one goodness of God is really communicated in different ways to His creatures, so also the unique mediation of the Redeemer does not exclude but rather gives rise to a manifold cooperation that is but a sharing in this one source. The Church does not hesitate to profess this subordinate role of Mary" (LG 62).

2. Associate

The term "associate" is largely a product of modern times and is intended to be a more generally acceptable term than Co-redemptrix in delineating Mary's function with respect to the Redemption worked by Christ her Son. It was championed by Pius XII, who used it in place of Co-redemptrix. Mary is the "noble associate of the Divine Redeemer" (Apostolic Constitution *Munificentissimus Deus*—On the Assumption).

This title was used by Vatican II as a substitute for Co-redemptrix: "The Blessed Virgin Mary was on this earth the virgin Mother of the Redeemer, and above all others and in a singular way the generous associate . . . of the Lord. She conceived, brought forth, and nourished Christ, she presented Him to the Father in the Temple, and she was united with Him by compassion as He died on the Cross. In this singular way she cooperated by her obedience, faith, hope, and burning love in the work of the Savior in giving back supernatural life to souls" (LG 61).

Although the word is admittedly vague with respect to what Mary actually did, it is a title that says something to contemporary people. An "associate" is someone who *works with* another—associate lawyer, associate professor, associate pastor. The associate *somehow* partakes in the work of the other. Thus, Mary actually shared in Christ's work of the Redemption. Indeed, she was an integral part of it—in God's plan it was through Mary that Christ would become man and be in a position to redeem humankind.

3. Blessed Mother

It is a cherished American custom to call the Mother of Jesus "our Blessed Mother." The following explanation was set forth by the Bishops of the United States in their Pastoral Letter on the Blessed Virgin Mary (nos. 70-71).

In many respects, this title can be explained in the same way as "Mediatrix." Still, it has its own special value. "Mother" belongs to the language of the transmission of life. The reference here is to our life in Christ. Saint Paul's familiar comparison likens the Church to a human body, with Christ as Head, and the faithful as its members. Like the Savior's parable of the vine and the branches, the image of the Church as "body of Christ" is a graphic reminder that the same life links members to Head, branches to Vine.

From earliest Christian times, the Church was regarded as "Mother Church." Gradually Mary's relationship to the sons and daughters of the Church came to be regarded also as that of "spiritual Mother." Physically mother of Christ the Head, Mary is spiritually mother of the members of Christ. She is mother of all human beings, for Christ died for all. She is especially the *Mother of the faithful*, or as Pope Paul VI proclaimed during the Second Vatican Council, she is "Mother of the Church."

It is important to understand what is meant by the title "Our Blessed Mother." Mary is spiritual mother of human beings not solely because she was physical mother of the Savior. Nonetheless, the full understanding of Mary's Motherhood of Jesus contains also the secret of her spiritual Motherhood of Christ's brothers and sisters. This secret is the truth already given in the Gospels and constantly stressed ever since in Christian thought and piety. Mary consented in *faith* to become the Mother of Jesus.

The Second Vatican Council was in the stream of the constant tradition of the Church when it said that Mary received the Word of God into her heart and her body at the Angel's announcement and thereby brought life to the world (LG 53). She conceived in her heart, with her whole being, before she conceived in her womb. First came Mary's faith, then her motherhood. Faith is the key also to the spiritual Motherhood of Mary. By her faith she became the perfect example of what the Gospels mean by "spiritual Motherhood."

In the preaching of the Savior, His "mother" is whoever hears God's word and keeps it. All who truly follow Christ become "mothers" of Christ, for by their faith they bring Him to birth in others.

As a perfect disciple, the Virgin Mary heard the Word of God and kept it, to the lasting joy of the Messianic generations who call her blessed. It is the Catholic conviction that in her present union with the risen Christ, our Blessed Mother is still solicitous for our welfare, still desirous that we become more like Jesus, her firstborn. The Mother of Jesus wishes all her other children, all men and all women, to reach that maturity of the fullness of Christ (Eph 4:13; Col 1:28).

4. Daughter of Zion

See p. 101.

5. Exemplar

The Second Vatican Council recognized Mary as a most excellent exemplar of the Church in the order of faith, charity, and perfect union with Christ (LG 63). This refers most especially to that interior disposition with which the Church, closely associated with her Lord, invokes Christ and through Him worships the eternal Father (SC 7).

The characteristics of this exemplarity of Mary are:

(1) *Attentive faith.* Mary received the Word of God with faith. This was the basis of all her actions as well as her prerogatives and privileges. The Church does the same, especially in the Liturgy when with faith she accepts, proclaims, and venerates the Word of God, distributes it to the faithful as the bread of life, and in the light of that Word examines the signs of the times and interprets and lives the events of history.

(2) *Prayer.* Mary prayed during her visit to Elizabeth (Lk 1:46-55), at Cana when she informed her Son of the wedding couple's need of wine (Jn 2:1-12), and before the coming of the Holy Spirit at Pentecost when she remained in prayer with the Apostles (Acts 1:14). The Church also prays, day after day presenting to the Father the needs of her children and praising the Lord unceasingly (SC 83).

(3) *Virgin-Mother.* Mary became a mother without human help, but solely by the power of the Holy Spirit (Lk 1:35). This was a miraculous Motherhood, set up by God as the exemplar of the fruitfulness of the Virgin-Church, which herself becomes a mother by the power of God in bringing forth children to the spiritual life through baptism.

(4) *Gift-Offering.* Mary offered Jesus in the Temple (Lk 2:22-35) and on Calvary (Jn 19:25). The Church offers the Eucharistic Sacrifice, the memorial of Christ's Death and Resurrection, every Sunday down through the ages.

However, Mary is not only an example for the whole Church in the exercise of Divine worship but also a teacher of the spiritual life for individual Christians. She is above all the example of that worship that consists in making one's life an offering to God. This is an ancient and ever new doctrine that each individual can hear again by heeding the Church's teaching and by meditating on Mary's "yes" to God (*"Let it be done to me as you say"*: Lk 1:38). For that "yes" is a lesson of obedience to the will of the Father, which is the way and means of one's sanctification.

6. Handmaid (Servant) of the Lord

The title "handmaid" or "servant" is the one applied by Mary to herself at the time of the Annunciation: *"I am the servant [handmaid] of the Lord. . . . He has looked with favor on His lowly servant"* (Lk 1:38, 48).

The Greek term used in the Gospel, *doule,* is the feminine form of a common Old Testament designation for "slave" or "servant" of God. It was a title of honor for God's messengers in the Old Testament and for Paul and the Apostles in the New.

Mary used it of herself to indicate her total openness to the work of salvation held out to her. She pledged her positive cooperation in the redeeming Incarnation. Hence, this title indicates certainty of God's transcendence and total obedience to His saving plan.

In this sense, Mary is in the line of God's servants: Israel, Abraham (Gn 18:3), and the Poor of Yahweh.

Finally, Mary's "handmaid" is an echo of the Servant of Yahweh par excellence, Jesus Christ—the suffering Servant Who became obedient to death in order to bring about God's salvation.

At the same time, the title "handmaid" highlights Mary's role as a model of all Christians. Each Christian is to be *"the servant of the Lord"* (Lk 1:38)—by humility, poverty, service to Christ, and courage in following the suffering Christ.

The title handmaid "places Mary among the lowly, the poor, and the sick. It places her at our level—indeed, at the lowest place among us. . . . Her social status was the most modest one, a woman of the people, we might say. She had no external qualities that distinguished her, even though a royal dynasty had ended right in her person. She belonged to the vast common multitudes. . . . 'Handmaid' teaches that we came from God and are subject to Him: 'He has looked with favor on His lowly servant.' He has endowed her with favors and brought her to supreme glory" (Pope Paul VI).

7. Help of Christians

From the very beginning, Christians have taken refuge in Our Lady in times of adversity—trials, heresies, persecutions, and wars—as shown by the 3rd-century prayer "We Fly to Your Patronage" (q.v.). The reason is not hard to determine and was spelled out by Pope Leo XIII:

"The Blessed Virgin was exempt from the stain of original sin and chosen to be the Mother of God. For this very reason she was associated with Him in the work of human salvation and enjoys favor and power with her Son greater than any human being or angel has attained or could attain.

"And since Mary's greatest joy is to grant her help and assistance to those who call upon her, there is no reason to doubt not only that she wishes to answer the prayers of the universal Church but also that she is eager to do so."

Hence, it was altogether natural for Mary to be given the title "Help of Christians" by the faithful of every century. It became an official title of Mary when it was inserted in the Litany of Loreto in 1571 by Pope Pius V in gratitude for the Christian victory over the Turkish forces at the Battle of Lepanto. It also commemorated Mary's role in overcoming the Albigensian Heresy and its fearful side effects that raged in the 12th century.

In 1815, Pope Pius VII established the liturgical feast of Our Lady Help of Christians in thanksgiving for his safe return to Rome after five years' captivity at Savona. It was assigned to May 24 for various local calendars, including that of Rome.

Although this feast has never become mandatory for the whole Church, it is celebrated in many places, especially under the impulsion of the Salesian Fathers. It is the patronal feast of Australia and New Zealand.

8. Immaculate Conception

See p. 190.

9. Mediatrix

See p. 319.

10. Mother of the Church

See p. 332.

11. Mother of God

See p. 332.

12. Mother of Mercy

One of the most cherished titles of Mary is that of "Mother of Mercy," which also appears in the Litany of Loreto. As a matter of fact, Saint Alphonsus claimed it was Mary who—in a vision to Saint Bridget—gave this title to herself: "I am the Queen of heaven and the Mother of Mercy. I am the joy of the just and the door through which sinners come to God.

"There are no sinners on earth so unfortunate as to be beyond my mercy. . . . There are no persons so abandoned by God that they will not return to Him and find mercy, if they invoke my aid. I am called by all the Mother of Mercy. It is my Son's mercy toward human beings that has made me merciful too. I am compassionate toward all and eager to help sinners."

This title goes back at least to the 3rd century. A new text of the prayer "We Fly to Your Patronage" (q.v.) has the word "mercy" in place of "patronage." From then on, many Saints have bestowed this title on Our Lady. She is also called "Mother of Mercy" in a widely-used prayer since the Middle Ages, "Hail Holy Queen." At the same time, many Saints have bestowed this title on Mary: Odo, Peter Damian, and Bernard, among others.

As Saint Thomas Aquinas said, "When the Blessed Virgin conceived the Eternal Word in her womb and gave Him birth, she obtained half the Kingdom of God. She became Queen of *Mercy* and her Son remained King of *Justice.*"

13. Queen of Peace

The invocation "Queen of Peace" was inserted in the Litany of the Blessed Virgin by Pope Benedict XV in 1917 when the world was being torn apart by war. The Pope specifically related this act to the long-hoped-for peace in that day: "May this pious and ardent invocation rise to Mary, the Mother of Mercy who is all-powerful in grace! . . . May her loving and most merciful solicitude be moved to obtain for this convulsed world the peace so greatly desired! And may the ages yet to come remember the efficacy of Mary's intercession and the greatness of her blessing to her supplicants!"

Thus, the title "Queen of Peace" is a logical outgrowth of the title "Help of Christians." By helping Christians, Mary enables them to overcome their adversaries and bring about peace. But this peace does not mean unpunished wrongdoing or unbridled freedom. It means an orderly living together, guided and commanded by the will of God. It also means orderly living within oneself in accord with God's will. As Queen, Mary brings to the world the presence of Christ's truth, justice, and love.

Mary brought forth the Prince of Peace (Is 9:5) amidst angelic chants of peace for all human beings. Peace is a blessing of Christ and does not come from the world; to pursue peace entails suffering and persecution (Mt 10:34-39). It is peace of heart that puts anxiety and fear to flight, since it is the fruit of the complete teaching brought us by the Holy Spirit and partakes of the joy of heavenly hope (cf. Jn 14:26-28).

Mary enables her clients to practice truth, justice, and love and so attain the inner peace of Christ for themselves. This is then manifested in a universal peace, without wars, disorders, or injustices, in which the Kingdom of Christ is propagated without barriers of any kind.

14. Seat of Wisdom

The title "Seat of Wisdom" is an ancient one whose beginnings can be seen in the early Fathers, like Augustine. It was reinforced by the Church's application of passages from the

Wisdom Books to Mary in the Liturgy: "The very words with which the Sacred Scriptures speak of Uncreated Wisdom and set forth His eternal origin, the Church, both in its ecclesiastical offices and in its Liturgy, has been wont to apply likewise to the origin of the Blessed Virgin, inasmuch as God, by one and the same decree, had established the origin of Mary and the Incarnation of Divine Wisdom" (Pius IX).

However, it was during the Middle Ages that this title took hold and became part of the Litany of the Blessed Virgin. Mary has this title because the Son of God, Who is called in Sacred Scripture the Word and Wisdom of God, once dwelt in her, and then after His birth from her was carried in her arms and seated on her lap in His first years. Hence, in Cardinal Newman's words, since she was "the human throne of Him Who reigns in Heaven, she is called the Seat of Wisdom. . . . For thirty continuous years [she] saw and heard Him . . . [and was] able to ask Him any questions that she wished explained, knowing that the answers she received were from the Eternal God."

Mary kept the Divine Mysteries in her heart (Lk 2:19-51). She came to know Jesus in a most singular way. Indeed, as Pius X stated, "sharing as she did the thoughts and the secret wishes of Christ, she may be said to have lived the very life of her Son. Hence nobody ever knew Christ so profoundly as she did, and nobody can ever be more competent as a guide and teacher of the knowledge of Christ."

Mary is the "throne of Wisdom," the "source of Wisdom," the "shrine of Wisdom," and the "sanctuary of Wisdom." Accordingly, she knows us and and our needs perfectly: "Nobody knows and comprehends so well as she everything that concerns us: what help we need in life; what dangers, public and private, threaten our welfare; what difficulties and evils surround us; above all how fierce is the fight we wage with the ruthless enemies of our salvation" (Leo XIII).

15. Complete List of Titles

Besides the major titles of Mary mentioned above, there are a host of others. Some are found in the Litany of the

Blessed Virgin. Others are given by various authors. Palmer gave the following titles in his book, *Mary in the Documents of the Church.*

Adam's Deliverance
Advocate of Eve
Advocate of Sinners
All Chaste
All Fair and Immaculate
All Good
Aqueduct of Grace
Archetype of Purity and Innocence
Ark Gilded by the Holy Spirit
Ark of the Covenant
Blessed among Women
Bridal Chamber of the Lord
Bride of the Canticle
Bride of the Father
Bride of Heaven
Bride Unbrided
Chosen before the Ages
Comfort of Christians
Conceived without Original Sin
Consoler of the Afflicted
Co-Redemptrix
Court of the Eternal King
Created Temple of the Creator
Crown of Virginity
Daughter of Men
David's Daughter
Deliverer of Christian Nations
Deliverer from All Wrath
Destroyer of All Heresies
Dispenser of the Gifts of the Redemption

Dispenser of Grace
Dove of Simplicity
Dwelling Place for Christ
Dwelling Place of God
Dwelling Place of the Illimitable
Dwelling Place of the Spirit
Dwelling Place Meet for God
Earth Unsown
Earth Untouched and Virginal
Eastern Gate
Ever Green and Fruitful
Ever Virgin
Eve's Tears Redeeming
Exalted above the Angels
Fleece of Heavenly Rain
Flower of Jesse's Root
Formed without Stain
Forth-bringer of the Ancient of Days
Forth-bringer of God
Forth-bringer of the Tree of Life
Fountain of Living Water
Fountain Sealed
Free from Every Stain
Full of Grace
Garden Enclosed
God's Eden
God's Olive Tree
God's Vessel
Handmaid of the Lord
Healing Balm of Integrity

Helper of All Who Are in Danger
Holy in Soul and Body
Hope of Christians
House Built by Wisdom
Immaculate
Immaculate Conception
Immaculate Heart
Immaculate Mother
Immaculate Virgin
Incorruptible Wood of the Ark
Inventrix of Grace
Inviolate
Joseph's spouse
Kingly Throne
King's Mother
Lady Most Chaste
Lady Most Venerable
Lamp Unquenchable
Life-giver to Posterity
Light Cloud of Heavenly Rain
Lily among Thorns
Living Temple of the Deity
Loom of the Incarnation
Market Place for Salutary Exchange
Mediatrix
Mediatrix and Counciliatrix
Mediatrix of All Graces
Mediatrix of Salvation
Mediatrix to the Mediator
Minister of Life
More Beautiful Than Beauty
More Glorious Than Paradise
More Gracious Than Grace
More Holy Than the Cherubim, the Seraphim and the Entire Angelic Host

Morning Star
Mother and Virgin
Mother of Christians
Mother of Christ's Members
Mother of God
Mother of Jesus
Mother of Men
Mother of the Mystical Body
Mother of Our Head
Mother of Wisdom
My Body's Healing
My Soul's Saving
Nature's Recreation
Nature's Restoration
Neck of the Mystical Body
Never-fading Wood
New Eve
Nourisher of God and Man
Olive Tree of the Father's Compassion
Only Bridge of God to Men
Our Own Sweet Mother
Paradise Fenced against the Serpent
Paradise of Innocence and Immortality
Paradise of the Second Adam
Paradise Planted by God
Patroness and Protectress
Perfume of Faith
Preserved from All Sin
Protectress from All Hurt
Queen of Creation
Queen of Heaven
Queen of Heaven and Earth
Queen of Martyrs
Queen Unconquered
Refuge of Sinners

Refuge in Time of Danger
Reparatrix
Reparatrix of Her Parents
Reparatrix of the Lost World
Rich in Mercy
Rose Ever Blooming
Sanctuary of the Holy Spirit
Scepter of Orthodoxy
Second Eve
Sister and Mother
Source of Virginity
Spotless Dove of Beauty
Star That Bore the Sun
Suppliant for Sinners
Surpassing Eden's Garden
Surpassing the Heavens
Surpassing the Seraphim
Sweet Flowering of Gracious Mercy
Tabernacle of God
Tabernacle of the Word
Temple Divine
Temple Indestructible
Temple of the Lord's Body

Throne of the King
Tower Unassailable
Treasure of the World
Treasure-house of Life
Treasury of Immortality
Undefiled
Undefiled Treasure of Virginity
Undug Well of Remission's Waters
Unlearned in the Ways of Eve
Unploughed Field of Heaven's Bread
Unwatered Vineyard of Immortality's Wine
Victor over the Serpent
Virgin
Virgin Inviolate
Virgin Most Pure
Virgin Mother
Wedded to God
Woman Clothed with the Sun
Workshop of the Incarnation

A. Buono

MARIAN TYPOLOGY

[128-130]

S<small>EE</small>   *Marian Symbols*

1. Nature and Purpose of Typology

TYPOLOGY comes under the heading of the interpretation and the senses of Sacred Scripture. There are three general senses of Scripture that have traditionally been utilized in the Church—two are authentic senses of Scripture and one is not.

(1) The *literal* or *grammatical* sense is the meaning conveyed directly and immediately by the words of the text when

they are interpreted in accord with the ordinary rules of language. It is also called the *historical* sense.

(2) The *spiritual* or *typical* sense is a meaning that goes beyond the literal sense but is based on it. Therefore, when a text has a typical sense, it really has *two* meanings. For example, the bronze serpent in the Old Testament (Nm 21:8f) served as a type of the saving power of Christ on the Cross (Jn 3:14). The only way that we know that a text has a typical sense is through revelation.

(3) The *accommodated* sense is not a true Biblical sense. It is an "accommodation" of the Scriptural text to a subject that neither the sacred writer nor the Holy Spirit meant to indicate. This sense may, however, be used for purposes of edification— and the New Testament writers, the Church Fathers, and even the Church in the Liturgy make splendid use of it. When used in the right way, typology serves to enhance the understanding of the subject in question.

The typology in this entry takes its start from the second sense just mentioned but is used in a very *broad way* that is equivalent to the third sense.

2. Old Testament Persons as Types of Mary

In Romans 5:14, Adam is called "that type of the man who is to come," that is, Christ, and in 1 Corinthians 10:11 the Israelites sojourning in the desert are taken as a type of the Christians sojourning on earth. Typology sees the foreshadowings of events and persons of the New Testament in the events and persons of the Old.

The Fathers of the Church took great delight in finding types—sometimes overdoing it. But the principle remains valid. The Fathers applied many person-types to Mary. They pointed among others to women who while far below her in holiness foreshadowed her as liberators of their fellow humans on earth: Sarah, Rachel, Miriam, Deborah, Jael, Judith, and Esther.

Sarah was the wife of Abraham to whom God had promised an innumerable posterity despite the fact that she was childless and far beyond child-bearing age. Through the power of God she brought forth a son, Isaac, who insured the continuation of God's saving plan (Gn 17:1—21:7). Sarah was thus a type of Mary by the superhuman manner of her childbearing. Just as Sarah gave birth to Isaac, head of the Chosen People, so Mary gave birth to Christ the Redeemer, Founder of the Children of God, the Church.

Rachel possessed an earthly beauty that drew Jacob to her and impelled him to serve her father Laban for 14 years so that he might win her as his wife (Gn 29:1-30). Hence, Rachel is a type of Mary's surpassing beauty of soul, which is extolled by the Church's age-old prayer: "You are all-beautiful, O Mary, and there is no stain of sin in you." Just as Rachel's beauty attracted Jacob, so Mary's beauty of soul captured the heart of God Who chose her to be the earthly Mother of His Son Jesus.

Miriam, the sister of Moses, saved him from the cruel death that the Pharaoh had decreed for all male Hebrew babies (Ex 2:1-8). She also possessed the gift of prophecy (Ex 15:20-21) and was at the head of the women as one of the leaders of the crossing of the Red Sea (Mi 6:4), afterward chanting the refrain to the magnificent hymn of thanksgiving (Ex 15:20-21). In like manner, Mary was endowed with the gift of prophecy and was the immaculately pure leader of all virgins. Associated with her Son in His conquest of Satan, she helped her children overthrow the bondage of sin and intoned a hymn of thanksgiving by her *Magnificat.*

Deborah, a prophetess and one of the greatest of the Judges of Israel (Jgs 4:4), was the inspirer of the Israelite reaction against the 20-year oppression of Jabin, Canaanite King of Hazor, carried out by Sisera. The tribes of Israel had not won a war for 175 years when she gathered together an army of 10,000 men and gave it to Barac, who put the enemy to flight (Jgs 4:4ff). Sisera took refuge in the home of Jael where he fell into an exhausted sleep and was executed by the Hebrew woman (Jgs 4:17ff). Deborah responded with her canticle of victory (Jgs 5:1ff).

Deborah is called the mother of Israel and Jael is acclaimed as blessed among women (Jgs 5:7, 24). They are thus types of Mary who through her Divine Son conquered Satan, relentless enemy of her people, became the Mother of the faithful, and is called blessed among women.

Judith was a widow of Israel, who combined great beauty with uncommon goodness of soul (Jdt 8:7-8). When her city of Bethulia was under siege by Holofernes and in danger of giving in, she rallied the people and outwitted the monarch, thus saving God's chosen. They blessed her with the words: "*You are the glory of Judah, the surpassing joy of Israel; you are the splendid boast of our people*" (Jdt 15:9), and she sang a song of praise to God.

The memorable words of praise directed at Judith by her people are directed to Mary by the Church, for she is the true glory of Judah and the surpassing joy of Israel. She crushed the head of Satan, the implacable enemy of the human race, and freed humanity from bondage forever. She also sang a song of praise to God.

Esther was Queen of King Ahasuerus (Est 2:17). By her great courage and skill she averted the extermination of the Jews that had been plotted by the wicked Haman. Filled with faith in God, Esther went before the king at the risk to her very life and pleaded for her people. Her charm and beauty saved her and the Hebrew people. Hence, Esther is a type of Mary who won God's love by the splendor of her goodness, drew Him into her heart, and saved her people from the devil by the Redeemer Whom she bore, while she became Queen of the World in the process.

3. Old Testament Objects as Types of Mary

Mary is also seen as foreshadowed by many of the objects of the Old Testament. All the praises heaped on the *kingdom of Israel* or *the Church* are applied to her. Jerusalem is itself a type of Mary: "*Glorious things are said of you, O city of God*" (Ps 87:3).

Mary is foreshadowed by the Garden of Eden, Noah's Ark, the Ark of the Covenant, Jacob's ladder, the rod of Aaron, Gideon's fleece, and the Temple of Solomon, among others.

The *Garden of Eden* as planted by God was a land of grace, a paradise of pleasure, where God placed the first man (Gn 2:8-10). This hallowed land is a type of Mary, watered by God with superabundant grace. This new Eden (Mary) is holier and more divine than the old Eden, which had Adam dwelling there. In Mary, it is God Who has made His dwelling, filling her with His grace.

Noah's Ark (Gn 6:14—8:19) was the instrument for safeguarding the earthly life of the human race. Mary—through her Son Jesus—is the instrument for safeguarding the eternal life of the human race. The Ark floated on the waters that were inundating the earth; Mary floated on the waters of concupiscence and sin. The earth was repeopled by those who took refuge in the Ark. Heaven is peopled by those who take refuge in Mary.

The Ark of the Covenant (Ex 26:33; 40:20) points to Mary in a variety of ways, as set forth by Saint Ambrose: "The Ark contained the Tablets of the Law; Mary contained in her womb the Heir of the Testament. The Ark bore the Law; Mary bore the Gospel. The Ark made the voice of God heard; Mary gave us the very Word of God. The Ark shone forth with the purest of gold; Mary shone forth both inwardly and outwardly with the splendor of virginity. The gold that adorned the Ark came from the interior of the earth; the gold with which Mary shone forth came from the mines of heaven."

Jacob's Ladder also foreshadows Mary. On the way to Mesopotamia, the patriarch Jacob had a dream one night. He saw a ladder extending from the earth to heaven, and by it Angels ascended and descended (Gn 28:12-15). Mary is the ladder by which the Son of God descended from heaven to earth and assumed human nature. And on this ladder He led all creatures back to union with the Father.

As the Lord commanded, the *rod (or staff) of Aaron* was brought into the Lord's presence in the Tent and put together with the rods of the eleven other heads of Israel's Tribes. It alone sprouted and gave forth fruit (with shoots and blossoms) despite the fact that it had no human help—no roots or nourishment (Nm 17:16-24). Mary is God's *rod* who became the living temple of the Holy Spirit and without human interven- tion carried to term and brought forth the blessed fruit that gives spiritual life to all—Jesus Christ.

Gideon's fleece also points to Mary. God used the fleece to give the Judge Gideon a sign that He was with him. On the first morning, dew was on the fleece alone while all the neigh- boring ground was dry. The next morning, the fleece was dry and the ground was wet (Jgs 6:36-40). Mary is God's fleece, and the dew that wets it in the silence of the night represents the descent of the Word of God into her most pure womb. Mary "conceived the Lord and was entirely imbued with Him as with a sweet dew, without any harm to her virginity" (Saint Ambrose).

The *Temple of Solomon* was the glory of the ancient world. The King adorned it lavishly, with gold, silver, rare wood, and precious stones for God was to reside there. Solomon placed within the Temple the Ark of the Covenant containing the Tablets of the Law (1 Kgs 16—17). In the new dispensation, God adorned Mary as His Temple—with all the riches of His grace and virtues. She is the Temple enclosing the real Holy of Holies within herself—she is the Temple of the Lord.

A. Buono

MARIOLOGICAL SOCIETIES   [971]

SEE   *Marian Classics*   *Marian Congresses*
       Marian Confraternities

THE growth of the science of Mariology (q.v.) has brought with it the spread of societies for fostering Marian studies. Most of the large Catholic countries now have such organiza- tions, which are open not only to those actively engaged in Marian teaching and Marian studies but also to any persons who wish to contribute to the aims of the societies.

Annual conventions of the societies feature lectures and discussions on Marian topics. They are then published *in Pro-*

ceedings. In the United States, the society is called the Mariological Society of America and it publishes a journal called *Marian Studies.*

A. Buono

MARIOLOGY

[971]

SEE *Magisterium (Documents of)*

MARIOLOGY is that part of the science of systematic theology that treats of the Mother of God. After the study of God Himself, no other is nobler and worthier than that of His Mother. This is so because next to God and the sacred Humanity of Christ, Mary holds the highest place among creatures in the order of grace and glory. Owing to her central position in the Divine Plan, the study of her mission and privileges will necessarily deepen our appreciation of the other phases of Catholic theology.

1. Division

The contents of the mariological tract may be logically divided as follows:

Part One—Mary's singular mission, namely, her Divine Motherhood, with its corollaries: her Spiritual Motherhood, her universal mediation, and her universal queenship. An introduction to this part would be a discussion of her unique predestination.

Part Two—Mary's prerogatives: Immaculate Conception, fullness of grace, freedom from actual sin, perpetual virginity, Mary's knowledge, her immunity from corruption, anticipated resurrection, and bodily Assumption.

2. Sources

Sacred Scripture and Tradition constitute the twofold source whence we may draw the various truths concerning Mary. They may be found therein either formally expressed (explicitly or implicitly) or only virtually.

(A) *Biblical* references to Mary are the Old Testament prophecies (Gn 3:15, Is 7:14, Jer 31:21, Mi 5:2-3), and particularly the New Testament accounts of the Annunciation (Lk 1:26-38), the Visitation (Lk 1:39-56), the Angel's apparition to Joseph assuring him of Mary's virginity (Mt 1:18-25), the Birth of our Lord (Lk 2:1-7), the purification of Mary (Lk 2:22-38), the Wedding Feast at Cana (Jn 2:1-11), Mary's Presence at Calvary (Jn 19:25-27), Saint Paul's reference to the Divine Motherhood (Gal 4:4), and Saint John's vision of the Woman clothed with the sun (Rv 12:1-18).

(B) By *Sacred Tradition* we mean the body of revealed truths not contained in the Bible, but transmitted from generation to generation under the guidance of the Holy Spirit and the Magisterium of the Church. These truths are communicated to us through the writings of the Fathers and Doctors of the Church, the theologians and Catholic writers of subsequent centuries, the liturgical books of the Church, etc.

3. Magisterium

The positive data furnished by both the Bible and Sacred Tradition must be interpreted in complete accordance with the ecclesiastical Magisterium, i.e., the Pope and the Bishops in communion with him.

It is the living Magisterium of the Church that constitutes the proximate norm of faith; it authoritatively interprets the genuine meaning of Divine revelation; it alone—not the theologians—has the final word on the subject.

4. Primary Principle

By "primary principle" we mean a fundamental truth that furnishes the ultimate reason for the various theses of a given science. Theologians disagree widely as to what is the primary principle of Mariology. According to the majority, the primary principle is the Divine Motherhood. Others say: Mary's role as Second Eve (or Co-redemptrix). A third group focuses on our Lady's bridal motherhood. The preference of not a few is: Mary as the Mother of the Whole Christ. O. Semmelroth opts for: Mary as type of the Church, and A. Müller favors: Mary's plenitude of grace.

Personally, we endorse the first opinion as being more in conformity with Pius XII's 1954 Encyclical *Fulgens corona* ("The Radiant Crown"), commemorating the centenary of the dogmatic definition of the Immaculate Conception.

5. Contemporary Mariological Movement

We refer here to the concerted efforts of Catholic scholars to promote a deeper appreciation of Mary's prerogatives, especially from a scientific point of view. The movement owes its inspiration primarily to the dogmatic definition of the Immaculate Conception in 1854 and to the numerous Marian Encyclicals of Leo XIII, followed by other important documents of Saint Pius X, Benedict XV, Pius XI, Pius XII, Paul VI, and John Paul II.

Another factor that has contributed considerably to the progress of serious Mariology has been the critical edition of many patristic and liturgical texts, e.g., the Oriental Patrology prepared by Graffin-Nau, the Berlin edition of the Greek Fathers, the Vienna edition of the Latin Fathers, the Blumebreves collection of medieval liturgical hymns, etc. These valuable sets have enabled scholars to eliminate a good deal of spurious documentation widely exploited in the past.

As an evidence of the vitality of Marian studies in recent years we may point to the many *Mariological Congresses*, both national and international, organized by the International Marian Academy headed by the late Charles Balic, O.F.M. (d. 1977); the founding of *Mariological Societies* in Belgium (1931), in France (1934), in Spain (1940), in Canada (1948), in the United States of America (1950), and finally in Germany (1952).

Mention should be made also of the various *Marian Libraries* that facilitate and stimulate research among students of Mariology. The more important of these are: the one kept at the International College of the Servites in Rome, and the one at the University of Dayton, Ohio, organized in 1943.

Finally, we must note the publication of scientific journals exclusively devoted to Mariology. The first to appear was *Marianum*, edited by the Servite Fathers in Rome since 1939. It was followed in 1951 by *Ephemerides Mariologicae*, published by the Claretian Fathers in Madrid. Both magazines publish occasional articles in English. Under this same head we may recall the annual proceedings of the Mariological Societies mentioned before. The more important of these are: *Etudes Mariales*, of the French Mariological Society, since 1935; *Estudios Marianos*, of the Spanish Mariological Society, since 1942; and *Marian Studies*, of the Mariological Society of America, since 1950. The last-mentioned item is available from the Marian Library at the University of Dayton, Ohio.

Even a superficial glance at the contemporary renaissance of Marian studies convinces us that Mariology has ceased to be a mere appendix to the theological tract on the Incarnation, as it was for centuries, and has become a highly important treatise in itself.

6. Bibliography

The literature on the various theological questions concerning Mary is quite extensive. Abundant information will be found in J. B. Carol, O.F.M. (ed.), *Mariology*, 3 vols. (Milwaukee, Wis.: Bruce Publ., 1954, 1957, 1961) and also in J. B. Carol, O. F. M., *Fundamentals of Mariology* (New York: Benziger Bros., 1956). The *New Catholic Encyclopedia* (1967) has a few informative entries on Mary. Generally reliable, though not up to date: Pohle-Preuss, *Mariology* (St. Louis, Mo.: Herder, 1926) and Scheeben-Geukers, *Mariology*, 2 vols. (St. Louis, Mo.: Herder, 1946-1947).

J. B. Carol

MARK (GOSPEL OF SAINT)   [124-127]

SEE   *Life of Mary*   *New Testament*

THE Marian episodes in the Gospels share in the revelatory character of the events of Christ's life as well as His words and deeds, which attained their greatest light with the Easter event. The latter became for the Apostles the hermeneutic criterion for understanding the Christian Mystery. Starting from the Easter event the apostolic communities accomplished a twofold journey. They passed from a Christology focused on the Paschal Mystery (cf. the kerygmatic discourses of Acts; 2:22-24; 3:13-15; 4:10-12; 5:30-32; 10:37-42; 13:23-31) to a Christology enlarged to include the other periods of Christ's life.

Mark announces Christ in the span of time from the Baptism to the Ascension. Matthew and Luke fill in the period of His Hidden Life with the Infancy Narratives. John contemplates Christ in His preexistence as the Word of God and in His relationship with the cosmos and the history of Israel. In this enlarged Christology, especially in responding to the problem of the origin of Jesus, we encounter Mary, His Virgin Mother. The interest in her does not arise because of properly Marian reasons but for reasons of a Christological order, that is, as part and consequence of the deepening of the Mystery of Christ.

Very little about Mary appears in Mark. When she does appear, it is in a context of the kenosis of her Son, Whose greatness is hidden. Thus, she appears to be linked with the familial clan that is hostile to Jesus (Mk 3:21) or that is seeking Him according to a natural logic (Mk 3:31f). In any case, she participates in a family without glory and incapable of explaining the wisdom of the young Rabbi from Nazareth (Mk 6:3).

Mark calls Jesus a *carpenter* and *the Son of Mary* (6:3). Contrary to Jewish custom, which calls a man the son of his father, this expression may reflect Mark's own faith that *God* is the Father of Jesus (Mk 1:11; 8:38; 13:32; 14:36). Thus, this text is compatible with the Virgin Birth. At the same time, Mark also refers to the *"brothers and sisters"* of the Lord (6:3; 15:40; 15:47; 16:1). In Semitic usage, the terms "brother" and "sister" are applied not only to children of the same parents but also to nephews, nieces, cousins, half-brothers, and half-sisters. Hence, this too does not take away the Virgin Birth.

In Mark, as in Paul (Gal 4:4), Mary demonstrates the human aspect of Christ, His humble condition bereft of privileges, and the conflict toward which He is heading. His Mother proclaims the reality of the Incarnation of the Son and His full acceptance of the risk of history. *A. Buono*

MATTHEW (GOSPEL OF SAINT) [124-127]

SEE *Infancy Narratives* *New Testament*

COMPARED with Luke, Matthew says little about Mary. He does mention her presence at events that mark the Infancy of Jesus, but he is extremely reticent in regard to her inward experience. We do not find in him an account of Mary's calling, nor expression of her reaction or her prayer following the announcement of the Incarnation. Mary certainly is present in his Gospel, but in a reserved and effacing manner.

Nevertheless, brief as the references to Mary's presence are, we cannot fail to detect, behind the persistence with which Matthew speaks of *"the Child and His Mother"* (2:11, 13, 20, 21), a more profound mystery, not of mere proximity but of a certain *community of destiny.* To grasp the full meaning of the restrained and allusive "Mariology" in Matthew, we should view his account against that of Luke and bear in mind its particular literary form and fundamental theological intent.

1. Analogies and Contrasts: The Two Accounts of the Infancy

Even cursory comparison of Matthew's and Luke's accounts of Jesus' Infancy reveals differences of perspective and literary form. Since he is addressing himself to a community more properly of Jewish origin, Matthew speaks of the Child Jesus through a type of literary structure that was very common in ancient Judaism: i.e., the *midrash,* a narrative form *in which Scripture serves to illuminate a present situation.* Accordingly, there appear in Matthew's account several parallels to comparable accounts about the infancy of Moses. This selection of literary form as well as the selection of episodes is made with a view to Matthew's general purposes, which is to show that Jesus of Nazareth truly is *the Messiah, "Son of David"* (1:1, 16) and the *"Son of the living God"* (16:16; 27:54).

In comparison with the first chapters of Luke, chapters 1—2 of Matthew offer less abundant material and narrations that are more schematic. And whereas Luke leaves the role of Joseph more or less in the shadow so as to bring into relief the role of Mary, the perspective that prevails in Matthew is just the reverse. He views and presents the Infancy of Jesus primarily from the standpoint of Joseph. It is Joseph who is summoned and guided by heavenly visions; it is he who gives Jesus His Name and who takes and leads *the Child and His Mother* where he is told to take them.

This difference of viewpoint is not surprising if we consider the kind of audience for whom Matthew intended his Gospel. Addressing himself to a community for whom the Davidic ancestry of the Messiah assumed primordial importance, he wanted *to show how, in actual fact, Jesus gained insertion into the Davidic line,* namely through being received and accepted by Joseph, son of David. Joseph, then, is not a figurehead. It was through him that Jesus could take His place by every legal right in the history and tradition of a people. And he was a *just man,* who acted *in service of the Child and His Mother,* under the prompting of the revelations received.

But while noting these differences between Matthew and Luke, we must be impressed by their *accord on a fundamental fact,* to wit the *virginal conception of Jesus,* sign both of His Divine origin and of His insertion in the chosen people. And behind a theologically different writing we can also perceive a goodly number of correspondences or equivalences in themes, which make it possible to elucidate the accounts one by the other. Among the principal correspondences are:

(a) Importance of revealed information for understanding the events and taking action (in Matthew, the dreams; in Luke, the apparitions).

(b) Universalism of Jesus' mission (in Matthew, coming of the Magi, then establishment of Jesus in Galilee, cf. 4:18: *"heathen Galilee"*; in Luke, prayer of Simeon).

(c) Prefiguration of the Passion (in Matthew, flight to Egypt and massacre of the infants of Bethlehem; in Luke, prophecy of the "sword" and Jesus' going up to Jerusalem at Passover time).

(d) Fulfillment of the Scriptures.

In point of fact, the two accounts offer two different yet complementary views on the Mystery of Jesus, already symbolically made known in the events of His Infancy.

2. Continuity and Rupture: Theology of Matthew 1—2

At the head of his Gospel Matthew places a stately title with highly meaningful overtones for a Jewish audience: *Book of the origin of Jesus Christ, son of David, son of Abraham* (1:1). *"Book of the origin of . . ."* points implicitly—without accentuation—to his history that began with the first man (Gn 5:1). *"Son of Abraham . . .":* Matthew at once shows his interest in the history of a people, as being the history of a choice and a Covenant in which God holds the initiative. At the center and apex of this history, to bring it to its completion, is *"Jesus Christ, Son of David . . ."* i.e., JESUS, THE MESSIAH, promised and awaited.

In this way Matthew introduces us to the deepest aspects of the Mystery of Jesus. He presents Him first as having roots in history, prepared by the slow human maturations of generations that preceded Him, and as recapitulating for His part the history of the chosen people (sojourn in Egypt and "exodus," parallelism to Moses). It is in Him that the history that began with Abraham finds its essential meaning and its fulfillment. But Matthew immediately shows us another dimension of the person of Jesus: His Divine origin and His transcendence. Jesus comes *from somewhere else.* No one begot Him, but *He is begotten* (1:16), and by none other than *the Holy Spirit* (1:20). He does not come simply as one among many: Abraham, David, the others. He bears in Himself the fullness of the Holy Spirit (cf. Is 11:2). He is the One chosen and consecrated to give a new and definitive meaning to the history of Israel, "because *He will save His people from their sins"* (1:21).

By the same token, Matthew proposes a rereading of the Scriptures, under the command of the same dialectic: continuity and rupture. We know the importance given to the Scriptures by the Jews to whom Matthew was addressing himself. Consequently, it is not unexpected to see him turning frequently to the Scriptures in order to show that Jesus is the One foretold in them and the One in Whom they are fulfilled. More particularly, Matthew fashions each of the five episodes of his narrative around a Scriptural citation. Sometimes the Scriptural text is woven into the episode (1:23; 2:6); other times it closes the presentation (2:15, 18, 23).

It is true that in the process Matthew may arrange the texts in his own way or give them a sense we did not anticipate. But this very arrangement is indicative of his purpose. For him, *the Scriptures must be reread in the light of Jesus.* Henceforth, it is Jesus Who becomes the norm for interpreting the Scriptures, which acquire in Him a new and plenary sense: *"You have heard the commandment. . . . What I say to you is . . ."* (5:21-22, 27-28, 31-32, 33-34, 38-39, 43-44).

3. Continuity and Rupture: Approach to the Mystery of Mary

The figure of Mary is drawn against this extremely rich and evocative background and along the lines of the same perspective, "continuity and rupture."

On the one hand, Mary appears as also being *in continuity with the chosen people*:

—with the long line of intermediaries (1:1-17) that prepared the coming of Jesus;

—with the women who stand out in Israel's history because of God's free and unmerited intervention in their behalf, beyond every anticipation and every frontier (Tamar, Rahab, Ruth, the wife of Uriah);

—by reason of the fact that in her was fulfilled historically the prophecy of Immanuel (Is 7:14; Mt 1:23), which conveyed all the Messianic hope of Israel;

—in continuity with the experience of Israel, which she relived in a close association with the destiny of her Son (sojourn in Egypt and "exodus");

—in continuity, or rather in communion, with all who one day would form the true family of Jesus: *"Whoever does the will of My heavenly Father . . ."* (12:50).

But Matthew emphasizes just as strongly the radical *break* that occurred in Mary by expressly linking her participation in the Mystery of Christ to a gift of God and the Spirit. For example, in his genealogy, in which the human initiative is given prominence, when it comes to Mary he writes: *"Mary, of whom was born Jesus Who is called the Messiah"* (1:16). By employing the passive *"of whom was born Jesus,"* Matthew introduces us to the heart of the Mystery: Jesus is the fruit of God's gift, of His exclusive initiative. He is the fruit of the Spirit (1:18, 20). But the wording is also apt in regard to Mary. Her part in making the Incarnation a reality was most especially a mystery of grace, fruit of the freely-bestowed love of God and communion in the action of the Spirit. More and better than anyone, Mary could say: *"By God's grace I am what I am. This grace of His to me has not proved fruitless"* (1 Cor 15:10).

Lastly, although Matthew stresses the role of Joseph, it is clear from his account that Joseph himself is *in the service of a greater Mystery,* that of "the Child and His Mother." Certainly, his vocation concerned first of all the mission of Jesus, but it also meant acceptance of Mary's singular vocation and her exceptional association with the destiny of Jesus. Joseph also lent himself to the Mystery that was taking place in Mary: *"Do not be afraid to take Mary home as your wife"* (1:20).

It is perhaps in this sense of an exceptional association of Mary with the destiny of Jesus that we should understand Matthew's rather surprising remark concerning the adoration of the Magi: *"They found the Child with Mary His Mother"* (2:11)—doubly surprising because of the not less surprising silence on the presence of Joseph. Is there an unspoken meaning here, or a theological intuition of Matthew, to the effect that Mary would be the one who offered Jesus to the contemplation and adoration of the Magi, symbolizing all who seek God and receive Him in faith? It is not impossible—a similar intuition has inspired many "Madonnas and Child" and icons—even though such an interpretation pertains more to a mystical reading of the text than to a reading that is strictly exegetical.

J. P. Prévost

MEDIATRIX [968-970]

SEE   *Communion of Saints*   *Intercession*
      Co-Redemptrix

A "MEDIATOR" is one who stands between two persons or groups of persons either to facilitate an exchange of favors or, more often, to reconcile parties at variance. As applied to Mary, the title "Mediatrix" dates back to the 6th century in the East, and to the 9th century in the West. Since the 17th century it has been widely used by Catholics everywhere. Let us say a word about its precise meaning and its endorsement by the Magisterium, Catholic Tradition, and the Liturgy.

1. Meaning

Our Lady may be styled "Mediatrix" either (a) because, as worthy Mother of God and full of grace, she occupies a "middle" position between God and His creatures; or (b) because, together with Christ and under Him, she cooperated in the reconciliation of God and humankind while she was still on earth; or (c) because she distributes the graces that God bestows on His children. In whichever of these three meanings it may be taken, Mary's mediation must always be understood as being secondary to, and dependent on, Christ's primary and self-sufficient mediatorial role. Since the second phase mentioned above coincides with Mary's function as Co-Redemptrix, which is treated elsewhere in this Dictionary, our attention will now be focused exclusively on the third phase, namely, the dispensation of graces through Mary.

When we say that Our Lady is Mediatrix as dispenser of graces, we mean that all favors and blessings granted by God to His rational creatures are granted in virtue of and because of her intervention. Her action here has a universal dimension; it involves all celestial and human beings with the sole exception of Christ and Mary herself. Those whose existence preceded the temporal existence of Our Lady (for example, the Angels, Adam and Eve, etc.) received all their graces in view of her future merits and intercession which were, of course, present to God from all eternity, and indeed with a logical priority to their predestination. It involves also every supernatural favor (sanctifying and actual grace), and even blessings of the temporal order bearing some relation to the supernatural order. Mary does not, of course, "produce" the sanctifying grace we receive through the Sacraments. And yet she is involved even here, in the sense that the actual grace we need to receive the Sacraments worthily is given to us because of her intervention.

Catholic Tradition frequently refers to Our Lady as being the "channel," "aqueduct," or "treasurer" of Divine grace. These are, of course, metaphors and hence not to be understood in a literal sense, as if Mary were the *physical* instrument of grace. She isn't. The manner in which she exercises her role is, specifically, by way of intercession. It is not necessary that we explicitly implore her intercession in our prayers. But whether we mention her or not, it is through her that we receive whatever we receive. Since she is our loving Mother in the supernatural realm, she knows our needs and wishes to help us in all of them; and since she is the Mother of God, her prayer on our behalf cannot but be most powerful and efficacious.

2. Magisterium

Papal documents have frequently portrayed Mary as Mediatrix of all graces. Worthy of specific mention is the trenchant statement of Leo XIII in his Encyclical *Octobri Mense* (*On the Rosary*, Sept. 22, 1891): "It may be affirmed with . . . truth and precision that, by the will of God, absolutely no part

of that immense treasure of every grace that the Lord amasses
. . . is bestowed on us except through Mary." All subsequent
Popes have substantially echoed the same refrain, some more
explicitly than others.

During the Second Vatican Council, Mary's mediatorial
role became the object of considerable discussion. A large number of bishops favored declaring the doctrine a Dogma of the
Faith. Others, e.g., the Dutch bishops, objected to even the use
of the word "Mediatrix" for fear of unnecessarily provoking a
non-Catholic reaction. Some cited the Pauline passage to the
effect that *"there is* one *mediator of God and man, the man
Christ Jesus"* (1 Tim 2:5)—forgetting that the same Saint Paul
who wrote those words, on another occasion referred to Moses
also as a mediator (Gal 3:19).

At any rate, after a lengthy argumentation pro and con,
the Council adopted the following innocuous text: "Therefore,
the Blessed Virgin is invoked by the Church under the titles of
Advocate, Auxiliatrix, Adjutrix, and *Mediatrix*" (LG 62). The
Council made it clear that it did not wish to settle legitimate
theological controversies, and that theologians were free to
continue adhering to different viewpoints (LG 54). The Council did stress that the titles just mentioned "are to be so understood that they neither take away nor add anything to the dignity and efficacy of Christ the one Mediator." And a bit further, we have this highly significant statement: "The unique
mediation of the Redeemer does *not* exclude but rather gives
rise among creatures to a manifold cooperation that is but a
sharing in this unique source" (LG 62). Indeed, the Angels, the
Saints, and the priests of the New Testament can all be regarded as mediators between God and humans in a true,
though secondary, sense.

3. Tradition

The early Fathers and ecclesiastical writers taught the
doctrine of Mary's mediation only implicitly, e.g., by stating
that she was the Second Eve, the mother of all the living, and
the Savior's associate in the process of our supernatural reconciliation. In the Middle Ages, it was mainly through the influ-

ence of Saint Bernard of Clairvaux (d. 1153) that our doctrine became familiar to an ever-widening sector in the Catholic Church. His words are clear and to the point: "God has willed that we should have nothing that did not pass through the hands of Mary." Later on, the Franciscan Saint Bernardine of Siena (d. 1444) was just as unequivocal: "I do not hesitate to say that she [Mary] has received a certain jurisdiction over all graces. . . . They are administered through her hands to whom she pleases, when she pleases, as she pleases, and as much as she pleases." In the 18th century the leading defender of this Catholic teaching was Saint Alphonsus Liguori (d. 1787) through his perennial "best-seller," *The Glories of Mary.* Among the prominent champions of the doctrine in more recent times, Msgr. J. Lebon, J. Bittremieux, and J. M. Bover, S.J., are particularly deserving of mention. At present, the doctrine is universally accepted, and Catholic theologians, with relatively few exceptions, deem it definable by the Magisterium as a dogma of faith.

4. Liturgy

Our Lady's prerogative as Mediatrix and dispenser of all graces is abundantly attested to in the liturgical books of the Eastern Church, e.g., the Byzantine, Coptic, Syriac, Armenian, and Chaldean. In the Latin Church we have the Office and Mass of *Mary Mediatrix of All* Graces, composed at the initiative of Cardinal D. J. Mercier, approved by Benedict XV in 1921, and originally celebrated by numerous dioceses and Religious Orders on May 31. When in 1954 Pius XII set that day aside for the observance of Our Lady's Queenship, the feast in honor of Mary's mediation was discontinued by some and transferred by others.

5. Bibliography

For more detailed information and literature on the subject, see: J. A. Robichaud, S.M., *Mary, Dispensatrix of All Graces,* in J. B. Carol, O.F.M. (ed.), *Mariology,* vol 2 (Milwaukee Wis., Bruce, 1957), pp. 426-460; M. O'Carroll, C.S.Sp.,

Theotokos (Wilmington, Del., M. Glazier, 1982), pp. 238-245; and our entry, *Mediatrix of All Graces*, in NCE 9 (1967).

J. B. Carol

MEDJUGORJE   [971]

SEE *Apparitions*   *Apparitions after Vatican II*

IN 1981, apparitions of Mary to six young people at Medjugorje, Yugoslavia, were reported. They first appeared in a hillside field and then in the village church of Saint James. Some reports indicated that the alleged visionaries saw, heard, and touched Mary during the visions and that they received several or all of ten secret messages related to world events and urging a quest for peace through prayer, penance, and conversion.

In March 1984, a commission appointed by Bishop Pavo Zanic of Mostar-Duvno reported that the authenticity of the apparitions had not been established nor had cases of reported healings been verified. A communique published in the official bulletin of the Archdiocese of Zagreb, dated January 29, 1987, announced that exploration of the events at Medjugorje was to be conducted on a national episcopal level. The Congregation of the Faith adhered to this decision.

While awaiting the outcome of the investigation by the national episcopal commission, pastors and faithful were exhorted to observe an attitude of prudence customary in such cases. The communique indicated that it was not permissible to organize pilgrimages and other manifestations motivated by the supernatural character attributed to the events at Medjugorje. Finally, legitimate devotion to Our Lady, recommended by the Church, was always to conform to the directives of the Magisterium, and especially those contained in the Apostolic Exhortation *Marialis Cultus* of Paul VI.

In 1990, the Vatican made a pronouncement banning Church-sponsored pilgrimages to Medjugorje. In 1996, Archbishop Tarcisio Bertone, secretary of the Congregation for the Doctrine of the Faith, wrote in a letter to a French bishop (who

had asked for clarification of the Church's position on Medjugorje): "From what was said, it follows that official pilgrimages
to Medjugorje, understood as a place of authentic apparitions
should not be organized." He indicated that his congregation
was still studying the alleged apparitions.

A. Buono

MEMORARE, THE (Remember, O Most Gracious Virgin Mary) [971]

SEE *Prayer(s) to Mary*

THE "Memorare" is a prayer to the Blessed Virgin Mary
named after its first word in Latin, which means "remember." The text reads as follows:

Remember, O most gracious Virgin Mary,
that never was it known
that anyone who fled to your protection,
implored your help or sought your intercession,
was left unaided.

Inspired with this confidence,
I fly to you, O Virgin of virgins, my Mother;
to you do I come,
before you I stand, sinful and sorrowful.
O Mother of the Word Incarnate,
despise not my petitions,
but in your mercy hear and answer me.

The monks of the Monastery of Citeaux in the 12th cen-
tury popularized the name "Our Lady." Saint Bernard of
Clairvaux (q.v.) was the client par excellence of Our Lady. His
sermons on Mary are famous and so are his catch-phrases: "Of
Mary there is never enough" and "Look at the star, call upon
Mary!"

Hence, when this prayer appeared in the 15th century, it
was quickly attributed to Saint Bernard. Another reason for
this spurious attribution was that the Frenchman who popu-

larized the prayer was the "poor priest" Claude Bernard (d. 1461). In reality, the prayer may have been based on a longer "Memorare" used by the Eastern Church.

No matter who the author was, the prayer is popular with devoted clients of Mary because of its simple yet eloquent fervor. Anyone who makes use of it cannot but be impregnated with the greatest sentiments of love for Mary, hope in her powerful intercession with God, and spiritual peace in every affliction. The prayer has spawned a longer version in verse by Saint Louis Grignion de Montfort (in the 18th century) as well as "Memorares" to Saint Joseph and other Saints.

A. Buono

MIRACULOUS MEDAL (Rue du Bac)   [971, 1146-1149]

SEE   *Appearances*   *Appearances after Vatican II*

1. Origin

IN 1830 the Virgin Mary appeared in the chapel of the motherhouse for the Daughters of Charity (located in Paris, at 140 on the street named Bac). The seer, *Catherine Labouré,* age 24, had entered the novitiate of the Congregation in April of that year.

During the first apparition, on the night of July 18-19, Catherine saw the Blessed Virgin seated in the choir of the chapel. The Blessed Virgin spoke at length to the novice kneeling at her feet and made several predictions that came true soon after or a few years later.

On November 27, 1830, Catherine again saw the Blessed Virgin. It was about five o'clock in the morning while she was making her meditation with the community. This time the Blessed Virgin appeared standing on a terrestrial globe, her arms extended downward to the globe, and from her open hands streamed bright rays of light. Round about this scene Catherine could read, in letters of gold, these words: *Mary conceived without sin, pray for us who have recourse to you.*

After a while, the apparition seemed to recede and Catherine could distinguish the letter M surmounted on a Cross and placed over the Hearts of Jesus and Mary. She then heard the Blessed Virgin say: *Have a medal struck on this model.*

Here lies the origin of the medal to which popular devotion soon gave the name Miraculous Medal, because of the many graces of all kinds obtained through it.

These apparitions of 1830 marked the beginning of a great period of religious acclaim to the Blessed Virgin conceived without sin. Twenty-four years later Pius IX declared belief in Mary's Immaculate Conception a dogma of the Catholic faith. And in 1858 the "Lady" of Massabielle revealed her identity in saying to Bernadette Soubirous: *"I am the Immaculate Conception."*

Found throughout the world in incalculable reproductions, the Miraculous Medal is a sort of catechesis by imagery, a vivid emblem of the history of salvation in Jesus Christ.

People still flock to the chapel on the *rue du Bac.* They come from all corners of the world to pray and hear the message of Mary preached. They have the added advantage of being able to venerate the body of Catherine Labouré, because in 1947 the Church numbered with the Saints the herald of Our Lady of the Miraculous Medal.

This humble nun, shrouded in silence, devoted the 45 years of her religious life to the needs of elderly, poverty-stricken men in her community at Reuilly (Paris). There she died, December 31, 1876.

J. Gonthier

2. Symbolism

1. Relevance of Symbols Today

The Miraculous Medal is not simply a mini-object but a *sign,* that is, something that points outside itself. In fact, the Medal is not a conventional sign either. It is a *symbol,* that is, a concrete "sign that evokes, by reason of a natural relationship, something absent or impossible to perceive" (A. Lalande). The inability to grasp the things signified impedes the understanding of the Miraculous Medal; one must go beyond the material datum.

Western culture has repressed and misconstrued symbols, regarding them as mere instruments of information (didactic forms to transmit ideas) or poetic expressions of an unreal world.

In our day, people are discovering that they are "symbolic beings," that is, they must transcend the phenomenal datum in order to discover the dimension of the signified without which they cannot live. They perceive that they live in a world of symbols, which "reveal the secrets of the unconscious, lead to the most hidden resources of activity, and open the spirit to the unknown and the infinite." Symbols constitute an irrepressible need for the historical dimension of human beings and hence an appeal to reality in more human terms.

It is precisely this type of language that the Blessed Mother utilized in the last century when she launched her Miraculous Medal through Catherine Labouré. And we must apply symbology to the reading of the Miraculous Medal so that it will speak to us even more eloquently. (The following observations are based on the four-volume French *Dictionary of Symbols* by J. Chevalier, Paris, 1974, which is also the source for the quotations.)

2. The Virgin in Light

—*The white clad and veiled Virgin*: virginity refers to an intact, sacred, untouchable being (even the veil is a language of consecration). Ever disposed to receive the Divine fecundity because she was totally open, "the Virgin Mother of God symbolizes the earth oriented toward the sun, so that it then becomes a transfigured earth, an earth of light."

—*The symbol of light*: "Her countenance [says Catherine] was all beauty. I could not describe it. . . ." The luminous rays streaming from her hands are the symbol of the graces that the Blessed Virgin transmits. In the Bible, *light* "constantly symbolizes *life, salvation,* and *happiness* given by God," while darkness is a "symbol of *evil, disgrace, punishment, perdition, and death.*" Flooded by light and radiant brightness, Mary is situated in the eschatological sphere, in the luminous region of the living. Light is interpreted by the Fathers as the symbol of the world of heaven and of eternity. As light in the Lord, Mary is the complete opposite of opacity and hypocrisy; she is total communication and authenticity.

3. The Triumphant Virgin

—*The hands with the rings.* We are interested not so much in the modern tone of this image (hands with many rings, which is the fashion today) as we are in the attitude indicated by the *extended hands.* Mary does not withhold anything for herself; she is not possessive but all-giving. Her hands are open to encounter and welcome. The rings indicate a bond of fidelity: they are a "sign of a covenant, a vow, a community, an associated destiny." As the Spouse of God, Mary is faithful even to human beings: she is the personification of the Covenant with God for a new world.

—*The serpent* "greenish in color with yellow spots," symbolizes—in the eyes of Jews and Christians—Satan and the powers of evil. He winds himself around the heel of the Virgin. This image gives us a dramatic vision of the world that is the theater and polygon of a no-holds-barred battle between good and evil. The serpent is the rival of human beings because he is at the beginning of the animal evolution; but he is also found in the human species itself because "he incarnates the inner psyche, the dark psychism, that which is rare, incomprehensible, and mysterious" (Jung). The Virgin vanquisher of Satan invites us to neutralize the zone of darkness that is in us and to eschew making peace with the powers of evil.

—The *globe* "can have a double significance: the geographic totality of the universe and the juridical totality of an absolute power. It is only in this second way that the globe is to be interpreted when it designates the limited territory over which the power of a personage is exercised: this power is itself limited; and it is this that the globe signifies." The globe beneath the Virgin's feet signifies her royal power over the world, over nations, and over every soul. In other words, everything belongs to Mary. Would not this fact constitute the foundation for social or personal consecration to her? However, we must not overlook the preceding gesture of the Virgin who holds the luminous globe in her hands:

"The triumphant Virgin, who offers and integrates the whole universe in this offering, represents the soul of the cosmic scientist who offers to God the whole cosmos integrated by the Risen Christ. Father Teilhard de Chardin in his classic work *The Mass on the World* has expressed these sentiments in his own way: they are the sentiments of the Virgin who offers the golden globe" (J. Guitton).

The consecration, as the acknowledgment of Mary's maternal and royal mission, is projected dynamically from the Virgin to God, supreme Lord and Father.

4. The Compassionate Virgin

—*The Cross* symbolizes the Crucifix. "More than being a figure of Christ, it is identified with His human history, that is, with His Person. The Cross in itself is recognized as 'the most totalizing symbol,' insofar as it is in relation with the other three basic symbols: the teacher, the circle, and the square. It has the function of synthesis and measure:

"In it heaven and earth come together . . . , time and space intersect. It is the symbol of the intermediary, the mediator, the one who is by nature permanent reunion of the universe and communication between earth and heaven, from top to bottom and from bottom to top."

—*Heart,* repeated twice on the back of the Miraculous Medal, refers to Jesus and to Mary in accord with traditional iconography. It has great evocative power: seat of sentiments (West) or of understanding (East), in the Biblical tradition the heart symbolizes the inner person, the affective life, and the center of one's being. Since the heart is the first organ formed and the last to die—observes Babua Ben Asher in the 18th century—to love God with all one's heart signifies to love Him until one's last breath.

The heart is an appeal to conscience to imitate Christ and Mary in choosing the way of love even to the total giving of self. In an age that creates constructions in iron and cement and that risks losing its sense of fraternity and responsibility, the hearts of the Miraculous Medal offer an indispensable therapy for the survival of humankind.

5. Triple Role toward Time

The symbolism of the Miraculous Medal remains open in its polyvalence of meanings and contents. But as a special symbol (that of medal), it plays a triple role toward the three moments of time: it *recalls* (past), *reveals* (present), and *protects* (future).

(a) The Miraculous Medal is a *memorial* insofar as it recalls an event of salvation. It fixes in metal the appearance of the Blessed Virgin to Catherine Labouré, that is, an encounter between time and eternity, between earth and heaven, an intervention of God, the Lord of History, through the mediation of Mary.

(b) The Miraculous Medal is the *word of revelation*, because it transmits a message: "The *front* manifests the light, God's irradiation on the one whom He has chosen as a prototype of the salvation proposed to all human beings in Jesus Christ, so that all will be light in His light. The *back* manifests the austere and hidden face of the message: love and the Cross, the resources of Salvation, illustrated by the Passion of Our Lord and the Compassion of Our Lady that all are invited to share" (R. Laurentin and P. Roche).

(c) The Miraculous Medal is the *sign of trust* in the Divine protection. It can be considered a reduction to tiny proportions of the defensive shield used by soldiers. It inspires us to live religiously and form a group identified by that sign of recognition.

This triple *communicative, revelatory,* and *protective* function of the Medal cannot be devalued.

The Miraculous Medal is extremely rich in symbols. We must know how to read and interpret them whether through a study of symbolism or through a contemplative non-intellectual attitude. We can regard it as a circumscribed oral space that assists the spirit to elevate itself and to concentrate on itself but above all to come into contact with the other world, with Mary, and with a story full of hope.

S. de Fiores

MONTH OF MARY   [971]

SEE   *Saturday of Our Lady*

THE month of May is the "month that the piety of the faithful has especially dedicated to Our Blessed Lady," and it is the occasion for a "moving tribute of faith and love that Catholics in every part of the world [pay] to the Queen of Heaven. During this month Christians, both in church and in the privacy of the home, offer up to Mary from their hearts an especially fervent and loving homage of prayer and veneration. In this month, too, the benefits of God's mercy come down to us from her throne in greater abundance" (Paul VI: *Encyclical Mense Maio: On the Month of May*, no. 1).

This Christian custom of dedicating the month of May to the Blessed Virgin arose at the end of the 13th century. In this way, the Church was able to Christianize the secular feasts that were wont to take place at that time. In the 16th century, books appeared and fostered this devotion.

The practice became especially popular among the members of the Jesuit Order—by 1700 it took hold among their students at the Roman College and a bit later it was publicly practiced in the *Gesù* Church in Rome. From there it spread to the whole Church.

The practice was granted a partial indulgence by Pius VII in 1815 and a plenary indulgence by Pius IX in 1859. With the complete revision of indulgences in 1966 and the decreased emphasis on specific indulgences, it no longer carries an indulgence; however it certainly falls within the category of the First General Grant of Indulgences.

This pious practice has been especially recommended by the Popes. Pius XII made frequent reference to it and in his great *Encyclical on the Sacred Liturgy* (*Mediator Dei*) characterized it as one of "other exercises of piety that although not strictly belonging to the Sacred Liturgy, are nevertheless of special import and dignity, and *may be considered in a certain way to be an addition to the liturgical cult*: they have been approved and praised over and over again by the Apostolic See and by the Bishops" (no. 182).

In his 1965 Encyclical, *Mense Maio,* Paul VI used the Month of Mary devotion as a means of obtaining prayers for peace. He urged the faithful to make use of this practice, which is "gladdening and consoling" and by which the Blessed Virgin Mary is honored and the Christian people are enriched with spiritual gifts" (no. 2).

There are no official prayers or rites for this practice. Many churches have a daily recitation of the Rosary in public or some other prayers in honor of Mary, including the crowning of Our Lady's statue. For private use, one can follow the format of a liturgy of the Word: entrance chant, opening prayer, Scripture reading, and brief reflection or homily, with a concluding prayer of invocation. The only *necessary element* is that Mary be honored in a special way.

A. Buono

MOTHER OF THE CHURCH

SEE   *Church and Mary*   *Vatican II and Mary*

MOTHER OF GOD   [495]

SEE   *Annunciation*

THE title "Mother of God" is not found as such in the writings of the New Testament. The first known mention is that of Saint Hippolytus of Rome (d. 235). Later, Nestorius, Patriarch of Constantinople (428), will dispute the attribution of this title to Mary because of his views on Christology. For him, the Son of God is *one* thing, the son of Mary *another*, in the sense that he sees in Christ two Persons: one Divine (the Logos), the other human (Jesus). Consequently, for Nestorius, Mary cannot be called "*theotokos*" (Mother of God), at least in the real sense demanded by the hypostatic union (the union of the two natures, the human and the Divine, in the *one* Person of the Word).

The Council of Ephesus (431) defends this unicity of person in Christ and condemns Nestorius and his followers. It approves, by acclamation, the second letter of Saint Cyril to Nestorius and through this approval officially confirms the attribution to Mary of the title Mother of God. The normative decision taken at Ephesus will be explicitly promulgated as dogma in 451 by the Council of Chalcedon.

1. Theological Content

As noted above, the title of Mother of God derives from Catholic teaching on the Incarnation of the Word. Mary conceives and brings forth, in His human nature, One Who is God from all eternity. Jesus is not God by the fact that He is conceived or born of Mary (this would not be a Mystery but an absurdity because it would make Mary mother of the Divine nature). Mary is Mother of God because from her own flesh she gives to the Word a human nature like hers. And just as in ordinary human generation the terminus of the parents' generative action is not the human nature produced but the person subsisting in this nature, so in the case of Mary: her maternal action reaches to the Person of the Word, Who by this very fact is truly her Son. Mary is "*theotokos*" because "*the Word was made flesh*" in her and through her.

This is laden with consequences that bring out the full import of the title Mother of God. If Jesus is sole Savior, only Mediator, and the Priest, Prophet, and King par excellence, it is as man, because His human nature from the first moment of its existence was *congenitally* united with the Divine nature in the Person of the Word. Mary's maternal action, under the power of the Holy Spirit, results in *One* Who, because *God-Man*, is the Savior, the Mediator, and the Priest, Prophet, and King of the New and definitive Covenant.

Mary, then, is Mother of the Savior in a sense much more profound than when we say of a woman that she is mother of a priest or of the president of a nation. The fact of being a priest or president of a nation does not result from the generative action of the parents but from a call or a consecration or an election, which affects a subject already "humanly" constituted. The same is true of an "hereditary" title, bestowed in virtue of *juridical* determinations that are completely extrinsic to generation as such. This is not the case here. The engendering to which Mary is called, with all the spiritual and physical resources of her being, could not but produce, ontologically and existentially, the Mediator par excellence, Whom she for her part is instrumental in constituting as such. This also indicates the depth of the association that exists here between Mary and the Holy Spirit, Who alone is capable of realizing in her such a wonder.

The reality of the Divine Motherhood explains the human and supernatural perfection of Mary. It is the only case in which a "Son" was able to "fashion" His Mother as He wanted her to be.

This Son is all-powerful. He could not but prepare for Himself a Mother worthy of Him, a "*worthy Mother of God*," totally devoted to her exceptional vocation: "Redeemed by reason of the merits of her Son and united to Him by a close and indissoluble tie, she is endowed with the high office and dignity of being the Mother of the Son of God and, in consequence, the beloved daughter of the Father and the temple of the Holy Spirit. Because of this sublime grace she far surpasses all creatures, both in heaven and on earth" (LG 53).

On a similar note: "The Father of mercies willed that the Incarnation should be preceded by its acceptance by her who was predestined to be the Mother of His Son, so that just as a woman contributed to death, so also a woman should contribute to life. This is true in outstanding fashion of the Mother of Jesus, who gave to the world Him who is Life itself and who renews all things and who [i.e., Mary] was enriched by God with the gifts that befit such a role" (LG 56).

Because of the "close and indissoluble tie" (LG 53) it forms between the Mother and her Son, the Divine Motherhood both calls for and explains "the cooperation absolutely beyond compare" that Mary brings "to the work of the Savior," a cooperation that makes her our Mother "in the order of grace" (LG 61).

2. The Divine Motherhood and History

In bringing a child into the world, every woman influences the course of history. But how much more in the case of Mary! She has a unique place in the sacred history of humankind because by embracing the Father's gift she plays a part in bringing us the One Who is the Beginning, the Center, and the End of this history. In the long line of generations, and the unfolding of God's plan, Mary stands as it were at the crossroads.

Mary, of the purest stock of Israel and the royal line of David, belongs to the People of God who are waiting for the Messiah. The Son of Mary *"will be great and will be called Son of the Most High. The Lord God will give Him the throne of David His father. He will rule over the house of David forever . . ."* (Lk 1:32-33). Clearly, Jesus too will be of Davidic descent (cf. 2 Sm 7:14, 16; Ps 2:7; 89:27-28).

Mary's question (*"How can this be since I do not know man?"*) provides the Angel an occasion to broach a new dimension: *"The Holy Spirit will come upon you and the power of the Most High will overshadow you; hence, the holy offspring to be born will be called Son of God"* (Lk 1:35). The "overshadowing" brings to mind the *"cloud,"* a word that is part of Biblical literature and connotes the effective presence of God (Ex 40:34-35; Nm 9:18-22; 10:34). Saying that the Child will be Holy indicates His privileged belonging to God (Is 6:3). For the Old Testament, the expression *"Son of God"* designates the Messiah (Ps 2:7; 2 Sm 7:14); here, however, the implication is not of a Divine protection in this Old Testament sense but of sonship proper.

Because Mary accepts a certain surmounting of her fore-fathers' Messianic conceptions, she enters into a new dimension of faith and introduces into our world the One through Whom we can accede to Divine sonship.

Mary's free acceptance, along with what is being accomplished in her "by the power of the Holy Spirit," gives our history its ultimate meaning in the plan of God that is realized in Jesus and by His work. Become one of us in this woman of our race, Mary of Nazareth, the Word of God dies on the Cross and rises again, the Living One forevermore. Through Him we partake of the life of the Spirit that He has come to give us so that we might have it in abundance.

A. Delesalle

MOTHERHOOD, SPIRITUAL   [968-970]

SEE   *Presence of Mary in the*   *Vatican II and Mary*
      Eucharist

AFFIRMATION of Mary's maternal role toward us is one of the capital points in chapter 8 of the Second Vatican Council's *Constitution on the Church (Lumen Gentium)*. In this chapter the title "Mother of human beings" (or "Mother of the faithful") synthesizes practically all aspects of Mary's activity in our behalf together with the sentiments she has for us.

1. A Slow Development

Even though we find in the first Christian centuries insights and assertions that tend toward the doctrine of Mary's spiritual motherhood (e.g., in Irenaeus, Epiphanius, Ambrose, and Augustine), the testimonies are sparse and occasional. One has to wait until the high Middle Ages to see the beginning of any real theological development of this Motherhood. Today, more and more, it is the pericope of John 19:25-27 (Mary on Calvary) that is seen as expressing the reality of Mary's spiritual motherhood toward the disciples of Jesus. But historically speaking, the pericope yielded its broader implications only very gradually.

We are here faced with a reality that was experienced spiritually by the Church and the faithful before it gained theological expression. The vital attitude of the Christian consciousness does not appear in this case as deriving from a truth received or discovered intellectually, by abstract reasoning. It presents itself as the progressive explication of what is implied in the presence and action of Mary upon our lives. This experience eventually found its best and universal expression in the analogy of motherhood (which in this case can only be "spiritual") with all that such a Mother/child relationship means both for Mary and for us.

The importance of this living experience is confirmed by a text of Vatican II: "The Church does not hesitate to profess this subordinate role of Mary. *She knows it through unfailing experience of it* and commends it to the *hearts* of the faithful, so that encouraged by this *maternal* help they may the more intimately adhere to the Mediator and Redeemer" (LG 62).

The context leaves no doubt that the Council was referring to Mary's role of Mother.

2. Content

When we call Mary "our Mother," we grasp instinctively the essential meaning of the title, since it evokes memories of a human experience that is universal and runs deep. But when it comes to explaining clearly and precisely the content of the title, the matter is not so simple. Primarily, this is due to the wealth of the content, including as it does practically all aspects of Mary's activity toward us. Hence, in the elucidation of the title these aspects must all be considered. (One way or another, all articles in this Dictionary that describe and explain Mary's mission are articles on her Spiritual Motherhood.)

Furthermore, Mary is our "Mother" in a way that is necessarily *analogical*. Theologians are well aware of what this imports, namely, certain limitations that have to be remembered, and a transcendence that also must be kept in mind. The limitations come from the obvious fact that as far as we are concerned we cannot apply to Mary all realities of natural mother-hood, since we are children of Mary not by the flesh (in this respect she is our sister by race) but "in the order of grace" (LG 61).

Nevertheless, if in certain ways Mary's Motherhood toward us says less than natural motherhood, in other ways it says much more. For example, the quality of our life as children of God, a life that Mary helps to obtain for us, ennobles and enriches incomparably our purely human life. And the perfection with which Mary dedicates herself to her maternal mission surpasses that of the best mothers on earth, plus the fact that Mary's maternal vocation is universal and calls for her forming a personal bond with each one of us.

From chapter 8 of the *Constitution on the Church (Lumen Gentium)* we can gather some essential characteristics of Mary's Motherhood.

(a) It is in and through service to her Son that Mary, during her life on earth, exercises her maternal activity toward us.

By the very fact that He Who is conceived in her on the day of the Annunciation is the Savior, Mary gives to the world "Him Who is Life itself and Who renews all things" (LG 56). But we must go much further.

The Council more than points out, in the wake of Tradition, the extent of Mary's maternal devotion to Jesus personally; it also notes that as servant of the Lord she is associated in a unique manner, and by Divine will, with the work of salvation accomplished by her Son: "Embracing God's salvific will with a full heart . . . [the Mother of Jesus] devoted herself totally as Handmaid of the Lord to the person and work of her Son, under Him and with Him . . . serving the Mystery of Redemption" (LG 56; cf. 61).

Mary's Spiritual Motherhood is coextensive with her service to Jesus the Savior. Everything she does for Him and with Him concerns us in our life as children of God: "She conceived, brought forth, and nourished Christ. She presented Him to the Father in the Temple, and was united with Him by compassion as He died on the Cross. In this singular way she cooperated by her obedience, faith, hope, and burning charity in the work of the Savior in giving back supernatural life to souls. Wherefore she is our Mother in the order of grace" (LG 61).

(b) Mary continues today to live her Spiritual Motherhood:

"This Motherhood of Mary in the order of grace, which began with the consent she gave in faith at the Annunciation and which she sustained without wavering beneath the Cross, lasts until the eternal fulfillment of all the elect. Taken up to heaven she did not lay aside this salvific duty, but by her constant intercession continued to bring us the gifts of eternal salvation" (LG 62).

But the Council does not finish by saying that Mary exercises this maternal function "by her constant intercession." It adds that her maternal love makes her "care for the brothers and sisters of her Son who still journey on earth . . ." (ibid.). We may take this as suggesting the personal character of Mary's relationship with each one of us, and not simply as expressing a general interest in us because we are always in need of prayer. The Council's words accord with the conviction we have when we ask Mary "to pray for us," a conviction that adds up to the certainty that she knows us, sees us, hears us.

This action of Mary is yet another expression of her total service to Christ, as the following shows.

(c) The purpose of Mary's maternal activity is to unite us with Christ so completely that each might say: "*The life I live now is not my own; Christ is living in me*" (Gal 2:20), so that Christ may be "*all in all*" (cf. Col 3:11).

Grace, after all, is the life of Christ in us, the life of Him "Whom God placed as the firstborn among many brothers and sisters (Rom 8:29), namely the faithful, in whose birth and education she cooperates with a maternal love" (LG 63).

Even though Mary's Divine Motherhood toward Jesus has to be distinguished from her Spiritual Motherhood toward us, the two must not be kept apart. The one (the Spiritual) derives from the other (the Divine) and is "explained" by it. Her Spiritual Motherhood is like an extension of the Divine because— according to a beautiful expression of Saint Louis-Marie

Grignion de Montfort—it consists in "forming us in Jesus Christ and Jesus Christ in us."

(d) Mary's maternal function toward us is entirely the fruit of Christ's saving action; it flows from it and depends on it in everything: "The maternal role of Mary toward us in no wise obscures or diminishes the unique mediation of Christ, but rather shows its power" (LG 60; cf. 61). The superabundance of Christ's Redemption lets Him make associates of the very ones He saves, and first of all, in a singular and universal manner, of His own Mother, whom He asks and gives the means to fulfill her maternal mission toward us.

(e) Additional point of note: Mary conceived the Word of God in her heart and flesh by the power of the Spirit Who overshadowed her (Lk 1:35). It is by the same power of the Spirit, soul of her soul and life of her life, that she attains the spiritual fecundity that makes her our Mother.

3. The Reciprocal Mother/Child Relation

Mary put all the spiritual and physical resources of her being into her vocation of Mother of Jesus. She does the same in regard to its extension, her Spiritual Motherhood toward us.

It is noteworthy that the Second Vatican Council uses the vocabulary of deep and tender affection when speaking of the relationship created between Mary and us. The Council says, for example, that *"by her maternal love she cares for the brothers and sisters of her Son . . ."* (LG 62). It speaks the same language in describing the attitude, or what should be the attitude, toward her, whether of the Church as a whole or of each one of us. Mary is "the object on the part of the Church, taught by the Holy Spirit, of *filial affection and piety,* such as it behooves one to have for a *most beloved Mother"* (LG 53). And although the Council cautions that "true devotion consists neither in sterile or transitory affection, nor in a certain vain credulity," but "proceeds from true faith," it immediately adds that such faith-inspired devotion *"moves us to love this Mother with a filial love . . ."* (LG 67).

True devotion, therefore, does not lapse into maudlin sentimentality or give primacy to the feelings. But if this danger does exist, it is not reason for denying or diminishing the importance of the fact that to grow mature in Christ we have need of Mary's maternal action, and this by will of the Lord. The living relationship which we for our part should try to maintain with Mary ought to involve in due proportion all the resources of our being, the affectivity not excepted—a point that also applies in regard to our relationship with Christ. The Spiritual Motherhood of Mary reminds us, among other things, of this affective dimension of our life as children of God.

To conclude we return to the source, the Gospel and the words of Christ on Calvary: *"Behold your son"*—*"Behold your Mother,"* and the words of Mary to the waiters at Cana: *"Do whatever He tells you."* These words she never tires of repeating to us, and she is with us every moment to help us, in a motherly way, to live them.   *A. Bossard*

MUNIFICENTISSIMUS DEUS   [966]

SEE   *Assumption*   *Feasts of Mary*
      Church and Mary   *Intercession*
      Cult of Mary   *Magisterium (Documents of)*
      Dormition, Holy Land   *Vatican II and Mary*
      and Mary, 2h

ON November 1, 1950, Pope Pius XII issued an Apostolic Constitution entitled *Munificentissimus Deus* ("The Most Bountiful God") in which he solemnly defined as a Dogma of Faith that the Blessed Virgin Mary was assumed body and soul into heaven. This Apostolic Constitution is thus a document of the solemn Magisterium of the Church, infallible in its dogmatic affirmation of the Assumption.

The whole document is in fact of great historical and doctrinal importance. It marks the end of very ardent wishes on the part of clergy and people to have the Dogma proclaimed and the beginning of a new fervor in Marian devotion, a new gem on the glorious forehead of the Queen of heaven.

The Pope states that petitions for such a proclamation began immediately after the definition of the Dogma of the Immaculate Conception in 1854. They grew steadily until they reached a crescendo at the beginning of his pontificate and gave birth to a worldwide movement. Hence, in 1946 he consulted the bishops of the world in the Encyclical *Deiparae Virginis* ("The Virgin Mother of God") asking for their thinking as well as that of the Catholic faithful entrusted to them.

The responses of the bishops and people were almost unanimously in favor of a definition of the Dogma. Indeed, they showed that the truth of the Assumption was part of the "sense of the faithful" throughout the centuries as indicated by the countless forms of devotions that had come into existence in its honor and especially the language of the Liturgy both in the East and in the West.

He goes on to say that the Fathers and Doctors of the Church echoed the voice of the Liturgy in feasts of the Assumption and spoke clearly about the glorification of the body of the Blessed Virgin as of a truth known and accepted by all the faithful from the earliest centuries. Theologians, too, among whom were the most brilliant and the most holy of them, agreed on this point. They demonstrated the harmony between the Faith and theological reason and the fitting character of this privilege. In doing so, they made use of facts, words, figures, and analogies that are found in Sacred Scripture.

Having heard the voice of the Universal Church, the Pope indicates that the moment has arrived that God has established for him to ratify this Dogma by his supreme authority. And he does so with the solemn majestic formula of definition, analogous to the one used by Pius IX for the Dogma of the Immaculate Conception:

"By the authority of Our Lord Jesus Christ, of the blessed Apostles Peter and Paul, and by our own proper authority we pronounce, declare, and define as Divinely revealed dogma that Mary, Immaculate Mother of God ever Virgin, after finishing the course of her life on earth, was taken up in body and soul to heavenly glory." *A. Buono*

- N -

NAME OF MARY [488]

SEE *Birth of Mary*   *Marian Titles*
    Life of Mary   *Marian Typology*

1. Name of Nine Persons in Scripture

THE name of Mary has the form *Myriam* in the Hebrew Old Testament and *Maryam* in the Aramaic, *Mariam* in the Greek translation of the Old Testament, and *Maria* in the Greek New Testament. It is the name held by eight other persons in the Bible besides the Mother of Jesus.

(1) The sister of Moses, usually called Miriam, whose song of praise after the crossing of the Red Sea is found in Exodus (15:20-21) and who is later punished for opposing Moses (Nm 12). (2) A woman descendant of Judah (1 Chr 4:17—although the text could be referring to a male descendant of Ezra with that name). (3) Mary Magdalene, the woman *"from whom seven devils had gone out"* (Lk 8:2). (4) Mary, the sister of Lazarus and Martha, who is portrayed as a devoted listener of Christ (Lk 10:38-42). (5) Mary, the mother of James and John, one of the witnesses of Jesus' crucifixion and of the empty tomb (Mk 15:40-47). (6) Mary, wife of Clopas (Jn 19:25), whom some identify with the woman in number 5. (7) Mary the mother of John Mark, in whose house Peter takes refuge after being freed from prison in Jerusalem (Acts 12:12). (8) A Christian at Rome who is greeted and praised by Paul in the Epistle to the Romans: *"My greetings to Mary, who has worked hard for you"* (16:6).

2. Meaning of This Name

Over the years more than seventy meanings have been attached to this name—most based on devotion rather than philology. Two such explanations have given rise to titles of Mary that are favorites among Catholics. The first is the explanation of Saint Jerome based on the Hebrew term for "sea" (*yam*) which produced *stilla maris,* meaning "drop of the sea"—that is, of that sea which is God. A copyist's error turned the phrase into *stella maris* meaning "Star of the Sea." It became a favorite name for Mary and part of the Marian literature through the Hymn *Ave Maris Stella* (Hail, Star of the Sea) (q.v.).

The second explanation is also the work of Saint Jerome. He proposed an alternative meaning based on the Aramaic *mar* which means "lord," although the form to be precise should have been *Marta*. This interpretation enjoyed wide acceptance and became the usual title applied to Mary in modern languages and meaning "lady": My Lady (*Madonna*) in Italian and Our Lady (*Notre Dame*) in French.

Modern philology, with its more precise tools, has been able to indicate three interpretations of Mary as more probable (there is no certainty as yet). The first connects the name with the Egyptian *mara* meaning "satiated, fat, or corpulent"— hence, in accord with Oriental feminine esthetic, *beautiful.* The second connects Mary with the Egyptian *mari* meaning "loved." The third relates it to the language of the inhabitants of Palestine, the Canaanites, which is akin to Hebrew.

This language is better understood today because of archeological expeditions that took place in Ugarit (Ras Shamra in Syria) in 1929. These brought to light the Ugaritic idiom that was spoken and written in those regions. In the tables that have been unearthed, the name *mrym* is well attested. It derives from the verb *rwm* and has the literal meaning of "high" or "lofty," hence "exalted" or "august." Therefore, Our Lady would be "The Exalted One" or "The Sublime One." This last seems to be the most probable of all—and it certainly fits Mary very well.

3. Feast of the Name of Mary

The liturgical feast of the Holy Name of Mary originated in Spain and was approved by the Holy See in 1513. Innocent XI extended its observance to the whole Church in 1683 in thanksgiving for the victory of John Sobieski, King of Poland, over the Turks, who were besieging Vienna and threatening the West. The feast was assigned to September 12, the date of the victory and only four days after the Feast of the Birth of Mary.

The feast remained in the Roman Calendar as a lesser Feast of Mary until the publication of the new *Roman Missal* revised in accord with the principles of the Second Vatican Council in 1970. It was then dropped from the universal calendar—as was the Feast (but not the Votive Mass) of the Holy Name of Jesus—because it duplicated the Feast of the Birth of Mary.

However, the 1975 edition of the *Roman Missal* added a Votive Mass of the Name of Mary that can be celebrated on open days.

In 1987, the new liturgical book *Collection of Masses of the Blessed Virgin Mary* (q.v.) was published by the Church. Among its 46 Masses that can be celebrated on open liturgical days is The Holy Name of the Blessed Virgin Mary (no. 21). It celebrates the Name of Mary as (1) a name of honor; (2) a holy name; (3) a maternal name; and (4) a name responsive to human need.

A. Buono

NATIONAL SHRINE OF THE IMMACULATE CONCEPTION [971]

SEE   *Immaculate Conception*

THE National Shrine of the Immaculate Conception in Washington, D.C., is the patronal church of the United States. It is the seventh largest religious building in the world and the largest Catholic church in the Western Hemisphere. It can house 6,000 persons (sitting and standing) and contains one of the largest mosaics in the world.

This shrine dedicated to the Patroness of America, Mary under her Immaculate Conception, was the result of the worldwide Marian movement that culminated in the definition of the Dogma of the Immaculate Conception by Pius IX in 1854.

The Sixth Provincial Council of Baltimore had, in 1846, requested the Holy See that Mary under the title of the Immaculate Conception be made patroness of the United States. The petition was granted in 1847.

In 1913, Bishop Thomas J. Shahan, fourth rector of the Catholic University of America, suggested the building of a national shrine of the Immaculate Conception. This, he hoped, would be a large and beautiful church in honor of Our Blessed Mother, erected by nationwide cooperation at the United States' capital and constituting a great hymn in stone.

The project was launched in 1913, and on September 23, 1920, Cardinal Gibbons laid the cornerstone on land adjoining the Catholic University of America. It turned out to be a long undertaking. Most of the crypt area and the foundations of the upper church were built by 1931. In 1954 work began on the upper church and it was sufficiently well along to permit the solemn dedication on November 20, 1959. Cardinal Spellman officiated in the presence of the largest ecclesiastical gathering in U.S. church history.

The church is built in a Byzantine-Romanesque style. It is 465 feet long and 238 feet wide, with the dome reaching a height of 254 feet and the campanile measuring 332 feet. The entire construction is suffused with Marian themes and Marian devotion.

The contributions of Catholics country-wide maintain the magnificent church, just as their offerings paid for its building in testimony to the place the Mother of God holds in the hearts and religious life of American Catholics.

Along with the many Washington visitors, of all faiths, who visit the Shrine while touring the capital, more and more groups are coming on pilgrimage even from distant dioceses, and focusing on Mary's Shrine as a place of prayer and inspiration.   *A. Buono*

NAZARETH

SEE   *Holy Land and Mary,* 2k

NEW EVE

SEE   *Marian Titles*

AFTER his fall and condemnation to death, Adam gave the woman *"taken from the man"* and *"built up"* by God (Gn 2:22) a name laden with hope. The name *Eve,* a transcription of the Hebrew *Hawah,* is in fact being used here as a derivative from the root *hay,* to live: *"The man called his wife Eve, because she became the mother of all the living"* (Gn 3:20). The author of the Biblical account cannot think *"woman"* without thinking *"life."* The *Septuagint* was not mistaken when it translated *Hawah,* Eve, by *"Zoé,"* the Greek word meaning *"life."*

With the light of the Christian faith, a new insight into the origins is offered us. To exalt the gift God made to us in Jesus Christ, Saint Paul shows by contrast the sad state in which humanity left to itself would be. But *"despite the increase of sin, grace has far surpassed it"* (Rom 5:20). Two types of man are set in opposition: *"The first man was of earth, formed from the dust, the second is from heaven"* (1 Cor 15:37). Paul pursues this parallel in several places. Christ at last appears as the second Adam, type of the new man created according to God in justice and truth (cf. Eph 4:24), source of grace (Rom 5:17-19) and life-giving spirit (1 Cor 15:45).

It is not until the first testimonies of Tradition that we find the new Eve mentioned in connection with the first Adam. Among the earliest and clearest witnesses is Saint Irenaeus, Bishop of Lyons, writing toward the second half of the 2nd century. Irenaeus could not support the opinion of Tatian that our first parents were damned. No, grace superabounded, and the human race was definitely restored: "It was right and necessary that Adam be restored in Christ . . . that Eve be restored in Mary, so that a Virgin, become advocate of a virgin, might erase and abolish the disobedience of a virgin by her obedience as Virgin."

With Tertullian, another symbolism is introduced, which reappears in Ambrose, Jerome, Augustine, and many others.

Christ is shown as falling into a sleep on the Cross and, during the sleep of the second Adam, from His side is born the Church, the new Eve, mother of the living. In the Latin tradition, we have to wait until the height of the Middle Ages before we see the title "Mother of the living" being applied not only to the Church but to Mary as well. Behind this attribution is the recognition of Mary's Spiritual Motherhood toward all humanity.

The Church and Mary are not the only ones to receive the name of Eve, or new Eve. Job's wife, who taunted him in his trials, received (among others) this appellation in an unfavorable sense. *"New Eve,"* therefore, did not always have the Marian sense that we habitually give it today.

In a letter to Pusey, in 1865, Newman speaks of this identification of Mary as the new Eve, calling it a rudimentary teaching that goes back to the earliest writings of the Church Fathers. The new Eve, he argues, could not be inferior to the first. If Eve had the interior supernatural gift of original justice from the first moment of her personal existence, then Mary, the second Eve, also must have had it from the first moment of her personal existence. The deduction strikes Newman as inevitable and means, quite literally, that Mary was conceived Immaculate.

Today, other qualities of the new Eve would also merit emphasis. Christian generations come and go and have had to contemplate in differing sociocultural contexts "the person and mission of Mary: New Woman and perfect Christian . . . outstanding type of womanhood" (MC 36). Whereas the first Eve let herself be enslaved by the devil, the New Eve experienced, increasingly, the freedom of soul given by the Spirit to those who hearken to Him. Her response to God's Word was complete. "Summing up in herself the most characteristic situations in the life of a woman as Virgin, Wife, and Mother" *(ibid.)*, Mary gave free and active consent to the event of the ages, which with the coming of her Divine Son, the New Adam, ushered in the New Creation.

J. Pintard

NEW TESTAMENT

SEE   *Annunciation*　　　　　*Life of Mary*
　　　 Cana　　　　　　　　 *Luke (Gospel of Saint)*
　　　 Cross (Mary at the)　　 *Mark (Gospel of Saint)*
　　　 Infancy Narratives　　　*Matthew (Gospel of Saint)*

REFERENCES in the New Testament to Mary, "*Mother of Jesus*," stand out not so much by their number as by their quality. The figure of Mary that emerges relates entirely to the first and fundamental Mystery proclaimed in the Gospels: the Incarnation of the Word of God. She is also seen for her part in fulfilling the hope of the Messianic community and exemplifying its response. These are the two aspects given special attention by the Evangelists in presenting Mary's role in the History of Salvation: On the one hand, *her relation to the Mystery of Jesus*, with which she was associated in an incomparable manner by her Motherhood; on the other, *her relation to the Mystery of Israel*. For Mary indeed is also the "*Daughter of Zion*," personification of the true Israel, the "small Remnant" from which was to be born the new Messianic people. Thanks to her acceptance of the Lord's message and her faithfulness, she stands forth, from amid the history of Israel, as the "Woman" of beginnings and fruitions.

1. The Mother of Jesus

The most common but also the most proper and significant designation by which the Evangelists refer to Mary is "*Mother of Jesus*" (Jn 2:1; Acts 1:14), or simply "*His Mother*" (Mk 3:31; Mt 1:18, 2:13, 20, 21; Lk 2:34, 48; Jn 2:5, 12; 19:25). She is the Mother of "*Jesus Who is called the Messiah*" (Mt 1:16). This simple title, by itself alone, expresses all the importance of Mary in the History of Salvation. She is forevermore indissociable from the Mystery of the Incarnation because in her "*the Word was made flesh*" (Jn 1:14).

Admittedly, it took the further reflection of the Church to bring out all the implications of this title. But already from the beginning, in the Gospel tradition, there is left no doubt as to the wealth and transcendence of its import. Matthew (as well as Luke) states clearly that this Motherhood is the work of the Spirit: *"It is by the Holy Spirit that she has conceived this Child"* (Mt 1:20; cf. Lk 1:35). Affirmed by two independent traditions, the *virginal conception* of Jesus was perceived by the first Christian communities as a sign of His Divine Sonship and a sign of God's total and absolutely free initiative in the Incarnation.

The Evangelists also give expression to another aspect of Mary's Motherhood—one that relates to the community of those who receive the Word of God in faith—and they do not fail to point out Mary's full communion in the demands of this new Motherhood. The account of the Annunciation (Lk 1:26-38) makes clear the importance of Mary's free response and her adherence *in faith* to the vocation announced to her. Mary consents to being the Mother of Jesus and, calling herself *"servant of the Lord,"* yields herself entirely to the Word of the Lord and accepts whatever this Motherhood might imply. In due course, Simeon lets her know of the connection between her vocation to Motherhood and the whole Messianic drama (Lk 2:34-35). Her Motherhood will have to pass through the trial of faith, amid a people divided on the subject of the very person and mission of Jesus. But from this trial, thanks to the Passion of Christ and Mary's faithfulness, there will be born the new Israel, the Church. Mary will also be the Mother of those who believe in Jesus (Jn 19:27).

2. Mary, Daughter of Israel and Daughter of Zion

Dogmatic theology may tend to accentuate the distance between Mary and us, between her faith and ours. But the authors of the New Testament present her as belonging completely to the people of Israel, her roots in her people not only by origin but also by her faith and in her prayer. The Evangelists depict her mainly as similar to her contemporaries, and from the moment that a community of believers begins to form around Jesus, they make sure to note Mary's presence in the midst of this new Israel in process of birth.

Speaking of Mary for the first time, Luke introduces her as most ordinary: *"to a town of Galilee named Nazareth . . . a virgin betrothed to a man named Joseph . . . the virgin's name was Mary"* (Lk 1:26-27). Everything, from her name and antecedents to her matrimonial situation, reveals Mary as belonging to the people of the promise. Daughter of Israel, Mary more than once shows her fidelity to observances of the Law. She consecrates to the Lord her firstborn Son; she presents the offering prescribed for the poor (Lk 2:22-25), and she brings Jesus to Jerusalem to celebrate the Passover *"according to the custom of the feast"* (Lk 2:41-42).

Additionally, in their description of Mary's role the authors of the New Testament make constant use of Old Testament symbols, as if to say that they saw in her the most perfect embodiment of Israel and the true *Daughter of Zion*. The variety of images and references harking back to the Old Testament builds to a remarkable convergence of purpose: namely, to show that the figure of Mary has to be understood in the light of the chosen people's history. Her vocation forms part of Israel's historic vocation, which however she brings to its crowning fulfillment.

Gabriel's greeting already carries an overtone of community. In Mary, it is the Daughter of Zion who is asked to rejoice in the salvation that is coming (Zep 3:14; Zec 9:9). The sign given her by the Angel (Lk 1:36-37) brings to mind the origins of her people. But henceforth it is Jesus Who is the true Son of the promise, and the new People of God will take form from the faith of Mary, just as formerly the chosen people was born of the faith of Abraham.

Elizabeth's blessing extols the faith of Mary by drawing an implicit comparison with great feminine figures of Israel's history (cf. Jdt 13). Mary's own canticle of thanksgiving is filled with the hopes and the faith of a chosen people in the God Who is faithful to His promises. And Mary's attitude at Cana (Jn 2:5) is not without parallel in what was the people's spontaneous reaction to the Covenant: *"Everything the Lord has said, we will do"* (Ex 19:8; 24:3, 7).

3. Mary, First Believer

For the Evangelists, Mary's true greatness lies less in the physical fact of her Motherhood than in her deep faith in the Word of God and her full communion in the Mystery of Christ: *"Blessed are they who hear the Word of God and keep it"* (Lk 11:28).

Rather than minimizing Mary's greatness, these words of Christ heap it with praise and give it its ultimate explanation. Mary is blessed because of her faith (Lk 1:45).

Not that Mary knew or understood everything beforehand. She has to ask Gabriel about the *"how"* of the vocation announced to her. In the Temple she *"marvels"* at the utterances of Simeon, and she confesses her "anxiety" over the conduct of Jesus. She will have to discover gradually the Mystery contained in His first public words *"Did you not know I had to be in My Father's house?"* (Lk 2:49). She has also to learn to accept the change in her simple life of Mother to Jesus, signaled by His addressing her as *"Woman"* (Jn 2:4; 19:26).

In all of these circumstances Mary is seen to be intent on receiving the Word of God and desirous of discovering its deeper meaning: *"Mary treasured all these things and reflected on them in her heart"* (Lk 2:19). Her *"fiat"* is unconditional adherence to the revelation made to her by Gabriel. At Cana, Mary promptly asks the waiters to heed the words of Jesus (Jn 2:5), thus effecting the transition to the new order of relations demanded by Jesus. Mary thus appears as the first of believers, wholly consecrated to the person and the work of Jesus. Her presence at the Cross shows the lofty degree of fidelity to a communion in the Mystery of Christ she has attained by her meditation on the prophecy of Simeon and the first public words of Jesus. In Mary, more than in any other disciple, the seed of the Word has been able to produce fruit a hundredfold (Mk 4:8).

4. Mary as Woman of Beginnings and Fruitions

Mary has a privileged place in the New Testament. Far from being episodic or incidental, her presence marks the most decisive moments in her people's history. And she is an integral part of the Mystery of Christ.

Mary is also present at Cana in Galilee, when Jesus performs *"the first of His signs"* (Jn 2:1-12): and her openness, in faith, to the words of Jesus (shown by her words *"Do whatever He tells you,"* Jn 2:5) gives rise to the first community of disciples. At the Cross, everything is not *"finished"* (Jn 19:28) until Jesus has formally announced her vocation to Motherhood toward the disciples: *"Woman, behold your son"* (Jn 19:26). With that, the Church is already being born, but it has not yet assumed her missionary scope. And here again, Mary is closely associated with the event that brings the Church to this scope. For she prays with the Apostles in wait for the Spirit (Acts 1:14), the Spirit Who had entered her on the day of the Incarnation to build in her the temple of flesh. This temple of flesh supersedes the temple of stone so as to form the Church into the Body of Christ by the gift of the Spirit.

In all these moments where the Gospel experiences its first beginnings and first fruitions, there also is found Mary, unfailingly and actively associated with the Mystery of Jesus and the Church.

J. P. Prévost

NOVENAS AND MARY   [971]

SEE *Communion of Saints*   *Intercession of Mary*
     Devotion(s)   *Miraculous Medal*
     Immaculate Conception   *Prayer(s) to Mary*

A NOVENA means nine days of public or private prayer for some special occasion or intention. It goes back to the nine days that the disciples and Mary spent together in prayer between Christ's Ascension and the Descent of the Holy Spirit on Pentecost Sunday (Acts 1:14).

To make a Novena means to persevere in prayer asking for some favor over a period of nine days in succession or nine weeks. It means fulfilling Our Lord's teaching that we must continue praying and never lose confidence. This confidence is based on Christ's words: *"Ask and you shall receive; seek and you shall find; knock and it shall be opened to you. For whoever asks, receives; whoever seeks, finds; whoever knocks, is admitted"* (Lk 11:9f).

Many Catholics make Novenas to Our Lady, the Mother of God and Queen of Heaven. In so doing, they are following the fervent recommendation of the Church issued through the lips of Pope Pius XI: "By persevering prayer let us make Mary our daily Mediatrix, our true Advocate. In this way, we may hope that she herself, assumed into heavenly glory, will be our Advocate before Divine Goodness and Mercy at the hour of our passing."

The Novena to the Immaculate Conception in preparation for the feast—which was indulgenced in 1764—seems to have been the oldest Marian Novena. There are now Novenas for every feast of Mary, with the Miraculous Medal Novena being the best-known. The purpose of these Novenas is not only to pray for favors from God through Mary but also to encourage people to pray frequently because prayer, after the Sacraments, is the richest source of God's grace.

After Vatican II, most of the Novenas were updated to accord with the Liturgical Year and to emphasize readings from the Word of God.

A. Buono

- O -

OCTOBRI MENSE

[971]

SEE   *Devotion(s)*   *Rosary*
      Intercession of Mary   *Value of Marian Devotion*

ON September 22, 1891, Pope Leo XIII issued an Encyclical entitled, *Octobri Mense* ("In the Month of October"), which summed up the basic reasons for devotion to Mary and presented a splendid praise of the Rosary.

Our Lady deserves all our trust for two reasons. First of all, she is the most powerful creature with Jesus because of her Motherhood and the closest creature to us because of her goodness. In her we see the natural intermediary with her Son, Whose infinite goodness draws us but Whose infinite justice fills us with dread.

In the second place, we see in Mary the dispensatrix of all graces in a kind of right that she acquired when she freely consented to cooperate in the Redemption and gave the world Jesus, the fount of our salvation, with Whom she effectively cooperated in the saving work:

"The eternal Son of God, about to take upon Himself our nature for the saving and ennobling of human beings, and about to consummate thus a mystical union between Himself and all humankind, did not accomplish His design without obtaining the free consent of her who was to become His Mother. She was the representative of all humankind, according to the illustrious and learned opinion of Saint Thomas, who says, that 'in the Annunciation was awaited the consent of the Virgin standing in the place of humankind.'

"With equal truth it may be said that of the great treasury of all graces given to us by Our Lord—*'for grace and truth came by Jesus Christ'* (Jn 1:17)—nothing comes to us except through the mediation of Mary, for such is the will of God. Thus as no one goes to the Father but by the Son, so no one goes to Christ except through His Mother."

Among the forms of devotion to this Divine Mother of human beings, the Rosary is one of the most pleasing to her and among the most efficacious for us.

The excellence of the Rosary stems from its internal composition, since it is a wonderful combination of the truths of the Mysteries of the Redemption and the most beautiful prayers. When it is well said, our faith is strengthened, our devotion is animated by renewed fervor, and our will is excited toward the good. This explains the favor that has been reserved for this devotion by the faithful, who have received help in the most grave dangers of the history of the Church.

Moved by these reasons, the Pope recommends that the faithful have recourse to the Rosary with trust and perseverance, uniting penance with prayer to obtain new and more extensive victories for the Church.

A. Buono

OLD TESTAMENT (MARY IN THE)   [128-130, 489]

SEE *Daughter of Zion*   *Queen*
     Marian Typology

MARY is not directly named in the Old Testament and no one has ever seriously claimed that any of the Prophets traced the personal characteristics of the Mother of Jesus of Nazareth. The same cannot be said if we speak of the Mother of Jesus Christ, Messiah-King.

1. The King in Israel

The discoveries and decipherings of the last two centuries have greatly altered our knowledge of the ancient Near East. In the light of this new understanding, the Old Testament appears as evidence of prophetic schools that preserved and developed the hope of a people in its national God, regarded as actively present in the person of its leaders.

At the beginning of the Biblical redactions Israel shares the hope of nations and desires a king, *"as other nations have,"* to judge it and save it by force of arms (1 Sm 8:5-20; 9:16). The king is the elect of God, Who communicates to His elect a Divine power and wisdom (1 Kgs 3:28). What is this action of the true God and how does it operate? The Bible unveils this little by little in the course of its composition.

Peoples of the ancient Near East distinguished the king from the judge—both provided with political functions—by the fact that kingship was dynastic. The dynastic reality best assured continuity of the State against the succession of individuals. The City-State arose, about 300 B.C., as a superior form of civilization. The capital offered services that the tribe, the camp, or the village did not offer: army, justice, accountability, all guaranteed in writing. The key to good functioning of these services was the king and his "house."

2. Role of the Queen-Mother and "Figures" of Mary

For the stability and prosperity of everyone's house the king's house had to function well, and it was in this point that the role of the *queen-mother* proved essential. As *wife* the queen is not without potential embarrassment to the security of the State: she can "divert" the king in every sense of the word and be a principle of dissension in the prevailing polygamy.

As *mother*, she is a principle of stability. Often her son owes her his throne, which she has obtained for him through her political sense and astuteness. Often, too, she acts as the king's regent. She understands the king and can say things to him that no one else could say. And the king can listen to her without misgivings since she has no interest except in him.

Accordingly, the oldest Biblical syntheses—the J "document" of the Pentateuch and the history of David's succession—reflect the problems of Solomon's court and record, from tradition or from experience, the role of the women denominated "figures of Mary." Under the action or by consent of Yahweh, God of Israel, they prepared the election and the coming of the Son of David.

The first head, Adam, has ignored the Word of God and listened to the word of the serpent, at the instigation of his wife. But it is to the descendant of *Eve,* wounded in the heel, that God promises to crush the head of the serpent. Sarah and Hagar both provide Abraham with a posterity, but *Sarah* obtains the inheritance for Isaac. God comforts and consoles but, without saying so, ratifies the manner in which *Rebekah* arranged for the passing of Esau's patriarchal blessing to Jacob. The same author who had affirmed God's active role in the birth of Eve's firstborn (*"I have produced*—or acquired—*a man with the help of the Lord"*: Gn 4) recalls God's special intervention in these births (Gn 30:2; cf. 20:17ff).

Again, Rachel is the preferred wife, but it is *Leah* who becomes the mother of Judah whom all nations will serve (Gn 49:10). And it is *Zipporah,* wife of Moses, who saves her husband by circumcising their son (Ex 4:24-26). Finally, it is *Bathsheba* who, with the help of the Prophet Nathan, obtains the crown from David for her son Solomon. She bows in homage to her husband David, but it is to her that her son Solomon bows (1 Kgs 2:19). Throughout the Books of Kings the name of the king's mother is carefully noted.

It will be left for the Prophet Isaiah to consolidate this line of development in the *Book of Immanuel* (6:1—9:6). The Book begins with the death of King Uzziah and ends with the accession to the throne of David by a child who receives human-Divine names: *God-Hero, Wonder-Counselor, Father-Forever, Prince of Peace.* It affirms the perpetuity of the Davidic dynasty against human plots to overthrow it (7:4-9).

The sign of this perpetuity is the birth of Immanuel: *God with-us.* The Prophet mentions not the father but the mother, the *Almah* who at that time was not yet the queen-mother. As we have seen in Israel, and as was said in regard to the Pharaoh in Egypt, it is on the mother that the special action of the national God falls with a view to the royal birth.

Micah also adopts this traditional sign of royal motherhood (5:2). With him, the salvific birth becomes a redemptive birth as well, since, in 4:10, it is the daughter of Zion who gives birth in pain in order to be redeemed from her enemies.

Jeremiah keeps the traditional doctrine that the king and his mother share in common both the glory (the crown) and the humiliation (13:18; 22:26). Finally, Ezekiel makes the mother of the last two kings of Judah, Jehoiakim and Zedekiah, the symbol of Israel: *"She is now without a strong branch, a ruler's scepter"* (19:14), even while he maintains the election of David (34:23ff; 37:25ff).

3. Messianic Hope and Mother of the Messiah

In the faith of Israel the Messianic hope continues bound to texts that associate the saving mission of the Messiah, Son of David, with a Divine action upon His Mother. After the fall of the monarchy the texts develop this theology by means of feminine figures.

It is the *ideal wife* that concludes the Book of Proverbs (ch. 31): by her intelligent activity she becomes the glory of her husband and the happiness of his house. It is the timid *Esther* who has the courage to confront Xerxes (Ahasuerus) for the salvation of her people. And the devout *Judith* it is who takes the bold decision by which the city is delivered.

These figures represent the better side of Israel and Judah, and no doubt enter into the faithful Jew's image of the Mother of the Messiah, bearer of total and definitive salvation. The Evangelists suppose them known whenever they speak of Mary simply as Mother of Jesus Christ.

For an understanding of the Mystery of the Incarnation it is perhaps the portrait of Wisdom, in Sirach 24, that is most laden with theology. In Proverbs 8, the Bible had shown that the true royal heir, *"by Whom kings reign,"* was a Wisdom born of God before all ages. In Sirach 24, it shows that this eternal Wisdom was planted by the Most High in the land of Israel (v. 12). She has her seat in the holy tent (Temple, v. 10), from which she derives growth and efflorescence prior to calling all nations. It was through Mary that the eternal Word willed to experience this growth and this planting.

H. Cazelles

OUR LADY OF THE CAPE (Quebec, Canada)
(Notre Dame du Cap)   [971]

IN all of North America there are few places of pilgrimage to the Virgin Mary as popular as the shrine of Our Lady of the Cape. Every year, especially in spring and summer, close to a million people make a special visit to this oasis of green space, this garden of peace, this old chapel dating from 1714, and above all to the miraculous statue twice crowned by papal delegates, in 1904 and 1954.

A Chosen Place . . .

To inspire such ardors of faith there must be something special. And there was, on this modest promontory along the majestic St. Lawrence. Apparitions? No, but two signs in which the people were not disappointed. The tiny parish of St. Mary Magdalen (named after the parish of the first proprietary who came from Châteaudun, France, in 1636) became a veritable place of pilgrimage to the Mother of God, initially in 1879 and then for good in 1888, under the special patronage of *Our Lady of the Most Holy Rosary.* An old Confraternity of the Rosary established there in 1694 had prepared the way for all this.

"Bridge of Rosaries" (1879)

Two priests of fervent faith, the pastor Father Desilets and his associate Father Duguay, brought an indifferent population to a remarkable spiritual reawakening, mostly through the simple devotion of the Rosary. In March 1879, the Virgin responded. It had been decided to build a larger church. But the stone for it was located on the other side of the river. The most economical means of transporting it was across the river, more than a mile wide, if it froze over. This winter there was no freezing. Father Desilets then made a vow to Mary not to demolish the old parish church but to dedicate it to Our Lady of the Rosary, if he obtained a bridge of ice.

His prayers were answered. "From the 18th of March to the 26th, 1897," according to a plaque unveiled at the centenary, "the parishioners of *Cap-de-la-Madeleine* transported stone for their new church, under the obvious protection of Our Lady of the Rosary, on the ice of the St. Lawrence as on a bridge, which they spontaneously named: Bridge of Rosaries." A shrine was in the making.

"Prodigy of the Eyes" (1888)

On the eve of the solemn consecration of the chapel to Our Lady, a most unusual phenomenon took place. The face of the statue of Mary, with the features of the "Miraculous Medal," came alive before three witnesses, Father Desilets, Father Frederic, O.F.M., and a handicapped man, Pierre Lacroix, all of whom swore until their dying day to the truth of the matter. "I saw very distinctly the eyes of the statue wide open (this statue with eyes cast down), but in a natural manner, and as though it were looking up above us," recalled one of the witnesses. This gaze of Mary no one could forget at the Cape.

Popular Fervor

It was actually from this time on that pilgrimages were formed, arriving by boat, by train, and by carriage. The people responded to the two calls of Mary. And the response has not ceased. Special favors and graces of conversion of life have been obtained there, according to the testimony of thousands who came, little by little, from all over North America. Pastoral ministry to so many people proved an enormous task. In 1902 the local bishop turned to the Congregation of Missionary Oblates of Mary Immaculate, who saw there a perfect opportunity for bringing the Gospel to the poor, to the common people, in a kind of *"Mission on the spot,"* an idea of their founder, Saint Eugene of Mazenod.

Since then, everything has grown: the "Gardens of the Virgin," an affecting place of prayer amid trimmed greenery and sparkling waters; the imposing basilica, dedicated in 1964; "Rosary groups" gathering to pray and meditate on the Rosary; and especially the great novena August 7 to 15, an immense popular mission with modern audiovisual aids, for crowds enthusiastic, ruddy-complexioned, singing . . . and fervent.

Bishops of the area have many times expressed their appreciation for what has come to pass at Our Lady of the Cape. The Shrine, there is no denying, has won a special place in the heart of the people, and that by means that go beyond the human. After the hesitations of the '60s, both the influx of visitors and the spiritual intensity revived and grew again. Noteworthy, among other things, is the pastoral ministry of intercessory prayer for the sick. At the Cape, through Mary, pilgrims of every age group, in a respite from their journey of life, rediscover the Lord Jesus, Who still declares: *"Repent and believe in the Gospel."*

A. Dumont

- P -

PARENTS OF MARY

SEE *Life of Mary*

SAINTS Joachim and Ann, both of the tribe of Judah of the royal house of David, are venerated by the Church as the parents of the Blessed Virgin Mary who was probably their only child. The other Mary mentioned in the Gospels as the sister of the Mother of God was, it is believed, her cousin; for this was a customary way of designating relatives in the East.

Saint Ann has been honored from early Christian times. Churches were dedicated to her honor, and the Fathers—especially of the Eastern Church—loved to speak of her sanctity and her privileges. She is often represented as teaching her little daughter to read the Scriptures.

Saint Joachim has been honored from time immemorial in the Churches of the East, and since the 6th century public devotion to him has been observed in all countries. However, as in the case of Saint Ann, the Gospel tells us nothing about his life.

Tradition, grounded on very old testimonies, informs us that Saints Joachim and Ann in their old age came from Galilee to settle in Jerusalem, and there the Blessed Mother of God was born and reared; there also they died and were buried. A church was built during the 4th century, possibly by Saint Helena, on the site of the home of Saints Joachim and Ann in Jerusalem.

In the new Liturgy, the Memorial of Ann and Joachim is celebrated on July 26.   *A. Buono*

POMPEII (Italy)   [971]

SEE *Crowning of an Image of the Blessed Virgin*

IN autumn of 1872, Bartolo Longo (a lawyer who was born at Latiano in Brindisi, Italy, on February 11, 1841, and died at

Pompeii on October 5, 1926) arrived at the plain of Pompeii to take care of the affairs of Countess Marianna Farnararo De Fusco. In that fertile agricultural region infested with robbers he also began to spread the Rosary among the sharecroppers of De Fusco and the farmers of the place.

With his wife's help, he inaugurated a confraternity of the Rosary and he had need of a picture of the Blessed Virgin before which the Rosary could be recited every day. He obtained one as a gift from a religious of the Monastery of the Rosary at Porta Medina, Sister M. Concetta de Litala, who had been holding it for the Dominican priest Alberto Radente. The latter had acquired it from a junk-shop dealer in Naples for a very small sum. The painting was of modest artistic merit and in very poor condition. It portrayed Our Lady of the Rosary, with Saint Dominic and Saint Catherine of Siena.

Arriving at Naples on November 13, 1875, the picture was provisionally exposed in a small declining chapel. But in that same month, Bartolo Longo received permission from the Bishop of Nola to build a new church.

Miracles were reported and pilgrimages began to frequent the place. Hence, in 1883, when the sanctuary was completed (and would be consecrated on May 8, 1891), Bartolo Longo entrusted the architect Rispoli with the construction of the throne of the Virgin and directed an appeal to the faithful: "In this place selected for its prodigies, we wish to leave to present and future generations a monument to the Queen of Victories that will be less unworthy of her greatness but more worthy of our faith and love."

Four years later saw the celebration of a threefold feast of the inauguration, the crowning, and the enthroning of the picture of Our Lady of the Rosary.

The picture, already summarily restored in 1875, was subjected in 1879 to a second and far more accurate retouching that stabilized the colors and the image. Finally, in 1965, at Rome, the cloth was renovated for a third time, at the hands of the Benedictine Monks. Moreover, before being returned to Pompeii (on April 25, 1965), the picture remained in the Vatican Basilica by express request of Paul VI.

During the homily (March 23, 1965), the Pope expressed the hope that "just as the image of the Virgin has been repaired and decorated . . ., so may the image of Mary that all Christians must have within themselves be restored, renovated, and enriched." At the end of the Mass, the Pope solemnly enthroned the Child and Madonna, placing on their heads two precious diadems that had been offered by the faithful.

Alongside the sanctuary of faith and Rosarian prayer, Bartolo Longo also caused to rise up in Pompeii a sanctuary of charity, with his multiple works and institutions (Orphanages, Sons of Prisoners, Daughters of Prisoners, Daughters of the Holy Rosary of Pompeii, and Dominican Tertiaries).

Most notable of all is the "Supplication to the Queen of Victories" that, begun at Pompeii on October 1883, is recited all over the world on May 8, and on the first Sunday in October.

On October 21, 1979, John Paul II went on pilgrimage to Pompeii and gazed out from the very balcony from which Bartolo Longo (in an intuition of faith on May 5, 1901) had "seen" gazing out "the white figure of the representative of Christ to bless the people calling for universal Peace."

On October 26, 1980, Bartolo Longo was beatified by John Paul II and termed the "man of the Madonna," and the "Apostle of the Rosary."

A. Rum.

PONTMAIN (France) [67]

SEE   *Apparitions*   *Apparitions after Vatican II*

1. In a Great Distress

IT is the darkest hour of the War of 1870. Prussian armies have invaded a large part of France, and the nation is in complete disarray. On the morning of January 17, 1871, Prussian troops are at the outskirts of Laval in the district of Mayenne. The city is preparing to pay the heavy military assessment levied against it: three million francs in gold. "The rout of fleeing soldiers is unimaginable. They are deaf to the command of officers. Two of them have been shot down in their tracks, but this example has had no effect on the others. In the 39 years that I have been in the service, never have I found myself in such a distressing situation," writes the Commander of the 16th Corps.

2. A Sign of Hope

Toward evening on January 17, Pontmain, a small town in the north of Mayenne, lies under a blanket of snow. People are anxious, but everybody is going about work as usual. In a barn in the middle of town two boys, Eugene and Joseph Barbedette, are helping their father pound stalks to feed to the horses. Some minutes before six o'clock in the evening, taking advantage of a break from work, Eugene leaves the barn and sees in the sky a "Lady" dressed in a dark-blue robe sprinkled with stars. She spreads her lowered hands in a gesture of welcome and smiles on him.

Joseph comes along a few moments later and also sees the Lady. But the father of the boys sees nothing. Undaunted, they call their mother, who also fails to see anything even after going back to the house for her eyeglasses. There is nothing to it, declare the parents, and the boys are to get on with work and then come in for supper. After a quick meal, the boys still see the beautiful Lady, so the Sisters of the school are called. Again, they see nothing. But two little girls with them do see the beautiful Lady and describe the star-studded blue robe, the dark veil, and the crown of gold.

3. Evening of Prayer

The town now gathers around the two small boys. Father Guérin, pastor of Pontmain for 35 years, is called and there, in the snow, a vigil of prayer ensues, a veritable dialogue with the Virgin. While the people are praying, the apparition grows and is covered and surrounded with stars. A large blue oval with four candles attached encloses it. The people kneel, some in the snow, some in the barn, whose small door is open. Sister Mary Edward, kneeling at the door, leads the Rosary.

The Lady becomes more beautiful and increases in size as prayer continues. The increase is harmoniously proportioned. The blue oval expands accordingly, and the stars surrounding the apparition seem to move aside to make way for the oval, ranging themselves two by two at the feet of the Lady. Those that spangle her robe multiply and the dark blue of the robe brightens.

4. Message of Hope

After recitation of the Rosary, the people sing the *Magnificat* "in the sonorous tone of the Bretons." A white banner then appears on which large letters of gold slowly form. The two small boys try to decipher them while prayer goes on. After some moments, they can read:

"PRAY, MY CHILDREN. GOD WILL ANSWER BEFORE LONG.
MY SON LETS HIMSELF BE MOVED. "

The message produces a strong emotional reaction in the crowd. After a momentary silence the pastor suggests they sing the hymn *"Mother of Hope."* The children leap for joy and clap their hands while repeating: "SEE HOW SHE SMILES! OH, HOW BEAUTIFUL SHE IS!" At the end of the hymn the banner bearing the inscription vanishes.

5. Sign of the Cross

The prayer of the people takes a penitential turn with the singing of the hymn:

"Gentle Jesus,
Pardon now our penitent hearts. . . ."

A sadness appears in the Virgin and is reflected in the children. A large red crucifix is then seen, surmounted by a placard bearing in beautiful red letters the name: JESUS CHRIST. The Virgin presents the crucifix to the children. The sadness seen in her makes a deep impression on Joseph. Later he will write:

"Her sadness was more than anyone can imagine. I saw my mother overwhelmed with grief when, some months later, my father died. You know what such grief in a mother's face does to the heart of a child. But, as I remember, what instinctively came to mind was the sadness of the Most Blessed Virgin, which must have been the sadness of the Mother of Jesus at the foot of the Cross that bore her dying Son."

6. "It's All Over . . ."

While all this is happening, the crowd continues to pray. Some moments later the red crucifix vanishes and the Virgin resumes her initial posture, arms extended downward. A small white Cross appears on each of her shoulders. The Lady smiles once more. At the suggestion of the pastor evening prayer is begun. People kneel where they happen to be, in the barn or in the snow. A large white veil appears at the feet of the Virgin, slowly lifts and gradually enshrouds her. When evening prayer is finished, the apparition vanishes. "IT'S ALL OVER," declare the two small boys. The time is about nine o'clock in the evening and everybody leaves for home.

7. Conclusion

This clear manifestation of the Mother of God tells us of her Son and renews our hope. There is no need to add anything, except perhaps to say that we ought to receive the message of Pontmain with the same joy and simplicity of soul as these villagers. Without fanfare or extraordinary demonstration, for two hours and more they prayed and listened to what the message meant for them.   P. Poulain

POOR OF YAHWEH AND MARY   [2619]

SEE   *Old Testament (and Mary)*

1. The Poor of Yahweh in Israel

THE idea of "the poor" in the Old Testament is one of total dependence on Yahweh. It represents a poverty of being not simply of money. Just as the Spirit of God worked on the primeval darkness to produce all that exists, so Yahweh worked on His poor to produce all that is good for them. It was Yahweh Who created a *land* for that people by driving out the inhabitants of Palestine before them. And it was Yahweh Who gave them the *Law* through Moses. In all these cases human power alone would have availed nothing.

As time went on, the Israelites forgot this lesson and in many cases depended on their own efforts. This availed them nothing but unfaithfulness to their God. The Prophets spoke of a *remnant* of Israel that would remain faithful and that would inherit the promises of Yahweh (Is 6:13; 37:31; Mi 4:6-7).

Gradually, this remnant became fused with the idea of the *anawim*, the "poor of Yahweh": "*In all the land, says the Lord, two thirds of them shall be cut off and perish, and one third shall be left. . . . They shall call upon My Name and I will hear them. I will hear them. I will say, 'They are My people,' and they shall say, 'The Lord [Yahweh] is my God' *" (Zec 13:8-9). The Psalmist spells this out when he says: "*The Lord loves His people, and He adorns the lowly [anawim:* the poor of Yahweh] *with victory*" (Ps 149:4).

The perfect example of the poor of Yahweh was the Prophet Jeremiah. He was wary of his calling to be a prophet, did not have the prophets' eloquence, rarely saw his message accepted, and suffered all kinds of privations and indignities. Yet his life became a symbol of all the poor of Yahweh who remain steadfast in hope and love: "*Sing to the Lord, praise the Lord, for He has rescued the life of the poor from the power of the wicked*" (Jer 20:13). By New Testament times, this remnant had become purified of sinful interests and completely open to and dependent on Yahweh.

2. Mary—the Poor of Yahweh Par Excellence

When Mary visited Elizabeth after the Annunciation, her cousin exclaimed, "*Blessed is she who trusted that the Lord's words to her would be fulfilled*" (Lk 1:45). By her acceptance of the Word of God about Jesus (Lk 1:38, 45), Mary is the first disciple of Christ.

Indeed, she is the spokeswoman for all Christ's disciples—but as the representative of the poor of Yahweh. "The great symphony of prayer that arose from the Church of the poor was a prelude to the *Magnificat*. The whole spiritual life of ancient times reached in Mary its apogee, its point of maturity. And each one of the *anawim*, each member of the true Israel, prepared for and proclaimed her" (Albert Gelin).

Thus, Mary was at the head of the New Testament community of pious ones that included Zechariah, Elizabeth, the shepherds at the crib, the afflicted, the widows and orphans as opposed to the proud and the self-sufficient who trusted in their own strength and showed no need of Yahweh.

Mary did not refuse the designation "blessed" for on that day she understood, as far as humanly possible, the unity of her life. She entered into the mystery of her vocation, and she committed herself wholeheartedly to the Divine adventure that far surpassed her own powers and in which she was the servant of the Lord.

Even more, she immortalized this adventure in the *Magnificat*, the "Hymn of the Poor of Yahweh." This is "more than a fabric woven of Old Testament quotations. In it we have the woman who has so identified herself with the *anawim* that, conscious of the newness of the Incarnation, she has become their perfect and living expression" (Albert Gelin).

The connection between the *Magnificat* and the Beatitudes has not gone unnoticed. The great Scripture scholar J. M. Lagrange has stated: "If it were possible to push that far the analysis of the human development [of Jesus], we could say that we can see in Him, as in so many others, something of the influence of His Mother." Listening to His Mother's words at Nazareth and noting her actions, Jesus must have come to love the poor of Yahweh whom He would later declare to be His disciples: *"Blessed are the poor in spirit: the Kingdom of God is theirs"* (Mt 5:3).

As the embodiment of trust and receptivity to Yahweh (outstanding qualities of the *anawim*), Mary is the link between the Old and the New Testaments, between the hope and promises of the Old Testament and the fulfillment in the Kingdom of God. She continues a certain style of Israelite piety and anticipates the spirit of the early Christians after Pentecost.

A. Buono

POPULAR RELIGION AND MARIAN PIETY   [971]

SEE   *Evangelization and Marian Piety*

THE Blessed Virgin has an important place in "popular religion," i.e., the religion of the masses, who generally are not the learned class and for whom the play of ideas represents nothing very real, especially in matters of faith.

What Paul VI said about popular piety in general in his Apostolic Exhortation on *Evangelization in the World (Evangelii Nuntiandi,* No. 48) has significant application here.

Doubtless, it is possible to see only the limits of popular (Marian) piety and the risk it runs of falling into superstition or "sectarian" bias. But pastoral love and respect for reality dictate a more judicious attitude toward this religious expression, "at once so rich and so vulnerable."

A positive approach to popular Marian piety requires above all that "one be sensitive to it, know how to perceive its interior dimensions and undeniable value, and be ready to help it to overcome its risks of deviation. When it is well oriented, this popular religiosity can be more and more for multitudes of our people a true encounter with God in Jesus Christ" (EN 48).

1. Richness

Popular religion is much more sensitive to persons, to lived experiences, and to feelings than it is to abstract formulations and general ideas. It has a better grasp of devotion to Mary than it has of the "great truths of faith."

For example, to many people the Incarnation, the notion of faith, even the "Word of God" remain abstractions. But the Virgin Mary receiving at Nazareth with joy and total trust the announcement of the birth of Jesus, Son of God, is something *real* and *true to life* for them.

Or again, the Mystery of the Motherhood of the Church and the Communion of Saints may not be understood in the abstract but it is exemplified in popular piety when it has recourse to Mary, our Mother, because she prays for us.

The same can be said about the "Sorrows of Mary and the Redemption"; "the Assumption and the 'last things' "; "the Immaculate Conception and grace.". . .

This does not mean that the Marian piety of the people is "symbolic mythology," an imaginative projection of revealed truth. The Gospels of Luke and John present Mary as a concrete person in whom *God Himself* was pleased "to personify" (to realize in exemplary fashion) the relations of love He offers to everyone personally and to humanity as a whole.

By its realism and its sensitivity to the actualities of life, personal or collective, "popular religion" is more in tune with the living God Who gives Himself to us in Jesus His Son— more, that is, than the abstract or obsessive dogmatic speculations of "demythologization. "

Other aspects of popular Marian piety could be examined in this more favorable light: e.g., importance of the prayer of petition as a means of educating in hope and evangelical childhood; the prayer of repetition as an expression of prayer of the heart, over and beyond words; the appreciation of sacred paintings and pictures, statues and medals, as an echo of the Incarnation; a feeling for concrete activity, often collective (pilgrimages, processions, etc.); and even the familiarity with miraculous "signs." In some way, this all "manifests a thirst for God that only the simple and poor can know . . . an acute awareness of the profound attributes of God: Fatherhood, Providence, loving and constant Presence" (EN 48).

This friendly view of popular piety requires from the spiritual shepherd, and the theologian, a certain humility and lowliness of heart. Only then can they minister to it on a constructive basis.

2. Limits

The risks of deviation in popular religion are obvious. The Second Vatican Council (LG 67) makes note of the "*gross ex-*

aggerations" of content and form that even falsify doctrine as well as the "*petty narrow-mindedness*" that obscures the figure and mission of Mary.

Paul VI reiterates the other deviations mentioned by the Council: "*vain credulity*, which substitutes reliance on merely external practices for serious commitment [and] . . . *sterile and ephemeral sentimentality*, so alien to the spirit of the Gospel that demands persevering and practical action. . . . The ultimate purpose of devotion to the Blessed Virgin is to glorify God and to lead Christians to commit themselves to a life that is in absolute conformity with His will" (MC 38-39).

It is clear that "true devotion proceeds from true faith" (LG 67). Devotions to Mary abound. Care must be exercised to keep them within the lines of discretion and their ultimate purpose. Sometimes a "recentering" may be in order, so that Marian piety remain "firmly rooted in the revealed Word and have solid dogmatic foundations" (MC 56).

Spiritual shepherds and theologians have a task of conducting the necessary "pedagogy of evangelization" (EN 48), based on the Gospel and related to the whole of faith and to daily life.

Paul VI also notes that popular religiosity "can even lead to the creation of sects and endanger the true ecclesial community" (EN 48). This is the harm—the split of the community—that can come from patronizing an "apparition" that has not been recognized or may even have been formally disapproved. The encounter between popular fervor and pastoral authority can then take a very delicate turn.

To repeat, popular religion is especially sensitive to persons and concrete life. Only some guidelines for dealing with it have been here proposed.

There is no question, however, that an immense task remains in the wake of Vatican II. It is the task of a "pastoral of Marian piety" that takes into account the values and strength of "popular religion" and does justice to the legitimate desires of the poor and lowly in this area of the faith.

J. Laurenceau

PRAYER(S) TO MARY   [971]

SEE | | |
|---|---|
| *Akathist Hymn* | *Magnificat* |
| *Angelus* | *Marian Classics* |
| *Communion of Saints* | *Marian Hymns* |
| *Devotion(s)* | *Mediatrix* |
| *Hail Holy Queen* | *Memorare* |
| *Hail Mary* | *Popular Religion and Marian* |
| *Intercession of Mary* | *Piety* |
| *Litany of the Blessed* | *Regina Caeli* |
| *Virgin* | *Rosary* |
| *Litany of Mary, Biblical* | *Stabat Mater* |
| *Liturgy* | *Sub Tuum* |

FROM the very beginning Christians have offered prayers to Mary, that is, called upon her, especially in times of adversity—trials, heresies, persecutions, and wars. The reason is not hard to determine and was spelled out by Pope Leo XIII:

"It has always been the habit of Catholics in danger and in arduous times to fly for refuge to Mary and to seek peace in her maternal goodness, which shows that the Catholic Church has always, and with justice, put all her hope and trust in the Mother of God. She who is associated with her Son in the work of the salvation of the human race has favor and power with Him greater than any other human or angelic creature has ever obtained or can obtain.

"And, as it is her greatest pleasure to grant her help and comfort to those who seek her, it cannot be doubted that she will deign, even anxiously, to receive the aspirations of the Universal Church" (Encyclical *Supremi Apostolatus* ["The Supreme Apostolic Office"], September 1, 1883).

1. Primitive Appeals to Mary's Help

Already in the first generation of Christians we see the singular honor and devotion accorded to Mary. The Angel of the Incarnation greets her with great respect as *"full of grace"* (Lk 1:28), and her cousin Elizabeth does likewise by the words *"Mother of my Lord"* (Lk 1:43).

The early Church attests that the model of the Virgin has become most significant for Christian piety. She does so through the profession of faith, which proclaims Christ as Son of God "born of the Virgin Mary" (this is the 2nd- century formula of the baptismal creed found in the various apocryphal works of the New Testament, e.g., the *Protevangelium of James*). The Church also does so in the Roman funeral monuments of the 2nd-3rd centuries, e.g., the frescoes in the Priscillian cemetery in which Isaiah points with his hand to the Mother of God seated with the Child Jesus in her arms.

The *Apostolic Tradition* of Hippolytus, which exerted a huge influence on the Eastern Liturgies, presents the primitive theme of the Virgin in the first part of the Eucharistic Prayer: "Sent from heaven into the bosom of the Virgin, conceived in her womb, He was made flesh and manifested Himself as [God's] Son, born from the Spirit and from the Virgin."

Mary thus finds a place in the Church's Eucharistic Celebration because of her connection with the Incarnation of the Son. A bit later, the Virgin, already associated with her Son in the economy of salvation, will find a place with Him in the Church's thanksgiving. She will be named before the Apostles in the *Communicantes* (Commemoration of the Saints) of the Roman Canon or after the Prophets in the chronological listing of the Eastern Anaphora. Hence, Mary is on the highest level of the heavenly Church and the first one whose memorial the earthly Church (represented by the Eucharistic Assembly) demands be celebrated.

By the 3rd century, the *Sub Tuum* comes into vogue, the first prayer to the Virgin Mother of God. It is a prayer for help in trials and sin. It stresses Mary's Divine Motherhood, her virginity, her holiness, and her powerful intercession in time of adversity.

By the 4th century, we have an illustration of the praying Madonna at the cemetery on the Nomentanian Way, that is, one who intercedes.

We also have the *Prayer to the Mother of God*, which is of patristic derivation: "Hope of all Christians; pacifier of the Divine Wrath; after God, sole refuge, light, strength, riches, glory of all who come to you; the one who assists her devotees in all their contingencies of soul and body; the one whose intercession with God is all-powerful and is put at the disposal of sinners."

2. From the 5th to the 11th Centuries

By the 5th century, the Akathist Hymn (or Prayer) has added a rich series of terms witnessing to Mary's help. And by the 6th-7th centuries the first part of the *Hail Mary* has been introduced into the Mass of the Annunciation.

In the 6th-century *Antiphonary* of St. Gregory the Great, we find texts derived from the Greek tradition, among which is the Antiphon: "Rejoice, O Virgin Mary; you have vanquished all heresies in the whole world," which is attributed to the Roman Victor the Blind. Allied to this there is the Antiphon that has become part of every Office of Our Lady: "Make me worthy of praising you, O holy Virgin; grant me strength against your enemies."

In the 7th century, in a hymn erroneously attributed to Saint Ambrose, there is a general invitation to pray to the Blessed Virgin: "Therefore, let us pray, O people, to the Virgin Mother of God that she may obtain for us peace and freedom."

At the same time, in Sermon II: "On the Birth of Saint Mary," composed for the new feast of the Assumption, we find the Antiphon that will be repeated in the Office of the Blessed Virgin and at the *Benedictus* of the Marian Office for Saturday: "Holy Mary, succor the miserable, help the weak, comfort the weeping; pray for the people, intervene for the clergy, and intercede for the devoted feminine sex."

Still in the 7th century, we find the first invocations of the Litany of Mary including the simple supplication "Holy Mary, pray for us" as well as the first prayers addressed to Mary by Saint Ildephonsus of Toledo, which then become part of the Mozarabic liturgical books.

In the 9th century the great liturgical reformer Alcuin of York composes a Sacramentary for private devotion that includes two votive Masses of the Blessed Virgin that were a prelude to the Office of Mary with prayers to Mary.

In the 10th century, prayers to the Virgin continue to be expressed in litanaic invocations and hymns. One example is the prayer of Odo of Cluny who customarily calls the Blessed Virgin "Mother of mercy." This passes on into the Litany of Loreto and ends up in the primitive text of the *Salve Regina Misericordiae*, "Hail, Queen of Mercy."

In the 11th century, beautiful prayers spring up such as the prayer of Fulbert of Chartres (d. 1028) that begins with the words: "Holy Virgin Mary, Queen of Heaven," as well as the *Salve Regina* ("Hail, Holy Queen") and the *Alma Redemptoris Mater* ("Mother Benign of Our Redeeming Lord"), which call upon Mary's powerful help.

3. From the 12th to the 16th Centuries

In the 12th century, the antiphon *Ave Regina Caelorum* ("Hail, O Queen of Heaven") celebrates the glory of the Queen of heaven, who gave birth to Christ, the Light of the world.

In the 14th century, the *Stabat Mater* ("At the Cross Her Station Keeping") is the great heart-shattering hymn of the sufferings of Compassion endured by the Blessed Virgin at the foot of the Cross. The *Angelus* ("The Angel of the Lord Declared unto Mary") commemorates the great moment of the Incarnation when, through Mary's "Yes," the Son of God became Man in her womb.

In the 15th century, there comes into being the present version of the *Litany of Loreto,* the Litany of the Mother of Christ and Virgin for the world, a Helper for us and a Queen for the Angels. At the same time, the *Rosary* receives its actual form, in which we ask the Blessed Virgin to unite with her own and immerse in the joys, sorrows, and victories of her Son: our poor sorrows, so that they will not be bitter; our poor victories, so that they may always be magnanimous. At the same epoch, there appears the touching popular prayer of the *Memorare* ("Remember . . .").

In the 16th century, the *Hail Mary* is finalized. The first part, which is in the Gospel, was most likely used as a prayer from the very 1st century and, as already mentioned, eventually appeared in an Entrance Antiphon of the Mass around the

6th century. It began to spread among the faithful beginning with the 12th century.

The second part ("Holy Mary . . ."), whose elements pre-existed in a separated state, was put together beginning with the 15th century and became current among the faithful a little after 1500.

The prayers to Mary mentioned above are only a few of the countless prayers composed in her honor throughout the centuries. They are, as it were, the most well known and quasi-official Marian prayers, and they have remained in the fore-front of prayers to Our Lady to the present time. (For classic prayers of the Saints to Mary, see p. 531.)

A. Buono

PREDESTINATION (OF MARY) [488-489]

SEE *Holy Spirit (and Mary)*   *Trinity (and Mary)*

BY "predestination" here we mean the act of the Divine Will determining Mary's existence, ordaining her to the be-atific vision and, as a means to that end, charging her with a specific mission. All mariologists agree that Mary's predestina-tion to be the Mother of God was purely gratuitous, i.e., un-merited. It is generally admitted, however, that Mary merited the Divine Motherhood in the order of *execution* (as the Schoolmen say); not in strict justice, but out of fittingness. That means that once God had decreed to bestow this preroga-tive on Mary, He endowed her with such degree of sanctity that she was "worthy" to become the Mother of God. Theolo-gians agree also that, since the terms "son" and "mother" are correlative, Mary was predestined *in one and the same decree with Christ*, as recent Popes have taught.

1. Two Theories

There is disagreement, however, as to whether Christ's and Mary's predestination "preceded" or "followed" the pre-destination of all others. (We must note, parenthetically, that in God there is no chronological "before" or "after"; every-thing is eternally present to Him. Besides, all are predestined by God from all eternity in *one, single decree*. Nevertheless, in this one, single decree the human mind distinguishes several virtual decrees, or better, several *logical* steps in the one decree, affecting the various persons according to the laws of reasonable order.) There are several theories on the subject, but for the sake of simplicity, we may reduce them to two as follows:

(A) The Thomists, or followers of Saint Thomas Aquinas (d. 1274), believe that God first predestined all human beings and Angels, and only "after" the prevision of Adam's sin were Christ and Mary predestined so as to restore the Divine Friendship lost by sin. Hence, in the present order of things, if Adam had not sinned, Christ and Mary would never have existed.

(B) The Scotists, or followers of Blessed John Duns Scotus (d. 1308), hold that Christ and Mary were predestined with a *logical priority* to all others, and hence regardless of Adam's sin or of any other factor. Does that mean that, if Adam had not sinned, Christ and Mary would have existed anyway? Many Scotists answer affirmatively; others say: We don't know for sure, since revelation seems to be silent on what God might have done *if* Adam had remained faithful. In either case, for the Scotists, the absolute and unconditional predestination of Christ and Mary remains unaffected.

2. Explanation of Scotistic Theory

The centuries-old controversy between Thomists and Scotists has never been settled by the Magisterium. However, the Scotistic viewpoint, which is now endorsed by a majority of writers, at least in its essential elements, is based on solid grounds. Thus Saint Paul states that Christ is the *"firstborn of all creation."* (Col 1:15). Since He was not the first to be born in the course of history, the reference must be to His priority in the mind of God. Again, *"all things have been created through Him and for Him"* (Col 1:16); *"He is above all creatures and in Him all things hold together . . . that in all things He may hold the primacy"* (Col 1:17-18). Saint Paul also says that *"those whom [God] has foreknown, He has also predestined to become conformed to the image of His Son, that He should be the firstborn among many brothers and sisters"* (Rom 8:29).

From these and similar Biblical passages we gather that Christ was the exemplary and final cause of our predestination and indeed of all creation. If so, He must have been the first to be predestined, according to the laws of metaphysics. We may add that the Scotistic thesis is also in harmony with the universally accepted philosophical principles: "That which is less noble is willed for the sake of that which is more noble" (cf. Saint Thomas, *Summa Theol.* 1, 65, 2). And again: "The better a thing is in its effects, the higher priority it enjoys in the intention of the agent" (cf. Saint Thomas, *Contra Gentiles* 2, 44, 1).

The Second Vatican Council made repeated references to the beautiful Pauline teaching concerning Christ's primacy and predestination but purposely abstained from taking sides in the theological debate.

Before his elevation to the throne of Peter, Cardinal Eugenio Pacelli summed up the Scotistic thesis rather neatly when he wrote: "When speaking of Mary . . . the first thought that comes to our minds is this: God looked upon her from all eternity, *before every other creature. . . . That is the mind of the Church* in attributing to Mary, with all the reservations demanded by faith, that which the author of Proverbs (8:22) has said of the Son of God: 'The Lord has possessed Me at the beginning of His ways, *before any other creature*' " (E. Pacelli, *Discorsi* . . . [Milan, 1939] 633). The sermon from which the above passage is taken was published twice with the author's approval *after* he became Pope Pius XII.

Bibliography

On the various other theories within the Thomistic and Scotistic Schools and their respective arguments, see J. B. Carol, O.F.M., *The Absolute Primacy and Predestination of Jesus and His Virgin Mother* (Chicago, Ill., Franciscan Herald Press, 1981), with further general information and an extensive bibliography. Also available and very useful: M. D. Meilach, O.F.M., *Mary Immaculate in the Divine Plan* (Wilmington, Del., M. Glazier Inc., 1981); and F. X. Pancheri, O.F.M. Conv., *The Universal Primacy of Christ* (Front Royal. Va., Christendom Publications, 1984). J. B. Carol

PRESENCE OF MARY IN
THE EUCHARIST
[487, 968-971]

SEE   *Co-Redemptrix*   *Liturgy*
       Cult of Mary   *Motherhood, Spiritual*

MARY cooperated in a singular way in the Savior's work of restoring supernatural grace to souls—she is a mother to us in the order of grace. By reason of this close connection with Christ and us, Mary could not be absent from our celebration of the Eucharist.

We must not see her presence there as the presence of Christ. The consecration effects the Real Presence of the Christ of Glory in the act of His Sacrifice under the appearances of bread and wine, with His Body and Blood, Soul and Divinity. Nothing of the kind is true in Mary's humanity. Yet the Presence of Jesus brings with it in some way the presence of His Mother.

The Christ Who becomes present on the altar is the same Christ Who took from Mary His Body and Blood of the Eucharistic Sacrifice that are given as nourishment to us. The reality of the Word made flesh can be perceived only in its twofold relation of Son: the one according to which He is eternally engendered by the Father and the one according to which He was begotten in time by Mary.

Hence, our faith in the Eucharistic Christ includes a background reference to His Mother according to the flesh: *Ave verum Corpus natum de Maria*—Hail true Body born of the Virgin Mary!

In addition, the real action that Christ exercises in the Eucharist brings with it the presence of those on whom His action is exercised, and whom He gathers together through it. This action, which transcends the limits of time and space, concerns in the first place Mary.

Inasmuch as she is the beneficiary, the first fruit of the Redemption, the first and perfect Christian, Mary lives in the glory of the life of her Son, because she does not cease to receive it from Him. This is in virtue of the unique and ever active offering by which He has *"forever perfected those who are being sanctified"* (Heb 10:14). Wherever Christ's Sacrifice is, there too is Mary, like the stream that cannot be cut off from its source.

Associated with the work of salvation, Mary retains her special place in God's plan of redemption. Her presence at the Cross is the guarantee of an ever active presence in the Eucharist of her Son. She can only exercise her mediation "interiorly" to the salvific action of Jesus, but wherever this action is, there too is the action of Mary!

Thus, at every Liturgical Celebration, Mary the Mother of God is with us as our Model, our Intercessor, and our Mother. And she is even more each of these things in the Marian celebrations. We should have frequent recourse to her and increase our devotion to her.

Each Marian liturgical celebration is also intended to give us a better understanding of Mary's part in our salvation, a true catechesis of Mary.

As the Liturgy honors Mary over the course of a year the Mysteries of Christ become present to us in their relationship with her.

A. Buono

PRESENTATION OF JESUS   [527]
(Lk 2:22-39)

SEE   *Finding in the Temple   Rosary*
       Luke (Gospel of Saint)

THE last two scenes of the Gospel of the Infancy in Luke are developed according to a calculated unity of setting and perspective. Both of them (Presentation and Finding of Jesus) take us to Jerusalem, and more specifically to the heart of the holy city, the Temple.

The theological importance of Jerusalem in Luke's Gospel is well known. The whole second half of his Gospel is dominated by the prospect of the Passion, which is to take place in

Jerusalem: *"As the time approached when He was to be taken up to heaven, Jesus resolutely set out for Jerusalem"* (9:51). Jerusalem is also where Luke places the appearances of the Risen Lord; there too will begin the preaching of salvation *"to the ends of the earth"* (Acts 1:8; cf. Lk 24:47).

For Luke, this twofold perspective is already present when Jesus first goes up to Jerusalem, the time when His parents come *"so that He could be presented to the Lord"* (2:22). On that occasion Simeon receives Him as Savior and Light of the nations, but not without looking ahead to the Messianic drama and the Passion.

1. "As It Is Written in the Law of the Lord . . ."

Even though Luke gives the impression of confusing the Mosaic prescriptions concerning a mother and child (*"their purification"*), his repeated mention of the *"Law of the Lord"* cannot be without design. Luke introduces and concludes his account with an explicit reference to the *"Law"* (2:22, 39). This same reference serves as refrain to the introduction (2:22, 23, 24): *"When the time of their purification according to the Law of Moses had been completed . . ."* (note the strict correspondence of the conclusion: *"When Joseph and Mary had fulfilled all the prescriptions of the Law of the Lord . . ."*—2:39).

This focusing on the Law is the more striking because it is not Luke's habitual preoccupation. No doubt he wants to underline the deeply religious faithfulness of the parents of Jesus, but even more *the belonging and consecration of Jesus to the Lord,* as firstborn Son par excellence. The law pertaining to firstborns (*"Consecrate to Me every firstborn that opens the womb among the Israelites. . . . It belongs to Me"*—Ex 13:2) is more than a law of purification; it is a reminder of what God has done for Israel, His *"son"*: *"Out of Egypt, I called My son"* (Hos 11:1).

When Mary and Joseph come to *"present Jesus to the Lord,"* they come acknowledging the twofold belonging of Jesus: to the chosen and consecrated people (cf. Dt 7:6) and to Him Whose beloved and "chosen" Son He was (Lk 9:35), the Firstborn par excellence. The numerous references to the Law of the Lord in the account of the Presentation have nothing to do with a concern for ritualism. They serve rather to express the two basic dimensions of the Mystery of Jesus: incarnation (He is fully son of Israel) and transcendence (He is *the First-born, consecrated to the Lord in unique and absolute manner*).

2. The Spirit Reveals Jesus

The Spirit, everywhere present in Luke's Gospel, plays here a paramount role in the revealing of the Mystery of Jesus: *"The Holy Spirit was upon him [Simeon]"* (2:25); *"it had been revealed to him by the Holy Spirit . . ."* (2:26); *"moved by the Holy Spirit he came now to the Temple"* (2:27). Such an outpouring of the prophetic Spirit already proclaims the inauguration of the Messianic age (Jl 3:1-5).

The Messianic hope preached by the Prophets was centered, like that of Simeon, on the coming of the *"Anointed of the Lord"* (2:26). The same Spirit Who had inspired the Prophets moves Simeon to identify Jesus as being this Anointed, this Messiah, Whom the Prophets had awaited and foretold: their hope has now become reality. With the intervention of Simeon, attention is henceforth drawn to the *mission* of Jesus and the manner in which He will achieve the *"consolation of Israel"* as well *as salvation* for *all peoples*.

3. The Mission of Jesus: From the "Consolation" of Israel to the Salvation of the Nations

The scene of the Presentation calls to mind the basic election and vocation of Israel. But it also marks the decisive transition from a national vision to a universalist vision of salvation. The salvation brought by Jesus supposes the Old Covenant and the hope of all who were waiting, like Simeon, for the *"consolation of Israel"* (cf. Is 40) or, like the Prophetess Anna, for the *"deliverance of Jerusalem."*

Beyond that, however, the coming of Jesus concerns all peoples and marks the inauguration of a new age: that of a Messianism without borders. *"For my eyes have witnessed Your salvation, displayed for all the peoples to see: a light of revelation to the Gentiles . . ."* (2:29-32). Jesus assumes entirely the mission of the Servant (Is 42:6; 49:6). He recalls to Israel the reason for its election and involves it as a consequence in the creation of the New Covenant, definitive and universal, the very one of Isaiah: *"I, the Lord, have called you . . . and set you as a Covenant of the people and a light for the nations . . ."* (Is 42:6).

4. The "Daughter of Zion" and the Messianic Drama

As is normal in the presence of a revelation or manifestation of Divine power (cf. Lk 1:21, 63; 2:18), Mary and Joseph are *"astonished"* at the words of Simeon. Their astonishment is the more understandable in the circumstance, given the exceptional importance and amplitude of the mission of Jesus predicted by Simeon. It is also an assent of faith to the mystery-laden destiny of their Son.

But the parents of Jesus are not yet at the end of their astonishment. The second prophecy of Simeon addresses Mary personally, speaking of her singular association with the mission of Jesus, and points to the Messianic drama that will take place in the very midst of Israel, around her person and the mission of Jesus: *"This Child is destined to be the downfall and the rise of many in Israel and to be a sign that will be opposed . . ."* (2:34).

Universal as is the salvation brought by Jesus, it will not make for unanimity; *"sign that will be opposed,"* it will provoke a crisis in Israel. Such will be the strange paradox of this chosen people, torn by the coming of the very One Whom it had expected and Who was to save it. But, at the same time, the salvation He brings will be the supreme sign of God's patience and His respect for the free will of human beings.

The twofold prophecy of Simeon refers to the whole Messianic drama and, in the person of Mary, is directed to the Daughter of Zion. In fact, the image of the *sword* and the *division of hearts* connotes the entire history of Israel, compounded of rebellions and communion, resistance and adherence, abandonments and returns. The mission of Jesus will not escape these contradictions but will even lead to deeper rifts, which culminate in the Passion.

In the course of this drama there appears, with a prominence altogether special, the figure of Mary, Daughter of Israel: "*And your own soul a sword shall pierce, that the thoughts of many hearts may be laid bare*" (Lk 2:35). Mary will bear in herself, with a sensitivity commensurate with her faith, the suffering caused by the drama that will take place in the midst of the people:

"It is with her vibrant person and in her heart of flesh that Mary bears the tragedy of her people. She bears it so really that she feels, more than anyone, all the repercussions of its drama, not only the joys of acceptance but also the pangs of refusal" (Pierre Benoit, O. P.).

Mary is involved, by exceptional title, in the revelation that has just been made concerning Jesus. Through her faith, her fidelity and her suffering, she will be associated with the "sign" that will make possible the transition of the old Israel to the new Israel: the Passion of her Son.

The Presentation in the Temple is the Fourth Joyful Mystery of the Rosary.

J. P. Prévost

PRESENTATION OF MARY

See   *Feasts of Mary*   *Holy Land and Mary, 2d*

PRIESTS AND MARY

See   *States of Life and Marian Devotion, 5*

PROTESTANTS AND MARY

See   *Ecumenism (Mary and)*

- Q -

QUEEN

[440, 2816]

SEE *Ad Caeli Reginam* *Feasts of Mary*
      Crowning of an Image *Old Testament (Mary in the)*
      of Mary

THE title of Queen is given to Mary by Christian Tradition from the beginning of the 4th century as an indication of her preeminence and power. Together with other royal titles it enters progressively into the usage of the people of God and eventually finds expression in the *Liturgy of the Hours (Hail Holy Queen, Queen of Heaven* . . .), in popular piety (Litany of the Blessed Virgin, 15th Mystery of the Rosary. . .), and in Christian iconography that frequently depicts Mary's coronation.

Attribution of the title of Queen goes on to become a common and accepted practice within the Church, to the point that Pius XII, in 1954, institutes the liturgical Feast of the Queenship of Mary. On that occasion also the Pope issues the principal document of the Magisterium concerning the royal dignity of Mary, the Encyclical *Ad Caeli Reginam* (October 11, 1954).

In recent years there has been a tendency to consider the royalty of Mary as pure symbol, and even a propensity to reject outright the concepts of *king, kingdom,* and *queen* for "sociological" reasons. Such concepts, it is said, are burdened with connotations of discredited authoritarian models that are outdated or in any case are contrary to human autonomy and democracy. In view of these tendencies it is important to come to a clear understanding of what makes up the Queenship of Mary as conceived in Christian Tradition. To this end, it should be studied in the light of God's sacred Word and in the light of what theologians are generally agreed on. At the same time, we must not neglect to relate it to contemporary culture.

1. The Teaching of Pius XII

The teaching of the Magisterium is summarized in the Encyclical *Ad Caeli Reginam.*

—*The Biblical foundations* are found in two texts of Saint Luke: "the words of the Angel Gabriel predicting that the Son of Mary would reign forever" (Lk 1:32-33), and "the words of Elizabeth, who greeted Mary with reverence and called her *'the Mother of my Lord.'*" These texts show "clearly that because of her Son's royal dignity, she [Mary] possessed a greatness and an excellence that set her apart."

—*Testimonies of the Fathers* are almost innumerable, and the Encyclical cites the most important ones.

—*Theological arguments*: the Divine Motherhood and Mary's association with the work of the Redemption are the two royal titles of Mary.

—*Nature and content.* Implicitly, *Ad Caeli Reginam* reprehends the tendency to make Mary a "king of the feminine sex" and clearly states the Christological principle that "Jesus Christ alone, God and Man, is King in the full, proper, and strict sense of the word." "The royalty of Mary is a participation in the royal dignity of Jesus Christ, but in a limited and analogical way." It includes three aspects or functions:

(a) *A preeminence, or primacy of excellence,* because the Blessed Virgin "surpasses in dignity all creation," according to the words of Saint Germanus: "Your honor and dignity surpass all creation; the Angels take second place to you in excellence."

(b) *A royal power,* which authorizes her to distribute the fruits of the Redemption: "The Blessed Virgin not only has been given the highest degree of excellence and perfection after Christ but also shares in the power that her Son and our Redeemer exercises over the minds and wills of human beings."

(c) *An inexhaustible efficacy of intercession with her Son and the Father.* "Mary has been made Queen of heaven and earth by God, exalted above all the choirs of Angels and all the Saints. Standing at the right hand of her only-begotten Son, Our Lord Jesus Christ, she pleads strongly for us with a mother's prayers, and what she seeks she finds, nor can she ask in vain."

The Encyclical does not say whether Mary shares in legislative, judicial, or executive power because—as Pius XII said—"even less than that of her Son, Mary's royal sovereignty must not be understood after the manner of modern political life. . . . Mary's royalty is a superterrestrial reality that nevertheless searches souls and touches them in their profoundest spiritual and immortal being" (Allocution of November 1, 1954).

2. The Teaching of the Post-Vatican II Liturgy

The Postconciliar Liturgy has elaborated on these ideas concerning the Queenship of Mary and has as it were provided a commentary on them. The Liturgy has (like the Council) continued to use the term King with reference to Christ and Queen with reference to Mary. In the Office for the Feast of the Birth of Mary (September 8) there are significant expressions of Mary's Queenship in the Latin Hymns for Morning Prayer, Daytime Prayer, and Evening Prayer.

In addition, the Solemnity of the Assumption continues to be the fullest celebration of Mary's Queenship with the Feast of the Queenship of Mary (August 22) as its festive prolongation.

However, the Queenship is explained with much more beauty and depth in the latest (March 25, 1981) Marian Rite to be promulgated by the Church: *The Order of Crowning an Image of the Blessed Virgin Mary.*

(a) *Biblical basis.* The Liturgy provides a Biblical basis for Mary's Queenship, rooting it (together with Christ's Kingship) in the Paschal Mystery, Christ's self-offering, Death, and Resurrection-Ascension. And this Mystery is itself ultimately rooted in Our Lord's words about reaching glory through humility and about the primacy of love and service.

This Paschal Mystery (abasement-exaltation) is prolonged in the members of Christ, especially Mary His Mother and perfect Follower. Her Passover is the Assumption, the moment of her final configuration to Christ.

(b) *Queenship of love and service.* Mary's Queenship is one of love and service not pomp and power, just as Christ's Kingdom is: *"My kingdom is not of this world"* (Jn 18:36); *"the Son of Man did not come to be served by others but to serve, to give His life as a ransom for the many"* (Mt 20:28).

On earth Mary was always humble, the servant of the Lord. She devoted herself totally to her Son and His work. With Him and under Him she served the Mystery of the Redemption. Assumed into heaven, she continues to manifest this love and service as a minister of piety by interceding with God for us so that all her children may attain salvation.

3. The Liturgy on the Reasons for Mary's Queenship

The rite thus pinpoints four reasons why Mary deserves to be Queen: She is (a) the Mother of the Son of God and the Messianic King; (b) the loving Associate of the Redeemer; (c) the perfect Follower (or Disciple) of Christ; and (d) the most excellent Member of the Church.

(a) *Mary is Queen because she is Mother of the Word Incarnate.* She gave birth to a Son Who at the very moment of conception was—by virtue of the hypostatic union of the human nature with the Word—even as man King of all things" (Pius XII, *Ad Caeli Reginam*, no. 26). And it was in this Incarnate Word that *"all things in heaven and on earth were created, things visible and things invisible, whether thrones or dominations, principalities or powers"* (Col 1:16).

Mary is Queen also because she is the Mother of the Messianic King. The Son she bore was characterized by the Angel in Messianic terms: *"He will be great and will be called Son of the Most High. The Lord God will give Him the throne of David His father. He will rule over the house of Jacob forever and His Kingdom will be without end"* (Lk 1:32f). Mary's Queenship is also indicated by Elizabeth's words to her: *"Who am I that the Mother of my Lord should come to me?"* (Lk 1:43).

(b) *Mary is Queen because she was associated wholeheartedly with Christ the Redeemer.* "By an eternal plan of God, the Blessed Virgin . . . is the new Eve and she played a great part in the work of salvation by which Christ Jesus, the new Adam, redeemed us and purchased us for Himself not with corruptible gold or silver but His Precious Blood (cf. 1 Pt 1:18-19) and made us into a Kingdom for our God (Rv 5:15)" (Rite).

(c) *Mary is Queen because she was the perfect Follower or Disciple of Christ.* Vatican II stressed this new theme taken from the New Testament: *"Be faithful even until death and I will give you the crown of life. . . . I will give the victor the right to sit with Me on My throne as I Myself won the victory and took My seat beside My Father on His throne"* (Rv 2:10; 3:21).

Basing itself on numbers 55-59 of the Council's *Constitution on the Church*, the Rite says: "Mary consented to the Divine plan and advanced in the journey of faith. She heard and kept the Word of God and faithfully preserved her union with the Son even to the Cross. She then persevered in prayer together with the Church and became proficient in the love of God."

(d) *Mary is Queen because she is the most excellent Member of the Church.* She is blessed among women and holds a preeminent place in the Communion of Saints for a twofold reason: her mission and her holiness. "Mary stands out in the chosen race, priestly people, and holy nation that is the Church because of the *singular mission* given her with regard to Christ and all members of His Mystical Body, and because of her *copious virtues and fullness of grace.* Therefore, she deserves to be called the Mistress of human beings and Angels and the Queen of all Saints" (Rite).

Indeed, Mary's glory reverberates even outside the Church. She is the daughter of Adam and Our Lady. She is thus not only the joy of Israel and the splendor of the Church but also the glory of the whole human race. Mary is the type of the modern woman (SEE Woman).

4. Keys for a Deeper Theological-Pastoral Understanding

Today people feel the need for subjecting the teaching concerning Mary's Queenship to further study so as to enrich it with the contributions of contemporary theology and to express it in terms consonant with present-day culture.

In order to arrive at a deeper theological-pastoral understanding that does not deny the traditional contents of Mary's Queenship but presents them in a broader and more significant vision for Christians today, the following points should be kept in mind.

A. *The Queenship of Mary must be inserted within the kingly status of the People of God.* The insertion of Our Lady's Queenship into the context of the kingly office of the People of God (1 Pt 2:9; Rv 1:6; 5:9; 20:4-6), while not detaching the person of Mary from the ecclesial community, helps us to understand the meaning of Marian Queenship and its challenges for contemporary Christians. In her quality as excelling Member of the Church, Mary the Queen proclaims "the royal character of the other human beings, which is founded on union with Christ" (M. Schmaus). Mary is not an isolated or alien figure. She is the one who in communion with all Christians participates in the very Kingship of Christ.

Speaking of the People of God's kingly function, the Second Vatican Council describes it as a power for deliverance and service (cf. LG 36).

Applying these indications to Mary, we find that she is Queen because in her life on earth she fulfilled by the grace of Christ a mission that she continues to fulfill even more in heaven—a mission that has three aspects.

(1) *Mary conquered the powers of evil*, conceding nothing to sin from the moment of her Immaculate Conception. Mary is the creature who had no part whatever with the way of sinners, in the sense that she was neither led astray nor divided by the influence of the devil (=divider). She was never under bondage to sin, which is a rift with God and with neighbor. In contrast to Eve, she heeded only the messenger of God and gave God's message her total consent. By her Assumption she already shares in Christ's victory even over the last enemy, death (1 Cor 15:26). And with Christ she works for the world's deliverance from sin.

(2) *Mary understood her life as a service*, in which consists royalty according to the Gospel (Lk 22:24-40). She did not construe her Divine Motherhood as expression of sovereignty but

declared herself *"servant of the Lord"* (Lk 1:38), worshiping the one God and completely given to service for His plan of salvation.

(3) *Mary accepted to render possible the realization of the Kingdom of God*, welcoming the Angel's message concerning the Davidic Messiah Who would reign forever over the house of Jacob (Lk 1:32-33). The oracle of Nathan (2 Sm 7:12-16), to which Luke's text refers, nourished Israel's hope. However, among the religious circles of the *anawim* (the Poor of Yahweh) to whom Mary belonged, that hope envisaged above all the Messianic benefits of the religious order, such as peace, justice, piety, and deliverance. In accepting the King-Messiah, the Blessed Virgin accepted the Kingdom of God, which her Son would then purify of every nationalistic interpretation.

B. *The Queenship of Mary must take on a deeper Gospel inspiration.* The Kingdom of God preached by Jesus has a logic that differs from that of the kingdoms of this world. Whereas worldly kingship is expressed by domination, imposition, and egoistic pursuits, the Kingship of Christ is manifested in the rejection of violence and in love and service of the truth, unto the total giving of self (Jn 18:36-37).

In its Gospel significance, the Kingdom of God is the sovereignty of the Lord in human life (Mt 7:21), sovereignty that implies Divine filiation, universal brotherhood, and acts of "power" like cures and miracles. Such a Kingdom is reserved for those who receive it in faith, with open heart, in poverty and suffering (Mt 5:3-10; 18:3-4).

In light of this, Mary is one who has inherited the Kingdom of God, because she shares in the power communicated by the Spirit for delivering the world from its evils (cures and conversions of life obtained at Marian shrines attest to this) and for bringing people to Divine filiation and Christian maturity. The discussion about Mary illumines the discussion about the Kingdom of God and vice versa.

C. *The Queenship of Mary must preserve its character of unique and maternal participation in Christ's kingly power.* If *"all power in heaven and on earth"* belongs to Christ (Mt 28:18), Mary was called to share in this power, in this authority and freedom of action, to be exercised in perfect union with the Father's will. The announcement of the Angel (Lk 1:32-33) suggests that the role that the queen-mother (the *Gebirah*) fulfilled in the Davidic kingdom was offered to Mary.

As the studies of H. Cazelles and G. F. Kirwin have shown, the *Gebirah* had a preeminence, i.e., an influence over the king and a common destiny with him. And she exercised an official function on the day of the king's marriage (Song 3:11). Applied to Mary, this means that she is "the associate of her Son born of God in His birth on earth, in His royal rule, in His glory" (H. Cazelles).

Mary is the *Gebirah* of the New Testament. As Mother of the King par excellence Whose Kingdom will have no end, she makes possible the marriage of the Word with humanity. She asks us to renew the Covenant with Christ (Jn 2:5), intercedes for us with her Son, and exercises a universal Motherhood toward disciples loved by Jesus (Jn 19:25-27).

D. *The Queenship of Mary must be harmonized with the legitimate demands of the modern mentality.* To be meaningful and acceptable to people of today, it must first be rid of every appearance of authoritarianism or the kind of influence that might seem to compromise human freedom. This requires a perception and a pointing out of the deeper meaning behind Biblical monarchy, which was "synonymous with hope in the realization of an ideal never verified in this world, the ideal of a just sovereign. In the thinking of peoples of the ancient East, justice did not consist so much in the impartial administration of the law as in the fact of providing help and protection to the needy, the weak and the poor. . . . Divine lordship is a lordship of love, and the glory of God is shown in His sovereign freedom to love and forgive" (W. Kasper).

In this context the Queenship of Mary is the opposite of oppression and servitude, because it means her participation in a work that rouses hope and is expressive of a merciful and furthering love.

People who say they are their own king, makers of their own destiny, still need someone—or some value—to inspire them. Today we accept the *leadership* of eminent persons who embody our values and influence the direction of social or personal life.

In connection with this, it may be recalled that in describing Jesus as King the first Christian generation made use of an historico-cultural analogy according to which the king was an absolute and indisputable point of reference, warranted by God Himself. Proclaiming Jesus "universal King" was equivalent to saying that all persons find in Him alone the true answer to the question of their own identity.

In like manner, Mary is Queen by exercising a role of *leadership* toward the People of God. Thanks to her prestige, her excellence as first Christian and type of the Church, she represents a necessary point of reference for the faithful. In her they can find the secret to their own royal identity as children of God and the model for giving the Lord an ever greater place in their life.

S. de Fiores—A. Buono

- R -

REDEMPTORIS MATER [495, 971]

SEE *Church and Mary*   *Marialis Cultus*
    Cult of Mary   *Signum Magnum*
    Magisterium (Documents of)   *Vatican II and Mary*

ON March 25, 1987, Pope John Paul II issued an Encyclical entitled, *Redemptoris Mater* ("The Mother of the Redeemer") concerning the Blessed Virgin in the life of the Church on her pilgrimage of faith. Nine days before its issuance, the Pope declared:

"This Encyclical represents essentially a 'meditation' on the revelation of the Mystery of Salvation, which was communicated to Mary at the dawn of the Redemption and in which she was called to participate and to collaborate in a wholly exceptional and extraordinary manner. It is a meditation that has repercussions on and in certain aspects deepens the Conciliar Magisterium . . . concerning the position that Mary Most Holy occupies in the Mystery of Christ and the Church.

"The reflections that flow from it soar over the Biblical horizon—from its beginnings to the symbolic visions of the Book of Revelation, which are filled with mystery—to the world that shall be. . . . The Christological nature of the discourse developed in the Encyclical is based on both the Ecclesial and the Mariological dimension. The Church is the Body of Christ mystically prolonged throughout the centuries. Mary of Nazareth is the Mother of the Church.

"Therefore, the Church 'looks' at Mary through Jesus, just as she 'looks' at Jesus through Mary. This mutuality enables us to continually deepen—together with the patrimony of the truths believed—the orbit of the 'obedience of faith' that earmarks the steps of the exalted Creature. . . . As the Servant, Mother, and Disciple of the Lord, Mary is the model, guide, and strength of the pilgrim People of God, especially during the most important stages of their journey throughout life."

The Pope presents Mary at the center of the economy of salvation, as the "Morning Star" and the dawn of the coming of the historical Christ and hence also of the passage from the second to the third Christian millennium. This millennium is now near, and the Church desires to initiate a spiritual and religious renewal of humanity for it.

In Part 1, the Pope closely follows the Biblical texts and especially the Gospel texts about Mary. He sketches an image corresponding to the will of God, as Mother of Christ, full of grace, blessed because of her faith and her obedience by which she accepted—from Nazareth to Calvary to the Upper Room—the Divine dispositions in her regard. These are essential traits that allow the profundity of the Mystery of Mary to be transparent in the Mystery of Christ.

In Part 2, the Pope considers Mary at the center of the Church as the People of God rooted in all nations of the earth and on the move toward a future condition of the human race, anticipated in Mary Immaculate and Assumed into heaven, who is thus the "Morning Star" even in regard to the eschatological goal of history. In the light of this goal and the universal vocation to attain it, the Pope illumines the historic pilgrimage of the Church and connects to it the problem of the unity of all Christians, which should be favored by a serene reflection on the Biblical data, tradition, and the teaching of the Church concerning Mary's mission. In the historical and eschatological perspective of the Church as the bearer of peace and the proclaimer of justice to the whole world, the Pope repeats and comments on the "Magnificat of the Pilgrim Church."

In Part 3, the Pope sums up in a felicitous formula the Christian tradition about Mary and Catholic teaching about the mission of Mary, Servant of the Lord in the service of all her brothers and sisters in need of redemption, in the life of the Church and of all Christians: her maternal mediation. He thus saves and indeed relaunches the term and concept of "mediation," which has been somewhat neglected in recent times because of the hypersensitivity of the Protestant world. At the same time, he emphasizes its substantial identification with the theme of "Motherhood."

Moreover, he repeats and confirms authoritatively what not only the Council but also Mariologists had indicated before and after Vatican II. The mediation of Mary (and analogically that of the Church and of the Saints) cannot but be understood as a participation in the work of the one Mediator Christ. His mediation does not receive any integration, any supplement, from the ministerial cooperation of Mary and of the Church, and instead manifests in it its unique excellence and power.

The Pope concludes by indicating the meaning of the Marian Year (1987-88) that he called. He wishes to emphasize the special presence of the Mother of God in the Mystery of Christ and His Church—in continuation of the Conciliar Mariology, which the Pope urges all to reread and reflect upon as sources of the doctrine of faith as well as the life of faith.

A. Buono

REGINA CAELI (QUEEN OF HEAVEN)   [971]

SEE   *Angelus*   *Prayer(s) to Mary*

THE *Regina Caeli* (Queen of Heaven) is an antiphon to the Blessed Virgin of unknown authorship that dates back to the 12th century. It replaces the Angelus during the Easter Season and is prescribed to be recited in the *Liturgy of the Hours* after Night Prayer from Holy Saturday to the Saturday after Pentecost. The text is as follows:

Queen of heaven, rejoice, alleluia:
For He Whom you merited to bear, alleluia,
Has risen, as He said, alleluia.
Pray for us to God, alleluia.
℣. Rejoice and be glad, O Virgin Mary, alleluia.
℟. Because the Lord is truly risen, alleluia.
Let us pray.
O God,
Who by the resurrection of Your Son,

Our Lord Jesus Christ,
granted joy to the whole world:
grant, we beg You,
that through the intercession of the Virgin Mary, His
    Mother,
we may lay hold of the joys of eternal life.
Through the same Christ our Lord.

A. Buono

RELICS OF MARY   [364]

R ELICS are the "remains" of a Saint—either the whole or part of the body (termed *real* relics) or objects that came in contact with the Saint (termed *representative* relics). Relics are venerated by the faithful with the approval of the Church (Council of Trent, Session XXV) because the bodies of the Saints while on earth were temples of the Holy Spirit and living members of Christ. The veneration may take the form of imitating the Saint's virtues or showing special respect for his or her relics. Ultimately, the respect is given not to the material objects but to the person of the Saint.

Thus, relics of the Saints are sacred objects. They are enshrined in altars, borne in procession, offered to the faithful in reliquaries to receive marks of veneration, and used in obtaining cures and other requests.

The practice of relics has been plagued by spurious relics. The Crusades especially paved the way for an endless stream of relics to make their way to Europe from the East. Splendid reliquaries were fashioned to hold them and shrines arose. This led to trafficking in relics, the exhibition of inauthentic or doubtful relics, and superstitious practices. Marian relics have suffered the same fate.

Since the Blessed Mother was assumed body and soul into heaven there can naturally be no relics of her body, except for parts of her hair. But there was nothing against finding objects that her body came into contact with. Hence, over the years various kinds of relics of Mary purporting to be authentic came to the fore. Many of them surfaced at the time of the Crusades.

However, there is little evidence to show that any of them are really what they are claimed to be. In this connection, the Church's approbation of any relics does not mean they are authentic. It simply means that they have not been shown to be inauthentic, and the Church allows their veneration in view of the good that will accrue to the faithful who use them properly—who direct their veneration *through the relics to Mary* herself.

We might cite some of the better relics:

- *Garment or girdle*—purportedly sent to the Emperor Marcian by Bishop Juvenal of Jerusalem in 452. It disappeared in 1453 when the Turks conquered the city, and parts of it are now said to be in the Monastery of Vatopedi on Mount Athos.

- *Hair*—parts of Mary's hair were claimed to be in the Messina Cathedral in Sicily, after being brought to Piazza, Sicily, by the Crusaders; various other places also claimed this relic.

- *House*—see entry "Loreto."

- *Letter*—supposedly sent by Mary to the first Christians of Messina. Investigation has shown that it was actually written by Constantine Laskaris in the 15th century.

- *Letter*—of Saint Ignatius of Antioch to Mary and her response turned out to be forgeries concocted in the 12th century.

In the final analysis, the most important "relic" of Mary that we have is a spiritual one—her abiding influence on Christians over the centuries and her comforting presence to us through her Divine Son.

A. Buono

RELIGIOUS AND MARY

SEE *States of Life and Mary, 4*

RESURRECTION AND MARY   [651-655]

SEE   *Joys of Mary*

1. The Risen Christ's Appearance to Mary

THE Gospels say nothing about a visit of Christ's Mother to the place of His Resurrection. Furthermore Mark (16:9) states that the Risen Lord appeared first to Mary Magdalen. Nonetheless since the 4th century the idea is found in the Fathers that the Risen Jesus appeared to His Mother. As John Paul II has indicated: All Catholics still think: "She must have been the first to share in the Mystery of the Resurrection." Indeed, he goes on to say that "it is certain that just as Mary, the first among the redeemed, was especially close to the Cross of her Son, so she also had a privileged experience of the Risen One" (*A Year with Mary*, pp. 142, 145).

The Byzantine Liturgy contains a text that refers to the popular idea that as the Annunciation was made to Mary through an Angel so the Resurrection was made known in the same way: "The Angel spoke to her who is full of grace, saying: 'Rejoice, pure Virgin; again I say, Rejoice; for your Son has risen from the dead on the third day, He Who has raised up the dead. You people, rejoice! Shine forth, new Jerusalem, shine forth, for the glory of the Lord has dawned upon you. Exult, Zion, and be glad! And you, pure Mother of God, be joyful at your Son's rising from the dead" (Easter Matins, 9th Ode).

There is also a legendary yet substantially accurate account that on the Saturday after Christ's death and His disciples' abandonment of Him, Mary was the only one to preserve intact her faith in the Divinity of her Son. As a result, she merited to receive an exceptional appearance of Jesus on that day.

2. Penetrating the Meaning of the Paschal Mystery through Mary

Pope John Paul II has also stated: "It is in Mary and with Mary that we are enabled to penetrate the meaning of the

Paschal Mystery, allowing it to bring forth in us the immense riches of its effects and its fruits of eternal life. It is in her and with her that we can do so, since she did not pass from sin to grace, as all of us have done, but through a singular privilege owing to the merits of Christ she was preserved from sin and began journeying toward the eternal Easter from the very first moment of her existence.

"Indeed, her whole life was an 'Easter,' a 'Passover'—a passage, a journey of joy—from the joy of hope at the moment of trial to the joy of possession after the triumph over death. Her human person, as we know through a solemn definition of the Church, has in the wake of the Risen One accomplished the Easter passage in soul and body from death to a glorious eternal life.

"Following Mary's example, we too are invited to welcome Christ, Who pardons us, redeems us, saves us, and works in us the Easter passage from death to life" (*A year with Mary,* pp. 148-149).

The Resurrection is the First Glorious Mystery of the Rosary.

A. Buono

REVELATION 12 [1138, 2853]

SEE *Daughter of Zion*

NOT all exegetes subscribe to the Marian interpretation of chapter 12 of the Book of Revelation. Without going into details, we can pinpoint a few factors that at least permit us to say that the Marian reading of this chapter is not arbitrary but has solid arguments in its favor. They are based on a paper prepared by Henri Cazelles ("The Maternal Function of Zion and Mary") for the Mariological Congress of Santo Domingo in 1956, and published in the multivolume and multilingual work *The Blessed Virgin Mary and the Contemporary Ecumenical Effort* (Rome: International Pontifical Marian Academy, 1967), Vol. 6: *Mary in Sacred Scripture,* pp. 165-178.

First, it should be remembered that like all other parts of the Bible, the Book of Revelation cannot be read in isolation. It must be read *both* in continuity with those that precede it (and by which it is influenced in borrowing from them a number of themes, symbols, etc.) and in relation to the concrete situation of the People of God at the time the Book was written. The Word of God always remained in contact with the reality of this People's life. And that life, notwithstanding the vicissitudes of a tumultuous history, experienced organic and continuous development right up to the fullness of time in Jesus Christ.

Consequently, recourse to the themes of the Old Testament utilized in this chapter 12 is indispensable for bringing out the aspect of continuity. But it is also necessary to interpret them with reference to the situation of the people of God to which they are addressed. This allows for more meaningful understanding of the themes and more concrete application.

The theme of the "double birth," presented in chapter 12 of Revelation with the male child of verse 5 and the rest of the offspring in verse 17, is already found in the Old Testament. Micah speaks of the royal birth of the Messiah (5:2), no doubt in connection with the prophecy of Isaiah 7:14; but he also mentions, in 4:9-10, another birth, "this one with pains, since there is question of deliverance and redemption" (H. Cazelles, *op. cit.*, p. 172).

In Isaiah 66, we have the same perspectives. Verse 7: "*Before she comes to labor, she gives birth; before the pains come upon her, she safely delivers a male child*," refers discreetly but really—according to Cazelles—to the birth of the royal heir (the Messiah). And this birth is characterized by the absence of "pains," whereas verse 8 has explicitly in mind the birth of a new *people* brought forth "*in one day*," but which does not exclude that Zion be "*in labor.*"

How should these Old Testament antecedents (here barely summarized) be used to elucidate the corresponding parts of chapter 12, and how does this chapter continue and make more specific the antecedents in question?

The "male child" of Isaiah 66:7 appears in verse 5: as "a boy" it is thus a question of the Messiah Who is to rule the nations (cf. Ps 2:9). But He is also presented as "*caught up to God and to His throne*," whereas the woman "*[flees] into the desert*" (v. 6). "With reference to the Gospel data, the birth and 'deliverance' of the male child are interpreted as the glorification of Christ in the presence of the Father" (H. Cazelles, *op. cit.*, p. 175).

If the thought is of Christ and His Mother, the latter, at the time when the author of Revelation writes, is no longer an anonymous woman, one still to come, or only the symbol of the people of Jerusalem or of Zion from which the Messiah was to be born. She has a name, and it is Mary.

This is not to say that the Church is absent here: "As a matter of fact, the author of Revelation does not limit the results of the painful birth to the glorification of Christ. He also sees, not in heaven but on earth, exposed to the onslaughts of the Beast, 'the rest of the offspring' (12:17). They are *those* who keep the Commandments of God and bear the testimony of Christ.

"In addition to Christ, with the Father, there are Christians on earth. The one and the others are the fruit of the painful birth of Calvary. Just as there is only one global offspring, namely, Christ and the rest of the woman's offspring (autès, the verse is very clear), so there is only one woman; it can only be Mary" (H. Cazelles, *op. cit.*, p. 176).

The reference to Calvary (which justifies the tenor of verse 2: the Woman "*was with Child and wailed aloud in pain as she labored to give birth*") and to the role that Mary plays in it explains why the author of Revelation 12 turns to Isaiah 66:8; it permits him to assign to Mary, Mother of the Messiah, "the function incumbent upon Zion as regards the Messianic people. This personalization was not arbitrary on his part" (*ibid.*).

In short, there is in Revelation 12 the final development in an entire work of personalization. Featured are the double birth and the motherhood of the Daughter of Zion toward the new People of God. In the end, we come to see that "it is through Mary that Zion has brought forth a new people and a numerous progeny. . . by the power of God and His Spirit" (*ibid.*, p. 178).   *A. Bossard*

ROSARY

SEE   *Adiutricem Populi*   *Laetitiae Sanctae*
      Hail Mary   *Sorrows of Mary*
      Joys of Mary

1. Content of the Rosary

THE complete *Rosary* is a prayer comprising 150 Hail Marys divided into 15 decades, each of which serves for meditating on a *Mystery* of Christ. All decades are preceded by an Our Father and concluded with Glory to the Father, and to the Son, etc. (Ordinarily, to "pray the Rosary" means to pray five of the 15 decades.)

The name *Rosary* is also given to the Rosary beads themselves, which are separated into groups of ten by larger individual beads. This instrument (beads, 14th century) grew out of a similar one that was used for counting Our Fathers. Recourse to beads or counters in repetitive prayer extends, however, beyond Christianity.

2. History of the Rosary

The history of the Rosary is very complex, since it has elements of all forms of Marian piety in the Middle Ages.

In the 12th century appears repetition of the Hail Mary in conjunction with the *five joys* of Mary: Annunciation, Nativity, Resurrection, Ascension, Assumption. Then came the *seven delights,* and gradually the *fifteen joys* answering to the 15 decades of the Psalter (150 psalms=150 Hail Marys).

In the 13th and 14th century, Franciscans and Servites spread devotion to the *Five Sorrows,* then to the *Seven Sorrows* of Mary.

About the same time, reaction to an overly historical tendency led to devotion to the *Seven Celestial Joys* of Mary.

In the 14th century the name *Rosary* could also mean a *florilegium,* a collection of thoughts or little poems. The name *Rosaries of Mary* was then given to whole series of stanzas (50, 150 . . .) rhyming with *Ave* and followed each by the *Ave Maria* of the Gospel.

Finally, the 15th century saw the appearance of two Marian Rosaries still prayed today:

(a) the Rosary of Dominic the Carthusian (St. Alban, near Trêves, about 1410): a succession of 150 Hail Marys to which were appended as many articulations of moments in the life of Christ and the Virgin Mary: ". . . and blessed is the fruit of your womb, *Jesus Christ, Whom at the announcement of the Angel you conceived by the Holy Spirit*," etc.;

(b) the "New Psalter of the Virgin" that Alain of Roche, a Dominican, began to preach at Douai in 1464. To him is owed the structure of three groups of Mysteries: Joyful, Sorrowful, and Glorious, corresponding to the fundamental aspects of the Mystery of Christ: Incarnation, Passion, and Resurrection.

This Marian prayer of Alain spread rapidly. Its popularity was largely the work of Confraternities of the Rosary, the first of which was established by Cologne Dominicans in 1475. The traditional list of 15 Mysteries, helped along by the invention of printing, became the norm between 1480 and 1500. All in all, what Alain preached is the Rosary of today.

3. Spirituality of the Rosary

Paul VI, recalling the traditional teaching of the Popes, spoke of the Rosary as a "compendium of the entire Gospel," a prayer "centered on the redemptive Incarnation," in which "the litany-like succession of Hail Marys becomes an unceasing praise of Christ, Who is the ultimate object both of the Angel's announcement and of the greeting of the Mother of John the Baptist: "Blessed is the fruit of your womb" (Lk 1:42). . . . The succession of Hail Marys constitutes the warp on which is woven the contemplation of the Mysteries. The Jesus that each Hail Mary recalls is the same Jesus Whom the succession of the Mysteries proposes to us" (MC 46).

Its recitation, if done in a relaxed and recollective manner, takes the nature of a *contemplative* prayer, a meditation "on the Mysteries of the Lord's life as seen through the eyes of her who was closest to the Lord" (MC 47).

To pray the Rosary is to contemplate with Mary the Lord made flesh, crucified, and raised for our salvation.

1.   The Annunciation
For the love of humility.

Mysteries of the Rosary

The Five
Joyful Mysteries

(For Mondays, Thursdays; Sundays in Advent, and from Epiphany to Lent.)

1. The Annunciation—*Luke 1, 28.*
2. The Visitation—*Luke 1, 42.*
3. The Nativity—*Luke 2, 7.*
4. The Presentation—*Luke 2, 28.*
5. Finding in the Temple—*Luke 2, 46.*

2.   The Visitation
For love of neighbor

4.   The Presentation
For the virtue of obedience.

3.   The Nativity
For the spirit of poverty.

5.   Finding in the Temple
For the virtue of piety.

1. Agony in the Garden
For true contrition.

The Five Sorrowful Mysteries

(For Tuesdays, Fridays, and every day during Lent.)

1. Agony in the Garden—Mark 14, 35.
2. Scourging at the Pillar—Mark 15, 15.
3. Crowning with Thorns—Mark 15, 17.
4. Carrying of the Cross—John 19, 17.
5. The Crucifixion—Luke 23, 33.

2. Scourging at the Pillar
For the virtue of purity.

4. Carrying of the Cross
For the virtue of patience.

3. Crowning with Thorns
For moral courage.

5. The Crucifixion
For final perseverance.

The Five Glorious Mysteries

(For Wednesdays, Saturdays, and for Sundays from Easter until Advent.)

1. The Resurrection—Mark 16, 6.
2. The Ascension—Mark 16, 19.
3. Descent of the Holy Spirit—Acts 2, 4.
4. Assumption of the B.V.M.—Gen. 3, 15.
5. Crowning of the B.V.M.—Apoc. 12, 1.

3. Descent of the Holy Spirit
For love of God.

1.   The Resurrection
For the virtue of faith

4.   Assumption of the B.V.M.
For devotion to Mary.

2.   The Ascension
For the virtue of hope.

5.   Crowning of the B.V.M.
For eternal happiness.

4. The Rosary as a Prayer of the Church

There can be little doubt that the Church regards the Rosary as a treasure and a prayer of its own. The last twelve Popes have all warmly recommended the recitation of the Rosary and gone out of their way to set aside October for recitation of the Rosary. Some of the reasons for this papal attitude are the following:

(1) *The Rosary is loved by the common folk.* Unfortunately, sometimes this love is expressed in ways that are inept or ill-conceived, but that does not take away from the reality of the love behind them. Ultimately, we might say, this love is based on a real understanding of the things of faith.

(2) *The Rosary fosters faith.* "The great power of the Rosary is that it makes a prayer of the Creed" (Cardinal Newman). It covers the entire range of the Mysteries of the Faith and enables us, so to speak, to hold our "entire Faith in the hand" (Cardinal Newman).

(3) *The Rosary is a humble prayer of petition.* Like every prayer it implies the recognition of a want or insufficiency and an appeal for God's help. The Rosary is *persistent prayer.* In the Gospel, Christ acknowledges and praises the poor and the humble who press their petitions until they are heard: like the Canaanite woman (Mt 15:21-28) or the widow in the parable of the corrupt judge (Lk 18:1-8). When repetition is the sign of deep distress together with a confidence that will not be disappointed, it is a sign of authentic prayer.

(4) *The Rosary has missionary power.* It combines petition with contemplation of the Mysteries of Christ. A prayer of this kind is an education in the Faith and one of the surest and most effective ways to conversion, which is totally the result of prayer.

(5) *The Rosary highlights Mary's maternal role.* It acquaints us with the Spiritual Motherhood of Mary and especially as regards her motherly role of educatrix in prayer. It teaches us to talk with Mary as we talk with our mother, opening our heart to her humility and love and so acquiring the attitude of soul fundamental for the Kingdom of God. We get close to Jesus and ultimately to the Father.

(6) *The Rosary has the rhythm of human life.* "The Rosary is marvelous in its simplicity and in its depth. . . . Against the background of the words 'Hail Mary' there pass before the eyes of the soul the main episodes in the life of Jesus Christ. They are composed altogether of the Joyful, Sorrowful, and Glorious Mysteries and they put us in living communion with Jesus through—we could say—His Mother's heart.

"At the same time our heart can enclose in these decades of the Rosary all the facts that make up the life of the individual, the family, the nation, the Church, and all humankind. They include personal matters and those of our neighbor, particularly persons who are closest to us. Thus in the simple prayer of the Rosary beats the rhythm of human life" (John Paul II).

5. The Rosary and the Liturgy

In response to some who over the years have asked that the Rosary be declared a liturgical prayer, Paul VI (MC 48) took up the question of the relationship between the Rosary and the Liturgy. The Rosary is as it were a broader spring from the ancient trunk of the Christian Liturgy, the Psalter of the Blessed Virgin, whereby the humble were associated in the Church's hymn of praise and universal intercession. However, this development occurred during the last period of the Middle Ages, a time when the liturgical spirit was in decline and the faithful were turning away from the Liturgy and toward a devotion to Christ's Humanity and to the Blessed Virgin Mary, a devotion favoring a certain external sentiment of piety.

Accordingly, liturgical celebrations and the pious practice of the Rosary are related but different. They must neither be set in opposition to one another nor considered as identical. Once the preeminent value of liturgical rites has been reaffirmed, it will be easy to appreciate the fact that the Rosary is a practice of piety that easily harmonizes with the Liturgy.

Like the Liturgy, the Rosary is of a community nature, draws its inspiration from Sacred Scripture, and is oriented toward the Mystery of Christ. The "commemoration" in the

Liturgy and the "contemplative remembrance" in the Rosary, although they exist on essentially different planes, have as their object the same salvific events wrought by Christ. The liturgical commemoration presents anew, under the veil of signs and operative in a hidden way, the great Mysteries of our Redemption. The "contemplative remembrance," by means of devout contemplation, recalls these same Mysteries to the mind of the person praying and stimulates the will to draw from them the norms of living.

Hence, it is apparent that the Rosary is an exercise of piety that draws its motivating force from the Liturgy and leads naturally back to it, if practiced in conformity with its original inspiration. Although the Rosary does not become part of the Liturgy, meditation on its Mysteries can be an excellent preparation for the Liturgy. By familiarizing the hearts and minds of the faithful with the Mysteries of Christ, the Rosary prepares them to celebrate those same Mysteries in the Liturgical Action. At the same time, it also becomes an echo of such Mysteries.

The Pope concludes by pointing out that the practice of reciting the Rosary during the celebration of the Liturgy is a mistake.

J. Laurenceau—A. Buono

RUE DU BAC

SEE *Miraculous Medal*

- S -

SABBATINE PRIVILEGE [971]

SEE *Carmel, Mount*   *Scapular of Mary*

THE so-called Sabbatine Privilege (from the Latin word for Saturday, *sabbatum*) refers to the pious belief that those who (1) wear the scapular of Our Lady of Mount Carmel, (2) observe chastity according to their state in life, and (3) daily recite the Little Office of the Blessed Virgin Mary or abstain from meat on Wednesdays and Saturdays or faithfully observe some other similar work will be aided "by Mary's unceasing intercession, devout pleadings, merits, and special protection—especially on Saturday, the day dedicated to the Holy Virgin."

The requirements and quoted words are those set forth by the Holy Office in 1613 referring to a privilege recorded in 1421 that purportedly went back to a Bull of John XXII in 1322. The Bull has been shown to be inauthentic.

Regardless of its inception, the privilege has become accepted by Church practice and was even mentioned with approval by Pius XII in 1950: "This most kind Mother will not be tardy in using her intercession with God to open the gates of heaven as soon as possible for those of her children who are expiating their faults in purgatory, a trust that is based on the promise known as the Sabbatine Privilege."

A. Buono

SAINT MARY MAJOR [971]

SEE *Feasts of Mary*   *Mother of God*
     Magisterium (Documents of)

1. The Triumphal Arch

"AFTER the Council of Ephesus (431) in which the Mother of Jesus was acclaimed as Mother of God, Pope Sixtus III erected at Rome on the Esquiline Hill a basilica ded-

413

icated to the honor of the holy Mother of God. It was afterward called Saint Mary Major and it is the oldest church in the West dedicated to the honor of the Blessed Virgin Mary." So states the *Roman Breviary.*

For its part, the *Roman Pontifical* observes that "Sixtus III constructed a basilica to Saint Mary, which was known from ancient times as that of Liberius." Joining these two accounts, we could say with Grisar that "the Liberian basilica, today called Saint Mary Major, was founded by Pope Liberius (352-366) and was restored and enlarged by Sixtus III."

The basilica of Saint Mary Major celebrates first of all Mary's Divine Motherhood. In fact, on the day after the Council of Ephesus—which vindicated against Nestorianism the true Divinity of Christ and the Divine Motherhood of Mary—Pope Sixtus III erected in the Liberian basilica a triumphal arch in honor of the Mother of God. He placed the simple dedication, which radiates on the blue enamel at the top of the arch itself—*Xystus Episcopus Plebi Dei* (Sixtus, Bishop of Rome, to the People of God).

"This great mosaic," states Armellini, "is a work of such brilliance as to appear to be not something earthly but something celestial; it is an enchanting spectacle, that overwhelms the exulting soul when it enters that temple, a monument to the triumphs of Mary, who overcomes all heresies."

2. Note on Art

In his *Note on Art*—composed for the 15th centenary of the Council of Ephesus and published in *Regina dei Cuori* (Queen of Hearts) in 1931—Father Oger, S.M.M., describes "the vast tapestry of mosaics that exists in front of the apse of the basilica." Having climbed up to the very scaffold where the mosaicists were doing some work of restoration, he admires "the imposing mass of the arch and the richness of that glorious monument" and he writes: "When light falls upon the enamel, the whole scene takes on a fantastic splendor, the relief corrects the harshness of the painting, and the Roman nobility of the physiognomy, the glowing visages of the Angels distributed everywhere, and the prevalence of white in the garments all produce an impression of grandiosity and of irresistible festivity."

Here is how the same Father Oger describes that mosaic in summary fashion: "The triumphal arch of Saint Mary Major extends over a length of 19 meters. The decoration, all in mosaic, is divided into four horizontal zones. At the center of the top zone, within a circle appears the throne of God; on the two sides of the circle are Saints Peter and Paul; above them are the symbols of the four Evangelists and below them is the dedication: 'Sixtus, Bishop of Rome, to the People of God.'

"In this same zone, the scene on the left represents the Annunciation, and the one on the right the Presentation of Jesus in the Temple. On the lower plane, the Adoration of the Magi is on the left, and on the right is an episode of the flight into Egypt.

"The third zone interprets the Slaughter of the Innocents on the left side, and on the right it has the Magi Kings before Herod.

"The last zone shows the sheep exiting from Jerusalem; on the left are the Israelites, those who are exiting from Bethlehem, and on the right the Gentiles."

3. Marian Shrine

Bypassing the legend of the "snow," we can say that Saint Mary Major was also called "Saint Mary at the Crib," because of the ancient "oratory at the crib" that was first located near the main altar and was later transferred to the "sistine" chapel, so called because it was constructed by Sixtus V (1585-1590).

Saint Mary Major also houses "the most celebrated icon" of Our Lady "Salus Populi Romani" (Health of the Roman People), attributed to Saint Luke. It has been crowned a few times: by Clement VIII (1592-1605), Gregory XVI (August 15, 1838), and finally Pius XII on November 1, 1954 (Marian Year for the centenary of the dogmatic definition of the Immaculate Conception), after Pius XII had proclaimed the Queenship of Mary with the Encyclical *Ad Caeli Reginam* and instituted the Feast of the Queenship of Mary.

Continuing with the description of the church, the mosaic of the apse basin sings of the Triumph of Mary (by Giacomo da Turrita), while the mosaics of the great middle nave (restored by Pius XI) are dedicated to the presentation of the Divine Motherhood in the Old Testament. They are like "a wonderful walk through Sacred Scripture," which consents to situate the Dogma of the Divine Motherhood of Mary "in the majestic perspective where, from the dawn to the end of time, the Divine Providence wishes to assign it" (Father Oger).

On November 12, 1964, in the basilica of Saint Mary Major, Paul VI prayed to the Madonna whom he had that day proclaimed "Mother of the Church." "With a spirit full of trust and filial love," he said, "we raise our glance to you, despite our unworthiness and our weakness. You who have given us Jesus, the source of grace, will not fail to help your Church, at this time when she is flowering because of the abundance of the gifts of the Holy Spirit and is committing herself with renewed zeal to her mission of salvation."

A. Rum

SALVE REGINA

SEE   *Hail Holy Queen*

SATURDAY OF OUR LADY   [971]

SEE *Collection of Masses of the   Month of Mary*
   Blessed Virgin Mary

THE practice of dedicating Saturday to Mary is very old. The reason for the choice of Saturday is based on a legendary yet substantially accurate account. On the Saturday after Christ's death and His disciples' abandonment of Him, Mary was the only one to preserve intact her faith in the Divinity of her Son. As a result, she merited to receive an exceptional appearance of Jesus *on that day*. Another explanation asserts that Divine Wisdom, becoming incarnate, *rested* (Saturday was the Sabbath=day of rest) in Mary as on a bed.

Hence, Saturday acquired its great Marian tone, and the existing fast on that day became associated with Mary. Today, the strongest trace of Mary's relationship with Saturday occurs in the Liturgy. Saturday is dedicated to Mary by a Mass or Office of the Blessed Virgin Mary. Through these liturgical acts, Christians exalt the person of Mary in the action that renews the sacrifice of Christ and in the action that prolongs His prayer.

This liturgical attribution of Saturday to Mary was largely the work of the great Alcuin (735-804), the Benedictine monk who was "Minister of Education" at the court of Charlemagne and who contributed in a decisive manner to the Carolingian liturgical reform. Alcuin composed six formularies for Votive (that is, devotional) Masses—one for each day of the week. And he assigned two formularies to Saturday in honor of Our Lady. The practice was quickly and joyously embraced by both clergy and laity.

Gradually, the "Mass of the Blessed Virgin on Saturday" became simply the "Mass of the Blessed Virgin" and was celebrated even on other days, whenever liturgical legislation permitted. (Many aged priests afflicted with diminishing sight were granted permission to celebrate daily this Marian Mass, which they had committed to memory.)

The liturgical reform of Vatican II did not abolish this traditional practice. It actually enriched the formularies with a greater variety of orations in accord with the spirit of the liturgical seasons and suggested the use of the weekday readings in place of the invariable liturgical readings once used. The present *Roman Missal* gives three common formularies of the Mass plus one each for the seasons of Advent, Christmas, and Easter.

In these texts Mary is seen as the image of the Church praying and as the model of the meditative hearing of God's Word. There are also references to her lowly condition as an innocent, free, and grateful *woman*; as a faithful and praying *witness*; and as a tender and attentive *mother*.

Hence, we can say that these new texts show respect for Marian devotion and insert it better into the annual liturgical cycle of Christ's Mysteries. Christ's eternal light shines its rays on His Mother who, remaining intact in her virginal glory, has irradiated the whole world. The virginity and motherhood of Mary are stressed in many ways. At the same time, there is no lack of appeal to Mary's intercession to save her people from sin and lead them to eternal life.

We might ask in what the newness of the Mass of Our Lady consists—especially when we recall that it now contains only three orations, since the readings are of the day and do not speak of Mary. The newness consists in a development of the ancient and daily "commemoration," with the petition that God may heed the constant intercession of Mary on our behalf.

Mary thus appears in the background, since the Eucharist is a thanksgiving for the redeeming work wrought by Christ. But the liturgical texts still bring out the exceptional traits of this creature of God—her dignity as the virgin Mother of Christ and Mother of all Christians, and the one for whom God has done great things. She shows that even now in her condition of glory, she does not cease to exercise a maternal function.

As we celebrate Christ's Passover, we commemorate the one who was intimately united with Him in His earthly life from conception to crucifixion, and is also united with Him in heavenly bliss. We commemorate the perfect model of today's believers and the image of what we shall be in the new life of heaven. (These same themes are found in the Saturday Office of the Blessed Virgin Mary.)

The Collection of Masses of the Blessed Virgin Mary (q.v.) contains 46 Marian Masses that can be celebrated on Saturday.

A. Buono

SCAPULAR OF MARY   [1145]

SEE *Devotion(s)*   *Popular Religion and Marian Piety*

1. Scapulars in General

SCAPULARS were the outgrowth of a desire on the part of monks to protect their habits while they were at work in the fields. The scapular was a strip of material with a hole inserted in the middle so that it could hang over the shoulders. Half of the material fell in front of the wearer and half protected the back of the habit. It usually matched the width and the length of the habit. Since it hung on the shoulder, it received the name scapular from the Latin word for shoulder, and it came to symbolize the gentle yoke of Christ. Later the scapular was shortened to become one of the most important parts of the religious habit.

When Third Orders of the Religious Orders arose in the 15th century, their members were required to wear the scapular. To make it possible for these people living in the world to do so easily, the scapular was reduced in size. By the 16th century, the scapular was miniaturized. It became made up of two small double squares of cloth (2 or 3 inches square), suspended from the shoulders by two strings or cords. The cloth was usually the same color as the habit and had an image of Our Lady or a symbol or aspect of the particular devotion it recalled (e.g., the Sacred Heart).

Scapulars became very popular even among lay Catholics since they were a way of manifesting a religious disposition of heart and mind and symbolized fellowship with others in dedication to a spiritual cause. They were *sacramentals*, giving the wearers God's protection through the intercession—in the name and merits of Christ—of the Church and the petition of the person by whom they were worn.

There are presently close to twenty scapulars connected with one religious Order or other and approved by the Church. The most popular five are the white scapular of the Trinity, the red of the Passion, the brown of Our Lady of Mount Carmel, the black of Our Lady of Sorrows, and the blue of the Immaculate Conception.

2. The Scapular of Our Lady

Among the scapulars approved by the Church there are eight Marian ones. Like most of the other scapulars, they owe their institution to a vision.

(1) *Scapular of the Hearts of Jesus and Mary* (WHITE). It originated in the Daughters of the Sacred Heart, a community that began in Antwerp in 1873. One part of the scapular contains an image of two Hearts and the implements of the Passion; the other has a red cross.

(2) *Scapular of the Immaculate Conception* (BLUE). It originated in a vision granted to Mother Ursula Benincasa, foundress of the Theatine Nuns in 1617. One part has the image of the Immaculate Conception and the other has the name of Mary.

(3) *Scapular of the Immaculate Heart of Mary* (WHITE). It was instituted by the Missionary Sisters of the Immaculate Heart in 1877. One part has the picture of the Heart of Mary, surrounded by flames, surmounted by a lily, encircled with roses, and pierced with a sword.

(4) *Scapular of Our Lady of Good Counsel* (WHITE). It is connected with the Augustinian friars and was approved in 1893. One part has an image of Our Lady of Good Counsel with the words "Mother of Good Counsel" and the other has the papal tiara and keys, with the words, "Follow her Counsel."

(5) *Scapular of Our Lady of Mount Carmel* (BROWN). This is the oldest and best known of the Marian Scapulars. It is often ornamented with pictures and owes its origin to Saint Simon Stock, an English Carmelite, who had a vision of Mary on July 16, 1251.

Our Lady showed him a large scapular and gave it to him as a signal grace for the Order. She promised that whoever died in it would not suffer everlasting punishment and would quickly be released from purgatory. This is known as the Sabbatine Privilege (q.v.). The scapular can be worn by anyone, and it has become one of the most widely practiced Marian devotions.

(6) *Scapular of Our Lady of Ransom* (WHITE). It is the scapular of a confraternity affiliated with the Mercedarian Order, which began as an Order to ransom Christian captives from the Moors. One part has the image of Our Lady of Ransom.

(7) *Scapular of Our Lady of Sorrows* (BLACK). It origi-nated in the Middle Ages with the Order of Servants of Mary. It has an image of Our Lady of Sorrows on it.

(8) *The Green Scapular.* This is not a scapular in the strict sense, being a single square of cloth hung around the neck by a single string. One side has the image of Our Lady on it and the other side has the image of her heart, with the words: "Immac-ulate Heart of Mary, pray for us now and at the hour of our death." It originated in Our Lady's appearances to Sister Jus-tine Bisquey-buru of the Daughters of Charity of Saint Vincent de Paul between 1840 and 1846 in France. It was instituted for the conversion of those without faith.

3. Reason for Modern Use of Scapulars

Ultimately, the reason for using scapulars lies in the Church's teaching about Mary's Motherhood of the Church and of the faithful as well as her intercessory role. Once the ne-cessity of living the essential Marian form of faith has been un-derstood, the symbol of the scapular or any other symbol adopted knowingly and spiritually vivified becomes an aid to faith and in some way renders effective what it signifies. Hence, the scapular is not a talisman or good luck charm. Rather it is a stimulus to faith and all that follows from it. So today, without any difficulty, many replace the scapular with a similar blessed medal. It is the commitment that matters.

The scapular is also a good reminder of the value of sym-bols in the lives of all human beings, especially in areas where love comes into play. The wedding ring, for example, is also a pure symbol, and it can be of gold or of any other metal. And those who understand that they should be grateful to bear with them the sign of a loved person will also understand the wis-dom of the Church in not deprecating these ancient symbols.

A. Buono

SECULAR INSTITUTES

SEE   *States of Life and Marian Devotion, 3*

SERVANT OF THE LORD

SEE   *Annunciation*   *Fidelity*
      Faith of Mary   *Marian Titles, 6*

THE Greek term used in Luke 1:38 is *doule*. Usually it means slave, even though it is most often translated in the Bible as servant—for example, 1 Samuel 25:41: "*Your maidservant would become a slave to wash the feet of my lord's servants.*"

Mary is not a servant or slave by social origin, nor even by force of circumstances. Yet Luke has Mary designate herself as such: "*I am the servant of the Lord.*" Does he want to convey the idea that Mary assumed this title, which was one of honor and glory in Israel? (Yahweh gave the title of "servant"—"*My servant*"—to one whom He called to collaborate with His plan, and kings were "servants" of Yahweh.) Does Luke mean that Mary deserves the title?

Or does he simply mean that Mary, spontaneously and of her own accord, puts herself at the service of her Lord, that she acknowledges Him as her sole Master, the only One Who has power over her? Luke would then be underlining Mary's faith: "*Let it be done to me according to your word.*"

Whatever the case, Mary's response expresses a fundamental attitude. Above all, traditional piety has seen in this consent a deep humility. But there is more. Enlightened by the Angel, fortified with a "comprehension," she accepts in all consciousness the "power" given her by authority of the Spirit to collaborate "here and now" in the realization of God's message.

Willingly, Mary assumes her "vocation" by an act which at the same time she knows will totally engage her future (See *Fidelity*). She accepts the task of "serving" God's purposes to the full, and she puts at His disposal her womanhood so that He Who is to come might come. Born of God, her Son will no more belong to her than she belongs to herself.

Mary's acceptance of her creaturely condition and the vocation that comes to her from on high has nothing of common servitude or passive submission. On the contrary, it is a veritable act of adoration expressing faith, love, surrender—and fulfillment of herself.

Step by step Mary lets herself be led and strives to place herself at the service of Jesus and His mission, a mission that in many respects proves disconcerting to His contemporaries. Her faith, together with her feminine intuition and her docility to the Holy Spirit, affords her a grasp of this unexpected form of Messianism. It also prepares her to make the adjustments her Son wants of her, including the adjustment in personal initiative as at Cana.

Mary, in short, learns more and more about Jesus in proportion as she puts herself at the service of His work, and does so entirely.

During Christ's public life, Mary maintains a tactful reserve, knowingly inconspicuous and self-effacing. But John notes her presence on Calvary, where in her own flesh she suffers from the suffering of the "flesh of her flesh" and pays the price of her *Fiat* ("Yes") yet ready and prepared to participate in a new birth, that of the Church.

By her participation in the accomplishment of God's plan, Mary has truly merited the title *"Servant of the Lord."* She is in the line of the great servants of God in the Old Testament. Having entered upon the condition of servant, she lives it so as to go beyond it by the perfection with which she devotes herself to her exceptional mission as Mother of the Savior. As a result, she opens the way for "servants" of the New Covenant, *"sons (and daughters) in the Son"*—the Servant par excellence—who live their service as *"children of the Father."*

"Thus Mary, a daughter of Adam, consenting to the word of God, became the Mother of Jesus, the one and only Mediator. Embracing God's salvific will with a full heart and impeded by no sin, she devoted herself totally as a servant of the Lord to the person and work of her Son, under Him and with Him, by the grace of almighty God, serving the Mystery of the Redemption" (LG 56).

A. Delessale

SERVANTS OF MARY

[971]

SEE   *Marian Classics*

THE list of the Servants of Mary is practically inexhaustible. The five described here were selected because of the influence they had and still have on the Marian devotion of the Church: Saint Ephrem for the East, Saint Bernard, Saint Louis-Marie Grignion de Montfort, Saint Alphonsus Liguori, and Saint Maximilian Kolbe.

1. Saint Ephrem the Syrian (306-373)

THE great Doctor of the Syrian Church was born about 306 at Nisibis in Mesopotamia, most probably of a very Christian family. He was tutored by the bishop of his native city, but his participation in the Council of Nicaea (325) no doubt is legendary, as are also his friendship with Saint Basil and his visits to the monks of Egypt. Ordained deacon of the church of Nisibis in 338, he declined to advance to the priesthood. When the Persians occupied Nisibis in 363, he fled with many other Christians to Edessa, which was Roman territory, and there founded a famous school of theology. Ephrem died in Edessa in 373. The Holy See declared him a Doctor of the Church in 1920 and inserted his feast in the calendar of the Universal Church.

The works of Saint Ephrem, written in Syriac, have come to us some in the original language and some in Armenian or Greek translations. Specialists have tried to separate what is authentic from what Eastern tradition falsely attributes to him.

As a commentator on Sacred Scripture, Saint Ephrem has a fondness for expressing himself in poetic form or in metric prose composed of verses having an equal number of syllables. Our distinctions of literary forms ill accord with the free style of Ephrem's poetry.

Saint Ephrem interests us for his great devotion to the Virgin Mary. But here again it is difficult to draw a line between the flights of his devotion, which is deep and often verbose, and the substance of his Marian theology. Frequently cited is this splendid strophe:

You alone, Jesus, and Your mother,
You are the only ones perfectly beautiful.
There is no taint in You,
nor is there any fault in Your Mother.

Some have wanted to see in this strophe an expression of the Immaculate Conception. Such a reading, by all indications, goes beyond the theological intent of the holy Doctor. The words should be taken for no more than a clear expression of Mary's purity of life, which reflected the holiness of her Son and the grace bestowed on the Mother of God.

Saint Ephrem is both an example and an inspirer of confident devotion, nourished by the Bible, toward her who gave us the Fruit of life and is for us the model of all Christian virtues. His hymn of praise to Mary deserves repeated reading and meditation:

Mary gave us a Fruit filled with sweetness
in place of the bitter fruit
that Eve plucked from the fatal tree;
and the whole world finds delight in Mary's Fruit.

The Virginal vine gave forth a grape
whose juice is delightful
and brings joy to the afflicted.
Eve and Adam overwhelmed with anguish
tasted of the drink of life
and drew consolation from it.

Holy in body, all-beautiful in soul, and pure in spirit,
sincere of mind and perfect in affections,
chaste, faithful, pure of heart, and proved in trial,
Mary was filled with all virtues.

H. Holstein

2. Saint Bernard (1090-1153)

SAINT Bernard is part of the whole Marian movement of his time, a movement in which the Cistercian Order is prominent. Entering Citeaux in 1113, he founds Clairvaux in 1115, which will give rise to 65 monasteries. The relatively limited place of Mary in his writings contrasts with the distinction she receives among his contemporaries and in subsequent Tradition. As Father Laurentin has said, "Bernard coined beautiful formulas of Marian belief destined to pass on to posterity, even though on some points he was a restraining influence."

His principal works on Mary are: the treatise *De Laudibus Mariae* (Praises of Mary: 4 homilies on *Missus est*, the Gospel of the Annunciation: Lk 1:26ff; 3 homilies for the Feast of the Purification; 3 homilies for the feast of the Annunciation; one homily for the Birth of Mary (Sermon of the *Aqueduct*); 5 homilies for the Assumption; one homily for the Octave of the Assumption (*Super Signum Magnum*); one for the Circumcision and the Presentation; one for Advent; and letter 174 to the Canons of Lyons on the new Feast of the Conception. Mary also receives greater or lesser mention in a number of other works.

Saint Bernard's Marian spirituality is liturgically centered. He views Mary in the context of the plan of salvation and tries to show the importance for the Christian life of the devotion we owe to the Mother of God. He presents the two following poles: the Mystery of the Incarnation, to which Mary brought her consent, and the Mystery of the Assumption.

Mary stands at the most intimate point of the encounter between God and us. Her Motherhood supervenes upon her Virginity without altering it. Her humility leads to her becoming the Mother of God and, at the same time, Queen, Mistress of the world, celestial Mediatrix with the Mediator, Mother of all peoples, Ladder of sinners, and Gate of heaven. Saint Bernard expresses the admiration of preceding centuries for the Virgin Mary and gives her "the memorable stamp that has prevailed in the West." Yet he does not feel constrained to add to the crown of Mary's privileges the ornament of the Immaculate Conception, telling himself that she has no need of a "false honor" not seen fit to be bestowed on her by the Universal Church of his day.

It is from Saint Bernard that subsequent tradition drew the very words of the *Memorare* ("Remember . . .") and the inspiration for the anthem *Inviolata* ("Inviolate . . .").

B. Billet

3. Saint Louis-Marie Grignion de Montfort (1673-1716)

LOUIS-MARIE Grignion was born on January 31, 1673, in Upper Britanny, at Montfort-sur-Meu, the name of which he took in honor of his Baptism. Youngest of 18 children, among whom were three priests and two nuns, he was educated at Rennes by the Jesuits, spiritual sons of Father Lallemant, then by the Sulpicians of the second generation, from whom he absorbed the deep spirituality of the French School. From 1700 to 1716 he was an itinerant missionary in some ten dioceses of the West. He died worn out at the age of 43, at Saint-Laurent-sur-Sèvre, leaving behind the beginnings of his Congregations: "The Daughters of Wisdom" and "The Company of Mary," whose developments were to come after his death. He was canonized by Pius XII on July 20, 1947.

This man gave one the impression of having benefited from a baptismal rebirth in the Pauline manner. He had the Apostle's visceral repugnance to evil and charismatic openness to life in the Spirit. Those who knew him as a child and growing boy say that he was "seized" by the Virgin right from his Baptism, like Saint Paul by Christ. Mystic union with Mary will be the "Divine milieu" of his spiritual life and his missionary apostolate.

This voyager, who traveled 16,000 miles on foot, seemed made for action, yet left a considerable body of writing, all of it penned with an eye to pastoral ministry. Among his 164 handwritten Canticles, totaling more than 20,000 lines, only 24 actually sing the praise of Mary. But her name appears in nearly all, invoked to promote conversion of life, spiritual practice, union with Christ, and perseverance.

His *Admirable Secret of the Most Holy Rosary* is a "digest" of the *Mystical Rose* by Antoninus Thomas, O.P. In this work Montfort shows the spiritual and apostolic power to be found in this very popular devotion, the Rosary. *Love of Eternal Wisdom*, in a sense a synthesis of his Christological spirituality, concludes with a solid chapter on devotion to Mary, put forward as a privileged means of achieving union with Jesus, Wisdom of God.

But Father Montfort's posthumous success throughout the world was owed to two other writings on Mary, which popularized the Montfortian way of living the devotion called servitude of Love.

One, a small work, was *The Secret of Mary*. Although it is in the form of a letter of spiritual direction, it deals more with a method of personal union with Jesus through Mary. The other, much larger and better known, and translated into some 50 languages, is *A Treatise on True Devotion to the Blessed Virgin*. Set forth here is a spiritual way for living in full the life of Christ with and through Mary. It is a work intended for all states of life. The overriding theme is the apostolic aspect of the Christian life.

Father Montfort was "driven" by the Gospel, which he lived to the letter. And it was in the Gospel—in the dependence of Jesus on Mary during His Hidden Life—that he found the model for our dependence on her. She molded the Head of the Body, and she molds the members as well. Baptism, in making us members of Christ, makes us children of Mary. Montfort's Act of Consecration acknowledges and has us live this filial relation.

The Act of Consecration, prepared by 30 years of true catechumenate, leads us to dependence and active imitation vis-à-vis Mary and Christ, considered as exemplars of the Divine image and resemblance within us. Commitment in theory is not enough. The state of consecration needs to be expressed in the actualities of daily life.

The spiritual attitude that Father Montfort urges upon the soul is called "adherence" in the French School. It is much more concerned with the interior disposition than the externality of our acts. That is why he is very flexible in regard to external Marian practices. But he is very insistent on four interior practices designed to ensure (1) openness to the Spirit *through* Mary, (2) familiarity of *mind with* the model of life, (3) consciousness of the maternal love *in* Mary, and (4) total commitment to service *for* Mary, and through her to service for Christ. This is the soul of all external activity, raised to the dignity of work for the Reign of God.

Montfort had the advantage (in France) of writing in the popular language of the 18th century. But his greatest advantage was that he could speak the language of personal mystic and missionary experience. This is what has made him the ecclesial classic of the Holy Servitude of Love the world over, wherever people are heard to say: "I have made the Consecration of Father Montfort."

O. Le Borgne

4. Saint Alphonsus Liguori (1696-1787)

BORN in Naples on September 27, 1696, Saint Alphonsus founded the Congregation of the Most Holy Redeemer in 1732. From 1762 to 1775 he was Bishop of Saint Agatha of the Goths. He died at Pagani, August 1, 1787. Canonized in 1839, he was declared Doctor of the Church in 1871 and Patron of Moralists and Confessors in 1950.

His whole life, characterized by deep devotion to Mary, is punctuated by interventions of the Mother of God who healed him of various illnesses and favored him with supernatural apparitions and communications. In gratitude he writes:

"Everything good that has happened to me: my conversion, my holy vocation, and so many other graces, I owe it all to your intervention. You know that I have wanted to see you loved by everyone as you deserve, and to make some return of gratitude for innumerable blessings. It is with this intention that I have tried, always and everywhere, in public and in private, to speak of you and to instill in all souls your beautiful and beneficial devotion" (Supplication preceding *The Glories of Mary*).

Echo and testimony of his devotion to Mary are also his canticles, especially the "O My Fair Hope." But his best known Marian work is *The Glories of Mary*, published in two volumes in 1750 and the product of long years of priestly care. Though well aware that cultured Naples, influenced by Widenfeld, Muratori, and the Jansenists, looked askance at Marian devotion, the Saint does not want to give a polemical tone to his book. He prefers a positive exposition that "will help the faithful to become enamored of Mary, through reading, without great fatigue or expense, and above all will provide priests with suitable material for preaching and spreading devotion to this most blessed Mother" (Introduction).

In his exhortation on the *Hail Holy Queen* (Volume I) and the Feasts of Mary (Volume II), Saint Alphonsus follows a tripartite pattern. He gives:

(1) A doctrinal part that highlights a privilege or title of Mary and supports it with references from the Fathers and theologians;

(2) An illustration or edifying story, such as to attract the popular imagination;

(3) A prayer that translates Marian doctrine into Marian devotion.

These three parts intend to show Mary as a living person, a loving mother, who intervenes in the life of sinful men and women: a mother who helps us overcome discouragement and leads us to the Sacraments and to the performance of Christian works of charity.

The Glories of Mary, an instant success, continues to enjoy great popularity. One might even say that it has been the "best-seller" of books on Mary: 800 printings in various languages.

Its exuberant style betrays its Southern origin and may not be wholly congenial to the more staid temperament of the Nordic. And there are testimonies and miraculous accounts that might fail to withstand the historian's critical scrutiny. But all in all, *The Glories of Mary* remains a masterpiece of prayer and contemplative theology that fell on a disintegrating society. Whereas Muratori failed in his attempt to purify

Marian devotion, Saint Alphonsus succeeded in revitalizing the devotion of the people by improving upon its spiritual tone and theological base. The Alphonsian method can serve as inspiration for workers in pastoral ministry who want to develop a popular Marian spirituality for our time.

S. de Fiores

5. Saint Maximilian Kolbe (1894-1941)

APOSTLE and theologian of the Immaculate Conception, this Polish religious, a Franciscan Conventual, founded in Rome in 1917 the *Militia Immaculatae* ("Mission of the Immaculate"). The goal of the Militia was "to bring to Christ the whole universe through the Immaculate." From 1927 to 1941, through the mass media—periodicals, newspapers, radio—he strove to show that consecration to the Immaculate was urgent for a world beset with every form of atheism.

His Marian teaching had its source in Lourdes, where he was struck by Mary's reply to Bernadette asking her name: "*I am the Immaculate Conception.*"

Father Kolbe reasoned as follows: At Lourdes Mary did not say "I am the one who was conceived immaculate." This expresses the Dogma of the Immaculate Conception proclaimed by Pius IX in 1854, four years before the apparitions at Lourdes. What Mary said was "I am the Immaculate Conception." Strictly speaking, only God can designate Himself as such. If Mary names herself in a way reminiscent of the way that belongs to God, it was because she stands as pure transparence of the Holy Spirit.

To the Spirit she owes the fact of having been immaculate in her conception, and she is such in view of being called to conceive the Son of God through the power of the Spirit. Because of the bond between Mary and the Holy Spirit, Father Kolbe concludes that to consecrate oneself to the Immaculate is to consecrate oneself formally and entirely to the Holy Spirit, Source of all gifts, "Soul of the Church," as Vatican II will say (LG 7). On this point we can say Father Kolbe was in his way a precursor of the Council.

This servant of Mary wanted to bear witness to his teaching in every way he could, death included. He had an ardent desire "to be ground to dust" for the Reign of the Divine Heart of Jesus through the Immaculate. God heard him to the letter. Maximilian was moved to volunteer to take the place of a father with a family who had been condemned to death by starvation in a bunker at Auschwitz. The offer was accepted, and he died dispatched by lethal injection, August 14, 1941, fifteen days after having been interned. His body was reduced to ashes the following day, the Feast of the Assumption. He was beatified October 17, 1971, by Pope Paul VI and was canonized October 10, 1982, by Pope John Paul II. His feast was assigned to August 14, the anniversary of his death.

H. M. Manteau-Bonamy

SHRINES (NATIONAL)   [971]

THE word shrine is usually applied to a place regarded as especially sacred. The sacred character may stem from many causes—for example, a tomb or relic, a statue or image, or the remembrance of some religious event that took place there. Hence, a shrine usually comes from some impetus of the people; it does not normally originate with the Church but is concerned with some facet of the Church—in the present case, the teaching on Mary.

The prayer expressed at a shrine is spontaneous, simple, in line with what are termed "devotions." When the original charism wanes, the shrine remains the seat of some memorable event for the people. It becomes part of *their Christian tradition*. This type of tradition thus has great importance in the life of a shrine; its authority is enough to establish the most original and disparate beliefs and practices. Here the Church enters the picture to officiate at the official worship conducted at the shrine—but it is always the popular religiosity that maintains the operation and the life of the shrine.

Except in rare cases of deviations, manifestations of prayer occasioned by shrines provide a necessary complement to the life of the Church. Over the years, shrines have contributed to saving certain values of the faith, avoiding schisms and heresies, maintaining the Christian identity of peoples, and nourishing their spirituality. All this would have to be acknowledged as being in some way the work of the Spirit.

Shrines may occur anywhere and they may be local, national, or international. The most famous Marian international shrines are treated in depth individually throughout the book. This article indicates the most popular national shrines (which are also international at times) and provides some details about most of them.

Algeria

Our Lady of Africa—A bronze, dark-colored statue of the Immaculate Conception with European features brought from France in 1840. It was placed in a basilica and in 1876 was crowned by the founder of the White Fathers, Cardinal Lavigerie, who also entrusted his Congregation to Mary's protection.

Argentina

Our Lady of Lujan—A 22-inch terra-cotta statue of the Immaculate Conception that arrived at this site outside Buenos Aires in 1630 under mysterious circumstances. A large basilica was built and the statue was moved to it in 1904. Patroness also of Uruguay and Paraguay.

Austria

Our Lady of Mariazell—A 10th-century statue of Mary that was enshrined in the Benedictine Monastery of the town in 1157.

Belgium

Our Lady of Beauraing—SEE Beauraing.

Bolivia

Our Lady of Copacabana—A statue of Mary made of plaster and wood by an Indian fisherman in thanksgiving for her protection. It was originally placed in a chapel near Lake Titicaca in northern Bolivia. Later a large church was built for it and it was crowned in 1925.

Brazil

Our Lady of Nazareth—A statue of Our Lady found by two hunters under a palm tree in northern Brazil. Devotion to it led to the growth of the city of Belém.

Our Lady Who Appeared—An originally headless wooden statue found by some fishermen in a river. It was given a head and placed in the village church in 1719. It was later moved to a new church near São Paulo and in 1929 Our Lady Who Appeared was named the Patroness of Brazil.

Canada

Our Lady of the Cape—SEE Our Lady of the Cape.

Saint Mary of the Hurons—Originally built in 1639 by Jerome Lalemant, S.J., as a shrine for Huron Indians, it was destroyed in 1649 by the Iroquois. It was rebuilt in 1925 and honors the martyrs John de Brébeuf and Gabriel Lalement.

Ceylon

Our Lady of Madhu—A shrine going back to the 17th century. It is frequented by both Christians and non-Christians.

England

Our Lady of Mount Carmel at Aylesford—This shrine is situated at a Carmelite friary that began in 1241, was dissolved in 1538, and was reestablished in 1949. Contains a statue of Our Lady Guardian of the Carmelites and the relics of Saint Simon Stock.

Our Lady of Walsingham—Shrine of the Annunciation founded in the 12th century with a chapel made according to the dimensions of the house of the Holy Family in Nazareth. Destroyed in 1738, it was revived at another site nearby in 1934, and its statue of Mary with Jesus on her knee was crowned in 1954.

France

Our Lady of La Salette—SEE La Salette.
Our Lady of Lourdes—SEE Lourdes.
Our Lady of the Miraculous Medal—SEE Rue du Bac.

Notre Dame Cathedral of Paris—Magnificent five-aisled cathedral built between the years 1163 and 1320 and containing among other things rich sculptural decorations of the life of Mary.

Notre Dame de Chartres—One of the greatest achievements of Gothic architecture, this cathedral erected in the 12th and 13th centuries is a marvel of sculpture and glass.

Germany

Our Lady of Altötting—Shrine located 60 miles from Munich in a chapel that was part of the imperial palace in 877, but the image of Our Lady dates back only to 1228.

Our Lady of Kevelaer—Located in the Lower Rhine, this shrine contains a picture of the statue of Our Lady of Consolation of Luxemburg. It was brought to its present spot by a soldier in 1642 and quickly gave rise to a great shrine.

Greece

The Holy Mountain of Our Lady (Mount Athos)—This ancient sacred mount contains three shrines of Our Lady: at Iviron, there is our Lady of Iviron; at Khilandar, the Three-handed Virgin; and at Vatopedi, the Consoling Virgin.

India

Our Lady of Bandel—Founded by the Portuguese in 1596, this shrine in Bengal houses a statue of Our Lady of Safe Travel.

Our Lady of Bandra—Founded in 1640, this shrine houses a statue of Our Lady of the Mount, which was crowned in 1954 when its church was also declared a lesser basilica.

Ireland

Our Lady of Knock—SEE Knock.

Our Lady of Limerick—A statue of Mary and her Child made in Flanders about 1622 and given to the Rosary Confraternity of Limerick. Since 1816 it has been housed in the Dominican church in Limerick and it was crowned in 1954.

Israel

Basilica of the Annunciation—SEE Holy Land and Mary, 2k.

Basilica of the Nativity—SEE Holy Land and Mary, 2c.

Church of the Dormition—SEE Holy Land and Mary, 2i.

Church of the Visitation—SEE Holy Land and Mary, 2a.

Italy

Basilica of Saint Mary Major (Rome)—This is the third of the Roman patriarchal basilicas; it was founded in 366 and dedicated to Mary in 435. SEE Saint Mary Major.

Holy House of Loreto—SEE Loreto.

Madonna of Saint Luke—Found in the chapel of the Church of Saint Mary Major in Bologna, this ancient image is venerated as Our Lady of Rome and is probably the most well-known of the images attributed to Saint Luke.

Our Lady of Perpetual Help (Rome)—Found at the Church of Saint Alphonsus, this shrine possesses one of the most famous Marian paintings, a 14th-century icon made on walnut wood and possibly stemming from Crete.

Our Lady of Tears (Syracuse)—SEE Syracuse.

Japan

Our Lady of Japan—This shrine in Nagasaki was erected in 1897 and commemorates the 17th-century Japanese martyrs. It was later made a cathedral and survived the atom bomb blast of 1945, although a chapel was destroyed.

Mexico

Our Lady of Guadalupe—SEE Guadalupe.

Philippines

Our Lady of Safe Travel—A statue transported from Mexico to Manila in 1626 and housed in different places. In 1929 it was solemnly crowned in Manila and then returned to its most usual place, Antipolo.

Our Lady of the Turumba—Statue of Our Lady of Sorrows found in the water in the 18th century and located at Pakil on the Laguna de Baie. "Turumba" is the name of a song in Mary's honor sung by the people who brought the statue to the church.

Poland

Our Lady of Czestochowa—SEE Czestochowa.

Portugal

Our Lady of Fatima—SEE Fatima.

South Africa

Our Lady of Shongweni—Statue of Mary Mediatrix of All Graces set on a hill near Durban.

Spain

Our Lady of Guadalupe of Estremadura—Statue claimed to have been bestowed on Saint Leander of Seville by Saint Gregory the Great. Mary was invoked by this title already in the 8th century.

Our Lady of Montserrat (Barcelona)—Sometimes called the Black Madonna, this statue was purportedly found by shepherds in the 9th century. It resides in the famed Benedictine Abbey.

Our Lady of the Pillar at Saragossa—The most famous of all Spanish shrines, linked to Saint James, and even the Blessed Mother herself who is said to have placed the statue in its shrine as Saint James rested.

Switzerland

Our Lady of the Hermits—Statue of Our Lady that was said to be the favorite of Saint Meinrad who was killed in the 9th century. It resides in a renowned Benedictine Monastery.

Uganda

Mary, Queen of Africa—Located at Koboko, this statue was crowned in 1954 and also contains a cross and a crescent— indicative of the veneration paid her by the Moslems.

United States

National Shrine of the Immaculate Conception—SEE National Shrine of the Immaculate Conception.

Our Lady of the Milk and Happy Delivery ("de la Leche y Buen Parto")—Shrine located near St. Augustine, Florida, which was begun in the 17th century. A new shrine was built in 1915 and is especially frequented by expectant mothers.

Our Lady of Victory (La Conquistadora)—Shrine begun in Santa Fe, New Mexico, in 1692 by Diego Vargas, in thanksgiving for his having retaken the city.

Vietnam

Our Lady of La Vang—Established in 1800 at Hué, where a vision had been reported, this shrine has become the most important in Vietnam, attracting thousands of pilgrims annually even under the Communist regime.

A. Buono

SIGNUM MAGNUM

SEE   *Magisterium (Documents of)*
   Marialis Cultus
   Redemptoris Mater

ON May 13, 1967, on the occasion of the 50th anniversary of Our Lady's appearances at Fatima, Pope Paul VI issued an Apostolic Exhortation entitled *The Great Sign (Signum*

Magnum). The document deals with two points of Marian doctrine and devotion: (1) the Biblical data concerning Mary, Handmaid of the Lord, Mother of the Church, Teacher of redeemed humankind, and Exemplar of dedication to the service of God and neighbor; (2) the true meaning of devotion to Mary in the teaching of the Church.

Among other things, *Signum Magnum* points out that Mary is highly honored by the Church with a special veneration, particularly in the Liturgy, not only as Mother of God who took part in the Mysteries of Christ but also as the Mother of the Church. It offers assurance that the liturgical reform (then in progress) will not be detrimental to the wholly singular veneration due to Mary and that the resultant greater veneration will in no way diminish the adoration offered to the incarnate Word as well as to the Father and to the Holy Spirit.

A. Buono

SINGLE PEOPLE AND MARY   [898-900, 971]

SEE   *States of Life and Marian Devotion*

IN their 1973 pastoral letter entitled, *Behold Your Mother*, the Bishops of the United States held Mary up as the model of single women too in her capacity as mother:

"Mary is model also for women who live a single life in the world. This can be a true vocation from God, freely chosen under the inspiration of grace, bringing with it the fruits of joy, personal holiness, and unselfish devotion to others. Many a young girl, on the death of her mother, has generously taken on herself the care of younger brothers and sisters to train them in the love of God.

"Others dedicated their lives to the service of their fellow human beings as nurses, teachers, and social workers. Many exercise an apostolate through personal example and influence, and through their work in Catholic lay organizations.

"All these devoted women share in the spiritual motherhood of the Mother of Jesus and, like her, find true happiness and fulfillment in doing God's will" (no. 145).

At the same time, everything said above of women applies equally to single men. They can take part in the very same activities and imitate Mary *the parent* by becoming spiritual fathers of those they help.

In addition, there are many other ways in which Mary is the model of all single people—most predominantly by her role as the quintessential disciple of Christ. Regardless of their state in life, all Christians can certainly imitate her virtues, the chief of which were enumerated by Paul VI in his Apostolic Exhortation *Marialis Cultus* on *Devotion to the Blessed Virgin Mary*: (1) holiness; (2) faith and docile acceptance of God's Word; (3) generous obedience; (4) true humility; (5) solicitous charity; (6) profound wisdom; (7) worship of God by fulfilling religious duties, by gratitude, by offering of self, and by prayer; (8) poverty reflecting dignity and trust in God; (9) attentive care for others; (10) delicate forethought; (11) virginal purity; and (12) strong and chaste married love.

Truly, as the author of the *Imitation of Mary* put it, "the Blessed Virgin's life contains lessons *for everyone*. If we study it, we learn how to live in prosperity and adversity, prayer and work, honors and humiliations." Furthermore, "in imitating her we imitate Jesus, King and incomparable Model of all virtue."

A. Buono

SISTER (MARY OUR)

BY her belonging to the human family Mary is our sister by race. The fact is obvious. Why, then, dwell on it? Not to prove the obvious but as a reminder to keep within reason our "idealization" of Mary. Despite her greatness and privileges, Mary did not escape the human order and we are less than true to her if we make her too distant, too far beyond reach.

1. Daughter of Adam

The Second Vatican Council speaks of the exceptional grace by which Mary "far surpasses all creatures, both in heaven and on earth." Then it immediately adds that "she belongs to the offspring of Adam and therefore is one with all those who are to be saved" (LG 53).

Paul VI, in his closing address to the Third Session of the Council, makes the same point when he says: "For all the abundance of wonderful prerogatives with which God endowed her to make her worthy of being the Mother of the Word incarnate, Mary is nonetheless near to us: a child of Adam like us, hence our sister by the bond of nature. . . ."

The way that the Bible presents Mary in her fundamental relation to Jesus should keep us from forgetting this aspect of hers. For Christ, the Word made flesh, to bear our human nature, Mary herself must be totally part of it (SEE *Old Testament, New Testament*).

The "privileges" of Mary themselves, properly understood, express the same thing. For example, belief in her Immaculate Conception is a strong statement of her belonging to the race of Adam and in need of redemption, since this privilege is how she was redeemed by her Son. So also the Assumption, which was an anticipation for her of something to which all of us are called (cf. LG 68), anticipation that accorded with her vocation and fidelity.

Whatever "happened" to Mary happened to one of us. That is why we can "read" in her, as in an open book, what God's love wants to realize in us, even if by different ways and to different degrees.

2. Simplicity and Proximity of Mary

Recognition of the fact that Mary is our sister also calls attention to the simple life she led and her remarkable closeness to us. The Evangelists could not pass over in silence the wounded astonishment of townsmen and kindred of Jesus when He embarked on His mission: "*Is this not the carpenter, the Son of Mary, a Brother of James and Joses and Judas and Simon? Are not His sisters our neighbors here?*" (Mk 6:3; cf. Mt 13:54-58; Lk 4:16, 22, 24; cf. also Mk 3:20-21; Mt 12:24-32; Lk 11:15-23). This astonishment shows that until then Jesus

had lived among them as one among many, doing nothing outwardly that could have *"revealed His glory"* (cf. Jn 2: 11).

The same is true of Mary, woman of the women of her village. If she cut a figure at all, it was mostly through mention of
the family clan and trade, both of which point to the "ordinary" character of the life and attitude of Jesus at Nazareth
before His public life. By all indications, Mary lived this extraordinary vocation of Mother of God unnoticed, within a
routine of the simplest kind.

It does not appear that things changed much for her, at
least outwardly, with the ministry of Jesus. If, as Vatican II observed, the Mother of the Divine Redeemer was generously associated with His work to a degree unparalleled, it was not in
spectacular fashion. Her intervention at Cana, so full of meaning and consequences, and her presence on Calvary are noted
by Saint John but go unmentioned by the Synoptic authors.

And if, in the Book of Acts, Luke, Evangelist of the Annunciation, intentionally shows us Mary in the Cenacle with
the Apostles waiting for the Holy Spirit after the Resurrection,
nowhere do we see her playing an official external role in the
beginning Church. But she is intensely present to the community of disciples, as simply—and as productively—as she had
been on various occasions when the Lord asked her to "serve."

All this in no way minimizes the exceptional greatness
and the universality of Mary's mission. But it asks us not to
overlook certain aspects. Mary lived her service to the Lord
and His brothers and sisters in a daily routine apparently, but
only apparently, commonplace. She lived it with the fullness of
a faith and love whose perfection never ceases to amaze us.
The simplicity and the "naturalness" of Mary, which were to
make her so close with all Jesus' brothers and sisters during
His earthly life, are not the least of the marvelous qualities it is
given us to admire in her. Her "greatness" would not be as perfect without them. Grace does not destroy nature but perfects
it.

Mary's glory, too, is our glory. Today we find it easy to see
Mary as "our mother" (SEE *Motherhood, Spiritual*). The reason
no doubt is that we instinctively find in her a closeness that is

loving, attentive, considerate and helpful. Though *"blessed among all women,"* she would not be so perfectly and so humanly "our Mother in the order of grace" (LG 61), did she not at the same time retain toward us the attitude and sentiments of a "sister by the bond of nature."

A. Bossard

SOLEMNITY OF MARY, MOTHER OF GOD

SEE   *Feasts of Mary*

SORROWS OF MARY   [494, 525ff, 2618]

SEE   *Cross (Mary at the)*   *Syracuse*
         Rosary

THE Liturgy celebrates on September 15, the day after the Feast of the Triumph of the Cross, a Feast in honor of Our Lady of Sorrows. This form of Marian piety goes back to the 14th century, but its roots are in the Gospel and in a rich spiritual tradition.

1. Gospel

"Near the Cross of Jesus there stood His Mother" (Jn 19:25). Mary's presence on Calvary was in keeping with an intention of God, since on the day of the Presentation the Holy Spirit had prompted Simeon to prophesy: *"This Child is destined to be . . . a sign that will be opposed—and your own soul a sword shall pierce"* (Lk 2:35).

From the Gospels we can infer other sorrows of Mary. For example: the inconvenience at the birth of Jesus when *"there was no room for them in the inn"* (Lk 2:7); the massacre of the infants of Bethlehem (Mt 2:16-18); the anxious search for Jesus until the third day (Lk 2:41-50); Jesus rejected and threatened with death first by His townsmen of Nazareth (Lk 4:28-30), then by the Jewish authorities of Jerusalem (Lk 11:53-54; 19:47-48, etc.); and certainly each episode of the Passion.

"Mary was intimately associated with the Mystery of Salvation accomplished by Christ, as Mother of the Suffering Servant of Yahweh," declares Paul VI (MC 7) alluding to Isaiah 53.

2. Compassion of Mary

Standing at the foot of the Cross with Mary is a very ancient aspect of Christian prayer.

Already at the time of the first "Fathers of the Desert" (4th-5th century) Abbot Poemen, questioned after coming out of an ecstasy, replied in a halting voice: "My mind was there with Blessed Mary, Mother of God, who was weeping over the Cross of the Savior. I too would like to weep with her always" (*Apothegms* 144).

About the same time Saint Ephrem the Syrian (373) writes a lamentation of Mary at the foot of the Cross where Jesus has just died, a poem still sung in the Syrian Rite at Vespers of Holy Saturday. Around the year 500 Romanos the Melodist composes a *Hymn of Mary at the Cross*, in which Jesus converses with His Mother and instructs her on the Mystery of the Cross.

In the West Saints Ambrose, Anselm, Bernard, and many others have meditated and preached on the Compassion of Mary. This spiritual theme became very popular in the 13th century, owing especially to Franciscan preachers and Servites of Mary. We have only to read, for illustration, the poignant *Plaint of the Madonna* by Jacopone da Todi (d. 1306).

O Son, Your soul has left You,
O Son of discouragement,
O Son of disappearance,
O Son Who was poisoned!
O Son bathed in red and white,
O Son without compare,
O Son, to whom shall I turn?
O Son, You have left me!

This was also the devotional climate and historical context that produced the *Stabat Mater Dolorosa* (SEE *Roman*

Missal, on September 15, and this article in the *Dictionary*), so dear to Mediterranean piety. The episode of the "Spasm" (swooning) of Mary, popularized by a work called *Meditations on the Life of Christ* (beginning of the 11th century), was gradually eliminated, Popes and theologians disapproving of it.

3. Sorrows of Mary

The devotion to the Sorrows of Mary appears toward the beginning of the 14th century. It is probable that Blessed Henry Suso (1295- or 1300-1366) and other "Rhenish mystics" of the Dominican Order were a contributing factor. From the central scene of Calvary meditation is extended to the whole Passion: from the arrest of Jesus to His burial. And so as to be in line with the very popular devotions to the *Five Joys* of Mary, one counts *five sorrows*; then *seven sorrows,* to correspond to the seven Hours of the daily Office and the *seven joys* of Mary.

With minor variations, the list of the *sorrows* of Mary suffered in the course of the Passion remained remarkably stable:

1. Jesus is arrested and struck.
2. Jesus is led to Pilate to be judged.
3. Jesus is condemned to death.
4. Jesus is nailed to the Cross.
5. Jesus gives up His spirit and dies on the Cross.
6. Jesus is taken down from the Cross.
7. Jesus is wrapped and laid in the tomb.

So as not to overlook anything of the Gospels, there was a parallel list of seven sorrows that included the infancy and childhood of Jesus:

1. The prophecy of Simeon ("a sword . . .").
2. The massacre of the Innocents and flight to Egypt.
3. Jesus lost in Jerusalem.
4. Jesus arrested and judged.
5. Jesus crucified and dying.
6. Jesus taken down from the Cross.
7. Jesus wrapped and laid in the tomb.

Another variation of this devotion was the life of Mary as she visited the places where her Son had lived and died (devotion inspired by the *Golden Legend* of Jacobus de Voragine).

The two lists of Mary's sorrows gave rise in the 14th century to all sorts of literary expression: Meditations, Prayers, Poems, etc. One image in particular—painted, then sculptured— caught the popular imagination, the *Pietà*, Mary holding on her knees the blood-stained body of Christ. It was the time of the Black Death with its terrible epidemics (1347-1350, 1358-1360, 1373-1375 . . .). All the greater, therefore, was the impact of these sorrowful themes of Marian devotion.

When, beginning in 1464, the Dominican Alain of Roche preached the *New Psalter of the Virgin Mary* (150 Hail Marys to be said every day), he recommended as a theme of meditation for the middle 50 the Passion of Our Lord and the Compassion of His Mother, from the Last Supper to the Burial. Confraternities of the Rosary (the first one in Cologne, 1475) made the meditations more specific, establishing a list of 15 Mysteries among which were *five sorrowful*: Agony, Scourging, Crowning with Thorns, Carrying of the Cross, and Crucifixion.

In 1482 a parish priest of Flanders, John de Coudenberghe, began to preach devotion to the *Seven Sorrows* under its present form:

1. The Prophecy of Simeon (Lk 2:34-35).
2. The Flight into Egypt (Mt 2:13-21).
3. The Loss of Jesus for Three Days (Lk 2:41-50).
4. The Ascent to Calvary (Jn 19:17).
5. The Crucifixion and Death of Jesus (Jn 19:18-30).
6. Jesus Taken Down from the Cross (Jn 19:39-40).
7. Jesus Laid in the Tomb (Jn 19:40-42).

The devotion brought into existence a *Confraternity of Our Lady of Sorrows*, which won approval from the Pope.

4. Spirituality

Mary's participation in the sufferings of Jesus the Savior is an important aspect of Marian spirituality that has been revitalized by Biblical theology.

The Second Vatican Council calls Mary "the exalted Daughter of Zion" (LG 55) and Paul VI, speaking in reference to the Presentation, characterizes Mary as "the one who performs a mission belonging to ancient Israel, and as the model for the new People of God" (MC 7).

Hence it is legitimate to think that in Mary on Calvary, her heart pierced with the sufferings of her Son, God "*fulfilled*" (cf. Jn 19:30) the mystery of the Woman—both Israel and the Church—"*wailing aloud in pain*" (Rv 12:2) to bring into the world, with the Risen Lord, "*the rest of her offspring*" (Rv 12: 17).

From this Biblical perspective sorrows and the joy of giving birth (compassion and spiritual motherhood) are inseparable, for Mary and for the Church.

With regard to our part in this Mystery, the Liturgy of September 15, recalling Colossians 1:24, speaks in point: "As we honor the compassionate love of the Virgin Mary, may we make up in our own lives whatever is lacking in the sufferings of Christ for the good of the Church" (Prayer after Communion).

J. Laurenceau

STABAT MATER
(At the Cross Her Station Keeping)

SEE   *Cross (Mary at the)*   *Sorrows of Mary*
       Prayer(s) to Mary

THE *Stabat Mater* (literally, "The Mother Was Standing") is a hymn consisting of 20 couplets in the Latin and describing with beauty and pathos the Sorrows of the Blessed Virgin at the Cross. It is thought to have originated in the 13th or 14th century, in an atmosphere of ardent Franciscan devotion to the crucified Jesus. It has been variously attributed to Pope Innocent III (d. 1216), Saint Bonaventure (d. 1274), or most often to Jacopone da Todi (d. 1306).

This hymn was introduced into the Liturgy gradually until 1727 when it was prescribed as a Sequence for the Mass of the Seven Sorrows of Mary on September 15 and on the Friday before Holy Week, as well as their corresponding Offices. The *Stabat Mater* has been retained as an optional Sequence for September 15 in the reformed *Roman Missal* and as the hymn for the Office of Readings, Morning Prayer, and Evening Prayer in the new *Liturgy of the Hours.*

The popularity of this world-famous writing is reflected by the more than sixty English translations that have been made and by its use in the popular devotion of the Stations of the Cross.

The compassion of Mary—her presence and participation in the Sacrifice of the Cross—is part of the Mystery of the Church sharing in and offering the sacrifice of Jesus for the salvation of the world.

At the Cross her station keeping,
Stood the mournful Mother weeping,
Close to Jesus to the last.

Through her heart, His sorrow sharing,
All His bitter anguish bearing,
Lo, the piercing sword has passed!

O, how sad and sore distressed
Was that Mother highly blessed
Of the sole-begotten One.

Christ above in torment hangs,
She beneath beholds the pangs
Of her dying glorious Son.

Is there one who would not weep
'Whelmed in miseries so deep

Christ's dear Mother to behold?

Can the human heart refrain
From partaking in the pain,
In that Mother's pain untold?

Bruised, derided, cursed, defiled,
She beheld her tender Child,
All with bloody scourges rent.

For the sins of His own nation
Saw Him hang in desolation
Till His Spirit forth He sent.

O sweet Mother! fount of love,
Touch my spirit from above,
Make my heart with yours accord.

Make me feel as you have felt.
Make my soul to glow and melt
With the love of Christ, my Lord.

Holy Mother, pierce me through.
In my heart each wound renew
Of my Savior crucified.

Let me share with you His pain,
Who for all our sins was slain,
Who for me in torments died.

Let me mingle tears with you,
Mourning Him Who mourned for me,
All the days that I may live.

By the Cross with you to stay,
There with you to weep and pray,
Is all I ask of you to give.

Virgin of all virgins blest!
Listen to my fond request:
Let me share your grief divine.

Let me, to my latest breath,
In my body bear the death
Of your dying Son divine.

Wounded with His every wound,
Steep my soul till it has swooned
In His very Blood away.

Be to me, O Virgin, nigh,
Lest in flames I burn and die,
In His awe-full judgment day.

Christ, when You shall call me hence,
Be Your Mother my defense,
Be Your Cross my victory.

While my body here decays,
May my soul your goodness praise,
Safe in heaven eternally.
Amen. Alleluia.

A. Buono

STATES OF LIFE AND MARIAN DEVOTION   [971]

SEE   *Devotion(s)*   *Motherhood, Spiritual*
       Family Life and Mary   *Single People and Mary*
       Imitation of Mary

"FIRST and perfect Disciple of Christ" (MC 35), Mary can be proposed as a model to be imitated by all. All Christians, however, must live their fidelity to the Lord within their personal vocation and the actual circumstances of their life. How can people called to "states of life" as diverse as those of the laity, members of the secular institutes, religious, and priests all take Mary as model?

1. A General Answer

First of all, it must be borne in mind that Mary is not a "model" for Christians in the sense that they should try to imitate her, literally, in every detail of her life. For many reasons this would be an impossibility. But Mary is "pattern" or "archetype" for the whole Church and for every one of the faithful through the perfection of her personal response to the call of the Lord in faith, hope, and supernatural love, a response that put her totally at the service of Christ and His brothers and sisters (SEE *Imitation of Mary*).

Moreover, Mary is not just model, but is present by her prayer and motherly attention in the life of the Church and the life of her Son's brothers and sisters (cf. LG 62). By reason of the perfect and unique character of her response to the Lord Mary constitutes an "exemplar" for all—"a permanent and universal exemplary value" (MC 33). At the same time, by her Spiritual Motherhood she also has each of us for children, who can and should live their filial relationship to her in a personal manner. Hence, no "state of life" can claim Mary for itself alone.

This said, it is interesting and useful to see how lay people, religious, members of secular institutes, and priests, with the characteristics of their state of life, can each find a model in Mary. Such a course, in fact, is not new but a tradition in the Church.

2. Lay People

The term laity refers to "all the faithful except those in Holy Orders and those in the state of religious life especially approved by the Church" (LG 31).

"The laity, by their very vocation, seek the Kingdom of God by engaging in temporal affairs and by ordering them according to the plan of God" (LG 31).

"Since the laity, in accordance with their state of life, live in the midst of the world and its concerns, they are called by God to exercise their apostolate in the world like leaven, with the ardor of the spirit of Christ" (AA 2).

The situation of Mary, with her vocation as Mother of God and Mother of all people, is certainly unique and irreducible to any other. If, nevertheless, one had to place her in a state of life according to present canonical distinctions, it would not be the priesthood, nor even that of religious, but that of the laity.

Consequently, in their resolve to live as children of God and disciples of Christ, Christian lay people need not have the slightest hesitation to seek an example in Mary: woman of her time and social environment, fully engaged in the "temporal affairs" that fell to her and perfectly ordering them according to God's plan. From her they can learn, or learn better, that by performing their daily tasks as a "service" committed to them by the Lord, they are already in the process of fulfilling the apostolic mission that is theirs in virtue of Baptism:

"The perfect example of this type of spiritual and apostolic life is the most Blessed Virgin Mary, Queen of Apostles. While leading the life common to all here on earth, one filled with family concerns and labors, she was always intimately united with her Son and in an entirely unique way cooperated in the work of the Savior" (AA 4).

The Council adds, in effect, that Christian lay people can and should count on Mary for help to make their activities more Christian and fruitful because "having been assumed into heaven, with her maternal charity she cares for these brothers and sisters of her Son who are still on their earthly pilgrimage until they are led into the happy homeland (cp. LG 62). All should devoutly venerate her and commend their life and apostolate to her maternal care" (AA 4).

3. Members of Secular Institutes

According to the Conciliar *Decree on the Adaptation and Renewal of Religious Life* (PC 11), "although Secular Institutes are not Religious Institutes they do involve a true and full profession of the Evangelical Counsels in the world, recognized by the Church." By the *Apostolic Constitution on Secular Institutes (Provida Mater* of February 2, 1947), Pius XII canonically sanctioned the life of Secular Institutes.

This means that today "the Church casts an arc between the two states—religious and secular—when it approves their synthesis in Secular Institutes: the closest union with the Lord in the life of the Evangelical Counsels and the closest relationship with one's brothers and sisters in the solidarity of effort and risk in the world. This is possibly the most important Christian design in our time" (H. U. von Balthasar).

On August 28, 1980, even John Paul II observed that this "state of consecrated life" is "a particular gift of the Holy Spirit to our time," capable of "offering an efficacious spiritual contribution for the future and opening new paths of universal value for the People of God." Therefore, he called upon "the maternal intercession of the Blessed Virgin" to grant "her gifts of light, wisdom, and decision-making in the search for better ways."

Reflecting upon the *"three conditions of fundamental importance"*—noted by the Pope in his discourse to the Secular Institutes—so that their members might have an effective mission (=to be *true disciples of Christ, competent in their own spheres, and capable of changing the world from within*), we easily see how and how much they can be helped by Mary's exemplarity and intercession to obtain light, wisdom, and decision-making.

Indeed, observes Paul VI (MC 37), the figure of the Virgin does not "disillusion any of the profound expectations of men and women of our time but offers them the perfect model of the disciple of the Lord: the disciple who builds up the earthly and temporal city while being a diligent pilgrim toward the heavenly and eternal city, the disciple who works for that justice which sets free the oppressed and for that charity which assists the needy; but above all, the disciple who is the active witness of that love which builds up Christ in people's hearts."

In this sense, Mary is truly the "perfect model" of all who belong to the Secular Institutes because she is the incomparable teacher of that *synthesis*—of that harmony of life—which is proper to Secular Institutes, "between the closest union with the Lord and the closest solidarity with one's brothers and sisters."

4. Religious

The personal holiness to which religious are called does not differ essentially from the holiness demanded of all Christians by reason of their Baptism. But the particular means that they employ and profess in order to attain it puts them in a somewhat different position as regards "temporal things" and lends special meaning to their way of living the realities of the Kingdom in this world. Religious put a certain distance between themselves and the possession and use of material things (vow of poverty). They give up the right to have a family of their own (vow of celibacy). They voluntarily limit the scope of their independence (vow of obedience).

In doing so they have no intention of denying or minimizing either the value of the things they renounce or their capacity to lead us to the Lord Who created them. They are only saying that these things are relative in comparison with the higher values of the Kingdom, to which they must be ordered and even sacrificed when the Lord asks it. What gives Religious Profession its true and deepest meaning is precisely that it consecrates the professed to the Lord and His Kingdom.

Although the Beatitudes, the *Magna Carta* of the Kingdom, are the program of life for all disciples of Christ, Religious have the mission, confirmed and approved by the Church, to proclaim the program more effectively by their way of life: "Religious, by their state of life, give splendid and striking testimony that the world cannot be transformed and offered to God without the spirit of the Beatitudes" (LG 31).

It is not hard to see why and in what way Mary is the perfect example of what Religious strive to become. The *end* they pursue—who has attained it more or better than Mary? Namely, total gift of self to the Lord, perfect "following of Christ," special witness to the values of the Kingdom. Everything in Mary, absolutely everything, was ordered to Christ and His mission. If anyone has been consecrated to Him exclusively and completely, it is Mary. If anyone has "followed" Him without fail, in love and giving of self, in detachment and obedience, it is she. If anyone has lived the Beatitudes and been imbued heart and soul with their spirit, it is she. Beyond all doubt, *that to which Religious aspire*, Mary, "perfect Disciple of Christ," attained better than anyone. And the witness that, for their part and in their way, it is the mission of Religious to bring, Mary brought in fullness.

The contemplation that they devote to Mary reminds them, clearly and indelibly, of the vocation to which they have been called, particularly the radical character of their option for Christ, expressed in their manner of life. Relying on Mary and the motherly help she never fails to offer, they progress more easily and more rapidly in their "following of Christ" as nearly as humanly possible.

"Therefore, let them beseech the Virgin Mary, gentle Mother of God, 'whose life is a model for all' (Saint Ambrose), that their number may daily increase and their salutary work be more effective" (PC 25).

As for the actual practice of their religious "state," some elucidations may be noted. Mary is certainly a model in the use of material things, in the obedience of faith, in total exclusive belonging to the Lord by her virginal consecration. But, to repeat, Mary's vocation is unique, and for that very reason surpasses all realizations of which we are capable.

Consider, for example, the virginal consecration of Mary. In her it was inseparable from the Divine Motherhood, to which moreover it was ordered. And this Motherhood, according to the Divine plan, called for her marriage with Joseph. Obviously, Mary's situation here is truly unique and "inimitable," for Religious as well as for any lay Christian. Even so, the virginity of Mary is an important element in the spiritual life of Religious. "Queen of Virgins" is one of the titles of Our Lady.

The title calls to mind the essential purpose of Mary's virginal consecration to the Lord Who is her Son, namely, a total belonging to God, which alone makes possible the fullness of a love that must assume the universal dimensions of supernatural love. The same purpose motivates the consecration of Religious, who can look to Mary for ground for their vow of celibacy and its spiritual fruitfulness. And in authentic devotion to Mary they can find a source of strength to maintain and live their fidelity to the renouncements that it entails.

Mary's example also reminds them that whatever the "objective" perfection of the means (e.g., vows) that they put into practice in their life, and whatever the value of these means for the Church and the world, they are only means. The *unum necessarium*, the one necessary thing, is Christ, the living Word of God in Whom all must believe with all their being, Whom all must follow according to their personal vocation to make it a life of the Beatitudes, beginning with that of faith: *"Blessed is she who believed that the Lord's words to her would be fulfilled"* (Lk 1:45). *"My mother and my brothers are those who hear the Word of God and keep it"* (Lk 8:21).

5. Priests

Mary and priests is another wide-ranging question, which it is not possible to do much more than touch on here.

First, a reminder: Although Mary participates more than anyone in the kingly, prophetic, and priestly character that Christ imparts to His people, she must be excluded from any kind of belonging to the "ministerial" priesthood properly speaking. For example, on Calvary Mary indeed is the "Virgin presenting offerings" (MC 20), but in the sense of the participation to which Christ calls all His disciples, participation unique and typical for the Church in her case, yet not participation in the ministerial sense, which in the presence of the Supreme Priest in the act of His Sacrifice would have been utterly superfluous.

It remains true that priests have a special ministry in the Church that presents certain analogies with that of Mary. They are ordained to enable Christ to continue His saving action in a manner adapted to the conditions of our earthly life. Through their ministry, accordingly, Christ makes Himself present in the world today, present in the reality of His redemptive Sacrifice to unite all human beings to Himself and form them into His Mystical Body, the Church.

Through Mary, the Word become flesh has made Himself present to our race in order to save it, and He has asked His

Mother to cooperate with all her being in the work of salvation by which He unites us to Himself in the Church, as members of His Body. And Mary, Mother of us all, Mother of the Church, continues to consecrate herself to the growth of the total Christ (SEE *Motherhood, Spiritual*).

Consequently, priests and Mary, each in their own way, are basically ordered to the same end, objectively associated in the same fundamental task, even though by very different kinds of action. And just as her special relationship and association with Christ implied for Mary the demand of a commensurate moral perfection, so with priests: their vocation summons them to a personal union with Christ corresponding to their character as instruments of the Savior in the exercise of the priestly ministry.

The priestly state, therefore, is a very strong supplementary reason for priests to contemplate Mary in order to learn from her how to put themselves totally at the service of Christ, of His Church, and of their fellow humans. And they do not deceive themselves if they think they have a kind of claim to special attention from Mary, in view of their specific mission and the obligations that go with it. Devotion to Mary is certainly not foreign to the spiritual life of the priest *qua* priest, as the Second Vatican Council so well indicated:

"Priests will always find a wonderful example of docility to the Holy Spirit in the Blessed Virgin Mary, who was led by the Holy Spirit to dedicate herself totally to the mystery of human Redemption. Let priests love and venerate with filial devotion and veneration this Mother of the Eternal High Priest, Queen of Apostles and Protectrix of their own ministry" (PO 18).

6. Different Situations of Life

The Christian life is the life of Christ in us. If we are to adapt to it and let it permeate and transform us, we have to begin with the actual conditions of our existence. To a certain extent, the particular aspect in which we view Our Lord—or Mary—at a given moment is conditioned by the situation of the moment. It is normal that in time of trial or mourning we turn to Christ and Mary on Calvary; that in moments of joy we make our own the Blessed Virgin's *Magnificat*; that young people considering their vocation turn to Our Lady of the Annunciation; that the mother of a family have a predilection for Mary in her exceptional motherhood, in her life in the home of Nazareth; that a widow think of her in her situation after the death of Joseph; that the elderly like to imagine her finishing her life on earth and looking forward to going home to the Father's house. Such "actualization" can give us a feel of Mary's closeness and her capacity to understand and help us (SEE *Mary Our Sister*).

But these resemblances between our life and hers, where they do exist, are always partial, and are not the principal reason that Mary is Our Lady for all age groups and all situations. It is rather that in every circumstance we can find help and support in her unbounded goodness, the woman whom the Lord Himself was pleased to give us for Our Mother.

A. Bossard — A. Rum

SUB TUUM (We Fly to Your Patronage)   [971]

SEE   *Intercession of Mary*   *Prayer(s) to Mary*

THE *Sub Tuum* is regarded as the oldest prayer of petition to the Blessed Virgin Mary. In 1917 an Egyptian papyrus was discovered containing what many believe is the original version of this prayer. Experts date the papyrus in the 3rd century, thus indicating that the *Sub Tuum* was already in existence in Egypt at the time. This was even before the Council of Nicaea in 325.

The prayer spread from Egypt—where Mary and Joseph fled with Jesus (Mt 2:13-15)—to other parts of the Christian world, and especially to Europe where it became a favorite of those devoted to Mary. This short but theologically rich prayer is like a cry out of the past, the Age of Persecution. It remains always relevant—in time of personal distress or worldwide disturbance.

We fly to your patronage,
O holy Mother of God;
despise not our petitions in our necessities,
but deliver us always from all dangers,
O glorious and blessed Virgin.

A. Buono

SYRACUSE (Sicily)   [67]

SEE *Apparitions*   *Apparitions after Vatican II*

BETWEEN August 29 and September 1, 1953, tears flowed
several times from the eyes of a plaster-cast image depicting the Immaculate Heart of Mary. The image was at the head of a young married couple's bed. Their names: Angelo Jannuso, a farm worker, and Antonina Giusto. They lived at 11 Garden Street, Syracuse (east coast of Sicily). Antonina, pregnant and suffering from attendant disorders, noticed first what was happening:

"To my great surprise, I saw tears flowing from the image. I called my sister-in-law and my aunt Antonina Sgarlata, who came and stood near me. I pointed out the tears to them. At first, all they could think of was hallucination, owing to my sickness. I insisted, and when they looked more closely, they also saw tears flowing from the eyes of the Madonna, which ran down her cheeks and fell on the head of the bed. Frightened, they went to the door and called for the neighbors to come. They, too, observed the phenomenon, which repeated itself at regular intervals. Throughout the day the crowd kept growing, and it became necessary to summon the police for help."

Besides Antonina, 188 other persons from diverse social categories, including police officers, testified to the fact of this weeping before an ecclesiastical tribunal.

The event was also caught by photographic lens on two negatives, and by two sequences of film that showed to everyone's amazement the formation, the flowing, and the dissipation of the tears.

A medical commission was named, which obtained and examined samples of the liquid and came to the following conclusion: "The appearance, the alkalinity, and the composition compel us to say that the examined liquid is similar to human lachrymal secretion."

Pontifical authority expressed itself in the memorable words of Pius XII, who also raised the question as to the significance of Mary's tears: "Admittedly, the Holy See has not at present rendered its judgment concerning the tears said to have been shed by one of her images in a humble workingman's home. Nevertheless, it is not without keen emotion that we have taken cognizance of the unanimous declaration by the Sicilian episcopate on the reality of this occurrence. There is no doubt that Mary is in heaven, eternally happy and beyond pain and grief; but she is not insensible.

"On the contrary, in heaven she maintains a constant love and pity for the troubled human race, to which she was given as Mother when, mournful and in tears, she stood at the Cross of Jesus. Does the world understand the mysterious language of these tears? The tears of Mary! On Golgotha they were tears of compassion for her Jesus and of sadness over the sins of the world.

"Does she now weep again for the renewed wounds inflicted on the Mysterious Body of Jesus? Or does she weep for so many of her children in whom error and sin have extinguished the life of grace, and who gravely offend the Divine Majesty? Or could they be tears of waiting for the return of others of her children, formerly faithful but today lured away by the false promises of enemies of God?" (Radio Message, October 17, 1954).

Since at Syracuse the Virgin neither appeared nor spoke, interpretation of the secret language of her tears remains problematical. At first they were seen as tears of sorrow over the inroads atheistic materialism was making among Christians. Soon other explanations were given: some general (sin in all its forms), some more particular (neglect of previous messages, threats to the sanctity of the family . . .).

The tears of Mary remain a mysterious and polyvalent symbol, by their nature open to various interpretations, depending on the times and circumstances. But any interpretation should be true to the spirit of the original meaning (compassion for Jesus, sorrow for the sins of the world). In that regard, her tears are a permanent message.

The Episcopal Conference of Sicily expressed a desire for a shrine to perpetuate the memory of the prodigy. This shrine is presently under construction. The designers are the French architects Michel Andrault and Pierre Parat, winners of a competition launched in 1955. The crypt was opened on August 28, 1968. On display there is the original image from which the tears flowed.

Every year the shrine attracts about a million visitors from all parts of the world. They are received by a pastoral team attentive to their needs and always available. The periodical "Madonna of the Tears" counts 90,000 subscribers and is published in six languages.

S. de Fiores

- T -

TEMPLE

SEE *Holy Land and Mary, 2l*

THEOTOKOS

SEE *Mother of God*

TOMB OF THE VIRGIN

SEE *Holy Land and Mary, 2m*

TRINITY (MARY AND) [488-501, 721-726]

SEE *Holy Spirit (and Mary)*   *Liturgy*

THE Second Vatican Council called attention to the fact that Mary is a created being of God (LG 53, 55, 60), but it also noted her election to "the high office and dignity of being the Mother of the Son of God and, in consequence, the Father's Daughter of predilection and Temple of the Holy Spirit" (LG 53).

Chapter 8 of the *Constitution on the Church (Lumen Gentium),* the chapter on the Blessed Virgin, begins by recalling the mystery of salvation planned and realized by the Father, the Son, and the Holy Spirit and with which was connected the "Woman," Mother of Christ (LG 52). It concludes with the words: "for the glory of the Most Holy and Undivided Trinity" (LG 69), indicating the supreme purpose of the Virgin Mary's existence and prayer.

Vatican II encouraged the cult toward Mary as promoting "the cult of adoration that is offered to the Incarnate Word, as well as to the Father and the Holy Spirit" (LG 66). In line with these words of the Council is Paul VI's observation: "It is

supremely proper that exercises of piety directed toward the
Virgin Mary should clearly express the Trinitarian and Christological note that is intrinsic and essential to them" (MC 25).

For Mariology to be characterized by the Trinitarian note,
it is imperative to begin, as Vatican II began, with the History
of Salvation. In the unfolding of this history, the Trinity appears in its "economic" and *ad extra* activity. According to the
Bible, salvation has a Trinitarian structure because it was
brought about by the God Who created the Covenant, Who
sent His Son as Savior in the fullness of time and, through
Him, disseminated the Spirit of filial adoption (Gal 4:4-5; Rom
8:16).

The Virgin Mary can be introduced into this soteriological
horizon (rather than a Hellenistic-style ontological framework)
because her relations with the Trinity then emerge from a
static conception and assume salvational significance. In like
manner, the cult toward Mary is inserted in the context of the
Christian cult, which is "by nature a cult rendered to the
Father, to the Son, and to the Holy Spirit, or, as the Liturgy
puts it, to the Father through Christ in the Spirit" (MC 25).

1. Mary and the Religious Experience of the Father

In the New Testament revelation the Father retains the
character of absolute principle and ultimate end. The plan of
salvation traces back to Him, and to Him is referred every
work of Christ in the Spirit (1 Cor 8:6; 15:28: Eph 1:3-14; Col
1:19-20). It is therefore necessary to insert Mary in the trajec-
tory of love that proceeds from the Father and returns to Him
as embracing the Church, the Mystical Body of Christ. This
reference to the Father entails notable advantages:

(a) Attention to the Father prevents us from making Mary
an absolute or independent being, as though existing by intrinsic necessity. Mary is a created being, dependent in everything
on her Creator, and she owes her presence in the Christian
Mystery to a free, unmerited choice by God. Any discussion of
Mary must guard against placing her outside God's plan of salvation. In the manner of the Second Vatican Council, we have
always to refer to the work and will of the Father, both in ex-

plaining Mary's global mission and in considering various episodes of her life: "God wishing in His supreme goodness . . ." (LG 52); "The Father of mercies willed . . ." (LG 56); "Since it has pleased God . . ." (LG 59).

Even the Motherhood of Mary, toward Christ and toward us, should be viewed as participating in and deriving from God's transcendent Fatherhood (cf. Eph 3:15). Better still, her Motherhood is a manifestation of the "maternal" care of God, Who is shown in Isaiah as both Father and Mother (cf. Is 49:15; 66:13).

(b) Brought into relation with the Father Who reveals Himself in the History of Salvation, Mary is seen as fulfilling a function of responsible service for the realization of God's salvific plan. Her prerogatives cease to be individualistic privileges specific to her person and assume a social dimension of salvation—prerogatives like being, for example, the Father's Daughter of predilection, or the Immaculate, and the Mother of God.

This, in fact, is the Biblical perspective of Saint Luke in describing Mary's calling. *"Full of grace"* (Lk 1:28), *"the Lord is with you"* (Lk 1:28), *"you have found favor with God"* (Lk 1:30) are expressions that reveal the Divine pleasure and a privileged theological status, but not of a static kind. They have a functional and ministerial significance: "Mary is termed *kecharitomene,* that is, full of that grace which she has received from God. She is the daughter of grace par excellence . . . and she is presented as the most singular expression composed intentionally so as to accentuate her role. Bypassing her personal data, Luke looks to the ministerial function of Mary, to her election, and to the intimation of a ministry of salvation" (E. Peretto).

(c) In this relation with the Father, Mary is also seen as the height of the people of Israel's preparation for receiving the Messiah. She is the Daughter of Zion who "stands out among the poor and humble of the Lord, such as confidently hope for and receive salvation from Him" (LG 55). In her deep religious experience Mary discovers the true physiognomy of God: holy, mighty, avenger of the poor, merciful, and faithful (Lk 1:46-

55). Above all, in her contact with Jesus, at least beginning with the Finding in the Temple, she perceives more and more that God is "Father."

(d) As Paul VI observes in *Devotion to the Blessed Virgin,* the Gospel shows a parallel between the words of Mary and those of the Father regarding the behavior to show toward Jesus, words she addressed to the servants at Cana: *"Do whatever He tells you"* (Jn 2:5). "These words, which at first sight were limited to the desire to remedy an embarrassment at the feast, are seen in the context of Saint John's Gospel to re-echo the words used by the people of Israel to give approval to the Covenant at Sinai (cf. Ex 19:8; 24:3, 7; Dt 5:27) and to renew their commitments (cf. Jos 24:24; Ez 10:12; Neh 5:12). And they are words that harmonize wonderfully with those spoken by the Father at the theophany on Mount Tabor: *Listen to Him* (Mt 17:5)" (MC 57).

(e) Lastly, the cult of the Virgin Mary calls us to adoration and love of the Father (LG 65). If the aim of Christians is to live as children of God, it is well to remember that the first passage in the New Testament to speak of Mary is directed toward Christ's mission of offering us filial adoption (Gal 4:4-5).

Living as "children of Mary," after the example of the beloved disciple (Jn 19:25-27), should be both a result and a support of an intense life as *children of God*, with all its implications. According to St. Louis-Marie de Montfort, devotion to Mary builds religious awareness of the Father: "To those who practice it faithfully, this devotion brings great interior deliverance, such as children of God enjoy. It removes from the soul every scruple and every hint of servile fear. It swells the heart with a holy trust in God that sees Him as our Father. And it inspires tender, filial love" (*Treatise on True Devotion to Mary,* no. 169).

2. Mary and Life in Christ

Christ is the center of the Father's plan of salvation (Eph 1:18-23). He is the one Savior, Lord, Revealer, and Mediator (Jn 4:42; 8:12; Heb 8:6; 1 Tm 2:5-6). He is also the moral Exemplar and Life for Christians (Rom 8:29; Col 3:3-4, 12-15; Jn 11:24; 14:6).

Concerning Mary's relation with Christ and the Christian life, some points should be noted:

(a) Christ is the living center of faith and catechesis. In the Mystery of Christ Mary is seen as an element and implication, her place willed by plan of God and progressively recognized by the Church. We have in some way to retrace the course of the first Christian communities, who discovered the person of Mary according as they developed their knowledge of Christ: "Through Jesus to Mary."

From a Christological view, the role of Mary consists in being "the venerable *Mother* of the Divine Redeemer, generously and in a singular way *associated with His work, humble servant* of the Lord," and now, "in the order of grace, our *Mother*" (LG 61). All these tasks or prerogatives put Mary in close relation with Christ and His work, and they prevent us from making her an independent or parallel being.

The Motherhood of Mary is not a purely biological function but an adherence of faith that makes Mary the first Christian, the first Disciple of Christ, and bestows on her a "glorious ministry" (Bossuet) designed to bring the world the Deliverer.

The Blessed Virgin's singular cooperation in the work of the Redemption does not put her on the same plane as the sole Mediator, for she is a created being redeemed by her Son. Spiritual Motherhood "flows forth from the superabundance of the merits of Christ, rests on His mediation, depends entirely on it, and draws all its power from it. In no way does it impede, but rather it fosters the immediate union of the faithful with Christ" (LG 60).

Accordingly, even as we portray Mary in her close and constant union with Christ and His work, we have scrupulously to respect the transcendence of the same Christ: "In the Virgin Mary everything is relative to Christ and dependent on Him" (MC 25).

(b) Devotion to Mary should be organically inserted "into the only worship that is rightly called *Christian*, because it takes its origin and effectiveness from Christ, finds its complete expression in Christ, and leads through Christ in the Spirit to the Father" (MC Introduction). This means that it should be principally lived in the Liturgy, whether by keeping the feasts of Mary or by drawing inspiration from her as "model of the spiritual attitude with which the Church celebrates and lives the Divine Mysteries" (MC 16).

Similarly, in a spirituality that sets direction to life's activities, the reference to Mary must not be separated from the relation to Christ, which for the Christian remains fundamental and characteristic. The lives of saintly men and women are witness that devotion to Mary does not constitute a second spiritual life but a "new way" of living in God. This is to say that the reign of Mary is in no way contrary to the reign of Christ but is totally directed toward it. For Saint Louis-Marie de Montfort, consecration to Mary is "perfect renewal of the vows and promises of holy Baptism" (*Treatise on True Devotion to Mary*, no. 120). Mary becomes for believers a living call to opt, like her, for Christ, to make her "yes" their own (Lk 1:38), and to renew their covenant with Christ, covenant of obedient love (Jn 2:5).

3. Mary and Walking in the Holy Spirit

The Holy Spirit is shown in the New Testament as the Divine Person Who "indwells" the Christian to renew the heart and make possible a life as child of God in liberty (from the flesh) and in love (Rom 5:5; 8:12-16; 1 Cor 12:13). Believers have therefore to walk in the Spirit and let themselves be led by Him (Gal 5:16-18; Rom 8:4), to the very transformation of their mortal bodies. For this truth of faith to be lived by Christians, it is imperative that the relation to Mary be formed so as to take account of the Holy Spirit.

(a) In the first place, to avoid every idle pneumatology and every tendency to substitute Mary for the Holy Spirit, we must identify the ties by which Mary is linked with the Paraclete. These are found in "the principal operations of the Spirit of Christ in the Mother of God" (Paul VI, Letter to Cardinal Suenens, May 13, 1975).

A spiritual reading of the Marian episodes in the New Testament leads one to see the Annunciation as Mary's anticipated Pentecost. The same expressions occur in the two scenes: *Divine power, Holy Spirit, come upon* (Lk 1:35; Acts 1:8). And both scenes are followed by a missionary ferment and charismatic communications (Lk 1:39-45; Acts 1:8; 4:31; 8:4-14). The Holy Spirit produces in Mary the virginal conception of Christ (Lk 1:35; Mt 1:20) and brings about in her the new heart spoken of by the Prophets (Ez 36:26-27; Jer 31:31), which makes possible a response of total faith (Lk 1:38).

To the inspiration of the Holy Spirit, Who has spoken by the Prophets, are likewise attributed the canticle of the *Magnificat* (Lk 1:46-55) and an understanding of the Divine Mystery (Lk 2:19, 51). Moreover, at the foot of the Cross Mary exercises a maternal and unitive function. This accords with the Johannine teaching that makes the Holy Spirit the principal agent of the rebirth by which we become children of God (Jn 3:5) and the principal agent of the unity of believers (Jn 14:16; 16:13-14). Like Mary, the Holy Spirit is part of the "legacy" bequeathed by the Lord (Jn 19:27-30).

In the Cenacle, Mary prays with the Apostles and disciples as they wait for the coming of the Spirit (Acts 1:14).

The glorious state of Mary in heaven is again the work of the Holy Spirit, Who raises bodies and makes them immortal and givers of life (1 Cor 15:42-45).

In this pneumatological view, Mary is not an obstacle or rival to the Holy Spirit. She is on the contrary a way for understanding this same Spirit and His operations.

(b) The cult of Mary has to be integrated with the larger horizon of life according to the Spirit. We need "to keep in mind that the action of the Mother of the Church for the good of the redeemed does not substitute for the omnipresent and universal action of the Holy Spirit and does not compete with it. Rather, Mary implores and prepares the way for the action of the Spirit. This she does by her *prayer* of intercession offered in accordance with the plan of God, Whom she now beholds in beatific vision. But she also does it by the direct influence of *example*, including the very important example of perfect docility to the inspirations of the Divine Spirit" [Paul VI, Letter to Cardinal Suenens, May 13, 1975].

As implied in these words of the Pope, there is a primacy of the Holy Spirit that needs to be respected and brought to attention. The Mystery of Pentecost must have priority in our life over the relation to Mary, because Christianity is first of all life in the Spirit and according to the Spirit (Rom 8:2-14; Gal 5:16-25).

Mary's own intercession has meaning only in the larger context of the Spirit's transcendent intercession (Rom 8:26-27). As for the tendency to substitute Mary for the Holy Spirit, this will not arise so long as the titles and prerogatives of Mary are seen for what they are, participation in the work performed by the Spirit in the Church: "It is therefore always in dependence on the Spirit that Mary leads souls to Jesus, fashions them in His image, inspires good counsels in them, and is the bond of love between Jesus and believers" (Paul VI).

On the pastoral side, it is not necessary "to redirect Marian devotion, so intense in the last hundred years, with the aim of making it more an ecclesial devotion to the Holy Spirit" (H. Muhlen). Nor should it simply be put to rest, a temptation, one fears, not always resisted. On the contrary, the cult of Mary should be considered as a zone or way of life *in* the Spirit, and at the same time a way of approach to the hiddenness of the Trinitarian Mystery and to Mary's Spiritual Motherhood.

Mary is the created being who was taken possession of by the Spirit and prepared by Him to become the virginal Mother of Christ the Messiah. She was the first Believer of the New Covenant. She is Mother of the faithful, revelatory image of the Spirit, and at the same time prototype of the living Church called to bring about the Kingdom of God in the world, through the Spirit.

In this connection, we must recognize the importance of the Catholic Charismatic Movement, which unexpectedly arose after the Council. Starting from the experience of the Spirit, the New Pentecostals relive the values of Christianity, such as the meditation of the word, the prayer of praise, the agape-communion, and the charisms of glossolalia and healing, but they also rediscover the figure of Mary in her relation to the Spirit.

Mary "orients" us to the "spiritual" life insofar as she is the Prototype of accepting the Spirit (Lk 1:28-38), whose Baptism she has received (Acts 1:5, 16) and by Whom she has been given the charism of tongues, understood as a conceptual form of contact with God or prayer of praise (Acts 2:4-13). The Marian experience at the heart of the Charismatic event is considered one of the most precious gifts of the Spirit (R. Laurentin).

4. Conclusion

The Trinitarian reference is extremely important for Mariology and the cult of Mary, if they are to find their rightful place and their true objective. Mary is the one to whom was revealed for the first time, even if in allusive terms, the Trinitarian Mystery of the Most High that by intervention of the Spirit gave birth to Christ, Son of God and transcendent Messiah (Lk 1:28-33).

As such, she can become for Christians a locus of encounter with the three Divine Persons and a locus of revelation for Their salvific work. With Mary as model, the Christian life becomes an itinerary to the Holy Trinity. The lives of Saints especially devoted to Mary are ample witness of this fact.

S. de Fiores

- U -

UNITED STATES AND MARY

SEE *National Shrine of the Immaculate Conception*

1. Marian Devotion before Independence

FROM their first coming to the New World, "American" Catholics have had the greatest devotion to Mary. Signs of it appear in the early explorations, the colonial period, and the attainment of independence. The Bishops of the United States have nicely sketched the salient features:

"Christopher Columbus' flagship was the *Santa Maria*. His successors planted the Christian cross with the Spanish flag across many territories that now fall within the United States. The names these pioneers gave to many cities in the South and West are an indication of their love of Mary.

"For example, they gave Los Angeles the full name *St. Mary Queen of the Angels of the Portiuncola*. When Menéndez landed in Florida in 1565 and founded the city of St. Augustine, the oldest city in the United States, one of his first acts was to have the chaplain, Father Mendoza, offer Mass in honor of Our Lady's Nativity. *Our Lady of La Leche* is still venerated there. In New Mexico the conquistadores paid tribute to the greater and fairer *La Conquistadora,* brought to Santa Fe in 1625.

"The French missionaries came from the north, down the St. Lawrence, and our maps still bear traces of their devotion to our Lady. Père Marquette explored the Mississippi with Louis Joliet in 1673 and called it *River of the Immaculate Conception.* Before him Saint Isaac Jogues (d. 1646) and his companions had brought the Christian faith and devotion to Mary to the region around the Great Lakes. Our Lady of the Martyrs' Shrine at Auriesville commemorates their witness.

"The England of penal times was an unlikely point of origin for an American colony where religious toleration would prevail and Catholics could publicly profess their faith, even their devotion to Saint Mary. Yet George Calvert, a convert to Catholicism and the first Lord Baltimore, was given a charter to found the crown colony of Maryland, where religious freedom would be guaranteed. When he died in 1632, his sons carried the project through.

"Their two ships, *The Ark* and *The Dove*, landed in Maryland (named for the queen), March 1634. Their Chaplain, Rev. Andrew White, S.J., recorded how the Catholics of the group consecrated the future colony to Our Lady of the Immaculate Conception. They called their first settlement and capital 'St. Mary's City,' and they named the Chesapeake 'St. Mary's Bay' " (*Behold Your Mother*, appendix).

2. Marian Devotion after Independence

On achieving nationhood, American Catholics showed their love and devotion even more. They chose Mary as the Patroness of the first American diocese and then of the whole country. They joined the worldwide Marian current that was part of the 19th century and they proclaimed Mary's name through the length and breadth of the land, assigning it to their parishes and other institutions.

"A son of Maryland, John Carroll, was the first bishop of the new United States. Consecrated bishop in 1790 on the feast of the Assumption, he placed his newly founded diocese of Baltimore under the patronage of Mary. In his first pastoral in 1792, he wrote: 'Having chosen her the special patroness of this Diocese, you are placed, of course, under her powerful protection and it becomes your duty to be careful to deserve its continuance by a zealous imitation of her virtues, and reliance on her motherly superintendence.' The Cathedral of Baltimore, which Bishop Carroll began, was dedicated at its completion in honor of the Assumption of Our Lady.

"The world-wide movement that resulted in the definition of the Immaculate Conception by Pius IX in 1854 had its influence on the American Church. The sixth provincial Council of Baltimore was held in 1846 under the presidency of Archbishop Samuel Eccleston, S.S., of Baltimore, with 23 of the country's 26 bishops in attendance. Their first decision (May 13, 1846) was to request the Holy See that Mary under the title of the Immaculate Conception be named patroness of the United States. This petition was granted by Pope Pius IX in the following year.

"In their pastoral of 1846 the bishops wrote: 'We take this occasion, brethren, to communicate to you the determination, unanimously adopted by us, to place ourselves, and all entrusted to our charge throughout the United States under the patronage of the holy Mother of God, whose Immaculate Conception is venerated by the piety of the faithful throughout the Catholic Church.'

"The example of devotion to Mary set by the pioneers led to a pattern among American Catholics. Cathedrals and churches and chapels too many to enumerate carry Mary's titles across the country. From St. Mary's Seminary, Baltimore, founded in 1791, to the present, the institutions of higher learning bearing Mary's name are manifold. *Notre Dame* and all its lovely variants have become titles for many institutions and for every sort of Catholic apostolic enterprise, e.g., Sodalities, Legion of Mary, and the Family Rosary, which has spread from America to all the world" (*Ibid.*).

This American devotion to the Mother of God culminated in the building of the great monument to the people's faith, the National Shrine of the Immaculate Conception (q.v.).

At the same time, American Catholics showed special devotion in liturgical Marian celebrations and special devotions (Feasts of Mary, especially the Immaculate Conception and the Assumption, Saturday Masses, May crownings and devotions, October Rosary recitations, and Novenas of the Miraculous Medal).

Before Vatican II, Marian devotions were the greatest category of nonliturgical pious practices among Catholics. They experienced a decline after the Council, but there are signs that some of the more popular devotions are coming back as they are brought into line with the Liturgy, in accord with the desires of the Church.

3. Marian Devotion Today

And there is one devotion that is still going strong—the recitation of the Rosary. Catholics were in the forefront of the Family Rosary Crusade pioneered for the last 40 years by Father Patrick Peyton with the slogan "The Family That Prays Together Stays Together." American movie stars gave their time and talents to broadcast live recitations of the Rosary all over the nation and the world. The movement is still strong and many Catholics are saying the Biblical Rosary and the Living Rosary—testifying to a vibrant devotion to Mary.

American organs of communication have also been involved in this devotion to Mary. After a brief period of inaction, they are now involved in a full-scale effort concerning all aspects of Mariology. The latest catechisms have implemented the Marian suggestions of Vatican II and the Popes. Catechetical and liturgical magazines have devoted whole issues to Mary. According to a noted Mariologist, Mary "is receiving sympathetic treatment in some segments of the women's movement, and also in liberation theology. There is a growing interest in Mary in ecumenical dialogue between the Churches, such as in the Lutheran-Roman Catholic Consultations that began discussing 'Mary and the Saints' in February 1984" (Eamon Carroll).

Finally, both scholarly works and popular books devoted to Mary are being published and distributed over the whole country. America's Marian orientation seems to be as strong as ever.

A. Buono

UPPER ROOM

SEE *Cenacle*

- V -

VALUE OF MARIAN DEVOTION [273, 971, 2030]

1. Force for Renewing Christian Living

CHRIST is the only way to the Father,[1] and the ultimate example to Whom the disciples must conform their own conduct,[2] to the extent of sharing Christ's sentiments,[3] living His life and possessing His Spirit.[4] The Church has always taught this and nothing in pastoral activity should obscure this doctrine. But the Church, taught by the Holy Spirit and benefiting from centuries of experience, recognizes that devotion to the Blessed Virgin, subordinated to worship of the Divine Savior and in connection with it, also has a great pastoral effectiveness and constitutes a force for renewing Christian living.

It is easy to see the reason for this effectiveness. Mary's many-sided mission to the People of God is a supernatural reality that operates and bears fruit within the body of the Church. One finds cause for joy in considering the different aspects of this mission, and seeing how each of these aspects with its individual effectiveness is directed toward the same end, namely, producing in the children the spiritual characteristics of the First-born Son. The Virgin's maternal intercession, her exemplary holiness and the divine grace that is in her become for the human race a reason for Divine hope.

The Blessed Virgin's role as Mother leads the People of God to turn with filial confidence to her who is ever ready to listen with a mother's affection and efficacious assistance. Thus the People of God have learned to call on her as the Consoler of the Afflicted, the Health of the Sick, the Refuge of Sinners, that they may find comfort in tribulation, relief in sickness and liberating strength in guilt. For she, who is free

[1] Cf. Jn 14:4-11
[2] Cf. Jn 13:15
[3] Cf. Phil 2:5
[4] Cf. Gal 2:20; Rom 8:10-11

from sin, leads her children to combat sin with energy and resoluteness. This liberation from sin and evil[5]—it must be repeated—is the necessary premise for any renewal of Christian living.

2. Imitates Mary's Virtues

The Blessed Virgin's exemplary holiness encourages the faithful to "raise their eyes to Mary who shines forth before the whole community of the elect as a model of the virtues." It is a question of solid, evangelical virtues: faith and the docile acceptance of the Word of God;[6] generous obedience;[7] genuine humility;[8] solicitous charity;[9] profound wisdom;[10] worship of God manifested in alacrity in the fulfillment of religious duties,[11] in gratitude for gifts received,[12] in her offering in the Temple[13] and in her prayer in the midst of the apostolic community;[14] her fortitude in exile[15] and in suffering;[16] her poverty reflecting dignity and trust in God;[17] her attentive care for her Son, from His humble birth to the ignominy of the Cross;[18] her delicate forethought;[19] her virginal purity;[20] her strong and chaste married love.

These virtues of the Mother will also adorn her children who steadfastly study her example in order to reflect it in their own lives. And this progress in virtue will appear as the consequence and the already mature fruit of that pastoral zeal which springs from devotion to the Blessed Virgin.

Devotion to the Mother of the Lord becomes for the faithful an opportunity for growing in Divine grace, and this is the ultimate aim of all pastoral activity. For it is impossible to honor her who is "full of grace"[21] without thereby honoring in oneself the state of grace, which is friendship with God, com-

[5] Cf. Mt 6:13
[6] Cf. Lk 1:26-28; 1:45, 11:27-28; Jn 2:5
[7] Cf. Lk 1:38
[8] Cf. Lk 1:48
[9] Cf. Lk 1:39-56
[10] Cf. Lk 1:29, 34; 2:19, 33, 51
[11] Cf. Lk 2:21-41
[12] Cf. Lk 1:46-49
[13] Cf. Lk 2:22-24
[14] Cf. Acts 1:12-14
[15] Cf. Mt 2:13-23
[16] Cf. Lk 2:34-35; 2:49; Jn 19:25
[17] Cf. Lk 1:48; 2:24
[18] Cf. Lk 2:1-7; Jn 19:25-27
[19] Cf. Jn 2:1-11
[20] Cf. Mt 1:18-25; Lk 1:26-38
[21] Cf. Lk 1:28

munion with Him and the indwelling of the Holy Spirit. It is this Divine grace that takes possession of the whole man and conforms him to the image of the Son of God.[22]

3. Unveils God's Plan

The Catholic Church, endowed with centuries of experience, recognizes in devotion to the Blessed Virgin a powerful aid for human beings as they strive for fulfillment. Mary, the New Woman, stands at the side of Christ, the New Man within Whose Mystery the mystery of human beings alone finds true light; she is given to us as a pledge and guarantee that God's Plan in Christ for the salvation of the whole person has already been realized in a creature: in her.

Contemplated in the episodes of the Gospels and in the reality that she already possesses in the City of God, the Blessed Virgin offers a calm vision and a reassuring word to modern persons, torn as they often are between anguish and hope, defeated by the sense of their own limitation and assailed by limitless aspirations, troubled in their mind and divided in their heart, uncertain before the riddle of death, oppressed by loneliness while yearning for fellowship, a prey to boredom and disgust. She shows forth the victory of hope over anguish, of fellowship over solitude, of peace over anxiety, of joy and beauty over boredom and disgust, of eternal vision over earthly ones, of life over death.

4. Leads to Christ

Let the very words that she spoke to the servants at the marriage feast of Cana, *"Do whatever He tells you,"*[23] be a seal on our Exhortation and a further reason in favor of the pastoral value of devotion to the Blessed Virgin as a means of leading men to Christ. Those words, which at first sight were limited to the desire to remedy an embarrassment at the feast, are seen in the context of Saint John's Gospel to re-echo the words used by the people of Israel to give approval to the Covenant at Sinai,[24] and to renew their commitments.[25] And

[22] Cf. Rom 9:29; Col 1:18
[23] Cf. Jn 2:5
[24] Cf. Ex 19:8; 24:3, 7; Dt 5:27
[25] Cf. Jos 24:24; Ezr 10:12; Neh 5:12

they are words that harmonize wonderfully with those spoken by the Father at the theophany on Mt. Tabor: *"Listen to Him"*[26] (MC 57).

Pope Paul VI

VATICAN II AND MARY [964-972]

SEE   *Church and Mary*   *Motherhood, Spiritual*

1. Chapter 8 of Lumen Gentium: History and Scope

AT the opening session of Vatican II in October 1962, it was decided that the *Church* would be the central theme of the Council. Everything would be studied in relation to the Church, Mary included. A schema on the mediation of Mary was presented without this reference. It was tabled.

At the next session, on October 16, 1963, after long and lively discussion, the following question was put to the assembly: "Are the Fathers in favor of adopting the schema on the Blessed Virgin Mary, Mother of the Church, and making it the final chapter of the schema *De Ecclesia* (On the Church)?" The vote taken and barely passing, work was begun along the lines proposed.

One point caused some misgiving for the Commission. That Mary be supereminent *member* of the Church, hence admired model for the Church and all its other members, well and good. But *Mother* of the Church, that was not traditional, and a new title would widen the rift that separates us from Protestants. Accepted was only an equivalent: "The Catholic Church, taught by the Holy Spirit, honors Mary with filial affection and piety as a most beloved Mother" (LG 53).

On November 21, 1964, Paul VI signed the Dogmatic Constitution *Lumen Gentium* and took the occasion to announce: "We proclaim Mary most holy *Mother of the Church*, i.e., of all the people of God, faithful and shepherds alike, who name her Mother most loving." He made explicit the Conciliar text.

[26] Cf. Mt 17:15

Paul VI reiterated this proclamation less than three years later, May 13, 1967, in his Apostolic Exhortation *The Great Sign (Signum Magnum)*: "We wish to call the attention of all the faithful once again to the close connection between Mary's Spiritual Motherhood—so well elucidated in the *Dogmatic Constitution on the Church (Lumen Gentium)*—and the devotion that the redeemed people consider it a duty to offer her under the title Mother of the Church. . . . This consoling truth, by free will of the supremely wise God, is an integral part of the mystery of human salvation. That is why it ought to be an object of faith for all Christians."

In the Encyclical *Redeemer of the Human Race (Redemptor Hominis)* of March 4, 1979, John Paul II, even as did the Council, dwells on the Church-Mary relation. He raised the question: "What does it mean to say that the Church is a mother and also what does it mean to say that the Church herself always, and particularly in our time, has need of a mother?" He finds the answer most suitably in the Council: "We owe a debt of gratitude to the Fathers of the Second Vatican Council, who expressed this truth in the *Constitution on the Church (Lumen Gentium)* with its rich Mariological doctrine. Paul VI, inspired by that teaching, proclaimed the Mother of Christ 'Mother of the Church,' and this title has become known far and wide."

2. Capital Points of Chapter 8

The chapter begins with a survey of Mary in the Divine plan of human salvation (nos. 52-54). As the title indicates, the Blessed Virgin Mary, Mother of God, is inscribed in the Mystery of Christ and the Church. Scripture and Tradition, especially patristic, define the role of Mary in the economy of salvation. Mary is prefigured in the preparation of Christ's coming (Old Testament) (no. 55). She begins the New Testament, at the Annunciation, where her faith, her Immaculate Conception, her Divine Motherhood move into focus (no. 56). Mary is a close associate in the work of salvation throughout the life of the Savior, her Son: Mother at Nazareth, Disciple from Cana to the Cross itself, where Jesus dying gives her as *Mother* to John (nos. 57-59).

The chapter then depicts Mary in her role in the life of the Church. Her mediation does not obscure or detract from that of the One Mediator (nos. 60-62). As the Model of the Church, her prayer is exemplary for ours (nos 63-65). Why and how honor her with special cult? She is the sign of eschatological hope (nos. 66-69): "Now still, exalted above all the Angels and Saints, the Mother of God continues to intercede before her Son, in communion with all the Saints, until all families of people . . . may be happily gathered together in peace and harmony into one People of God for the glory of the Most Holy and Undivided Trinity" (no. 69). So ends chapter 8 and the *Dogmatic Constitution Lumen Gentium.*

3. Mary in Other Documents of the Council

(a) *Constitution on the Sacred Liturgy*: "In celebrating the annual cycle of Christ's Mysteries, holy Church honors with especial love the Blessed Mary, Mother of God, who is joined by an inseparable bond to the saving work of her Son. In her the Church holds up and admires the most excellent fruit of the Redemption, and joyfully contemplates, as in a faultless image, that which she herself desires and hopes wholly to be" (SC 103).

(b) *Decree on the Apostolate of the Laity*: "The Most Blessed Virgin Mary is the perfect example of this type of spiritual and apostolic life. While leading the life common to all here on earth, one filled with family concerns and labors, Mary was always intimately united with her Son and in an entirely unique way cooperated in the work of the Savior. Now, assumed into heaven, 'with her maternal love she cares for the brothers and sisters of her Son who are still on their earthly pilgrimage and remain involved in dangers and difficulties until they are led into the happy homeland' (LG no. 62). All should devoutly venerate her and commend their life and apostolate to her maternal care" (AA 4).

(c) *Decree on the Appropriate Renewal of Religious Life*: "Through the intercession of the Blessed Virgin Mary, gentle

Mother of God, 'whose life is a model for all' (Saint Ambrose), religious (both men and women) will experience continual increases and bear most abundant fruits of salvation" (PC 25).

(d) *Decree on Priestly Formation*: Priests "should love and honor with filial trust the Blessed Virgin Mary, who was given as Mother to His disciple by Jesus as He was dying on the Cross" (OT 8).

(e) *Decree on the Ministry and Life of Priests*: "Priests will always find a wonderful example of docility (to the Holy Spirit) in the Blessed Virgin Mary. Led by the Holy Spirit, she dedicated herself totally to the mystery of human redemption (cf. LG 65). Mother of the Eternal High Priest, Queen of Apostles, Protectrix of their own ministry, she has a right to the filial devotion of priests, to their veneration and their love" (PO 18).

(f) *Decree on the Missionary Activity of the Church*: "It was at Pentecost that the 'acts of the apostles' began (through the coming upon them of the Holy Spirit), just as Christ was conceived when the Holy Spirit came upon the Virgin Mary, and just as Christ was moved to begin His ministry when the same Holy Spirit descended upon Him while praying" (AG 4).

4. Marian Contribution of the Council

The Council, while remaining true to a tradition that stretches from the Apostles, revolutionized our way of thinking about Mary, at least in the West. Before Vatican II we said: Jesus, Mary, and the Church in such a way that Mary stood out from a Church formed of sinful, albeit redeemed, members. Mary was above, by the privilege of her Immaculate Conception. As a consequence, she was seen as Mediatrix between the Church and her Son, sole Mediatrix before Him, as Jesus is sole Mediator between the Father and redeemed humanity.

The Council enabled us to define the Mary-Church relation more accurately, so that now we say: there is Jesus and the Church, the Head and the Mystical Body. Mary is a member of the Church, supereminent member to the point of being Model and Mother. In this family, of which Jesus is the Head, she is the Mother and the other members, her children. As Jesus was conceived in Mary by the Holy Spirit, so all members of the Church are reborn by the same Spirit, Mary included. But in her case, this happened at conception and not, as with us, through sacramental Baptism.

Because of this fact her union with the Holy Spirit rested in her very being, a special union formed by grace of God and designed for her role as Spiritual Mother of the Church. It is therefore without further dependence on the Spirit that she exercises her maternal mediation in behalf of the Church and without compromise to the unique Mediation of her Son. Thanks to this union with the Spirit, she never ceases by her intercession and her action to unite the members with the Head, and the last word we have of her in the Gospel is and will always be in point: *"Do whatever He tells you"* (Jn 2:5).

Where the Church is, there is Mary, first and always. Where Mary is, there is the Holy Spirit, "Soul of the Church" (cf. LG 7). Where the Holy Spirit is, there is Christ, Son of the Father, our One Savior and Mediator.

"Thus, the universal Church is seen as a people that derives its unity from the unity of the Father and the Son and the Holy Spirit" (LG 4).

H. H. Manteau-Bonamy

VIRGIN BIRTH

SEE *Virginal Conception*

VIRGINAL CONCEPTION [496-507, 510]

SEE *Annunciation*   *Virginity, Perpetual*
Infancy Narratives

MARY conceived Jesus without *"knowing man,"* remaining a virgin. Two of the Gospels testify to this, and the oldest professions of faith declare it: *"I believe . . . in Jesus Christ, . . . Who was conceived by the Holy Spirit, born of the Virgin Mary, and became man."*

The Protestant Reformers of the 16th century—Luther, Zwingli, Calvin, etc.—continued to teach and preach, without apology, the virginity of Mary, Mother of Jesus. The virginal conception of Jesus is very closely linked with the Mystery of the Incarnation.

1. Testimony of the Gospels

The Gospels of Matthew and Luke both in effect say the same thing: *"Before they came together, Mary was found to be with child through the Holy Spirit"* (Mt 1:18); *"The Holy Spirit will come upon you and the power of the Most High will overshadow you"* (Lk 1:35).

Between these two testimonies the similarities are striking, notwithstanding a difference of context and style.

(a) The conception of Jesus is the work of the Holy Spirit. Joseph is only the legal ("adoptive") father of Jesus.

(b) The conception takes place while Mary and Joseph are only *"promised in marriage."* But at the moment of birth they are living together in marriage.

(c) Jesus is born at the time of King Herod, in Bethlehem, city of David.

(d) After the birth of Jesus, Joseph and Mary take up residence in Nazareth.

"On the historical level, the exegete can certify the existence of belief in such a [virginal] conception, not only in the communities of Matthew and Luke but even in an earlier tradition, source of their common documentation. It is probable that the theme first circulated among Judeo-Christian groups, like the church of Matthew itself, groups familiar with Jewish accounts of miraculous births and receptive to a substantiation of the virginity" (C. Perrot).

2. Reality of the Virginal Conception

For some modern exegetes the virginal conception of Jesus is only a figurative or "symbolic" expression of a theological truth: that Jesus is the Son of God. Without going into details, we will make a few remarks concerning this crucial question for Marian piety.

(a) It is true that Matthew 1—2 introduces Biblical symbols, particularly in the account of the Magi: the star, gold, incense, and myrrh. But the virginal birth of the Messiah, far from being clearly foretold by the Prophets (the Hebrew text of Isaiah 7:14 says: *"Behold, the young woman shall be with child"*), created on the contrary a difficulty as to His Davidic legitimacy. Joseph was to overcome it by legally recognizing Jesus as *"son of David."* Therefore, Judeo-Christians were not at all predisposed to invent the virginal conception of Jesus.

(b) Luke, at the beginning of his Gospel, says expressly that he is going to speak of *"events that have been fulfilled in our midst, precisely as they were transmitted to us by those who from the first were eyewitnesses"* (Lk 1:1-2). Consequently, in his account of the Annunciation he is attesting to what he believes to be a real fact, one that could be a serious problem with Greek minds. Interwoven, to be sure, are numerous Biblical allusions: Daughter of Zion, the cloud over the Tabernacle where the glory of God dwells, the miraculous birth of Isaac, among others. And it is almost impossible to determine if these allusions are part of the event itself or of its presentation made by Mary, by the Johannine tradition, or by Luke himself. But there is no doubt that the virginal conception and Mary's act of faith are affirmed by Luke.

(c) Our belief in the reality of the virginal conception, based on the testimony of the Gospels, is of the same order as our belief in the Resurrection of Jesus. A purely symbolic interpretation throws out all the objective reality of the testimony received by the original Church and all the radical newness of the Mystery of Jesus-Savior (cf. 1 Cor 15:14: *"If Christ has not been raised, our preaching is useless and so is your faith"*). God could not have meant to make dupes of those who believed the Apostolic testimony. God really intervened in an exceptional manner, for the Incarnation of His Son.

3. Significance of the Virginal Conception

Like Mary, the Church will never cease to meditate on this singular event, i.e., to pursue its full significance in the light of sacred history recorded in the Bible.

(a) *"Nothing is impossible with God"* is reminiscent of Isaac's miraculous birth (Lk 1:37; Gn 18:14). The *Magnificat* recalls the canticle of Anna, the barren one, after Samuel's birth. The virginal conception of Jesus is the major instance of these miraculous births produced by the Almighty Power of God to save His people.

Salvation comes from God alone and not from human powers. The very name of *Jesus* indicates as much, for it means *God saves.*

In this respect the virginity of Mary is a sign of the radical human poverty before God, Who saves by His grace (cf. Lk 18:26-27). Poverty of the heart is the secret of hope.

God is absolute master of life. This was Abraham's fundamental act of faith: *"Without weakening in his faith, he thought of his own body, which was as good as dead . . . and of the dead womb of Sarah. Yet he never questioned or doubted God's promise. . . . The words 'It was credited to him' were written not for him alone but also for us. For our faith will be credited to us also if we believe in Him Who raised Jesus our Lord from the dead"* (Rom 4:19-24). Virginal birth and Resurrection are two miracles of life that only God can do through His Spirit, *"Who gives life."*

(b) *"He will be called the Son of God"* (Lk 1:35), *"a Son to Whom they will give the name Emmanuel, God-with-us"* (Mt 1:23). The virginal conception is a *sign,* amazingly plain, of the personal Mystery of Jesus, Who has no other father than God. His first words in the Temple, according to Luke, were: *"Did you not know that I had to be in My Father's house?"*, after Mary had said to Him: *"Your father and I have been searching for you"* (Lk 2:48-49).

He prays to God, addressing Him as *"Abba"* (Mk 14:36), equivalent to *Papa,* or *Daddy,* and the Jews charge Him with *"calling God His own Father"* (Jn 5:18). The virginal conception was for Mary and for Joseph—and remains for us—the *sign* that makes it possible with our human understanding to grasp something of the Mystery of God the Son.

(c) *"Through the power of the Holy Spirit." "The Holy Spirit will come upon you."* The role given to the Holy Spirit is similarly rich in meaning. Greek theologians see in it a reflection of the eternal generation of the Son in the love of the Father. Virginal Incarnation, Pentecost, and Sacraments are conjointly the work of the Holy Spirit, work of the eternal love of the Father and the Son.

(d) *"Blessed is she who believed."* In announcing it to Mary—and to Joseph—God offers the virginal conception of Jesus for their assent of faith. The supernatural birth then becomes the central object and, in a way, the measure of their faith in God the Savior. Of us, too, God asks the free and permanent assent of our faith so that Jesus may grow in us by the working of the Holy Spirit.

Mary's faith in the virginal conception is the model par excellence of the Church's faith in the Divine work of salvation.

J. Laurenceau

VIRGINITY, PERPETUAL   [496-507, 510]

SEE   *Infancy Narratives*   *Virginal Conception*

IN calling Mary "ever virgin," Tradition is saying that after conceiving Jesus in virginity Mary always remained a virgin, abstaining from all conjugal relations. This also implies that the birth of Jesus left intact the virginity of His Mother.

1. The Gospels

The Gospels furnish no argument against this teaching:

Luke says: *"Mary gave birth to her firstborn son"* (2:7). This makes allusion to the legal prescriptions concerning the first male child of a family, even if there were no other children.

Matthew declares: *"Joseph had no relations with [Mary] at any time before she bore a Son, Jesus"* (1:25). The Semitic locution *before . . .* or *until . . .* makes no judgment about the future. Thus: *"Michal was childless until the day of her death"* (2 Sm 6:23).

The Gospels on several occasions speak of *"brothers of Jesus,"* for example, James and Joseph (Mt 13:55). But these are sons of another Mary, expressly named *"the mother of James and Joseph"* (Mt 27:56), who cannot be identified with the Mother of Jesus and who is always named *after* Mary Magdalene.

Besides, in the Semitic world the name *brothers* often was given to relatives and confederates. Abraham says to his nephew Lot: *"We are brothers"* (Gn 13:8).

In fact, the episode of the Finding in the Temple and especially the episode on Calvary where Jesus entrusts His Mother to a disciple (Jn 19:25-27) seem to imply that Mary had no other children. But in any case, the very ancient Tradition of Mary's perpetual virginity was never historically questioned at a time when the memory of *"brothers of Jesus"* was still much alive.

2. Tradition

The Protevangelium of James, a legendary account written between 150 and 200, relates that when Joseph became the husband of Mary he was old and a widower with several children. This indicates that belief in Mary's perpetual virginity already was widespread and attempts were being made to counter the objection of *"brothers of Jesus."*

Origen (d. 254) strongly defends the virginity of Mary, before and after the birth of Jesus. He cannot accept that Mary, after being lavished with the Holy Spirit at the Annunciation, could have had other children. For him, "Jesus is the beginning of chastity for men, Mary of chastity for women."

Tertullian (d. 220/230) is an exception. Although asserting the virginal conception, he allows himself to be carried away by his polemic against Docetists and Gnostics. He thus presents the birth of Jesus as a normal event and His Mother as having had several children, without citing any tradition in support.

About 350-375, in the context of an ascetical renewal, Zeno of Verona expresses the traditional belief of the Church: "How great a Mystery! The Virgin Mary conceived inviolate. After the conception, a virgin gave birth. After the birth, a virgin she remained."

Saint Ambrose, Saint Jerome, and Saint Augustine were ardent defenders of the perpetual virginity of Mary, model of consecrated women.

Thereafter, the Tradition is firm and continuous, and the letter of Pope Siricius against Bishop Bonosus attests to the official teaching of the Church, which "repudiates in no uncertain terms the idea that any other child came from the same virginal womb of which Christ was born according to the flesh."

A surprising thing for many Catholics is that the leading Protestant reformers of the 16th century—Luther, Zwingli, and Calvin among them—asserted and preached Mary's perpetual virginity, as Max Thurian has shown.

3. Significance

That there were no other children born of Mary after Jesus was not enough to say that Mary remained *ever virgin.*

Tradition was guided by a sort of spiritual intuition concerning Mary's inmost life.

Mary's question in the account of the Annunciation is not decisive. *"How can this be, since I do not know man?"* can be understood of a factual situation that obtained at the moment when God's Word was about to be fulfilled.

Saint Augustine was the first, in 401, to put forward the idea that Mary had made a vow of virginity *before the Annunciation.* But he may have been swayed by a certain distrust of things carnal.

The ritual purity of the Essenes, which is sometime adduced, seems to have been quite foreign to evangelical chastity.

Another interpretation is possible, which one writer gives as follows: "When Mary and Joseph, after miraculous conception, decided on a life of virginity, their motive was to put themselves entirely and exclusively at the service of Jesus, and to renounce everything that might conceivably divert or distract them from playing their full part in His mission. Their motive was not lack of esteem for the married life (unthinkable in Judaism) or even the prizing of continence as a higher ideal than the consummation of marriage. Their choice was motivated exclusively by the fact of the virginal conception, by the desire to serve *this* Child. . . .

"The virginal conception itself, being a word of God to man, was both an invitation and a call, to her who was to be the Mother of the Lord. What possible response could Mary have made except that of exclusive dedication to the work of Him Who is mighty, Who had done such great things for her? . . . Certainly, it is not so much because of her physical virginity as because she gave Jesus the undivided love of her soul that the Church extols her as *Virgo veneranda, Virgo praedicanda, Virgo fidelis* [Virgin most venerable, Virgin most renowned, Virgin most faithful]" (John McHugh).

Mary continued *"as she was when the Lord called her"* and she always kept her virginity *so as to "live in undivided devotion to the Lord"* (1 Cor 7:17-35).

The decision of Mary and Joseph to observe continence comports with Luke's allusions to the Presence of God's glory in Mary as in a new Temple (cf. Lk 1:35), a new Ark of the Covenant. Behind the legends of the *Protevangelium of James* we detect an intuition of the connection between Mary's consecrated virginity and the Temple. Indeed, the traditional bond in Jewish literature between continence and nearness to God reached its perfection in Mary's perpetual virginity and the celibacy consecrated to "the Bridegroom Who is coming."

Tradition and the teaching of the Magisterium hold that Mary's physical virginity was preserved in the birth of Jesus. This physical virginity is to be viewed as a concrete sign both of the total joy brought by the Immanuel and of Mary's voluntary consecration to virginity.

The logic of the Incarnation and the Sacraments does not dissociate the spiritual and the corporal.

To understand the deep reasons for Mary's lifelong virginity is at the same time to perceive the greatness of a total response to the Word that God speaks to us in Jesus Christ.

J. Laurenceau

VISITATION

SEE   *Feasts of Mary*   *Magnificat*
       Infancy Narratives

EVERYTHING in the scene of Mary's Visitation to Elizabeth is motion and excitement. Mary's "*haste*," her greeting to Elizabeth, John's "*leaping for joy*," Elizabeth's exclaim-
ing with loud cry and Mary's thanksgiving are so many show-
ings of the Spirit's action that accompanies the inauguration of
the Messianic age. But the scene of the Visitation is not only a
scene of transition; it also marks a major advance in revealing
the Messiah, Who receives for the first time, in the Gospel of
Luke, the title "*Lord*."

1. The Word of God Is Effective

The account of the Visitation, which Luke has conceived
in close continuity with the two preceding announcements of
the births of John and Jesus, serves in the first instance to
demonstrate the effectiveness of God's Word. The announcement to Zechariah, like that to Mary, has to do with an approaching motherhood, and it is this sign that Mary goes "*in
all haste*" to rejoice over with Elizabeth. This motherhood is
also the event that Elizabeth celebrates in receiving her as "*the
Mother of my Lord*." The Word of God is herein fulfilled.

Elizabeth expressly recognizes the fulfillment in proclaiming Mary's fundamental blessedness: "*Blessed is she who believed that the Lord's words to her would be fulfilled*" (1:45). In
addition, and on the level of action properly speaking, we are
made to see in the account the fulfillment of the word spoken
to Zechariah concerning John: "*. . . He will be filled with the
Holy Spirit even from His mother's womb . . .*" (1:15).

2. Prophetic Consecration of John

In the Old Testament there is the prophetic *consecration*
of Jeremiah while still in his mother's womb (Jer 1:5). Here in
a similar consecration, the mere presence of the Messiah is
enough to evoke from John, at the moment of Mary's greeting,

a reaction of *joy.* The reaction is the culminating point in the first part of the Visitation narrative, a reaction most appropriate to the Messianic age and the introduction of God's eschatological salvation (cf. Jn 8:56 and Rv 19:7). It is also an expression of the exceptional bond between John and Jesus: *"It is the bridegroom who has the bride. The groom's best man waits there listening for him and is overjoyed when he hears his voice"* (Jn 3:29).

Like Jeremiah, John is invested with the prophetic spirit. Through words of his mother *"filled with the Holy Spirit"* (1:41), he is exercising his prophetic function: *"And you, O child, shall be called a prophet of the Most High . . ."* (1:76), designating Jesus as *"Lord."*

3. A New Revelation concerning Jesus

The whole burden of Luke's account centers on the Mystery of Jesus. This is made the more evident by a certain solemnity with which he endows Elizabeth's utterances in regard to Mary. Elizabeth is *"filled with the Holy Spirit."* She cries out *"in a loud voice"* (like the liturgical acclamations, it is a profession of faith in the presence of the Lord: cf. 1 Chr 16:4, 5, 42). She uses the title *"Lord,"* which will be the title par excellence of the risen Son of God (Acts 2:36; Jn 20:13; Phil 3:8). She speaks a double blessing: *"Blessed are you among women and blessed is the fruit of your womb"* (1:42). The words project the holiness of the Child carried by Mary and echo the predictions of Gabriel: *"He will be great and will be called the Son of God"* (1:32, 35).

4. "Blessed Is She Who Believed . . ."

At the same time, Elizabeth makes known to us the Mystery of Mary and the basic reason why she is blessed. The Mystery of Mary stems entirely from the privileged bond of her motherhood, which unites her with the *"fruit of [her] womb"* (1:42). To capture the spirit of Elizabeth's greeting, the translation ought to read: *"Blessed are you among women BECAUSE blessed is the fruit of your womb."* The blessedness, the holiness, of the Son is reflected in the Mother. Better still, the Son is cause of the Mother's holiness. In the estimation of the Evangelists and the first Christians, there is not a more beautiful title for Mary than this one: *"Mother of Jesus"* (cf. Jn 2:1), *"Mother of my Lord."*

But it is a motherhood first received in faith. Mary is most of all a believer, a woman who has given a total *yes* to God's Word, unlike Zechariah who doubted.

It is this faith of Mary that Elizabeth extols: *"Blessed is she who believed that the Lord's words to her would be fulfilled"* (1:45). Luke sees no opposition between Mary's motherhood and her hearing of the Word of God (cf. 11:27-28). On the contrary, he associates one with the other.

5. Mary's Thanksgiving

The scene of the Visitation is extended in Mary's personal act of thanksgiving, the *Magnificat*. Mary gives praise for the intervention of God, *her Savior*, in the stupendous motherhood that is coming to pass within her: *"God Who is mighty has done great things for me"* (1:49).

But Mary's vision does not stop at herself. It moves over the whole history of Israel, and her thanksgiving takes on the accents of a whole people singing the great deeds of its God. This woman, *"blessed above all women"* (cf. Jdt 13:18), belongs entirely to the history of Israel, the long line of men and women who have experienced and extolled the salvation of God. Like them, Mary sings praise to the God faithful to His Covenant, faithful to the Promise made the Fathers.

6. Mary, Ark of the Covenant

The Angel's words to Mary suggest a parallel between Mary and the Ark of the Covenant. Mary was filled with the Divine presence as the Ark was with the glory of Yahweh. But in the scene of the Visitation this association is brought out more emphatically:

—Whereas the people of Jerusalem hold festival for the return of the Ark (2 Sm 6:12), Elizabeth cries out *"in a loud voice"* (an expression that always occurs in liturgical context where the Ark of the Covenant is concerned: cf. above, no. 3), and the child in her womb leaps *"for joy."*

—Elizabeth's question to Mary: *"Who am I that the mother of my Lord should come to me?"* (1:43) recalls that of David before the Ark: *"How can the Ark of the Lord come to me?"* (2 Sm 6:9).

—Mary's coming to Elizabeth is a source of blessing, just as was the coming of the Ark for the house of Obededom (2 Sm 6:11).

—The mention of *"about three months"* confirms this link with 2 Samuel 6 since the Ark of the Covenant remained for three months with Obededom.

A notable proponent of this identification is René Laurentin. But it has recently been minimized, if not questioned, by John McHugh. While the identification may not be absolutely necessary, it has more than one support in the text, and the analogy it suggests is confirmed by the light it sheds on the role of Mary in the scene of the Visitation. What the Ark of the Covenant could only *signify* (and solely in a purely local way), Mary makes a reality, and in a personal way: she is an *effective sign* of God's presence with His people.

The Visitation is the Second Joyful Mystery of the Rosary.

J. P. Prévost

- W -

WAY OF THE CROSS

Sᴇᴇ   *Holy Land and Mary, 2n*

WOMAN   [726]

Sᴇᴇ   *Cana*   *Servant of the Lord*
      Cross (Mary at the)

1. Mary as the Perfect Woman

ACCORDING to Saint John's Gospel, Jesus twice addresses His Mother as "Woman" (Jn 2:4; 19:26). This can
indicate that Mary represents and personifies the Messianic
people. It can also be referred, at the Cross, to the New Eve,
Mother of the living, who, in a quasi-spousal relationship with
the New Man, contributes to the birth of the New people of
God in the Spirit.

"According to the prophecy of Genesis 3:15, the Woman
was destined to be an ally of God in the struggle against the
devil. She was to be the Mother of the One Who would crush
the head of the enemy. Nevertheless, in the prophetic perspective of the Old Testament, this offspring of the Woman Who
was to conquer the spirit of evil seemed to be necessarily a
man.

"Herein intervenes the wondrous reality of the Incarnation. The offspring of the Woman Who fulfills the prophecy is
not a simple man. He is indeed fully human, thanks to the
Woman whose Son He is, but at the same time He is true God.
The Covenant established at the beginnings between God and
the Woman takes on a new dimension. Mary enters into this
Covenant as the Mother of God.

"In order to respond to the image of the woman who had
committed the sin, God gives rise to an image of a perfect
Woman, who receives a Divine Motherhood. The new Cove-

nant goes far beyond the exigence of a simple reconciliation. It raises the Woman to a height that no one could have imagined" (John Paul II, January 4, 1984).

2. Mary's Womanhood

The term also suggests the personal dimension of Mary as mature and responsible woman, accepting completely her situation and vocation. She is the "woman of Israel," her roots in her people and its history.

She is "woman" in the strongest sense of the word because she acts as an adult. We see her assuming her responsibilities at the Annunciation, the event that will forever shape her destiny. She does not boast of her privilege, and does not lavish an exclusive love on her Son that would tend to keep Him to herself. On the contrary, mindful of the mission of Jesus, she wants Him to proceed: *"They have no more wine"* (Jn 2:3). During His Public Life, she remains in the background but she is present at the Hour of the Cross. She does not take offense when reminded to make the adjustments that every mother must make as her child grows and matures, adjustments that in her case assume an exceptional dimension because of the Person of her Son. To the natural dimensions of the mother-son relation are added those of faith, over and above the bonds of the flesh. Her "dispossession" even extends to accepting the death of Jesus on the Cross for the salvation of the world.

In Mary, therefore, one does not find jealous guarding of her Son. She knows that He does not belong to her. He belongs to all. Mary is not trapped by the possessive attitude that inhibits development of mother and child alike. Her existence is centered, not on herself but on the Son Who gives it all its meaning. This attitude is the source of a genuine personal life for Mary, with a sense of responsibility and freedom that can, when necessary, take the initiative (cf. Lk 1:38; Jn 2:3). She gives herself in service to her Son and finds her freedom by allowing Jesus to have His.

Mary is the consummate woman because, along with her exceptional vocation of virgin, wife, and mother, she takes upon herself in its entirety her feminine condition, expressing its proper qualities of intuition, refinement, sensitivity, and attention to others and their needs. This is one reason why the Christian people have a quasi-instinctive trust and confidence in her.

Finally, the person of Mary as woman is considered in its simplicity, strength, and true "humanness." In his Apostolic Exhortation on *Devotion to the Blessed Virgin Mary*, Paul VI sets forth some orientations for rediscovering the person of Mary as a woman of faith and an active and responsible woman: "The picture of the Blessed Virgin presented in a certain type of devotional literature cannot easily be reconciled with today's life style, especially the way women live today. . . . In consequence of these phenomena some people are becoming disenchanted with devotion to the Blessed Virgin and finding it difficult to take as an example Mary of Nazareth because the horizons of her life, so they say, seem rather restricted in comparison with the vast spheres of activity open to mankind today" (MC 34).

"The Virgin Mary has always been proposed to the faithful by the Church as an example to be imitated not precisely in the type of life she led, and much less for the sociocultural background in which she lived and which today scarcely exists anywhere. She is held up as an example to the faithful rather for the way in which, in her own particular life, she fully and responsibly accepted the will of God, because she heard the Word of God and acted on it and because charity and a spirit of service were the driving force of her actions. She is worthy of imitation because she was the first and most perfect of Christ's disciples. All of this has a permanent and universal exemplary value" (MC 35; cf. 37).

3. Mary and the Modern Woman

In a magnificent 1973 Pastoral Letter entitled *Behold Your Mother*, the Bishops of the United States dealt with Mary in various aspects of the life of Christians today. They pointed her out as the model of all real feminine freedom and stressed her part in the emancipation of womanhood and in foreshadowing the role of Christian women in contemporary Church and society.

"According to the Gospels, Christ showed an enlightened attitude toward women: in His conversation with the Samaritan woman at the well; in His friendship with Martha and Mary, especially in defense of Mary's preference to listen to His words, rather than wait upon Him; in His behavior toward the Syro-phoenecian woman with the sick daughter (Mk 7:29); and in His appearance as risen Lord to Mary Magdalene, whom He sends to announce the Good News to His Apostles. These incidents, interpreted in their cultural context, give us a basis for a genuine emancipation and liberation of womanhood.

"The dignity that Christ's redemption won for all women was fulfilled uniquely in Mary as the model of all real feminine freedom. The Mother of Jesus is portrayed in the Gospel as *intelligent* (the Annunciation, 'How can this be?'); *apostolic* (the visit to Elizabeth); *inquiring and contemplative* (the Child lost in the Temple); *responsive and creative* (at Cana); *compassionate and courageous* (at Calvary); a woman of *great faith*. These implications in the lives of Jesus and Mary need to be elaborated into a sound theology on the role of Christian women in the contemporary Church and society" (nos. 141-142).

Pope Paul VI sketched such a Marian theology in his 1974 Apostolic Exhortation on *Devotion to the Blessed Virgin*. He set forth the role of Mary and modern woman: she is a mirror of the expectations of the women of our day (MC 37).

(1) The modern woman is anxious to participate with decision-making power in the affairs of the community. She can thus contemplate with intimate joy Mary, "who, taken into dialogue with God, gives her active and responsible consent, not to the solution of a contingent problem, but to that event of world importance which is the Incarnation."

(2) The modern woman lives in a world that extols the value of marriage but looks down on virginity as counterproductive. By realizing that Mary's choice of the state of virginity in God's plan prepared her for the Mystery of the Incarnation, she can thus "appreciate that Mary's choice was not a rejection

of the values of the married state but a courageous choice that she made in order to consecrate herself totally to the love of God."

(3) The modern woman lives in a world where self-assurance is important. She can thus note with pleasant surprise "that Mary of Nazareth, while completely devoted to the will of God, was far from being a timidly submissive woman or one whose piety was repellent to others. On the contrary she was a woman who did not hesitate to proclaim that God vindicates the humble and the oppressed and removes the powerful people of this world from their privileged positions (cf. Lk 1:51-53)."

(4) The modern woman wishes to support the liberating energies of people and of society. She can thus recognize in Mary, "who stands out among the poor and the humble of the Lord, a woman of strength, who experienced poverty and suffering, flight and exile (cf. Mt 2:13-23)."

In the light of the above observations, it is possible for modern Christians to arrive at a better understanding of Mary as the model for women today. To do so, of course, they must be aided by the reading of the Scriptures, carried out under the guidance of the Spirit, and by the discoveries of the human sciences and the different situations of the world today.

A. Delesalle—A. Buono

WORDS OF MARY   [722, 2619]

SEE *Annunciation*   *"Fiat" in the Name of Humanity*
  Cana   *Life of Mary*
  Cross (Mary at the)   *Magnificat*

IN line with the Gospel's reticence about a great part of Mary's life, it recounts very few of the words spoken by Our Lady. What it does preserve for us can be set forth in seven phrases or words, counting the *Magnificat* as one. The New Testament includes only seven instances where Mary's words are recorded. Six brief phrases plus the slightly longer *Magni-*

ficat, her song of praise recorded in the first chapter of Luke's Gospel, are all that remain of Mary's wisdom. Few though they be, these seven phrases or "words" of Mary—like Christ's seven famous words on the Cross—give us a glimpse into the very soul of the speaker.

Jesus said *"Each man speaks from his heart's abundance"* (Lk 6:45). And it is out of the overflowing treasure of thoughts and sentiments in her heart that Mary speaks. Her words are filled with meaning and sum up essential traits of her personality and religious functions—as is indicated in the various entries of the Dictionary that deal with one or other of these words. They can thus provide fitting meditation material concerning Our Lady.

1. First Word: Childlike Wonder

"How can this be since I do not know man?" (Lk 1:34).

Mary speaks these words at Nazareth when the Archangel Gabriel announces to her that she is to be the Mother of God. Her immediate reaction to such great news is not one of self-acclaim or personal glory but one of honest amazement. How can God's call to motherhood be accomplished since she is still a virgin?

This first Marian phrase or "word" shows her innate honesty. In her relationship with God, there is no room for dissembling or for hiding her true feelings. She freely expresses her amazement, her consternation, her simplicity. Still, in a childlike way, Mary is quick to accept God's invitation. She does not flee or hide from the challenge. She seeks clarification only so that right action may follow. She acts with her eyes open.

2. Second Word: Obedient Service

"I am the servant of the Lord" (Lk 1:38).

As soon as the Archangel assures Mary that her virginity will remain intact since this unparalleled event will come about through the almighty power of God, she has no reservation whatever. She immediately identifies her state in relation to God—a devoted servant ready to provide zealous service.

This second word shows that Mary is totally open to God's will for her. The term "servant" in Greek is the feminine form of a common Old Testament designation for slave or servant of God. The whole phrase thus testifies to Mary's certainty of God's transcendence and her unflagging obedience to His saving plan. At the same time it brings out Mary's humility, selflessness, and commitment to true poverty.

3. Third Word: Scriptural Knowledge

"*Let it be done to me as you say*" (Lk 1 :38).

Mary now goes further, putting her understanding into action. She consents to have take place in her what Gabriel has proclaimed. At this historic moment the Son of God becomes man. Mary thus sets into operation the tremendous events called for in God's redeeming plan.

This third word illustrates the depth of Mary's understanding and knowledge of God. Once assured of what is entailed in God's call, she never hesitates.

Such a faith can only stem from an active involvement in and meditation on the Scriptures that detail God's promises and their fulfillment in the history of the chosen people. It points to Mary's familiarity with the Messianic tradition faithfully handed down over the centuries among the deeply devout segment of God's people.

4. Fourth Word: Joyful Praise

"*My soul proclaims the greatness of the Lord . . .* " (Lk 1:46-55).

In a visit to her cousin Elizabeth in the hill country of Jerusalem, Mary responds to the older woman's greeting of praise with a poetic passage in praise of the God Who has done such great things for her. This is Mary's *Magnificat*, one of the most beautiful hymns of praise ever voiced.

The *Magnificat* is filled with allusions to the great deeds God worked for His chosen people in the Old Testament. And it points to still greater things to come, beginning with the magnificent event in which Mary herself is taking part, the Incarnation of the Son of God.

We could weave a whole theology out of the splendid lines and ideas contained in this poem. It pinpoints Mary's keen mind, understanding spirit, joyous heart, concern for others, and love for God. It sets her apart as a woman of unshakable faith, unwavering hope, and uncommon love.

The poem is also reminiscent of several Old Testament hymns of praise—those of Miriam, Hannah, and Judith. In time the glorious words credited to Judith would be applied to Mary by the Church: *"You are the glory of Jerusalem, the surpassing joy of Israel; you are the splendid boast of our people"* (Jdt 15:10).

5. Fifth Word: Gentle Authority

"Son, why have You done this to us? You see that Your father and I have been searching for You in sorrow" (Lk 2:48).

Twelve years after the birth of Jesus, Mary is unwittingly separated from Him during a trip to Jerusalem. After a frantic search that must have conjured up many imagined evils, she finally finds Him on the third day in the Temple and voices her anguish.

This fifth word brings out Mary's gentleness and her acceptance of the responsibility and authority God has given her. Her Son is still bound to respect her and Joseph, but the whole tenor of the thought goes even further.

This word shows that Mary shares the common lot of all human beings, experiencing trials and anxiety. She faces obscurity in her faith, seeing indistinctly as in a cloudy mirror. In other words, her faith, like our own, obeys the law of human progress.

6. Sixth Word: Tender Charity

"They have no more wine" (Jn 2:3).

Some twenty years later, at a wedding in Cana of Galilee, Mary notices that the young bridal couple has run out of wine—a distinct embarrassment at that time. She immediately intercedes with her Son by telling Him what has happened.

This sixth word demonstrates the greatness of Mary's heart. She attends to every detail and she knows what she has to do. Her faith in her Son precedes and prepares for the miracle or sign that will be worked.

Mary thus shows her awareness that she is destined to play a role in the creation of the new People of God, the Messianic community that will form around Jesus beginning at this first sign at Cana. Her role is to point their way to Jesus by preparing them through this miracle for the acceptance of His signs.

7. Seventh Word: Deep Faith

"*Do whatever He tells you*" (Jn 2:5).

After informing Jesus of the bridal couple's problem at Cana, Mary turns to the waiters and bids them do whatever Jesus should tell them. Her words correspond to the words of the chosen people when they promised to adhere to the Covenant of the Lord: "*Everything the Lord has said, we will do*" (Ex 19:8); "*Then tell us what the Lord, our God, tells you; we will listen and obey*" (Dt 5:27).

In this seventh word, Mary expresses the faith of the whole people disposed to receive the revelation brought by Jesus.

8. Words of Light and Life

In addition to revealing her personality and her role, Mary's words hold special meaning for us. As the servant of God, she is the model for all Christians, since we are all called to be servants of God. Meditation on her words and on her life will inevitably open up ways in which we too can grow in our servanthood.

If we are wise, we will follow the advice of the Book of Proverbs to "reject not your mother's teaching. Bind them upon your heart forever; fasten them around your neck . . . " (Pr 6:20-23).

A. Buono

- Y -

YOUTH AND MARY

[971]

SEE   *States of Life and Marian Devotion*

1. Mary, Their Model

MARY may legitimately be held up as the model of youth. All the virtues that make her the model of all disciples of Christ also make her the model of all youthful disciples.

But she is the model of youth in an even more important way. She shows *by her life* how youth can serve God, for it was as a youth of 14 or 16 that she was called by God to be the Mother of the Redeemer of the human race—a role that she freely accepted and that far transcended the role of any other youth (except her Son) in the history of the world.

Young people, adolescents in particular, will find in Mary the totally unselfish person, the brave young woman who could face and accept the hidden future bound up with being Virgin and Mother of the Messiah. According to the customs of her time and people, Mary was probably no more than 14 when her parents arranged her marriage, and Joseph about 18. God asked great things of them both and they responded to His call with dedicated love (*Behold Your Mother*, no. 143).

In this respect Mary put her stamp on the world's history—she helped make the world a better place by bringing into the world the One Who guided the human race into a way of life that was positive, giving, God-oriented, and dedicated to service of others. Today's youth can imitate her in this in their own way.

Many young people today are eager to make the world into a better place, where justice and peace and love will prevail. The great obstacles still remain human greed and selfishness, all the deadly sins that bring turmoil and agony to so many suffering human beings. The succession of wars that grow in horror as technology improves, the oppression of underprivileged people at home and abroad, the imbalance between rich and poor countries are evils that become even more intolerable, when men would seem to have such great potential and when modern communications have so shrunk the information.

Only God can change men's hearts; only with the help of His grace can the enemies of mankind be conquered. Only those men and women will make an impact on society and change the world for the better, who make themselves powerful, effective instruments of God by lives of faith, hope and love, giving themselves completely to God in order that in and through them He may accomplish His great designs (*Behold Your Mother*, no. 144).

2. Mary, Their Mother and Intercessor

But Mary is more than merely a model; she is also a Mother and Intercessor for youth—indeed she is a very human school of perfection for them. She can guide and educate all the young people of our generation who are assailed by so many profanations, tempted by so many false attractions of permissive immorality, and perhaps skeptical about the beauty and the possibility of innocence, as well as the dignity of the body and the soul and the delicate rapport that distinguishes and unites them.

Mary represents for youth the inspired reminder and the hope of Christ's words, the beatitude promised to the pure of heart, that of seeing God present everywhere. May she ever come to their aid.

A. Buono

APPENDICES

1

MARIAN CELEBRATIONS OF THE LITURGICAL YEAR

(Homilies or Meditation in the spirit of "Marialis Cultus")

1. IMMACULATE CONCEPTION (December 8), solemnity: "Joint celebration of the Immaculate Conception of Mary, of the basic preparation for the coming of the Savior, and of the happy beginning of the Church without spot or wrinkle" (MC 3).

—Readings: Gn 3:9, 15-20 (The Fall and God's promise)
          Eph 1:3-6, 11-12 (The Divine plan of salvation)
          Lk 1: 28-36 (The Annunciation)

—Commentary: *See* Immaculate Conception
                Ineffabilis Deus
                Ad Diem Illum Laetissimum
                Annunciation
                Lourdes
                Miraculous Medal

2. FOURTH SUNDAY OF ADVENT: "It recalls the ancient prophecies concerning the Virgin Mother and the Messiah and includes readings from the Gospel concerning the imminent birth of Christ and His Precursor" (MC 3).

—Readings:

	Year A	Year B	Year C
	Is 7:10-14	2 Sm 7:1-5, 8-11, 16	Mi 5:1-4
	Rom 1:1-7	Rom 16:25-27	Heb 10:5-10
	Mt 1:18-24	Lk 1:26-38	Lk 1:39-45

—Commentary: *See* Old Testament   Annunciation
                 Marian Typology   Visitation
                 Immanuel   Matthew (Gospel of)

3. MARY MOTHER OF GOD (January 1), solemnity: Celebrates "the part played by Mary in the mystery of salvation," exalts "the singular dignity that this mystery brings to the 'holy Mother,' " renews "adoration to the newborn Prince of Peace," and implores from God, through Mary's intercession, "the supreme gift of peace" (MC 5).

—Readings: Nm 6:22-27 (The Lord's blessing)
          Gal 4:4-7 (The adoption of children)
          Lk 2:16:21 (Visit of the shepherds and the circumcision
             of Jesus)

—Commentary: *See* Mother of God   Annunciation
                   Queen   Immanuel

4. PRESENTATION OF THE LORD (February 2), feast: "Joint commemoration of the Son and of the Mother," that is, "a celebration of
a Mystery of salvation accomplished by Christ, a Mystery with which
the Blessed Virgin was intimately associated as the Mother of the
Suffering Servant of Yahweh, as the one who performs a mission belonging to ancient Israel, and as the model for the new People of
God, which is ever being tested in its faith and hope by suffering and
persecution" (MC 7).

—Readings: Mal 3:1-4 (The temple and the oblation)
            Heb 2:14-18 (The redemption accomplished by Christ)
            Lk 2:22-40 (The presentation of Jesus in the temple)

—Commentary: *See* Presentation of the Lord
                   Holy Land and Mary
                   Infancy Narratives
                   Sorrows of Mary

5. OUR LADY OF LOURDES (February 11), optional memorial.

—Readings: Is 66:10-14 ("As a mother comforts her son")
            Jn 2:1-11 (The wedding at Cana)

—Commentary: *See* Lourdes
                   Immaculate Conception
                   Apparitions
                   Apparitions after Vatican II

6. ANNUNCIATION OF THE LORD (March 25), solemnity: "A joint
feast of Christ and of the Blessed Virgin: of the Word, Who becomes
'Son of Mary' (Mk 6:3), and of the Virgin, who becomes Mother of
God" (MC 6).

—Readings: Is 7:10-14 ("The virgin shall be with child, and bear a
            son")
            Heb 10:4-10 ("A body you have prepared for me")
            Lk 1:26-38 ("You shall conceive and bear a Son")

—Commentary: *See* Annunciation of the Lord   Loreto
                   "Fiat"   Mother of God
                   Full of Grace   Saint Mary Major

7. VISITATION (May 31), feast: "The Liturgy recalls the Blessed Virgin Mary carrying her Son within her, and visiting Elizabeth to offer
charitable assistance and to proclaim the mercy of God the Savior"
(MC 7).

—Readings: Zep 3:14-18 ("Shout for joy, O daughter of Zion! sing joyfully, O Israel!")
    Or: Rom 12:9-16 ("Look on the needs of the saints as your own; be generous in offering hospitality")
    Lk 1:39-47 (Mary visits Elizabeth)

—Commentary: *See* Daughter of Zion
    Visitation
    Infancy Narratives
    Servant of the Lord

8. IMMACULATE HEART OF MARY (Saturday after the Solemnity of the Sacred Heart of Jesus), memorial: It expresses "tendencies that have emerged in contemporary devotion" (MC 8).

—Readings: Is 61:9-11 ("I rejoice heartily in the Lord")
    Lk 2:41-51 ("Your father and I have been searching for You in sorrow")

—Commentary: *See* Immaculate Heart of Mary
    Faith of Mary
    Finding of Jesus in the Temple
    Devotion(s)

9. OUR LADY OF MOUNT CARMEL (July 16), optional memorial: "Originally celebrated by a particular religious family, but . . . today, by reason of the popularity [it has] gained, it can truly be considered ecclesial" (MC 8).

—Readings: Zec 2:14-17 ("I am coming to dwell among you")
    Lk 2:15-19 (The adoration by the shepherds: God reveals Himself to the poor)

—Commentary: *See* Carmel, Mount
    Holy Land and Mary
    Apparitions

10. DEDICATION OF SAINT MARY MAJOR (August 5), optional memorial.

—Readings: Rv 21:1-5 ("This is God's dwelling among men")
    Lk 11:27-28 ("Blest are they who hear the word of God and keep it")

—Commentary: *See* Saint Mary Major
    Church and Mary
    Mother of God
    Motherhood, Spiritual

11. ASSUMPTION (August 15), solemnity: "It is the feast of [Mary's] destiny of fullness and blessedness, of the glorification of her immaculate soul and of her virginal body, of her perfect configuration to

the Risen Christ; a feast that sets before the eyes of the Church and of all mankind the image and the consoling proof of the fulfillment of their final hope" (MC 6).

—Readings: (a) Mass of the Vigil:
1 Chr 15:3-4, 15, 16; 16:1-2 (The transferral of the Ark)
1 Cor 15:54-57 ("O death, where is your victory?")
Lk 11:27-28 (Blest is your Mother!)

(b) Mass of the Day:
Rv 11:19; 12:1-6, 10 ("A woman clothed with the sun")
1 Cor 15:20-26 ("Christ the first fruits and then . . . all those who belong to Him")
Lk 1:39-56 ("God Who is mighty has done great things for me; . . . He has raised the lowly")

— Commentary: *See* Assumption   Queen
                Death of Mary   Revelation
                Munificentissimus Deus

12. QUEENSHIP OF MARY (August 22), memorial: "The Solemnity of the Assumption is prolonged in the celebration of the Queenship of the Blessed Virgin Mary, which occurs seven days later. On this occasion we contemplate her who, seated beside the King of Ages, shines forth as *Queen and intercedes as Mother*" (MC 6).

—Readings: Is 9:1-6 ("A child is born to us . . .")
         Lk 1:28-36 (The Annunciation)

—Commentary: *See* Queen   Annunciation
             Ad Caeli Reginam   Mother of God
             Coronation of Mary   Litany of the Blessed
                                      Virgin

13. BIRTH OF MARY (September 8), feast. It commemorates a salvific event: "Mary the hope of the entire world and the dawn of salvation" (MC 7).

—Readings: Mi 5:1-4 ("She who is to give birth . . .")
         Or: Rom 8:28-30 ("Those whom He foreknew He predestined")
         Mt 1:1-16, 18-23 (The ancestors of Jesus)

—Commentary: *See* Birth of Mary   New Eve
             Parents of Mary   Old Testament
             Daughter of Zion   Marian Typology

14. OUR LADY OF SORROWS (September 15), memorial: "A fitting occasion for reliving a decisive moment in the History of Salvation and for venerating, together with the Son lifted up on the Cross, His suffering Mother" (MC 7).

—Readings: Heb 5:7-9 (The Passion of Christ)
          Jn 19:25-27 (Mary at the foot of the Cross)
          Or: Lk 2:33-35 ("You yourself shall be pierced with a
          sword")

—Commentary: *See* Sorrows of Mary
                Finding of Jesus in the Temple
                Infancy Narratives
                Cross (Mary and)

15. OUR LADY OF THE ROSARY (October 7), memorial: A truly "ecclesial" celebration (MC 8).

—Readings: Acts 1:12-14 (The Apostles and Mary in the Cenacle)
          Lk 1:28-36 (Annunciation)

—Commentary: *See* Rosary   Church and Mary
                Adiutricem Populi   Sorrows of Mary
                Laetitiae Sanctae   Joys of Mary
                Octobri Mense

16. PRESENTATION OF MARY (November 21), memorial. It proposes a "lofty and exemplary" value and carries on a venerable tradition "having [its] origin especially in the East" (MC 8).

—Readings: Zec 2:14-17 ("Rejoice, O daughter Zion! See, I am coming")
          Mt 12:46-50 ("There are My mother and My brothers")

—Commentary: *See* Presentation of Jesus   Imitation of Mary
                Infancy Narratives   Apocrypha and Mary
                Holy Land and Mary

17. OUR LADY OF GUADALUPE (December 12), feast: A commemoration "connected with local devotions" that has "acquired a wider popularity and interest" (MC 8).

—Readings: Zec 2:14-17 ("Rejoice, O daughter Zion! See, I am coming")
          Lk 11:27-28 ("Blest are they who hear the word of God
          and keep it")

—Commentary: *See* Guadalupe   Shrines (National)
                Apparitions   Apparitions after Vatican II

LOCAL CELEBRATIONS

18. OUR LADY MEDIATRIX OF ALL GRACE (May 8), optional memorial.

—Readings: Est 8:3-8 (Misfortune strikes my people . . .)
    Jn 2:1-11 (The wedding at Cana: the Mother of Jesus was there)

—Commentary: *See* Motherhood, Spiritual   Intercession
    Church and Mary   Trinity (Mary and)
    Mediatrix

19. MARY, MOTHER OF THE CHURCH (October 11), optional memorial.

—Readings: Rv 21:1-3 ("He shall be their God Who is always with them")
    Jn 19:25-27 ("There is your Mother")

—Commentary: *See* Church and Mary   Motherhood, Spiritual
    Homily of Paul VI . . .   New Eve

20. OUR LADY OF THE MIRACULOUS MEDAL (November 27), optional memorial.

—Readings: Rv 2:19; 11:19; 12:1-5, 14-17 ("A great sign appeared in the sky")
    Jn 2:1-11 (Jesus begins His miracles in Cana of Galilee)

—Commentary: *See* Miraculous Medal   Apparitions
    Immaculate Conception   Novenas and Mary

2

MONTH OF MARY
"Behold Your Mother"

I — MARY IN THE WORD OF GOD

1. A first sketch of the person of Mary

   See *Old Testament:*
   > 1. The role of the queen-mother and "figures" of Mary
   > 2. Messianic hope and the Mother of the Messiah

   Example/commitment of life: Pilgrimage to the Holy Land (no. 1). See also *Life of Mary; Words of Mary.*

2. A positive portrait of Woman

   See *New Eve:*
   > 1. Eve mother of the living
   > 2. The new Adam and the new Eve
   > 3. The thought of the Fathers of the Church

   Example/commitment of life: Every woman can see herself in Mary. See also *Woman.*

3. Mary inserted in her people

   See *Daughter of Zion:*
   > 1. The Daughter of Zion in the Old Testament
   > 2. Mary, daughter of Israel and Daughter of Zion (See *New Testament*, no. 2)

   Example/commitment of life: The behavior of *Joseph*, a just man. See also *Life of Mary.*

4. Vocation of Mary

   See *Annunciation:*
   > 1. A revelation concerning the Mystery of Jesus
   > 2. A revelation concerning the vocation of Mary
   > 3. Fulfillment of the promises made to Israel

   Example/commitment of life: Let us meditate on the *Hail Mary*. See also *Infancy Narratives.*

5. Mary, woman of faith

   See *Faith of Mary:*
   > 1. Faith illumination and faith adherence
   > 2. Mary's path of faith

   Example/commitment of life: The *fidelity* of the Blessed Virgin in the words of John Paul II. See also *Knowledge of Mary; Redemptoris Mater.*

510

6. Mary, servant of the Lord

See *Servant of the Lord:*
   1. Mary, humble servant of the Lord
   2. For the realization of the Divine plan

Example/commitment of life: Let us recall the servant of the Lord by reciting the *Angelus*. See also *Marian Titles, 6.*

7. Mary, Ark of the Covenant

See *Visitation:*
   1. The word of God is effective
   2. Prophetic consecration of John
   3. A new revelation concerning Jesus
   4. "Blessed is she who believed . . ."
   5. Mary's thanksgiving
   6. Mary, Ark of the Covenant

Example/commitment of life: Let us contemplate the Mystery of Mary under the guidance of the *Akathist Hymn*. See also *Catechism of the Catholic Church and Mary; Immanuel.*

8. The Magnificat: Mary's song of religious hope

See *Magnificat:*
   1. Text and source of the Magnificat
   2. Movement of the Magnificat:
      a. The present of the personal experience
      b. An experience open to the future
      c. From yesterday to today

Example/commitment of life: Let us relive the *Joys of Mary*. See also *Poor of Yahweh and Mary; Resurrection and Mary.*

9. The prediction of a mysterious and tragic future: the sword of sorrow

See *Presentation of Jesus:*
   1. "As it is written in the law of the Lord . . ."
   2. The Spirit reveals Jesus
   3. The mission of Jesus
   4. The "Daughter of Zion and the Messianic drama"

Example/commitment of life: Let us participate in the *Sorrows of Mary*. See also *Infancy Narratives; Cross (Mary at the).*

10. The anticipated experience of the Paschal Triduum

See *Finding in the Temple:*
   1. Anticipation of the Paschal Mystery
   2. Jesus reveals and declares Himself
   3. Mary's faith

Example/commitment of life: Let us take our inspiration from Mary in every existential situation (See *States of Life* . . .). See also *Knowledge of Mary.*

11. The Virgin of the beginnings

See *Cana:*
1. A new reading: Cana and the experience of Sinai and the Covenant
2. The Mother of Jesus and the beginning of signs

Example/commitment of life: See "Lay people" in *States of Life* . . . See also *Intercession of Mary.*

12. Behold your Mother!

See *Cross (Mary at the):*
1. The hour of Jesus and the hour of the Woman
2. The "accomplishment" of all things and Mary's oblation
3. The gathering into one of God's dispersed children and the Motherhood of Mary.
4. Reception by the disciple and Reception by the Church
5. Fountain of life and the community of the redeemed

Example/commitment of life: Mary's grieving message at *La Salette.* See also *Sorrows of Mary.*

13. The woman clothed with the sun

See *Revelation 12*
1. Marian interpretation
2. Ecclesiological interpretation

Example/commitment of life: The apparitions at *Rue du Bac.* See also *Apparitions after Vatican II.*

II—MARY IN THE THEOLOGICAL REFLECTION OF THE CHURCH

14. Mary, Mother of God

See *Mother of God:*
1. Theological content
2. The Divine Motherhood and history

Example/commitment of life: The basilica of *Saint Mary Major.* See also *Dogmas, Marian, 1.*

15. Mary ever Virgin

See *Virginal Conception:*
1. Testimony of the Gospels
2. Reality of the virginal conception
3. Significance of the virginal conception

Or: *Virginity, Perpetual:*
    1. The Gospels
    2. Tradition
    3. Significance

Example/commitment of life: Religious in the path of the Virgin (*Religious and Mary*). See also *Dogmas, Marian, 1.*

16. The Immaculate Conception

See *Immaculate Conception:*
    1. Mary, all-holy
    2. Immaculate from conception
    3. The definition of 1854
    4. Conclusion

Example/commitment of life: The Virgin appears at *Lourdes.* See also *Ad Diem Illum Laetissimum.*

17. Assumption to heavenly glory

See *Assumption:*
    1. Content of the dogma
    2. The meaning of the Assumption for Mary
    3. The Assumption and us

Example/commitment of life: The message of *Fatima.* See also *Fulgens Corona.*

18. Mary Our Mother

See *Motherhood, Spiritual:*
    1. A slow development
    2. Content
    3. The reciprocal Mother/child relationship

Example/commitment of life: Our Lady of *Guadalupe.* See also *Devotion(s).*

19. The one who prays for us

See *Intercession of Mary:*
    1. Confidence in Mary's prayer
    2. Ground for this confidence
    3. Does Mary's prayer influence God?

Example/commitment of life: The shrine of *Loreto.* See also *Adiutricem Populi.*

20. Mary in relation to the Church

See *Church and Mary:*
    1. Mary—prototype of the Church
    2. Mary—member of the Church
    3. Mary—Mother of the Church

Example/commitment of life: Our Lady of *Czestochowa.* See also *Homily of Paul VI. . . .*

21. Mary reigns with Christ forever

See *Queen:*
1. Teaching of Pius XII
2. The teaching of the Post-Vatican II Liturgy
3. The Liturgy on the reasons for Mary's Queenship
4. Keys for a deeper theological-pastoral understanding

Example/commitment of life: The *Salve Regina,* a Marian prayer. See also *Ad Caeli Reginam.*

22. Humble and raised above all creatures

See *Sister (Mary Our):*
1. Daughter of Adam
2. Simplicity and proximity of Mary

Example/commitment of life: The message of *Carmel.* See also *Full of Grace.*

III—WELCOMING MARY INTO ONE'S LIFE

23. A true devotion to Mary

See *Devotion(s):*
1. Devotion
2. Devotions
3. Devotion and devotions to Mary

Example/commitment of life: *Saint Ephrem,* poet of Mary. See also *Cult of Mary.*

24. Celebrating Mary in the Liturgy

See *Liturgy:*
1. Prayer to God with Mary
2. Prayer to God in honor of Mary
3. Prayer to Mary

Example/commitment of life: *Saint Bernard* and *Marian Doctors.* See also *Presence of Mary in the Eucharist.*

25. Taking inspiration from Mary's example

See *Imitation of Mary:*
1. Take Mary as a model
2. Be formed by Mary and by the Holy Spirit

Example/commitment of life: *Maximilian Kolbe,* knight of Mary. See also *Words of Mary.*

26. Contemplating Mary's countenance

See *Icons and Images of Mary:*
1. "Born of a woman"
2. In the West
3. In the East
4. Today

Example/commitment of life: A statue of Mary weeps at *Syracuse*. See also *Imitation of Mary*.

27. Evangelization with Mary

See *Evangelization and Marian Piety:*
   1. Union with Jesus-Savior
   2. Power of the Spirit
   3. Motherhood of the Church
   4. A few corollaries

Example/commitment of life: *Alphonsus Liguori,* Mary's chanter. See also *Marian Classics*.

28. Popular expressions of devotion to Mary

See *Popular Religion and Marian Piety:*
   1. Richness
   2. Limits

Example/commitment of life: *Litany of the Blessed Virgin* a simple and trusting prayer. See also *Litany, Biblical*.

29. With Mary toward the separated brothers and sisters

See *Ecumenism (Mary and):*
   1. "Mary Mother of God" at the Council of Ephesus
   2. Mary in the Western controversy between Catholics and Protestants
   3. Mary in Eastern Christianity
   4. Toward a conciliar community

Example/commitment of life: *Apparitions,* sign of Mary's presence. See also *Judaism and Mary*.

30. Mary, way to the Trinity

See *Trinity (Mary and):*
   1. Mary and the religious experience of the Father
   2. Mary and life in Christ
   3. Mary and walking in the Holy Spirit

Example/commitment of life: Daily recitation of the *Rosary*. See also *New Testament*.

31. Consecration to Mary

See *Consecration:*
   1. To consecrate, to consecrate "oneself"
   2. Consecration to Mary
   3. Consecrating others to Mary

Example/commitment of life: *Saint Louis-Marie Grignion de Montfort,* apostle of consecration to Mary. See also *Novenas and Mary*.

THE LECTIONARY OF THE COMMON OF THE BLESSED VIRGIN AND MARY'S PLACE IN THE LITURGICAL YEAR

FIRST READINGS

1.	*1.*	Gn 3:9, 15-20	*Descendance from Eve*	Immac. Con.; 1 Lent A; 10 Ord. B
2.	*2.*	Gn 12:1-7	*The promise to Abraham*	2 Lent A
3.	*3.*	2 Sm 7:1 16	*The throne of David*	4 Advent B
4.	*4.*	1 Chr 15:3 ....16; 16:1-2	*The ark of the covenant*	Assumption (Vigil)
5.	*5.*	Prv 8:22-31	*Jesus, Son of Mary, Wisdom*	Presentation of Mary; Trinity C
6.	*6.*	Sir 24:1-12	*Wisdom among human beings*	2 Christ.
7.	*7.*	Is 7:10-14	*The virgin will conceive*	Annunciation; 4 Advent A
8.	*8.*	Is 9:1................6	*A son is given us*	Queenship; Christmas eve
9.	*9.*	Is 61:9-11	*The seed from the earth*	Immac. Heart; Consec. of Virg; Rel. Prof.
10.	*10.*	Mi 5:1-4	*The one who is to give birth*	Birth; 4 Advent C
11.	*11.*	Zec 2:14-17	*I will dwell among you*	O.L. of Mt. Carmel

SECOND READINGS

12.	*1.*	Acts 1:12-14	*The Apostles and Mary*	7 East. A; O.L. Rosary; (Mir. Medal)
13.	*2.*	Rom 5:12, 17-19	*Mary, Mother of new Adam*	1 Lent A
14.	*3.*	Rom 8:28-30	*The first-born of many brothers*	Birth; 17 Ord. A
15.	*4.*	Gal 4:4-7	*Born of a woman*	Ded. M. Maj.; M. Mother of God; Catechumen.
16.	*5.*	Eph 1:3-6, 11-12	*God's eternal choice*	Immac. Con.; 2 Christ.
17.	*6.*	Rv 11:19; 12:1 ... 10	*A sign in the sky*	Assumption
18.	*7.*	Rv 21:1-5	*The new Jerusalem*	5 East. C; Child. Fun.

PSALMS AND CANTICLES

19.	*1.*	Ps 45:11-17	*The Queen*	Assump.; Presentation
20.	*2.*	Ps 113:1-8	*The poor raised from the mud*	Ded. M. Maj; Queenship
21.	*3.*	1 Sm 2:1 8	*Canticle of Hannah*	Immac. Heart

22.	*4.*	Lk 1:46-55	*Magnificat*	O.L. Mt. Carmel; O.L. Rosary; O.L. Guad.
23.	*5.*	Jdt 13:18, 19, 20	*Blessed are you above all women*	O.L. Lourdes; M. Mediat.

GOSPELS

24.	*1.*	Mt 1:1-16.......23	*The announcement to Joseph*	Birth; 4 Advent A; Christ. Eve; S. Joseph
25.	*2.*	Mt 2:13-15, 19-23	*The Holy Family*	H. Family; Refugees
26.	*3.*	Mt 12:46-50	*Who is My mother?*	Comm. BVM; Tues. 16 Ord. Wk.
27.	*4.*	Lk 1:28-36	*The Annunciation*	Im. Concep.; Annunciation; Queenship; 4 Advent B; O.L. Rosary; Rel. Prof.
28.	*5.*	Lk 1:39-47	*The Visitation*	Visitation; Assumption (39-56); 4 Advent C
29.	*6.*	Lk 2:1-4	*Birth of Jesus*	Christ. Eve; Ded. M. Major (17)
30.	*7.*	Lk 2:15-19	*Adoration of the Magi*	Comm. BVM; Christ. Dawn; Present. of Mary
31.	*8.*	Lk 2:27-37	*Simeon's prophecy*	O.L. Sorrows (33-35)
32.	*9.*	Lk 2:41-52	*Jesus found in Temple*	H. Fam. C (22-40); Immac. Heart
33.	*10.*	Lk 11:27-28	*Happy is Jesus' Mother*	Assumption Vig.; Marriage; O.L. Guad.
34.	*11.*	Jn 2:1-11	*Wedding at Cana*	O.L. Lourdes
35.	*12.*	Jn 19:25-27	*Mary at the Cross*	O.L. Sorrows; Good Fri.; Mary Mediatrix

4

BIBLICAL READINGS OF CELEBRATIONS
WITH A MARIAN CHARACTER

FIRST READINGS

36.	*12.*	*1.* Is 49:13-15	*Can a woman forget?*	O.L. Consolation (Luxem.); 8 Ord. A
37.	*13.*	*2.* Is 52:7-10	*He ransoms Jerusalem*	Christ. Day
38.	*14.*	*3.* Is 60:1-6	*The Lord's glory over Jerusalem*	Epiphany
39.	*15.*	*4.* Is 66:10-14	*As a mother comforts her children*	O.L. Guad.; 14 Ord. C
40.	*16.*	*5.* Zep 3:14-18	*Rejoice, daughter Zion*	Visit.; Thanksgiv., Presentation of Lord
41.	*17.*	*6.* Mal 3:1-4	*Offering of Judah and of Jerusalem*	Presentation of Lord

SECOND READINGS

42.	*8.*	*1.* Rom 12:9-16	*Rejoice with those who rejoice*	Visitation
43.	*9.*	*2.* 1 Cor 15:20-26	*Christ, the first to rise*	Assumption
44.	*10.*	*3.* 2 Cor 1:3-7	*He comforts us in our distress*	O.L. Consolation (Luxem.)
45.	*11.*	*4.* Heb 1:1-6	*Today I have begotten You*	Christ. Day
46.	*12.*	*5.* Heb 2:14-18	*He partook the human condition*	Presentation of Lord
47.	*13.*	*6.* Heb 5:7-9	*The passion of Christ*	O.L. Sorrows
48.	*14.*	*7.* Heb 10:4-10	*I come to do Your will*	Annunciation

GOSPELS

49.	*13.*	*1.* Mt 2:1-12	*Adoration of the Magi*	Epiphany
50.	*14.*	*2.* Mt 13:54-58	*His Mother is called Mary*	Joseph the Worker
51.	*15.*	*3.* Mk 3:31-35	*The Mother and brothers of Jesus*	10 Ord. B; Rel. Prof.
52.	*16.*	*4.* Jn 1:1-18	*The Word became flesh*	Christ. Day; Christ. Init.

OTHER "MARIAN" READINGS
FROM THE SUNDAY AND WEEKDAY LECTIONARIES

FIRST READINGS

53. *18.*	*1.*	Gn 22:1-18	*The blessing promised to Abraham*	Thurs. I 13 Ord.
54. *19.*	*2.*	Gn 28:10-17	*The vision of Jacob*	Mon. I 14 Ord.
55. *20.*	*3.*	Ex 3:1-18	*The burning bush*	Wed. I 15 Ord.
56. *21.*	*4.*	Nm 24:15-17	*Balaam's prophecy*	Mon. 3 Advent
57. *22.*	*5.*	1 Kgs 8:1-7, 9-13	*Dedication of the Temple*	Mon. II 5 Ord.
58. *23.*	*6.*	Sir. 51:17-20	*Thanksgiving for Wisdom*	Sat. I 8 Ord.
59. *24.*	*7.*	Is 11:1-10	*A shoot from the stump of Jesse*	Tues. I Advent
60. *25.*	*8.*	Zec 9:9-12	*The Messiah King and the daughter of Zion*	14 Ord. A

SECOND READINGS

61. *15.*	*1.*	Col 1:21-24	*Sharing Christ's Passion*	Sat. I 22 Ord.; Mon. I 23 Ord.
62. *16.*	*2.*	Phil 4:5-8, 9	*The model of Christian life*	27 Ord. A

GOSPELS

63. *17.*	*4.*	Mk 6:1-6	*The carpenter, Son of Mary*	15 Ord. B
64. *18.*	*5.*	Lk 4:21-30	*The Son of Joseph*	5 Ord. C
65. *19.*	*6.*	Lk 10:38-42	*Martha and Mary*	16 Ord. C
66. *20.*	*7.*	Jn 6:41-51	*We know His mother*	19 Ord. B
67. *21.*	*8.*	Jn 16:20-22	*The joy of the woman who gives birth*	Fri. 6 East.

CELEBRATING ADVENT AND CHRISTMAS WITH MARY

ADVENT

4th Sunday

A Is 7:10-16   The virgin shall be with Child and bear a Son
   Rom 1:1-7   Jesus was descended from David, according to the
                flesh
   Mt 1:18-24   It is by the Holy Spirit that she has conceived this Child

B 2 Sm 7:1-16 The promise made to David
   Rom 16:25-27 The mystery hidden for many ages
   Lk 1:26-38   You shall bear a Son. He shall rule over the house of
                David

C Mi 5:1-4   Bethlehem, from you shall come forth the One Who is
                to be ruler of Israel
   Heb 10:5-10 A body you have prepared for Me
   Lk 1:35-45   Who am I that the mother of my Lord should come to
                me?

DECEMBER 17
   Mt 1:1-17   It was of Mary that Jesus was born

DECEMBER 18
   Mt 1:18-24   The angel's announcement to Joseph

DECEMBER 19
   Lk 1:5-25   The angel's announcement to Zechariah

DECEMBER 20
   Is 7:10-14   The virgin shall be with Child
   Lk 1:26-38   You shall conceive and bear a Son

DECEMBER 21
   Song 2:8-14 The beloved and her lover
Or: Zep 3:14-18 Shout for joy, O daughter Zion
   Lk 1:39-45   Blessed is she who trusted

DECEMBER 22
   1 Sm 1:24-28 The magnificat of Hannah, mother of Samuel
   Lk 1:46-56   The magnificat of Mary

DECEMBER 23
   Lk 1:57-66   Birth of John the Baptist

DECEMBER 24
   1 Sm 7:1 ... 16 A house for the Ark of the Covenant
   Lk 1:67-79   The canticle of Zechariah

CHRISTMAS

DECEMBER 25: CHRISTMAS VIGIL

Mt 1:1-25   It was of Mary that Jesus was born

Midnight

Lk 2:1-14   Mary gave birth to her first-born Son

Dawn

Lk 2:15-20   The shepherds found Mary and Joseph, and the Baby lying in a manger

During the Day

Jn 1:1-18   The Word became flesh and made His dwelling among us

DECEMBER 28

Mt 2:13-18   Take the Child and His Mother and flee to Egypt

DECEMBER 29

Lk 2:22-25   The Presentation of Jesus in the Temple

DECEMBER 30

Lk 2:36-40   Encounter with the prophetess Anna

DECEMBER 31

Jn 1:1-18   The Word became flesh and made His dwelling among us

JANUARY 1: *Mary Mother of God*

See Appendix 1

2nd SUNDAY AFTER CHRISTMAS

Sir 24:1-4, 8-12   Canticle of wisdom

JANUARY 6 or 2nd SUNDAY AFTER CHRISTMAS: *Epiphany*

Mt 2:1-12   They found the Child with Mary His Mother

7. DEVELOPMENT OF THE CULT OF MARY IN THE ROMAN LITURGY

PRAYERS OF THE ROMAN MISSAL	FEASTS OF THE BLESSED VIRGIN	DEVOTION OF THE CHURCH
		3rd c. *Sub Tuum* (in Egypt)
		4th c. Akathist Hymn, in East
5th c. (beg.) *Communicantes* of the Roman Canon	5th c. Dedication of St. Mary Major weekdays of Advent and Christmas	431 Council of Ephesus
	6th c. Holy Mary, Mother of God	
7th c. Embolism of Our Father *Gelasian Sac.*	7th c. Presentation (Purification); Annunciation Assumption	8th c. *Ave Maris Stella*
11th c. Creed introduced at Mass Preface of Assumption (St. Gall)	Birth	11th c. *Alma Redemptoris Mater; Salve Regina* (priv. recit.); *Ave Maria: Gaude Virgo Maria.*
	11th c. Compassion of O.L.	
12th c. Mention of Mary in the *Confiteor*	Masses of BVM on Saturday Visitation	12th c. *Ave Regina Caelorum; Regina Caeli*
13th c. *Suscipe Sancta Trinitas* (Receive, O holy Trinity)	14th c. Presentation of Mary *Stabat Mater* (1306)	14th c. Black Death (1348-1350)
	16th c. O.L. of Rosary (1563)	15th c. Rosary of Alain de la Roche (1475)
	17th c. O.L. of Sorrows (Sept. 15)	16th c. Victory of Lepanto (1571)
	18th c. O.L. of Mt. Carmel (1726); O.L. of Guadalupe (1754)	19th c. Marian apparitions: Rue du Bac (1830); La Salette (1846); Lourdes (1858); Pontmain (1871); Knock (1879)
	19th c. Immaculate Conception (1854)	
20th c.	20th c. O.L. of Lourdes (1907)	20th c. Fatima (1917); Beauraing (1932); Banneux (1933)
New Eucharistic Pr. and New Prefaces (1969); Common of BVM (1970); Collection of Masses of BVM (1987)	Immac. Heart of Mary (1944) Queenship of Mary (1954)	Definition of Assumption (1950) Vatican II (1962-65)

COLLECTION OF MASSES OF THE BLESSED VIRGIN MARY

ADVENT

1. THE BVM, CHOSEN DAUGHTER OF ISRAEL

RI(a)   Gn 12:17   *God speaks to our ancestors*
RI(b)   2 Sm 7:1-5, 8b-11, 16 *The Lord will give Him the throne of David His father*
G   Mt 1:1-17   *Genealogy of Jesus Christ*

2. THE BVM AND THE ANNUNCIATION OF THE LORD

RI(a)   Is 7:10-14; 8:10c *The Virgin will conceive*
RI(b)   Is 11:1-5, 10   *A shoot shall come forth from the stump of Jesse*
G(a)   Lk 1:26-38   *You will conceive and bear a Son*
G(b)   Mt 1:18-23   *What is conceived in her is of the Holy Spirit*

3. THE VISITATION OF THE BVM

RI(a)   Zep 3:14-18a *The Lord, the King of Israel, is among you*
RI(b)   Song 2:9-14   *See, my lover comes leaping across the mountains*
RI(c)   Zec 9:9-10   *Rejoice greatly, O daughter Zion*
G   Lk 1:39-56   *Why should I be honored with a visit from the Mother of my Lord?*

CHRISTMAS SEASON

4. HOLY MARY, MOTHER OF GOD

RI   Gal 4:4-7   *God sent His Son, born of a woman*
G   Lk 2:15b-19   *The shepherds found Mary and Joseph, and the Baby, lying in the manger*

5. THE BVM, MOTHER OF THE SAVIOR

RI(a)   Is 9:1-3, 5-6   *A Son is given to us*
RI(b)   Mi 5:1-4a   *This is the time when she who is in labor is to give birth*
G   Lk 2:1-14   *A Savior is born for you*

6. THE BVM AND THE EPIPHANY OF THE LORD

RI   Is 60:1-6   *The glory of the Lord shines upon you*
G   Mt 2:1-12   *Entering the house, they saw the Child with Mary, His Mother*

7. THE BVM AND THE PRESENTATION OF THE LORD

RI   Mal 3:1-4   *The Lord Whom you seek will come to His Temple*
G   Lk 2:27-35   *A sword will pierce your very soul*

8. OUR LADY OF NAZARETH

I

RI	Gal 4:4-7	*God sent His Son, born of a Woman, born under the Law*
G(a)	Lk 2:22, 39-40	*They returned to their own home of Nazareth. The Child grew to maturity, and He was filled with wisdom*
G(b)	Lk 2:41-52	*Jesus went down with them and came to Nazareth, where He was subject to them*

II

RI	Col 3:12-17	*May the fullness of Christ's message live within you*
G	Mt 2:13-15, 19-23	*He went and lived in a town called Nazareth*

9. OUR LADY OF CANA

RI	Ex 19:3-8a	*Whatever the Lord has spoken, we will do*
G	Jn 2:1-11	*Do whatever He tells you*

LENT

10. HOLY MARY, DISCIPLE OF THE LORD

RI	Sir 51:13-18, 20-22	*My heart delighted in wisdom*
G(a)	Lk 2:41-52	*The Mother of Jesus treasured all these things in her heart*
G(b)	Mt 12:46-50	*Extending His hands toward His disciples, He said: Here are My Mother and My brothers*
G(c)	Mk 3:31-35	*Whoever has done the will of God is My brother, My sister, and My Mother*

11. THE BVM AT THE FOOT OF THE CROSS I

RI(a)	Rom 8:31b-39	*God did not spare His own Son*
RI(b)	Col 1:21-24	*In my flesh I fill up what is lacking in the sufferings of Christ*
G	Jn 19:25-27	*There by the Cross of Jesus stood His Mother*

12. THE BVM AT THE FOOT OF THE CROSS II

RI(a)	Jdt 13:17-20	*You have averted our ruin before our God*
RI(b)	Gn 22:1-2, 9-13, 15-18	*You have not withheld your only Son*
Or	Heb 5:7-9	*He learned obedience and became the source of eternal life*
G	Jn 19:25-27	*There by the Cross of Jesus stood His Mother*

13. THE COMMENDING OF THE BVM

RI	2 Mc 7:1, 20-29	*Because of her hope in the Lord, this admirable mother bore their deaths with honor*

G   Jn 19:25-27   *Woman, this is your son*

14. THE BVM, MOTHER OF RECONCILIATION

RI   2 Cor 5:17-21 *On behalf of Christ we implore you to be reconciled to God*

G   Jn 19:25-27   *This is your son. This is your Mother*

EASTER SEASON

15. THE BVM AND THE RESURRECTION OF THE LORD

RI   Rv 21:1-5a   *I saw the new Jerusalem, as beautiful as a bride dressed for her husband*

G   Mt 28:1-10   *Tell His disciples that He has risen*

16. HOLY MARY, FOUNTAIN OF LIGHT AND LIFE

RI   Acts 2:14a, 36-40a, 41-42 *Everyone must be baptized in the Name of Jesus Christ*

G(a)   Jn 12:44-50   *I, the light, have come into the world*

G(b)   Jn 3:1-6   *What is born of the Spirit is spirit*

17. OUR LADY OF THE CENACLE

RI   Acts 1:6-14   *You will receive the power of the Holy Spirit*

G(a)   Lk 8:19-21   *My Mother and My brothers are those who hear the Word of God and put it into practice*

G(b)   Lk 24:44-53   *Stay in the city, until you are clothed with power from on high*

18. THE BVM, QUEEN OF THE APOSTLES

RI   Acts 1:12-14; 2:1-4 *With one heart the disciples continued in steadfast prayer with Mary, the Mother of Jesus*

G   Jn 19:25-27   *Woman, this is your son. This is your Mother*

ORDINARY TIME—SECTION 1

19. HOLY MARY, MOTHER OF THE LORD

RI(a)   1 Chr 15:3-4, 15-16; 16:1-2 *Mary, whose womb bore the Lord, is hailed as the ark of the Lord*

RI(b)   Ex 3:1-8   *Your blessed and fruitful virginity is like the bush that Moses saw on Horeb: though on fire, the bush was not consumed*

G   Lk 1:39-47   *Blessed is the fruit of your womb*

20. HOLY MARY, THE NEW EVE

RI(a)   Rv 21:1-5a   *I saw the new Jerusalem, as beautiful as a bride all dressed for her husband*

RI(b)   Rom 5:12, 17-19 *Where sin increased, there grace abounded all the more*
Or   Eph 1:3-6, 11-12 *Before the world was made, God chose us in Christ*
G(a)   Lk 1:26-38   *Hail, full of grace*
G(b)   Jn 2:1-11   *The Mother of Jesus said to the attendants: Do whatever He tells you*

21. THE HOLY NAME OF THE BVM

RI   Sir 24:17-21 *Remembrance of me is a legacy to future generations*
G   Lk 1:26-38   *The Virgin's Name was Mary*

22. HOLY MARY, HANDMAID OF THE LORD

RI   1 Sm 1:24-28; 2:1-2, 4-8 *I stood praying to the Lord, and the Lord granted my request*
G   Lk 1:26-38   *Behold, the handmaid of the Lord*

23. THE BVM, TEMPLE OF THE LORD

RI(a)   1 Kgs 8:1, 3-7, 9-11 *A cloud filled the Temple of the Lord God*
RI(b)   Rv 21:1-5a *Here God lives among His people*
RI(c)   Gn 28:10-17 *This is nothing else but the house of God and the gate of heaven*
G   Lk 1:26-38   *The power of the Most High will overshadow you*

24. THE BVM, SEAT OF WISDOM

RI(a)   Prv 8:22-31 *Mary, seat of wisdom*
RI(b)   Sir 24:1-4, 18-21 *Mary, seat of wisdom*
G   Lk 10:38-42   *Mary chose the better part*

25. THE BVM, IMAGE AND MOTHER OF THE CHURCH I

RI   Gn 3:9-15, 20 *I will put enmity between your offspring and her offspring*
G   Jn 19:25-27   *Woman, this is your son. This is your Mother*

26. THE BVM, IMAGE AND MOTHER OF THE CHURCH II

RI   Acts 1:12-14 *With one heart the disciples continued in steadfast prayer with Mary, the Mother of Jesus*
G   Jn 2:1-11   *The Mother of Jesus was there. And His disciples believed in Him*

27. THE BVM, IMAGE AND MOTHER OF THE CHURCH III

RI   Rv 21:1-5a *I saw the new Jerusalem, as beautiful as a bride all dressed for her husband*
G   Lk 1:26-38   *He will rule over the house of Jacob for ever*

28. THE IMMACULATE HEART OF THE BVM

RI   Jdt 13:17-20; 15:9 *You are the highest honor of our race*
G(a)   Lk 11:27-28 *Blessed is the womb that bore You*
G(b)   Lk 2:46-51 *The Mother of Jesus treasured all these things in her heart*

29. THE BVM, QUEEN OF ALL CREATION

RI(a)   Is 9:1-3, 5-6 *The dominion of the Lord is boundless*
RI(b)   Zec 9:9-10 *Rejoice greatly, O daughter Zion*
Or   1 Cor 15:20-26 *As members of Christ all people will be raised, Christ first, and after Him all who belong to Him*
G   Lk 1:26-38 *You will conceive and bear a Son*

ORDINARY TIME—SECTION 2

30. THE BVM, MOTHER AND MEDIATRIX OF GRACE

RI   Est 8:3-8, 16-17a *How can I bear to see the evil that is to befall my people?*
G   Jn 2:1-11 *The Mother of Jesus said to Him: They have no wine*

31. THE BVM, FOUNTAIN OF SALVATION

I

RI   Ez 47:1-2, 8-9, 12 *I saw water flowing from the Temple, and all who were touched by it were saved*
G   Jn 19:25-27 *One of the soldiers pierced His side with a lance, and immediately there came out blood and water*

II

RI   Song 4:6-7, 9, 12-15 *Fountain of the garden, well of living water*
G   Jn 7:37-39a *Streams of living water shall flow from His heart*

32. THE BVM, MOTHER AND TEACHER IN THE SPIRIT

RI(a)   Prv 8:17-21, 34-35 *Whoever finds me, finds life*
RI(b)   Is 56:1, 6-7 *My house will be called a house of prayer for all the peoples*
G(a)   Mt 12:46-50 *Extending His hands toward the disciples, He said: Here are My Mother and My brothers*
G(b)   Jn 19:25-27 *Woman, this is your son. This is your Mother*
G(c)   Mk 3:31-35 *Whoever has done the will of God is My brother, my sister, and My Mother*

33. THE BVM, MOTHER OF GOOD COUNSEL

RI(a)   Is 9:1-3, 5-6 *The Wonderful Counselor is given to us*

RI(b) Acts 1:12-14; 2:1-4 *With one heart the disciples continued in steadfast prayer with Mary, the Mother of Jesus*

G Jn 2:1-11 *The Mother of Jesus said to the attendants: Do whatever He tells you*

34. THE BVM, CAUSE OF OUR JOY

RI(a) Zec 2:14-17 *Rejoice and be glad, Daughter of Zion*

RI(b) Is 61:9-11 *I exult for joy in the Lord*

G(a) Lk 1:39-47 *As soon as Elizabeth heard Mary's greeting, the infant leaped in her womb*

G(b) Jn 15:9-12 *May My joy be within you*

35. THE BVM, PILLAR OF FAITH

RI Jdt 13:14, 17-20 *You have brought to nothing the enemies of your people*

G Lk 11:27-28 *Blessed is the womb that bore You*

36. THE BVM, MOTHER OF FAIREST LOVE

RI Sir 24:17-21 *I am the Mother of fairest love*

G Lk 1:26-38 *Hail, full of grace*

37. THE BVM, MOTHER OF DIVINE LOVE

RI Sir 24:9-12, 18-21 *I am the Mother of Divine Hope*

G Jn 2:1-11 *The Mother of Jesus was at the wedding feast with Him*

38. HOLY MARY, MOTHER OF UNITY

RI(a) Zep 3:14-20 *At the proper time I will gather you together*

RI(b) 1 Tim 2:5-8 *There is one Mediator between God and humanity, Christ Jesus, Himself human*

G(a) Jn 11:45-52 *He will gather together in unity the scattered children of God*

G(b) Jn 17:20-26 *May they be completely one*

ORDINARY TIME—SECTION 3

39. HOLY MARY, QUEEN AND MOTHER OF MERCY

I

RI Est C: 12, 14-15, 25, 30 (Vulg. 4:17n, p-r, aa-bb, hh-kk) *Queen Esther prays for her people*

G Jn 2:1-11 *The Mother of Jesus was at the wedding feast with Him*

II

RI	Eph 2:4-10	*God is rich in mercy*
G	Lk 1:39-55	*The Lord has mercy on those who fear Him in every generation*

40. THE BVM, MOTHER OF DIVINE PROVIDENCE

RI	Is 66:10-14	*As a mother comforts her child, so will I comfort you*
G	Jn 2:1-11	*The Mother of Jesus was there. And the disciples of Jesus believed in Him*

41. THE BVM, MOTHER OF CONSOLATION

RI(a)	Is 61:1-3, 10-11	*The Spirit of the Lord sent me to comfort the brokenhearted*
RI(b)	2 Cor 1:3-7	*God comforts us that we might comfort others in their sorrows*
G(a)	Mt 5:1-12	*Blessed are those who mourn, for they shall be comforted*
G(b)	Jn 14:15-21, 25-27	*I shall ask the Father, and the Father will give you another Advocate to be with you for ever*

42. THE BVM, HELP OF CHRISTIANS

RI(a)	Rv 12:1-3, 7-12ab	*A great sign appeared in the sky*
RI(b)	Gn 3:1-6, 13-15	*I will put enmity between you and the Woman*
G	Jn 2:1-11	*This was the first of Jesus' signs*

43. OUR LADY OF RANSOM

RI	Jdt 15:8-10; 16:13-14	*The hand of the Lord strengthened me*
G	Jn 19:25-27	*Woman, this is your son*

44. THE BVM, HEALTH OF THE SICK

RI	Is 53:1-5, 7-10	*He bore our sufferings Himself*
G	Lk 1:39-56	*Why should I be honored with a visit from the Mother of my Lord?*

45. THE BVM, QUEEN OF PEACE

RI	Is 9:1-3, 5-6	*The dominion of the Lord is boundless in a peace that has no end*
G	Lk 1:26-38	*You will conceive and bear a Son*

46. THE BVM, GATE OF HEAVEN

RI(a)	Rv 21:1-5a	*I saw the new Jerusalem as a bride all dressed for her husband*
RI(b)	Gn 28:10-17	*This is nothing else but the house of God and the gate of heaven*
G	Mt 15:1-13	*Look, the Bridegroom comes. Go out to meet Him*

CLASSIC PRAYERS OF THE SAINTS TO MARY

In addition to the traditional quasi-official prayers to Mary found throughout this Dictionary (see pp. 374ff), there are classic prayers of the Saints to Our Lady. Of these the following are among the best known.

Mary, Vessel of God's Mysteries

MARY, you are the vessel and tabernacle containing all mysteries. You know what the Patriarchs never knew; you have experienced what was never revealed to the Angels; you have heard what the Prophets never heard. In a word, all that was hidden from preceding generations was made known to you; even more, most of these wonders depended on you. — *Saint Gregory Wonderworker (d. 270)*

Mary, Our Hope

BLESSED Virgin, immaculate and pure, you are the sinless Mother of your Son, the mighty Lord of the universe. You are holy and inviolate, the hope of the hopeless and sinful; we sing your praises. We praise you as full of every grace, for you bore the God Man. We all venerate you; we invoke you and implore your aid.

Holy and immaculate Virgin, rescue us from every need that presses upon us and from all the temptations of the devil. Be our intercessor and advocate at the hour of death and judgment. Deliver us from the fire that is not extinguished and from the outer darkness.

Make us worthy of the glory of your Son, O dearest and most kind Virgin Mother. You indeed are our most secure and only hope for you are holy in the sight of God, to Whom be honor and glory, majesty and power forever. —*Saint Ephrem of Edessa (d. 373)*

Mary, Mother of Grace

IT BECOMES you to be mindful of us, as you stand near Him Who granted you all graces, for you are the Mother of God and our Queen. Help us for the sake of the King, the Lord God and Master Who was born of you. For this reason you are called "full of grace."

Remember us, most holy Virgin, and bestow on us gifts from the riches of your graces, Virgin, full of grace. —*Saint Athanasius (d. 373)*

Mary, Mother of Mercy

BLESSED Virgin Mary, who can worthily repay you with praise and thanksgiving for having rescued a fallen world by your generous consent? What songs of praise can our weak human nature offer in your honor, since it was through you that it has found the way to salvation?

Accept then such poor thanks as we have to offer, unequal though they be to your merits. Receive our gratitude and obtain by your prayers the pardon of our sins. Take our prayers into the sanctuary of heaven and enable them to bring about our peace with God.

May the sins we penitently bring before Almighty God through you be pardoned. May what we beg with confidence be granted through you. Take our offering and grant our request; obtain pardon for what we fear, for you are the only hope of sinners. We hope to obtain the forgiveness of our sins through you. Blessed Lady, in you is our hope of reward.

Holy Mary, help the miserable, strengthen the discouraged, comfort the sorrowful, pray for your people, plead for the clergy, intercede for all women consecrated to God. May all who venerate you, feel now your help and protection. Be ready to help us when we pray, and bring back to us the answers to our prayers. Make it your continual care to pray for the People of God, for you were blessed by God and were made worthy to bear the Redeemer of the world, Who lives and reigns forever.

—Saint Augustine (d. 430)

Mary, Mother and Virgin

HAIL, Mother and Virgin, imperishable Temple of the Godhead, venerable treasure of the whole world, crown of virginity, support of the true Faith upon which the Church is founded throughout the whole world.

Mother of God, you enclosed under your heart the infinite God, Whom no space can contain. Through you the Most Holy Trinity is adored and glorified, demons are banished, and our fallen nature is again assumed into heaven. Through you the human race, held captive in the bonds of idolatry, arrives at the knowledge of truth.

Hail, through whom kings rule, through whom the Only-begotten Son of God has become a star of light to those who were sitting in darkness and in the shadow of death!   *—Saint Cyril of Alexandria (d. 444)*

Mary, Model of Life in the Spirit

I ASK and beg you, holy Virgin, that from this Spirit Who brought Jesus to birth in you I too may receive Jesus. Let my soul receive Him from this Spirit Who caused your flesh to conceive Him. May I love Jesus in this Spirit in Whom you yourself worshiped Him as your Lord and contemplated Him as your Son.   *—Saint Ildephonsus of Toledo (d. 677)*

Mary, Life of Christians

WHO could know God, were it not for you, most holy Mary? Who could be saved? Who would be preserved from dangers? Who would receive any grace, were it not for you, Mother of God, full of grace?

What hope could we have of salvation, if you abandon us, O Mary, who are the life of Christians?   —*Saint Germanus of Constantinople (d. 732)*

Mary, Cause of Our Joy

HAIL Mary. full of grace, the Lord is with you. I salute you, O Cause of our Joy, through whom the sentence of our condemnation has been revoked and changed into one of blessings. Hail, temple of God's glory, sacred home of the heavenly king! You are God's reconciliation with the human race. Hail, Mother of our joy and gladness! You are indeed blessed, because out of all women you alone have been found worthy to be the Mother of your Creator. All generations call you blessed.

O Mary, if I put my trust in you, I shall be saved; if I am under your protection, I have nothing to fear. For being your servant means possessing salvation, which God grants only to those whom He wills to save.

O Mother of mercy, appease your beloved Son. While on earth, you occupied only a small part of it. However, now that you have been raised above the highest heavens, the whole world regards you as the intercessor of all nations.

We implore you, therefore, O holy Virgin, to grant us the help of your prayers with God, which prayers are dearer to us than all the treasures of the earth. They render God propitious to us in our sins and obtain for us a great abundance of graces, including the grace to receive pardon for our sins and the grace to practice virtue. Your prayers check our enemies, confound their plans, and triumph over their efforts.

—*Saint Andrew of Crete (d. 740)*

Mary, Hope of Christians

HAIL Mary, hope of Christians, hear the prayer of a sinner who loves you tenderly, who honors you in a special manner, who places in you the hope of his salvation. I owe you my life.

You obtain for me the grace of your Divine Son. You are the sure pledge of my eternal happiness. I entreat you, deliver me from the burden of my sins, take away the darkness of my mind, destroy the earthly affections of my heart, defeat the temptations of my enemies, and rule all the actions of my life so that with you as guide I may arrive at the eternal happiness of heaven.   —*Saint John Damascene (d. 754)*

Mary, Mother of God

YOUR name, O Mother of God, is filled with all graces and Divine blessings. You have contained Him Who cannot be contained, and nourished Him Who nourishes all creatures. He Who fills heaven and earth, and is the Lord of all, was pleased to be in need of you, for it was you who clothed Him with that flesh which He did not have before. Rejoice, then, O Mother and handmaid of God!

Rejoice, because you have made Him a debtor Who gives being to all creatures. We are all God's debtors, but He is a debtor to you. That is why, O most holy Mother of God, you have greater goodness and greater charity than all the other Saints, and have freer access to God than any of them, for you are His Mother. Remember us, we beseech you, in our miseries, who celebrate your glories and know how great your goodness is.

—Saint Methodius (d. 847)

The Mother of God Is Our Mother

O BLESSED Lady, you are the Mother of Justification and those who are justified; the Mother of Reconciliation and those who are reconciled; the Mother of Salvation and those who are saved. What a blessed trust, and what a secure refuge! The Mother of God is our Mother. The Mother of the One in Whom alone we hope and Whom alone we fear is our Mother! . . .

The One Who partook of our nature and by restoring us to life made us children of His Mother invites us by this to proclaim that we are His brothers and sisters. Therefore, our Judge is also our Brother. The Savior of the world is our Brother. Our God has become—through Mary—our Brother. *—Saint Anselm of Canterbury (d. 1086)*

Mary, Beloved of the Trinity

H OLY Virgin Mary, there is none like you among women born in the world. Daughter and handmaid of the heavenly Father, the Almighty King. Mother of our Most High Lord Jesus Christ! Spouse of the Holy Spirit! Pray for us to your most holy Son, our Lord and Master.

Hail, holy Lady, most noble Queen, Mother of God, Mary ever Virgin! You were chosen by the heavenly Father, Who has been pleased to honor you with the presence of His most holy Son and Divine Paraclete. You were blessed with the fullness of grace and goodness.

Hail, Temple of God, His dwelling-place, His masterpiece, His handmaid. Hail, Mother of God, I venerate you for the holy virtues that, through the grace and light of the Holy Spirit, you bring into the hearts of your clients to change them from unfaithful Christians to faithful children of God. *—Saint Francis of Assisi (d. 1126)*

Mary, Our Advocate

O BLESSED Lady, you found grace, brought forth the Life, and became the Mother of salvation. May you obtain the grace for us to go to the Son. By your mediation, may we be received by the One Who through you gave Himself to us. May your integrity compensate with Him for the fault of our corruption; and may your humility, which is pleasing to God, implore pardon for our vanity. May your great charity cover the multitude of our sins; and may your glorious fecundity confer on us a fecundity of merits.

Dear Lady, our Mediatrix and Advocate, reconcile us to your Son, recommend us to Him, and present us to your Son. By the grace you found, by the privilege you merited, by the Mercy you brought forth, obtain for us the following favor, O blessed Lady.

May the One Who—thanks to you—came down to share our infirmity and wretchedness make us share—again thanks to you—His glory and beatitude: Jesus Christ, your Son, our Lord, Who reigns in heaven and is blessed forever!   —*Saint Bernard of Clairvaux (d. 1153)*

Mary, Mother of Sacred Healing

Radiant Mother of sacred healing, O Mary, you poured salve on the lamentable wounds that Eve caused to torment our souls. For your salve is your Son, and you destroyed death forever, giving rise to life. Pray for us to your Child, O Mary, Star of the Sea.

You are the source of life, sign of gladness, and sweetness of all unfailingly flowing delights. Pray for us to your Child, O Mary, Star of the Sea.

Glorify the Father, the Spirit, and the Son. Pray for us to your Child, O Mary, Star of the Sea.   —*Saint Hildegard of Bingen (d. 1179)*

Mary, Our Queen

MARY, our Queen, Holy Mother of God, we beg you to hear our prayer. Make our hearts be filled with Divine grace and resplendent with heavenly wisdom. Render them strong with your might and rich in virtue. Pour down upon us the gift of mercy so that we may obtain the pardon of our sins. Help us to live in such a way as to merit the glory and bliss of heaven. May this be granted us by your Son Jesus Who has exalted you above the Angels, has crowned you as Queen, and has seated you with Him forever on His refulgent throne.

—*Saint Anthony of Padua (d. 1231)*

Dedication to Mary

VIRGIN full of goodness, Mother of mercy, I entrust to you my body and soul, my thoughts, my actions, my life and my death.

O my Queen, help me, and deliver me from all the snares of the devil. Obtain for me the grace of loving my Lord Jesus Christ, your Son, with a true and perfect love, and, after Him, O Mary, to love you with all my heart and above all things.   —*Saint Thomas Aquinas (d. 1274)*

For a Happy Death

HOLY Virgin, I beg of you, when my soul shall depart from my body, be pleased to meet and receive it.

Mary, do not refuse me then the grace of being sustained by your sweet presence. Be for me the ladder and the way to heaven, and finally assure me of pardon and eternal rest.   —*Saint Bonaventure (d. 1274)*

Favor with God

"DO NOT fear, Mary, you have found favor with God" (Lk 1:30). Fear not, Mary, for you have found, not taken grace, as Lucifer tried to take it. You have not lost it, as Adam lost it. You have found favor with God because you have desired and sought it. You have found uncreated Grace: that is, God Himself became your Son, and with that Grace you have found and obtained every uncreated good.

—*Saint Albert the Great (d. 1280)*

Petition to Mary

MOST chaste Virgin Mary, I beg of you, by that unspotted purity with which you prepared for the Son of God a dwelling of delight in your virginal womb, that by your intercession I may be cleansed from every stain.

Most humble Virgin Mary, I beg of you, by that most profound humility by which you deserved to be raised high above all the choirs of Angels and Saints, that by your intercession all my sins may be expiated.

Most amiable Virgin Mary, I beg of you, by that indescribable love which united you so closely and inseparably to God, that by your intercession I may obtain an abundance of all merits.   —*Saint Gertrude (d. 1334)*

In Praise of Mary

O MARY, Mary, temple of the Trinity. O Mary, bearer of fire. O Mary, dispenser of mercy. O Mary, restorer of human generation, because the world was repurchased by means of the sustenance that your flesh found in the Word. Christ repurchased the world with His Passion, and you with your suffering of mind and body.

O Mary, peaceful ocean. O Mary, giver of peace. O Mary, fruitful land. You, O Mary, are that new plant from which we have the fragrant flower of the Word, Only-begotten Son of God, because this Word was sown in you, O fruitful land. You are the land and the plant.

O Mary, vehicle of fire, you bore the fire hidden and veiled beneath the ash of your humanity. O Mary, vase of humility, in which there burns the light of true knowledge with which you lifted yourself above yourself and yet were pleasing to the eternal Father; hence He took and brought you to Himself, loving you with a singular love.

With this light and fire of your charity and with the oil of your humility, you inclined His Divinity to come into you—although He was first drawn to come to us by the most ardent fire of His inestimable charity. . . .

Today I ardently make my request, because it is the day of graces, and I know that nothing is refused to you, O Mary. Today, O Mary, your land has generated the Savior for us. O Mary, blessed are you among women throughout the ages!   —*Saint Catherine of Siena (d. 1380)*

Prayer of Self-Commendation to Mary

O holy Mary, my Lady, into your blessed trust and safe keeping and into the depths of your mercy I commend my soul and body this day, every day of my life, and at the hour of my death. To you I entrust all my hopes and consolations, all my trials and miseries, my life and the end of my life. By your most holy intercession and by your merits, may all my actions be directed and disposed according to your will and the Will of your Divine Son.   —*Saint Aloysius Gonzaga (d. 1591)*

Offering to Mary

MOST holy Mary, Virgin Mother of God, most unworthy though I am to be your servant, yet moved by your motherly care for me and longing to serve you, I choose you this day to be my Queen, my Advocate, and my Mother. I firmly resolve ever to be devoted to you and to do what I can to encourage others to be devoted to you.

My loving Mother, through the Precious Blood of your Son shed for me, I beg you to receive me as your servant forever. Aid me in my actions and beg for me the grace never by word or deed or thought to be displeasing in your sight and that of your most holy Son. Remember me, dearest Mother, and do not abandon me at the hour of death.

—*Saint Francis de Sales (d. 1622)*

The Spirit of Mary

HAIL MARY, beloved Daughter of the eternal Father. Hail Mary, wonderful Mother of the Son. Hail Mary, faithful Spouse of the Holy Spirit. Hail Mary, my dear Mother, my loving Lady, my powerful Queen. You are all mine through your mercy, and I am all yours. Take away from me all that may be displeasing to God. Cultivate in me everything that is pleasing to you.

May the light of your faith dispel the darkness of my mind, your deep humility take the place of my pride; your continual sight of God fill my memory with His presence; the fire of the charity of your heart inflame the lukewarmness of my own heart; your virtues take the place of my sins; your merits be my enrichment and make up for all that is wanting in me before God.

My beloved Mother, grant that I may have no other spirit but your spirit, to know Jesus Christ and His Divine Will and to praise and glorify the Lord; that I may love God with burning love like yours.

—*Saint Louis de Montfort (d. 1716)*

Mary, Hope for Salvation

MOST holy and immaculate Virgin, my Mother, you are the Mother of my Lord, the Queen of the world, the advocate, hope, and refuge of sinners. I, the most miserable among them, come to you today. I venerate you, great Queen, and thank you for the many graces you have bestowed on me. I thank you especially for having saved me so many times from the punishment of God that I deserved.

I love you, most lovable Lady. By the love that I have for you, I promise ever to serve you, and to do as much as I can to make you loved by others.

I put all my hope in you, my entire salvation. Receive me as your servant, Mother of mercy, and cover me with the mantle of your protection. Since you are so powerful with God, free me from all temptations, or, at least, obtain for me the grace to overcome them until death.

I ask of you a true love for Jesus Christ. Through you I hope to die a good death. My Mother, by the love you have for God, I beg you to help me always, and most of all at the last moment of my life. Do not leave me until you see me safe in heaven. I hope to thank and praise you there forever.

—*Saint Alphonsus Liguori (d. 1787)*

Mary, Our Model in Suffering

O MARY, you became my Mother at the height of suffering and trials. Hence, I must have a great and complete trust in you. Whenever I am subjected to trials at the hands of creatures and am exposed to temptation and desolation of soul, let me take refuge in your Heart, my Good Mother, and call upon you for help.

Do not let me perish but give me the grace to be submissive and confident in trials after your example. Let me suffer with love. Let me stand, like you, at the foot of the Cross, if that is the Will of your dear Son.

Never will a child perish who is devoted to Mary. O good Mother, have mercy on me. I give myself entirely to you so that you may give me to your dear Son, Whom I desire to love with all my heart. Bestow on me, good Mother, a heart burning with love for Jesus.

—Saint Bernadette (d. 1879)

Mary, Help of Christians

MARY, powerful Virgin, you are the mighty and glorious protector of the Church. You are the marvelous help of Christians. You are awe-inspiring as an army in battle array. You have destroyed heresy in the world. In the midst of our anguish, our struggle, and our distress, defend us from the power of the enemy, and at the hour of our death receive our soul in heaven.   *—Saint John Bosco (d. 1888)*

Mary, Our Guide to Heaven

VIRGIN full of grace, I know that at Nazareth you lived modestly, without requesting anything more. Neither ecstasies, nor miracles, nor other extraordinary deeds enhanced your life, O Queen of the Elect.

The number of the lowly, "the little ones," is very great on earth. They can raise their eyes to you without any fear. You are the incomparable Mother who walks with them along the common way to guide them to heaven.

Beloved Mother, in this harsh exile, I want to live always with you and follow you every day. I am enraptured by the contemplation of you and I discover the depths of the love of your Heart. All my fears vanish under your Motherly gaze, which teaches me to weep and to rejoice!

—Saint Theresa of the Child Jesus (d. 1897)

Consecration to Our Lady

IMMACULATE Virgin, grant that I may praise you with my total commitment and my personal sacrifice. Grant that I may live, work, suffer, be consumed, and die for you.

Grant that I may contribute to an ever greater exaltation of you. May I render more glory to you than anyone has ever rendered to you in the past. Grant that others may surpass me in zeal for your exaltation and that I may in turn surpass them. Thus, in a noble emulation, your glory may always increase, in accord with the desire of the One Who exalted you above all creatures.

In you God is glorified more than in all His Saints. Through you God has created the world, and through you He has called me into existence.

Make me worthy to praise you, O Immaculate Virgin.

—Saint Maximilian Kolbe (d. 1941)

10
SELECT CHRONOLOGY OF MAJOR MARIAN EVENTS IN THE CHURCH

30/50	The apostolic preaching (some of which is recorded in the early speeches in the Acts of the Apostles—2:14-21; 3:12; 13:15ff) says not a word about Mary and practically nothing about Christ's earthly life. Reasons: (1) Mary was known to all the faithful of Palestine; (2) her major role in Jesus' life had been carried out during his early years when there were no disciples to know about it; and (3) the role of women in general was always played down in the East of that era.
54/57	Saint Paul provides the first allusion to Mary from among the apostolic preaching—in the Letter to the Galatians (4:4): "God sent His Son *born of a woman*."
65	Saint Mark sketches a portrait of Mary as the Mother of Jesus (3:31ff; 6:3).
70/80	Saint Matthew presents Mary as associated with Jesus in His birth in accord with Old Testament prophecies (including her virginal conception)—a singular role which puts her in a personal relationship with the Spirit (1:16-23; 2:11).
70/80	Saint Luke portrays Mary as the servant of the Lord, daughter of Zion, and closest follower of Christ—who hears God's Word and keeps it (1:38, 48; 2:19, 51; 11:28).
70/80	Saint Luke (in Acts) makes mention of Mary gathered in prayer with the Apostles in the Upper Room and so hints at her role in the formation of the Church (1:14).
90/100	Saint John portrays Mary as united with Jesus in life (2:1-11) and at His death (19:25) and as His dying gift to His followers (19:26-27).
90/100	The Book of Revelation puts the finishing touches to the primitive Church's image of Mary, which focuses on her concrete fidelity, deep faith, ecclesial role, and singular grace. Mary is the servant par excellence, who did nothing other than accept, fashion, and offer Jesus (12:1-17).
100/200	An inscription (found under Saint Peter's Basilica) portrays Mary as Protectrix for the departed and their Mediatrix.
110/115	Saint Ignatius of Antioch gives five references to Mary as a Virgin and Mother.

120	The *Odes of Solomon* mentions the Virgin who gives birth.
145	Aristedes of Athens cites Mary in a credal formula.
150/200	Inscription of Abercius, Bishop of Hieropolis, alludes to Mary's virginity, holiness, and relationship to Eucharist.
150	Saint Justin Martyr is the first to write fully about Mary and he makes use of the Eve-Mary typology.
150	The *Protevangelium of James* is the first work to show an independent interest in Mary. It is the "Gospel of Mary."
150/202	Saint Irenaeus of Lyons attributes to Mary a necessary role in the Redemption.
162	The *Sybilline Oracles* speaks admiringly of Mary.
bef. 200	First paintings of Mary are inscribed on the catacombs.
200/300	The *Sub Tuum*, the most ancient Marian prayer recorded, is composed, emphasizing Mary's powerful intercession.
200/300	Inscriptions in Greek, Hebrew, Aramaic, Syrian, and Armenian at the site of the Basilica of the Annunciation offer evidence that devotion to Mary was practiced.
200	Composition of *The Obsequies of the Virgin,* a work written in Syria alluding to the assistance of Mary.
217	The Church of Santa Maria in Trastevere (Saint Mary across the Tiber) is founded at Rome.
250	Saint Cyprian of Carthage stresses the confidence that Christians should have in Mary and extols her virginity.
300	The *Akathist Hymn* is introduced in the East.
350/400	At Constantinople, Bishop Severian of Gabala issues an official and public invitation for prayers to Mary.
350/390	Saint Gregory of Nyssa diffuses throughout the Middle East a Marian prayer that is a forerunner of the Hail Mary. He also chronicles the first apparition of Mary recorded—to Saint Gregory the Wonderworker.
350/370	Saint Ephrem calls upon Mary's powers of mediation.
350	Saint Justina voices the earliest recorded invocation to Mary for help (reported later by Saint John Chrysostom).
350	Mary is frequently called Theotokos.
352-366	Saint Mary Major is founded by Pope Liberius I.
360(?)	St. Epiphanius evokes Mary's Assumption.

370	Earliest known Liturgy of Mary is composed in Syria.
370	Saint Ambrose holds Mary up as a model of women and a type of the Church.
392	Pope Saint Siricius, in a letter to Bishop Anysius, upholds Mary's perpetual virginity.
394	Saint Augustine proclaims Mary free from original sin and extols her status as Virgin and Mother.
400/500	A temple of Isis (an Egyptian nature goddess) at Soissons (France) is dedicated to the Blessed Virgin Mary.
400/500	The Feast of the Commemoration of the Virgin is instituted in various places in Europe.
400/500	The Feast of the Annunciation is celebrated in Byzantium.
400/500	The Feast of the Hypapante (that is, Encounter between Christ and Simeon) is celebrated.
400	Earliest copy of the *Transitus* of Mary is written.
420	In a meeting with Saint Augustine the Pelagian movement spreads belief in the Immaculate Conception.
431	Mary is given the title *Theotokos* (Mother of God) by the Council of Ephesus—led by Saint Cyril of Alexandria.
432	The church of Saint Mary Major in Rome is restored, enlarged, and dedicated by Pope Sixtus III.
440/461	Mary is introduced into the texts of the Mass. In the *Leonine Sacramentary*, Saint Leo the Great adds to the Canon (Eucharistic Prayer) the reference to Mary: "In communion with and venerating in the first place the glorious ever-Virgin Mary, Mother of God. . . ."
451	The Council of Chalcedon calls Mary Mother of God.
451	The empress Pulcherria of Byzantium sets about collecting the relics of Mary.
470	A Basilica is dedicated to Mary in Salonika.
500/600	The Parthenon—the celebrated temple of Athena, located on the Acropolis at Athens—is dedicated to Mary.
500/600	The church of Saint Mary Antiqua in Rome is consecrated.
520/556	The Syrian poet Saint Romanos the Melodist reaches new heights in composing four greatly used Marian hymns.
534	Pope John II, in a letter to the Senate at Constantinople, declares that Mary is "truly the Mother of God."

543	The church of Saint Mary in Jerusalem is dedicated.
550/600	Theoteknos, Bishop of Livias, provides the earliest affirmation of belief in Mary's bodily assumption.
550	The Feasts of the Birth of Mary, the Presentation of Jesus, and the Dormition are celebrated in Byzantium.
550	The first completely Marian interpretation of Revelation 12 is given by the Greek philosopher Oecumenius.
553	The Second Council of Constantinople reiterates the Dogma of the Divine Motherhood and mentions Mary's perpetual virginity.
580(?)	Saint Gregory of Tours provides the first theological formulation of the Assumption.
600/800	The *Gospel of Pseudo-Matthew* appears in the West.
600/700	The Marian antiphon *Ave Maris Stella* is composed.
600/650	The Feast of the Purification (February 2) is celebrated at Rome (more as a Feast of Christ than as one of Mary).
600/636	Saint Isidore of Seville, last Father in the West, writes knowingly about Mary.
610	Byzantine Emperor Heraclius has the image of Mary placed on the masts of his fleet.
649	The (non-Ecumenical) Council of the Lateran declares the perpetual virginity of Mary.
650/675	The Feast of the Annunciation (March 25) is celebrated at Rome (more as a feast of Christ than as one of Mary).
650	The Feast of the Assumption (August 15) is celebrated at Rome and goes on to become the principal Marian Feast.
675/700	The Feast of the Birth of Mary is celebrated at Rome (stemming from the dedication of the church of Mary's Nativity at Jerusalem, celebrated since the 5th century).
680(?)	Saint Germanus of Constantinople states that no one is saved without Mary.
680/681	The Third Council of Constantinople reaffirms Mary's Divine Motherhood.
700/749	Saint John Damascene, last Father in the East, gives the clearest teaching on the Immaculate Conception up to his day.
700/740	Saint Andrew of Crete (the most prolific Marian writer of all the Fathers) invokes Mary as "Help of Christians."

700/733	Saint Germanus of Auxerre formulates the idea that we "seek God through Mary."
705/707	Pope John VII is called "servant of the Mother of God."
750	The *Legend of Theophilus* is translated into Latin.
787	The Second Council of Nicaea defines the liceity of the cult rendered to images of Mary.
800/900	The Feast of the Conception of Saint Ann is instituted at Byzantium.
800/900	The Feast of the Conception of Mary begins to be propagated in the West.
800	The Gospel of Mary's Nativity makes its appearance.
before 804	The Benedictine monk Alcuin composes Masses of Our Lady on Saturday, which become part of the Missal in 875.
814	Emperor Charlemagne, after a life characterized by devotion to Mary, is buried with a statue of Mary placed on his heart in accord with his request.
845/860	Saint Paschasius Radbert upholds the Virgin Birth, the Assumption (only of the soul), and a form of Mary's Immaculate Conception.
before 851	The *story of the Birth of Mary* is composed, most likely by Saint Paschasius Radbert.
869/870	The Fourth Council of Constantinople renews approval of the "cult rendered to images of Mary."
876	Charles the Bold obtains what is believed the dress of Mary.
900/1000	The antiphon *Regina Caeli* is composed.
900/1000	The *Little Office of the Blessed Virgin Mary* is introduced.
900/1000	The *Transitus* stories about Mary's passing from this world are translated into Latin.
945	The title "Mother of Mercy" spreads throughout the West after it is mentioned in the *Life of Odo* by John of Salerno.
975	Saturdays are devoted to the Blessed Virgin Mary.
976	The abbey of Montserrat is founded in Spain and goes on to become a famous Marian shrine.
1000/1100	The Feast of Mary's Compassion is introduced.
1000/1100	The *Hail Holy Queen* is composed and perfectly suits the attitude of medieval Christians toward Mary.
1000/1100	The Cathedral of Notre Dame de Chartres is begun.

1000	Hroswitha of Gandersheim, a Benedictine nun, writes versions of the *Legend of Theophilus* and the *Gospel of James*—presenting Mary as the powerful Queen of Heaven.
1050/1150	The antiphon *Alma Redemptoris Mater* is composed, probably by Herman the Cripple.
1050/1093	Saint Anselm of Canterbury composes inspiring works about Mary (including three famous prayers) that go on to exert a tremendous effect on the Middle Ages.
1050/1072	Saint Peter Damian sets forth the connection between the Eucharist and Mary—and also promotes the Little Office.
1080/1124	Eadmer writes *The Conception of the Blessed Virgin Mary,* the best exposition of the doctrine up to the time.
1100/1200	The *Life of Mary* is spread to the West.
1100/1200	The Litany of the Blessed Virgin Mary begins to take shape.
1100/1150	The Hail Mary makes its appearance (the second part will be added only in the 15th century).
1100/1150	One of the greatest Marian mosaics is placed in the Cathedral at Torcello, Italy.
1100/1135	The Benedictine Rupert of Deutz is the first to interpret the Song of Songs entirely with respect to Mary.
1120/1150	Saint Bernard of Clairvaux expounds a Biblically centered Marian spirituality and coins beautiful Marian formulas.
1120/1130	Dominic of Evesham writes *Miracles of the Blessed Virgin.*
1120	Anselm the Younger collects the miracle stories about Mary in his popular book *Miracles of the Blessed Virgin Mary.*
1130	The church of Our Lady of Walsingham is built in England.
1140	The Benedictine historian William of Malmesburg writes the influential book *Miracles of the Blessed Virgin Mary.*
1150/1164	Saint Elizabeth of Schonau has visions of Mary assumed into heaven more actively than in the Dormition scenes, thus inspiring artists of the Middle Ages to depict the Assumption more dynamically.
1150	The first Dormition scene in the West is contained in the Senlis Cathedral in France.
1150	The church of La Martorana is built in Palermo in honor of Mary and exhibits a beautiful Dormition painting.
1160/1205	The Church of Notre Dame at Laon is built.
1163/1235	The Church of Notre Dame in Paris is built.

1194/1220	The Cathedral of Chartres is rebuilt.
1200/1250	The Church at Coutances is built.
1200	The Church of Notre Dame at Mantes is built.
1215	The Fourth Lateran Council mentions the Divine and Virginal Motherhood of Mary in the "Profession of the Catholic Faith against the Albigensians and other Heretics."
1220	The Church of Notre Dame at Amiens is built.
1223/1224	Caesar of Heisterbach states in the *Dialogus Miraculorum* that Mary protects Cistercian monks with her mantle.
1230/1280	Saint Albert the Great writes extensively on Mary and uses the title "Mother of the Church."
1250/1300	The anonymous *Mariale Super Missus Est* sets forth extravagant claims about Mary's spiritual and secular gifts.
1250/1274	Saint Thomas Aquinas evolves a theological doctrine on Mary that is free of all gross exaggerations.
1250/1274	Saint Bonaventure is the first to coin the word hyperdulia to identify the type of veneration given to Mary.
1251	Saint Simon Stock receives the Scapular from Mary.
1260/1306	Jacopone da Todi writes the *Laude,* which includes much Marian teaching. He also composes the *Stabat Mater.*
1260	Notre Dame de Chartres is dedicated.
1260	Cimabue paints a Madonna for Santa Trinita, Florence.
1265/1308	Blessed Duns Scotus is the first to set forth cogent reasons for the doctrine of Mary's Immaculate Conception.
1269	The *Angelus* becomes a popular devotion.
1274	The Second Council of Lyons professes that the Son of God was born in time from the ever-Virgin Mary.
1278/1350	The Church of Santa Maria Novella in Florence is built.
1280/1300	Beginnings of the custom of dedicating May to Mary (rooted in 7th-9th century Eastern practice).
1296	The Holy House is discovered in Loreto.
1296	The Church of Santa Maria del Fiore in Florence is begun.
1300/1400	The Feast of Mary's Presentation is instituted.
1300	The Legend of Mary's girdle spreads to the West.
1314/1321	In the *Divine Comedy,* Dante sketches a theology of Mary in action that is restrained yet gives Our Lady her just honor and glory—showing that he is the "supreme poet of Mary."

1326	Oriel College is founded at Oxford and dedicated to Mary.
1340/1373	Saint Bridget of Sweden reveals her visions of Mary that become very influential in the Church.
1355	The Church of Saint Mary at Nuremburg is begun.
1372	The Feast of the Purification is instituted in the West.
1376/1383	The Feast of Mary's Scapular is instituted.
1379	Saint Mary's College is founded at Oxford.
1384	The icon of Our Lady, which has been traced to the 5th and 8th centuries, is brought to Czestochowa, Poland.
1389	The Feast of the Visitation is recognized.
1400-1500	The prayer *Memorare* is composed.
1400-1450	Johannes Herolt writes the *Miracles of the B.V.M.*
1409/1411	John Lydgate composes the *Life of Our Lady*.
1410/1444	Saint Bernardine of Siena writes about the 7 Words of Mary.
1418	Thomas a Kempis, in *The Imitation of Christ*, emphasizes recourse to Mary in the spiritual life.
1420/1447	Saint Colette of Corbie reveals her visions of Mary.
1423	The Feast of the Sorrows of Mary is established.
1438/1445	The Council of Florence firmly professes that the Son of God became man through Mary.
1439	The Council of Basle defines the doctrine of the Immaculate Conception (but this has only significative value since it comes after Pope Eugene IV has repudiated this Council).
1440	Eton College dedicated to Mary is established.
1457	The *Little Office of the Blessed Virgin Mary* is printed.
1470/1471	Martin Schongauer makes engravings of the *Life of Mary*.
1470	The Dominican Alan Rupe writes on *The Utility of Mary's Psalter* upholding the power of the Rosary with Mary.
1471	Louis XI asks all the people of France to recite the Hail Mary each day on their knees for the peace of their country.
1475	The first Confraternity of the Rosary is established.
1492	The *Salve Regina* is the first Christian prayer recited in the New World—by Columbus and his men on San Salvador.
1495	The Rosary is approved by Pope Alexander VI.
1496/1501	Michelango completes the world-renowned *Pieta*—a sculpture of Mary with her dead Son in her lap.

1500/1510	Albrecht Dürer produces a woodcut *Life of Christ*.
1507	Pilgrimages to the shrine of Loreto are approved.
1518	Titian paints his *Assumption* at Frari, Venice.
1521	Martin Luther publishes a work entitled *The Magnificat,* a Commentary on the Gospel canticle that is regarded as one of the most beautiful texts about the Blessed Virgin.
1531	The Blessed Virgin appears to Juan Diego at Guadalupe.
1538	The Shrine of Our Lady of Walsingham is destroyed.
1543	Martin Luther affirms the Immaculate Conception.
1558	The Litany of Loreto in honor of Mary is published.
1547	The Council of Trent affirms that Mary is regarded as immune from every actual fault, even the slightest.
1550/1617	Francis Suarez establishes the first systematic Mariology with Volume IX of his *Opera Omnia*.
1555	Pope Paul IV in the Constitution *Cum Quorumdam* attests to Mary's virginity before, during, and after Christ's birth.
1563	The Council of Trent reaffirms the liceity of the cult of the images of Mary.
1563	The Hail Mary is introduced into the Divine Office.
1567	Pope Saint Pius V affirms Mary's sinlessness.
1573	The Feasts of the Expectation of the Virgin and of Our Lady of Victory and the Rosary are established.
1577	Saint Peter Canisius writes the *Incomparable Virgin Mary,* the first important Mariological work after the Reformation.
1600/1700	The Feast of Our Lady of Sorrows is instituted.
1600/1629	Pierre de Bérulle, founder of the "French School of Spirituality," renews devotion to Mary.
1601	The Litany of the Blessed Virgin is prescribed for the Universal Church by Pope Clement VIII.
1630/1657	Jean Jacques Olier, founder of the Sulpicians, applies mystical language to Marian concepts in a novel way.
1644	The Feast of the Most Pure Heart of Mary is established.
1670	The *Mystical City of God* by Maria de Agreda de Jesus is published posthumously.
1680	Saint John Eudes composes the first full-length book on the Heart of Mary, *The Admirable Heart of Mary*.

1683	The Feast of the Holy Name of Mary is extended to the Universal Church.
1690	Pope Alexander VIII upholds Mary's perfect sinlessness.
1700-1716	Saint Louis-Marie Grignion de Montfort preaches devotion to Mary and writes about Marian spirituality.
1716	The Feast of the Rosary is extended to the whole Church.
1716	Alexander de Rouville publishes *The Imitation of Mary*, patterned after *The Imitation of Christ*.
1726	The Feast of Our Lady of Mount Carmel is instituted.
1750	Saint Alphonsus Liguori publishes *The Glories of Mary*, which goes on to become a classic.
1754	Our Lady of Guadalupe is declared Patroness of Mexico.
1800-1850	Multiplication of foundations of Marian Religious Orders and publication of abundant Marian literature.
1815	The invocation "Help of Christians" is added to the Litany of the Blessed Virgin.
1815	The Feast of Mary Help of Christians is established.
1824	Catherine Emmerich has a vision of Mary's house at Ephesus.
1830	Our Lady appears to Saint Catherine Laboure and asks for the Miraculous Medal to be struck.
1836	Jean Claude Colin founds the Society of Mary.
1842	Saint Louis-Marie Grignion de Montfort's *True Devotion* is discovered, with its emphasis on Holy Slavery to Mary.
1845	Cardinal Newman defends true devotion to Mary but deplores excesses.
1846	The Immaculate Conception is declared Patroness of the United States.
1846	Our Lady appears at La Salette.
1849	Pope Pius IX writes the first Encyclical concerning Mary *Ubi Primum*, which stresses her Immaculate Conception.
1854	The Dogma of the Immaculate Conception is solemnly defined by Pope Pius IX in the Bull *Ineffabilis Deus*.
1858	Our Lady appears to Saint Bernadette at Lourdes.
1871	Our Lady appears at Pontmain.
1875	Devotions to the Sacred Heart of Mary are forbidden.

1879	The beginnings of the Shrine of Our Lady of the Cape in Canada are laid.
1879	Our Lady appears on a chapel wall at Knock, Ireland.
1883-1902	Leo XIII, "the Pope of the Rosary," issues 11 encyclicals on the Rosary and Mary, calling her Mediatrix of all Graces, Mother of the Redeemed and Guardian of the Faith, and Mediatrix with the Mediator (Christ), and advocating devotion to her as the salvation of society.
1883	The invocation "Queen of the Most Holy Rosary" is added to the Litany of the Blessed Virgin.
1890	Saint Theresa of Lisieux expresses deep devotion to Mary.
1900	Our Lady of Guadalupe is proclaimed Patroness of the Americas.
1904	Pope Saint Pius X in the Encyclical *Ad Diem Illud* develops the theological bases for Mary's Mediatorship of grace.
1907	The Feast of Our Lady of Lourdes is established.
1913	The cornerstone is laid for the National Shrine of the Immaculate Conception in Washington, D.C.
1917	Our Lady appears to three small children at Fatima.
1918	The invocation "Queen of Peace" is added to the Litany of the Blessed Virgin.
1918	In the Decree *Sunt Quo*, the Congregation of the Holy Office praises the custom of calling Mary "Co-Redemptrix."
1918	In the Apostolic Letter *Inter Sodalicia*, Pope Benedict XV sets forth the role of Mary in Christ's redeeming sacrifice.
1921	The Legion of Mary is established in Dublin.
1923	In the Apostolic Letter *Explorata Res*, Pope Pius XI affirms Mary's role in the Redemption wrought by Christ.
1927	Devotions to "Mary the Priest" are forbidden.
1931	The Feast of the Divine Motherhood is established.
1932/1933	Our Lady appears at Beauraing, Belgium.
1933/1934	Pope Pius XI speaks of Mary's contributions to Christ's redemptive work. He portrays her as associated with this work not only in Bethlehem as Mother of God but also at Calvary and treats all the principal Mariological themes.
1937	Our Lady appears at Banneux, Belgium.

1941	The practice of promising graces to those who wear a medal without any other obligation on their part is censured.
1942	Pope Pius XII dedicates the world to the Immaculate Heart of Mary in keeping with her wish expressed at Fatima.
1943	In the Encyclical *Mystici Corporis,* Pope Pius XII outlines the role played by Mary in human salvation and explains how she is spiritually the Mother of Christ's members.
1944	The Feast of the Immaculate Heart of Mary is established.
1946	Pope Pius XII writes the Encyclical *Deiparae Virginis Mariae* on the possibility of defining the Assumption.
1947	In the Encyclical *Mediator Dei,* Pope Pius XII deals with Mary in the Liturgy.
1950	A Marian Year is proclaimed.
1950	The Dogma of Mary's Assumption is solemnly defined by Pope Pius XII in the Bull *Munificentissimus Deus.*
1950	The invocation "Queen assumed into heaven" is added to the Litany of the Blessed Virgin.
1951	Pope Pius XII writes the Encyclical *Ingruentium Malorum* on the spiritual power of Mary's Rosary.
1953	The plaster-cast image depicting the Immaculate Heart of Mary in Syracuse, Sicily, is seen to be weeping.
1954	In the Encyclical *Fulgens Corona,* Pope Pius XII proclaims a Marian Year to commemorate the centenary of the definition of the Immaculate Conception.
1954	In the Encyclical *Ad Caeli Reginam,* Pope Pius XII proclaims the Queenship of Mary and establishes it as a Feast.
1957	In the Encyclical *Pelerinage de Lourdes,* Pope Pius XII commemorates the centenary of Mary's appearances at Lourdes.
1959	In the Encyclical *Gratia Recordati,* John XXIII calls Mary "the cause of salvation for the whole human race."
1964	The Second Vatican Council in the *Dogmatic Constitution on the Church,* Chapter eight, sets forth for the first time a Conciliar synthesis of teaching concerning the position that Mary holds in the Mystery of Christ and the Church.
1964	Pope Paul VI declares Mary "Mother of the Church."
1965	In the Encyclical *Mense Maio,* Pope Paul VI urges prayer during Mary's month of May.

1966	In the Encyclical *Christi Matri,* Pope Paul VI urges prayer for peace during October.
1967	On the 50th anniversary of Mary's appearances at Fatima, Pope Paul VI issues the Apostolic Exhortation *Signum Magnum* on the meaning and purpose of devotion to Mary.
1969	The *Roman Missal* of Paul VI is published with a revised Marian approach based on Mary's role in the Mystery of Christ and the Church. Some minor feasts are eliminated but many more prayers and readings are added for the feasts and memorials that remain.
1970	The *Liturgy of the Hours* is published with a revised Marian approach. It makes much use of the Magnificat, Marian antiphons, hymns, and readings.
1973	The U.S. Bishops publish the Pastoral Letter entitled *Behold Your Mother,* to proclaim the preeminent position of Mary "in the Mystery of Christ and the Church" and to restore the ancient love of Christendom for Christ's Mother.
1974	Pope Paul VI issues the Apostolic Constitution *Marialis Cultus,* which treats at length of liturgical Marian piety, popular Marian devotion, indicates the criteria for deciding which Marian practices are completely valid and for introducing new ones, and concludes with the theological and pastoral value of devotion to Mary.
1975	The revised *Roman Missal* (2nd ed.) includes Votive Masses of "Mary Mother of the Church" and "Holy Name of Mary."
1978	Archbishop Karol Wojtyla of Krakow is elected Pope. He takes the name John Paul II and dedicates his pontificate to Mary, taking the motto *Totus Tuus* ("All Yours, O Mary").
1980	The invocation "Mother of the Church" is added to the Litany of the Blessed Virgin.
1981	The Congregation of Divine Worship publishes a new Marian Litany in the *Rite for Crowning an Image of Mary.*
1982	Pope John Paul II visits Fatima and consecrates the world anew to the Immaculate Heart of Mary.
1983	Pope John Paul II mentions at Lourdes the eventuality of an exceptional celebration of the second-millennium of Mary's birth.

1987   Pope John Paul II proclaims a Marian Year (June 7, 1987 to August 15, 1988) and issues the Encyclical *Redemptoris Mater* ("Mother of the Redeemer") concerning the position that Our Lady holds in the Mystery of Christ and the Church.

1987   The Latin Edition of the *Collection of Masses of the Blessed Virgin Mary* is published along with a partial English Edition—for use on open days.

1992   The complete English Edition of the *Collection of Masses of the Blessed Virgin Mary* is published in two volumes: *I: Sacramentary* and *II: Lectionary*.

1994   The *Catechism of the Catholic Church* is published, and it succinctly sets forth the Church's teaching about the Blessed Virgin Mary.

1995   The Mass of "The Blessed Virgin Mary, Star of the Sea" is approved for use in the United States in special circumstances.

1995   The invocation "Queen of families" is added to the Litany of the Blessed Virgin.

1996   The rank of the celebration of the Immaculate Heart of the Blessed Virgin Mary on Saturday following the Second Sunday after Pentecost is changed from optional memorial to *obligatory memorial.*